Lecture Notes in Computer Sci

Commenced Publication in 1973
Founding and Former Series Editors:
Gerhard Goos, Juris Hartmanis, and Jan van Leeuwen

For further volumes:
http://www.springer.com/series/7410

Joaquin Garcia-Alfaro · Georgios Lioudakis
Nora Cuppens-Boulahia · Simon Foley
William M. Fitzgerald (Eds.)

Data Privacy Management and Autonomous Spontaneous Security

8th International Workshop, DPM 2013, and
6th International Workshop, SETOP 2013
Egham, UK, September 12–13, 2013
Revised Selected Papers

 Springer

Editors

Joaquin Garcia-Alfaro
Telecom SudParis
Evry
France

Simon Foley
University College Cork
Cork
Ireland

Georgios Lioudakis
National Technical University of Athens
Athens
Greece

William M. Fitzgerald
IDA Ovens
EMC Information Systems International
Cork
Ireland

Nora Cuppens-Boulahia
Telecom Bretagne
Cesson Sévigné
France

ISSN 0302-9743   ISSN 1611-3349   (electronic)
ISBN 978-3-642-54567-2   ISBN 978-3-642-54568-9   (eBook)
DOI 10.1007/978-3-642-54568-9
Springer Heidelberg New York Dordrecht London

Library of Congress Control Number: 2014934122

LNCS Sublibrary: SL4 – Security and Cryptology

Printed on acid-free paper

Springer is part of Springer Science+Business Media (www.springer.com)

Foreword from the DPM 2013 Program Chairs

This volume contains the proceedings of the 8th Data Privacy Management International Workshop (DPM 2013), held in Egham, UK, at Royal Holloway, University of London, during September 12–13, 2013, in conjunction with the 18th annual European research event in Computer Security (ESORICS 2013) symposium. It includes a revised version of the papers selected for presentation at the workshop. Previous issues of the DPM workshop were held in 2012 in Pisa (Italy), 2011 in Leuven (Belgium), 2010 in Athens (Greece), 2009 in Saint Malo (France), 2007 in Istanbul (Turkey), 2006 in Atlanta (USA), and 2005 in Tokyo (Japan).

The aim of DPM is to promote and stimulate the international collaboration and research exchange on areas related to the management of privacy-sensitive information. This is a very critical and important issue for organizations and end-users. It poses several challenging problems, such as translation of high-level business goals into system level privacy policies, administration of sensitive identifiers, data integration and privacy engineering, among others.

In response to the call for participation, 46 submissions were received. Each submission was evaluated on the basis of significance, novelty, and technical quality. All submissions went through a careful anonymous review process (three or more reviews per submission) aided by 49 Technical Program Committee members and 31 additional referees. In the end, 13 full papers, accompanied by five short papers, were presented at the event. The final program also included three invited talks by Steven J. Murdoch (University of Cambridge), Emil Lupu (Imperial College London), and John Borking (former Privacy Commissioner and Board Member of the Dutch Data Protection Authority in The Hague). Our special thanks to Steven, Emil, and John for accepting our invitation and for their presence during the event and talks.

We would like to thank everyone who helped at organizing the event, including all the members of the Organizing Committee of both ESORICS and DPM 2013. In particular, we would like to highlight and acknowledge the tremendous efforts of the ESORICS 2013 General Chair Keith Mayes and his team. Thank you Keith for all your help and support with DPM. Our gratitude goes also to Pierangela Samarati, Steering Committee Chair of the ESORICS Symposium, for all her arrangements to make possible the satellite events. Our special thanks to the General Chairs of DPM 2013, Josep Domingo-Ferrer and Maryline Laurent, as well as Steering Committee member Guillermo Navarro-Arribas, for their unconditional help since the beginning of this event. Last but by no means least, we thank all the DPM 2013 Program Committee members, additional reviewers, all the authors who submitted papers, and all the workshop attendees.

Finally, we want to acknowledge the support received from the sponsors of the workshop: Institute Mines-Telecom, CNRS Samovar UMR 5157, Telecom SudParis, UNESCO Chair in Data Privacy, and National Technical University of Athens.

January 2014

Joaquin Garcia-Alfaro
Georgios Lioudakis

8th International Workshop on Data Privacy Management—DPM 2013

Program Committee Chairs

Joaquin Garcia-Alfaro   Telecom SudParis, France
Georgios Lioudakis   National Technical University of Athens, Greece

Workshop General Chairs

Josep Domingo-Ferrer   Universitat Rovira i Virgili, Spain
Maryline Laurent   Telecom SudParis, France

Program Committee

Esma Aimeur   Université de Montreal, Canada
Michel Barbeau   Carleton University, Canada
John Borking   Borking Consultancy, The Netherlands
Jens-Matthias Bohli   NEC Laboratories Europe, Germany
Ana Cavalli   Telecom SudParis, France
Frederic Cuppens   Telecom Bretagne, France
Nora Cuppens-Boulahia   Telecom Bretagne, France
Roberto Di Pietro   Roma Tre University of Rome, Italy
Nicola Dragoni   Technical University of Denmark, Denmark
Christian Duncan   Quinnipiac University, USA
David Evans   University of Derby, UK
Sara Foresti   Università degli Studi di Milano, Italy
Sebastien Gambs   University of Rennes 1, France
Flavio D. Garcia   Radboud University Nijmegen, The Netherlands
Paolo Gasti   New York Institute of Technology, USA
Francesca Gaudino   Baker & McKenzie Law Firm, Italy
Stefanos Gritzalis   University of the Aegean, Greece
Marit Hansen   Unabhängiges Landeszentrum für Datenschutz,
    Germany
Artur Hecker   Telecom ParisTech, France
Jordi Herrera   Autonomous University of Barcelona, Spain
Iakovos Venieris   National Technical University of Athens, Greece
Dimitra Kaklamani   National Technical University of Athens, Greece
Panos Kampanakis   Cisco Systems, USA
Georgia Kapitsaki   University of Cyprus, Cyprus

Sokratis Katsikas	University of Piraeus, Greece
Evangelos Kranakis	Carleton University, Canada
Jean Leneutre	Telecom ParisTech, France
Giovanni Livraga	Università degli Studi di Milano, Italy
Javier Lopez	University of Malaga, Spain
Brad Malin	Vanderbilt University, USA
Sotirios Maniatis	Hellenic Authority for Communications Privacy, Greece
Chris Mitchell	Royal Holloway, UK
Refik Molva	Eurecom, France
Krish Muralidhar	University of Kentucky, USA
Guillermo Navarro-Arribas	Autonomous University of Barcelona, Spain
Silvio Ranise	Fondazione Bruno Kessler, Italy
Kai Rannenberg	Goethe University Frankfurt, Germany
Indrajit Ray	Colorado State University, USA
Yves Roudier	Eurecom, France
Mark Ryan	University of Birmingham, UK
Claudio Soriente	ETH Zürich, Switzerland
Alessandro Sorniotti	IBM Research, Switzerland
Traian M. Truta	Northern Kentucky University, USA
Yasuyuki Tsukada	NTT Communication Science Laboratories, Japan
Jens Weber	University of Victoria, Canada
Lena Wiese	University of Göttingen, Germany
Yanjiang Yang	Institute for Infocomm Research, Singapore
Nicola Zannone	Eindhoven University of Technology, The Netherlands
Melek Önen	Eurecom, France

Steering Committee

Josep Domingo-Ferrer	Universitat Rovira i Virgili, Spain
Joaquin Garcia-Alfaro	Telecom SudParis, France
Guillermo Navarro-Arribas	Autonomous University of Barcelona, Spain
Vicenç Torra	Artificial Intelligence Research Institute, Spain

Additional Reviewers

Achilleas Achilleos	Christian Kahl
Ahmad Sabouri	David Galindo
Alessio Di Mauro	David Nuñez
Ana Nieto	Elisa Costante
Anderson Morais	Eugenia Papagiannakopoulou
Anis Bkakria	Fatbardh Veseli
Aouadi Mohamed	Flavio Lombardi

Foreword from the SETOP 2013 Program Chairs

These are the proceedings of the 6th International Workshop on Autonomous and Spontaneous Security (SETOP 2013).

The purpose of this workshop is to bring together researchers to explore challenges in the automated configuration of security. In this volume you will find papers on a range of topics related to authentication and authorization, mobile security and vulnerabilities.

The workshop program also included invited talks by Steven Murdoch (University of Cambridge, UK) on "Quantifying and Measuring Anonymity" and by Emil Lupu (Imperial College London) on "Pervasive Autonomous Systems: Challenges in Policy based Adaptation and Security."

As with previous years, SETOP was a satellite workshop of the European Symposium on Research in Computer Security (ESORICS). We are grateful to the ESORICS 2013 Organizing Committee for agreeing to host SETOP-2013 and especially to ESORICS General Chair Keith Mayes for his assistance and support.

We are grateful to the many people who contributed to the success of the workshop. The members of the Program Committee and external reviewers. The Publications Chair, William Fitzgerald assembled the workshops proceedings and ensured its timely publication.

Finally, the workshops would not be possible without the authors who submitted papers, the presenters, and attendees.

We hope you enjoy reading the proceedings.

Nora Cuppens-Boulahia
Simon Foley

6th International Workshop on Autonomous and Spontaneous Security—SETOP 2013

Program Committee Chairs

Research Track

Simon Foley	University College Cork, Ireland
Nora Cuppens-Boulahia	Telecom Bretagne, France

Industrial Track

Edgardo Montes de Oca	Montimage, France

Workshop General Chairs

Ana Cavalli	Telecom SudParis, France
Frédéric Cuppens	Telecom Bretagne, France

Publicity and Publication Chair

William Fitzgerald	University College Cork, Ireland

Webmaster

Said Oulmakhzoune	Telecom Bretagne, France

Program Committee

Fabien Autrel	Telecom Bretagne, France
Gildas Avoine	Catholic University of Louvain, Belgium
Michele Bezzi	SAP Research, France
Christophe Bidan	Supelec, France
Carlo Blundo	University of Salerno, Italy
Joan Borrell-Viader	UAB, Spain
Jordi Castella-Roca	Rovira i Virgili University, Spain
Iliano Cervesato	Carnegie Mellon University, Qatar
Stelvio Cimato	Università degli Studi di Milano, Italy
Mauro Conti	Università di Padova, Italy
Ernesto Damiani	Università degli Studi di Milan, Italy
Sabrina De Capitani di Vimercati	Università degli Studi di Milano, Italy

Josep Domingo-Ferrer   Rovira i Virgili University, Spain
William Fitzgerald   University College Cork, Ireland
Sara Foresti   Università degli Studi di Milano, Italy
Jerome Francois   University of Luxembourg, Luxembourg
Joaquin Garcia-Alfaro   Telecom SudParis, France
Stefanos Gritzalis   University of the Aegean, Greece
Olivier Heen   Technicolor, France
Wei Jiang   Missouri University of S&T, USA
Sokratis Katsikas   University of Piraeus, Greece
Florian Kerschbaum   SAP Research, France
Evangelos Kranakis   Carleton University, Canada
Marie Noelle Lepareux   Thales, France
Javier Lopez   University of Malaga, Spain
Giovanni Livraga   Università degli Studi di Milano, Italy
Wissam Mallouli   Montimage, France
Guillermo Navarro-Arribas   Autonomous University of Barcelona, Spain
Marie Nuadi   EADS-Cassidian, France
Andreas Pashalidis   K.U. Leuven, Belgium
Nicolas Prigent   Supelec, France
Yves Roudier   Eurecom, France
Thierry Sans   Carnegie Mellon University, Qatar
George Spanoudakis   City University London, UK
Radu State   University of Luxembourg, Luxembourg
Ari Takanen   Codenomicon, Finland
Bachar Wahbi   Percevio, France

Steering Committee

Ana-Rosa Cavalli   Telecom SudParis, France
Frédéric Cuppens   Telecom Bretagne, France
Nora Cuppens-Boulahia   Telecom Bretagne, France
Jean Leneutre   Telecom ParisTech, France
Yves Roudier   Eurecom, France

Contents

Keynote Address

Quantifying and Measuring Anonymity 3
  Steven J. Murdoch

Data Privacy Management

Performance Evaluation of Primitives for Privacy-Enhancing
Cryptography on Current Smart-Cards and Smart-Phones 17
  Jan Hajny, Lukas Malina, Zdenek Martinasek, and Ondrej Tethal

Practical Packing Method in Somewhat Homomorphic Encryption 34
  Masaya Yasuda, Takeshi Shimoyama, Jun Kogure,
  Kazuhiro Yokoyama, and Takeshi Koshiba

Collaborative and Privacy-Aware Sensing for Observing Urban Movement
Patterns 51
  Nelson Gonçalves, Rui José, and Carlos Baquero

Parallel Implementation of GC-Based MPC Protocols
in the Semi-Honest Setting 66
  Mauro Barni, Massimo Bernaschi, Riccardo Lazzeretti,
  Tommaso Pignata, and Alessandro Sabellico

Privacy Analysis of a Hidden Friendship Protocol 83
  Florian Kammüller and Sören Preibusch

Anonymous and Transferable Electronic Ticketing Scheme 100
  Arnau Vives-Guasch, M. Magdalena Payeras-Capellà,
  Macià Mut-Puigserver, Jordi Castellà-Roca, and Josep-Lluís Ferrer-Gomila

Privacy-Preserving Publish/Subscribe: Efficient Protocols
in a Distributed Model 114
  Giovanni Di Crescenzo, Brian Coan, John Schultz, Simon Tsang,
  and Rebecca N. Wright

Privacy-Preserving Processing of Raw Genomic Data 133
  Erman Ayday, Jean Louis Raisaro, Urs Hengartner, Adam Molyneaux,
  and Jean-Pierre Hubaux

Using Search Results to Microaggregate Query Logs Semantically 148
  Arnau Erola and Jordi Castellà-Roca

Legal Issues About Metadata Data Privacy vs Information Security   162
Manuel Munier, Vincent Lalanne, Pierre-Yves Ardoy, and Magali Ricarde

Privacy-Preserving Multi-Party Reconciliation Secure in the Malicious Model . . .   178
Georg Neugebauer, Lucas Brutschy, Ulrike Meyer, and Susanne Wetzel

Differentially Private Smart Metering with Battery Recharging   194
Michael Backes and Sebastian Meiser

AppGuard – Fine-Grained Policy Enforcement for Untrusted Android
Applications.   213
*Michael Backes, Sebastian Gerling, Christian Hammer, Matteo Maffei,
and Philipp von Styp-Rekowsky*

Autonomous and Spontaneous Security

Reference Monitors for Security and Interoperability in OAuth 2.0.   235
*Ronan-Alexandre Cherrueau, Rémi Douence, Jean-Claude Royer,
Mario Südholt, Anderson Santana de Oliveira, Yves Roudier,
and Matteo Dell'Amico*

Remote Biometrics for Robust Persistent Authentication   250
Mads I. Ingwar and Christian D. Jensen

Classifying Android Malware through Subgraph Mining   268
Fabio Martinelli, Andrea Saracino, and Daniele Sgandurra

Introducing Probabilities in Contract-Based Approaches
for Mobile Application Security   284
*Gianluca Dini, Fabio Martinelli, Ilaria Matteucci, Andrea Saracino,
and Daniele Sgandurra*

Advanced Detection Tool for PDF Threats   300
Quentin Jerome, Samuel Marchal, Radu State, and Thomas Engel

Enforcing Input Validation through Aspect Oriented Programming.   316
Gabriel Serme, Theodoor Scholte, and Anderson Santana de Oliveira

Lightweight Cryptography for Embedded Systems – A Comparative
Analysis   333
*Charalampos Manifavas, George Hatzivasilis, Konstantinos Fysarakis,
and Konstantinos Rantos*

Short Papers

A Simulation of Document Detection Methods and Reducing False Positives
for Private Stream Searching   353
Michael Oehler and Dhananjay S. Phatak

Dynamic Anonymous Index for Confidential Data   362
   Guillermo Navarro-Arribas, Daniel Abril, and Vicenç Torra

Are On-Line Personae Really Unlinkable?.   369
   Meilof Veeningen, Antonio Piepoli, and Nicola Zannone

On the Privacy of Private Browsing – A Forensic Approach   380
   Kiavash Satvat, Matthew Forshaw, Feng Hao, and Ehsan Toreini

Privacy-Preserving Trust Management Mechanisms from Private Matching
Schemes   390
   Oriol Farràs, Josep Domingo-Ferrer, and Alberto Blanco-Justicia

Author Index   399

Keynote Address

Quantifying and Measuring Anonymity

Steven J. Murdoch[✉]

University of Cambridge Computer Laboratory, Cambridge, UK
Steven.Murdoch@cl.cam.ac.uk
http://www.cl.cam.ac.uk/~sjm217/

Abstract. The design of anonymous communication systems is a relatively new field, but the desire to quantify the security these systems offer has been an important topic of research since its beginning. In recent years, anonymous communication systems have evolved from obscure tools used by specialists to mass-market software used by millions of people. In many cases the users of these tools are depending on the anonymity offered to protect their liberty, or more. As such, it is of critical importance that not only can we quantify the anonymity these tools offer, but that the metrics used represent realistic expectations, can be communicated clearly, and the implementations actually offer the anonymity they promise. This paper will discuss how metrics, and the techniques used to measure them, have been developed for anonymous communication tools including low-latency networks and high-latency email systems.

1 Introduction

Anonymous communication systems seek to hide patterns visible in communications to obscure relationships between people and the activities they carry out, typically over the Internet. Such systems have become increasingly popular as a result of the Internet developing into an important tool in the support and promotion of human rights. Examples of uses include the publication of videos showing human rights abuses, journalists soliciting information on government corruption, and law enforcement agencies monitoring websites operated by organized crime.

In all these examples there are motivated individuals who would want to discover the identity of the users of the anonymous communication system. Therefore it is of critical importance that the level of protection that the anonymous communication system provides is well understood. Overestimating the level might result in users putting themselves at unacceptable amounts of risk; underestimating the level might result in users avoiding using a system unnecessarily.

The task of measuring the level of anonymity offered by anonymous communication tools is challenging particularly because of the narrow safety margins which they necessarily offer. A system operating perfectly can only hide the real sender or receiver of a message within the ranks of the users of that system. An attacker who wants to de-anonymise a user can often also take into account

J. Garcia-Alfaro et al. (Eds.): DPM 2013 and SETOP 2013, LNCS 8247, pp. 3–13, 2014.
DOI: 10.1007/978-3-642-54568-9_1, © Springer-Verlag Berlin Heidelberg 2014

auxiliary information collected through means other than monitoring the anonymous communication system.

For example, suppose a company discovers that a whistleblower has leaked documents, sent through an anonymous communication system, proving that management have authorised the bribing of government officials. If that anonymous communication system only had a million users that day, then there are at most a million candidates for who leaked the document. Intersecting the set of users of the system with the set of people who had access to the documents in question might leave only a handful of possibilities. Even a small amount of information disclosed by the anonymous communication system could leave the whistleblower singled out.

In contrast, encryption systems draw their strength from the large number of possible keys that could have been used to encrypt the information – far more than the number of users of the system. Adding to the key length imposes a linear cost to users of the system but increases the time needed to attack the system exponentially. As a result, modern encryption systems have a very large safety margin and so even serious weaknesses in encryption algorithms rarely have a practical effect on their security.

Therefore research on anonymous communication systems has focussed on improving security through increasing their number of users and decreasing the information disclosed to an observer. However, achieving either of these goals typically comes at a significant cost to users by reducing network capacity. As a result, it is not feasible to achieve the same safety margins that encryption systems offer and so it is important to develop ways to accurately measure the level of protection offered by anonymous communication systems. Then appropriate design choices can be made to provide the right trade-off between performance and security.

2   Email Mixes

One of the early applications of anonymous communication technology was to email. In a scheme proposed by Chaum [2] a user selects one or more "mixes" as a path through which his message should be sent. Messages are encrypted by a sender under multiple layers of public-key encryption (Fig. 1). Outside each layer of encryption is the address of the next mix, which allows messages to be routed. This mix can remove the next layer of encryption, and will find the address of the next mix in the path to which the message should be sent. Once the message reaches the last mix in the path, the plaintext of the message will be available along with the address of the ultimate destination of the message.

Each mix will see the immediate source of the message and the immediate destination. Therefore the first mix will know the sender's address but not the recipient's, and the last mix will know the recipient's address, but not the sender's. Similarly, someone observing messages flowing through the network will not be able to match incoming messages to outgoing messages based on the content because a decryption operation is carried out at each step which only

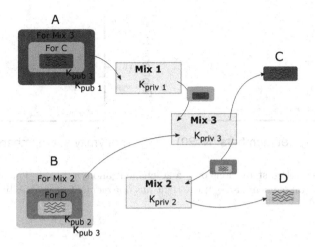

Fig. 1. A two-hop mix network. A is sending a message to C, via Mix 1 then Mix 3. B is sending a message to D via Mix 3 then Mix 2

a specific mix has the private key necessary to perform, and message lengths are fixed. Messages are also delayed at each mix, for a random period of time or until a particular number of messages have been received by a mix (or some combination of these) so as to complicate matching based on the time messages are sent and received.

In this way, the email mix network provides "unlinkability" [6] to messages because the attacker should not be able to link which messages entering the mix network correspond to which messages leaving the mix network. The mix network can also be seen to offer anonymity to its users – for each message leaving the network it should not be possible to establish its sender and for each message entering the network it should not be possible to establish its recipient. An attacker does however know a list of possible candidate senders for each message which leaves the network – the "sender anonymity set". Similarly there is a "recipient anonymity set" for each message sent.

2.1 Measuring Anonymity

Much of the research on email mixes has focussed on how to quantify the anonymity provided. Berthold et al. [1] proposed to simply count the size ("cardinality") of the anonymity set: a larger list of candidates for the true sender or receiver corresponds to better anonymity. By taking the logarithm of the set size, base 2, this quantity can be expressed in bits. An ideal anonymous communication system will have an anonymity set size of the number of users and the probability of each user being the sender or recipient of a particular message will be equal. Looking at the anonymity set as a probability distribution over possible senders/receivers of a message, the ideal anonymous communication system produces the uniform distribution.

6   S.J. Murdoch

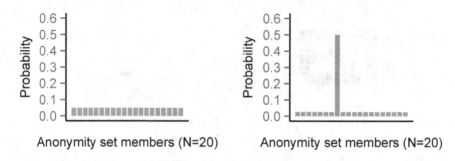

Fig. 2. Two possible distributions over a 20-element anonymity set. The left distribution is uniform (all elements at $\frac{1}{20}$); the right has one element at probability $\frac{1}{2}$ and the others at $\frac{1}{38}$

However real anonymous communication systems will not achieve this ideal. It is typically possible to distinguish senders from recipients by observing the direction of flow of data. Also by taking into account that it will be unlikely (for usability reasons) that mixes will delay messages for a long period of time, not every possible sender/recipient will be equally likely the true sender/recipient. In an extreme case an attacker may know that a single user may almost certainly be the sender of a message yet based on cardinality this system is indistinguishable from an ideal one of the same size, as shown in Fig. 2.

For this reason, other proposed metrics take into account the unevenness of the probability distribution. One such metric is the "degree of anonymity" proposed by Reiter et al. [7]. Although originally developed for analysing a system for anonymising web traffic it can equally be applied to email mixes. The 6 point scale is described in Table 1.

The degree of anonymity metric differentiates between the two anonymity set distributions of Fig. 2. The left graph shows that users are beyond suspicion whereas the right is barely probable innocence. For all reasonable purposes, the left graph corresponds to a better system so taking into account the unevenness of the distribution has produced a better metric, but ignoring the cardinality of the set has a weakness too.

For example, an anonymity set probability distribution over 101 senders, with the most likely sender having probability 0.01 and others probability 0.0099 offers possible innocence. Whereas an uniform anonymity set probability distribution over 4 senders has each sender assigned a probability of 0.25. Although the latter system has a better degree of anonymity, the probability of an attacker successfully identifying a user is much higher than the former.

It therefore follows that both cardinality and unevenness of distribution should be taken into account, and so Shannon entropy was proposed as a metric by Serjantov and Danezis [8]. Here, if the probability that user i was the true sender is p_i, and there are N members of the anonymity set, then the entropy

Table 1. The 6-point degree of anonymity scale

	Degree	Attacker observation
Best anonymity	Absolute privacy	No evidence whether or not a sender sent any message
	Beyond suspicion	A sender sent a message, but all senders are equally likely to have sent any message
	Probable innocence	A sender is no more likely to have been the originator of a message than to not have been
	Possible innocence	A sender has a nontrivial probability of not being the originator of a message
	Exposed	The originator has been identified
Worst anonymity	Provably exposed	The originator has been identified and the identity can be proven to others

of the anonymity set S is:

$$H(S) = -\sum_{i=1}^{N} p_i \log_2 (p_i)$$

For the probability distributions in Fig. 2, the left distribution has entropy ≈ 4.32 bits (the same as the cardinality, in bits – $\log_2(20)$), but the right distribution only has entropy ≈ 3.12. The anonymity set discussed above, of 101 senders with one at probability 0.01 and others at 0.0099, gives entropy 6.66 bits (only $10^{-5}\%$ less than the entropy of the uniform distribution over 101 senders). Whereas the uniform distribution over 4 senders is 2. We can see that entropy takes into account both cardinality and unevenness, and also gives similar values to similar distributions, but it is still possible to find examples which raise the question of whether entropy is the best metric.

For example, in Fig. 3 the two very different distributions have the same entropy. However, from the perspective of an attacker the anonymity might be very different. The de-anonymisation of communications is seldom used as an end in itself, but rather to guide further investigation. An attacker analysing the left distribution would need to investigate 10 senders before getting a 50 % probability of having found the right sender. In contrast the attacker could achieve the same goal with the right distribution after trying only one user.

One way of differentiating between the two distributions is to note that the number of users is rarely under direct control of the system designer so a reasonable metric could examine the ratio between the security of the ideal system for a given user base to the actual security achieved for the same user base. This metric was proposed as the "degree of anonymity" by Diaz et al. [3], but to differentiate from the Crowds degree in Table 1 we will use the term "nor-

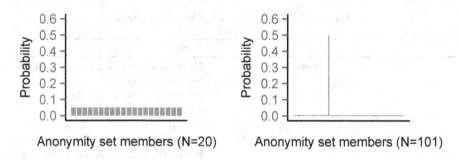

Fig. 3. Two possible distributions. The left graph is the same as in Fig. 2 – the uniform distribution over 20 senders. The right diagram is a probability distribution over 101 senders, with one having probability $\frac{1}{2}$ and the others having probability $\frac{1}{200}$. Both have entropy $\log_2(20) \approx 4.32$

malized entropy" to refer to the Diaz degree. Where H(S) is the entropy of the anonymity set S and N is the cardinality of the anonymity set, the normalized entropy is defined as:

$$d(S) = \frac{\mathrm{H}(S)}{\log_2(N)}$$

However, even when the sizes and entropy of the anonymity sets are the same there may be questions as to which distribution is better. For example, the two distributions in Fig. 4 have the same entropy (≈ 3.12) and cardinality (20) and therefore the same normalized entropy. They also have the same degree of anonymity – probable innocence. The left distribution has one sender at probability $\frac{1}{20}$ and the other 19 at $\frac{1}{38}$. The right distribution has 5 senders at probability $\frac{a}{5}$ and the other 15 at $\frac{1-a}{15}$ where $a \approx 0.86$ is the solution to the equation defined by Tóth et al. [9]:

$$a \log_2\left(\frac{a}{5}\right) + (1-a) \log_2\left(\frac{1-a}{15}\right) = \frac{\log_2\left(\frac{1}{2}\right)}{2} + \frac{19 \log_2\left(\frac{1}{38}\right)}{38}$$

Considering an attacker able to investigate one possible sender, the left distribution is worse for privacy, with a 50 % chance that the attacker will succeed compared to 17.2 % for the right. On the other hand an attacker able to investigate 5 senders will succeed in the left distribution with probability 61 % but 86 % with the right distribution. Tóth et al. [9] proposed using min-entropy – $- \log_2\left(\max_i p_i\right)$ to quantify the minimum security achieved by any user, which matches the effective security in the case of an attacker able to investigate one sender. Under this metric the left distribution gives 1 bit and the right gives ≈ 2.54 bits.

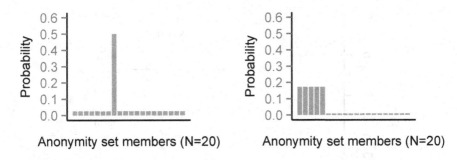

Fig. 4. Two possible distributions, with identical cardinality ($\approx$ 4.32 bits), entropy ($\approx$ 3.12 bits) and normalized entropy ($\approx$ 0.72)

In fact, cardinality, entropy and min-entropy are all special cases of Rényi entropy, for $\alpha = 0$, $\alpha \rightarrow 1$ and $\alpha \rightarrow \infty$ respectively where:

$$\mathrm{H}_\alpha(S) = \frac{1}{1-\alpha} \log_2 \left(\sum_{i=1}^{N} p_i^{\,\alpha} \right)$$

Figure 5 shows $\mathrm{H}_\alpha(S)$ over a range of α for the anonymity set distributions in Figs. 3 and 4. As expected, cardinality depends only on the number of senders and min-entropy depends only on the probability of the most-likely sender. For many values of α there can be a conceivable model of the attacker in which the $\mathrm{H}_\alpha(S)$ will make sense as a metric for anonymity. For example H_0 will be the number of questions that the attacker needs to ask if a question can eliminate half of the candidates; $\mathrm{H}_{\rightarrow 1}$ will be the same if the attacker can choose questions which will eliminate an arbitrary subset of the anonymity set. $\mathrm{H}_{\rightarrow \infty}$ represents the security if the attacker can investigate one user.

3   Low-Latency Anonymous Communication Systems

As we have seen above, metrics implicitly define a threat model in terms of the attacker's strategy. Measuring the security of a network according to a metric also requires defining the attacker's capabilities. For email mixes the attacker capability commonly assumed is "global-passive" – the attacker can monitor the entire network but cannot interfere with network traffic nor view the internal processing of any mix. There is debate as to whether this is appropriate as few attackers can monitor the entire Internet, and computer security is not good enough to ensure that email mixes are not compromised. However where the global-passive model fails is the analysis of low-latency general-purpose anonymous communication system.

The leading low-latency anonymous communication system is Tor [4]. It is capable of anonymising any TCP-based protocol, and it introduces very low levels of delay compared to email mixes (milliseconds rather than days). It therefore has much wider applicability and so has far more users than any email mix. Users

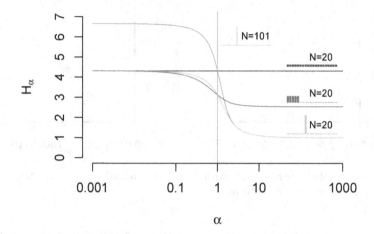

Fig. 5. Rényi entropy for four anonymity set distributions for a range of α

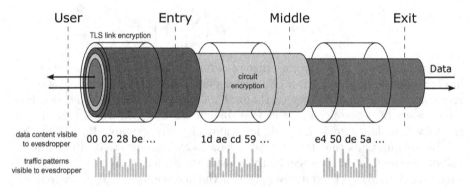

Fig. 6. Use of encryption in Tor. Telescoping circuit encryption shares keys between the user and each of the nodes in the circuit. On top of the circuit encryption, TLS authenticated encryption is performed on a link basis. Together, the circuit and link encryption ensure that incoming and outgoing traffic on a node cannot be linked based on content, but it may be linkable based on timing patterns

send traffic through the network by building a "circuit" through 1 or more (usually 3) Tor nodes, with nested layers of symmetric encryption, to fulfil a similar purpose as the nested public-key encryption of email mixes. Symmetric keys are negotiated with authenticated Diffie-Hellman key agreement. On top of the circuit-level encryption, TLS tunnels are maintained between each pair of Tor nodes which are exchanging traffic.

Figure 6 shows how encryption is performed in Tor. Unlike email mixes however, Tor does not attempt to make all messages the same length as others. This is because TCP network traffic is highly variable and maintaining a constant rate of traffic would either dramatically reduce the maximum bandwidth of the network or add a massive amount of overhead. Therefore, like any other proposed low-latency general-purpose anonymous communication system, an attacker monitoring the entire Internet would be able to correlate network connections entering and leaving the network.

Since analysing a low-latency anonymous communication network under the global-passive model leads to the conclusion that any system is insecure, metrics assuming the global-passive model do not help guide the design of low-latency anonymous communication systems intended to defend against other threat models. It is therefore advantageous to directly measure the probability that the user's security will be compromised, under the assumptions of the actual attackers' capabilities, rather than using proxies for this probability such as the various types of entropy.

This is the approach used by Murdoch and Watson [5] to analyse the security of Tor directly, against an adversary who wishes to insert malicious nodes into the network so as to de-anonymize users. The goal of this analysis was to discover which of proposed schemes, for selecting Tor nodes in a circuit, is more secure. One candidate scheme was to select from nodes uniformly at random and another is that a user would select nodes with a probability weighted proportional to how much bandwidth that node has available. While the uniform selection had a higher entropy, the bandwidth-weighted scheme had better security.

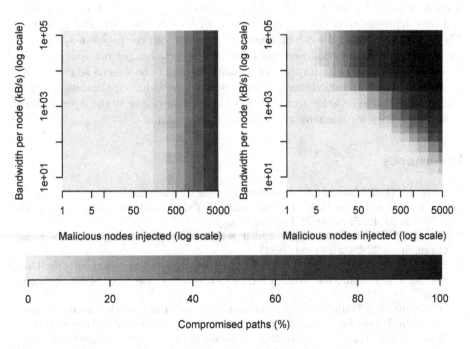

Fig. 7. Probability of path compromise for two different circuit selection algorithms – uniform on left and bandwidth weighted on right

The result can be seen in Fig. 7. In these figures, each point shows a particular attacker strategy in terms of the number of malicious nodes added and the bandwidth given to each node. The colour shows what proportion of circuits will be compromised as a result. The attacker capabilities are represented as a line on the graph, showing what is the maximum investment possible: in this case the attacker has a bandwidth budget of 100 MB/s and can distribute this over a small number of high-bandwidth nodes or a large number of low-bandwidth nodes. The left graph shows the uniform-selection scenario, where the optimum attacker strategy will be to have a large number of low-bandwidth nodes resulting in 80 % of circuits compromised. In contrast, the right shows the bandwidth weighted scenario where no matter how the attacker allocates resources, no more than 20 % of circuits will be compromised.

4   Conclusions

The above examples have shown a few examples from the wide variety of metrics for anonymous communication networks. These range from the discrete levels of the anonymity degree through various types of entropy then to directly quantifying the probability of user compromise. Each has their own advantages in terms of how easy they are to calculate for a given system, how simple a summary they provide, how versatile they are in terms of possible attacker models, and how representative the measurement is of the practical security provided. The narrow safety margins which necessarily follow from the problem-space that anonymous communication systems exist in poses challenges not only for system design but also quantification of security. Some of the lessons learnt by the anonymous communication community may be more widely applicable, and it is likely that much knowledge from other fields can contribute to the development of better metrics for anonymous communication systems.

References

1. Berthold, O., Pfitzmann, A., Standtke, R.: The disadvantages of free MIX routes and how to overcome them. In: Federrath, H. (ed.) Anonymity 2000. LNCS, vol. 2009, pp. 30–45. Springer, Heidelberg (2001)
2. Chaum, D.: Untraceable electronic mail, return addresses, and digital pseudonyms. Commun. ACM **24**(2), 84–90 (1981)
3. Díaz, C., Seys, S., Claessens, J., Preneel, B.: Towards measuring anonymity. In: Dingledine, R., Syverson, P.F. (eds.) PET 2002. LNCS, vol. 2482, pp. 54–68. Springer, Heidelberg (2003)
4. Dingledine, R., Mathewson, N., Syverson, P.: Tor: the second-generation onion router. In: Proceedings of the 13th USENIX Security Symposium (August 2004)
5. Murdoch, S.J., Watson, R.N.M.: Metrics for security and performance in low-latency anonymity systems. In: Borisov, N., Goldberg, I. (eds.) PETS 2008. LNCS, vol. 5134, pp. 115–132. Springer, Heidelberg (2008)

6. Pfitzmann, A., Hansen, M.: A terminology for talking about privacy by data minimization: anonymity, unlinkability, undetectability, unobservability, pseudonymity, and identity management (Aug 2010), http://dud.inf.tu-dresden.de/literatur/Anon_Terminology_v0.34.pdf, v0.34
7. Reiter, M., Rubin, A.: Crowds: anonymity for web transactions. ACM Trans. Inf. Syst. Secur. 1(1), 66–92 (1998)
8. Serjantov, A., Danezis, G.: Towards an information theoretic metric for anonymity. In: Dingledine, R., Syverson, P.F. (eds.) PET 2002. LNCS, vol. 2482, pp. 41–53. Springer, Heidelberg (2003)
9. Tóth, G., Hornák, Z., Vajda, F.: Measuring anonymity revisited. In: Liimatainen, S., Virtanen, T. (eds.) Proceedings of the Ninth Nordic Workshop on Secure IT Systems. pp. 85–90 (November 2004)

Data Privacy Management

Performance Evaluation of Primitives for Privacy-Enhancing Cryptography on Current Smart-Cards and Smart-Phones

Jan Hajny[1]([⊠]), Lukas Malina[1], Zdenek Martinasek[1], and Ondrej Tethal[2]

[1] Cryptology Research Group, Department of Telecommunications,
Brno University of Technology, Brno, Czech Republic
{hajny,crypto}@feec.vutbr.cz
http://crypto.utko.feec.vutbr.cz
[2] OKsystem, Prague, Czech Republic
tethal@oksystem.cz

Abstract. The paper deals with the implementation and benchmarking of cryptographic primitives on contemporary smart-cards and smart-phones. The goal of the paper is to analyze the demands of today's common theoretical cryptographic constructions used in privacy-enhancing schemes and to find out whether they can be practically implemented on off-the-shelf hardware. We evaluate the performance of all major platforms of programmable smart-cards (JavaCards, .NET cards and MultOS cards) and three reference Android devices (a tablet and two smart-phones). The fundamental cryptographic primitives frequently used in advanced cryptographic constructions, such as user-centric attribute-based protocols and anonymous credential systems, are evaluated. In addition, we show how our results can be used for the estimation of the performance of existing and future cryptographic protocols. Therefore, we provide not only benchmarks of all modern programmable smart-card platforms but also a tool for the performance estimation of privacy-enhancing schemes which are based on popular zero-knowledge proof of knowledge protocols.

Keywords: Cryptography · Privacy · Benchmark · Primitives · Proof of knowledge protocols · Smart-cards · Smart-phones

1 Introduction

With the increasing number and complexity of electronic services and transactions, the role of cryptography becomes more and more important. While the classical cryptographic algorithms for ensuring data confidentiality, authenticity and integrity are mostly well analyzed [1,2], the modern cryptographic primitives which are used as the building blocks of many advanced privacy-enhancing schemes remain theoretical and without any evaluation on real-world devices. Therefore, the goal of this paper is to identify the most frequent cryptographic primitives, which are being used in, e.g., digital identity protection

J. Garcia-Alfaro et al. (Eds.): DPM 2013 and SETOP 2013, LNCS 8247, pp. 17–33, 2014.
DOI: 10.1007/978-3-642-54568-9_2, © Springer-Verlag Berlin Heidelberg 2014

schemes, attribute-based authentication schemes and credential schemes, and analyze these primitives on commercially available devices.

For our benchmarks, we chose mobile and personal devices. The reason is that these devices are becoming the most popular ones for personal electronic transactions. For user authentication, eIDs and access control, the smart-cards are already the most preferred devices. For Internet transactions, the mobile phones and tablets are becoming the best choice for many users today. Thus, we chose smart-cards, mobile phones and tablets as the platforms for our benchmarks. We ran the benchmarks on all major programmable smart-card platforms, namely on JavaCards [3], .NET cards [4] and MultOS cards [5]. We chose Android as the platform for the smart-phone and tablet benchmarks because Android, together with Apple iOS, is the preferred operating system for mobile devices worldwide [6].

1.1 Related Work

We consider classical cryptographic constructions, such as RSA signatures, DSA signatures, hashes and symmetric block ciphers, to be well analyzed according to their speed on low-performance devices. A complex analysis of modern symmetric encryption algorithms is provided in [1]. Here, a selection of 12 block ciphers is evaluated on 8-bit microcontrollers. Furthermore, the paper [2] deals with the benchmarking of modern hash functions. A selection of 15 hashes (some of them in more versions) was evaluated on 8-bit microcontrollers. These rigorous benchmarks can be taken as a rich source of information when implementing the classical cryptographic systems.

On the other hand, there is a lack of information when someone needs to implement advanced privacy-enhancing schemes which employ provably secure protocols such as Σ-protocols [7], proof of knowledge (PK) protocols [8] or cryptographic commitments [9]. In fact, there are many theoretical cryptographic schemes which use these constructions without any analysis of implementability. The most well-known examples are group signature schemes [10], verifiable encryption schemes [11], anonymous credential systems [12] and Vehicular Ad-hoc Networks (VANETs). Unfortunately, only little information about the performance of these protocols can be inferred from the implementation papers [14,15]. These papers usually provide information about the overall performance of the schemes, but little about the performance of the building blocks used. Other papers [13,16] present only partial information. Since the building blocks are usually shared among many privacy-enhancing schemes, the information about their performance would be very useful for the evaluation of many unimplemented schemes and newly emerging theoretical constructions.

1.2 Our Contribution

In this paper, we provide benchmarks of selected cryptographic primitives on all major smart-card platforms and three Android devices. We chose the cryptographic primitives which are commonly used in modern privacy-enhancing schemes and which have not been evaluated on resource-limited devices yet. These primitives are described in Sect. 2. The testing environment is described in Sect. 3. The actual benchmarks are included in Sect. 4. Finally, short analysis of results and the examples of how to use our results for the performance estimation of novel schemes is provided in Sects. 4.3 and 4.4.

2   Cryptographic Constructions

We briefly introduce the cryptographic constructions selected for benchmarking in this section. We chose the constructions and protocols which are often used in privacy-enhancing schemes. These constructions work as the building blocks and are modularly used in many today's schemes (such as IBM's Idemix [17], Microsoft's U-Prove [18], HM12 [19], etc.). These and similar schemes are further used in many privacy-enhancing applications (such as access control services, inter-vehicular communication, electronic IDs, e-cash) whose description is out of scope of this paper.

2.1   Classical Algorithms

We call well-known cryptographic algorithms, such as block ciphers, digital signatures and hash functions, the classical algorithms. These algorithms are usually provided directly by the API (Application Programming Interface) of almost all smart-cards and smart-phones. The examples of most common classical algorithms are DES [20], 3DES, AES [21] block ciphers and RSA [22], DSA [23] digital signatures and MD5 [24], SHA-1, SHA-2 [25] hash functions.

2.2   Commitment Schemes

A cryptographic commitment scheme can be used in scenarios where a user is required to bind to a number (e.g., a secret key) without disclosing it. There are two properties which must be fulfilled. They are the *hiding property* and the *binding property*.

- **Hiding property**: it is difficult[1] to learn the secret number from the knowledge of the commitment.
- **Binding property**: once committed to a number, the user cannot change it without changing the commitment.

Discrete Logarithm Commitment Scheme. Mostly, the DL commitment scheme works with the subgroup $\mathbb{Z}_q^*$ of a multiplicative group $\mathbb{Z}_p^*$. The subgroup $\mathbb{Z}_q^*$ is defined by a generator g of order q in $\mod p$, where q and p are large primes and q divides $p - 1$. The same group is used in the Digital Signature Algorithm (DSA) [23]. Numbers g, q, p are system parameters which are made public. To commit to a number $w < q$, a user computes $c = g^w \mod p$. The user can later decide to open the commitment by making w public.

---

[1] It is either impossible or computationally unfeasible.

Pedersen Commitment Scheme. The systems parameters g, q, p, used in the DL commitment scheme, can be also used in the Pedersen scheme [9]. Additionally, one more generator h is used. It is important that $\log_g h \bmod p$ is unknown to the user. The commitment to a secret number w is computed as $c = g^w h^r \bmod p$ where r is a random number smaller than q chosen by the user. The user can later decide to open the commitment by making (w, r) public.

2.3 Proof of Knowledge of Discrete Logarithm Protocols

The proof of knowledge (PK) protocols can be used by a Prover to give a proof of knowledge of discrete logarithm $(PKDL)$. Using the proof of knowledge protocol, the Prover is able to convince a Verifier that he knows $w = \log_g c \bmod p$ from the aforementioned DL commitment without actually disclosing the secret value w. In the CS notation [8], which we use throughout the paper, the protocol is denoted as $PK\{w : c = g^w \bmod p\}$. The most used practical $PKDL$ protocol for general groups, called Schnorr protocol [26], is recalled in Fig. 15 in Appendix.

2.4 Proof of Discrete Logarithm Equivalence

Using the proof of knowledge protocols, it is easy to give a proof that two different DL commitments c_1, c_2 were constructed using the same exponent w, so that $w = \log_{g_1} c_1 = \log_{g_2} c_2 \bmod p$. For this type of proof, the proof of discrete logarithm equivalence $(PDLE)$ protocols can be used. The protocol is then denoted as $PK\{w : c_1 = g_1^w \bmod p \wedge c_2 = g_2^w \bmod p\}$. A practical example based on the Schnorr protocol is recalled in Fig. 16 in Appendix.

2.5 Signatures and Other Derived PK Protocols

In the last three sections, we introduced simple cryptographic primitives which are very often used as the building blocks in more advanced schemes. In our examples, we described very simple protocols only. Nevertheless, these protocols can be modularly combined in much more complex systems. For example, the proof of knowledge protocols can be adapted to the proofs of knowledge of DL representation of a public value c with respect to multiple generators $g_1, g_2, \ldots, g_i$. Such a protocol is described in CS notation as $PK\{(w_1, w_2, \ldots, w_i) : c = g_1^{w_1} g_2^{w_2} \ldots g_i^{w_i} \bmod p\}$. Also, PK protocols can be used for proving the knowledge and equivalence of discrete logarithms of different representations. The protocol $PK\{(w_1, w_3) : c_1 = g_1^{w_1} g_2^{w_2} g_3^{w_3} \wedge c_2 = g_1^{w_2} g_3^{w_3} \bmod p\}$ is a simple example in CS notation. The number of possible variations is unlimited. The work [8] can be taken as a fundamental reference for the construction of PK protocols.

By using the Fiat-Shamir heuristic [27], all the PK protocols can run non-interactively. Then, a hash $\mathcal{H}$ of all protocol parameters is used. All protocols shown in the Appendix are non-interactive. This adaptation leads to signature schemes. By taking our simple $PKDL$ protocol from Sect. 2, we can get a digital signature protocol where w works as a private key. The protocol uses a hash function $\mathcal{H}$ of the message and all protocol parameters. For reference, the signature proof of knowledge protocol (SPK) is depicted in Fig. 17 in Appendix. All PK protocols can be easily adapted to signatures using this approach [27].

In previous sections, we considered only examples based on the simple DSA group [23]. But also different groups can be used in PK protocols (e.g., RSA group [22], Okamoto-Uchiyama (OU) group [28], etc.). Still, the atomic operations of these protocols remain the same. Namely, modular arithmetic, random number generation and hash functions are used. That is the reason why we implemented these atomic operations in our benchmarks. Based on their performance, we can compute the actual performance of PK protocols and subsequently the performance of advanced systems based on PK protocols.

3   Selected Devices and Benchmark Settings

This chapter contains the information about the benchmark settings and about the software/hardware we used.

3.1   Selected Devices

The evaluation of cryptographic primitives was carried out using all major smart-card platforms, namely JavaCards [3], .NET cards [4] and MultOS cards [5]. Furthermore, we implemented the benchmark tests on the Android platform, namely on Android smart-phones and an Android tablet.

JavaCards. JavaCard platform [3] provides a development and runtime environment for applications (called applets) written in Java. In our benchmarks, we used Oberthur Technologies ID-One Cosmo V7.0-A [29,30] and Gemalto TOP

Table 1. The specification of the JavaCards used in our benchmarks.

	Software specifications	
Card type	Oberthur ID-One V7.0-A	Gemalto TOP IM GX4
Type	JavaCard	JavaCard
Transfer protocol	T=0, T=1	T=0, T=1
Asymmetric crypto	RSA upto 2048, EC upto 521 b	RSA upto 2048 bits
Symmetric crypto	DES, 3DES, AES	3DES, AES
Hash	SHA1, SHA2	SHA1
	Hardware specifications	
Chip	Atmel AT90SC256144RCFT	S3CC9TC
CPU	8/16 bit	16 bit
Internal/External clock	40 MHz/3.4 MHz	Unknown
RAM memory	8 kB	10 kB
ROM/EEPROM	256 kB/144 kB	384 kB/74 kB
Temperature range	−25 °C to +85 °C	−25 °C to +85 °C
Modular arithmetic API	No	No

Table 2. The specification of the .NET cards and the MultOS cards used in bench-marks.

	Software specifications		
OS type	.NET	MultOS	MultOS
Card type	.NET V2+	ML2-80K-65	ML3-36K-R1
Asymmetric crypto	RSA 2048 bits	RSA 2048, EC 384 bits	RSA 2048, EC 512 bits
Symmetric crypto	3DES, AES	DES, 3DES, AES	DES, 3DES, AES
Hash	SHA1, SHA2, MD5	SHA1, SHA2	SHA1, SHA2
	Hardware specifications		
Chip	SLE 88CFX4000P	SLE66CLX800PEM	SLE78CLXxxxPM
CPU	32 bit	16 bit	16 bit
Internal/External clock	66 MHz/10 MHz	30 MHz/7.5 MHz	33 MHz/7.5 MHz
RAM memory	16 kB	702 + 9604 B	1088 + 960 B
ROM/EEPROM	80 kB/400 kB	236 kB/78 kB	280 kB/60 kB
Temperature range	$-25\ °C$ to $+85\ °C$	$-25\ °C$ to $+85\ °C$	$-25\ °C$ to $+85\ °C$
Modular API	No	Yes	Yes

IM GX4 [31] cards. The hardware specification of these cards is described in Table 1.

.NET Smart-Cards. .NET smart-card platform [4] provides very similar features as JavaCards for applications developed using any language of the .NET framework. In our benchmarks, we used the Gemalto .NET V2+ cards. The hardware specification of these cards is described in Table 2.

MultOS Smart-cards. The last smart-card platform we used for benchmarking is the MultOS platform [5]. In comparison to JavaCard and .NET cards, MultOS allows the development of applications in both high level languages (Java and C) and assembly language. This provides developers with much wider opportunities and better access to hardware. In particular, only the MultOS cards allow the direct big-integer modular operations through the default API. The hardware specification of MultOS ML2-80K-65 and ML3-36K-R1 cards is described in Table 2.

Mobile Devices. The Android devices form a different group which is incomparable to smart-cards. While smart-cards are very resource-limited devices with extremely low RAM and slow CPUs, the mobile phones and tablets resemble more classical PCs. They have strong CPUs with frequency over 1 GHz and enough RAM (hundreds of megabytes). Still, these devices are extremely mobile and very popular for personal electronic transactions. Due to this reason, we included them to our benchmarks. The hardware of selected Android devices is described in Table 3.

Table 3. The specification of the Android devices used in our benchmarks.

		Software specifications	
Device type	Samsung Galaxy S i9000	Samsung Galaxy Nexus I9250M	ASUS TF 300T
Android version	v2.1 (Eclair)	v4.0 (ICS)	v4.0 (ICS)
		Hardware specifications	
Chip	Cortex-A8	Dual-core Cortex-A9	Quad-core Cortex-A9
Frequency	1 GHz/45 nm	1.2 GHz/45 nm	1.2 GHz/45 nm
GPU	PowerVR SGX540	PowerVR SGX540	ULP GeForce
RAM memory	512 MB	1024 MB	1024 MB
ROM/Storage	2 GB/8(16) GB	2 / 16 GB	2 GB/16(32) GB

3.2 Measured Operations and Keylengths

In the Sect. 2, we showed the cryptographic commitments and proof of knowledge
protocols. We included only simple examples to illustrate these primitives. Nevertheless, these basic constructions can be modularly compiled into advanced
systems. The discrete logarithm commitments, proof of knowledge of discrete
logarithm protocols and proofs of discrete logarithm equivalence protocols are
the building blocks of many complex modern systems [17–19]. But still, even
the complex systems are based on the same atomic operations as the primitives
selected by us. It can be observed from Sect. 2 that only random number generation, hash functions and big-integer modular arithmetic operations are needed
for all selected protocols. Namely, the following operations are required.

- **RNG - Random Number Generation**: on all platforms and devices, we
  measured the time of generation of large random numbers of length 160 bits
  (**RNG_160** operation) and 560 bits (**RNG_560** operation).

- **Hash Functions**: on all platforms and devices, we measured the time of
  computation of following hash functions.
  - **SHA1_4256**: SHA1 of 4256 bit random data[2]
  - **SHA1_7328**: SHA1 of 7328 bit random data
  - **SHA1_20000**: SHA1 of 20000 bit random data
  - **SHA2_8448**: SHA2 of 8448 bit random data
  - **SHA2_14592**: SHA2 of 14592 bit random data
  - **SHA2_20000**: SHA2 of 20000 bit random data

- **Big-Integer Modular Arithmetic Operations**: it can be observed from
  our cryptographic overview in Sect. 2 that the proof of knowledge protocols
  heavily rely on arithmetic operations in groups where the discrete logarithm
  operation is hard to compute. Namely, modular operations with moduli in
  orders of thousand bits are required. These operations are usually available

---

[2] The size of data hashed reflects the requirements of PK protocols.

on the PC platform in the form of BigInt libraries (such as OpenSSL, Bouncy Castle, etc.). Unfortunately, these libraries are missing on smart-cards. Only the MultOS platform supports direct modular operations. Thus, the following operations were implemented and measured on all selected platforms and devices. The bit-lengths of moduli and operands were selected according to the most popular group sizes in cryptography (1024 and 2048 bit modulus).

- **MExp1024_160:** Modular Exponentiation with 1024 b modulus and 160 b exponent
- **MExp1024_368:** Modular Exponentiation with 1024 b modulus and 368 b exponent
- **MExp2048_160:** Modular Exponentiation with 2048 b modulus and 160 b exponent
- **MExp2048_560:** Modular Exponentiation with 2048 b modulus and 560 b exponent
- **MMult1024:** Modular Multiplication with 1024 b modulus and operands
- **MMult2048:** Modular Multiplication with 2048 b modulus and operands

- **Big-Integer Arithmetic Operations**: additionally to modular operations, some non-modular (plain) big-integer operations were implemented as they are contained in PK protocols which operate in hidden order groups.
  - **Mult320**: Multiplication of two 320 b numbers
  - **Sub400**: Subtraction of two 400 b numbers

Although the above selected bit-length combinations do not include all the variants used in today's cryptographic schemes, they represent a sample which can be further interpolated to get the estimation of other bit-lengths. Thus, an estimate of smart-card performance of any new protocol, which is based on above operations, can be created.

3.3   Benchmark Environment

The hardware selected for our benchmarks is described in Sect. 3. The operations measured on the hardware are listed in the previous Sect. 3.2. We measured the time necessary for the computation of each operation 25 times. We present the arithmetic mean of these values. The resulting time does not include the time of communication with the device (sending inputs and receiving results). The code was implemented by a single person on smart-cards and by a single person on Android devices. Thus, the influence of different programming styles is eliminated. We tried to use the default API of our cards as much as possible. To increase the speed of computation, we used the RSA encryption method to implement modular exponentiation. For many operations (e.g., for modular arithmetic), only some cards, namely those running MultOS, were providing the necessary interface. On the rest, we had to implement our methods.

4   Benchmark Results

We divided our results into a smart-card section and an Android section. The graphs in the next two sections show the time in milliseconds of the operations specified in the Sect. 3.2 above.

4.1   Benchmarks on Smart-card Devices

Figures 1, 2, 3, 4, 5, 6 and 7 show the time in milliseconds of operations specified in captions.

4.2   Benchmarks on Android Mobile Devices

Figures 8, 9, 10, 11, 12, 13 and 14 show the time in milliseconds of operations specified in captions.

4.3   Results Analysis

Smart-Cards. It was possible to implement all required operations on all selected cards with the exception of MultOS ML2-80K-65 card which is lacking the support of SHA2 and 2048 b modular exponentiation. In many operations, the JavaC-

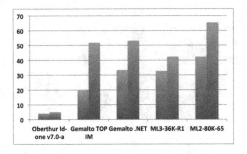

Fig. 1. RNG_160 (blue) and **RNG_560** (red)

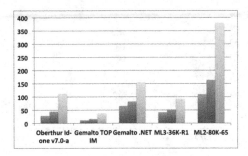

Fig. 2. SHA1_4256 (blue), **SHA1_7328** (red) and **SHA1_20000** (green)

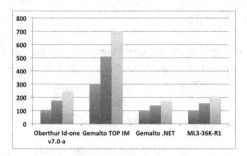

Fig. 3. SHA2_8448 (blue), SHA2_14592 (red) and SHA2_20000 (green)

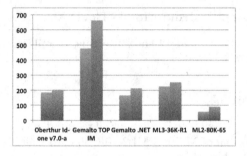

Fig. 4. MExp1024_160 (blue) and MExp1024_368 (red)

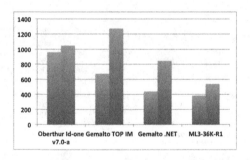

Fig. 5. MExp2048_160 (blue) and MExp2048_560 (red)

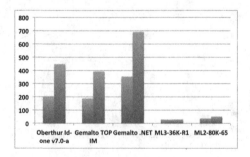

Fig. 6. MMult1024 (blue), MMult2048 (red)

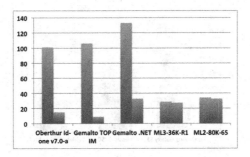

Fig. 7. Mult320 (blue) and Sub400 (red)

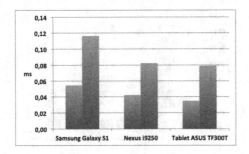

Fig. 8. RNG_160 (blue) and RNG_560 (red)

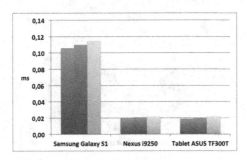

Fig. 9. SHA1_4256 (blue), SHA1_7328 (red) and SHA1_20000 (green)

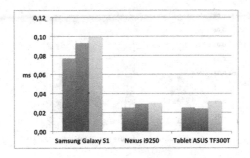

Fig. 10. SHA2_8448 (blue), SHA2_14592 (red) and SHA2_20000 (green)

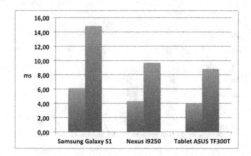

Fig. 11. MExp1024_160 (blue) and MExp1024_368 (red)

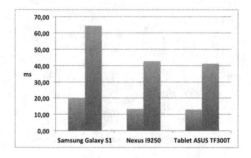

Fig. 12. MExp2048_160 (blue) and MExp2048_560 (red)

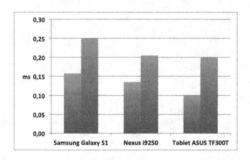

Fig. 13. MMult1024 (blue), MMult2048 (red)

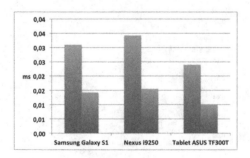

Fig. 14. Mult320 (blue) and Sub400 (red)

ard Oberthur ID-one v7.0a is very fast (in particular, in random number generation and 1024 b modular exponentiation). Often, the bit-length of inputs (cryptographic group size) does play a significant role, for example in the case of modular exponentiation. Thus, we recommend to plan ahead before implementing and
choose the right balance between speed and security (group size). Even with modern smart-cards, operations in 2048 b groups might be too demanding. When implementing complex privacy-enhancing schemes, operations in 2048 b groups would
be probably too slow. Also, a big difference among cards appears when the modular multiplication and non-modular operations are needed. This is the case of
all PK protocols where a group with unknown order is used (such as RSA group
[22], OU group [28]). Then, the MultOS cards are much faster than the rest due to
their direct support of these operations in API, in particular due to their built-in
support of accelerated modular multiplication.

Android Devices. It is no surprise that most operations are several hundred
times faster on Android devices than on smart-cards. All primitives can be
easily implemented on Android. Due to the high performance, we recommend
using larger (and safer) 2048-bit groups and more recent primitives (e.g., SHA-2
instead of SHA-1 or MD5).

4.4   Performance Estimation of Selected Protocols and Schemes

Using the results of our benchmarks, we estimated the theoretical performance of
the protocols introduced in the Sect. 2 and of some well-known privacy-enhancing
schemes like Idemix of IBM [13], U-Prove of Microsoft [18] and HM12 [19]. All
protocols are evaluated using 1024 bit groups and 160 bit secrets. All the scheme
estimates include only the time of operations needed for proving the ownership
of an anonymous token (we use the same approach as in [13]) and do not include
any communication/management overhead. Furthermore, we used the closest
bit-length of inputs. Thus, the numbers in Table 4 should be considered estimates
only.

   We created the estimates using our implementation of atomic operations.
From the knowledge of the construction of the advanced protocols and the knowledge of performance of underlying operations, we were able to predict the performance of protocols. To find out the correctness of our estimates, we compared
our results with existing, real implementations. Since they use smart-cards of different specifications, the comparison is rough only. The IBM's Idemix has been
previously implemented on JavaCards [13]. The proving protocol of the 1280 bit
version took 7.5 s. Our estimates of the 1024 b version are 4.5 and 9.4 s, depending on the concrete type of our JavaCard. The Microsoft's U-Prove scheme has
been implemented on the MultOS platform [5]. The proving protocol took 0.55
s on an unspecified MultOS-family card. Our estimates on our MultOS cards are
0.63 and 0.82 s, depending on the concrete type of the MultOS card. Based on
these results, we consider our estimates highly accurate. Using our benchmarks,
it is possible to easily predict the approximate time of newly designed protocols
or cryptographic schemes.

Table 4. Performance estimation based on benchmarks.

	Time in ms							
	S1	**S2**	**S3**	**S4**	**S5**	**A1**	**A2**	**A3**
$c = g^w$ (DL commitment)	186	476	165	226	58	6	4	4
$c = g^w h^r$ (Pedersen commitment)	580	1161	717	513	195	12	9	8
$PK\{w : c = g^w\}$	325	830	433	352	222	15	10	9
$PK\{w : c_1 = g_1^w \wedge c_2 = g_2^w\}$	529	1494	646	605	313	30	20	18
$SPK\{w : c = g^w\}(m)$	354	842	498	393	332	15	10	9
Idemix	4519	9433	7270	4219	4208	153	100	91
U-Prove	837	1618	1295	827	633	13	9	8
HM12	2540	6016	3312	2509	1467	102	68	62

Glossary:
S1: Oberthur Technologies ID-One Cosmo V7.0-A
S2: Gemalto TOP IM GX4
S3: Gemalto .NET V2+
S4: MultOS ML2-80K-65
S5: MultOS ML3-36K-R1
A1: Samsung Galaxy S i9000 (smart-phone)
A2: Samsung Galaxy Nexus I9250M (smart-phone)
A3: ASUS TF 300T (tablet)

5 Conclusion

In this paper, we provide the performance evaluation of modern cryptographic primitives on smart-cards and mobile devices. In particular, selected atomic operations which are the core of many privacy-enhancing protocols and schemes are implemented on all major programmable smart-card platforms and on the Android platform. The results can be used for the evaluation of many existing and newly appearing schemes. Using the results of implementation of all operations used in PK protocols, it is possible to predict the performance of any protocol or scheme which is composed of DL-based commitments and/or DL-based proof of knowledge protocols. In particular, it is possible to predict the performance of very popular computational zero-knowledge protocols.

Even with the fastest smart-cards on the market, it is quite difficult to achieve reasonable execution times. Though, with the right choice of hardware, in particular, with hardware-accelerated cards, it is possible.

We showed our performance estimates of today's most preferred privacy-enhancing anonymous credential schemes on all 8 devices. When compared to existing implementations, we almost match the real performance when similar hardware is used. Thus, our benchmarks can be used by cryptography designers to easily predict the performance of their protocols and schemes before implementing on smart-cards and Android devices.

Acknowledgment. This research work is funded by projects SIX CZ.1.05/2.1.00/03. 007; the Technology Agency of the Czech Republic projects TA02011260 and TA03010818; the Ministry of Industry and Trade of the Czech Republic project FR-TI4/647.

Appendix

Simple examples of Proof of Knowledge (PK) protocols. All operations are in a group $\mathbb{Z}_p^*$ of order q where discrete logarithm is hard to compute and l_1, l_2 are security parameters. More information about PK protocols in [8].

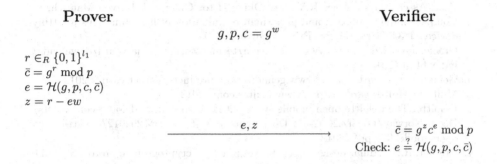

Prover

$r \in_R \{0,1\}^{l_1}$
$\bar{c} = g^r \bmod p$
$e = \mathcal{H}(g, p, c, \bar{c})$
$z = r - ew$

Verifier

$g, p, c = g^w$

$\xrightarrow{\quad e, z \quad}$

$\bar{c} = g^z c^e \bmod p$
Check: $e \overset{?}{=} \mathcal{H}(g, p, c, \bar{c})$

Fig. 15. Schnorr's proof of knowledge of discrete logarithm protocol $PK\{w : c = g^w\}$.

Prover

$r \in_R \{0,1\}^{l_1}$
$\bar{c}_1 = g_1^r \bmod p$
$\bar{c}_2 = g_2^r \bmod p$
$e = \mathcal{H}(g_1, g_2, p, c_1, c_2, \bar{c}_1, \bar{c}_2)$
$z = r - ew$

Verifier

$c_1 = g_1^w, c_2 = g_2^w, g_1, g_2, p$

$\xrightarrow{\quad e, z \quad}$

$\bar{c}_1 = g_1^z c_1^e \bmod p$
$\bar{c}_2 = g_2^z c_2^e \bmod p$
Check: $e \overset{?}{=} \mathcal{H}(g_1, g_2, p, c_1, c_2, \bar{c}_1, \bar{c}_2)$

Fig. 16. Proof of discrete logarithm equivalence $PK\{w : c_1 = g_1^w \wedge c_2 = g_2^w\}$.

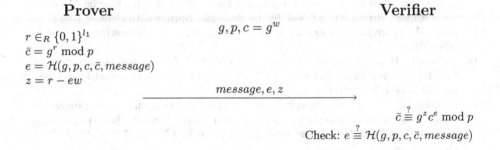

Prover

$r \in_R \{0,1\}^{l_1}$
$\bar{c} = g^r \bmod p$
$e = \mathcal{H}(g, p, c, \bar{c}, message)$
$z = r - ew$

Verifier

$g, p, c = g^w$

$\xrightarrow{\quad message, e, z \quad}$

$\bar{c} \overset{?}{=} g^z c^e \bmod p$
Check: $e \overset{?}{=} \mathcal{H}(g, p, c, \bar{c}, message)$

Fig. 17. Schnorr's signature $SPK\{w : c = g^w\}(message)$.

References

1. Eisenbarth, T., et al.: Compact implementation and performance evaluation of block ciphers in attiny devices. In: Mitrokotsa, A., Vaudenay, S. (eds.) AFRICACRYPT 2012. LNCS, vol. 7374, pp. 172–187. Springer, Heidelberg (2012)
2. Balasch, J., Ege, B., Eisenbarth, T., Gérard, B., Gong, Z., Güneysu, T., Heyse, S., Kerckhof, S., Koeune, F., Plos, T., Pöppelmann, T., Regazzoni, F., Standaert, F.X., Assche, G.V., Keer, R.V., van Oldeneel tot Oldenzeel, L., von Maurich, I.: Compact implementation and performance evaluation of hash functions in attiny devices. IACR Cryptology ePrint Archive (2012)
3. Oracle: Javacard. http://www.oracle.com/technetwork/java/javacard/downloads/index.html (2013)
4. Gemalto: .net card. http://www.gemalto.com/products/dotnet_card/ (2013)
5. MultOS: Multos card. http://www.multos.com (2013)
6. Deloitte: The deloitte open mobile survey 2012. http://www.deloitte.com/assets/Dcom-Norway/Local%20Assets/Documents/Publikasjoner%202012/deloitte_openmobile2012.pdf (2012)
7. Cramer, R.: Modular design of secure, yet practical cryptographic protocols. Ph.D. thesis, University of Amsterdam (1996)
8. Camenisch, J., Stadler, M.: Proof systems for general statements about discrete logarithms. Technical report (1997)
9. Pedersen, T.P.: Non-interactive and information-theoretic secure verifiable secret sharing. In: Feigenbaum, J. (ed.) CRYPTO 1991. LNCS, vol. 576, pp. 129–140. Springer, Heidelberg (1992)
10. Chaum, D., Van Heyst, E.: Group signatures. In: Proceedings of the 10th Annual International Conference on Theory and Application of Cryptographic Techniques, EUROCRYPT'91, pp. 257–265. Springer, Heidelberg (1991)
11. Stadler, M.A., Fujisaki, E., Okamoto, T.: A practical and provably secure scheme for publicly verifiable secret sharing and its applications. In: Nyberg, K. (ed.) EUROCRYPT 1998. LNCS, vol. 1403, pp. 32–46. Springer, Heidelberg (1998)
12. Camenisch, J.L., Lysyanskaya, A.: An efficient system for non-transferable anonymous credentials with optional anonymity revocation. In: Pfitzmann, B. (ed.) EUROCRYPT 2001. LNCS, vol. 2045, p. 93. Springer, Heidelberg (2001)
13. Bichsel, P., Camenisch, J., Groß, T., Shoup, V.: Anonymous credentials on a standard java card. In: Proceedings of the 16th ACM Conference on Computer and Communications Security, CCS '09, pp. 600–610. ACM, New York (2009)
14. Mostowski, W., Vullers, P.: Efficient u-prove implementation for anonymous credentials on smart cards. In: Rajarajan, M., Piper, F., Wang, H., Kesidis, G. (eds.) SecureComm 2011. LNICST, vol. 96, pp. 243–260. Springer, Heidelberg (2012)
15. Hajny, J.: Anonymous authentication for smartcards. Radioengineering 19(2), 363–368 (2010)
16. Malina, L., Hajny, J.: Accelerated modular arithmetic for low-performance devices. In: 34th International Conference on Telecommunications and Signal Processing, pp. 131–135. IEEE (2011)
17. Camenisch, J., et al.: Specification of the identity mixer cryptographic library. Technical report. http://domino.research.ibm.com/library/cyberdig.nsf/1e4115aea78b6e7c85256b360066f0d4/eeb54ff3b91c1d648525759b004fbbb1?OpenDocument (2010)
18. Paquin, C.: U-prove cryptographic specification v1.1. Technical report. http://research.microsoft.com/apps/pubs/default.aspx?id=166969 (2011)

19. Hajny, J., Malina, L.: Unlinkable attribute-based credentials with practical revocation on smart-cards. In: Mangard, S. (ed.) CARDIS 2012. LNCS, vol. 7771, pp. 62–76. Springer, Heidelberg (2013)
20. FIPS: Data encryption standard. In: Federal Information Processing Standards Publication, FIPS PUB 46, 46–2 (1977)
21. FIPS: Advanced encryption standard (aes). In: Federal Information Processing Standards Publication, FIPS PUB 197, pp. 1–47 (2001)
22. Rivest, R., Shamir, A., Adleman, L.: A method for obtaining digital signatures and public-key cryptosystems. Commun. ACM **21**, 120–126 (1978)
23. National Institute of Standards and Technology (U.S.) : Digital Signature Standard (DSS) [electronic resource]. U.S. Deptartment of Commerce, National Institute of Standards and Technology, Gaithersburg (2009)
24. Rivest, R.: The md5 message-digest algorithm. http://www.ietf.org/rfc/rfc1321.txt (1992)
25. FIPS: Secure hash standard (shs) (2012)
26. Schnorr, C.P.: Efficient signature generation by smart cards. J. Cryptol. **4**, 161–174 (1991)
27. Fiat, A., Shamir, A.: How to prove yourself: practical solutions to identification and signature problems. In: Odlyzko, A.M. (ed.) CRYPTO 1986. LNCS, vol. 263, pp. 186–194. Springer, Heidelberg (1987)
28. Okamoto, T., Uchiyama, S.: A new public-key cryptosystem as secure as factoring. In: Nyberg, K. (ed.) EUROCRYPT 1998. LNCS, vol. 1403, pp. 308–318. Springer, Heidelberg (1998)
29. Id-one cosmo v7.0: Technical report, French Network and Information Security Agency (Agence Nationale de la Scurit des Systmes dInformation (ANSSI)). http://www.ssi.gouv.fr/IMG/certificat/anssi-cc-cible_2009-36en.pdf (2009)
30. Atmel: At90sc256144rcft datasheet. http://datasheet.elcodis.com/pdf2/104/7/1040758/at90sc256144rcft.pdf (2007)
31. NIST: Gemxpresso r4 e36/e72 pk—multiapp id 36k/72k—top im gx4. http://csrc.nist.gov/groups/STM/cmvp/documents/140-1/140sp/140sp771.pdf (2009)

Practical Packing Method in Somewhat Homomorphic Encryption

Masaya Yasuda[1](✉), Takeshi Shimoyama[1], Jun Kogure[1],
Kazuhiro Yokoyama[2], and Takeshi Koshiba[3]

[1] Fujitsu Laboratories Ltd., Kamikodanaka 4-chome,
Nakahara-ku, Kawasaki 211-8588, Japan
{yasuda.masaya,shimo-shimo,kogure}@jp.fujitsu.com
[2] Department of Mathematics, Rikkyo University, Nishi-Ikebukuro,
Tokyo 171-8501, Japan
kazuhiro@rikkyo.ac.jp
[3] Division of Mathematics, Electronics and Informatics,
Graduate School of Science and Engineering, Saitama University, 255 Shimo-Okubo,
Sakura, Saitama 338-8570, Japan
koshiba@mail.saitama-u.ac.jp

Abstract. Somewhat homomorphic encryption is public key encryption supporting a limited number of both additions and multiplications on encrypted data, which is useful for performing fundamental computations with protecting the data confidentiality. In this paper, we focus on the scheme proposed by Lauter, Naehrig and Vaikuntanathan (ACM CCSW 2011), and present two types of packed ciphertexts based on their packing technique. Combinations of two types of our packing method give practical size and performance for wider computations such as statistical analysis and distances. To demonstrate its efficiency, we implemented the scheme with our packing method for secure Hamming distance, which is often used in privacy-preserving biometrics. For secure Hamming distance between two binary vekoshiba@mail.saitama-u.ac.jpctors of 2048-bit, it takes 5.31 ms on an Intel Xeon X3480 at 3.07 GHz. This gives the best performance in the state-of-the-art work using homomorphic encryption.

Keywords: Somewhat homomorphic encryption · Ring-LWE assumption · Packed ciphertexts · Secure Hamming distance

1 Introduction

Homomorphic encryption is public key encryption with the additional property that it supports some operations on encrypted data. This gives a useful method in performing meaningful computations with protecting the data privacy. The recent development of cloud storage and computing allows users to outsource their data to cloud services. On the other hand, new privacy concerns for both individuals and business have risen (see [10]). With homomorphic encryption,

J. Garcia-Alfaro et al. (Eds.): DPM 2013 and SETOP 2013, LNCS 8247, pp. 34–50, 2014.
DOI: 10.1007/978-3-642-54568-9_3, © Springer-Verlag Berlin Heidelberg 2014

users send their data in encrypted form to the cloud, and the cloud still can perform computations on encrypted data. Since all data in the cloud are in encrypted form, the confidentiality of users' data is preserved irrespective of any actions in the cloud. Therefore this encryption would give a powerful tool to break several barriers to the adoption of cloud services for various uses.

In cryptography, homomorphic encryption schemes proposed before 2000 can only support simple operations such as either additions or multiplications on encrypted data (see [12,18,26] for examples), and hence the applications of these schemes are very limited (typical applications of additive schemes are electronic voting and cash). The first scheme supporting both additions and multiplications is the BGN scheme [3] proposed in 2005, which is based on pairings on elliptic curves. However, the BGN scheme can handle a number of additions but one-depth multiplications on encrypted data. In 2009, Gentry in [15] proposed a concrete construction for a fully homomorphic encryption (FHE) scheme, which supports arbitrary operations on encrypted data. After Gentry's breakthrough work, a lot of FHE schemes have been proposed (see [6–8,14,15] for examples), and FHE has strongly been expected to be applied to various areas, mainly including cloud computing. However, currently known FHE schemes are impractical (see [11,16,17] for implementation results), and it is believed to need a long way for the use in real life.

In this paper, we focus on somewhat homomorphic encryption (SHE), which is known as a building block for the FHE construction. Although SHE can support only a limited number of both additions and multiplications, it is much faster and more compact than FHE. Therefore SHE can give a practical solution in wide applications, and it is coming to attention to research on applications with SHE schemes (see [22], and also [4] for recent work). However, compared to the other privacy-preserving techniques, (somewhat) homomorphic encryption has a difficulty on the performance and the size. For the problem, we present a new technique in SHE, and demonstrate its efficiency in a concrete application.

1.1   Our Contributions

We summarize our main contributions as follows:

– The special message encoding enables us to reduce both the encrypted data size and the performance in several computations. In their work [22], Lauter, Naehrig and Vaikuntanathan introduce an SHE scheme based on the ring learning with errors (ring-LWE) assumption and present some message encoding techniques, which give efficient computations of private statistic on encrypted data. In this paper, we present a new packing method in the same scheme, which can be considered as an extension of their techniques. Our extension is to give two types of packed ciphertexts (see Sect. 3.1), and to make use of the homomorphic structure of the scheme for wider computations over packed ciphertexts (see Sect. 3.2). In particular, our packing method gives a practical performance for the inner product, the Hamming and the Euclidean distances on encrypted data.

- To demonstrate the efficiency, we apply the SHE scheme with our packing method to privacy-preserving biometrics, in which secure Hamming distance is used to measure the similarity of two biometric feature vectors. Our implementation results show that our packing method gives faster performance compared to the state-of-the-art prior work using homomorphic encryption (see Sect. 4.5 and Table 1).

1.2 Comparison with the Other Packing Methods

Smart and Vercauteren in [29] propose the polynomial-CRT (Chinese Remainder Theorem) packing method, which is useful to perform SIMD (Single Instruction - Multiple Data) operations on encrypted data. The polynomial-CRT packing method is applied in the work [17] for evaluating the AES circuit homomorphically in a leveled FHE scheme of [6]. Furthermore, while the polynomial-CRT packing method can be applied only in ring-LWE based schemes, Brakerski, Gentry and Halevi in [6] extend SIMD notions to the standard LWE based scheme of [8] using the packing method of [27]. Our packing method cannot be applied for SIMD operations, but it is very easier to handle and much more efficient for evaluating fundamental computations compared to the packing methods as introduced above. However, it would be more interesting by combining ours and the polynomial-CRT packing method.

NOTATION. For two integers z and d, let $[z]_d$ denote the reduction of z modulo d included in the interval $[-d/2, d/2)$ (the reduction of z modulo d included in the interval $[0, d)$ is denoted by $z \bmod d$ as usual). For a vector $\boldsymbol{a} = (a_1, a_2, \ldots, a_n)$, let $||\boldsymbol{a}||_\infty$ denote the ∞-norm defined by $\max_i |a_i|$. We let $\langle \boldsymbol{a}, \boldsymbol{b} \rangle$ denote the inner product of two vectors $\boldsymbol{a}$ and $\boldsymbol{b}$. Finally, we let $\lg(q)$ denote the logarithm value of an integer q with base 2.

2 Preliminaries: Somewhat Homomorphic Encryption

In this section, we give the basic construction of the SHE scheme proposed in the work of [22], which is a slightly modification of Brakerski and Vaikuntanathan's scheme [7,8]. The security of the scheme is based on the polynomial LWE assumption described in [7, Sect. 2], which is a simplified version of the ring-LWE assumption of [24].

2.1 Construction

We need the following four parameters (according to an application scenario, these parameters should be appropriately chosen):

n : an integer of 2-power, which defines the base ring $R := \mathbb{Z}[x]/(f(x))$ with the cyclotomic polynomial $f(x) = x^n + 1$ of degree n. This parameter is often called the lattice dimension.

q : a prime number with $q \equiv 1 \mod 2n$, which defines the base ring $R_q :=$ $R/qR = \mathbb{F}_q[x]/(f(x))$ for a ciphertext space.

t : an integer with $t < q$ to determine a plaintext space $R_t := \mathbb{F}_t[x]/(f(x))$.

σ : the parameter to define a discrete Gaussian error distribution $\chi := D_{\mathbb{Z}^n,\sigma}$ with the standard deviation σ. In practice, we take $\sigma = 4 \sim 8$.

Key Generation. We choose an element $R \ni s \leftarrow \chi$, and then sample a random element $a_1 \in R_q$ and an error $R \ni e \leftarrow \chi$. Set $\mathsf{pk} = (a_0, a_1)$ with $a_0 := -(a_1 \cdot s + t \cdot e)$ as the public key and $\mathsf{sk} = s$ as the secret key.

Encryption. For a plaintext $m \in R_t$ and $\mathsf{pk} = (a_0, a_1)$, the encryption samples $R \ni u, f, g \leftarrow \chi$ and compute the 'fresh' ciphertext given by

$$\mathsf{Enc}(m, \mathsf{pk}) = (c_0, c_1) = (a_0 u + tg + m, a_1 u + tf) \in (R_q)^2,$$

where $m \in R_t$ is considered as an element of R_q in the natural way.

Decryption. For a ciphertext $\mathsf{ct} = (c_0, \ldots, c_\xi) \in (R_q)^{\xi+1}$ (note that the homomorphic multiplication defined below makes the ciphertext length longer)., the decryption with the secret key $\mathsf{sk} = s$ is computed by

$$\mathsf{Dec}(\mathsf{ct}, \mathsf{sk}) := [\tilde{m}]_q \mod t \in R_t,$$

where $\tilde{m} = \sum_{i=0}^{\xi} c_i s^i \in R_q$ For the secret key vector $s := (1, s, s^2, \ldots)$, we can also write $\mathsf{Dec}(\mathsf{ct}, \mathsf{sk}) = [\langle \mathsf{ct}, s \rangle]_q \mod t$.

Homomorphic Operations. Let $\mathsf{ct} = (c_0, \ldots, c_\xi)$, $\mathsf{ct}' = (c'_0, \ldots, c'_\eta)$ be two ciphertexts. The homomorphic addition "$+$" is computed by component-wise addition of ciphertexts, namely, we have

$$\mathsf{ct} \dotplus \mathsf{ct}' := (c_0 + c'_0, \ldots, c_{\max(\xi,\eta)} + c'_{\max(\xi,\eta)}) \in R_q^{\max(\xi,\eta)+1},$$

by padding with zeros if necessary. Similarly, the homomorphic subtraction is computed by component-wise subtraction. Furthermore, the homomorphic multiplication "$*$" is computed by

$$\mathsf{ct} * \mathsf{ct}' := (\hat{c}_0, \ldots, \hat{c}_{\xi+\eta}),$$

where we consider $\mathsf{ct}, \mathsf{ct}'$ as elements of $R_q[z]$ by an embedding map $(R_q)^r \ni (v_0, \ldots, v_{r-1}) \mapsto \sum_{i=0}^{r-1} v_i z^i \in R_q[z]$ for any $r \geq 1$, and compute

$$\sum_{i=0}^{\xi+\eta} \hat{c}_i z^i := \left(\sum_{i=0}^{\xi} c_i z^i \right) \cdot \left(\sum_{i=0}^{\eta} c'_i z^i \right) \in R_q[z].$$

2.2 Correctness

By correctness, we mean that the decryption can recover the operated result over plaintexts after some homomorphic operations over ciphertexts. It follows from the proof of [22, Lemma 3.3] that the homomorphic operations over ciphertexts correspond to the ring structure of the plaintext space R_t, namely, we have

$$\mathsf{Dec}(\mathsf{ct} \dotplus \mathsf{ct}', \mathsf{sk}) = m + m' \in R_t,$$
$$\mathsf{Dec}(\mathsf{ct} * \mathsf{ct}', \mathsf{sk}) = m \times m' \in R_t,$$

for ciphertexts $\mathsf{ct}, \mathsf{ct}'$ corresponding to plaintexts m, m', respectively. However, the scheme merely gives SHE (not FHE), and its correctness holds under the following condition (see the proof of [22, Lemma 3.3]):

Lemma 1 (Condition for Correct Decryption). *For a ciphertext* ct, *the decryption* $\mathsf{Dec}(\mathsf{ct}, \mathsf{sk})$ *recovers the correct result if* $\langle \mathsf{ct}, s \rangle \in R_q$ *does not wrap around mod* q, *namely, if* $|| \langle \mathsf{ct}, s \rangle ||_\infty$ *is smaller than* $q/2$.

3 Practical Packing Method

For reduction of both the size and the performance, Lauter, Naehrig and Vaikun-tanathan in [22] introduce some message encoding techniques. Their main tech-nique is to encode integers in a single ciphertext so that it enables us to efficiently compute their sums and products over the integers (see [22, Sect. 4.1]). Their idea is to break an integer M of at most n bits into a binary vector $(M_0, \ldots, M_{n-1})$, create a polynomial given by (note that n is the lattice dimension parameter described in Sect. 2)

$$\mathsf{pm}(M) := \sum_{i=0}^{n-1} M_i x^i \tag{1}$$

of degree $(n-1)$, and finally encrypt M as $\mathsf{ct}_{\mathrm{pack}}(M) := \mathsf{Enc}\,(\mathsf{pm}(M), \mathsf{pk})$, where we consider $\mathsf{pm}(M)$ as an element of R_t for sufficiently large t. Note that we have $\mathsf{pm}(M)|_{x=2} = M$ for any integer M of n bits. For two integers M, M' of n bits, the homomorphic addition of $\mathsf{ct}_{\mathrm{pack}}(M)$ and $\mathsf{ct}_{\mathrm{pack}}(M')$ gives the polynomial addition $\mathsf{pm}(M) + \mathsf{pm}(M')$ on encrypted data by the correctness of the scheme, and it also gives the integer addition $M + M'$ since $\mathsf{pm}(M) + \mathsf{pm}(M')|_{x=2} = M + M'$. However, the integer multiplication $M \cdot M'$ causes a problem since the polynomial multiplication $\mathsf{pm}(M) \cdot \mathsf{pm}(M')$ has larger degree than n in general. Their solution is to encode integers of at most n/d bits if we need to perform d times homomorphic multiplications over ciphertexts. Their solution is acceptable in computing low degree multiplications such as the standard deviation.

3.1 Definition of Our Packing Method

In contrast to their packing method, we present a new packing method for encod-ing vectors (of course, our method is easily applied for encoding integers as their work). Our idea is based on theirs, and our packing method can be considered as an extension of their technique. Unlike their technique, we give two types of packed ciphertexts in order to make use of the ring structure of the plaintext space R_t for wider computations over packed ciphertexts. While their method only gives efficient private statistic such as the mean and the standard deviation, our method gives wider computations such as basic statistical analysis and distances. Now, let us define our packing method for encoding vectors.

Definition 1. *For a vector $A = (A_0, A_1, \ldots, A_{n-1})$ of length n, we define two types of packed ciphertexts as follows:*

(i) *As the Eq. (1), set* $\mathsf{pm}_1(A) := \sum_{i=0}^{n-1} A_i x^i$. *For sufficiently large t, we consider the above polynomial to be an element of R_t, and then we define* $\mathsf{ct}_{\mathrm{pack}}^{(1)}(A) := \mathsf{Enc}\left(\mathsf{pm}_1(A), \mathsf{pk}\right)$ *as the packed ciphertext of the first type. This type is almost same as given in* [22].

(ii) *Unlike the first type, set* $\mathsf{pm}_2(A) := -\sum_{i=0}^{n-1} A_i x^{n-i}$. *As the second type, we define* $\mathsf{ct}_{\mathrm{pack}}^{(2)}(A) := \mathsf{Enc}\left(\mathsf{pm}_2(A), \mathsf{pk}\right)$.

By the above definition, we always pack a vector of length n into a single ciphertext irrespective of types. Hence, compared to coefficient-wise encryption, our method considerably reduces the encrypted data size.

3.2   Computations Over Packed Ciphertexts

Due to two types of our packing method, we can efficiently perform some meaningful computations over packed ciphertexts. We begin with the following result on an efficient computation of the inner product:

Proposition 1 (Secure Inner Product). *For two vectors A, B of length n, let ct denote the ciphertext given by the homomorphic multiplication of $\mathsf{ct}_{\mathrm{pack}}^{(1)}(A)$ and $\mathsf{ct}_{\mathrm{pack}}^{(2)}(B)$. Let m_0 denote the constant term of the decryption result $\mathsf{Dec}(\mathsf{ct}, \mathsf{sk}) \in R_t$. Then we have $m_0 \equiv \langle A, B \rangle \bmod t$. In other words, the constant term of the decryption result gives the inner product of two vectors A and B for sufficiently large t.*

Proof. Since the homomorphic operations over ciphertexts correspond to the ring structure of the plaintext space R_t (see Sect. 2.2), the decryption result $\mathsf{Dec}(\mathsf{ct}, \mathsf{sk})$ is equal to the polynomial multiplication $\mathsf{pm}_1(A) \times \mathsf{pm}_2(B)$ in R_t.

Set $A = (A_0, \ldots, A_{n-1})$ and $B = (B_0, \ldots, B_{n-1})$. Then

$$\mathsf{pm}_1(A) \times \mathsf{pm}_2(B) = \left(\sum_{i=0}^{n-1} A_i x^i\right) \times \left(-\sum_{j=0}^{n-1} B_j x^{n-j}\right)$$

$$= -\sum_{i=0}^{n-1} A_i B_i x^n + \text{(the other terms)}$$

$$= \langle A, B \rangle + \text{(non-constant terms)}$$

in R_t since $x^n = -1$. This completes the proof of this proposition.   □

Proposition 1 shows that our packing method enables us to compute the inner product of two vectors of length n by only one time homomorphic multiplication over packed ciphertexts. Actually, in Definition 1, we take two types of our packing method so that the result of Proposition 1 holds. Note that our packing method specializes in $R = \mathbb{Z}[x]/(x^n + 1)$. In the following, we present some fundamental examples of the possible computations, and describe how to compute them over packed ciphertexts (in particular, our packing method gives an efficient computation of the Hamming and the Euclidean distances):

Basic Private Statistic. For n integers $A_0, \ldots, A_{n-1}$, we set $A = (A_0, \ldots, A_{n-1})$ and pack integers A_i's into the packed ciphertext $\mathsf{ct}_{\mathrm{pack}}^{(1)}(A)$ of the first type, and/or $\mathsf{ct}_{\mathrm{pack}}^{(2)}(A)$ of the second type. In the following, we give how to compute some basic private statistic over packed ciphertexts:

Sum, and Mean For the sum of n integers $A_0, \ldots, A_{n-1}$ on encrypted data, we need to define two polynomials

$$C_1 := -\sum_{i=0}^{n-1} x^{n-i} \text{ and } C_2 := \sum_{i=0}^{n-1} x^i,$$

which can be precomputed in implementation. For the packed ciphertext $\mathsf{ct}_{\mathrm{pack}}^{(1)}(A)$, let ct denote the ciphertext given by the homomorphic multiplication $\mathsf{ct}_{\mathrm{pack}}^{(1)}(A) * C_1$, where we consider C_1 as an element of R_q and the homomorphic multiplication is computed in the same way as in Sect. 2. From a similar argument in the proof of Proposition 1, the constant term of the decryption of the ciphertext ct gives the sum $\sum_{i=0}^{n-1} A_i$ since the homomorphic multiplication $\mathsf{ct}_{\mathrm{pack}}^{(1)}(A) * C_1$ corresponds to the multiplication $\mathsf{pm}_1(A) \times C_1$ in R_t and its polynomial is equal to

$$\left(\sum_{i=0}^{n-1} A_i x^i\right) \times \left(-\sum_{j=0}^{n-1} x^{n-j}\right) = \sum_{i=0}^{n-1} A_i + \text{(non-constant terms)}.$$

Similarly, for $\mathrm{ct}^{(2)}_{\mathrm{pack}}(\boldsymbol{A})$, the homomorphic multiplication $\mathrm{ct}^{(2)}_{\mathrm{pack}}(\boldsymbol{A}) * C_2$ also gives the sum $\sum_{i=0}^{n-1} A_i$ over packed ciphertexts. For the mean $M := \dfrac{\sum_{i=0}^{n-1} A_i}{n}$, we have no efficient division on encrypted data. Therefore, after we compute the sum over packed ciphertexts as described above and decrypt it, we divide the sum by n over plaintexts as in [22].

Variance, and Standard Deviation While the mean is the average of a set of numbers, the variance is a measure of the dispersion around the mean. The variance is denoted by σ^2 (the standard deviation is denoted by σ as in Sect. 2), and it is $\sigma^2 = \dfrac{\sum_{i=0}^{n-1} (A_i - M)^2}{n}$ which can be rewritten as

$$\sigma^2 = \frac{1}{n} \sum_{i=0}^{n-1} A_i^2 - M^2. \tag{2}$$

Given two packed ciphertexts $\mathrm{ct}^{(1)}_{\mathrm{pack}}(\boldsymbol{A})$ and $\mathrm{ct}^{(2)}_{\mathrm{pack}}(\boldsymbol{A})$, it follows from Proposition 1 that the homomorphic multiplication $\mathrm{ct}^{(1)}_{\mathrm{pack}}(\boldsymbol{A}) * \mathrm{ct}^{(2)}_{\mathrm{pack}}(\boldsymbol{A})$ gives the sum of squares $\sum_{i=0}^{n-1} A_i^2$ on encrypted data. After we compute the mean M and the sum of squares $\sum_{i=0}^{n-1} A_i^2$ over two packed ciphertexts $\mathrm{ct}^{(1)}_{\mathrm{pack}}(\boldsymbol{A})$ and $\mathrm{ct}^{(2)}_{\mathrm{pack}}(\boldsymbol{A})$ and decrypt them, we can derive σ^2 by computing the expression (2) over plaintexts. The standard deviation is defined as the square root of the variance. To obtain σ, we take the square root over plaintexts after computing the variance σ^2 as described above.

Basic Statistical Analysis. Let $(X, Y) = (X_0, Y_0), \ldots, (X_{n-1}, Y_{n-1})$ be a pair of two variables with n independent integer sample pairs (X_i, Y_i). Consider $\mathrm{ct}^{(i)}_{\mathrm{pack}}(\boldsymbol{X})$ and $\mathrm{ct}^{(i)}_{\mathrm{pack}}(\boldsymbol{Y})$ for $i = 1, 2$, where $\boldsymbol{X} = (X_0, \ldots, X_{n-1})$ and $\boldsymbol{Y} = (Y_0, \ldots, Y_{n-1})$ denote two vectors of length n. We give how to compute basic statistical analysis over packed ciphertexts.

Covariance The covariance measures the linear relationship between two variables X and Y, and its formula is written as

$$\mathrm{cov}(X, Y) = \frac{1}{n-1} \sum_{i=0}^{n-1} (X_i - M_X)(Y_i - M_Y),$$

where M_X (resp. M_Y) denotes the mean of the variable X (resp. Y). Its alternative expression is given by

$$\mathrm{cov}(X, Y) = \frac{1}{n-1} \left(\sum_{i=0}^{n-1} X_i Y_i - n M_X M_Y \right). \tag{3}$$

By Proposition 1 and the above arguments, the inner product $\sum_{i=0}^{n-1} X_i Y_i$ and two means M_X and M_Y can be efficiently computed. After computing the inner product $\sum_{i=0}^{n-1} X_i Y_i$ and two means M_X, M_Y over packed ciphertexts and decrypt them, we derive the covariance $\mathrm{cov}(X, Y)$ by computing the expression (3) over plaintexts.

Correlation The correlation examines the relationship between two variables. It is written as $r(X, Y) = \dfrac{\mathrm{cov}(X, Y)}{\sigma_X \sigma_Y}$, where σ_X (resp. σ_Y) denotes the standard deviation of the variable X (resp. Y). We can efficiently compute the covariance $\mathrm{cov}(X, Y)$ and two standard deviations σ_X, σ_Y over packed ciphertexts, and hence we can also compute the correlation.

Basic Distances. For two vectors $\boldsymbol{A}$ and $\boldsymbol{B}$ of length n, we give how to compute some basic distances over packed ciphertexts as follows:

Hamming Distance The Hamming distance between two strings of same length is the number of positions at which the corresponding symbols are different. It is often used to search for similar words, or to measure the similarity of two feature vectors mainly in biometric authentication. For two binary vectors $\boldsymbol{A}, \boldsymbol{B}$ of length n, the Hamming distance is computed by $d_H(\boldsymbol{A}, \boldsymbol{B}) = \sum_{i=0}^{n-1} A_i \oplus B_i = \sum_{i=0}^{n-1} (A_i + B_i - 2A_i B_i)$, where $\oplus$ denotes the XOR operation. Hence the Hamming distance over packed ciphertexts is computed by

$$\underbrace{\mathrm{ct}_{\mathrm{pack}}^{(1)}(\boldsymbol{A}) * C_1}_{\sum A_i} \dotplus \underbrace{\mathrm{ct}_{\mathrm{pack}}^{(2)}(\boldsymbol{B}) * C_2}_{\sum B_i} \dotplus \underbrace{(-2\mathrm{ct}_{\mathrm{pack}}^{(1)}(\boldsymbol{A})) * \mathrm{ct}_{\mathrm{pack}}^{(2)}(\boldsymbol{B})}_{-2 \sum A_i B_i} \qquad (4)$$

from Proposition 1 and the above arguments. In particular, the above equation tells us that it requires only two times homomorphic additions and three times homomorphic multiplications to compute the Hamming distance between two binary vectors of length n over packed ciphertexts $\mathrm{ct}_{\mathrm{pack}}^{(1)}(\boldsymbol{A})$ and $\mathrm{ct}_{\mathrm{pack}}^{(2)}(\boldsymbol{B})$. For example, in the case $n = 2048$ which we take in Sect. 4 below, our packing method gives us a powerful efficiency (cf. in coefficient-wise encryption, we need at least $n = 2048$ times homomorphic multiplications in this case).

Euclidean Distance The Euclidean distance is an ordinary distance between two points. For two non-binary vectors $\boldsymbol{A}, \boldsymbol{B}$ of length n, the Euclidean distance is the square root of the value $\sum_{i=0}^{n-1} (A_i - B_i)^2 = \sum_{i=0}^{n-1} (A_i^2 + B_i^2 - 2A_i B_i)$. By Proposition 1, the computation

$$\mathrm{ct}_{\mathrm{pack}}^{(1)}(\boldsymbol{A}) * \mathrm{ct}_{\mathrm{pack}}^{(2)}(\boldsymbol{A}) \dotplus \mathrm{ct}_{\mathrm{pack}}^{(1)}(\boldsymbol{B}) * \mathrm{ct}_{\mathrm{pack}}^{(2)}(\boldsymbol{B}) \dotplus (-2\mathrm{ct}_{\mathrm{pack}}^{(1)}(\boldsymbol{A})) * \mathrm{ct}_{\mathrm{pack}}^{(2)}(\boldsymbol{B})$$

gives us the value $\sum_{i=0}^{n-1} (A_i - B_i)^2$ over packed ciphertexts. Therefore, after we compute $\sum_{i=0}^{n-1} (A_i - B_i)^2$ over packed ciphertexts and decrypt it, we can derive the Euclidean distance by taking the square root.

Remark 1. In the use of homomorphic encryption, it is difficult to perform computations such as the median and the 1-norm on encrypted data since we can not compare two values without the decryption.

4   Application to Privacy-Preserving Biometrics

In this section, we apply the SHE scheme with our packing method to a concrete application, and demonstrate the efficiency. As an application example, we take privacy-preserving biometric authentication. We begin with its background and related work.

4.1   Background and Related Work

Biometrics authentication (or biometrics) is to identify clients by their physical characteristic such as fingerprint, iris, vein and DNA. Compared to the commonly used ID/password authentication, it has the advantage that clients do not remember their long and complex password, and its use is rapidly expanding (see [30]). On the other hand, concerns for the privacy and the security are also increasing. In particular, it is important to protect *templates*, which are stored biometric feature data, since once leaked templates can be neither revoked nor replaced. There are three main approaches for privacy-preserving biometrics (see [1] or [20]).

(1) *Feature transformation approach*, in which biometric feature data are transformed to random data by using a client-specific key. Cancelable biometrics and biohashing are typical. This approach is practical in performance, but it is no longer secure if the client's key is leaked.

(2) *Biometric cryptosystem approach* is based on error-correcting codes, and includes fuzzy vault and fuzzy commitment. Since this approach needs to have strong restriction of authentication accuracy, both practical and security issues are controversial.

(3) *Homomorphic encryption approach*, in which the privacy of biometric feature data are protected by homomorphic encryption, and the similarity of two feature data is measured on encrypted data by metrics such as the Hamming and the Euclidean distances. As long as the secret key is securely managed by a trusted party, it enables biometric authentication system to be considerably secure. However, the performance and the encrypted data size are main issues.

Related Work on Homomorphic Encryption Approach. We focus on the homomorphic encryption approach, and summarize its previous work. In 2006, Schoenmakers and Tuyls in [28] proposed secure computations suitable for privacy-preserving biometrics using the Paillier scheme [26], which is additively homomorphic. In 2010, Osadchy et al. in [25] designed a new face recognition algorithm and proposed an efficient secure face identification system, called *SCiFI*, with the Paillier scheme and the oblivious transfer protocol. Their secure two-party computation is based on the work of [21]. In SCiFI, a feature vector extracted from face image is always represented as a binary vector of 900-bit, and the Hamming distance is used as a metric to compare two feature vectors. Their implementation showed that it took 310 ms to compute secure Hamming distance with the Paillier scheme of a 1024-bit modulus. Currently, SCiFI is known as one of the state-of-the-art privacy-preserving biometric authentication systems suitable for real life. In 2011, Blanton and Gasti in [2] developed secure protocols for iris and fingerprints. Their secure computation is similar to SCiFI, but they use the DGK scheme [13], which is an additive one with shorter ciphertexts than the Paillier scheme. In their protocol, an iris feature vector is always represented as a binary vector of 2048-bit and the Hamming distance is used as in SCiFI. Their implementation showed that it took 150 ms to compute secure Hamming distance with the DGK scheme of a 1024-bit modulus. Finally, in our preprint paper [31], we proposed a new secure protocol with the SHE scheme based on ideal lattices. Its protocol is based on the work of [19], and involves three parties unlike SCiFI and the protocol of [2]. Due to a similar packing method as presented in this work, it took 18.10 ms to compute secure Hamming distance of two feature vectors of 2048-bit with the SHE scheme of a 4096 lattice dimension. This is about 8 times faster than the protocol of [2] when we ignore the PC performance.

4.2   Secure Protocol with Our Packing Method

Using the SHE scheme with our packing method, we give a secure protocol based on our previous work [31] (we remark that in [31] we use the SHE scheme based on ideal lattices, which is not different in this work). As in the work of [31], our protocol involves three parties, a client server $\mathcal{C}$, a computation server $\mathcal{S}$ with a database D, and finally an authentication server $\mathcal{A}$. In our protocol, we assume that the authentication server $\mathcal{A}$ is a trusted party to manage the secret key sk of the SHE scheme. Furthermore, we assume that biometric data are always represented as binary vectors of 2048-bit for various biometrics, and we will not refer how to generate feature vectors. In the following, we give our secure protocol of biometric authentication with ID:

Setup Phase The authentication server $\mathcal{A}$ generates the public key pk and the secret key sk of the SHE scheme (see Sect. 2 for the key generation, and see also Sect. 4.3 for suitable key parameters), and distributes only pk to both the client server $\mathcal{C}$ and the computation server $\mathcal{S}$.

Enrollment Phase

1. The client server $\mathcal{C}$ generates a feature vector $\boldsymbol{A}$ from client's biometric data such as fingerprints, encrypts $\boldsymbol{A}$ into a packed ciphertext $\mathsf{ct}_{\mathrm{pack}}^{(1)}(\boldsymbol{A})$ of the first type, and sends only $\mathsf{ct}_{\mathrm{pack}}^{(1)}(\boldsymbol{A})$ with client's ID to the computation server $\mathcal{S}$.

2. The computation server $\mathcal{S}$ stores $\mathsf{ct}_{\mathrm{pack}}^{(1)}(\boldsymbol{A})$ in D as a template.

Authentication Phase

1. As in the enrollment phase, the client server $\mathcal{C}$ generates a feature vector $\boldsymbol{B}$ from client's biometric data, encrypts $\boldsymbol{B}$ into a packed ciphertext $\mathsf{ct}_{\mathrm{pack}}^{(2)}(\boldsymbol{B})$ of the second type, and sends only $\mathsf{ct}_{\mathrm{pack}}^{(2)}(\boldsymbol{B})$ with client's ID to the computation server $\mathcal{S}$.

2 The computation server $\mathcal{S}$ extracts the template $\text{ct}^{(1)}_{\text{pack}}(\boldsymbol{A})$ corresponding to client's ID from the database D. Then $\mathcal{S}$ computes secure Hamming distance ct_H defined by (4) in Sect. 3.2 over packed ciphertexts $\text{ct}^{(1)}_{\text{pack}}(\boldsymbol{A})$ and $\text{ct}^{(2)}_{\text{pack}}(\boldsymbol{B})$, and sends only ct_H to $\mathcal{A}$.

3. The authentication server $\mathcal{A}$ decrypts ct_H with the secret key sk to obtain the Hamming distance $d_H(\boldsymbol{A}, \boldsymbol{B})$. Finally, the server $\mathcal{A}$ returns the authentication result 'OK' (resp. 'NG') if $d_H(\boldsymbol{A}, \boldsymbol{B}) \leq T$ (resp. otherwise), where T denotes a pre-defined threshold.

Feature of Our Protocol. Our secure protocol could have the following feature:

- *Confidentiality* (the computer server $\mathcal{S}$ does not learn any information about clients' biometric data): All data in $\mathcal{S}$ are in encrypted form, and especially, our protocol is secure against the hill climbing attack as long as the secret key is securely managed by the authentication server $\mathcal{A}$. Therefore we hope that we could use the cloud as $\mathcal{S}$ for outsourcing storage of templates and computation resources of secure Hamming distance. The use of cloud computing would reduce the cost in adopting biometric authentication.
- *Template protection* (the identity theft is hard even if a template is stolen): When a malicious client steals a template $\text{ct}^{(1)}_{\text{pack}}(\boldsymbol{A})$, he can not know $\boldsymbol{A}$ without sk. Furthermore, when he sends $\text{ct}^{(1)}_{\text{pack}}(\boldsymbol{A})$ to $\mathcal{S}$ instead of $\text{ct}^{(2)}_{\text{pack}}(\boldsymbol{B})$ in the authentication phase, the authentication would fail with very high probability due to our asymmetric packing methods (it would be hard to compute the Hamming distance between $\boldsymbol{A}$ and $\boldsymbol{A}$ without the packed ciphertext $\text{ct}^{(2)}_{\text{pack}}(\boldsymbol{A})$ of the second type, and hence he could not obtain scores smaller than T).
- *Availability* (the use of multiple client servers is easy): Once the authentication server $\mathcal{A}$ distributes pk to multiple client servers, they can start to use the system (cf. symmetric key encryption).

4.3   Choosing Key Parameters

As remarked in Sect. 2, key parameters (n, q, t, σ) of the SHE scheme should be appropriately chosen in order to achieve both the security and the correctness of the scheme according to an application scenario. We consider secure Hamming distance as the scenario in this section. The method to choose key parameters is based mainly on the work of [22].

Correctness. We first need to consider the correctness. For two binary vectors $\boldsymbol{A}$ and $\boldsymbol{B}$ of 2048-bit, let ct_H denote a ciphertext of secure Hamming distance defined by the Eq. (4) over packed ciphertexts $\text{ct}^{(1)}_{\text{pack}}(\boldsymbol{A})$ and $\text{ct}^{(2)}_{\text{pack}}(\boldsymbol{B})$. It follows from Lemma 1 that the correctness for the ciphertext ct_H is satisfied if

$$\|\langle \text{ct}_H, \boldsymbol{s} \rangle\|_\infty < q/2. \tag{5}$$

By the correctness of the scheme, the element $\langle \mathsf{ct}_H, s \rangle$ is equal to

$$\left\langle \mathsf{ct}_{\mathrm{pack}}^{(1)}(A), s \right\rangle \cdot \langle C_1, s \rangle + \left\langle \mathsf{ct}_{\mathrm{pack}}^{(2)}(B), s \right\rangle \cdot \langle C_2, s \rangle - 2 \left\langle \mathsf{ct}_{\mathrm{pack}}^{(1)}(A), s \right\rangle \cdot \left\langle \mathsf{ct}_{\mathrm{pack}}^{(2)}(B), s \right\rangle$$

in the ring R_q (see the proof of [22, Lemma 3.3]). When we set U to be an upper bound of the ∞-norm size $||\langle \mathsf{ct}, s \rangle||_\infty$ for any fresh ciphertext $\mathsf{ct} \in (R_q)^2$, the above equation on the element $\langle \mathsf{ct}_H, s \rangle$ gives an inequality $||\langle \mathsf{ct}_H, s \rangle||_\infty \leq 2nU + 2nU^2$ by the fact that $||\langle C_i, s \rangle||_\infty = ||C_i||_\infty = 1$ for $i = 1, 2$ and $||\langle \mathsf{ct}_{\mathrm{pack}}^{(1)}(A), s \rangle||_\infty$, $||\langle \mathsf{ct}_{\mathrm{pack}}^{(2)}(B), s \rangle||_\infty \leq U$ (we also use the fact that $||a+b||_\infty \leq ||a||_\infty + ||b||_\infty$ and $||a \cdot b||_\infty \leq n \cdot ||a||_\infty ||b||_\infty$ for any two elements $a, b \in R_q$). As in the work of [22], we take U to be the value $2t\sigma^2\sqrt{n}$, which is an experimental estimation (see the proof of [22, Lemma 3.3] for details). Then we have $||\langle \mathsf{ct}, s \rangle||_\infty \leq 2nU + 2nU^2 \approx 8n^2t^2\sigma^4$. Therefore, by the inequality (5), we estimate that the correctness for the ciphertext ct_H is satisfied if

$$16n^2t^2\sigma^4 < q, \tag{6}$$

which condition gives a lower bound of the prime q for the correctness.

Chosen Parameters. Next we consider to take concrete parameters. As in the work [22], we take $\sigma = 8$ to make the SHE scheme secure against the combinatorial attack. We also set $t = 2048$ as the plaintext space parameter, which is enough to compute the Hamming distance of two binary vectors of 2048-bit. Furthermore, we need $n \geq 2048$ in order to pack a binary vector A or B of length 2048 into a single ciphertext with our packing method (see Definition 1). When we take $n = 2048$, the equality (6) tells us that the correctness for the ciphertext ct_H is satisfied if $q > 2^{60}$. Then let us fix

$$(n, q, t, \sigma) = (2048, 61\text{-bit}, 2048, 8). \tag{7}$$

Security Level of Chosen Parameters. Finally, we consider the security of parameters (7). The security of the scheme relies on the polynomial LWE assumption of [7]. According to the analysis in the work of [22] (their analysis is based on the methodology of Lindner and Peikert [23]), the security of the assumption is determined by the root Hermite factor δ derived from the relation $c \cdot q/\sigma = 2^{2\sqrt{n \lg(q) \lg(\delta)}}$, where c is the constant determined by the attack advantage, and we assume $c = 3.758$ (see [22, Appendix A] for details). For parameters (7), we have $\delta \approx 1.0050$ by the above relation. According to recent work [9], the factor $\delta \approx 1.005$ is estimated to have more than 80-bit security with an enough margin (the authors in [22] estimate that similar parameters $(n, q, t, \sigma) = (2048, 58\text{-bit}, 1024, 8)$ as (7) have 120-bit security level). Therefore we conclude that parameters (7) satisfy both the enough security and the correctness.

Table 1. A comparison with related work using homomorphic encryption

Protocols (feature vector size)	Performance of secure hamming	Size increase rate by encryption[†] (cipher. size)	Homomorphic encryption scheme
SCiFI [25] (900-bit)	$310\,\mathrm{ms}^{(a)}$	2048 times (230 KByte)	Paillier-1024 (additive scheme)
Protocol of [2] (2048-bit)	$150\,\mathrm{ms}^{(b)}$	1024 times (262 KByte)	DGK-1024 (additive scheme)
Previous work[‡] [31] (2048-bit)	$18.10\,\mathrm{ms}^{(c)}$	about 80 times (19 KByte)	ideal lattices-4096 (SHE)
This work (2048-bit)	$\mathbf{5.31\,ms}^{(c)}$	**about 120 times (31 KByte)**	**ring-LWE-2048 (SHE)**

[†]denotes the ratio of (encrypted feature vector size)/(plain feature vector size)
[‡]uses a similar packing method as in this work
(a)on an 8 core machine of 2.6 GHz AMD Opteron processors with 1 GByte memory
(b)on an Intel Core 2 Duo 2.13 GHz with 3 GByte memory
(c)on an Intel Xeon X3480 at 3.07 GHz with 16 GByte memory

4.4   Implementation Results

For parameters (7), we implemented the SHE scheme with our packing method for secure Hamming distance given by the Eq. (4). Our experiments ran on an Intel Xeon X3480 at 3.07 GHz with 16 GByte memory, and we used our software library written with assembly language x86_64 for computations in the base ring $R_q = \mathbb{F}_q[x]/(x^n + 1)$ of the ciphertext space. In particular, we implemented the Karatsuba multiplication and the Montgomery reduction algorithms for efficient multiplication in R_q. The sizes and the performances are shown as follows (see [22, Sect. 1.2 or Sect. 5] for a comparison):

- The size of $\mathsf{pk} = (a_0, a_1) \in R_q^2$ is $2n \cdot \lg(q) \approx 31$ KByte, and the size of $\mathsf{sk} = s \in R_q$ is $n \cdot \lg(q) \approx 16$ KByte. A fresh ciphertext has two elements in the ring R_q, and hence its size is $2n \cdot \lg(q) \approx 31$ KByte.
- The key generation (excluding the prime generation) ran in 1.89 ms, packed encryption irrespective of types took 3.65 ms, secure Hamming distance over packed ciphertexts took 5.31 ms, and finally the decryption took 3.47 ms. In our implementation, it took about 0.001 ms (4,837 clock cycles) to compute one polynomial addition, and it also took about 1.56 ms (4,793,850 clock cycles) to compute one polynomial multiplication in the ring R_q. For secure Hamming distance ct_H, we implemented the computation

$$\mathsf{ct}_H = \mathsf{ct}_{\mathrm{pack}}^{(1)}(A) * C_1 + \mathsf{ct}_{\mathrm{pack}}^{(2)}(B) * C_2 + (-2\mathsf{ct}_{\mathrm{pack}}^{(1)}(A)) * \mathsf{ct}_{\mathrm{pack}}^{(2)}(B)$$
$$= -\frac{1}{2}\left\{\left(2\mathsf{ct}_{\mathrm{pack}}^{(1)}(A) - C_2\right) * \left(2\mathsf{ct}_{\mathrm{pack}}^{(2)}(B) - C_1\right) - C_1 * C_2\right\},$$

whose size is $3n \cdot \lg(q) \approx 46.5$ KByte (we did not use the relinearization technique described in [22, Sect. 3.2.3] for reducing ring elements of a ciphertext).

It mainly requires only one time homomorphic multiplication when we pre-compute C_1, C_2 and $C_1 * C_2$.

4.5   Comparison with Related Work

In Table 1, we give a comparison of our protocol with related work described in Sect. 4.1 on the performance and the encrypted data size for secure Hamming distance (all encryption schemes are estimated to have more than 80-bit security). Table 1 shows that our protocol has the best performance in the state-of-the-art work. Due to our packing method, our protocol is much faster and more compact than SCiFI [25] and the protocol of [2] using additively homomorphic encryption. In particular, our protocol is about 30 times faster and about 8 times shorter than the protocol of [2]. Furthermore, Table 1 shows that compared to the SHE scheme based on ideal lattices, the ring-LWE based SHE scheme is about 3 times faster but about 1.5 times longer. Note that the ring-LWE based scheme only needs 2048 lattice dimension to achieve 80-bit security while the ideal lattices based scheme needs 4096 lattice dimension. When we use 2048 lattice dimension in the ideal lattices based scheme, the performance is almost same as in this work.

Finally, let us compare our protocol with one using the BGN scheme [3]. The BGN scheme uses pairing computations on elliptic curves for its homomorphic multiplication. As well described in [22, Sect. 1.2], the homomorphic multiplication in the BGN scheme is very slower than that in lattice-based encryption such as the ring-LWE and the ideal lattices schemes. Furthermore, we can not use our packing method in the BGN scheme, and hence it needs 2048 homomorphic multiplications for secure Hamming distance between two vectors of 2048-bit. Even if we use very fast implementation taking 1 ms for one pairing computation, it takes about 2048 ms ≈ 2 s. Therefore we estimate that our protocol is much faster than the BGN scheme.

References

1. Belguechi, R., Alimi, V., Cherrier, E., Lacharme, P., Rosenberger, C.: An overview on privacy preserving biometrics. http://cdn.intechopen.com/pdfs/17038/InTech-An_overview_on_privacy_preserving_biometrics.pdf
2. Blanton, M., Gasti, P.: Secure and efficient protocols for iris and fingerprint identification. In: Atluri, V., Diaz, C. (eds.) ESORICS 2011. LNCS, vol. 6879, pp. 190–209. Springer, Heidelberg (2011)
3. Boneh, D., Goh, E.-J., Nissim, K.: Evaluating 2-DNF formulas on ciphertexts. In: Kilian, J. (ed.) TCC 2005. LNCS, vol. 3378, pp. 325–341. Springer, Heidelberg (2005)
4. Boneh, D., Gentry, C., Halevi, S., Wang, F., Wu, D.J.: Private database queries using somewhat homomorphic encryption. In: Jacobson, M., Locasto, M., Mohassel, P., Safavi-Naini, R. (eds.) ACNS 2013. LNCS, vol. 7954, pp. 102–118. Springer, Heidelberg (2013)

5. Brakerski, Z., Gentry, C., Halevi, S.: Packed ciphertexts in LWE-based homomorphic encryption. In: Kurosawa, K., Hanaoka, G. (eds.) PKC 2013. LNCS, vol. 7778, pp. 1–13. Springer, Heidelberg (2013)
6. Brakerski, Z., Gentry, C., Vaikuntanathan, V.: (Leveled) fully homomorphic encryption without bootstrapping. In: Innovations in Theoretical Computer Science-ITCS 2012, pp. 309–325. ACM (2012)
7. Brakerski, Z., Vaikuntanathan, V.: Fully homomorphic encryption from ring-LWE and security for key dependent messages. In: Rogaway, P. (ed.) CRYPTO 2011. LNCS, vol. 6841, pp. 505–524. Springer, Heidelberg (2011)
8. Brakerski, Z., Vaikuntanathan, V.: Efficient fully homomorphic encryption from (standard) LWE. In: Foundations of Computer Science-FOCS 2011, pp. 97–106. IEEE (2011)
9. Chen, Y., Nguyen, P.Q.: BKZ 2.0: better lattice security estimates. In: Lee, D.H., Wang, X. (eds.) ASIACRYPT 2011. LNCS, vol. 7073, pp. 1–20. Springer, Heidelberg (2011)
10. Cloud Security Alliance (CSA), Security guidance for critical areas of focus in cloud computing. https://cloudsecurityalliance.org/csaguide.pdf, December 2009
11. Coron, J.-S., Mandal, A., Naccache, D., Tibouchi, M.: Fully homomorphic encryption over the integers with shorter public keys. In: Rogaway, P. (ed.) CRYPTO 2011. LNCS, vol. 6841, pp. 487–504. Springer, Heidelberg (2011)
12. Cramer, R., Gennaro, R., Schoenmakers, B.: A secure and optimally efficient multi-authority election scheme. In: Fumy, W. (ed.) EUROCRYPT 1997. LNCS, vol. 1233, pp. 103–118. Springer, Heidelberg (1997)
13. Damgård, I., Geisler, M., Krøigård, M.: Homomorphic encryption and secure comparison. J. Appl. Crypt. 1(1), 22–31 (2008)
14. van Dijk, M., Gentry, C., Halevi, S., Vaikuntanathan, V.: Fully homomorphic encryption over the integers. In: Gilbert, H. (ed.) EUROCRYPT 2010. LNCS, vol. 6110, pp. 24–43. Springer, Heidelberg (2010)
15. Gentry, C.: Fully homomorphic encryption using ideal lattices. In: Symposium on Theory of Computing-STOC 2009, pp. 169–178. ACM (2009)
16. Gentry, C., Halevi, S.: Implementing gentry's fully-homomorphic encryption scheme. In: Paterson, K.G. (ed.) EUROCRYPT 2011. LNCS, vol. 6632, pp. 129–148. Springer, Heidelberg (2011)
17. Gentry, C., Halevi, S., Smart, N.P.: Homomorphic evaluation of the AES circuit. In: Safavi-Naini, R., Canetti, R. (eds.) CRYPTO 2012. LNCS, vol. 7417, pp. 850–867. Springer, Heidelberg (2012)
18. Goldwasser, S., Micali, S.: Probabilistic encryption and how to play mental poker keeping secrete all partial information. In: Symposium on Theory of Computing-STOC 1982, pp. 365–377. ACM (1982)
19. Hattori, M., Matsuda, N., Ito, T., Takashima, K., Yoneda, T.: Provably-secure cancelable biometrics using 2-DNF evaluation. J. Inf. Process. 20(2), 496–507 (2012)
20. Jain, A.K., Nandakumar, K., Nagar, A.: Biometric template security (review article). EURASIP J. Adv. Sig. Process 2008, 1–17 (2008)
21. Jarrous, A., Pinkas, B.: Secure hamming distance based computation and its applications. In: Abdalla, M., Pointcheval, D., Fouque, P.-A., Vergnaud, D. (eds.) ACNS 2009. LNCS, vol. 5536, pp. 107–124. Springer, Heidelberg (2009)
22. Lauter, K., Naehrig, M., Vaikuntanathan, V.: Can homomorphic encryption be practical?. In: ACM Workshop on Cloud Computing Security Workshop-CCSW 2011, pp. 113–124. ACM (2011)

23. Lindner, R., Peikert, C.: Better key sizes (and Attacks) for LWE-based encryption. In: Kiayias, A. (ed.) CT-RSA 2011. LNCS, vol. 6558, pp. 319–339. Springer, Heidelberg (2011)

24. Lyubashevsky, V., Peikert, C., Regev, O.: On ideal lattices and learning with errors over rings. In: Gilbert, H. (ed.) EUROCRYPT 2010. LNCS, vol. 6110, pp. 1–23. Springer, Heidelberg (2010)

25. Osadchy, M., Pinkas, B., Jarrous, A., Moskovich, B.: SCiFI - a system for secure face recognition. In: IEEE Security and Privacy, pp. 239–254. IEEE Computer Society (2010)

26. Paillier, P.: Public-key cryptosystems based on composite degree residuosity classes. In: Stern, J. (ed.) EUROCRYPT 1999. LNCS, vol. 1592, pp. 223–238. Springer, Heidelberg (1999)

27. Peikert, C., Vaikuntanathan, V., Waters, B.: A framework for efficient and composable oblivious transfer. In: Wagner, D. (ed.) CRYPTO 2008. LNCS, vol. 5157, pp. 554–571. Springer, Heidelberg (2008)

28. Schoenmakers, B., Tuyls, P.: Efficient binary conversion for paillier encrypted values. In: Vaudenay, S. (ed.) EUROCRYPT 2006. LNCS, vol. 4004, pp. 522–537. Springer, Heidelberg (2006)

29. Smart, N.P., Vercauteren, F.: Fully homomorphic SIMD operations. Des. Codes. Cryptogr. **71**, 57–81 (2014)

30. U.S. Department of Homeland Security, Privacy impact assessment for the biometric storage system. http://www.dhs.gov/xlibrary/assets/privacy/privacy_pia_cis_bss.pdf, 28 March, 2007

31. Yasuda, M., Shimoyama, T., Kogure, J., Yokoyama, K., Koshiba, T.: Packed homomorphic encryption based on ideal lattices and its application to biometrics. In: Cuzzocrea, A., Kittl, C., Simos, D.E., Weippl, E., Xu, L. (eds.) CD-ARES Workshops 2013. LNCS, vol. 8128, pp. 55–74. Springer, Heidelberg (2013)

Collaborative and Privacy-Aware Sensing for Observing Urban Movement Patterns

Nelson Gonçalves[1], Rui José[2], and Carlos Baquero[1(✉)]

[1] HASLab, INESC Tec & Universidade do Minho, Braga, Portugal
goncalvesnelson@gmail.com, cbm@di.uminho.pt
[2] Centro Algoritmi, Universidade do Minho, Braga, Portugal
rui@dsi.uminho.pt

Abstract. The information infrastructure that pervades urban environments represents a major opportunity for collecting information about Human mobility. However, this huge potential has been undermined by the overwhelming privacy risks that are associated with such forms of large scale sensing. In this research, we are concerned with the problem of how to enable a set of autonomous sensing nodes, e.g. a Bluetooth scanner or a Wi-Fi hotspot, to collaborate in the observation of movement patterns of individuals without compromising their privacy. We describe a novel technique that generates Precedence Filters and allows probabilistic estimations of sequences of visits to monitored locations and we demonstrate how this technique can combine plausible deniability by an individual with valuable information about aggregate movement patterns.

Keywords: Privacy · Mobility traces · Bloom filters · Vector clocks

1 Introduction

The ubiquity of the information technology infrastructure that increasingly pervades urban environments constitutes a major opportunity for sensing Human activity. The large scale collection of such data may give new insights into the dynamics of city life and the digital fingerprint of the urban environment.

Wi-fi and Bluetooth hotspots are particularly interesting for that purpose. Given their widespread presence and their inherent communication with personal devices, they can easily be leveraged as general purpose platforms for massive sensing and actuation in urban spaces. However, this huge potential has been undermined by the overwhelming privacy risks that are associated with such forms of large scale sensing. Given that many detectable devices would be personal devices, their presence at a particular location is a reliable representation

Financed by the ERDF – European Regional Development Fund through the COMPETE Programme (operational programme for competitiveness) and by National Funds through the FCT – Fundação para a Ciência e a Tecnologia (Foundation for Science and Technology) within project "FCOMP - 01-0124-FEDER-022701".

J. Garcia-Alfaro et al. (Eds.): DPM 2013 and SETOP 2013, LNCS 8247, pp. 51–65, 2014.
DOI: 10.1007/978-3-642-54568-9_4, © Springer-Verlag Berlin Heidelberg 2014

of the presence of the respective owner. Consequently, a record of Bluetooth or Wi-Fi sightings holds the potential to become a large scale tracking system capable of detecting the presence, movements and patterns of individuals.

In this research, we are concerned with the problem of how to enable a set of autonomous sensing nodes, e.g. a Bluetooth scanner or a Wi-Fi hotspot, to collaborate in the observation of movement patterns of individuals without compromising their privacy. Our approach is based on a stochastic technique that can characterize the sequence of presences in the monitored areas, with a para-meterized fidelity that protects user privacy. Our Precedence Filters algorithm combines properties found on counting bloom filters and vector clocks, providing a solid approach to the detection of sequences of presences. It enables us to provide probabilistic answers to questions such as: *"Are the individuals in this art gallery likely to have visited a given art museum first?"* or, in a shopping mall, *"Which shops are visited most likely after the movie theater? and before the theater?"*. The data collection system can be calibrated in a way that each individual (actually its MAC address pseudonym) has a given chance, say 50 %, of not having been in a reported location or done a given reported transition, thus protecting its privacy and supporting plausible deniability.

To support the evaluation of the approach, we compare the accuracy of the causality traces estimated by the application of the algorithm with the ground truth corresponding to the causality traces generated from perfect information about node transitions. The evaluation confirms the expectations that a higher fidelity on collective movement patterns can be supported by lower fidelity in the individual traces.

2   Related Work

Anonymity. Tang et. al [19] describe a sensing method through which personal devices can become anonymous sensors reporting the number of nearby devices without compromising their own or other peoples privacy. In this case, individuals do not need to be sensed, and this work demonstrates how given a specific sensing goal, it can be possible to devise a technique that limits the collected information to those goals and thus significantly improves the privacy vs utility tradeoff. The use of pseudonyms is perhaps the most obvious way to achieve anonymity when individuals need to be identified in subsequent observations. However, using the same pseudonym for a long time makes it easy for an attacker to gather enough history on an individual to infer its habits or true identity. This is particularly true for spatial data. Previous work has shown how anonymous location traces can easily be re-identified by considering the likely home address of a person [13] or the Home/Work location pair [10].

To try to mitigate this issue, Beresford and Stajano in [4] proposed an idea which relied upon pseudonym exchange. They introduced two new concepts: *mix zone* and *application zone*. The aim is to conceal information in the *mix zone* so that users can safely change pseudonyms when getting in and out of these zones. Based on a different concept, *k-anonymity*, Gruteser and Grunwald [11] were the first to investigate anonymity as a method to attain location privacy. According to them, a subject is considered to be k-anonymous with regard to location information, if and only if she is indistinguishable from at least $k - 1$ other subjects with respect to a set of *quasi-identifier* attributes. Bigger values of k correspond to higher degrees of anonymity.

Mokbel et al. in [18] use the *k-anonymity* concept as well. They presented the Casper framework which consists of two main components, a location anonymizer and a privacy-aware query processor. The location anonymizer blurs the location information about each user according to that user's defined preferences (minimum area A_{min} in which she wants to hide and minimum value for k). The query processor adjusts the functionality of traditional location-based databases to be privacy-aware. It does so by returning cloaked areas instead of exact points when queried for location information.

Our technique can be described as a form of anonymity, but because we never register any individual identifier, the technique is not prone to re-identification attacks that could compromise the entire trace of previous locations of an individual.

Obfuscation. Obfuscation based techniques usually degrade the "quality" of the information in order to provide privacy protection. Even tough this may seem comparable to what *k-anonymity* based techniques do, there is a key difference: obfuscation based techniques allow the actual identity of the user to be revealed (thus making it suitable for applications that require authentication or offer some sort of personalization [15]). Duckam and Kulik [7] were the ones who introduced the idea of obfuscation for location privacy. They talk about three distinct types of imperfection that can be present in spatial information: Inaccuracy - lack of correspondence between information and reality. E.g. "Paris is in Spain"; Imprecision - lack of specificity. E.g. "Paris is in Europe"; Vagueness - using fuzzy borderlines [8]. E.g. "Paris is in Western Europe". Any of these types of imperfection can be used to obfuscate an individual's location. Another example of an obfuscation based approach was shown by Ardagna et al. in [2] and later improved in [1,3]. Their obfuscation process numerically represents a relative accuracy loss in a location measurement.

Even though there are several techniques that allow reducing the quality of raw location information, we found no approach that allows for the characterization of device sighting sequences with adjustable fidelity.

3   System Model

The model in which we base our work assumes the existence of a network of heterogeneous and autonomous nodes that collaborate in the tracking process. While we may consider various types of sensing nodes, for the remainder of this paper we will assume the use of Bluetooth devices. In this case, our sensing node would be some sort of Bluetooth scanner with the ability to discover nearby devices and obtain information about their MAC address, the timestamp of the sighting, among others.

Our model does not impose restrictions on the type of information collected by the scanners or how it is used by the local node. We do, however, want to limit the information that each node is going to share with the rest of the system to the minimum information possible that is still able to support the detection of movement patterns. We need to be able to detect the same device on different nodes, and for this specific purpose we will only use the device's MAC address.

In their everyday life and depending on their specific needs, people visit several different places. For instance, a person P_1 wants to buy a new laptop. To do so, she visits store S_1 which does not have the model she wants. She then visits store S_2 which is out of stock and afterwards store S_3 where the price is a little steep. She ends up buying the laptop in store S_4. To represent this behavior we introduce the concept of *mobility traces*. A mobility trace is simply the representation of the places visited in the order by which they were visited. In this specific case, the mobility trace of P_1 is $MT_{P_1} = \{S_1, S_2, S_3, S_4\}$. Our mechanism, *Precedence Filters*, allows the recording of information relative to the individual traces of people, in a manner compatible with plausible deniability. That information can later be processed to obtain more accurate data about the habits of the aggregate of all individuals. For instance, in this example, the order in which the stores were visited might be an indicator of their popularity.

Whenever a device is sensed, the sighting node records that event locally. This information is then used in the computation of device transitions between the system's multiple nodes. The place where that computation occurs depends on the system's architecture. Our mechanism can be deployed in either centralized or decentralized architectures. In a centralized system configuration, the computation has to be done in the server since only it has enough information to do so. Each node only shares its local information with the server. On the other hand, with a decentralized architecture, nodes can do the processing locally. The local information each node possesses is shared with the other nodes, thus allowing all the nodes to have access to the data. Both models have advantages and disadvantages. For instance, the centralized approach is not fault tolerant, if the server crashes the tracking system stops working. Compared to the centralized version, the decentralized model also has greater availability as a result of the information redundancy. However, as a consequence of the exchange of information between all the nodes, the decentralized scenario has a bigger burden on the network.

In order to achieve the goal we set ourselves, and taking into account the constrains presented by our model, our solution is based upon the following set of assumptions:

- Even though we cannot make assumptions about how each individual node will handle the observed Bluetooth addresses, our solution should never require the Bluetooth address or any other information that could uniquely identify individuals to ever leave the sensing node.
- No system element should, at any given time, have all the information necessary to accurately determine the path of a single individual.

– There are no communication failures in the system and the exchange of information between any two nodes is faster than the time it takes for a person to move between them, i.e., when a person goes from node A to node B, node B must already have the information that she was in A.

4   Precedence Filter Algorithm

This section describes the behavior of Precedence Filters. However, to do so, we must first do a brief overview of the techniques in which they are based, namely Counting Bloom Filters [9] and Vector Clocks [12,17].

4.1   Bloom Filters

Bloom Filters (BFs) were created in 1970 [5] by B.H. Bloom. They are a simple and space efficient data structure for set representation where membership queries are allowed. Bloom Filters allow false positives but do not allow false negatives, i.e, when querying a filter about the existence of an element in a given set, if the answer is no, then the element is definitely not in the set, but if the answer is yes, the element might be in the set.

A Bloom Filter for representing a set of n items $S = \{x_1, x_2, x_3, \ldots, x_n\}$ is traditionally implemented using an array of M bits, all initially set to 0. Then, k independent hash functions are used $\{h_1, h_2, \ldots, h_k\}$, each one mapping the element of the set into a random number uniformly distributed over the range $\{1, \ldots, M\}$. For each element x of the set ($x \in S$) the bits of the positions $h_i(x)$ are all set to 1 for $1 \leq i \leq k$. A location can be set to 1 multiple times. Due to the independence of the hash functions, nothing prevents collisions in the outputs. In extreme cases it is possible to have $h_1(x) = h_2(x) = \ldots = h_k(x)$. To prevent this, we use the variant of Bloom Filters presented in [6] which partitions the M bits among the k hash functions, creating k slices of $m = M/k$ bits. This ensures that each item added to the filter is always described by k bits. Given a Bloom Filter BF_S, checking if an element $z \in BF_S$, consists in verifying whether all $h_i(z)$ are set to 1. If they aren't, then z is definitely not present on the filter. Otherwise, if all the bits are set to 1, then it is assumed that z belongs to BF_S although that assumption might be wrong. This false positive probability exists because the tested indices might have been set by the insertion of other elements. Figure 1 illustrates such an example.

The false positive probability P can be obtained using equation $P = p^k$, where p is the ratio between the number of set bits in the slice and the slice size m. The fill ratio p can be obtained through equation $p = 1 - \left(1 - \frac{1}{m}\right)^n$.

Furthermore, given a maximum false positive probability P, and the number n of distinct elements to store, equations $k = log_2\left(\frac{1}{P}\right)$ and $m = \frac{n*|lnP|}{k*(ln2)^2}$ can be used to estimate the optimal number of bits required by a Bloom Filter to store those n elements, $M = m * k$.

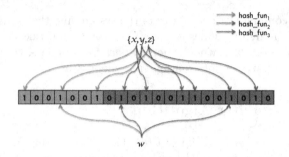

Fig. 1. Bloom filter with $k = 3$, $M = 21$ and $m = 7$, containing elements $\{x, y, z\}$. Querying for the presence of element w yields a false positive.

Counting Bloom Filters. Counting Bloom Filters (CBFs) were presented in [9]. In a Counting Bloom Filter, each position is a small counter rather than a single bit. When an item is inserted the corresponding counters are incremented, and when the item is deleted the same counters are decremented. We just have to choose sufficiently large counters, in order to avoid counter overflow.

4.2   Vector Clocks

In order to better understand how Vector Clocks work, we must first comprehend the concept of causality. Causality is a relation through which we can connect two events, a first event (known as the *cause*) and a second one (the *effect*).

In the context of Distributed Systems, causality is expressed using the *happens-before* relation [14] denoted by the → symbol. For instance, given 2 events, $x \rightarrow y$, reads as x happened-before y, and means y might be a consequence of x.

Vector Clocks were introduced by Colin Fidge [12] and Friedemann Mattern [17] in 1988 and are a practical implementation of the *happens-before* concept. In this algorithm, each process P_i has a vector of integer values $VC_i[1..n]$ where n is the number of processes, maintained by the following set of rules:

1. In the beginning, all the positions from the vector are set to 0.
2. Each time the state of a process P_i changes (send, receive or internal event), it must increment the value $VC_i[i]$, i.e, ($VC_i[i] = VC_i[i] + 1$).
3. Each time a process P_i sends a message, its vector VC_i is sent.
4. When a process P_i receives a message m, it must update its vector using the formula:
   $\forall x : VC_i[x] = max(VC_i[x], m.VC[x])$, where $m.VC$ symbolizes the vector clock attached to m.

Vector Clocks are able to accurately represent the causality relation and the partial order it defines. Given any two distinct events x and y:

$$\forall(x, y) : (x \rightarrow y) \Longleftrightarrow (VC_x < VC_y)$$

Where $VC_x < VC_y$ stands for:

$$(\forall k : VC_x[k] \le VC_y[k] \wedge (\exists k : VC_x[k] < VC_y[k]))$$

4.3 Precedence Filters

By applying some of the previously mentioned general constructs of distributed systems to the mobility sensing scenario, Bluetooth scanners can be treated as processes and device sightings as state transition events. Precedence Filters (PFs) are based upon this idea and provide accurate mobility information, at a macroscopic level, without neglecting individual privacy. Precedence Filters can be seen as a vector clock [12,17] implementation, whose difference is the use of Counting Bloom Filters [9] (one for each node in the system) by the PFs instead of integers (one per process) used by vector clocks.

With that in mind, Precedence Filters work as follows: supposing we have a set of Bluetooth scanners (nodes) S, each node $n \in S$ has a Precedence Filter PF_n. That PF is in turn composed of a map of *Counting Bloom Filters*, one for each node $z \in S$. We use notation PF_n^z to refer to the CBF for scanner z belonging to PF_n.

All CBFs are initially set to 0, use the same set of hash functions K and have the same fixed size $M = m * k$. Once calculated, the value M cannot be changed. This limitation has to do with ensuring that the same device is correctly identified across the several nodes (upon detection it will be mapped to the same indices). Precedence Filters can also be seen as a matrix where the number of rows is equal to the number of nodes in the system and the number of columns is equal to M.

Each time a node n detects a device d, its Precedence Filter PF_n is updated according to the following set of rules:

1. Using the set of hash functions K, the node n calculates the set of indices I_d. I_d consists on the output from the K hash functions regarding device d, $I_d = \bigcup_{f \in K} f(d)$.
2. Node n sends the set of indices I_d to all other nodes in S.
3. Each one of the z nodes belonging to Z ($Z = S\backslash\{n\}$) replies with a set of tuples $R_z^{I_d}$. R_z contains the previously required I_d along with the set of values that each of the CBFs belonging to PF_z had stored in those indices, $R_z^{I_d} = \{(i, PF_z^z[i]) \mid \forall i \in I_d\}$.
4. Upon the reception of the replies from the other nodes, node n updates its own indices I_d on the CBFs relative to the other nodes with the maximum value received, $PF_n^z[i] = \max(R_z^{I_d}[i]), \forall z \in Z, \forall i \in I_d$, where $R_z^{I_d}[i] = v \Rightarrow (i, v) \in R_z^{I_d}$.
5. Lastly, n updates the indices I_d on its own CBF (PF_n^n). For each index $i \in I_d, PF_n^n[i] = \max(PF_n^s[i]) + 1, \forall s \in S$. By adding 1 to the maximum value stored in the other nodes, the current node "dominates" them in the operation that returns the causality between the visited places. In other words, this is the key to obtaining the order in which the places were visited.

This set of rules allows the Precedence Filters to record information about the precedence of the locals visited by a device. Given a set of indices I_d for device d and any pair of scanners x and y, we say that the sighting of d in x precedes the one in y, $x \rightsquigarrow y$ if:

$$x \rightsquigarrow y \iff PF_x[I_d] < PF_y[I_d]$$

Where $PF_x[I_d] < PF_y[I_d]$ stands for:

$$\forall i \in I_d : PF_x^x[i] < PF_y^y[i]$$

Mobility traces, used in our model to describe the behavior of individuals, characterize a total order between the places visited. This means that it is always possible to establish an order between any two places in the mobility trace. However, being based upon the happens-before relation [14], Precedence Filters represent partial orders. In this particular case, for each of the nodes/locations, they can only "remember" the last time each device was sighted in a given place. For instance, given the mobility trace

$$MT_P = \{S_1, S_2, S_1, S_3, S_2, S_4, S_1\}$$

where scanners S_1 and S_2 are visited more than once, in the best case scenario PFs can obtain $CT_P = \{S_3, S_2, S_4, S_1\}$, which we will refer as a *causality trace*. This is a consequence of the irreflexivity and antisymmetry properties from the happens-before relation. However, we can look at this as a feature of Precedence Filters, a sort of automatic data degradation. It ensures that the length of the record of sightings for any device has an upper bound equal to the number of scanners in the tracking system.

The level of privacy offered by Precedence Filters can be further customized by adjusting the CBFs' false positive ratio P. The higher the ratio, the greater the inaccuracy of the PFs. The occurrence of false positives in the CBFs results in the appearance of *fictitious transitions*, i.e., the causal trace obtained from querying the filters, contains transitions which are non-existent in the original trace. This property also makes unfeasible the use of sets of indexes as pseudonyms as indexes can be shared by different devices. These properties are what allow individual users to plausibly deny the fidelity of the data extracted from Precedence Filters.

Ignoring constant and logarithmic factors, the communication and space storage scalability of the technique is dominated by the number of scanners S and the expected number of devices to monitor, D. Each scanner needs to store state that is linear with the number of devices $O(D)$. One should note however, that due to lossy compression only a fraction of the bit size of a MAC address is needed, with smaller fractions for higher privacy (and lower fidelity). As a whole, the system stores state $O(SD)$, and this would be the server state for a centralized setup. Each time a device is sighted at a given scanner, its network link will have a communication load of $O(S)$ and induce $O(1)$ communication in other scanner links, as it collects logarithmic information on a constant number of positions k at all other scanners. Thus, the maximum communication load induced per sighting is linear on the number of scanning sites.

5   Metrics and Data Sets

To assess the estimation quality of Precedence Filters we compared the set of transitions obtained from querying the Precedence Filters with the set of transitions obtained from the causality traces (baseline), which were themselves obtained from mobility traces. For instance, given the mobility trace $MT_P = \{S_1, S_2, S_2, S_1, S_3\}$, we calculate its causality trace according to the happens-before relation (that only contains last sighting in each place), $CT_P = \{S_2, S_1, S_3\}$. Then we extract the set of transitions, denoted $\mathcal{T}$, from that causality trace, $\mathcal{T}(CT_p) = \{(S_2, S_1), (S_2, S_3), (S_1, S_3)\}$. Each transition is a two location tuple where the first location causally precedes the second. In our scenario, that means the device was seen in the first location before being sighted at the second location. This set of transitions is then finally compared to a similar set of transitions obtained from the PFs, $\mathcal{T}(PF)$.

Metrics. To support the evaluation of Precedence Filters, we used two different metrics. The *individual* metric which measures the false probability of statements like the following – " individual X visited location S_1 before visiting location S_2". For each user u, this is done by calculating the cardinality of the difference between the transitions belonging to the causality trace $(\mathcal{T}(CT_u))$ and the transitions extracted from the Precedence Filter $(\mathcal{T}(PF_u))$, according to Eq. 1.

$$\frac{\#((\mathcal{T}(CT_u) \bigcup \mathcal{T}(PF_u)) \setminus (\mathcal{T}(CT_u) \bigcap \mathcal{T}(PF_u)))}{\#(\mathcal{T}(PF_u))} \tag{1}$$

The individual metric calculates the relative amount of incorrect information (information that is on the CTs and not on the PFs and *vice-versa*) returned by the Precedence Filters. However, given the assumption that the exchange of information between nodes is faster than people, our system never forgets information, i.e., $\mathcal{T}(CT) \subseteq \mathcal{T}(PF)$. Therefore, Eq. 1 can be simplified, resulting in Eq. 2.

$$\frac{\#(\mathcal{T}(PF_u) \setminus \mathcal{T}(CT_u))}{\#(\mathcal{T}(PF_u))} \tag{2}$$

The *global* metric quantifies the inaccuracy of information regarding the relative weight of specific transitions. This enables us to establish the relative importance of each type of transition, i.e., to know the inherent error in statements like - "2 % of the transitions are from Restaurant Y to Cafe Z". Assuming that, U represents the universe of all users, $\mathcal{A}_{PF} = \biguplus_{u \in U} \mathcal{T}(PF_u)$ and $\mathcal{A}_{CT} = \biguplus_{u \in U} \mathcal{T}(CT_u)$ are respectively the multiset union of all transitions in the Precedence Filters and in the Causality Traces and that $\mathcal{A}[t]$ is multiset composed only of the t transitions in $\mathcal{A}$, the global metric for each transition

$t \in \mathcal{A}$ is calculated according to Eq. 3. For each transition, we calculate the absolute difference between its relative weight in the Precedence Filter and its relative weight in the actual Causality Traces. Then we divide that number by its weight on the Precedence Filters. This gives us the relative error of the relative weight of the transition.

$$\frac{\left| \frac{\#\mathcal{A}_{PF}[t]}{\#\mathcal{A}_{PF}} - \frac{\#\mathcal{A}_{CT}[t]}{\#\mathcal{A}_{CT}} \right|}{\#\mathcal{A}_{PF}[t]} \tag{3}$$

Real Data Set. To evaluate the PFs' performance we used a real data set with information about Bluetooth sightings by static nodes. This data set was taken from Leguay et al.'s work [16]. To collect this information, the authors handed out a set of Bluetooth enabled devices called *iMotes* to a group of users who carried them in their day-to-day. Additionally, the authors installed Bluetooth scanners in several places with the purpose of registering the sightings of *iMotes*. The dataset contains 18 static nodes and 9244 distinct device IDs, 6439 of which have been sighted only once and were therefore removed. This leaves us with 2805 devices, whose average mobility trace size is approximately 4 and maximum size is 11. Figure 2(a) shows the distribution of total and distinct sightings for all scanners. As expected, not all places have the same popularity, some are more visited than others, thus the bigger number of Bluetooth sightings.

Synthetic Data Set. Still in the context of evaluating the PF's performance, we built a synthetic trace generator. Our motivation came from the need to simulate scenarios with arbitrary number of locations and users.

In a first approach, we tried fitting the statistic distribution of the real data set using a negative exponential distribution. This would have allowed us to choose an arbitrary number of sensors, users and trace length. However, after evaluation with Pearson's Chi-Square test, it turned out to be a bad fitting.

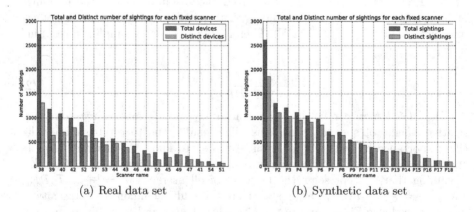

(a) Real data set   (b) Synthetic data set

Fig. 2. Number of total and distinct device sightings across the scanners

This might be solvable by switching to a more complex distribution function. Instead we chose to work with the empiric distribution. On this second approach, it was decided to use the same number of sensors as the real data set, i.e. 18. This allowed us to simulate the popularity of each sensor/place using the number of sightings from the real data set as weights. The larger the number of sightings at a sensor, the bigger its weight is, and the more likely it is to be chosen. Each node is defined by two parameters, unique sightings and total sightings. We only made use of the latter. The use of *replication*[1] enabled us to create a simpler and less error prone simulator, capable of producing as many users as we want, as well as mobility traces with arbitrary length. The downside of not using the unique number of sightings is that we are assuming that even though places have different weights, they are the same for everyone, i.e. everyone has the same probability of choosing a given place, everyone is an "average" person.

Figure 2(b) shows the synthetic distribution obtained using the approach mentioned above. As expected the results are very similar but not a perfect match. There is a correlation between the number of total and unique sightings which stems from the use of the "average" person model. Also, the curve from the synthetic data set is smoother, it does not suffer from the "noise" inherent to raw real data.

6   Evaluation

Using the metrics and data sets previously mentioned, we tested the Precedence Filter's inaccuracy across several scenarios, varying both the number of devices and the length of the mobility traces. Furthermore, each of the scenarios was tested with multiple different settings for the Counting Bloom Filter's maximum false positive probability. A good performance is reflected through high inaccuracy values for individual information together with low values for global inaccuracy.

As can be seen in Figs. 3, 4, 5 and 6, by increasing the false positive probability of CBFs, inaccuracy increases as well. Inaccuracy is manifested via the occurrence of fake (visible on PFs only) transitions, i.e., *fictitious transitions*. As the false probability increases, so does the percentage of fake transitions. This is easily explainable. In Bloom Filters, false positives denote elements wrongfully considered as belonging to the set. Given that in PFs Bloom Filters are used to record device sightings, the occurrence of false positives generates fake device sightings, which in turn give origin to fictitious transitions.

As previously explained, both data sets use 18 scanning nodes, what differs is the number of devices and the length of the mobility traces. To describe the parameters of each scenario, the following notation is used in the captions: Synthetic/Real-[*number of devices*]-[*maximum trace length*]-[*average trace length*].

---

[1] In statistics, replication is the repetition of an experiment or observation in the same or similar conditions.

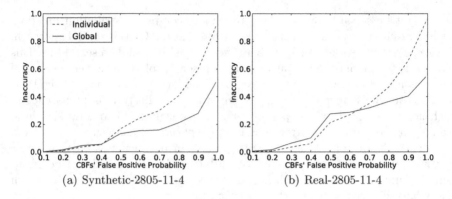

Fig. 3. Comparison between real and synthetic data set, with same parameters

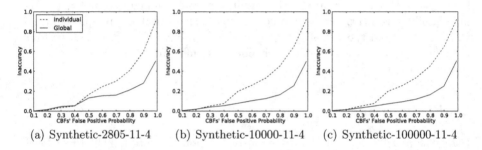

Fig. 4. Synthetic data sets with increasing number of devices

Figure 3 shows the comparison between a synthetic data set and the real data set. This synthetic data set will serve as the baseline for all tests because it simulates both the number of devices and trace length found in the real data set. Our technique performs better with data from the synthetic data set (Fig. 3(a)) than it does with data from the real one (Fig. 3(b)). This is a consequence of the average person simplification we did for the synthetic data sets. Figure 2 shows that while the number of total sightings is approximately equal in both data sets, the number of unique sightings is usually bigger in synthetic data set. This means that the real data set has a greater number of repeated sightings by user, which in turn means that the average length of the causality traces is smaller, i.e., even if both data sets have the same number of users and similar sized mobility traces, the causality traces in the real data set are smaller, explaining the worse performance of our technique.

For both these data sets, there is a point where the individual accuracy is greater than the global one, however, when the individual inaccuracy is approximately 50 %, the global inaccuracy is higher than what is desirable. This is a result of the low number of individuals and small mobility trace sizes of both data sets, as supported by Figs. 4, 5 and 6.

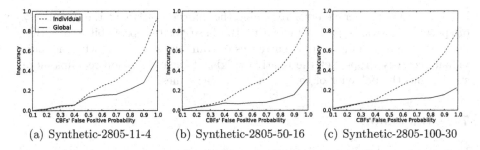

(a) Synthetic-2805-11-4   (b) Synthetic-2805-50-16   (c) Synthetic-2805-100-30

Fig. 5. Synthetic data sets with increasing trace sizes

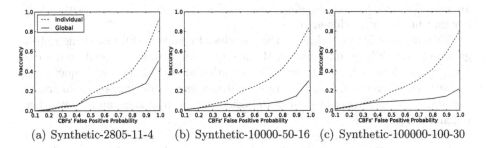

(a) Synthetic-2805-11-4   (b) Synthetic-10000-50-16   (c) Synthetic-100000-100-30

Fig. 6. Synthetic data sets with increasing number of devices and trace sizes

Keeping the length of mobility traces constant, Fig. 4 shows that Precedence Filter's global inaccuracy drops by increasing the number of devices to 10^4, and then again, although little, by increasing that number to 10^5. In both scenarios, for a false positive probability of 0.8, PFs provide global inaccuracy below 20 % while ensuring that in average, 50 % of the information about any given individual is incorrect.

Keeping the same number of devices, while increasing the length of the mobility traces also improves the Precedence Filter's global accuracy, as depicted in Fig. 5. For instance, Fig. 5(c) shows that by increasing the average and maximum values for mobility traces respectively to 30 and 100, our technique offers a global error of about 15 %, while providing 50 % of inaccuracy for individual information. Increasing both the number of devices and the length of the mobility traces yields the better results, which is not surprising given both the previous results.

In a scenario with 10^5 users whose maximum and average mobility trace sizes are respectively 100 and 30, depicted in Fig. 6(c), our technique has a global inaccuracy a little higher than 10 % while providing an individual inaccuracy of 50 %. This means that, on average, half of the information about individual transitions is wrong, which we consider to be a value compatible with plausible deniability. To recap, our technique registers information user transitions. Each user has a set of transitions, and the individual metric measures, in average, the percentage of those which are fictitious/false. The global metric, on the other hand, returns the average error regarding the information about the popularity of specific transitions/paths. Increasing the false positive probability of CBFs increases the total number of occurrences of transitions, which is why the individual accuracy drops; yet the relative weight of each transition remains more stable, thus the behavior of the global inaccuracy lines.

7   Conclusion

Vast amounts of collective movement patterns could be harnessed and put to good use in city planning, ad placement, and traffic congestion prevention. The limitations are no longer of a technological nature and suitable infrastructures are often in place that could allow mass sensing. Our stance is that privacy is a key limiting factor in this area.

We have presented a technique that provides Precedence Filters. Using aggregation of probabilistic information about sequences of visits to monitored locations, this technique is able to reveal information about the relative frequency of transitions. In practice, frequent transitions can lead to optimizations in transportation systems, discount policies in businesses and museums, and many other potential applications.

To evaluate the technique we first had to define and propose new metrics to analyze trace estimation quality. Evaluation was based on a robust trace driven simulation, from a real mobility dataset, complemented with simulations over longer synthetic traces that allowed a comprehensive analysis of the long term properties, for higher numbers of users and longer traces.

The resulting technique is highly adjustable in the degree of privacy and degradation of fidelity that is required in each potential setting. An important overall property is the ability to give good quality collective traces from lower quality individual traces. This brings the best of both worlds, high individual privacy and good collective statistics.

References

1. Ardagna, C.A., Cremonini, M., Damiani, E., De Capitani di Vimercati, S., Samarati, P.: Location privacy protection through obfuscation-based techniques. In: Barker, S., Ahn, G.-J. (eds.) Data and Applications Security 2007. LNCS, vol. 4602, pp. 47–60. Springer, Heidelberg (2007)
2. Ardagna, C.A., Cremonini, M., De Capitani di Vimercati, S., Samarati, P.: A middleware architecture for integrating privacy preferences and location accuracy. In: Venter, H., Eloff, M., Labuschagne, L., Eloff, J., von Solms, R. (eds.) New Approaches for Security, Privacy and Trust in Complex Environments, pp. 313–324. Springer, Boston (2007)
3. Ardagna, C.A., Cremonini, M., De Capitani di Vimercati, S., Samarati, P.: An obfuscation-based approach for protecting location privacy. IEEE Trans. Dependable Secure Comput. 8(1), 13–27 (2011)
4. Beresford, A., Stajano, F.: Location privacy in pervasive computing. IEEE Pervasive Comput. 2(1), 46–55 (2003)

5. Bloom, B.H.: Space/time trade-offs in hash coding with allowable errors. Commun. ACM **13**(7), 422–426 (1970)
6. Chang, F., Chang, F., chang Feng, W.: Approximate caches for packet classification. In: In IEEE INFOCOM, pp. 2196–2207 (2004)
7. Duckham, M., Kulik, L.: A formal model of obfuscation and negotiation for location privacy. In: Gellersen, H.-W., Want, R., Schmidt, A. (eds.) PERVASIVE 2005. LNCS, vol. 3468, pp. 152–170. Springer, Heidelberg (2005)
8. Duckham, M., Mason, K., Stell, J., Worboys, M.: A formal approach to imperfection in geographic information. Comput. Environ. Urban Syst. **25**(1), 89–103 (2001)
9. Fan, L., Cao, P., Almeida, J., Broder, A.Z.: Summary cache: a scalable wide-area web cache sharing protocol. In: IEEE/ACM Transactions on Networking, pp. 254–265 (1998)
10. Golle, P., Partridge, K.: On the anonymity of home/work location pairs. Pervasive Comput. **5538**, 390–397 (2009)
11. Gruteser, M., Grunwald, D.: Anonymous usage of location-based services through spatial and temporal cloaking. In: Proceedings of the 1st International Conference on Mobile Systems, Applications and Services, pp. 31–42. ACM (2003)
12. Fidge, C.J.: Timestamps in message-passing systems that preserve the partial ordering. Aust. Comput. Sci. Commun. **10**(1), 56–66 (1988)
13. Krumm, J.: Inference attacks on location tracks. In: LaMarca, A., Langheinrich, M., Truong, K.N. (eds.) Pervasive 2007. LNCS, vol. 4480, pp. 127–143. Springer, Heidelberg (2007)
14. Lamport, L.: Time, clocks, and the ordering of events in a distributed system. Commun. ACM **21**, 558–565 (1978). doi:10.1145/359545.359563
15. Langheinrich, M.: Privacy by design principles of privacy-aware ubiquitous systems. In: Abowd, G.D., Brumitt, B., Shafer, S.A.N. (eds.) Ubicomp 2001. LNCS, vol. 2201, pp. 273–291. Springer, Heidelberg (2001)
16. Leguay, J., Lindgren, A., Scott, J., Friedman, T., Crowcroft, J.: Opportunistic content distribution in an urban setting. In: Proceedings of the 2006 SIGCOMM Workshop on Challenged Networks, pp. 205–212. ACM (2006)
17. Mattern, F.: Virtual time and global states of distributed systems. In: Workshop on Parallel and Distributed Algorithms (1988)
18. Mokbel, M., Chow, C., Aref, W.: The new casper: query processing for location services without compromising privacy. In: Proceedings of the 32nd International Conference on Very Large Data Bases, pp. 763–774. VLDB Endowment (2006)
19. Tang, K.P., Keyani, P., Fogarty, J., Hong, J.I.: Putting people in their place: an anonymous and privacy-sensitive approach to collecting sensed data in location based applications. In: SIGCHI Conference on Human Factors in Computing Systems, vol. 8, pp. 93–102. ACM (2006)

Parallel Implementation of GC-Based MPC Protocols in the Semi-Honest Setting

Mauro Barni[1], Massimo Bernaschi[2], Riccardo Lazzeretti[1(✉)],
Tommaso Pignata[1], and Alessandro Sabellico[2]

[1] Information Engineering and Mathematical Science Department,
University of Siena, Siena, Italy
barni@dii.unisi.it, {riccardo.lazzeretti,pignata.tommaso}@gmail.com,
[2] Institute of Applied Computing, National Research Council of Italy, Rome, Italy
{massimo.bernaschi,a.sabellico}@gmail.com

Abstract. Parallel computing offers the chance of improving the efficiency of Garbled Circuit technique in multi-party computation protocols. We propose two different types of parallelization: fine-grained, based on the parallel evaluation of gates, and coarse grained, based on the parallelization of macro-blocks. To analyze the efficiency of parallel implementation, a biometric scenario, having an intrinsically parallel nature, is considered. Moreover our approach is compared to previous works by using a privacy preserving implementation of AES encryption. We show that both fine-grained and coarse-grained solutions provide significant runtime improvements. Better results are obtained by the coarse-grained parallelization, which, however, can be exploited only when the same block is used more than once in parallel, whereas fine-grained parallelization can be applied to any garbled circuit.

Keywords: Parallel computing · Multi-party computation · Signal processing in the encrypted domain · Garbled circuits

1 Introduction

Rapid technological advances in multi-party signal processing have given rise to a variety of new signal processing applications for which security aspects can no longer be dealt with by classical cryptographic methods. The classical security model is targeted toward protecting the communication of two trusted parties against a potentially malevolent third party. In such cases, it is sufficient that secure cryptographic primitives are applied on top of transmission and processing modules. In an increasing number of applications, however, the classical security model is no longer adequate since at least one of the parties involved in the communication, distribution or processing of the data may not be trustworthy.

Multi-Party Computation (MPC) provides a clever way to process data without revealing any details about the data itself during the processing. When the to-be-processed data is a signal [11,20], MPC is customarily referred to as

J. Garcia-Alfaro et al. (Eds.): DPM 2013 and SETOP 2013, LNCS 8247, pp. 66–82, 2014.
DOI: 10.1007/978-3-642-54568-9_5, © Springer-Verlag Berlin Heidelberg 2014

S.P.E.D. (Signal Processing in the Encrypted Domain), since signal protection is usually achieved by encrypting the signals and processing them in encrypted form. Possible applications of MPC are virtually endless. For example, a database server may be untrustworthy [1], creating the need to hide the content of queries to the database server, while still allowing the query to be resolved. As another example, we may consider a remote diagnosis service [4,21], where a non-trusted party is tasked with processing sensitive medical data without leaking the private data of the patient (including the diagnosis results). The use of MPC for biometric identification and access control is also gaining popularity since it permits to protect the privacy of the biometric owners in client server applications. Many types of biometries have been addressed in S.P.E.D. analysis, including: face recognition [10], fingerprinting identification [2,3], iris identification [23], etc. Besides the scenarios already outlined, we also recall user preferences [12], watermarking [9], digital rights management [14].

In a two-party computation (2PC) protocol, two players, usually referred to as Alice and Bob, are interested in cooperating to evaluate a given public function $z = f(x; y)$, where x and y are the inputs owned by Alice and Bob respectively, and where neither Alice nor Bob wants to disclose her/his inputs to the other party. At the end of the protocol, the output will be available to one party between Alice and Bob, or to both of them. Yao's Garbled Circuits theory (GC) [30,31] is one of the most used approaches to private computing. In its seminal work, Yao showed that any polynomial size functionality $f(\cdot)$ can be evaluated privately in a constant number of rounds, with polynomial communication and computational overhead. GC allows the evaluation of the binary circuit implementing $f(x, y)$ on input bits privately owned by Alice and Bob, so that the final result is available to one of them (or both), whereas intermediate values cannot be discovered by any of the parties. Yao's protocol has long been thought to be of theoretical interest only due to its complexity. However, recent works have shown several ways to improve GCs efficiency, making them usable even in practical scenarios. Parallel evaluation of circuits is surely one of such methods, however even though it is known that GC can benefit from parallelization, no benchmark analysis has been provided before.

In this paper we describe two ways whereby parallel computing can significantly improve the GC efficiency. Parallel computing has been used in scientific applications for decades in fields like fluid dynamics, material science, weather forecasts. Recently, due to the difficulties of further reducing the clock rate of the processors, all CPU vendors are investing, for the sake of better performance, on multi and many-core architectures, so parallel processing is becoming common practice in many other fields. Due to specific features of GC, briefly recalled in Sect. 2, parallel processing of GC requires a paradigm that entails an overhead as limited as possible for the management of parallel tasks.

Related Work. Several implementations of GC have been already proposed, starting from Fairplay [24], FairplaySPF [27], Tasty [15], etc. To the best of our knowledge, currently, the most efficient implementation in the semi-honest setting is the one presented in [16].

Recently also some parallel implementations have been proposed. In [29], GPU is used for parallel implementation of specific operations needed by the GC protocol, whereas [13] uses GPU processors for GC implementation in the malicious setting.

Our Contribution. In this paper we demonstrate that GC can take advantage of parallel computation, especially when the representation of the required functionality results in a very large circuit. We address two different types of parallelization: the first one, fine-grained parallelization, is based on the parallelization of the single gates composing a circuit, while the second one, coarse-grained parallelization, is based on macro-blocks parallelization. The proposed solutions are evaluated by running them on multi-core processors. In particular, we resort to *threads* for parallel processing of GC since they run very efficiently on modern CPUs and offer all the synchronization mechanisms required to prevent race conditions in the evaluation of GC. For our tests a biometric identification scenario has been chosen, for its high parallel nature. Moreover, to compare our results to previous implementations, a privacy preserving implementation of AES encryption [8] has been tested as well.

Outline. In Sect. 2 the basis of the GC scheme is presented; in Sect. 3 we present our parallel implementations, whose application to privacy preserving biometric scenarios and AES encryption is presented in Sect. 4, together with the obtained results and a security analysis. Finally some conclusions are provided in Sect. 5.

2   Preliminaries

Garbled circuit (GC) is an elegant method for secure function evaluation of boolean circuits. The general idea of GCs, going back to Yao [30,31], is to encrypt (*garble*) each wire and gate with a symmetric encryption scheme.

Yao's Protocol. At a high-level, Yao's GC protocol works as follows: in the setup phase, the *constructor* (Bob) generates an encrypted version of the function f (represented as boolean circuit), called *garbled circuit* $\widetilde{f}$. To that purpose, he assigns to each wire w_i of f two randomly chosen garbled values $\widetilde{w}_i^0, \widetilde{w}_i^1$ (symmetric keys) of t bits each (security parameter set equal to $t = 80$ for short-term security), that correspond to the respective values 0 and 1. Note that $\widetilde{w}_i^v$ does not reveal any information about the plain value v as both keys look random. Then, for each gate of f, the constructor creates helper information in form of a *garbled table* $\widetilde{T}_i$ that allows to decrypt only the output key from the gate's input keys. Each table is used to find the correct value of the output wire of the gate given a specific value on each of the garbled gate's input wires. By expressing the functionality of a given gate as $\gamma = G(\alpha, \beta)$, where $\alpha \in \{0, 1\}$ and $\beta \in \{0, 1\}$ are the input wires of the gate while $\gamma \in \{0, 1\}$ is the gate's output wire, then the garbled computation table is a random permutation of $E_{\widetilde{w}^\alpha}\left(E_{\widetilde{w}^\beta}(\widetilde{w}^\gamma | check)\right)$ for all the four possible input pairs, (α, β), using some symmetric encryption function $E_{key}(\cdot)$ and appending a *check* sequence to the garbled output that helps the identification of the correct row.

The garbled circuit $\tilde{f}$, consisting of the garbled tables generated from the gates, is sent to the *evaluator* (Alice). Later, in the online phase, Alice obliviously obtains the garbled values $\tilde{x}$ and $\tilde{y}$ corresponding to the plain inputs x and y of Alice and Bob, respectively. To convert a plain input bit y_i of Bob into its garbled version, Bob simply sends the key $\tilde{y}_i^{y_i}$ to Alice. Similarly, Alice must obtain the garbled secret $\tilde{x}_i^{x_i}$ corresponding to her input bit x_i, avoiding that Bob learns x_i. This can be achieved by running, possibly in parallel, for each bit x_i of x, a 1-out-of-2 *Oblivious Transfer (OT)* protocol [25]. OT is a cryptographic protocol taking as input Alice's choice bit $b = x_i$ and Bob's strings $s^0 = \tilde{x}_i^0$ and $s^1 = \tilde{x}_i^1$. The protocol guarantees that Alice obtains only the chosen string $s^b = \tilde{x}_i^{x_i}$ while Bob learns no information on $b = x_i$. Afterwords, Alice evaluates the garbled circuit $\tilde{f}$ on $\tilde{x}, \tilde{y}$ by evaluating the garbled gates one-by-one decrypting the rows of the associated tables, where the correct decryption is identified by the *check* sequence. Finally, Alice obtains the corresponding garbled output values $\tilde{z}$ which can be decrypted into the corresponding plain output $z = f(x, y)$.

OT implementation. To efficiently implement OT, the following techniques are used:

Pre-computing OT [6] allows moving computation and communication burden to the setup phase, where both parties run the OT protocol on random inputs. This makes secrets generation independent from circuit execution. Then, in the more time-critical online phase, Alice and Bob use those random inputs to mask their real inputs with a one-time pad. OT secrets, that have been produced in the offline phase, are "consumed" by retrieving them from the files, where they have been stored by the offline generator procedure. The same secret is never used twice in the same or other circuits.

Extending OT efficiently [17] allows for the reduction of the computation complexity during the setup phase by replacing n parallel OTs of t-bit-strings with t parallel OTs of t-bit strings performed in the opposite direction, followed by other computations that extends the number of OT.

Implementation over elliptic curves permits the implementation of efficient OT protocols, evaluating n parallel OTs of ℓ-bit strings, implemented efficiently with the protocol of [25] over *elliptic curves*. The use of elliptic curves allows to perform operations on and transmit shorter cyphertexts with respect to group Z_n. Unfortunately the computation complexity of the protocol increases, but the communication complexity reduction results in a significant decrease of the execution time, since communication between parties is a critical component of the execution.

Optimized GCs. While Yao's GC formulation does not take into account the problem of the efficiency, many improvements have been proposed in the last years. The principal improvements can be summarized as follows.

First of all for efficient implementation of GC, a random oracle $H(\cdot)$ is used. It is usually instantiated with a suitably chosen cryptographic hash function such as SHA-256 [26]. Hence symmetric encryption of the gate rows is performed as

$$E_{\widetilde{w}^\alpha}\big(E_{\widetilde{w}^\beta}(\widetilde{w}^\gamma|check)\big) = (\widetilde{w}^\gamma|check) \oplus H(\widetilde{w}^\alpha|\widetilde{w}^\beta|s) \tag{1}$$

where s is a gate identifier.

The *point and permute* technique [24] allows the evaluator to decrypt directly the correct row, resulting in a double advantage: only a single call to the encryption function for each gate is needed during evaluation and the *check* sequence is no longer necessary, reducing the dimension of the garbled tables. The idea is to associate a single permutation bit $\pi_i \in \{0,1\}$ to each wire i. The garbled value associated to the wire is $\widetilde{w}^i|c_i$, where $c_i = b_i \oplus \pi_i$. Each row of the garbled table is hence computed as $(\widetilde{w}^\gamma|c^\gamma) \oplus H(\widetilde{w}^\alpha|\widetilde{w}^\beta|s)$ and the rows of the garbled tables are permuted according to the input permutation bits. In such a way, during evaluation, the correct row is directly selected by observing c^α and c^β.

Another important improvement is the *free-XOR* technique [19]. Garbled XOR gates require no garbled table and negligible computation. A global key Δ is randomly chosen and the secrets for each wire i are generated so that $\widetilde{w}_1^i = \widetilde{w}_0^i \oplus \Delta$. The output wire of a XOR gate having input wires α and β is computed as $(\widetilde{w}^\gamma|c^\gamma) = (\widetilde{w}^\alpha|c^\alpha) \oplus (\widetilde{w}^\beta|c^\beta)$.

Finally Garbled Row Reduction [28] can also be used to reduce the size of non-XOR gates by eliminating a row in each garbled table, resulting in a $\approx 25\,\%$ reduction of non-XOR gate garbling, transmission and evaluation times.

Our implementation. To evaluate the benefits provided by parallel evaluation, we implemented our version of GC tools. Our C++ implementation of Garbled Circuits relies on the object-oriented paradigm to guarantee reusable code and consistent modules interaction. absence does not compromise the comparison between the sequential GC implementation and the parallel implementations.

We consider that by using the extending OT technique, blocks of 1 million OTs are precomputed and stored, so that when a given number of OT are evaluated online, the same number of precomputed OTs are picked, used and removed from the memory. In our implementation we evaluate $\approx$200000 offline OTs in a second. It is important to underline that we consider the function f that Alice and Bob are going to jointly evaluate, to be known before they have the input values, hence garbling and garbled circuit transmission can also be performed in the setup phase.

3   Circuit Parallelization

As mentioned above, many recent works have improved the efficiency of GC. Hereafter, we demonstrate that the evaluation of GC can also take advantage from parallel execution. Parallel processing can be used for both OT, where bits are independent from each other, and processing of those gates that, depending on the circuit, can be garbled/evaluated in any order.

With respect to other GC implementations, in OT parallelization, we have parallelized secrets generation, by computing multiple bits at the same time and the protocol used to securely exchange secrets, the Bellare-Micali protocol [7], whose computation is divided in offline and online phases. Gate parallelization strongly depends on the characteristics of the to be evaluated function, so a flexible and low-overhead parallelization technique is required. *Threads* fulfill both requirements: on multi-processor or multi-core systems, they can concurrently be assigned to each processor or core running a thread of the same process (or task) and the time required to create and synchronize them is much lower with respect to standard processes. *Threads* are supported at both language (e.g., Java) and operating system level (*pthreads* in Unix-like OS and *winthreads* in Windows). In the present work we resort to *pthreads* programmed in C++ and the resulting GC evaluation engine runs seamlessly under Unix and Mac OS. Porting to Windows is possible simply by replacing the calls to *pthreads* with invocation of *winthreads* primitives.

Two different kinds of parallelization are considered: fine-grained, corresponding to classic parallelization of single gates evaluation and our new subdivision of the circuit into layers, where with layer we intend a subset of the circuit's gates that can be evaluated independently from other gates by Garbler and Evaluator; and coarse-grained, considered here for the first time where macro blocks composing the circuit are parallelized. Inside each macro block, gates can again be evaluated in parallel.

3.1 Fine-Grained Parallelization

In fine-grained parallelization, the gates of the circuit are subdivided into layers, such that all the gates in the same layer can be evaluated in parallel. No special attention is needed during circuit design, that is performed as usual. Later, the circuit is parsed, so that the gates are sorted to ease the parallel execution. The gates connected only to input wires are placed in layer 0. Then the gates having, at least, one input wire coming from a gate in layer 0 are placed in layer 1. The procedure is then iterated on all the gates, placing a gate having input wires obtained as output from two gates respectively already in layers i and j, in layer $\max(i, j) + 1$. In the end of the scanning procedure, all the gates of the circuit are grouped in layers. Almost contemporaneously to us, a similar scheme for gate parallelization has been proposed also in [13], although their target platform are the Graphics Processing Units (GPU).

It is important to underline that the sorted circuit can be garbled and evaluated sequentially or by using threads that permit the parallel elaboration of gates in the same layer. This permits a sequential execution from a single core system, while in multi core systems, to prevent from incurring in a slow down caused by an insufficient work load for each thread, there is a minimum number of gates per thread that can be executed in parallel. If the number is lower than the threshold the execution is serialized. If we indicate with Δt the time that can be saved by running the level in parallel, we have the condition $\Delta t = S_t - (P_t + C) > 0$ if

$S_t - P_t > C$ where P_t is the execution time in parallel, S_t is the serial execution time and C is the overhead introduced by the management of the threads (creation, synchronization, etc.).

Having different garbling/evaluation procedures, we analyze separately the parallelization of XOR gates and non-XOR gates. Thanks to [19], circuits are designed to reduce the number of non-XOR gates and, as a result, XOR gates are usually the most common gate type (e.g., in our circuits 74 %, on average). As expected, the computational burden necessary to execute them is less than that required by other gates. Nevertheless for large circuits there is such a high number of XOR gates per level to justify parallelization on this phase. As a matter of fact, we obtain a good speedup when executing in parallel XOR gates for large circuits. Non-XOR gates are generic gates that can have an arbitrary number of inputs and any truth table (usually plain gates are often used to execute AND, OR operations with 2 inputs). That class of gates has a major impact on computation time since, for each gate, it is necessary to cipher its truth table associated to the possible secrets' combinations on inputs. The ciphering requires the execution of a SHA-256 hash function and several XOR operations on the gate secret inputs. For non-XOR gates we have parallelized only the creation and the ciphering of the truth table. This is in charge of the Garbler that afterward sends the result through the communication channel. NOT gates, that can be also evaluated for free, are not very expensive in computational terms and also relatively few even for large circuits. As a consequence, we did not develop a parallel procedure for the execution of NOT gates.

In our solution we resort to CPU *threads* for parallelization since the grain of the computation hardly justifies the usage of hundreds of relatively slow cores like those available in a GPU. CPU *threads* have a very low creation overhead and can be managed in a dynamic way depending on the features of the circuit under evaluation (*i.e.*, the number of gates in each layer).

3.2   Coarse-Grained Parallelization

A macro block parallelization presents many advantages, but requires some substantial changes in the protocol. The possibility of dividing a circuit in blocks makes the circuit representation easier, since the developer can design and test small parts of the circuit. Moreover, there is no need to repeat the design of identical parts of the circuit, as often happens in protocols where the same operation is repeated on different inputs. Finally this solution reduces the overhead introduced by thread management, since, while in fine-grained parallelization in each layer a thread is created and then destroyed for each gate, here a thread is created for groups of gates.

To design a circuit by using macro blocks it is necessary to define also secret inputs and outputs, besides the classical evaluator and garbler inputs and outputs. A secret input is a sequence of bits, obtained as output from another macro block, that can not be revealed to either the garbler and the evaluator. In practice, secret inputs/outputs are used to connect different blocks. Obviously, in the design phase, particular attention must be paid to the dimension of secret inputs and outputs to avoid inconsistency problems. For a good design, it can be useful to handle the evaluator and garbler input association phase by using one or more blocks that accept plain inputs and return the associated secrets.

During garbling it is important to use the same global key Δ for all the circuits, then garbling is performed as usual, paying attention to the pair of input secrets. Obviously, if the same macro-block is used more than once in the circuit (with different secret inputs), each instance needs to be garbled independently from the others, because, as usual, if the same garbled circuit is evaluated twice with different inputs, the security of the protocol is compromised. Garbling of macro blocks that can be processed in parallel is assigned to different threads.

Evaluation is performed as usual, the only change consists in the requirement of storing the secrets obtained as outputs of a block to assign them to the inputs of another block. Macro blocks that can be evaluated in parallel are assigned to different threads.

Even if blocks evaluated in parallel can be different, when the same block is garbled/evaluated multiple times in parallel, the operations performed by the threads can be driven together, because they perform the same operation on different values. Beyond the easy design and the parallelization, this solution results in another, non negligible, advantage: the file containing the description of a macro block that is garbled/evaluated multiple times in parallel is read only once, reducing the memory load.

4   Analysis

To provide an analysis of the benefits introduced by the parallel evaluation we consider a biometric matching problem and AES encryption of a large amount of data. For both scenarios, we compare the sequential implementation to the parallel implementations (fine-grained, coarse grained and coarse-grained with fine-grained parallelization inside the blocks). We show how the results change as a function of the number of available threads and the time needed by each phase of the computation. Finally we provide a security analysis of the two implementations.

4.1   Iris Identification

As first example, we consider the iris identification protocol proposed in [23], modified so that the final result is the index of the best match, if exceeding a given threshold, instead of a simple answer that specifies if the tested biometry is in the database or not. The parameters are chosen according to the original paper and their values are specified during the description.

In such protocol, the biometric server, Bob, has an iris gallery which stores the iris features $\{X_1, \ldots, X_n\}$ of $n = 1023$ members. X_i is a binary vector denoted as $(x_{i,1}, \ldots, x_{i,\ell})$, where $\ell = 2048$. The user, Alice, provides a probe $q = (q_1, \ldots, q_\ell)$ and evaluates the GC which produces a match if there exists at least an $i \in \{1, \ldots, n\}$ such that $d(q, X_i) < \varepsilon$ for a similarity threshold ε. $d(q, X_i)$ is a modified Hamming Distance (HD) defined below:

$$d(q, X_i) := \frac{D(q, X_i)}{M(q, X_i)} = \frac{||(q \otimes X_i) \cap mask_q \cap mask_{X_i}||}{||mask_q \cap mask_{X_i}||}, \qquad (2)$$

where $\otimes$ denotes XOR, $\cap$ AND, and $|| \cdot ||$ the norm of the binary vector; $mask_q$ and $mask_{X_i}$ are the corresponding binary masks that zero out the unusable portion of the irises due to occlusion by eyelids and eyelash, specular reflections, boundary artifacts of lenses, or poor signal-to-noise ratio. Considering that masks do not disclose sensitive information about the subjects, as demonstrated in [23], a common mask can be used. Mask filtering is performed in the plain domain on all the irises by Alice and Bob and together they can compute the distances

$$d'(q, X_i) := \frac{HD(mask(q), mask(X_i))}{||CM||}, \qquad (3)$$

where HD$(\cdot)$ denotes the Hamming distance and $mask(\cdot)$ is the masking function with the common mask, identified by CM.

At this point, given an acceptance threshold ε, the index of the best match can be obtained as $\arg\min(\varepsilon, \{d'(q, X_i)\}_{i=1}^n)$. If the return value is equal to 0 there is no match. We underline that, for simplicity, we can reformulate the problem as

$$\arg\min(||CM||\varepsilon \ , \ \{HD(mask(q), mask(X_i))\}_{i=1}^n). \qquad (4)$$

The protocol can be implemented by the circuit shown in Fig. 1, where the Hamming distance is computed by XOR gates between the two inputs and a COUNTER circuit [5], whereas the argMIN tree is implemented as in [18]. The circuit is composed by approximately 6.3 millions of gates, 1.1 millions of which are non-free gates.

While fine-grained parallelization is applied on a single circuit implementing Fig. 1, segmented in 356 layers, coarse-grained parallelization needs subdivision into sub-blocks. We can identify the following blocks, whose composition is shown in Fig. 2:

– n *Garbler input interfaces* for Bob's iris templates, each one converting one ℓ-bit long input in ℓ t-bit long secrets;
– 1 *Evaluator input interface* for Alice's iris template query, converting one ℓ-bit long input in ℓ secrets;
- 1 *Garbler input interface* for acceptance threshold ε, converting one $\lceil \log_2 \ell \rceil$-bit long input in $\lceil \log_2 \ell \rceil$ secrets;
– n *Hamming distances*, each one having 2 inputs composed by ℓ secrets and 1 output composed by $\lceil \log_2 \ell \rceil$ secrets;
- 1 *argMIN tree*, having n inputs represented with $\lceil \log_2 \ell \rceil$ secrets and returning an index represented with $\lceil \log_2 n + 1 \rceil$ bits (output interface is included in the block).

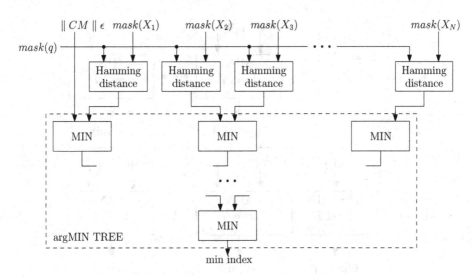

Fig. 1. Iris identification scheme.

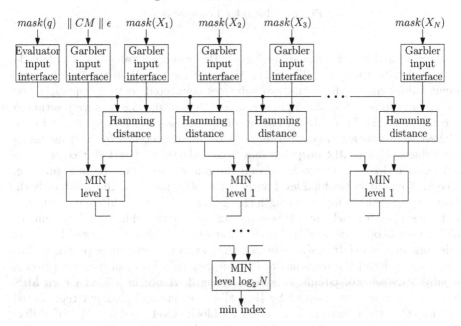

Fig. 2. Block subdivision of iris identification scheme for coarse-grained parallelization.

The index of the best match is obtained by a reverse argMIN tree having $\lceil \log_2 n + 1 \rceil$ levels and $n + 1$ inputs, where the input_0 is the threshold and the input_i is the output of the i-th Hamming distance. The i-th level ($i = 0 \ldots \lceil \log_2 n + 1 \rceil - 1$) is composed by $\lceil \frac{n+1}{2^{i+1}} \rceil$ MIN blocks. Each MIN selector circuit in level 0 outputs the secret relative to the minimum value together with

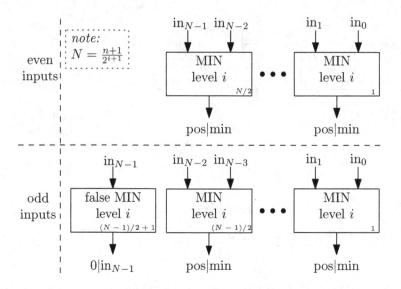

Fig. 3. Subtree level composition

a secret related to a bit signaling whether the minimum value is in the left (1) or in the right (0) input. The other MIN selector circuit in the tree has two input values coming from the two sub-trees connected to their inputs. These values are composed by the highest sub-tree's input and the relative position in the sub-tree. The MIN selector circuit outputs the secrets corresponding to the highest value concatenated with the subtree index, preceded by a bit assuming the value 0 whether the output comes from right subtree or 1 if it comes from left subtree. In such a way, we obtain the relative index of the new sub-tree. The MIN circuit in the final level outputs the plain index to Alice, Bob or both. Considering that the input bitlength changes at each level, a different circuit has to be described for each level. It is important to note that if in a level the number of k inputs is odd, we need $k/2$ MIN selectors, but if k is even, $(k-1)/2$ max selectors are needed. In the second case the last value needs to be propagated to the next level and the bit 0 has to be concatenated. This can be done through a *false* MIN selector circuit, as shown in Fig. 3. Hence in a level i each MIN block has 2 inputs represented by $\lceil \log_2 \ell \rceil + i$ secrets and 1 output represented by $\lceil \log_2 \ell \rceil + i + 1$ secrets. The final MIN block (level $\lceil \log_2 n + 1 \rceil - 1$) differs from the others because its output is composed by $\lceil \log_2 n + 1 \rceil$ bits.

It is important to note that all the sub-circuits placed in the same level in Fig. 2 (input interfaces, HDs, MINs of level i) can be evaluated in parallel. Moreover only a description file for each block type is necessary.

We suppose that server and client perform garbling, OT precomputation and transmission of the garbled circuit offline, to provide the most efficient computation when real data is available. As already mentioned, OT precomputation is performed by using the OT extension protocol that, in our case, performs

Table 1. Runtimes (in seconds) of iris identification protocol by using sequential implementation (S), fine-grained (FG) parallelization, coarse-grained parallelization (CG), or both. 8 cores have been used in parallel implementations.

	Phase	S	FG	CG	CG+FG
Offline	Garbling	9.772	3.475	2.175	1.860
	OT Prec.	0.010	0.010	0.010	0.010
	Garbled table Tx	1.701	1.314	0.036	0.690
Online	Bob's secret Tx	0.338	0.378	0.130	0.158
	Alice's secret Tx	0.002	0.003	0.002	0.002
	Evaluation	3.437	2.899	1.019	1.765

$\approx$1.000.000 OTs offline in about 5 s, hence the OT precomputation runtime reported in the table is the portion of the time referred to 2048 OTs (the same implementation is used for all the solutions). Tests have been performed on a system with two Intel Xeon E5-2609@2.4 GHz with 10 Mbytes of cache and 16 Gbyte of RAM connected to a Fast Ethernet network (100 Mb/s.). Each ES-2609 has four cores, hence the total number of available cores is eight.

Table 1 shows the different implementation runtimes needed for each element of the protocol when 8 threads are used (except for sequential implementation). During the offline phase the same OT precomputation protocol has been used for all the solutions. We can easily observe that all the parallel solutions provide better runtimes with respect to the sequential solution. As expected, the parallelization of the single gates introduces a management overhead greater than the one introduced by macroblock parallelization. On the other hand, the use of gate parallelization inside parallelized macroblocks produces worst results with respect to the coarse-grained parallelization, but the solution is still preferable than fine grained parallelization.

Figure 4 shows the offline, online and total runtimes of the different implementations as a function of the number of threads. We can see that the performance increase with the number of threads, especially in the solutions that rely on coarse grained parallelization having a trend that is inversely proportional to the number of threads used. Indeed the results are affected by the number of cores available and their turnover due to the system inactivity time. We can observe that, having 8 cores, there is no more improvement if more than 16 threads are used.

4.2 AES Encryption

As a second test case, we evaluate our solution on the commonly used circuit for oblivious 128 bit AES encryption[1] [8]. This circuit is often used as benchmark in MPC implementations for boolean functions, due to its relatively random

---

[1] Boolean circuit description kindly provided by Benny Pinkas, Thomas Schneider, Nigel P. Smart and Stephen C. Williams.

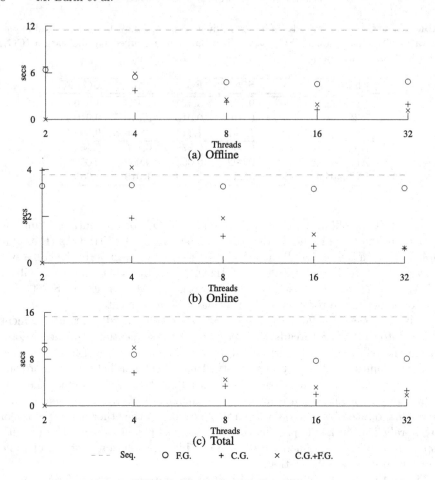

Fig. 4. Iris execution times.

Table 2. Runtimes (in seconds) of AES encryption protocol by using sequential implementation (S) and fine-grained (FG) parallelization. 8 cores have been used in parallel implementations. We run Huang et al. implementation in the same hardware used for our tests.

	Phase	S	FG	Huang et al.
Offline	OT Prec.	0.001	0.001	0.540
	Garbling	0.133	0.082	0.898
	Garbled table Tx	0.039	0.044	
Online	Bob's secret Tx	0.000	0.000	0.038
	Alice's secret Tx	0.013	0.002	0.086
	Evaluation	0.066	0.017	0.311

structure and large size. The idea is to encrypt a value known by Alice by using an encryption key known by Bob.

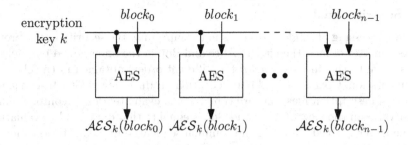

Fig. 5. Two-party computation of 128-bit AES on large amount of data.

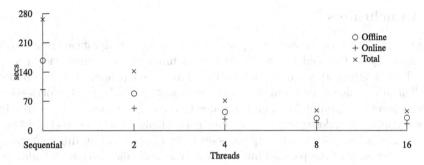

Fig. 6. Multiple AES execution times.

Here we are interested to compare our sequential and fine-grained implementations to the one described in [16]. The obtained results are shown in Table 2.

For a single AES implementation, macroblock parallelization cannot be used, anyway fine-grained parallelization guarantees better results than sequential implementation. To compare our solution to other implementations, we run Huang et al. code [16] on the same computer used for our tests, obtaining results worse than ours. Again we can also observe that fine-grained parallelization offers better performance than serial execution.

To extend our analysis, we used the AES circuit as a block in a coarse grained parallelization of a circuit encrypting more than 128 bits provided by Alice by using the 128 bit encryption key of Bob, as shown in Fig. 5.

For our tests we imagine to encrypt a gray-scaled image of size 256×256 pixels, hence $n = 4096$ AES encryption blocks are evaluated in parallel by using coarse-grained parallelization. Considering that associating a secret to an input available on the evaluator side is more expensive than associating a secret to an input available on the garbling side, Alice, having $256 \times 256 \times 8$ input bits, acts as garbler, whereas Bob, having 128 input bits, acts as evaluator. In Fig. 6 we can observe the offline, online and total runtime of the protocol. As expected, parallel evaluation of AES blocks provides a significant improvement, confirming again that runtime decreases as $\approx 1/threads$ and by using 16 threads each AES takes less than 4 ms online.

4.3 Security Analysis

Parallel processing of single gates does not compromise the security of the protocol. As a matter of fact, the view of Alice and Bob in the fine-grained parallelization is equal to the one (except for the different order) obtained in the classical implementation. Coarse grained parallelization produces many GCs from a small number of description files that are combined to evaluate a more complex functionality. Again the view of Alice and Bob is equal to that obtained by evaluating a single larger garbled circuit in the common sequential implementation. Hence, being the security for Yao's protocol in the semi-honest model demonstrated in [22], also security of parallel implementations is granted.

5 Conclusions

In this paper we have shown that parallel processing can significantly improve the efficiency of Garbled Circuit technique in multi-party computation protocols. Two different types of parallelization have been proposed. Fine-grained parallelization allows the parallel evaluation of any garbled circuit processed to identify layers containing independent gates that can be evaluated concurrently. Coarse grained parallelization is based on the parallelization of macro-blocks and can be used whenever the same block is evaluated in parallel on different data.

The efficiency of the parallel implementations has been analyzed by addressing a biometric scenario, having an intrinsic parallel nature, and AES encryption. We demonstrated that both fine-grained and coarse-grained solutions provide significant runtime improvements. Macroblock parallelization is preferable when allowed by the intrinsic nature of the application, such as in a biometric identification scenario, otherwise gate parallelization can be used. The joint use of both techniques, by evaluating in parallel macroblocks, whose gates are still processed in parallel, results in a slight improvement.

Considering the results provided in this paper, efficient circuits for parallel GC evaluation could have different shapes with respect to circuits for classical sequential GC. By using coarse-grain parallelization a circuit designer is no more focused on the development of a whole optimized circuit, but to design blocks that can be evaluated in parallel, even if some gates can be superfluous. In fine-grained parallelization, even if reducing the number of non-XOR gates is still important, sometimes circuits with more gates can be evaluated more efficiently than others if they are characterized by a high level of parallelization. For example, having 8 threads available, the parallel evaluation of 4 gates can be more efficient than the sequential evaluation of only two gates. An accurate analysis of this issue is left for future research.

To extend our analysis, we are interested to apply our solutions to Garbled Circuits in a malicious setting and running the protocols on GPUs.

References

1. Agrawal, R., Srikant, R.: Privacy-preserving data mining. ACM Sigmod Rec. **29**(2), 439–450 (2000)

2. Barni, M., Bianchi, T., Catalano, D., Di Raimondo, R., Donida Labati, R., Failla, P., Fiore, D., Lazzeretti, R., Piuri, V., Piva, A., Scotti, F.: A privacy-compliant fingerprint recognition system based on homomorphic encryption and fingercode templates. In: IEEE Fourth International Conference on Biometrics: Theory, Applications and Systems, BTAS 2010 (2010)
3. Barni, M., Bianchi, T., Catalano, D., Di Raimondo, R., Donida Labati, R., Failla, P., Fiore, D., Lazzeretti, R., Piuri, V., Piva, A., Scotti, F.: Privacy-preserving fingercode authentication. In: 12th ACM Workshop on Multimedia and Security, MM&Sec 2010 (2010)
4. Barni, M., Failla, P., Lazzeretti, R., Sadeghi, A.-R., Schneider, T.: Privacy-preserving ECG classification with branching programs and neural networks. IEEE Trans. Inf. Forensics Secur. **6**(2), 452–468 (2011)
5. Barni, M., Guajardo, J., Lazzeretti, R.: Privacy preserving evaluation of signal quality with application to ECG analysis. In: Second IEEE International Workshop on Information Forensics and Security, WIFS 2010 (2010)
6. Beaver, D.: Precomputing oblivious transfer. In: Coppersmith, D. (ed.) CRYPTO 1995. LNCS, vol. 963, pp. 97–109. Springer, Heidelberg (1995)
7. Bellare, M., Micali, S.: Non-interactive oblivious transfer and applications. In: Brassard, G. (ed.) CRYPTO 1989. LNCS, vol. 435, pp. 547–557. Springer, Heidelberg (1990)
8. Daemen, J., Rijmen, V.: The Design of Rijndael: AES-The Advanced Encryption Standard. Springer, Heidelberg (2002)
9. Deng, M., Bianchi, T., Piva, A., Preneel, B.: An efficient buyer-seller watermarking protocol based on composite signal representation. In: Proceedings of the 11th ACM Workshop on Multimedia and Security, pp. 9–18. ACM (2009)
10. Erkin, Z., Franz, M., Guajardo, J., Katzenbeisser, S., Lagendijk, I., Toft, T.: Privacy-preserving face recognition. In: Goldberg, I., Atallah, M.J. (eds.) PETS 2009. LNCS, vol. 5672, pp. 235–253. Springer, Heidelberg (2009)
11. Erkin, Z., Piva, A., Katzenbeisser, S., Lagendijk, R.L., Shokrollahi, J., Neven, G., Barni, M.: Protection and retrieval of encrypted multimedia content: when cryptography meets signal processing. EURASIP J. Inf. Secur. **2007**, 17 (2007)
12. Erkin, Z., Veugen, T., Toft, T., Lagendijk, R.I.: Generating private recommendations efficiently using homomorphic encryption and data packing. IEEE Trans. Inf. Forensics Secur. **7**(3), 1053–1066 (2012)
13. Frederiksen, T.K., Nielsen, J.B.: Fast and maliciously secure two-party computation using the GPU. In: Jacobson, M., Locasto, M., Mohassel, P., Safavi-Naini, R. (eds.) ACNS 2013. LNCS, vol. 7954, pp. 339–356. Springer, Heidelberg (2013)
14. Barni, M., Lazzeretti, R., Orlandi, C.: Processing encrypted signals for DRM applications. In: Hartung, F., Kalker, T., Lian, S. (eds.) Digital Rights Management: Technology, Standards and Applications. CRC Press, Boca Raton (2013, To appear)
15. Henecka, W., Kögl, S., Sadeghi, A.-R., Schneider, T., Wehrenberg, I.: TASTY: tool for automating secure two-partY computations. In: ACM Computer and Communications Security (CCS'10), pp. 451–462 (2010). http://www.trust.rub.de/tasty/
16. Huang, Y., Evans, D., Katz, J., Malka, L.: Faster secure two-party computation using garbled circuits. In: USENIX Security Symposium. http://MightBeEvil.org (2011)
17. Ishai, Y., Kilian, J., Nissim, K., Petrank, E.: Extending oblivious transfers efficiently. In: Boneh, D. (ed.) CRYPTO 2003. LNCS, vol. 2729, pp. 145–161. Springer, Heidelberg (2003)

18. Kolesnikov, V., Sadeghi, A.-R., Schneider, T.: How to combine homomorphic encryption and garbled circuits. In: Signal Processing in the Encrypted Domain-First SPEED Workshop-Lousanne, 100 p. (2009)

19. Kolesnikov, V., Sadeghi, A.-R., Schneider, T.: Improved garbled circuit building blocks and applications to auctions and computing minima. In: Garay, J.A., Miyaji, A., Otsuka, A. (eds.) CANS 2009. LNCS, vol. 5888, pp. 1–20. Springer, Heidelberg (2009)

20. Lagendijk, R.L., Erkin, Z., Barni, M.: Encrypted signal processing for privacy protection: conveying the utility of homomorphic encryption and multiparty computation. IEEE Signal Process. Mag. **30**(1), 82–105 (2013)

21. Lazzeretti, R., Guajardo, J., Barni, M.: Privacy preserving ECG quality evaluation. In: Proceedings of ACM Workshop on Multimedia and Security (MM&SEC). ACM (2012)

22. Lindell, Y., Pinkas, B.: A proof of YAO's protocol for secure two-party computation. J. Cryptology **22**(2), 161–188 (2009). Preliminary version at http://eprint.iacr.org/2004/175

23. Luo, Y., Samson, S.C., Pignata, T., Lazzeretti, R., Barni, M.: An efficient protocol for private iris-code matching by means of garbled circuits. In: Special Session on Emerging Topics in Cryptography and Image Processing, International Conference on Image Processing (ICIP) (2012)

24. Malkhi, D., Nisan, N., Pinkas, B., Sella, Y.: Fairplay – a secure two-party computation system. In: USENIX Security Symposium (Security'04). http://www.cs.huji.ac.il/project/Fairplay (2004)

25. Naor, M., Pinkas, B.: Efficient oblivious transfer protocols. In: ACM-SIAM Symposium on Discrete Algorithms (SODA'01), pp. 448–457. Society for Industrial and Applied Mathematics (2001)

26. NIST. US Department of Commerce, National Institute of Standards and Technology (NIST): Federal Information Processing Standard Publication 180-2, Announcing the SECURE HASH STANDARD (August 2002). http://csrc.nist.gov/publications/fips/fips180-2/fips180-2withchangenotice.pdf

27. Paus, A., Sadeghi, A.-R., Schneider, T.: Practical secure evaluation of semi-private functions. In: Abdalla, M., Pointcheval, D., Fouque, P.-A., Vergnaud, D. (eds.) ACNS 2009. LNCS, vol. 5536, pp. 89–106. Springer, Heidelberg (2009). http://www.trust.rub.de/FairplaySPF

28. Pinkas, B., Schneider, T., Smart, N.P., Williams, S.C.: Secure two-party computation is practical. In: Matsui, M. (ed.) ASIACRYPT 2009. LNCS, vol. 5912, pp. 250–267. Springer, Heidelberg (2009)

29. Pu, S., Duan, P., Liu, J.-C.: Fastplay–a parallelization model and implementation of smc on cuda based gpu cluster architecture. Technical report, Cryptology ePrint Archive, Report 2011/097, 2011 (2011)

30. Yao, A.C.: Protocols for secure computations. In: Proceedings of the 23rd Annual Symposium on Foundations of Computer Science, pp. 160–164 (1982)

31. Yao, A.C.: How to Generate and Exchange Secrets. In IEEE Symposium on Foundations of Computer, Science (FOCS'86), pp. 162–167 (1986)

Privacy Analysis of a Hidden Friendship Protocol

Florian Kammüller[1]([⊠]) and Sören Preibusch[2]

[1] Middlesex University, London, UK
f.kammueller@mdx.ac.uk
[2] Microsoft Research, Cambridge, UK
spr@microsoft.com

Abstract. Friendship relations are a defining property of online social networks. On the one hand, and beyond their cultural interpretation, they sustain access control mechanisms and are privacy-enhancing by limiting the proliferation of personal information. On the other hand, the publicity of friendship links is privacy-invasive. We outline a distributed authentication protocol based on hidden friendship links that has been suggested in earlier work. We then investigate its formalisation and, using model-checking, we carry out a mechanised analysis of the protocol that enables the revision and rectification of the earlier version. We thus demonstrate more generally how model-checking and epistemic logic can be used for the detection of privacy and security vulnerabilities in authentication protocols for social networks.

1 Introduction

In this paper, we present a formal analysis of a protocol that offers the possibility to declare friendships for social network as hidden. This protocol has been designed by one of the authors [PB09]. Friendship lists conform to the friend of a friend (FOAF) ontology [FOA10,BM10] a machine readable description of persons, their activities and their relations to other people and objects. In social networks users advocate and promote own and others' networks. Therefore, public lists of friends – FOAF lists – are published on social networks sites. Friendship relations can have a negative impact on privacy since inference about unpublished friendship links becomes possible if a linked friend publishes personal information.

In a distributed environment, like social networks without a central control, the security control over these FOAF lists cannot be guaranteed by a centralized unit but should be self-administered. This motivates a distributed procedure and format to specify lists of friends and control access and distribution of those. Users may publish public lists of friends themselves but for privacy it is necessary that also hidden friends are available to validate communications. The paper [PB09] suggests a solution to this problem by proposing a public key based protocol. Public and hidden friendship relations can be encoded uniformly in

J. Garcia-Alfaro et al. (Eds.): DPM 2013 and SETOP 2013, LNCS 8247, pp. 83–99, 2014.
DOI: 10.1007/978-3-642-54568-9_6, © Springer-Verlag Berlin Heidelberg 2014

one public FOAF file with no need to serve different friends lists based on the credentials a requesting client presents.

However, further analysis of the friendship protocol shows there are possibilities to undermine the security and privacy that is intended to be granted by it. We provide a formal analysis of this protocol using the modelchecker MCMAS for belief logic that is well suited for this kind of tasks as it can model knowledge of principals involved in a protocol.

Often protocols are only secure within certain given boundaries and under certain strong assumptions. These assumptions need to be verified again in a new scenario like social networks since privacy is an issue there and has not been a central concern in classic security protocols. Verification techniques for classic security protocols, i.e., formal modeling and automated verification, are likely to be beneficial in this new scenario. Formal specification of security protocols leads naturally to a mechanical analysis with model-checking tools. Security protocols are a good application area for this technology providing analysis and re-engineering possibilities, e.g. [KMPS12]. Fewer case studies exist for privacy related protocols and also more generic security scenario analysis, e.g. insider threats [KP13]. The current work adds to the body of work exploring the boundaries of such formal analyses.

In this paper, we investigate the hidden friendship protocol for social networks for security and privacy vulnerabilities (Sects. 2 and 3). We expose a replay attack on the originally proposed protocol enabling illicit data access. The technique we are using for the analysis is a specific extension of classic model checking given by the modelchecker MCMAS [LQR09] which implements a so-called epistemic logic of beliefs (Sect. 3.2). Epistemic logic quite naturally gives rise to expressing privacy in social networks because we can formally express that some outsider, like the intruder, does *not know* certain facts like hidden friendship relations (Sect. 4). A mechanised verification using MCMAS reveals that the intruder I can successfully impersonate legitimate friend B encoded in a FOAF list; moreover, privacy is violated in proximity to this attack (Sect. 5). We are able to patch the security weakness by requiring further authentication steps.

2   The Hidden Friendship Protocol

2.1   Hidden Friendship Relations Increase Privacy Doubly

Friendship relations are a defining property of online social networks [BP09]; they empower users to create links with fellow members on the network. Besides their (culture-dependent) social interpretation, these friendship links also sustain higher-level access control mechanisms. Private photo collections or extended profile information can be specified to be inaccessible, but for a member's friends. In restricting access to user-generated content, friendship relations are privacy enhancing.

Typically, friendship relations are a canonical type of relationship, potentially refined into more specialised forms of links, such as kinship or romantic relationships. Online social network operators often have a business interest in making a member's ties to other users public. Whilst some networks provide their members with the ability to configure whether and to whom their list of friends should be visible, the global market leader Facebook abolished the ability to hide one's list – provoking harsh criticism [Fac09]. As a result, the social graph of this network has now become practically world-readable.

In addition to a user's profile with self- and foreign-generated content, her group membership and friendship relations are a most valuable resource for extracting information from a network. The codified and consciously self-established nature of friendship links allows for easy extraction and useful mining in an automated manner. From a marketer's perspective, friendship links are helpful in identifying opinion-leaders and potential lead-users. There is also an understanding that socio-demographics propagate along links and allow to infer blank attribute values such as a user's nationality or age with high confidence [ZG09].

Friendship relations can have a negative impact on privacy since inference about unpublished friendship links becomes possible if a linked friend publishes personal information. Hidden friendship relations mitigate this dual privacy nature as they allow *selective hiding* of one's connections [PB09]. A hidden friendship relation is understood to carry the same rights for the two parties involved as does a public friendship relation. The difference is that knowledge of the existence of this friendship link is confined to the friends alone. The requirement of symmetry and the desire for reflexivity will be assumed for public and hidden friendship relations alike.

Repeatedly articulated concerns from a network's user base following changes in their friends' lists visibility settings are an indicator online users actually want to decide for themselves how visible their cliques are (Fig. 1 and [Fac09]). As another example, prior to an overhaul of the MySpace profile pages [MyS08], all member pages displayed the complete list of friends. As a result, a plethora of stylesheet (CSS) snippets was available from third-parties to visually hide one's friends – without actually removing it from the HTML markup.

Whilst it is conceptually easy to implement selectively hidden friendship relations in a *centralised* online social network such as today's mainstream Web platforms, the implementation becomes less straightforward when moving towards a distributed social network without a superordinate body to provide authentication and enforce access controls. In a centralised network, the operator is typically aware of a user's credentials who has previously logged in. These can be matched against permission settings defined by other users and equally stored on this central server. Hidden friendship relations then becomes an issue of delivering request-specific views on a user's list of friends; a hidden friendship link will not be included in the list unless it involves the requesting party.

Contribution. This first application of epistemic logics to online privacy and security scenarios demonstrates, how existing software engineering techniques can uncover and heal potential vulnerabilities in social access control protocols. To the best of our knowledge, we pioneer model-checking for protocol verification in the context of privacy on the social and semantic Web.

Attacker Model. We assume Dolev-Yao channels, that is all communication channels can be overheard, messages intercepted, and new fake messages sent.

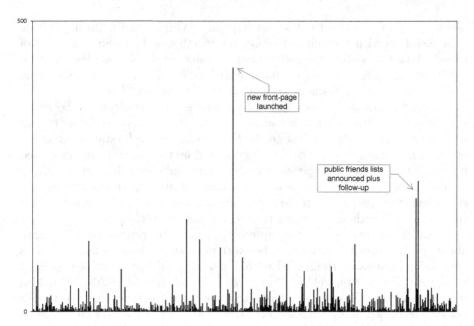

Fig. 1. Number of comments solicited by postings on the editorial blog of a medium-sized German social network operator over the entire year 2006. Two subsequent postings announcing friends lists will be publicly visible by default attracted 195 and 225 comments respectively. A similarly controversial topic had only been the relaunch of the frontpage of the social network.

The latter point includes what is commonly known as *spoofing*: messages can be sent with fake sender addresses. An attacker has a finite ability to store messages and files. We also assume that untrustworthy people can join the social network, that is, attackers are normal members of the social network. Moreover, we assume secure keys and the usual cryptographic infrastructure for distributed systems as described next.

2.2 Self-Published Lists of Friends in Decentralised Architectures

In a truly *distributed* scenario, there will be no central authority to store and manage authorisation credentials, and neither will it be possible to rely on such a centralised body to authenticate users. Whilst distributed scenarios appeal per se as they provide stronger privacy and allow users to remain in control of their digital assets [Fed11], design for distributed access control is also a pragmatic approach. On the move, mobile device users may be unable to connect to a central server when connectivity is unavailable or prohibitively expensive, including opportunity costs such as latency. Users shall be able to grant and to deny access to resources locally, without having to delegate to a central service. Notwithstanding, users may wish to delegate subsequent authorisation requests. A typical application would be spontaneous encounters during which media files are shared between portable devices.

We envision a usage scenario for hidden friendship relations that does not rely on a central authority for authentication and authorisation. All the same, we do not deny there is an infrastructure of centrally provided commodity services such as email providers, Web hosters, cloud storage, certificate authorities, and connections to which may be established opportunistically. Also, we assume that fundamental Internet infrastructure such as a domain name system are available and can be relied upon.

In a peer-to-peer environment, friendship links shall be encoded in *self-published lists of friends*. Any given user should be able to draft a list of her friends and publish it as a resource on the Web, under a given URL. We envision that a user's existing personal information management infrastructure, such as Outlook, may act as a tool and data source to generate such a public list of friends. Entries in the public list of friends would then correspond to contact details in the private database, where more information may be held. On the semantic Web, the FOAF standard [FOA10] has emerged as a machine-readable format for publishing profile information about oneself along with links to FOAF files from other people, marked as friends.

We envision deployment for situations like the following: Alice and some close colleagues are having an after-work party at the pub. She wants to share photos with them she has shot during a recent hike. Access should be limited to people Alice lists in her FOAF file. Colleagues she has listed will find that their mobile devices can retrieve the media files from Alice's camera directly via Bluetooth. To protect their privacy (and her own), Alice has decided not to list some of her contacts under their real names but to hide their identity so that others will not become aware of their relationship. From this point of view, hidden friendship relations can also be seen as an analogy to the BCC recipient header in emails.

2.3   Lists of Friends Encode Secret and Public Friendship Relations

The FOAF standard describes a vocabulary one can use to describe oneself and people as well as things (in a broad sense) one is connected to in an XML document. In the wild, FOAF files exhibit a range of depth regarding the degree of detail the author has gone into. An example of a FOAF file is presented at the end of this section. FOAF files can be merged into more comprehensive FOAF files by matching the data items published across these different files concerning the same person or thing.

To leverage the potential of FOAF as a single contact and profile base data repository, we expect that public and hidden links to other people will be stored in the same public FOAF file. The difference in visibility is semantic rather than presentational or syntactic. This unified storage opens the route for uniform treatment of both links, although some restrictions remain.

To emphasise the conceptual level of the hidden friendship protocol and to abstract from the various rendering formats for the same semantic information, we will subsequently use a condensed notation for FOAF files instead of an XML-like syntax.

```xml
<?xml version="1.0" encoding="utf-8"?>
<rdf:RDF xmlns:rdf=
    "http://www.w3.org/1999/02/22-rdf-syntax-ns#"
        xmlns:foaf="http://xmlns.com/foaf/0.1/"
        xmlns:dc="http://purl.org/dc/terms/">

<foaf:PersonalProfileDocument rdf:about=""
 dc:available="2013-02-15T13:00Z"
 dc:issued=2013-02-15T13:00Z">
  <foaf:primaryTopic rdf:resource="#soeren" />
  <dc:creator rdf:resource="#soeren" />
  <foaf:maker rdf:resource="#soeren" />
  <dc:source rdf:resource=
    "http://preibusch.de/projects/hidden-friends/
    samples/soeren.foaf" />
</foaf:PersonalProfileDocument>

<foaf:Person rdf:ID="soeren">
    <foaf:name>Soeren Preibusch</foaf:name>
    <foaf:title>Mr</foaf:title>
    <foaf:mbox rdf:resource=
      "mailto:spr@microsoft.org"/>
    <foaf:homepage rdf:resource= "http://preibusch.de/"/>

    <foaf:knows><foaf:Person>
        <foaf:name>Alice Allington</foaf:name>
        <foaf:mbox>aallington@example.com</foaf:mbox>
        </foaf:Person></foaf:knows>

    <foaf:knows><foaf:Person>
        <foaf:name>Bob Burnsteen</foaf:name>
        <foaf:mbox>bburnsteen@example.com</foaf:mbox>
        </foaf:Person></foaf:knows>

    <foaf:knows><foaf:Person>
        <foaf:nick>UwKjv2KIV4FFWoB827G7</foaf:nick>
        </foaf:Person></foaf:knows>

    <foaf:knows><foaf:Person>
        <foaf:nick>VIlYvMmw8viTZdfEMIGW</foaf:nick>
        </foaf:Person></foaf:knows>

    <foaf:knows rdf:ID="Dg3SloiNr5X6UFfIOqLP" />

    <foaf:knows rdf:resource=
        "mailto:F.Kammueller@mdx.ac.uk"/>
</foaf:Person>
</rdf:RDF>
```

3   Protocol Steps

3.1   Notation for Formal Verification

Users A, B, C and so forth engage in public and hidden friendship relations.

Intruder I, different from the users noted above, will try to impersonate them to fraudulently access restricted resources by misusing their credentials.

FOAF files noted $foaf$, will be published by users. The original author of a FOAF file will be noted in subscript, so that $foaf_A$ will be A's FOAF file. A user's FOAF file is made up by profile information about the author, which will be condensed to an identifier or name, $name_A$ for simplicity. More generally, such an identifier could be a URI, such as an email address, as suggested by the FOAF specification.

Friend entries in FOAF files are an unordered set made up of users' names such as $name_C$ (in the case of public friendship relations) and of tokens that do not reveal the identity of the respective hidden friend, noted $K_{B \to A}$ for a token in $foaf_A$ produced by B and sent to A to be recorded for later authentication of B to A.

Points in time will be referred to as $R|t$ which denotes the resource R such as a FOAF file at the time t. We may write $foaf_A|t_0$ to refer to A's FOAF file at the time t_0 which may evolve to $foaf_A|t_1$.

We will use the compact notation

$$foaf_A = (name_A, t, \{name_C, name_D, K_{B \to A}\})$$

for A's FOAF file published at time t that lists her public friends C and D as well as the token $K_{B \to A}$ provided by B as a hidden friend. The time-stamp t is to be read as the date this FOAF file was published (i.e. made available online for public retrieval) rather than the time it was actually retrieved.

   The listing shown in Sect. 2.3 shows a sample FOAF file which will be used as a demonstration example. Using the condensed notation, this file can be represented as

$$foaf_S = (\text{``Soeren Preibusch''}, \texttt{"2013-02-15T13:00Z"},$$
$$\{\text{``Alice Allington''}, \text{``Bob Burnsteen''}, K_{X \to S}, K_{Y \to S}, \dots\})$$

with X and Y being hidden friends who only the author of this FOAF file knows (besides X and Y, respectively).

   Note that for both hidden and public friendship links, there are varying levels of verbosity: combining different semantic Web technologies, RDF and the more specialised vocabulary FOAF in this case, equivalent semantic links may be encoded differently.

Cryptographic Assumptions. We assume a public key infrastructure, i.e. public/private key pairs are available to all principals. The hidden friendship entries

$K_{A \to B}$ are public keys of A for the friendship with B. The corresponding private key is written as $K_{A \to B}^{-1}$. For public and private key we assume that they are inverse functions, i.e., for any number n we have that $K_{A \to B}^{-1}(K_{A \to B}(n)) = n$.

3.2   Establishing a Hidden Friendship Relation

Establishing a hidden friendship relation according to the procedure described in [PB09] is depicted in the Figs. 2 and 3.

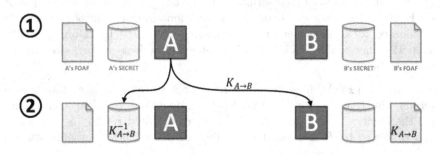

Fig. 2. A creates key pair $K_{A \to B}$, $K_{A \to B}^{-1}$ sending former to B while keeping the latter in his secret storage [PB09]. Public friends are not shown here.

(i) A and B want to share some media files privately.

(ii) B sets up $foaf_B$ under url_B, listing C and D as public friends:
$foaf_B = (name_A, t_2, \{name_C, name_D\})$

(iii) B becomes a hidden friend with A by putting the friendship-specific public key $K_{A \to B}$ into her $foaf_B$. Prior to that, B has received this $K_{A \to B}$ from A who has just generated a new key pair when the hidden friendship was set up (see Fig. 2). It is A that holds the corresponding private key $K_{A \to B}^{-1}$ in its secret data storage. Dually, A herself replicates this expansion of her FOAF file with $K_{B \to A}$ sent to her by B as is depicted in Fig. 3. We now have

$$foaf_B = (name_B, t_3, \{name_C, name_D, K_{A \to B}\})$$

and A's friendship list contains $K_{B \to A}$ which A received from B. A holds $K_{A \to B}^{-1}$, B holds $K_{B \to A}^{-1}$. The FOAF files $foaf_A$ and $foaf_B$ are publicly readable with all their content therein.

3.3   Using a Hidden Friendship Relation

We consider now the case where B wants to retrieve media from A with whom he has a hidden friendship relation according to [PB09]. The state when B makes his request is described by $foaf_A$ and $foaf_B$, established as described above.

(iv) B wants to retrieve media from A. In making a request for it, he sends along $foaf_B$ which contains $name_B$ and $K_{A \to B}$.

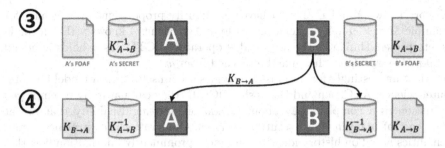

Fig. 3. B creates pair $K_{B \to A}$, $K_{B \to A}^{-1}$ sending former to A while keeping the latter in his secret storage [PB09].

(v) A receives B's request and extracts $name_B$ from it.

(vi) A then applies her secret key $K_{A \to B}^{-1}$ to verify $K_{A \to B}$. On success, B will be granted access to the file.

4   Temporal and Epistemic Logics

Verification in computer science has two major challenges: abstraction and automation. Abstraction is necessary to make properties of models decidable. Many properties of reactive systems are most naturally expressed using some notion of time. Temporal logics – enabling the statement like "at some time in the future a certain event occurs" are a particularly well suited abstraction to express many system properties. The expressivity of temporal logics has found newborn attention since the advent of model checking as a primary method for mechanical verification.

Security protocol verification is one of the almost legendary application fields for model checking since Gavin Lowe has found an attack on the Needham-Schroeder protocol using the FDR model-checker [Aug95]. It is remarkable, how-·ever, that the FDR does not primarily use temporal logics. There, protocols are rather abstracted as sequential processes (in CSP) communicating according to the protocol description, principals synchronizing by incoming or outgoing messages. Messages encode communication content and enable verification of cryptographic assumptions.

In the very early days, the BAN logic already used the idea of establishing "knowledge" of the principals in a protocol session in order to analyse whether a protocol achieved its goal by inferring whether a principal "believes" in the authenticity of his partner [BAN90]. The BAN logic implements protocol engineering knowledge in a logical framework in an ad hoc manner but there are also logical foundations for belief logics. Besides temporal logics, there are other so-called modal logics that feature *knowledge* or *belief* as their modal operator: *epistemic* logics [Sta06]. Equal to other modal logics, the world is modelled as a directed graph over states. Epistemic logic additionally has a set of *agents* whose knowledge is defined by the propositions of each world. The modal operators,

K (for "knows") and B (for "believes"), quantify propositions over agents, for example $M, w \vdash K(A, p)$ means in world $w \in M$ agent A knows p. The formula is interpreted, similar to the universal A operator in CTL*, as: p holds in w and all possible worlds w' that may be reached from w.

Most interestingly for us, epistemic logics are a useful logical model for computer science. As Cohen and Dams show [CD07] they can naturally be employed to reason in a complete way about notion of indistinguishability that are at the heart of many modern security analyses. Observational equivalence, agent semantics based on history identity, and most prominently information flow theory can be axiomatised [Dam11]. Not surprisingly, BAN and its successor SVO can be embedded in epistemic logics [CD07].

Moreover, epistemic logics can be verified by model checking [LQR09] – as one might guess by its resemblance to other modal logics. Another reason why epistemic logic is well suited – as we will point out in the following section – is that the focus of security protocols slightly shifts when they are used for privacy.

Epistemic logic quite naturally gives rise to expressing privacy in social networks because we can formally express that some outsider, like the intruder, does *not know* certain facts like relationships between principals.

The epistemic logic model checker MCMAS, http://www-lai.doc.ic.ac.uk/mcmas/, contains an expressive subset of CTL* augmented with epistemic logic. Thereby, temporal properties may be specified together with properties containing "knows" statements. For example, we can express that if Bob has connected to Alice then the Intruder knows that Alice and Bob are hidden friends.

```
BconnectedA -> K(Intruder, AknowsB);
```

The evident advantages lie first of all in the natural expression of the privacy related statements. Second, as sketched below, we can also express the "lack" of knowledge by formalising that an intruder does not know x. For example, we can express that the Intruder does not know about Alice's and Bob's hidden friendship if they do not communicate.

```
AG(!BconnectedA -> !K(Intruder, AknowsB));
```

4.1 Protocol Modelling for the Epistemic Model Checker MCMAS

For mechanised verification, we turn the protocol flow from Sect. 3.2 into a MCMAS model (see listing shown in Sect. 2.3), with A and B as well as an intruder I as agents—the atom in MCMAS for a participant in a protocol. In Fig. 4 the specification of the actor for Alice and Bob are shown and explained in the following. The full MCMAS source code of our model is available at https://sites.google.com/site/floriankammueller/home/resources/hidden_friendship_mcmas.ispl.

The protocol steps for A and B – called Alice and Bob in the model – and their state evolution are given in Fig. 4. Agent progress through the protocol is described by the Evolution sections. State variables such as access (declared under Vars) are assigned new values (e.g. true) conditional upon the truth of

```
Agent Alice
  Vars:
    initialpermission : { none };
    currentpermission: { accesstoB, accesstoI, none };
  end Vars
    Actions = { wait, openaccessB, openaccessI, sendfoaftoB };
  Protocol:
    currentpermission = none : { wait };
    currentpermission = accesstoB : { openaccessB };
    currentpermission = accesstoI: { openaccessI };
  end Protocol
  Evolution:
    currentpermission = accesstoB if
      (Environment.foafcontainsKAB = true and Bob.Action = sendfoaftoA);
    currentpermission = accesstoI if
      (Environment.foafcontainsKAB = true and Intruder.Action = sendfoaftoA);
  end Evolution
end Agent

Agent Bob
  Vars:
    initialconnection   : { none };
    currentconnection: { alice, none };
  end Vars
  Actions = { wait, sendfoaftoA };
  Protocol:
    currentconnection = none : { sendfoaftoA };
    currentconnection = alice : { wait };
  end Protocol
  Evolution:
    currentconnection = alice if (Alice.Action = openaccessB);
  end Evolution
end Agent

Agent Environment
  Obsvars:
-- check that currently sent foaf file has K_AB in it
    foafcontainsKAB: boolean;
  end Obsvars
  Evolution:
    (foafcontainsKAB = true) if (Bob.Action = sendfoaftoA);
  end Evolution
end Agent
```

Fig. 4. MCMAS model for the original protocol flow: agent definitions for Alice and Bob, and Environment. Environment allows using global state.

an appended predicate (if ...) over the agent's own and its communication partner's state variables and actions.

Which actions are valid at any given protocol step are defined in the Protocol section and depends on the agent's own state and on the observables of the environment it is embedded in. The agent called Environment is a standard construction in MCMAS that allows to share state variables between agents. The following section considers the attack properties that we can express on this model and that MCMAS can proof automatically for us.

5   Attacks on the Hidden Friendship Protocol

There are two attacks on the hidden friendship protocol: a *security attack*, during which the intruder tries to break the access control mechanism built on top of the friendship relations; a *privacy attack*, during which the intruder learns who the involved parties of a hidden friendship are. The security attack and the privacy attack are closely intertwined.

5.1   Security Attack: Breaking the Access Control

We will consider a security attack successful when an intruder I fraudulently impersonates a friend of A and thereby gains access to restricted resources of A that A had not intended for I. It corresponds to the breach of the protocol requirement that only friends should get access.

A mechanised verification using MCMAS reveals that the intruder I can successfully impersonate the legitimate requester B.

Intuitively, A bases her authorisation decision on receiving the name and the hidden friendship token by a valid user, but the token is world-readable and A does not verify that this name is indeed authentic. I can successfully impersonate B by simply replaying B's $foaf_B$. The entry in the $foaf_B$ is the public key $K_{A \to B}$ but it does not carry any proof that this key belongs to B or I.

The intruder can observe the exchange of $foaf_A$ and $foaf_B$ as we assume a Dolev-Yao model in which all communication channels are visible. This is insufficient to get neither of $K_{A \to B}$ nor $K_{B \to A}$ since these are not identifiable in a FOAF file without the corresponding secret key. However, this does not matter. Although the intruder cannot identify the precise key $K_{A \to B}$, he knows that the key is contained in $foaf_B$. Therefore, he can just *replay* the $foaf_B$ to A and thereby get access.

The MCMAS source code for the agent Intruder is contained in Fig. 5. We introduce the following central propositions to later express attack goals.

```
IhiddenfriendA if Intruder.IwithA = true;
BconnectedA if (Bob.currentconnection = alice);
AadmittedB if (Alice.currentpermission = accesstoB);
AknowsB if (Alice.currentpermission = accesstoB and
            Bob.currentconnection = alice);
```

```
Agent Intruder
Vars:
  initialstate: { noKey };
  currentstate: { noKey, seenfoafB, seenfoafA };
-- I manages to connect with A
  IwithA: boolean;
end Vars
  Actions = { listen, sendfoaftoA, sendfoaftoB };
Protocol:
  currentstate = noKey: { listen };
  currentstate = seenfoafA: { sendfoaftoA };
  currentstate = seenfoafB: { sendfoaftoB };
end Protocol
Evolution:
  currentstate = seenfoafA if (Bob.Action = sendfoaftoA);
  currentstate = seenfoafB if (Alice.Action = sendfoaftoB);
  IwithA = true if (Alice.Action = openaccessI);
end Evolution
end Agent
```

Fig. 5. Agent definition for the intruder.

The security attack can be checked by the following assertions that are all checked true when applying the MCMAS tool to the model.

```
EF(IhiddenfriendA);
AF(BconnectedA -> IhiddenfriendA);
AF(AadmittedB -> IhiddenfriendA);
```

The security attack shows that it is possible for the Intruder to become a friend with Alice. It also shows that if B has connected to A or if A had admitted B access, then this attack will always be successful.

To heal this vulnerability of the hidden friendship protocol [PB09], we need to introduce authentication when B wants to access A. Sending $foaf_B$ and thus proving possession of the dedicated public key $K_{A \to B}$ is not sufficient in the presence of a Dolev-Yao attacker as we have seen in the attack.

Instead, requester B could present proof that he knows the private key $K_{B \to A}^{-1}$ that corresponds to $K_{B \to A}$ (and thereby proving his identity) by generating a fresh signature with it. We propose to amend the fourth step of the protocol, i.e. step (iv) in Sect. 3.3. Instead of

$$B \to A | t_1 : (name_B, t_0, \{K_{A \to B}\}) = foaf_B$$

we shall have:

$$B \to A | t_1 : \left(name_B, t_0, K_{B \to A}^{-1}(t_1), \{K_{A \to B}(K_S)\}\right) = foaf_B.$$

When A receives this request she uses the key $K_{B \to A}$ in her $foaf_A$ received from B in the Establishment phase (see Sect. 3.2) to first restore the time stamp

$$K_{B \to A}(K_{B \to A}^{-1}(t_1)) = t_1$$

and then verify its timeliness, i.e., $|t_1 - \text{current time}| \leq \epsilon$ where ϵ is a threshold. The threshold ϵ must be chosen such that it admits reasonable latency in distributed systems while being small enough to exclude successful observation and replay by an Intruder. Assuming synchronised clocks this simple authentication mechanism authenticates B to A and avoids the replay attack within the boundaries of reasonable assumptions, e.g. times for threshold ϵ. After authentication, A's data must be encrypted with session key K_S before allowing B the download. The session key K_S has been communicated to A in a form only readable to A by encrypting it with the public key $K_{A \to B}$ in B's possession.

5.2 Privacy Attack: Breaking the Secrecy of Hidden Friendship Relations

We will consider a privacy attack successful when an intruder I achieves to learn $name_B$ from $K_{B \to A}$. It corresponds to the breach of the protocol requirement that knowledge about who participates in a hidden friendship relation should be kept to them.

There are two possible scenarios for I to learn the identity of A and B. First, by monitoring updates in $foaf_A$ and $foaf_B$ to correlate the additions of $K_{B \to A}$ and $K_{A \to B}$ respectively; second, by iteratively removing $K_{X \to B}$ entries from $foaf_B$ during replay to A (i.e., the security attack), to observe which entry corresponds to $K_{A \to B}$.

The first attack variant does not scale and it also fails if I misses some of the updates in the FOAF files or is unable to correlate them. This could happen if I records too few or too many updates, some of the latter may be deliberately introduced noise. The second attack variant requires prior knowledge whom to target. The set of potential hidden friends must be small. Further, the intruder has to mount the attack in both directions, identifying both $K_{B \to A}$ and $K_{A \to B}$ to successfully learn the identity of the users.

In summary, both attack variants require a history of FOAF files that can be diff'ed. Diffing cannot be represented in a modelchecker like MCMAS. Because MCMAS is a CTL model-checker, it supports boolean expressions to construct temporal formulae, but it does not allow temporal operators within the former. That is, one cannot write (`foafAlice_hBA = false`) and `X((foafAlice_hBA = true))` in MCMAS, to specify that an intruder has observed a change in the FOAF files as it happened. Instead, we specified that I piggy-backs the security attack, with $X\,knows\,Y$ to be true iff X is hidden friend with Y.

```
BconnectedA -> K(Intruder, AknowsB);
AadmittedB -> K(Intruder, AknowsB);
AG(!BconnectedA -> !K(Intruder, AknowsB));
```

As soon as I is able to observe interactions between A and B, the intruder necessarily breaches the privacy of their relationship. However, the intruder is *not necessarily* successful, because it could be impossible for him to observe the required anterior interactions. The above properties are all checked true automatically by MCMAS with respect to the specification given in the previous section. The last one is also a sanity check that the model is not trivial: the original idea of protecting hidden friendships by anonymous public keys does work unless a life connection between two hidden friends is observed by a Dolev-Yao attacker.

Although potential hidden friends can conceal and encrypt their communication, their FOAF files are necessarily public. Safeguards against aforementioned attacks are therefore limited to classical authentication mechanisms. For large populations, the privacy attack would be beyond our threat model as it requires powerful means of surveillance.

6   Conclusions and Perspectives for Discussion

Hidden friendship relations provide means to ground access control on reciprocally stated interpersonal relationships without revealing the identity of the partners. Implementation in centralised infrastructures can leverage existing authentication mechanisms and a global view of access rights. In distributed scenarios, however, a user's identity is harder to establish, especially as we focus on peer-to-peer solutions.

We have provided a more formal statement of the hidden friendship protocol to make it amenable for automated verification by model checking tools. MCMAS, a model checker for epistemic logic was chosen as it allows to capture confidentiality through a modal knowledge operator. As a result of the analysis, we found the previous protocol version [PB09] had been too naïve and was vulnerable to security and privacy attacks. We were able to patch the security weakness by requiring authentication and a session key. The privacy weaknesses were discovered to be a side-effect of the security vulnerability.

Our protocol specification and the subsequent analysis with MCMAS add to the existing body of model-checking case studies, in particular in the area of epistemic logics and privacy (as opposed to confidentiality), for which few previous studies exist. We also demonstrate the usefulness of mechanised verification for privacy and security in the social and semantic Web.

However, challenges remain. Formalisation of privacy properties turned out difficult, even with epistemic logic at hand. Regarding the protocol, keeping the interaction between the two parties minimal is challenging. Also, it remains to be shown that the extended protocol still allows delegation of authorisation decisions to third parties such as media hosting services that hold shareable content on users' behalf. Eventually, the more sophisticated the features of hidden friendship, the less likely their implementation and the possibility for unified management of both hidden an public friendship links.

As a result of the presentation at the workshop some interesting suggestions for future work have been made. A possibility that we plan to address are comparative formalisations of the extended protocol in the dedicated protocol analysis tools AVISPA [ABB+05] and ProVerif [BS11]. Both tools support expression of cryptographic primitives like public key infrastructure and are suitable to examine the cryptographic extension proposed in the current paper. Moreover, the ProVerif tool enables the statement of observable equivalence based on bisimulation relations since it is an implementation of the applied π-calculus. This additional feature would enable experimenting with a mechanized analysis of privacy properties of the extended version of the protocol.

References

[ABB+05] Armando, A., et al.: The AVISPA tool for the automated validation of internet security protocols and applications. In: Etessami, K., Rajamani, S.K. (eds.) CAV 2005. LNCS, vol. 3576, pp. 281–285. Springer, Heidelberg (2005). http://www.avispa-project.org/publications.html

[Aug95] Lowe, G.: An attack on the needham-schroeder public-key authentication protocol. Inf. Process. Lett. **56**, 131–133 (1995)

[BAN90] Burrows, M., Abadi, M., Needham, R.: A logic of authentication. ACM Trans. Comput. Syst. **8**, 18–36 (1990)

[BM10] Brickley, D., Miller, L.: FOAF Vocabulary Specification 0.97. Namespace document, January 2010

[BP09] Bonneau, J., Preibusch, S.: The privacy jungle: on the market for data protection in social networks. In: The Ninth Workshop on the Economics of Information Security (WEIS 09), March 2009

[BS11] Blanchet, B., Smyth, B.: ProVerif 1.85: Automatic Cryptographic Protocol Verifier, User Manual and Tutorial (2011)

[CD07] Cohen, M., Dam, M.: A complete axiomatization of knowledge and cryptography. In: Proceedings of the 22nd IEEE Symposium on Logic in Computer Science (LICS 2007), 10–12 July 2007, Wroclaw, Poland, pp. 77–88. IEEE Computer Society (2007)

[Dam11] Dam, M.: A little knowledge goes a bit further. invited talk. In: Annual Meeting of Priority Program RS3 – Reliably Secure Software Systems (2011)

[Fac09] Facebook. Updates on your new privacy tools (2009)

[Fed11] Federated Social Web Europe. Federated social architectures and protocols, privacy on the federated social web (2011)

[FOA10] FOAF project. The Friend of a Friend (FOAF) project (2010)

[KMPS12] Kammüller, F., Mapp, G., Patel, S., Sani, A.S.: Engineering security pro tocols with modelchecking – radius-sha256 and secured simple protocol. In: International Conference on Internet Monitoring and Protection, ICIMP'12 (2012)

[KP13] Kammüller, F., Probst, C.W.: Invalidating policies using structural information. In: Workshop on Research in Insider Threats WRIT'13 - IEEE CS Security and Privacy Workshops, SPW (2013)

[LQR09] Lomuscio, A., Qu, H., Raimondi, F.: MCMAS: a model checker for the verification of multi-agent systems. In: Bouajjani, A., Maler, O. (eds.) CAV 2009. LNCS, vol. 5643, pp. 682–688. Springer, Heidelberg (2009)

[MyS08] MySpace. Profile 2.0 launch - check it out :) (2008)

[PB09] Preibusch, S., Beresford, A.R.: Establishing distributed hidden friendship relations. In: Seventeenth International Workshop on Security Protocols (2009)

[Sta06] Stanford Encyclopedia of Philosophy. Epistemic logic (2006)

[ZG09] Zheleva, E., Getoor, L.: To join or not to join: the illusion of privacy in social networks with mixed public and private user profiles. In: Proceedings of the 18th International Conference on World Wide Web (WWW '09), pp. 531–540. ACM, New York (2009)

Anonymous and Transferable Electronic Ticketing Scheme

Arnau Vives-Guasch[1], M. Magdalena Payeras-Capellà[2],
Macià Mut-Puigserver[2], Jordi Castellà-Roca[1][(✉)],
and Josep-Lluís Ferrer-Gomila[2]

[1] Departament d'Enginyeria Informàtica i Matemàtiques,
Universitat Rovira i Virgili, Av. Països Catalans 26, 43007 Tarragona, Spain
{arnau.vives,jordi.castella}@urv.cat
[2] Dpt. de Ciències Matemàtiques i Informàtica, Universitat de les Illes Balears,
Ctra. de Valldemossa, km 7,5., 07122 Palma de Mallorca, Spain
{mpayeras,macia.mut,jlferrer}@uib.es

Abstract. Electronic tickets demonstrate, without the use of paper, the possession of an authorization or access to a determined service. In this scenario, some security requirements must be accomplished. Moreover, some determined services should guarantee the anonymity of the users in the system. In addition to these requirements, the transferability of a ticket from one user to another (without involving a third party) is useful but also generates other issues to be solved in terms of security, as several attacks could be performed. In this article we present an electronic ticketing system with anonymity and transferability based on the use of group signatures, giving a solution to enable linkability between several group signatures, and also proving their ownership with the use of Zero-Knowledge Proofs (ZKPs).

Keywords: E-ticketing · E-commerce · Transferability · Privacy · Security

1 Introduction

Information technologies (IT) are being extended progressively in our society. Users can access online services regardless of place and time. For example, they can purchase a movie or theater ticket online. Nonetheless, in some cases, they have to print the ticket to access to the service. In other words, the process is not completely electronic because a printed ticket is required.

Thanks to the introduction of smartphones, all the processes can be performed electronically. These devices offer a good computation power, high storage capacity, and also different communication technologies, such as Near Field Communication (NFC). All these features can be available on a small device. That allows mobility and flexibility and makes the system perfectly suitable for management, e-ticketing and e-payment schemes [5]. Electronic tickets can be

J. Garcia-Alfaro et al. (Eds.): DPM 2013 and SETOP 2013, LNCS 8247, pp. 100–113, 2014.
DOI: 10.1007/978-3-642-54568-9_7, © Springer-Verlag Berlin Heidelberg 2014

defined as a representation of the owner's rights to act as a user of a determined service, preserving the same requirements as the ones offered in paper
format. We would like to emphasize the following properties: anonymity and
transferability.

In the same way as paper tickets, electronic tickets have different properties
according to the services where they are used. These services can be classified by
the anonymity offered. For instance, a plane e-ticket cannot be anonymous: the
identity of the passenger is a fixed parameter that is part of the e-ticket. In the
e-tickets with revocable anonymity, the beneficiary can use the ticket demonstrating its possession but without any need of identification. This modality
helps to avoid fraud related to the reuse of e-tickets. E-tickets with non-revocable
anonymity are not linked to a user at all. The user who owns this e-ticket is the
one who can use this service. The verification phase of the e-ticket should check
if it has previously been used. For that reason, we need some kind of centralized
verification. This alternative would not be applied when we are talking about
reusable e-tickets (e.g. monthly tickets), with which many uses can be given by
the same user.

Regarding the transferability property, there are several e-ticket sales and
distribution companies that allow the e-ticket transfer[1,2]. Nonetheless, the typical transfers of e-tickets are performed through a central service and are non-
anonymous. Moreover, recent studies in related fields incorporate transferability
as a desired requirement [2,11]. We would like to transfer an electronic ticket in
the same way that we can transfer a paper ticket, i.e. anonymously and without
the participation of a central service. In such system, we should note that we
are giving the rights linked to that ticket to another user when we transfer a
ticket. In some cases, it needs a change in the beneficiary role, because some
service parameters are affected: the right to transfer, the service disposal and
the beneficiary identity. According to the right to transfer, the tickets can be
granted to another user with (resale) or without any counterpart (loan).

We can find new systems using cryptographic techniques that enable the
online e-ticket issue and verification [3,6,8,10,12,13].

These actions are really important if the users purchase the electronic tickets
before their use, and the e-ticket is not able to be used everywhere with an online
connection to a central database. In [13] a recent implementation of electronic
tickets over mobile devices with NFC technology has been performed. Another
example is the InMoDo system (Mobile Phone as a Ticket)[3], which has been
adopted by the Swedish national train company, among others.

In some concrete systems, the receiver of an electronic ticket uses smartcards
to carry it. This is the case of Oyster card for public transport in London. This
system was designed in order to make the scanners work independently when
the central system connectivity was down.

---

[1] http://www.ticketmaster.com/transfer
[2] https://www.e-ticket.lu
[3] http://inmodo.com/

1.1   Contribution

A complete survey in this field can be found in [9]. The previous proposals already analysed use a central service that synchronizes the transfer of e-tickets between the users and does not allow revocable anonymity. Thus, the main goal of our contribution is to preserve the security properties of (a) revocable anonymity, where the identity of users could be only revealed in case of misbehaviour, (b) transferability, where the electronic tickets can be transferred as a resale or loan without the collaboration of a central service, and (c) short-term linkability, where the user can easily demonstrate that she is the same user at both moments of receiving the ticket and later transferring it. This can be achieved by using the same cryptographic technique, short-term linkability with group signatures. By fulfilling these security requirements, they could allow to deploy transferable electronic ticketing in real scenarios.

1.2   Document Organization

First, Sect. 2 details a brief background explaining the cryptographic techniques. In Sect. 3, we explain all the system proposal with its desired properties, the entities and the phases. The security analysis is performed in Sect. 4, and in Sect. 5, we finally state the conclusions and future work.

2   Background

We use the short group signature (BBS) scheme [1] in order to verify that a user is a correct member of a certain group of users. Next, we introduce the main definitions related to the BBS signature, both the group signatures scheme and the Zero-Knowledge Proof (ZKP) of the group signatures.

2.1   Group Signatures Scheme

In this section we specify the procedures ($KeyGen_G$, $Sign_G$, $Verify_G$, $Open_G$, $SignLinkable_G$, $VerifyLinkable_G$) to be further used in the protocol with their parameters. $KeyGen_G$, $Sign_G$, $Verify_G$ and $Open_G$ are constructed from the same BBS scheme [1]. Both $SignLinkable_G$ and $VerifyLinkable_G$ have also been constructed in [7]. Consider bilinear groups G_1 and G_2 with respective generators g_1 and g_2.

Definition 1 *The q-**Strong Diffie-Hellman** problem (q-SDH). Given two cyclic groups G_1 and G_2 of prime order p, two randomly chosen generators $g_1 \in G_1$ and $g_2 \in G_2$ of their respective groups, with an isomorphism $\psi : G_2 \rightarrow G_1$ where $g_1 = \psi(g_2)$, the q-SDH problem is a hard computational problem where the (q+2)-tuple $(g_1, g_2, g_2^{\gamma}, g_2^{\gamma^2}, ..., g_2^{\gamma^q}) \in G_1 \times G_2^{q+1}$ is the input and the pair $(g_1^{\frac{1}{x+\gamma}}, x) \in G_1 \times \mathbb{Z}_p$ is the output, for some $x \in \mathbb{Z}_p^*$ such that $x + \gamma \neq 0$.*

Definition 2 The Decision Linear Diffie-Hellman problem (DLIN).
Given a cyclic group G_1 of order p, and taking $u, v, h, u^a, v^b, h^c \in G_1$ as input, where $u, v, h \in G_1$ randomly chosen generators, and random $a, b, c \in \mathbb{Z}_p$, and output yes if $a + b = c$ and no otherwise.

Suppose that the SDH assumption holds on (G_1, G_2), and that the DLIN assumption holds on G_1. The scheme uses a bilinear map $e : G_1 \times G_2 \to G_T$ and a hash function $H : \{0,1\}^* \to \mathbb{Z}_p^*$. The public values are $g_1, u, v, h \in G_1$ and $g_2, w \in G_2$. Here $w = g_2^\gamma$ for some secret $\gamma \in \mathbb{Z}_p$. The functions are:

- $KeyGen_G(n)$. This algorithm takes a parameter n as input, which is the number of members of the group. The algorithm has the following steps:
  1. select a random value $h \xleftarrow{R} G_1 \backslash \{1_{G_1}\}$ and $gmsk = (\xi_1, \xi_2)$ where $\xi_1, \xi_2 \xleftarrow{R} \mathbb{Z}_p^*$, and set $u, v \in G_1$ such that $u^{\xi_1} = v^{\xi_2} = h$;
  2. select $\gamma \xleftarrow{R} \mathbb{Z}_p^*$ and set $w = g_2^\gamma$; and
  3. generate for each user $\mathcal{U}_i$, $1 \leq i \leq n$, an SDH tuple (A_i, x_i) by performing: select $x_i \xleftarrow{R} \mathbb{Z}_p^*$ and set $A_i \leftarrow g_1^{1/(\gamma + x_i)}$. The parameter γ is the private master key of the group key issuer.
- $Sign_G(gpk, gsk[i], M)$. Given a group public key $gpk = (g_1, g_2, h, u, v, w)$, a private user's key $gsk[i] = (A_i, x_i)$ and a message $M \in \{0,1\}^*$, compute and output a signature of knowledge $\sigma = (T_1, T_2, T_3, c, s_\alpha, s_\beta, s_x, s_{\delta_1}, s_{\delta_2})$. Note that the tuple (T_1, T_2, T_3) is the linear encryption of A, that is: $(T_1, T_2, T_3) = (u^\alpha, v^\beta, Ah^{\alpha+\beta})$ for $\alpha, \beta \xleftarrow{R} \mathbb{Z}_p$. There are also some helper values $\delta_1 \leftarrow x\alpha$ and $\delta_2 \leftarrow x\beta$. The parameter c is the self-generated challenge (hash of the information in the commit information of the proof of knowledge). Finally, $(s_\alpha, s_\beta, s_x, s_{\delta_1}, s_{\delta_2})$ are the response values of the proof of knowledge.
  1. select $\alpha, \beta \xleftarrow{R} \mathbb{Z}_p$ and compute the linear encryption of A: $(T_1, T_2, T_3) \leftarrow (u^\alpha, v^\beta, Ah^{\alpha+\beta})$ together with the helper values $\delta_1 \leftarrow x\alpha$ and $\delta_2 \leftarrow x\beta$;
  2. select $r_\alpha, r_\beta, r_x, r_{\delta_1}, r_{\delta_2} \xleftarrow{R} \mathbb{Z}_p$ and compute the values $R_1 \leftarrow u^{r_\alpha}$, $R_2 \leftarrow v^{r_\beta}$, $R_3 \leftarrow e(T_3, g_2)^{r_x} \cdot e(h, w)^{-r_\alpha - r_\beta} \cdot e(h, g_2)^{-r_{\delta_1} - r_{\delta_2}}$, $R_4 \leftarrow T_1^{r_x} \cdot u^{-r_{\delta_1}}$, $R_5 \leftarrow T_2^{r_x} \cdot v^{-r_{\delta_2}}$
  3. compute the challenge: $c \leftarrow H(M, T_1, T_2, T_3, R_1, R_2, R_3, R_4, R_5)$
  4. compute the values $s_j \leftarrow r_j + cj$ for $j \in \{\alpha, \beta, x, \delta_1, \delta_2\}$
  5. output $\sigma \leftarrow (T_1, T_2, T_3, c, s_\alpha, s_\beta, s_x, s_{\delta_1}, s_{\delta_2})$.
- $Verify_G(gpk, M, \sigma)$. Given a group public key $gpk = (g_1, g_2, h, u, v, w)$, a message M and a group signature $\sigma = (T_1, T_2, T_3, c, s_\alpha, s_\beta, s_x, s_{\delta_1}, s_{\delta_2})$, verify that σ is a valid signature of the message.
  1. re-derive R_1, R_2, R_3, R_4, R_5: $\tilde{R}_1 \leftarrow u^{s_\alpha}/T_1^c$, $\tilde{R}_2 \leftarrow v^{s_\beta}/T_2^c$, $\tilde{R}_3 \leftarrow e(T_3, g_2)^{s_x} \cdot e(h, w)^{-s_\alpha - s_\beta} \cdot e(h, g_2)^{-s_{\delta_1} - s_{\delta_2}} \cdot (e(T_3, w)/e(g_1, g_2))^c$, $\tilde{R}_4 \leftarrow T_1^{s_x}/u^{s_{\delta_1}}$, $\tilde{R}_5 \leftarrow T_2^{s_x}/v^{s_{\delta_2}}$
  2. checks that $c \overset{?}{=} H(M, T_1, T_2, T_3, \tilde{R}_1, \tilde{R}_2, \tilde{R}_3, \tilde{R}_4, \tilde{R}_5)$.
- $Open_G(gpk, gmsk, M, \sigma)$. This algorithm is used in order to trace a signature to a concrete signer inside the group. It is only available for the group manager, as she is the holder of the $gmsk$ master key and knows all the pairs (A_i, x_i). Given a group public key $gpk = (g_1, g_2, h, u, v, w)$, the group

master private key $gmsk = (\xi_1, \xi_2)$, a message M and a signature $\sigma = (T_1, T_2, T_3, c, s_\alpha, s_\beta, s_x, s_{\delta_1}, s_{\delta_2})$, it proceeds as follows. First, recover the user's A by performing $A \leftarrow T_3/(T_1^{\xi_1} \cdot T_2^{\xi_2})$. If the elements $\{A_i\}$ of the user's private keys are given to the group manager, then she can look up the user index corresponding to the identity A recovered from the signature.

- $SignLinkable_G(gpk, gsk[i], M', \sigma, \alpha, \beta)$. Given a group public key gpk, a private user's key $gsk[i]$, a new message M', a previous signature σ, and the values α, β used for that signature, compute and output a signature σ'. In order to use this procedure correctly, it is defined as follows:
  - First use: standard $Sign_G(gpk, gsk[i], M)$ obtaining a group signature σ and using (α, β).
  - Further uses: $SignLinkable_G(gpk, gsk[i], M', \sigma, \alpha, \beta)$:
    1. use the same pair (α, β) producing the same linear encryption of A as in the first time: $(T_1, T_2, T_3) = (u^\alpha, v^\beta, Ah^{\alpha+\beta})$; and
    2. given a message M', sign the message and output a signature $\sigma' \leftarrow (T_1, T_2, T_3, c', s'_\alpha, s'_\beta, s'_x, s'_{\delta_1}, s'_{\delta_2})$ where $c' \leftarrow H(M', T_1, T_2, T_3, R'_1, R'_2, R'_3, R'_4, R'_5) \in \mathbb{Z}_p$.

  It becomes trivial to verify that several signatures are produced by the same user, as the information (T_1, T_2, T_3) is public in the same signature. In addition, the random values $(r_\alpha, r_\beta, r_x, r_{\delta_1}, r_{\delta_2})$ must be different from the previous times, that is: $(r_\alpha' \neq r_\alpha, r_\beta' \neq r_\beta, r_x' \neq r_x, r_{\delta_1}' \neq r_{\delta_1}, r_{\delta_2}' \neq r_{\delta_2})$ in order not to reveal information.

- $VerifyLinkable_G(\sigma, \sigma')$. This algorithm takes two signatures σ and σ' as input and outputs $true$ or $false$ depending on whether the signatures have been produced by the same signer's pseudonym: $(T_1 \overset{?}{=} T_1', T_2 \overset{?}{=} T_2', T_3 \overset{?}{=} T_3')$.

2.2   ZKP of the Group Signatures Scheme

In our proposal, both standard and linkable group signatures are used, as they enable to verify the internal message information as well as to verify that determined signatures related to the same event or e-ticket belong to the same *anonymous* user. Despite these advantages, the signatures are generated by the same user, and the verifications can be performed *offline*, that is, the verifier does not take a role during the signature generation, so this verification needs to be performed. Then we detail the procedures $ZKP_GCommit$, $ZKP_GResponse$ and $ZKP_GVerify$:

- $ZKP_GCommit(M^*)$. This procedure is performed by the user that wants to demonstrate (prover) to another user (verifier) that she is the right holder of the ticket. This part is the commitment, the first procedure. Given a public group key $gpk = (g_1, g_2, h, u, v, w)$, a group private key for the user $gsk[i] = (A_i, x_i)$ and a signed message $M^* = (M, \sigma)$ where $\sigma = (T_1, T_2, T_3, c, s_\alpha, s_\beta, s_x, s_{\delta_1}, s_{\delta_2})$, it generates the commitment $m' = (T_1, T_2, T_3, R'_1, R'_2, R'_3, R'_4, R'_5)$ as output.

1. we have to demonstrate the ownership of the values $(\alpha, \beta, x, \delta_1, \delta_2)$ that have been generated by the signature of M^*, keeping then the resulting values with the linear encryption of A: $(T_1, T_2, T_3) = (u^\alpha, v^\beta, Ah^{\alpha+\beta})$;

2. the values $r_\alpha', r_\beta', r_x', r_{\delta_1}', r_{\delta_2}' \xleftarrow{R} \mathbb{Z}_p$ are selected and then the following values are generated:
   - (a) $R_1' \leftarrow u^{r_\alpha'}$; $R_2' \leftarrow v^{r_\beta'}$;
   - (b) $R_3' \leftarrow e(T_3, g_2)^{r_x'} \cdot e(h, w)^{-r_\alpha'-r_\beta'} \cdot e(h, g_2)^{-r_{\delta_1}'-r_{\delta_2}'}$;
   - (c) $R_4' \leftarrow T_1^{r_x'} \cdot u^{-r_{\delta_1}'}$; $R_5' \leftarrow T_2^{r_x'} \cdot v^{-r_{\delta_2}'}$.

3. the output $m' = (T_1, T_2, T_3, R_1', R_2', R_3', R_4', R_5')$ is generated.

- $ZKP_G Response(m', c')$. This procedure is the second part of the ZKP, where the user responds to the challenge of the verifier given a first commitment. Given a commitment m' where $m' = (T_1, T_2, T_3, R_1', R_2', R_3', R_4', R_5')$ and a challenge c' given by the verifier, the prover generates the response $s' = (s_\alpha', s_\beta', s_x', s_{\delta_1}', s_{\delta_2}')$ where their values are given by: $s_j' \leftarrow r_j' + c'j$ for $j \in \{\alpha, \beta, x, \delta_1, \delta_2\}$

- $ZKP_G Verify(m', c', s')$. This part is performed by the verifier to check that the commitment, challenge and response of the ZKP match. Given a commitment m' where $m' = (T_1, T_2, T_3, R_1', R_2', R_3', R_4', R_5')$, a challenge c' given by the verifier, and the response $s' = (s_\alpha', s_\beta', s_x', s_{\delta_1}', s_{\delta_2}')$ provided by the prover, the verifier checks

1. $u^{s_\alpha'} \stackrel{?}{=} T_1^{c'} \cdot R_1'$; $v^{s_\beta'} \stackrel{?}{=} T_2^{c'} \cdot R_2'$;

2. $e(T_3, g_2)^{s_x'} \cdot e(h, w)^{-s_\alpha'-s_\beta'} \cdot e(h, g_2)^{-s_{\delta_1}'-s_{\delta_2}'} \stackrel{?}{=} (e(g_1, g_2)/e(T_3, w))^{c'} \cdot R_3'$;

3. $T_1^{s_x'} \cdot u^{-s_{\delta_1}'} \stackrel{?}{=} R_4'$; $T_2^{s_x'} \cdot v^{-s_{\delta_2}'} \stackrel{?}{=} R_5'$.

3 Description of the System

In this section, we describe our system proposal. First of all, the security requirements to achieve are briefly introduced in Sect. 3.1. Then, the details of the protocol are presented in Sect. 3.2.

3.1 Requirements

We can classify e-ticket requirements into two categories [9]. On the one hand, we have security requirements, and on the other hand we have functional requirements for e-tickets.

The desired main security requirements for our proposal are:

- Authenticity: the generated ticket is demonstrably genuine.
- Non-repudiation: the issuer of the ticket cannot deny its generation.
- Integrity: the ticket cannot be modified after its issue.
- Revocable anonymity: the ticket is anonymous, but if the user performs an unauthorized use, then it can be identified.
- Short-term linkability: different movements of a same user, although anonymous, cannot be traced between them, in order to avoid generation of profiles. However, a user could demonstrate being the same user in determined movements of a same journey/action, or to demonstrate ownership of an action.

– Non-overspending: the ticket cannot be used more times than the established in the issue.
– Transferability: the ticket can be transferred to other users, without losing any of the requirements previously stated.

The functional requirements considered are the following:

– Validity time: the ticket can be valid until an established time.
– Online/Offline: ticket verification can require (or not) a connection to the Internet or a centralized system for checking.

3.2   Details of the Protocol

There are three main entities in the system, User ($\mathcal{U}$), Issuer ($\mathcal{I}$) and Service provider ($\mathcal{P}$), and also a Group Manager $\mathcal{M_G}$ that only interacts in case of conflict. There are six phases: *Ticket Issue*, between $\mathcal{I}$ and $\mathcal{U}$; *Ticket Transfer (first time)*, between two users $\mathcal{U}_1$ and $\mathcal{U}_2$; *Ticket Transfer (following 'k' times)*, also between two users $\mathcal{U}_1$ and $\mathcal{U}_2$; *Ticket Verification (standard)*, between $\mathcal{U}$ and $\mathcal{P}$; *Ticket Verification (transferred)*, also between $\mathcal{U}$ and $\mathcal{P}$; and finally the *Revocation of anonymity* phase, which is only used in case of conflict, and which can be called by the Group Manager $\mathcal{M_G}$.

Ticket Issue. In this protocol, $\mathcal{U}$ receives a valid ticket from $\mathcal{I}$ in order to be later used, or transferred. It works as follows:

1. $\mathcal{I}$ generates and sends a random value $n_\alpha \xleftarrow{R} \mathbb{Z}_p$;
2. $\mathcal{U}$:
   (a) selects the service Sv;
   (b) generates $V^* = (V, \widehat{V})$, where $V = (Sv, n_\alpha, \mathsf{flag\_issue})$ and $\widehat{V} = Sign_G(gpk, gsk[i], V)$ is the group signature;
   (c) sends V^* to $\mathcal{I}$;
3. $\mathcal{I}$:
   (a) verifies the group signature: $Verify_G(gpk, V, \widehat{V})$;
   (b) generates the ticket information: $T = (Sn, V, Ti, Tv, Tc)$ where the ticket includes V received from $\mathcal{U}$, Sn as the ticket serial number, Ti as the date of issue, Tv as the validity time, and Tc as the terms and conditions;
   (c) signs the ticket: $T^* = Sign_\mathcal{I}(T)$ where this signature could be a standard RSA-like signature; and
   (d) sends the ticket T^* to $\mathcal{U}$;
4. $\mathcal{U}$ verifies the signature of T^*.

Ticket Transfer (First Time). In this protocol, $\mathcal{U}_1$ transfers the original ticket to $\mathcal{U}_2$ by giving the permission to use it with a group signature which is linked to the commitment of the issued ticket V^*. It works as follows:

1. $\mathcal{U}_1$:
   (a) generates a commitment $m_{\beta_0} = ZKP_GCommit(\mathsf{T}^*)$; and
   (b) sends the commitment and the ticket $(m_{\beta_0}, \mathsf{T}^*)$;
2. $\mathcal{U}_2$:
   (a) verifies the information and signature of T^*: $Verify_\mathcal{I}(\mathsf{T}^*)$;
   (b) verifies the group signature: $Verify_G(gpk, \mathsf{T.V}, \mathsf{T.\widehat{V}})$;
   (c) generates a random value $n_{\lambda_0} \overset{R}{\leftarrow} \mathbb{Z}_p$; and
   (d) generates the first *challenge* with the number of transferred times $k = 0$ and the agreed *price* for the transfer: $c_{\beta_0} = H(n_{\lambda_0}, k = 0, price,$ flag_transfer) and sends it;
3. $\mathcal{U}_1$:
   (a) generates the response $s_{\beta_0} = ZKP_GResponse(m_{\beta_0}, c_{\beta_0})$;
   (b) generates a random value $n_{\beta_0} \overset{R}{\leftarrow} \mathbb{Z}_p$; and
   (c) sends $(s_{\beta_0}, n_{\beta_0})$;
4. $\mathcal{U}_2$:
   (a) verifies the response: $ZKP_GVerify(m_{\beta_0}, c_{\beta_0}, s_{\beta_0})$; and
   (b) generates $\mathsf{W_0}^* = (\mathsf{W_0}, \widehat{\mathsf{W_0}})$ where $\mathsf{W_0} = (n_{\beta_0}, \mathsf{T}^*, $ flag_transfer$)$ and its group signature $\widehat{\mathsf{W_0}} = Sign_G(gpk, gsk[i], \mathsf{W_0})$ and sends it;
5. $\mathcal{U}_1$:
   (a) verifies the group signature: $Verify_G(gpk, \mathsf{W_0}, \widehat{\mathsf{W_0}})$; and
   (b) generates $\mathsf{X_0}^* = (\mathsf{X_0}, \widehat{\mathsf{X_0}})$ where $\mathsf{X_0} = \mathsf{W_0}^*$ and $\widehat{\mathsf{X_0}}$ is a group signature which is linkable only to V^*:
   $\widehat{\mathsf{X_0}} = SignLinkable_G(gpk, gsk[i], \mathsf{W_0}^*, \widehat{\mathsf{V}}, \alpha, \beta)$, and sends it;
6. $\mathcal{U}_2$:
   (a) verifies the group signature: $Verify_G(gpk, \mathsf{X_0}, \widehat{\mathsf{X_0}})$ and
   (b) verifies that the two signatures have been performed by the same user: $VerifyLinkable_G(\mathsf{T.\widehat{V}}, \widehat{\mathsf{X_0}})$. $\mathsf{X_0}^*$ works as a transfer agreement of the ticket of the user $\mathcal{U}_1$ to the user $\mathcal{U}_2$.

Ticket Transfer (Following 'k' Times). In this protocol, $\mathcal{U}_1$ transfers the (already transferred in the past) ticket $\mathsf{X_{k-1}}$ to $\mathcal{U}_2$ by giving the permission to use it with a group signature which is linked to the commitment of the ticket previously received.

1. $\mathcal{U}_1$:
   (a) generates a commitment $m_{\beta_k} = ZKP_GCommit(\mathsf{X_{k-1}})$; and
   (b) sends the commitment and ticket $(m_{\beta_k}, \mathsf{X_{k-1}})$;
2. $\mathcal{U}_2$:
   (a) verifies the information and signature of T^*: $Verify_\mathcal{I}(\mathsf{T}^*)$, the group signature: $Verify_G(gpk, \mathsf{V}, \widehat{\mathsf{V}})$, and the linkability of the two group signatures of the beginning of the first transfer:
   $VerifyLinkable_G(\widehat{\mathsf{X_0}}, \mathsf{T.\widehat{V}})$;
   (b) for each transfer $\forall i \in [0, k)$, verifies the group signatures
   $Verify_G(gpk, \mathsf{X_i}, \widehat{\mathsf{X_i}})$ and $Verify_G(gpk, \mathsf{W_i}, \widehat{\mathsf{W_i}})$, and checks the linkability of $VerifyLinkable_G(\widehat{\mathsf{X_i}}, \widehat{\mathsf{W_{i-1}}})$ if $i > 0$;

    (c) generates a random value $n_{\lambda_k} \xleftarrow{R} \mathbb{Z}_p$; and

    (d) generates the first *challenge*: $c_{\beta_k} = H(n_{\lambda_k}, k, price, \mathsf{flag\_transfer})$ (with the price agreed for the transfer) and sends it;

3. $\mathcal{U}_1$:

    (a) generates the response $s_{\beta_k} = ZKP_G Response(m_{\beta_k}, c_{\beta_k})$;

    (b) generates a random value $n_{\beta_k} \xleftarrow{R} \mathbb{Z}_p$; and

    (c) sends $(s_{\beta_0}, n_{\beta_0})$;

4. $\mathcal{U}_2$:

    (a) verifies the response: $ZKP_G Verify(m_{\beta_k}, c_{\beta_k}, s_{\beta_k})$; and

    (b) generates $\mathsf{W_k}^* = (\mathsf{W_k}, \widehat{\mathsf{W_k}})$ where $\mathsf{W_k} = (n_{\beta_k}, \mathsf{X_{k-1}}, \mathsf{flag\_transfer})$ and its group signature is $\widehat{\mathsf{W_k}} = Sign_G(gpk, gsk[i], \mathsf{W_k})$ and sends it;

5. $\mathcal{U}_1$:

    (a) verifies the group signature: $Verify_G(gpk, \mathsf{W_k}, \widehat{\mathsf{W_k}})$; and

    (b) generates $\mathsf{X_k}^* = (\mathsf{X_k}, \widehat{\mathsf{X_k}})$ where $\mathsf{X_k} = \mathsf{W_k}^*$ and $\widehat{\mathsf{X_k}}$ is a group signature which is linkable only to $\mathsf{W_{k-1}}^*$:
$\widehat{\mathsf{X_k}} = SignLinkable_G(gpk, gsk[i], \mathsf{W_k}^*, \widehat{\mathsf{W_{k-1}}}, \alpha, \beta)$, and sends it;

6. $\mathcal{U}_2$:

    (a) verifies the group signature: $Verify_G(gpk, \mathsf{X_k}, \widehat{\mathsf{X_k}})$; and

    (b) verifies that the two signatures have been performed by the same user: $VerifyLinkable_G(\widehat{\mathsf{X_k}}, \widehat{\mathsf{W_{k-1}}})$. $\mathsf{X_k}^*$ works as a transfer agreement of the ticket of the user $\mathcal{U}_1$ to the user $\mathcal{U}_2$.

Ticket Verification (Standard). This protocol is used when no transfer has been performed since its issue. Here, $\mathcal{U}$ shows the ticket to $\mathcal{P}$ in order to be verified to receive the associated service. It works as follows:

1. $\mathcal{U}$ sends the ticket T^* to $\mathcal{P}$;

2. $\mathcal{P}$:

    (a) verifies the information and signature of T^*; and

    (b) generates a random value $n_\gamma \xleftarrow{R} \mathbb{Z}_p$ and sends it back;

3. $\mathcal{U}$ generates $\mathsf{Y}^* = (\mathsf{Y}, \widehat{\mathsf{Y}})$ where $\mathsf{Y} = (n_\gamma, \mathsf{T.Sn}, \mathsf{flag\_spend\_standard})$ with a group signature which is linkable only to V^*:
$\widehat{\mathsf{Y}} = SignLinkable_G(gpk, gsk[i], \mathsf{Y}, \widehat{\mathsf{V}}, \alpha, \beta)$;

4. $\mathcal{P}$:

    (a) verifies the group signature: $Verify_G(gpk, \mathsf{Y}, \widehat{\mathsf{Y}})$ and that the two signatures are generated by the same user:
$VerifyLinkable_G(\mathsf{T.\widehat{V}}, \widehat{\mathsf{Y}})$; and

    (b) store $\mathsf{T.Sn}$ in $\mathcal{P}$'s centralized database.

Ticket Verification (Transferred). This protocol is used when some transfer has been performed since its issue. Here, $\mathcal{U}$ shows the ticket to $\mathcal{P}$ in order to be verified and receive the associated service. It works as follows:

1. $\mathcal{U}$ sends the transferred ticket $X_k{}^*$ to $\mathcal{P}$;
2. $\mathcal{P}$:
   (a) verifies the information and signature of $X_k{}^*$: $Verify_{\mathcal{I}}(T^*)$ and
       $Verify_G(gpk, X_k, \widehat{X_k})$. The service provider $\mathcal{P}$ can detect if the ticket has
       been transferred or not depending on its content;
   (b) verifies that the two signatures which are included into the ticket have
       been generated by the same user: $VerifyLinkable_G(\widehat{X_0}, T.\widehat{V})$.
   (c) for all the transfers, $\forall i \in [0, k]$: verify all the group signatures
       $Verify_G(gpk, X_i, \widehat{X_i})$ and $Verify_G(gpk, W_i, \widehat{W_i})$, and also the linkability
       of $W_{i-1}{}^*$: $VerifyLinkable_G(\widehat{X_i}, \widehat{W_{i-1}})$ where needed; and
   (d) generates a random $n_\gamma \xleftarrow{R} \mathbb{Z}_p$ and sends it back;
3. $\mathcal{U}$ generates $Y^* = (Y, \widehat{Y})$ where $Y = (n_\gamma, T.Sn, flag\_spend\_transferred)$ and its
   linkable group signature to $W_k{}^*$ as follows:
   $\widehat{Y} = SignLinkable_G(gpk, gsk[i], Y, \widehat{W_k}, \alpha, \beta)$;
4. $\mathcal{P}$:
   (a) verifies the group signature: $Verify_G(gpk, Y, \widehat{Y})$ and that the two signa-
       tures are generated by the same user:
       $VerifyLinkable_G(\widehat{W_k}, \widehat{Y})$ where the ticket receiver has then to demon-
       strate that is the same user both in the transfer and verification phases;
       and
   (b) store $T.Sn$ in $\mathcal{P}$'s centralized database.

Revocation of Anonymity. To spend an e-ticket, any user has to do a new
signature at the 3rd step of the ticket verification phase. In case of controversy
(such as a e-ticket overspending case), the group manager $\mathcal{M_G}$ could take part
in the resolution of the controversy and revoke the anonymity of the signer that
misbehaved by calling the $Open_G$ procedure.

4   Security and Transferability of the System

In this section we discuss the security properties of our protocol. The discussion
is organized in four propositions that state the security features of the scheme.
Then the respective claims discuss and provide evidence to support propositions'
arguments. This discussion does not provide any demonstration of the security
of the cryptographic primitives and does not pretend to be a formal analysis of
the security of the protocol, but it substantiates the security properties of the
protocol. The common security properties of authenticity, non-repudiation and
integrity, which are based on the security of the signature scheme used by $\mathcal{I}$,
are attested in the Proposition 1, then revocable anonymity in Proposition 2,
non-overspending in Proposition 3 and, finally, Proposition 4 is devoted to the
requirement of transferability.

Proposition 1. *The proposed e-ticketing system preserves authenticity, non-repudiation and integrity of the e-ticket.*

Claim 1. It is computationally infeasible to make a new fraudulent e-ticket.

Security Argument. A valid e-ticket has the form $T^* = (T, Sign_{\mathcal{I}}(T))$. Then, the first step that $\mathcal{P}$ does when an e-ticket is received is the verification of the signature. The Ticket Verification protocol will continue only if this verification is positive; otherwise, $\mathcal{P}$ refuses $\mathcal{U}$'s request. Thus, making a new fraudulent valid e-ticket would be equivalent to breaking the signature scheme, which would be computationally infeasible as we have supposed that $\mathcal{I}$ uses a secure signature scheme.

Claim 2. The issuer $\mathcal{I}$ can not deny the emission of a valid e-ticket.

Security Argument. A valid e-ticket has $\mathcal{I}$'s signature and the signature scheme used is secure. Consequently, the identity of the issuer is associated to the ticket i.e. the signature is a non-repudiation evidence of origin.

Claim 3. The content of the e-ticket cannot be modified.

Security Argument. Suppose that someone modifies the content of the ticket, then a new $\mathcal{I}$'s signature has to be generated over the modified content; otherwise, the e-ticket will not pass the verification i.e. it will not be valid. Again, if it is computationally infeasible to forge $\mathcal{I}$'s signature, it is infeasible to modify the content of the e-ticket.

Proposition 2. *The e-ticketing system described in Sect. 3 is anonymous. The offered service is revocable anonymous.*

Claim 4. The protocol to get an e-ticket is anonymous.

Security Argument. The user establishes a connection with the ticket issuer $\mathcal{I}$ in order to receive the e-ticket. This connection could be established through an anonymous channel like TOR [4], guaranteeing then the user's privacy. There are current contributions[4] that have implemented TOR for mobile devices with Android. Additionally, the user does not use any personal authentication method to get the e-ticket. $\mathcal{I}$ generates and sends the e-ticket to $\mathcal{U}$ if she accredits to be member of the group of users by producing a valid group signature over a challenge sent by $\mathcal{I}$. The $Verify_G(V)$ procedure performed by $\mathcal{I}$ cannot identify the user.

Claim 5. An e-ticket has revocable anonymity.

Security Argument. A valid e-ticket does not have any information related to the user's identity. The e-ticket is generated by $\mathcal{I}$ who does not know the user's identity as we have discussed in the previous claim. The only item inside the e-ticket that can identify the user is the group signature V and only the group manager $\mathcal{M_G}$ can reveal this information by performing $Open_G(gpk, gmsk, M, \sigma)$, because it is the only entity that knows $gmsk$. Therefore, e-tickets can be spent anonymously but the anonymity can be revoked by $\mathcal{M_G}$. $\mathcal{M_G}$ plays the role of a trusted third party, thus it will only do that by law enforcement.

---

[4] http://sourceforge.net/apps/trac/silvertunnel/wiki/TorJavaOverview

Claim 6. In spite of the anonymity of the e-ticket, a fake user cannot spend an e-ticket impersonating another user.

Security Argument. In order to spend the e-ticket, the legitimate $\mathcal{U}$ has to prove the ownership of the e-ticket by means of a linkable signature Y with the element V, placed inside the e-ticket. An illegitimate $\mathcal{U}$ cannot perform properly the $SignLinkable_G$ operation: the fraud will be detected because the $VerifyLinkable_G()$ operation performed at the ticket verification protocol will warn $\mathcal{P}$ about this impersonation attack.

Proposition 3. *The protocol controls overspending.*

Claim 7. If the ticket is only validated by one $\mathcal{P}$, the verification can be offline and $\mathcal{P}$ can control any overspending attempt.

Security Argument. $\mathcal{P}$ maintains a database with the serial numbers of the e-tickets already validated (i.e used). $\mathcal{P}$ can check both the issuer's signature and whether the e-ticket has not been spent before by using the information stored in the database. So the provider does not need to contact any party during the validation of an e-ticket.

Claim 8. If the ticket is validated with several providers, all $\mathcal{P}$'s must then be connected and share a database of spent tickets.

Security Argument. The set of providers maintains a shared database with the serial numbers of the e-tickets that have been already validated. The contents of this database are used by the providers to decide if they accept and validate a new ticket. So the provider does not need a connection with the issuer during the verification of an e-ticket, but the set of providers must share a database instead, so that the overspending can then be detected and the identity of the overspender can be revealed by the group manager through the $Open_G(gpk, gmsk, M, \sigma)$ procedure.

Proposition 4. *Users can transfer their e-ticket to other users making use of the proposed scheme. The transferability operation among users preserves the security properties no matter how many transfers of the e-ticket have been made.*

Claim 9. A transferred e-ticket can guarantee authenticity, non-repudiation and integrity properties as a non-transferred e-ticket.

Security Argument. During a transfer, the format of the e-ticket is not substantially altered. Only a new group signature of the new owner is added to the e-ticket so that the properties of the signature keep authenticity, non-repudiation and integrity of the transferred e-ticket since the discussion of the Proposition 1 is already valid.

Claim 10. A transferred e-ticket preserves the anonymity of its owner.

Security Argument. During a transfer, the owner of the e-ticket proves its ownership with a ZKP operation in order not to disclose her identity. The receiver of the transferred e-ticket includes a new group signature in it, so her identity is similarly protected in the same way, as we see in the step 4 of the ticket verification protocol (transferred version).

Claim 11. A transferred ticket cannot be overspent.

Security Argument. The overspending detection procedure described in Proposition 3 is also valid for transferred e-tickets as well as the anonymity revocation which can be made using $Open_G(gpk, gmsk, M, \sigma)$ because this property relies on the verification made by $\mathcal{P}$ on the serial number of the e-ticket stored in the database. The transfer of any e-ticket does not change its serial number.

5 Conclusions

We have presented a proposal for an electronic ticketing system which guarantees the anonymity for their users and also allows the transferability of the tickets between them through payment or loan.

The proposed scheme is anonymous, as in the ticket issue protocol, a group signature scheme has been used, which allows the issuer to verify that the user belongs to a valid group of users, yet cannot identify which one she is. If the user tries to commit fraud, the group manager can revoke her anonymity.

Moreover, the protocol introduces the requirement of ticket transferability between two users. This property aims to increase the system flexibility since users can share their tickets with friends or they can give them to other users. To do that, we use a linkable group signature scheme. With this technique, group signatures from the users involved in the transfer operation are used in order to generate a ticket transfer agreement, which could be further used as an evidence proof in case of any conflict between the parties. As future work, the main goal will be to develop and evaluate the performance of the protocol in a mobile platform, in order to check its feasibility.

Disclaimer and Acknowledgements. This work was partially supported by the Spanish Ministry of Science and Innovation [eAEGIS TSI2007-65406-C03-01, ARES--CONSOLIDER INGENIO 2010 CSD2007-00004, Audit Transparency Voting Process IPT-430000-2010-31, CO-PRIVACY TIN2011-27076-C03-01, ICWT TIN2012-32757, BallotNext IPT-2012-0603-430000]; and the Government of Catalonia [2009 SGR1135]. The authors are solely responsible for the views expressed in this paper, which do not necessarily reflect the position of UNESCO nor commit that organization.

References

1. Boneh, D., Boyen, X., Shacham, H.: Short group signatures. In: Franklin, M. (ed.) CRYPTO 2004. LNCS, vol. 3152, pp. 41–55. Springer, Heidelberg (2004)
2. Canard, S., Gouget, A.: Anonymity in transferable e-cash. In: Bellovin, S.M., Gennaro, R., Keromytis, A.D., Yung, M. (eds.) ACNS 2008. LNCS, vol. 5037, pp. 207–223. Springer, Heidelberg (2008)

3. Chen, Y.-Y., Chen, C.-L., Jan, J.-K.: A mobile ticket system based on personal trusted device. Wirel. Pers. Commun. Int. J. **40**(4), 569–578 (2007)

4. Dingledine, R., Mathewson, N., Syverson, P.: Tor: the second-generation onion router. In: Proceedings of the 13th USENIX Security Symposium (2004)

5. Ghiron, S., Sposato, S., Medaglia, C., Moroni, A.: NFC ticketing: a prototype and usability test of an NFC-based virtual ticketing application. In: Workshop on Near Field Communication 2009, NFC '09, pp. 45–50. IEEE, February 2009

6. Heydt-Benjamin, T.S., Chae, H.-J., Defend, B., Fu, K.: Privacy for public transportation. In: Danezis, Ge, Golle, P. (eds.) PET 2006. LNCS, vol. 4258, pp. 1–19. Springer, Heidelberg (2006)

7. Isern-Deyà, A.P., Vives-Guasch, A., Mut-Puigserver, M., Payeras-Capellà, M., Castellà-Roca, J.: A secure automatic fare collection system for time-based or distance-based services with revocable anonymity for users. Comput. J. **56**, 1198–1215 (2012)

8. Jorns, O., Jung, O., Quirchmayr, G.: A privacy enhancing service architecture for ticket-based mobile applications. In: Availability, Reliability and Security, Vienna, Austria, pp. 374–383, ARES 2007 - The International Dependability Conference, vol. 24, April 2007

9. Mut-Puigserver, M., Payeras-Capellà, M.M., Ferrer-Gomila, J.-L., Vives-Guasch, A., Castellà-Roca, J.: A survey of electronic ticketing applied to transport. Comput. Secur. **31**(8), 925–939 (2012)

10. Quercia, D., Hailes, S.: Motet: mobile transactions using electronic tickets. In: Proceedings of the Security and Privacy for Emerging Areas in Communications Networks, vol. 24, pp. 374–383, Greece, Sept. 2005

11. Sunitha, N., Amberker, B., Koulgi, P.: Transferable e-cheques: an application of forward-secure serial multi-signatures. In: Ao, S.-I., Rieger, B., Chen, S.-S. (eds.) Advances in Computational Algorithms and Data Analysis. Lecture Notes in Electrical Engineering, vol. 14, pp. 147–157. Springer, Netherlands (2009)

12. Vives-Guasch, A., Castellà-Roca, J., Payeras-Capella, M., Mut, M.: An electronic and secure automatic fare collection system with revocable anonymity for users. In: Advances in Mobile Computing & Multimedia (MoMM) (2010)

13. Vives-Guasch, A., Payeras-Capellà, M.M., Mut-Puigserver, M., Castellà-Roca, J., Ferrer-Gomila, J.L.: A secure e-ticketing scheme for mobile devices with near field communication (NFC) that includes exculpability and reusability. IEICE **E95–D**(1), 78–93 (2012)

Privacy-Preserving Publish/Subscribe: Efficient Protocols in a Distributed Model

Giovanni Di Crescenzo[1]([⊠]), Brian Coan[1], John Schultz[2],
Simon Tsang[1], and Rebecca N. Wright[3]

[1] Applied Communication Sciences, Basking Ridge, NJ, USA
{gdicrescenzo,bcoan,stsang}@appcomsci.com
[2] Spread Concepts, Bethesda, MD, USA
jschultz@spreadconcepts.com
[3] Rutgers University, New Brunswick, NJ, USA
rebecca.wright@rutgers.edu

Abstract. We consider the problem of modeling and designing efficient and privacy-preserving publish/subscribe protocols in a distributed
model where parties can act as publishers or subscribers or both, and
there are no brokers or other types of parties. The problem is particularly challenging as privacy demands on such protocols come with efficiency limitations; most notably, the publisher must send messages as
long as the publications to all parties, and the cryptographic techniques
to perform the publish/subscribe match need to be based on asymmetric
cryptographic operation which are known to be less efficient than their
symmetric counterpart.

Our main result is a distributed publish/subscribe protocol which
addresses and essentially nullifies the impact of both efficiency limitations, without sacrificing the required privacy properties. Our construction is based on very efficient design of a novel cryptographic tool, of
independent interest, called 'hybrid conditional oblivious transfer protocol', as it resembles hybrid encryption, where asymmetric encryption is
only used to transfer a short key, which enables (much more efficient)
symmetric encryption of a long message.

1 Introduction

Publish/subscribe protocols address the problem of publishing data items to
interested participants. They come in many different formulations and variations, as well surveyed in [1]. In this paper's formulation of the problem, a
publish/subscribe protocol can be considered a distributed protocol between
multiple participants who can, at any given time, act as subscribers (with subscription keywords, called interests) or publishers (with data items and related
publication keywords, called topics). The publisher would like to distribute a
data item to the subscribers if there is a match between the data item's topics
and a subscriber's interests, with no help from brokers or other types of parties. These protocols find applications in a large number of areas, and are of

J. Garcia-Alfaro et al. (Eds.): DPM 2013 and SETOP 2013, LNCS 8247, pp. 114–132, 2014.
DOI: 10.1007/978-3-642-54568-9_8, © Springer-Verlag Berlin Heidelberg 2014

interest in essentially every area where distributed systems are used. In most applications, however, privacy is a sensitive issue that may even deter from the implementation or use of a publish/subscribe system. For instance, in finance, a publish/subscribe system assisting a market maker could allow subscribers to submit their interest in companies and publishers to issue data relative to companies; however, by revealing company names and data from either the subscribers or the publishers, it may not only impact participants' privacy but also significantly alter the market's pricing process and overall integrity.

In this paper we investigate the modeling and design of distributed publish/subscribe protocols which preserve the privacy of subscribers' interests and of publishers' data items and topics. We start by observing that such privacy demands come with at least two main efficiency limitations. First, while in non-private publish/subscribe protocols, a publisher can send data items only to matching subscribers, this cannot happen in protocols with privacy demands, as this would reveal the subset of matching subscribers (and thus, information about their interests) to the publisher. In fact, we make the rather discouraging observation that the publisher must send a message at least as long as the data item to each of the subscribers, regardless of whether the publication matches their interests or not. Second, computing which subscribers are entitled to data items can be shown, using well-known fundamental results in cryptography [2], to require asymmetric cryptographic operations, which are well-known to be less efficient than their symmetric counterparts, the difference being significant in applications with high data arrival rates, which are not uncommon publish/subscribe scenarios. In particular, general solutions from the area of secure function evaluation protocols (e.g., [3,4]) suffer from similar inefficiency drawbacks.

Our Contribution. We design a publish/subscribe protocol that not only addresses the mentioned efficiency limitations, but achieves desirable privacy and efficiency properties. Specifically, our protocol satisfies a highly desirable set of requirements: publication correctness (i.e. subscribers obtain a data item if their subscription predicate is satisfied by their interests and the data item's topics), privacy of interests (i.e., against a malicious adversary corrupting the publisher), privacy of topics and data items (i.e., against an honest-but-curious adversary corrupting even all the subscribers), and efficiency (i.e., the publication, which is the real-time part of the protocol, only requires a small rate of public-key cryptography operations per item). We overcome the two efficiency limitations as follows: first, we perform cryptographic processing of data items only once for all subscribers, by encrypting the data item once and distributing the key only to matching subscribers; then, we minimize the use of asymmetric cryptographic operations in distributing the encrypting key by using a novel hybrid cryptographic primitive (i.e., starting with asymmetric cryptographic operations and then continuing with symmetric ones for the rest of the protocol lifetime). Specifically, our protocol uses new constructions for conditional oblivious transfer (COT) protocols [5], called *hybrid COT protocols*, where the first execution of such a subprotocol requires asymmetric cryptography operations, while all remaining ones, when based on the same private inputs, do not. We prove privacy properties using a natural adaptation of the real/ideal security definition approach (frequently used in cryptography), and show that our protocol leaks no information to the publisher or to all subscribers. We also describe measurements of the protocol's publication latency, which, for large and practical parameter ranges, is only a small (≤ 8) constant slower than a distributed publish/subscribe system with no privacy. Our techniques for hybrid COT protocols can also be extended to more general conditions than equality.

Related Work. Some papers have proposed interesting publish/subscribe protocols with some security or privacy properties (e.g., [6–11]). All these papers fall short of meeting our combined functionality and privacy requirements for a mixture of reasons, including a different set of security and/or privacy requirements (i.e., they often require privacy against intermediate routing nodes or privacy only against one party, or rely on trusted broker parties). None of these papers proves privacy properties in a formal, cryptographic model for private publish/subscribe protocols. Our previous paper in the area [12] proposes a solution with privacy provable in a cryptographic model but in a different participant model (i.e., using an intermediate broker to achieve even greater efficiency). We could not find any paper studying hybrid COT protocols; the seemingly closest paper [13] first studied a related problem about precomputing 1-out-of-2 oblivious transfer protocols, which is however different in at least 2 important ways (i.e., it is about 1-out-of-2 oblivious transfer instead of equality-based COT, and it performs several oblivious transfers in the preprocessing phase instead of one). Equality-based COT protocols were already presented in [5, 14–17], which however did not consider the problem of designing hybrid constructions. The COT concept is a variant of oblivious transfer, which was first introduced by [18].

2   Models and Definitions

We detail models and definitions of interest during our investigation of private and distributed publish/subscribe protocols: data, participant, network and protocol models and correctness, privacy and efficiency requirements.

Data Model. We consider the following data objects or structures. The *data items* to be published are digital documents and are represented as binary strings of length ℓ_d. To each data item, we associate d publication keywords, also denoted as *topics*, taken from a set, called the *dictionary*, known to all parties, and assumed, for simplicity, to be the set of all ℓ_t-bit strings. To each party, we associate c subscription keywords, also denoted as *interests*, taken from the dictionary. Moreover, each party has a *public file* to post information accessible by all other participants (as for a public-key infrastructure in cryptography). Finally, each party has a list of all other system participants. For simplicity, length and number variables ℓ_d, ℓ_t, d, c are defined as system parameters with value known to all parties; however, smaller values can be accommodated by simple padding techniques. Data items and associated topics are assumed to be either generated by or streamed to a publisher, at possibly high rate. Although we target high data arrival rates, we only deal with scenarios where an execution of the publish/subscribe protocol ends before the next data item is streamed to a publisher. Generalizations to other data arrival scenarios are possible, but not further discussed in this paper.

Participant and Network Model. We consider a distributed model with $n+1$ participants $P_1, \ldots, P_{n+1}$, all assumed to be *efficient* (i.e., running in probabilistic polynomial-time in a common security parameter, denoted in unary as 1^σ). Two participant roles are possible at any given time; specifically, a participant can act as a *publisher*, also denoted as P, when it publishes a data item to all other participants; or can act as a *subscriber*, also denoted as S_i, for $i \in \{1, \ldots, n\}$, when it posts its interests or receives another party's publication. Each participant is able to communicate with all others and post on its own public file (also implicitly defining a communication channel with all other parties) . We consider a confidential and authenticated network (this assumption is without loss of generality as parties can use a security protocol like TLS) with no loss of transferred data or of party connectivity.

Protocol Model. A publish/subscribe protocol includes the following subprotocols:

Init: participants $P_1, \ldots, P_{n+1}$, may interact and/or post messages on their public files to initialize their data structures and/or cryptographic keys. Formally, on input security parameter 1^σ, protocol Init returns public and secret outputs for all parties.

Subscribe: Party P_i, for $i \in \{1, \ldots, n+1\}$, acting as a subscriber, posts its updated subscription (based on its latest set of interests) on its public file, without interacting with any other party. Formally, on input security parameter 1^σ, a party index $i \in \{1, \ldots, n+1\}$, and a set of interests $int_1, \ldots, int_c$, algorithm Subscribe returns a public and a secret output, where the public output is posted on P_i's public file.

Publish: Party P_i, for $i \in \{1, \ldots, n+1\}$, acting as a publisher, distributes the data item to the subscribers (i.e., all remaining n participants) based on the data item's topics and on the other participants' subscriptions. In terms of distribution strategy, we consider a protocol that follows the so-called 'push mode': as soon as a new data item arrives, along with its topics, it is processed by the publisher towards the subscribers. Formally, on input security parameter 1^σ to all parties, and a data item m and a set of topics $top_1, \ldots, top_d$ as private inputs of publisher P, protocol Publish returns a private output for the i-th subscriber, for $i \in \{1, \ldots, n+1\}$, which is either empty or equal to the data item m. Generalizations to other distribution strategies, like the so-called 'pull mode', are possible but not further discussed in this paper.

Requirements. We now briefly describe publication correctness, privacy and efficiency requirements. Let σ be a security parameter. A function over the set of natural numbers is *negligible* if for all sufficiently large $\sigma \in \mathcal{N}$, it is smaller than $1/p(\sigma)$, for any polynomial p. We say that a subscriber S_i is *entitled* to data item m if at least one of subscriber S_i's interests $int_1, \ldots, int_c$ is equal to any one of the topics $top_1, \ldots, top_d$ associated with m. We address publish/subscribe protocols that satisfy the following classes of requirements.

Correctness. The probability of the following two events is negligible in the security parameter: (a) after executing Init and Subscribe, S_i is entitled to m but does not receive m as output from Publish; (b) after executing Init and Subscribe, S_i is not entitled to m but S_i receives m as output from Publish. Formally, for each data item m and associated topics $top_1, \ldots, top_d$, each subscriber S_i with interests $int_1, \ldots, int_c$, the probability ϵ that, after an execution of Init on input 1^σ, an execution of Subscribe on input $int_1, \ldots, int_c$, and an execution of Publish on input $m, top_1, \ldots, top_d$, one of the following two events happens, is negligible in σ: (a) at least one of subscriber S_i's interests $int_1, \ldots, int_c$ is equal to at least one of the topics $top_1, \ldots, top_d$ but S_i's output at the end of the publication subprotocol is $\neq m$; (b) at least one of subscriber S_i's interests $int_1, \ldots, int_c$ is equal to at least one of the topics $top_1, \ldots, top_d$ but S_i's output at the end of the publication subprotocol is $= m$.

Privacy: We consider two privacy requirements: against a potentially malicious publisher, and against a coalition of honest-but-curious subscribers (i.e., subscribers who follow the protocol but can perform arbitrary computation at the end in their attempt to violate privacy properties). First, consider an efficient and potentially malicious publisher; we require that after an execution of protocols Init, Subscribe and Publish, any such participant learns no additional information about the subscribers' interests. Second, consider a coalition of efficient and honest-but-curious subscribers who did not subscribe to a data item m; we require that after an execution of protocols Init, Subscribe and Publish, any such coalition learns no additional information about the data item or its associated topics.

Towards a formal definition, we recall the notions of computational indistinguishability and participant's view. Two distribution ensembles $\{D_\sigma^0 : \sigma \in \mathcal{N}\}$ and $\{D_\sigma^1 : \sigma \in \mathcal{N}\}$ are *computationally indistinguishable* if for any efficient algorithm A, the quantity $|\text{Prob}[\,x \leftarrow D_\sigma^0 : A(x) = 1\,] - \text{Prob}[\,x \leftarrow D_\sigma^1 : A(x) = 1\,]|$ is negligible in σ (i.e., no efficient algorithm can distinguish if a random sample came from one distribution or the other). A participant's *view* in a protocol (or a set of protocols) is the distribution of the sequence of messages, inputs and internal random coins seen by the participant while running the protocol (or the set of protocols).

We use a natural adaptation of the real/ideal privacy definition framework, which is commonly used in the cryptography literature. A formal definition for the privacy requirement according to this framework goes, briefly speaking, as follows. For any efficient (i.e., probabilistic polynomial time) adversary Adv corrupting one of the two party types (i.e., either a publisher P or some subset of all subscribers $S_1, \ldots, S_n$), there exists an efficient algorithm Sim (called the *simulator*), such that Adv's view in the "real world" and Sim's output in the "ideal world" are computationally indistinguishable, where these two worlds are defined as follows. In the *real world*, runs of the Init subprotocol, Subscribe algorithm and Publish subprotocol are executed, while *Adv* acts as the corrupted participant(s). In the *ideal world*, each run of the Init subprotocol, Subscribe algorithm and Publish subprotocol is replaced with an 'ideal execution' that does not reveal any additional information, in addition to system parameters, inputs and outputs intended by the publish/subscribe functionality. Thus, we define these ideal executions of Init, Subscribe and Publish as follows:

1. Ideal-Init, on input security parameter 1^σ, returns all system parameters and a *done* string to all participants.
2. Ideal-Subscribe, on input a sequence of c interests $int_1, \ldots, int_c$ from a subscriber S_i, returns a *done* string to S_i.
3. Ideal-Publish, on input a data item m and a sequence of d topics $top_1, \ldots, top_d$ of known length from a publisher P, returns the data item m to each subscriber S_i for which at least one of S_i's interests is equal to at least one of the topics $top_1, \ldots, top_d$, and a *done* string to all remaining subscribers and publisher P.

Efficiency: The protocol's *latency* is measured as the time taken by a sequential execution of subprotocol Init, algorithm Subscribe, and subprotocol Publish (as a function of σ and other system parameters). The protocol's *communication complexity* (resp., *round complexity*) is defined as the length (resp., number) of the messages, as a function of σ and other system parameters, exchanged by publisher and subscribers during subprotocols Init, Publish. Even if we will mainly focus our efficiency analysis on publication latency, our design targets minimization of all the mentioned efficiency metrics.

We observe that in any protocol satisfying privacy against the publisher, the latter cannot tell if a subscriber receives the data item or not. Because this holds regardless of the distribution of the data item's content, it also holds for random data items, which cannot be compressed. We thus obtain the following

Proposition 1. In any publish/subscribe protocol in our model, satisfying privacy against the publisher, in the Publish protocol, the publisher needs to send at least ℓ_d bits to each subscriber.

Although we have focused our formalization on the correctness, privacy and efficiency properties, we note that our design has targeted a number of additional *security* properties, which are however obtained using well-known techniques. Specifically, properties like *confidentiality* of the communication between all participants, message *sender authentication*, message *receiver authentication*, and *communication integrity* protection, can be immediately obtained by using a security protocol like TLS.

3   Hybrid Conditional Oblivious Transfer

In this section we formally define the notion of hybrid COT protocols, and then design one such protocol for the equality condition, under the intractability of the Decisional Diffie-Hellman problem.

Equality Conditional Oblivious Transfer (eq-COT): Definition. Informally, an eq-COT protocol is a 2-party protocol where a sender wants to privately transfer a message to a receiver in a way that the only leaked information is the sender's message when the equality predicate evaluates to 1 with private inputs from sender and receiver. Here, we slightly adapt the formal definition from [5] to consider the equality predicate and to more easily express the hybrid COT definition later. Then an eq-COT protocol is a pair (Alice,Bob) of probabilistic polynomial algorithms where Alice's (respectively, Bob's) private input is a string x_a (resp., x_b); m_a denotes Alice's message, m_b denotes Bob's output at the end of the protocol, and the following requirements hold: *(Transfer Correctness)* if $x_a = x_b$ then the probability that $m_b \neq m_a$ is negligible; if $x_a \neq x_b$ and m_a is uniformly distributed, then the distribution of m_b is uniform and independent from m_a; *(Privacy against Bob)* if $x_a \neq x_b$ then for any efficient adversary *Adv* corrupting Bob, the protocol's communication transcript reveals no information to *Adv* about m_a; *(Privacy against Alice)* for any efficient adversary *Adv* corrupting Alice, the protocol's communication transcript reveals no information to *Adv* about whether $x_a = x_b$ or not.

Hybrid Equality Conditional Oblivious Transfer (h-eq-COT). Informally, an h-eq-COT protocol is a 2-party, 2-phase, protocol that allows Alice to perform an eq-COT of an arbitrary number of messages to Bob, as follows. In a first phase, called *h-eq-COT protocol, asymmetric phase*, Alice and Bob execute a single preliminary eq-COT of a κ-bit random symmetric key k_a, based on asymmetric cryptography techniques, where k_a denotes Alice's input and k_b denotes the key received by Bob at the end of this phase. In a second phase, called *h-eq-COT protocol, symmetric phase*, Alice and Bob execute an eq-COT of a message m_a, based on symmetric cryptography techniques, where Alice takes as input k_a, m_a and Bob takes as input k_b and receives m_b at the end of this phase. That is, in all symmetric phase executions of the eq-COT protocol Alice and Bob take as input the symmetric key returned at the end of the preliminary eq-COT protocol (i.e., the same key if $x_a = x_b$ or random and independent keys otherwise.) The formal definition of an h-eq-COT protocol is derived by extending the one for an eq-COT protocol and is omitted here.

Our h-eq-COT Protocol. Similarly to almost all known efficient 1-out-of-2 oblivious transfer (OT) protocols (e.g., [16,17,19]), we base our hybrid COT protocol on an encryption scheme with suitable malleability and/or homomorphism properties. In particular, we use the Decisional Diffie-Hellman problem [20] and its properties, as done in El-Gamal encryption [21] and in the 1-out-of-2 OT protocol from [19], the latter is well known to have especially the latter having desirable security and performance properties.

Informally speaking, the h-eq-COT protocol can be described as follows. First, in the preliminary eq-COT protocol, Bob posts an asymmetric encryption of string x_b, where the encryption scheme used allows Alice to later manipulate this encryption and transform it, without knowing x_b, into an encryption of $k_b = k_a(x_b/x_a)^r \bmod p$, for some random value r, where k_a is Alice's input secret key. In this way, if $x_b = x_a$, Bob receives an encryption of $k_b = k_a$, which he can decrypt; while if $x_b \neq x_a$, Bob receives an encryption of a random key k_b independently distributed from k_a. More formally, this preliminary eq-COT protocol goes as follows:

1. Using a public random source, Alice and Bob uniformly and independently choose σ-bit primes p, q such that $p - 1$ is a multiple of q, a generator g for the q-order subgroup G_q of Z_p, and a random key $k_h \in \{0, 1\}^\kappa$ that defines an efficiently invertible map $M_{\kappa,p}$ from $\{0, 1\}^\kappa$ to G_q
2. Bob computes $x_b' = M_{\kappa,p}(k_h, x_b)$, where $x_b' \in G_q$
3. Bob randomly chooses $r_0, r_1 \in Z_q$, computes $h = g^{r_0} \bmod p$, $u = g^{r_1} \bmod p$ and $v = h^{r_1}(x_b') \bmod p$ and sends (h, u, v) to Alice
4. Alice computes $x_a' = M_{\kappa,p}(k_h, x_a)$, where $x_a' \in G_q$; randomly chooses $k_a \in \{0, 1\}^\kappa$ and computes $k_a' = M_{\kappa,p}(k_h, k_a)$, where $k_a' \in G_q$; and randomly chooses $s_0, s_1 \in Z_q$
5. Alice computes $w = g^{s_0} u^{s_1} \bmod p$ and $z = h^{s_0}(v/x_a')^{s_1} \cdot k_a' \bmod p$ and sends w, z to Bob
6. Bob computes $k_b' = z w^{-r_0} \bmod p$, and $k_b = M_{\kappa,p}^{-1}(k_h, k_b')$, for $k_b \in \{0, 1\}^\kappa$
7. Bob returns: k_b.

At any later time, to perform an eq-COT transfer of any message m, Alice uses key k_a and Bob uses key k_b, and both use an arbitrary symmetric encryption scheme, denoted as (KG,E,D), where E (resp., D) is the encryption (resp., decryption) algorithm. Alice can just perform a symmetric encryption of data item m based on k_a and Bob would be able to decrypt the right item whenever $k_b = k_a$, which holds whenever Alice's private input x_a is equal to Bob's private input x_b. For efficiency purposes, we use another session key so that Bob does not need to decrypt the (potentially long) message when the decryption is not successful. More formally, this preliminary eq-COT protocol goes as follows:

1. Alice randomly chooses a session key $skey_a \in \{0, 1\}^\kappa$
2. Alice computes an encryption of message m as $M = E(skey_a, m_a)$, and values $c = E(k_a, skey_a)$ and $tag = E(skey_a, 0^\kappa)$, and sends (M, c, tag) to Bob
3. Bob computes $skey_b = D(k_b, c)$ and checks if $tag = E(skey_b, 0^\kappa)$;
   if not, Bob returns: $\perp$.
   if yes, Bob computes $m_b = D(skey_b, M)$ and returns: m_b.

We also designed variants of the above constructions based on [16,17], but we omit them here, as they seemed slightly less efficient.

Properties. Building on results from [5,19,21], we obtain the following properties for the above h-eq-COT protocol:

1. If Alice and Bob are honest, and $x_a = x_b$, then at the end of the protocol the value m_b obtained by Bob is equal to the value m_a transferred by Alice.
2. If Alice is honest, and $x_a \neq x_b$, then for any polynomial-time adversary Adv corrupting Bob, at the end of the protocol, Adv learns no additional information about Alice's input x_a or the message m_a.

3. The message (h, u, v) from Bob to Alice can be efficiently simulated by returning a random triple from $(G_q)^3$, and the simulated triple is computationally indistinguishable from the same triple in the real execution assuming the intractability of the Decisional Diffie-Hellman problem. This implies that any polynomial-time adversary corrupting Alice does not learn anything about x_b.

4. When $x_a = x_b$, the messages (w, z) and (M, c, tag) sent by Alice to Bob can be efficiently simulated against an adversary corrupting Bob and having x_b as input and obtaining m_b as output, and the simulation's output is distributed exactly as in the real execution;

5. When $x_a \neq x_b$, the messages (w, z) and (M, c, tag) sent by Alice to Bob can be efficiently simulated against an adversary corrupting Bob and having x_b as input, and the simulation's output is computationally indistinguishable from the same messages in the real execution, assuming the security of the used encryption scheme (KG,E,D).

Proof of properties. We now sketch a proof of properties 1-5 of our h-eq-COT protocol.

Proof of property 1. To see that property 1 is satisfied, we prove two facts: (a) if Alice and Bob are honest and $x_a = x_b$ then at the end of h-eq-COT, asymmetric phase, it holds that $k_b = k_a$; (b) if Alice and Bob are honest and $k_a = k_b$ then at the end of h-eq-COT, symmetric phase, it holds that $m_b = m_a$.

To prove (a), observe that $x_a = x_b$ implies $x'_a = x'_b$ and thus

$$z = h^{s_0}(v/x'_a)^{s_1} \cdot k'_a = h^{s_0}(h^{r_1} x'_b/x'_a)^{s_1} \cdot k'_a = h^{s_0 + r_1 s_1} \cdot k'_a = g^{r_0 s_0 + r_0 r_1 s_1} \cdot k'_a \bmod p.$$

Then we have that

$$w^{-r_0} = (g^{s_0} u^{s_1})^{-r_0} \bmod p = g^{-r_0 s_0 - r_0 r_1 s_1} \bmod p,$$

from which we see that $k'_b = zw^{-r_0} \bmod p = k'_a$, which implies that

$$k_b = M^{-1}_{\kappa,p}(k_h, k'_b) = M^{-1}_{\kappa,p}(k_h, k'_a) = k_a.$$

To prove (b), observe that $k_a = k_b$ implies that

$$skey_b = D(k_b, c) = D(k_a, c) = D(k_a, E(k_a, skey_a)) = skey_a$$

and therefore $E(skey_b, 0^\kappa) = E(skey_a, 0^\kappa)$ and

$$m_b = D(skey_b, M) = D(skey_a, M) = D(skey_a, E(skey_a, m_a)) = m_a.$$

Proof of Property 2 (Sketch). Similarly as for property 1, we can show that when $x_a \neq x_b$, for any h, u, v sent by an adversary playing as Bob, we have that $k'_b = k'_a \cdot (x'_b/x'_a)^{s_1} \bmod p$, for some $x'_b = vh^{-r_1} \bmod p$. Since s_i is random, we have that k'_b is random and independent from k'_a, and thus cannot be used by *Adv* to obtain any information about m_a or x_a from the message (M, c, tag) sent by Alice.

Proof of Property 3 (Sketch). This property follows by the observation that the (u, v) is an El-Gamal encryption of x_b' and thus the well-known fact that the tuple (g, h, u, v) is computationally indistinguishable from a random tuple from $(G_q)^4$.

Proof of Property 4 (Sketch). To prove this property, we now show a simulator *Sim* that, when $x_a = x_b$, efficiently simulates the messages (w, z) and (M, c, tag) sent by Alice to Bob, and using x_b and m_b as input, and show that the simulation's output is distributed exactly as in the real execution.

Sim generates (w, z) exactly as Alice does, with the only apparent difference that it uses x_b instead of x_a. *Sim* can do that since it has the exact same inputs k_a and x_a as Alice, and we are considering the case $x_a = x_b$. Specifically, *Sim* randomly chooses $s_0, s_1 \in Z_q$, and $k_a \in \{0, 1\}^\kappa$, and generates w, z as $w = g^{s_0} u^{s_1} \bmod p$ and $z = h^{s_0} (v/x_b')^{s_1} \cdot k_a' \bmod p$, where $x_b' = M_{\kappa, p}(k_h, x_b)$ and $k_a' = M_{\kappa, p}(k_h, k_a)$.

Analogously, *Sim* generates (M, c, tag) exactly as Alice does, with the only apparent difference that it uses m_b instead of m_a. *Sim* can do that since it has the exact same inputs k_a and m_a as Alice, and we are considering the case $x_a = x_b$, which implies that $m_a = m_b$.

Proof of Property 5 (Sketch). To prove this property, we now show a simulator *Sim* that, when $x_a \neq x_b$, efficiently simulates the messages (w, z) and (M, c, tag) sent by Alice to Bob, using x_b as input, and show that the simulation's output is computationally indistinguishable from the same messages in the real execution, assuming the security of the used encryption scheme (KG,E,D).

Sim generates w, z as two random and independent values in Z_p. By using an analogue property of the oblivious transfer protocol from [19], we obtain that the output of this simulation is equally distributed to the same pair in the real execution.

Moreover, *Sim* generates (M, c, tag) as encryptions of random messages of the same length of the messages encrypted in the real execution. By a standard hybrid argument, this triple is computationally indistinguishable from the triple generated in the real execution, assuming the security of the used encryption scheme (KG,E,D).

4   A Distributed Publish/Subscribe Protocol

In this section we describe our distributed publish/subscribe protocol. We start with a formal statement of the properties of our protocol, then discuss the known and new cryptographic primitives used in the protocol, and give an informal description, a detailed description, and a proof of the properties of our protocol.

Theorem 1. In the model of Sect. 2, there exists (constructively) a distributed publish/subscribe protocol satisfying the following properties: (1) publication correctness with error negligible in security parameter σ; (2) privacy against any efficient adversary corrupting a publisher P, under the hardness of the Decisional

Diffie-Hellman problem; (3) privacy against any efficient and honest-but-curious adversary corrupting an arbitrary subset of subscribers, under the security of the symmetric encryption scheme (KG,E,D) used; (4) non-interactive subscription; (5) one-message publication.

An important claim of our paper is that our protocol, in addition to satisfying Theorem 1, has highly desirable publication latency. In our testing experiments we verified that for a large domain of practical parameter values, the publication latency of our protocol remains within a small constant factor (i.e., 8) worse than the publication latency of a protocol performing the same functionality but offering no privacy guarantee. An example chart for these results is described at the end of this section.

4.1 Informal Description

Our goal is to design a distributed publish/subscribe protocol where the subscription phase is non-interactive (i.e., each subscriber simply posts a message on its public file), the publication protocol requires a single message from publisher to subscribers, and where the publisher is allowed to be malicious and the subscribers are allowed to collude in their attempt to violate the privacy requirements, as specified in Sect. 2.

A high-level view of our protocol can be given as follows. During the initialization subprotocol, the parties agree on common cryptographic parameters using publicly available randomness. During the subscription phase, a subscriber simply runs an asymmetric encryption algorithm to compute an encryption of each one to its interests, and posts such encryptions on its public file. During the publication phase, a publisher sends a single message to all subscribers so that this message, combined with the instructions run by a subscriber, form a conditional oblivious transfer of the data item to be published. Here, the condition is the subscription predicate (i.e., at least one of the subscriber's interests is equal to at least one of the data item's topics). This is reduced to running, for each (data item topic, subscriber interest) pair, an equality-COT where the condition is equality between the data item topic and the subscriber's interest in this pair.

Now, a main goal in the design of our protocol is to minimize the use of asymmetric cryptographic primitives, which are well known to be less efficient than their symmetric counterpart. Specifically, to minimize this efficiency degradation, we use them in a way that is reminiscent of the very practical 'hybrid encryption' approach, where an asymmetric encryption scheme is only used once per communication session to establish the key for a symmetric encryption scheme, and the latter is used for all message encryptions required in the future. Then, we realize a 'hybrid' equality-COT protocol where for each publisher and subscriber, the first of such transfers for a given (data item topic, subscriber interest) pair is performed using asymmetric primitives and all following ones for the same pair re-use the symmetric key established during the first one, using memoization. Then we use an hybrid equality-COT, as described in Sect. 3, which uses: (1) for

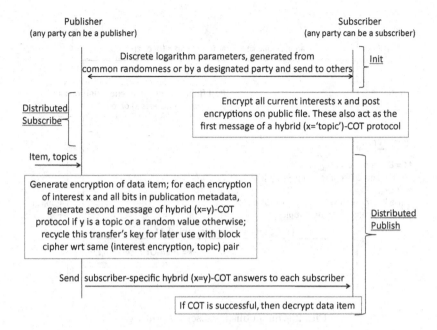

Fig. 1. Informal description of our publish/subscribe protocol

the symmetric part, an equality-COT based on symmetric encryption; and (2) for the asymmetric part, El-Gamal encryption [21] and a novel variant of the most efficient known oblivious transfer protocol [19]. Using asymmetric encryption helps, among other things, avoiding low-entropy guessing attacks on the subscribers' interests and publisher's topics.

An informal pictorial description of our protocol can be found in Fig. 1.

4.2 Detailed Description

We proceed with a formal description of our distributed publish/subscribe protocol (see Fig. 2 for a pictorial description).

Protocol Preliminaries: A point-to-point secure communication protocol such as TLS is assumed to be used for all exchanged communication.

Init: In the initialization subprotocol, parties $P_1, \ldots, P_{n+1}$ run the following instructions:

1. Let ρ be a sufficiently long random string available to all parties; if such a string is not available, $P_1, \ldots, P_{n+1}$ run a multi-party key-agreement protocol to generate one
2. $P_1, \ldots, P_{n+1}$ use ρ to generate the triple (p, q, g) as defined in the initialization subprotocol of the h-eq-COT protocol

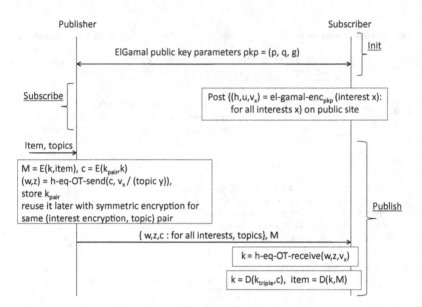

Fig. 2. Our publish/subscribe protocol

Subscribe: Recall that a subscriber S_i's subscription is formally represented as a sequence of c interests $int_1, \ldots, int_c$, for some integer $c \geq 1$. To subscribe, S_i runs the following instructions:

1. For $j = 1, \ldots, c$,
   let int_j denote subscriber S_i's jth interest
   S_i uses triple (p, q, g) to compute a value h_j and an asymmetric encryption (u_j, v_j) of int_j, as done in h-eq-COT protocol, asymmetric phase, step 1
   S_i sets $ip_j = (h_j, u_j, v_j)$
2. S_i posts $(ip_1, \ldots, ip_c)$ on its public file

Publish: We assume that a participant, acting as a publisher P, somehow originates a new data item m, associated with a number d of topics. In the Publish subprotocol, involving P and all remaining participants, acting as subscribers $S_1, \ldots, S_n$, the following instructions are repeated for each subscriber $S_i, i = 1, \ldots, n$.

1. P computes a random key $k_p \in \{0,1\}^\kappa$, and an encryption of data item m as $M = E(k_p, m)$, and sends M to S_i
2. P computes $tag = E(k_p, 0^\kappa)$, and sends tag to S_i
3. For $h = 1, \ldots, d$,
   for $j = 1, \ldots, c$,
   each current interest pseudonym ip_j from C_i, where $j = 1, \ldots, c_p$,
   if P and S_i had not yet executed the key transfer for this
   (interest encryption (u_j, v_j), topic top_h) pair,

P randomly chooses $k_{pair,p} \in \{0,1\}^\kappa$

P uses the h-eq-COT protocol, asymm. phase, to transfer $k_{pair,p}$ to S_i

let $k_{pair,s,i}$ be the key received by S_i at the end of this subprotocol

P uses the h-eq-COT protocol, symm. phase, to transfer k_p to S_i,
    where P uses $k_{pair,p}$ and S_i uses $k_{pair,s,i}$ as additional input

let $k_{s,i}^{h,j}$ be the key received by S_i at the end of this subprotocol

if P and S_i had already executed the key transfer for this
(interest encryption (u_j, v_j), topic top_h) pair,
    P uses the h-eq-COT protocol, symm. phase, to transfer k_p to S_i,
        where P uses $k_{pair,p}$ and S_i uses $k_{pair,s,i}$ as additional input

let $k_{s,i}^{h,j}$ be the key received by S_i at the end of this subprotocol

4. S_i checks if $tag = E(k_{s,i}^{h,j}, 0^\kappa)$ for some $h \in \{1, \ldots, d\}$ and $j \in \{1, \ldots, c\}$

5. if yes, then S_i computes $m = D(k_{s,i}^{h,j}, M)$ for the found h, j values, and returns: m; else S_i returns: $\bot$

In the rest of this section we discuss why our protocol satisfies publication correctness, privacy and efficiency properties, as defined in Sect. 2.

4.3 Properties: Correctness, Privacy and Efficiency

Publication Correctness: To prove that our protocol satisfies this requirement, we need to show the facts (a) and (b) as from the requirement definition.

To see that fact (a) is satisfied, assume that one of subscriber S_i's interests, denoted as int_h, is equal to one of the data item's topics, denoted as top_j. Then, by Property 1 of the h-eq-COT protocol, when run on input top_j as Alice's input and int_h as Bob's input, the key $k_{s,i}^{h,j}$ received by S_i, when playing as Bob, is equal to the key k_p sent by P, when playing as Alice, and used to encrypt the data item m as M. Accordingly, S_i can successfully decrypt M and receive the data item m with probability 1.

To see that fact (b) is satisfied, assume that all of subscriber S_i's interests are different from all of the data item's topics. Then, by Property 2 of the h-eq-COT protocol, when run on input a topic as Alice's input and an interest as Bob's input, all keys $k_{s,i}^{h,j}$ received by S_i, when playing as Bob, are random and independent from the key k_p sent by P, when playing as Alice, and used to encrypt the data item m as M. Accordingly, S_i can successfully decrypt M and receive the data item m with probability smaller than $(cd)\delta(\sigma)$, for some negligible function δ, which is negligible in σ.

Privacy. Our protocol achieves privacy against an efficient and potentially malicious adversary that corrupts the publisher and against an efficient and honest-but-curious adversary that corrupts any subset of the subscribers. Accordingly, we divide the proof of this property into these two cases. In both cases, the simulation of the Init protocol directly follows from the simulatability properties of the key agreement protocol used (if necessary). Thus, we only focus on the simulation of the output of the Subscribe algorithm and of the Publish subprotocol.

Here, in both cases, which we now discuss, we show the existence of an efficient simulator algorithm that simulates Adv's view.

Adv corrupts P: In this case, the simulation mainly follows from the simulation specified in Property 3 of our h-eq-COT protocol. Specifically, assume an efficient adversary, denoted as Adv, corrupts the publisher P. For any such Adv, we show a simulator Sim that produces a view for Adv in the ideal world (while posing as P) that is computationally indistinguishable from Adv's view in the real world (while posing as P), during the execution of the Init, Subscribe and Publish protocols.

To simulate Adv's view from the subscription phase, Sim invokes the ideal Subscribe functionality, which only returns a *done* string to P. Then, the messages posted by the subscribers on their public file are generated by Sim as in the simulation specified in Property 3 of our h-eq-COT protocol.

To simulate Adv's view in the Publish subprotocol, on input the data item m and topics $top_1, \ldots, top_d$, Sim invokes the ideal Publish functionality, which returns a *done* string to P, and then runs Adv on input $m, top_1, \ldots, top_d$ to obtain P's messages to all subscribers. If P does not return such a message, then Sim simply halts.

The proof that Sim's simulation in the ideal world is computationally indistinguishable from Adv's view in the real world, follows from Property 3 of our h-eq-COT protocol, which holds under the intractability of the Decisional Diffie-Hellman problem.

Adv Corrupts an Arbitrary Subset of Subscribers: In this case, the simulation mainly follows from the simulation specified in Properties 4 and 5 of our h-eq-COT protocol. Specifically, assume an efficient and honest-but-curious adversary, denoted as Adv, corrupts a subset of subscribers, or even all of them. For any such Adv, we show a simulator Sim that produces a view for Adv in the ideal world (while posing as the corrupted subscribers) that is computationally indistinguishable from Adv's view in the real world. To simulate the output of the Subscribe algorithm, given as input interests $int_1, \ldots, int_c$ for each corrupted subscriber, Sim does the following. It invokes the ideal Subscribe functionality, which only returns a *done* string to all subscribers. Then it invokes the corrupted subscribers to directly obtain the message they post on their public file. Finally, it simulates the messages posted by the uncorrupted subscribers on their public file, exactly as done in the previous case; that is, again using the simulation specified in Property 3 of our h-eq-COT protocol.

Finally, to simulate the Publish subprotocol, Sim invokes the ideal Publish functionality, possibly obtaining (or not) data item m as output for the corrupted subscribers, depending on whether at least one of the topics $top_1, \ldots, top_d$ is equal to at least one of the interests $int_1, \ldots, int_c$ or not, for each specific subscriber in the corrupted subset. In the former case, Sim has to simulate the strings (w, z) and (M, c, tag) sent by P and can use data item m to do that perfectly, by running P's algorithm. Specifically, Sim runs the simulator as specified in Property 4 of our h-eq-COT protocol. In both cases, Sim can simulate the strings sent to the subscribers by P as part of each execution of the h-eq-COT protocol by running the simulator as specified in Property 4 of our h-eq-COT protocol, where it is also proved that the simulation from Sim is equally distributed to Adv's view in the real world.

In the latter case, Sim has to again simulate the strings (w, z) and (M, c, tag) sent by P but does not have data item m this time. However, Sim can run the simulator as specified in Property 5 of our h-eq-COT protocol. Here, the proof that the simulation from Sim in the ideal world is computationally indistinguishable from Adv's view in the real world, follows from Property 5 of our h-eq-COT protocol, which holds under the security of the encryption scheme used.

Efficiency. By inspection, we verify that in our publish/subscribe protocol the subscription is non-interactive, in that each subscriber only posts a message on its public file (which is from then on readable by any publisher), and the publication only requires a single message from a publisher to all subscribers. Our protocol's efficient communication complexity is also easy to verify.

It remains of interest to evaluate the publication latency metric, under varying parameter values. We implemented both our protocol, denoted as P3.0, and another publish/subscribe protocol, called P0, that only addresses communication privacy and integrity properties using the TLS protocol on all messages between parties, and does not address any privacy on interests, topics or data items between publisher and subscribers.

We note that in P0 the publisher only communicates to the matching subscribers, while this cannot happen in P3.0 or otherwise its privacy property would be violated, due to Proposition 1. Thus, it is of interest to ask whether we can avoid the communication overhead of sending an encryption of the data item to all subscribers, especially in applications where the data item is large. Accordingly, we also implemented a protocol, denoted as P3.1, as the following variant of P3.0:

1. During the Publish subprotocol, the publisher sends the encryption $E(k, m)$ of the data item to a third party, called *repository server*, together with a random value $t = E(k, nonce)$, acting as an access token.
2. The publisher runs the same, previously defined, Publish subprotocol, this time publishing token t instead of a data item
3. All subscribers that received key k and token t send t to the repository server
4. If the repository server receives a valid access token from a subscriber, he sends to this subscriber the associated encryption $E(k, m)$ of the data item
5. The subscriber uses k to retrieve the data item.

We performed testing on a collection of 6 Dell PowerEdge 1950 processors and one Dell PowerEdge 2950 processor. Subscribers were divided in 4 groups of size 25 each, and each group was run on a PowerEdge 1950 processor. The publisher was run on a dedicated 1950 processor, the third party was run on dedicated 1950 processor, and the testing control was run on the 2950 processor. All initialization, subscription, and publication traffic was run over a dedicated gigabit Ethernet LAN. Testing control and collection of timing measurement traffic was isolated on a separate dedicated gigabit Ethernet LAN.

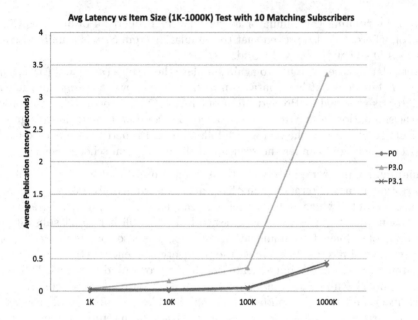

Fig. 3. Publication latency measurements for P3.0, P3.1, and P0

We compared P3.0. P3.1 and P0 against three sets of parameters, each test with a publication rate of 1 item per second, with values 1 K, 10 K, 100 K, and 1000 K bytes for data items, with 10 matching subscribers and 10 topics per item. (see Fig. 3). Tests were run dozens of times over a period of several weeks and results were consistently the same over all the runs (i.e. there is nothing stochastic in the experiments). A resulting performance chart can be found in Fig. 3.

In particular, we observe that the performance of the P3.0 protocol is always within a small constant (e.g., ≤ 8) of the performance of P0. This is remarkable, in light of the fact that P3.0 sends information to all participants (to safeguard privacy against the publisher), while P0 is only sending the data item to the interested participants. Our protocol P3.1, employing a repository server, has performance very close to that of P0 (in other words, it achieves high performance and moderately satisfactory privacy properties, but at the cost of having to trust the repository server).

5   Conclusions

We formally defined a distributed model for publish/subscribe protocols where participants can act as publishers or as subscribers in any given publication transaction. In this challenging model, we showed that solutions with provable privacy and efficiency are possible. In particular, two inherent efficiency limitations (the use of asymmetric cryptography operations and the fact that data items need to be sent to all subscribers) can be mitigated to have only a very small impact on performance, allowing private solutions with efficiency comparable to non-private solutions. This is achieved without the need of a broker (as required in our recent solution [12]). Our approach, based on a novel cryptographic primitive (i.e., hybrid conditional oblivious transfer protocols), can also be generalized to more elaborate publish/subscribe conditions.

Acknowledgements. Many thanks go to Jim Burns and Jonathan Stanton for useful technical conversations. This work was supported by the Intelligence Advanced Research Projects Activity (IARPA) via Department of Interior National Business Center (DoI/NBC) contract number D12PC00520. The U.S. Government is authorized to reproduce and distribute reprints for Governmental purposes notwithstanding any copyright annotation hereon. Disclaimer: The views and conclusions contained herein are those of the authors and should not be interpreted as necessarily representing the official policies or endorsements, either expressed or implied, of IARPA, DoI/NBC, or the U.S. Government.

References

1. Eugster, PTh, Felber, P., Guerraoui, R., Kermarrec, A.-M.: The many faces of publish/subscribe. ACM Comput. Surv. **35**(2), 114–131 (2003)
2. Impagliazzo, R., Rudich, S.: Limits on the provable consequences of one-way permutations.In: Proceedings of the ACM STOC, pp. 44–61 (1989)
3. Yao, A.C.-C.: Protocols for secure computations. In: Proceedings of the IEEE FOCS 1982, pp. 160–164 (1982)
4. Goldreich, O., Micali, S., Wigderson, A.: How to play any mental game or a completeness theorem for protocols with honest majority. In: Proceedings of the ACM STOC, pp. 218–229 (1987)
5. Di Crescenzo, G., Ostrovsky, R., Rajagopalan, S.: Conditional oblivious transfer and timed-release encryption. In: Stern, J. (ed.) EUROCRYPT 1999. LNCS, vol. 1592, pp. 74–89. Springer, Heidelberg (1999)
6. Raiciu, C., Rosenblum, D.S.: Enabling confidentiality in content-based publish/subscribe infrastructures. In: Proceedings of the SecureComm 2006, pp. 1–11 (2006)
7. Minami, K., Lee, A.J., Winslett, M., Borisov, N.: Secure aggregation in a publish/subscribe system. In: Proceedings of the WPES 2008, pp. 95–104 (2008)
8. Shikfa, A., Onen, M., Molva, R.: Privacy-preserving content-based publish/subscribe networks. In: Gritzalis, D., Lopez, J. (eds.) SEC 2009. IFIP AICT, vol. 297, pp. 270–282. Springer, Heidelberg (2009)
9. Tariq, M.A., Koldehofe, B., Altaweel, A., Rothermel, K.: Providing basic security mechanisms in broker-less publish/subscribe systems. In: Proceedings of the ACM DEBS, pp. 38–49 (2010)
10. Ion, M., Russello, G., Crispo, B.: Supporting publication and subscription confidentiality in pub/sub networks. In: Jajodia, S., Zhou, J. (eds.) SecureComm 2010. LNICST, vol. 50, pp. 272–289. Springer, Heidelberg (2010)
11. Choi, S., Ghinita, G., Bertino, E.: A privacy-enhancing content-based publish/subscribe system using scalar product preserving transformations. In: Bringas, P.G., Hameurlain, A., Quirchmayr, G. (eds.) DEXA 2010, Part I. LNCS, vol. 6261, pp. 368–384. Springer, Heidelberg (2010)

12. Di Crescenzo, G., Burns, J., Coan, B., Schultz, J., Stanton, J., Tsang, S., Wright, R.N.: Efficient and private three-party publish/subscribe. In: Lopez, J., Huang, X., Sandhu, R. (eds.) NSS 2013 LNCS, vol. 7873, pp. 278–292. Springer, Heidelberg (2013)
13. Beaver, D.: Precomputing oblivious transfer. In: Coppersmith, D. (ed.) CRYPTO 1995. LNCS, vol. 963, pp. 97–109. Springer, Heidelberg (1995)
14. Di Crescenzo, G.: Private selective payment protocols. In: Frankel, Y. (ed.) FC 2000. LNCS, vol. 1962, pp. 72–89. Springer, Heidelberg (2001)
15. Di Crescenzo, G.: Privacy for the stock market. In: Syverson, P.F. (ed.) FC 2001. LNCS, vol. 2339, pp. 259–278. Springer, Heidelberg (2002)
16. Aiello, W., Ishai, Y., Reingold, O.: Priced oblivious transfer: how to sell digital goods. In: Pfitzmann, B. (ed.) EUROCRYPT 2001. LNCS, vol. 2045, pp. 119–135. Springer, Heidelberg (2001)
17. Lipmaa, H.: Verifiable homomorphic oblivious transfer and private equality test. In: Laih, C.-S. (ed.) ASIACRYPT 2003. LNCS, vol. 2894, pp. 416–433. Springer, Heidelberg (2003)
18. Michael, O.: Rabin: How to exchange secrets with oblivious transfer. Technical report TR-81, Aiken Computation Lab, Harvard University (1981)
19. Moni, N., Pinkas, B.: Efficient oblivious transfer protocols. In: Proceedings of the SODA 2001, pp. 448–457 (2001)
20. Diffie, W., Hellman, M.E.: New directions in cryptography. IEEE Trans. Inf. Theory **22**(6), 644–654 (1976)
21. El Gamal, T.: A public key cryptosystem and a signature scheme based on discrete logarithms. IEEE Trans. Inf. Theory **31**(4), 469–472 (1985)

Privacy-Preserving Processing
of Raw Genomic Data

Erman Ayday[1]([✉]), Jean Louis Raisaro[1], Urs Hengartner[2], Adam Molyneaux[3],
and Jean-Pierre Hubaux[1]

[1] École Polytechnique Fédérale de Lausanne, Lausanne, Switzerland
erman.ayday@epfl.ch
[2] University of Waterloo, Waterloo, Canada
[3] Sophia Genetics, Lausanne, Switzerland

Abstract. Geneticists prefer to store patients' aligned, raw genomic data, in addition to their variant calls (compact and summarized form of the raw data), mainly because of the immaturity of bioinformatic algorithms and sequencing platforms. Thus, we propose a privacy-preserving system to protect the privacy of aligned, raw genomic data. The raw genomic data of a patient includes millions of short reads, each comprised of between 100 and 400 nucleotides (genomic letters). We propose storing these short reads at a biobank in encrypted form. The proposed scheme enables a medical unit (e.g., a pharmaceutical company or a hospital) to privately retrieve a subset of the short reads of the patients (which include a definite range of nucleotides depending on the type of the genetic test) without revealing the nature of the genetic test to the biobank. Furthermore, the proposed scheme lets the biobank mask particular parts of the retrieved short reads if (i) some parts of the provided short reads are out of the requested range, or (ii) the patient does not give consent to some parts of the provided short reads (e.g., parts revealing sensitive diseases). We evaluate the proposed scheme to show the amount of unauthorized genomic data leakage it prevents. Finally, we implement the proposed scheme and assess its practicality.

Keywords: Genomics · Privacy · Bioinformatics · Raw genomic data

1 Introduction

Genomics holds great promise for better predictive medicine and improved diagnoses. However, genomics also comes with a risk to privacy [4] (e.g., revelation of an individual's genetic properties due to the leakage of his genomic data). An increasing number of medical units (pharmaceutical companies or hospitals) are willing to outsource the storage of genomes generated in clinical trials. Acting as a third party, a biobank could store patients' genomic data that would be used by the medical units for clinical trials. In the meantime, the patient can also benefit from the stored genomic information by interrogating his own genomic

J. Garcia-Alfaro et al. (Eds.): DPM 2013 and SETOP 2013, LNCS 8247, pp. 133–147, 2014.
DOI: 10.1007/978-3-642-54568-9_9, © Springer-Verlag Berlin Heidelberg 2014

data, together with his family doctor, for specific genetic predispositions, sus-
ceptibilities and metabolical capacities. The major challenge here is to preserve
the privacy of patients' genomic data while allowing the medical units to operate
on specific parts of the genome (for which they are authorized).

We can put the research on genomic privacy in three main categories: (i) re-
identification of anonymized genomic data [12,13,17,18], (ii) cryptographic algorithms to protect genomic data [6–9,14,16], and (iii) private clinical genomics
[11]. To the best of our knowledge, none of the existing works on genomic privacy addresses the issue of private processing of aligned, raw genomic data (i.e.,
sequence alignment/map files), which is crucial to enable the use of genomic
data in clinical trials.

Sequence alignment/map (SAM and its binary version BAM) files are the *de
facto* standards used to store the aligned[1], raw genomic data generated by next-
generation DNA sequencers and bioinformatic algorithms. There are hundreds
of millions of short reads (each including between 100 and 400 nucleotides) in
the SAM file of a patient. Typically, each nucleotide is present in several short
reads in order to have sufficiently high coverage of each patient's DNA.

In general, geneticists prefer storing aligned, raw genomic data of the patients
(i.e., their SAM files), in addition to their variant calls (which include each
nucleotide on the DNA sequence once, hence is much more compact) due to
the following reasons: (i) Bioinformatic algorithms and sequencing platforms
for variant calling are currently not yet mature, and hence geneticists prefer to
observe each nucleotide in several short reads. (ii) If a patient carries a disease,
which causes specific variations in the diseased cells (e.g., cancer), his DNA
sequence in his healthy cells will be different from those diseased. Such variations
can be misclassified as sequencing errors by only looking at the patient's variant
calls (rather than his short reads). And (iii) due to the rapid evolution of genomic
research, geneticists do not know enough to decide which information should
really be kept and what is superfluous, hence they prefer to store all outcome of
the sequencing process as SAM files.

In this paper, we propose a privacy-preserving system for the storage, retrieval
and processing of the SAM files. In a nutshell, the proposed scheme stores the
encrypted SAM files of the patients at a *biobank* and it provides the requested
range of nucleotides (on the DNA sequence) to a medical unit (for a genetic
test) while protecting the patients' genomic privacy. It is important to note that
the proposed scheme enables the privacy-preserving processing of the SAM files
both for individual treatment (when the medical unit is embodied in a hospital)
and for genetic research (when the medical unit is embodied in a pharmaceutical company). The main contributions of this paper are summarized in the
following:

1. We develop a privacy-preserving framework for the retrieval of encrypted
   short reads (in the SAM files) from the biobank without revealing the scope
   of the request to the biobank.

---

[1] Alignment is with respect to the reference genome, which is assembled by the
scientists.

2. We develop an efficient system for obfuscating (i.e., masking) specific parts of the encrypted short reads that are out of the requested range of the medical unit (or that the patient prefers to keep secret) at the biobank before providing them to the medical unit.
3. We show the benefit of masking by evaluating the information leak to the medical unit, with and without the masking is in place.
4. We implement the proposed privacy-preserving system by using real genomic data, evaluate its efficiency, and show its practicality.

2   Genomic Background

The DNA sequence data produced by DNA sequencing consists of millions of short reads, each typically including between 100 and 400 nucleotides (A,C,G,T), depending on the type of sequencer. These reads are randomly sampled from a human genome. Each read is then bioinformatically treated and positioned (aligned) to its genetic location to produce a so-called SAM file. There are hundreds of millions of short reads in the SAM file of one patient.

The privacy-sensitive fields of a short read are (i) its position with respect to the reference genome, (ii) its *cigar string* (CS), and (iii) its content (including the nucleotides from $\{A, T, G, C\}$).

A short read's position denotes the position of the first aligned nucleotide in its content, with respect to the reference genome. The position of a short read is in the form $L_{i,j} = \langle x_i | y_j \rangle$, where x_i represents the chromosome number ($x_i \in [1, 23]$ as there are 23 chromosomes in the human genome) and y_j represents the position of its first aligned nucleotide on chromosome x_i ($y_j \in [1, 240M]$ as the maximum number of nucleotides on a chromosome is around 240 million). The cigar string (CS) of a short read expresses the variations in the content of the short read. The CS includes *pairs* of nucleotide lengths and the associated operations. The operations in the CS indicate some properties about content of the short read such as which nucleotides align with the reference, which are deleted from the reference, and which are insertions that are not in the reference (without revealing the content of the short read). Finally, the content of a short read includes the nucleotides. We provide more details about the SAM files in [5].

There are several types of DNA variations in the human genome, among which the *single nucleotide polymorphism* (SNP) is the most common. A SNP is a position in the genome holding a nucleotide that varies between individuals. Recent discoveries show that the susceptibility of a patient to several diseases can be computed from his SNPs [1]. Thus, we focus on the SNPs of a patient when evaluating the information leakage in Sect. 6.

3   Overview of the Proposed Solution

We assume that the sequencing and encryption of the genomes are done at a *certified institution* (CI), which is a trusted entity. Short reads are encrypted after the sequencing, and encrypted SAM files of the patients are stored at a biobank (for security, efficiency, and availability). We note that a private company (e.g., cloud storage service) or the government could play the role of the biobank. When a *medical unit* (MU) requests a specific range of nucleotides (on the DNA sequence of one or multiple patients) for a genetic test, the biobank provides all the short reads that include at least one nucleotide from the requested range. We assume that an MU is a broad unit consisting of many sub-units (e.g., physicians or specialized clinics) that can potentially request nucleotides from any parts of a patient's genome. To avoid the biobank from associating the conducted genetic tests with the patients, we hide both the real identities of the patients (using pseudonyms) and the types of the conducted tests from the biobank.[2] We hide the types of the conducted tests from the biobank by permuting the positions of the short reads, and then using order preserving encryption (OPE) on the positions of the short reads. OPE is a deterministic encryption scheme whose encryption function preserves numerical ordering of the plaintexts [3].

As each short read includes between 100 and 400 nucleotides, some short reads that are provided to the MU might include information out of the MU's requested range of genomic data, as in Fig. 1. Similarly, some provided short reads might contain privacy-sensitive SNPs of the patient, hence the patient might not give consent to reveal such parts, as in Fig. 2. Therefore we mask such parts of the encrypted short reads at the biobank, without decrypting them using an efficient algorithm.

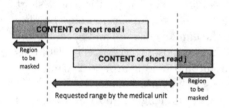

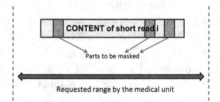

Fig. 1. Parts to be masked in the short reads for out-of-range content.

Fig. 2. Parts to be masked in a short read based on patient's consent. The patient does not give consent to reveal the dark parts of the short read.

The cryptographic keys of each patient are stored on a *masking and key manager* (MK) by using the patient's pseudonym (hence the participation of the patient is not required in the protocol).[3] The MK can also be embodied in the government or a private company. To avoid the MK from associating the

---

[2] Knowing the MU (e.g., the name of the hospital) the biobank could de-anonymize an individual using other sources (e.g., by associating the time of the test and the location of the MU with the location patterns of the victim).

[3] Following our discussions with geneticists and medical doctors, we conclude that the patient's involvement in the genetic tests is not desired for the practicality of the protocol (e.g., when a pharmaceutical company conducts genetic research on thousands of patients).

genetic tests with the patients, we do not reveal the identities of the MUs or the patients to the MK.

4 Threat Model

We consider the following models for the attacker:

• A curious party at the biobank (or a hacker who breaks into the biobank), who tries (i) to infer the genomic sequence of a patient from his stored genomic data and (ii) to associate the type of the genetic test (e.g., the disease for which the patient is being tested, which can be inferred from the nucleotides requested by the MU) with the patient being tested.

• A curious party at the MK (or a hacker who breaks into the MK), who tries (i) to infer the genomic sequence of a patient from his stored cryptographic keys and the information provided by the biobank and (ii) to associate the type of the genetic test with the patient being tested.

• A curious party at an MU, who can be considered either as an attacker who hacks into the MU's system or a disgruntled employee who has access to the MU's database. The goal of such an attacker is to obtain the private genomic data of a patient for which it is not authorized.

We assume that the biobank, the MK, and the MUs honestly follow the protocols and provide correct information to the other parties. Finally, collusion between the parties (i.e., the biobank, the MK, and an MU) is not allowed in our threat model and we assume that laws could enforce this.

5 Privacy-Preserving Processing of Raw Genomic Data

5.1 Cryptographic Keys and Encryption of the Short Reads

We represent the position of a short read ($L_{i,j} = \langle x_i | y_j \rangle$) as a 35-bit number, where the first 5 bits represent the chromosome number (x_i) and the remaining 30 bits represent the position of the short read in the corresponding chromosome (y_j). If the positions of the short reads were encrypted following this representation, the biobank could infer the approximate positions of the short reads as a result of using OPE.

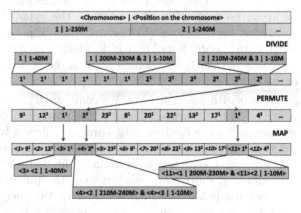

Fig. 3. Division, permutation and mapping of the positions on the whole genome.

To avoid this, we first divide the positions on the whole genome into parts of equal lengths, permute these parts, and then modify the positions in each part based on the permutation. In Fig. 3, we show such an example, in which the positions on the genome are divided into parts of length 40 million (totaling 75 parts as there are 3 billion nucleotides in the human genome). For example, chromosome 1 is divided into 6 parts $(1^1, 1^2, \ldots, 1^6)$, where the last part includes positions from both the first and second chromosomes. After division, all parts are permuted and mapped to different positions. As a result of the new mapping, the new position of a short read at $L_{i,j} = \langle x_i | y_j \rangle$ becomes $\mathfrak{M}(L_{i,j}) = \langle k \rangle \langle x_i | y_j \rangle$, where $\mathfrak{M}(.)$ is the mapping function for patient P, and k is the mapping of the corresponding part. For example, the position of a short read located in the first part of the first chromosome (part 1^1 in Fig. 3) becomes $\mathfrak{M}(L_{i,j}) = \langle 3 \rangle \langle x_i | y_j \rangle$ after the permutation and mapping. Thus, for each patient, we re-define the positions of the short reads based on this new positioning, before encrypting the positions of the short reads using OPE. By doing so, we also change the ordering of the encrypted positions of the short reads. As a consequence, a curious party at the biobank cannot infer which part of the patient's genome is queried by the MU from the stored (encrypted) positions of the short reads. Finally, we assume that the MK keeps the mapping table $\mathfrak{M}_P$ (showing the mapping of each part in each chromosome) for each patient. Note that as the permutation is done differently for each patient, the biobank cannot infer if two different patients are having a similar genetic test.

The different parts of each short read are encrypted as follows: (i) The positions of the short reads are encrypted using order preserving encryption (OPE), (ii) the cigar string (CS) of each short read is encrypted using a semantically secure symmetric encryption function (SE), and (iii) the content of each short read is encrypted using a stream cipher (SC). We note that an SC also provides semantic security, and although we really need an SC for the encryption of the content, one can also use an SC for the encryption of the CS.

We represent the key used for the semantically secure encryption scheme between two parties i and j as $K_{i,j}$. The symmetric OPE key that is used to encrypt the positions of the short reads of patient P is represented as K_P^O. Further, the master key of patient P, which is used to generate the keys of the SC is represented as M_P. We denote $K_P^{C_{i,j}}$ as the SC key used to encrypt the content of the short read whose position is $L_{i,j}$ (where $C_{i,j}$ represents the content of the short read with position $L_{i,j}$). We compute $K_P^{C_{i,j}} = \mathrm{H}(M_P, \mathcal{F}(L_{i,j}, S_{i,j}), L_{i,j})$, where $L_{i,j}$ is the (starting) position of the corresponding short read (on the DNA sequence), $S_{i,j}$ is a random salt to provide different keys for the short reads with the same positions, and H is a pseudorandom function. Moreover, $\mathcal{F}(L_{i,j}, S_{i,j})$ is a function that generates a *nonce* from the position and the random salt of the corresponding short read. We represent the public-key encryption of message m under the public key of i as $\mathcal{E}(\mathcal{K}_i, m)$, the encryption of message m via a semantically secure symmetric encryption function (SE) using the symmetric key between i and j as $\mathrm{E_{SE}}(K_{i,j}, m)$, and the OPE of message m using the OPE key of P as $\mathrm{E_{OPE}}(K_P^O, m)$. Furthermore, we represent the SC encryption of the

Figure 4(a) — Position and content (nucleotide level):

Position (on Ref.)	9	10	11	12	13	14	16	17	*	*	21	22	23	24	25	26	27	28
Content of SR in the SAM file	a	t	g	T	A	A	A	T	G	C	T	A	T	G	C	G	A	G
Decrypted nucleotides	T	G	C	T	A	A	A	G	G	C	T	G	A	T	G	G	C	A

Binary rows (bit level):

Plaintext content in binary	0 0 0 1 1 1 0 1 0 0 0 0 0 0 0 1 1 1 1 0 0 1 0 0 0 1 1 1 1 0 1 1 0 0 1 1
Key stream	1 0 0 0 1 1 0 0 1 0 0 1 0 0 0 1 1 1 1 0 0 1 1 0 1 1 1 0 0 1 0 0 1 1 0 0
Encrypted content (XOR)	1 0 0 1 0 0 0 1 1 0 0 1 0 0 0 0 0 0 0 0 0 0 1 0 1 0 0 1 1 1 1 1 1 1 1 1
Masking vector	1 1 1 1 1 1 0 0 0 0 0 0 0 0 1 1 0 0 0 0 1 1 1 1 1 1 1 1 1 1 1 1 1 1 1 1
Random masking string	0 1 1 0 0 1 0 0 0 0 0 0 0 0 1 0 0 0 0 0 0 0 1 1 0 1 1 0 0 1 0 0 1 0 1 1
Masked enc. content (XOR)	1 1 1 1 1 1 0 1 1 0 0 1 0 0 1 0 0 0 0 0 0 0 0 1 1 1 1 1 1 0 1 1 0 1 0 0
Decrypted binary content (XOR)	0 1 1 1 1 0 0 1 0 0 0 0 0 0 1 1 1 1 1 0 0 1 1 1 0 0 0 1 1 1 1 1 1 0 0 0

(a)

(b) Encoding format of the nucleotides:

Encoding nucleotides	
A	00
T	01
C	10
G	11

(b)

(c) Properties of the corresponding short read:

	CS of the SR before masking	3S3M1D2M2I3N8M
Properties of the SR	Position of the SR	12
Input parameters	Requested range of nucleotides	10-20
	Non-consented positions	{3,5,11,17,21}
Output parameters	CS of the SR after masking	3O3M1D1M1O2I3N8O

(c)

Fig. 4. Illustrative example for the encryption, masking and decryption of the content of a short read (SR). (a) Content of the SR (the 2 stars between positions 17 and 21 represent the positions at which the SR has insertions, G and C), its binary representation, the key stream to encrypt the corresponding content, and the format of the encrypted content. Furthermore, following the discussion in Sect. 5.2, we illustrate the masking process considering the range of the requested nucleotides and the patient's consent (in (c)). Finally, we show the format of the decrypted binary content. (b) Encoding format of the nucleotides. (c) Properties of the corresponding short read. We provide more details about different letters in the CS in [5].

$E_{OPE}(K_P^O, POSITION)$	$E_{SE}(K_{P,CI}, CS)$	$E_{SC}(K_P^{C_i}, CONTENT)$	RAND.SALT

Fig. 5. Format of an encrypted short read. The size of each field is discussed in Sect. 7.

content of a short read as $E_{SC}(K_P^{C_{i,j}}, C_{i,j})$, where $C_{i,j}$ represents the content of the short read at $L_{i,j}$. In Fig. 4(a), we illustrate how the content of a short read is translated to plaintext bits and encrypted using SC (by XOR-ing the content with the key stream). Finally, in Fig. 5, we illustrate the format of an encrypted short read.

We assume that the certified institution (CI), where the patient's DNA is sequenced and analyzed, has K_P^O, M_P, and $K_{P,CI}$ ($K_{P,CI}$ is used to encrypt the CSs of the short reads) for the initial encryption of the patient's genomic data. These keys are then deleted from the CI after the sequencing, alignment, and encryption. We also assume that for each patient P, the MK stores K_P^O, M_P, and $K_{P,CI}$ along with the mapping table $\mathfrak{M}_P$ (as discussed before). Finally, the MU only stores the public key of the MK, $\mathcal{K}_{MK}$.

5.2   Proposed Protocol

Typically, a specialist at the MU (e.g., a physician at the hospital or a specialized clinic connected to the hospital) requests a range of nucleotides (on the DNA sequence of one or more patients) from the biobank (either for a personal genetic test or for clinical research). For simplicity of the presentation, we assume that the request is for a specific range of nucleotides of patient P. We illustrate the connections between the parties that are involved in the protocol in Fig. 6(a). In the following, we describe the steps of the proposed protocol (these steps are also illustrated in Fig. 6(b)).

• **Step 1:** The patient (P) provides a sample (e.g., his saliva) along with his permission to the certified institution (CI) for sequencing.
• **Step 2:** The CI does the sequencing and constructs the SAM file of the patient. The short reads of the patient are also encrypted at the CI (as discussed in Sect. 5.1).
• **Step 3:** The CI sends the encrypted SAM file to the biobank along with the corresponding pseudonym of the patient. The CI also sends K_P^O, M_P, $K_{P,CI}$, and the mapping table $\mathfrak{M}_P$ for patient P directly to the MK via a secure channel (we do not illustrate this step in Fig. 6). We note that the first 3 steps of the protocol are executed only once.
• **Step 4:** A specialized sub-unit at the MU requests nucleotides from the range $[R_L, R_U]$ (R_L being the lower bound and R_U being the upper bound of the requested range) on the DNA sequence of patient P for a genetic test. We note that an access control unit stores the authorizations (i.e., access rights) of the original request owners (e.g., specialist at a hospital) to different parts of the genomic data. In our setting, the MU checks the access rights of the original request owner before forwarding the request to the biobank. Once, the MU verifies that the original request owner has the sufficient access rights to the requested range of nucleotides, the MU generates a one-time session key $K_{MK,MU}$, which will be used for the secure communication between the MU and the MK. The MU encrypts this session key with the public key of the MK to obtain $\mathcal{E}(\mathcal{K}_{MK}, K_{MK,MU})$.

The MU encrypts the lower and upper bounds of the requested range with $K_{MK,MU}$ to obtain $\mathrm{E_{SE}}(K_{MK,MU}, R_L \| R_U)$ and sends the corresponding request to the biobank along with the pseudonym of the patient P, the identification of the MU[4], $\mathcal{E}(\mathcal{K}_{MK}, K_{MK,MU})$, and $\mathrm{E_{SE}}(K_{MK,MU}, \Omega_P)$, where Ω_P is the pseudonymized consent of the patient.[5] The MK uses this pseudonymized consent Ω_P to generate the masking vectors (as in Step 9).

---

[4] We reveal the real identity of the MU to the biobank to make sure that the request comes from a valid source.
[5] Ω_P denotes the positions on the patient's genome for which the patient does not give consent to the original request owner (e.g., specialized sub-unit at the MU).

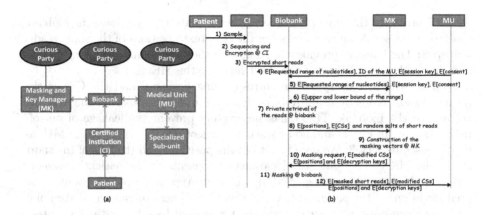

Fig. 6. (a) Connections between the parties in the proposed protocol. (b) The operations and message exchanges in the proposed protocol.

- **Step 5:** Once the biobank verifies that request comes from a valid source[6], it forwards $\mathrm{E}_{\mathrm{SE}}(K_{MK,MU}, R_L\|R_U)$, and $\mathrm{E}_{\mathrm{SE}}(K_{MK,MU}, \Omega_P)$, along with the pseudonym of the patient, and the encrypted session key $\mathcal{E}(\mathcal{K}_{MK}, K_{MK,MU})$ to the MK.
- **Step 6:** The MK decrypts the session key to obtain $K_{MK,MU}$ and decrypts the request ($\mathrm{E}_{\mathrm{SE}}(K_{MK,MU}, R_L\|R_U)$) to obtain R_L and R_U. As we discussed before, the position of a short read is the position of the first aligned nucleotide in its content. Let Γ be the maximum number of nucleotides in a short read. Then, the short reads with position in $[R_L - \Gamma, R_L - 1]$ might also include nucleotides from the requested range ($[R_L, R_U]$) in their contents. Thus, the MK re-defines the lower bound of the request as $R_L - \Gamma$ in order to make sure that all the short reads (which include at least one nucleotide from the requested range of nucleotides) are retrieved by the biobank.

Next, the MK determines where $(R_L - \Gamma)$ and R_U are mapped to following the mapping table $\mathfrak{M}_P$ of patient P (as discussed in Sect. 5.1). If both $(R_L - \Gamma)$ and R_U are on the same part (e.g., in Fig. 3), then the MK computes the range of short read positions (to be retrieved by the biobank) as $[\mathfrak{M}(R_L - \Gamma), \mathfrak{M}(R_U)]$, where $\mathfrak{M}(.)$ is the mapping function for patient P. Otherwise (if they are not on the same part), due to the permutation of the parts, the MK generates multiple ranges of short read positions to make sure all short reads including at least one nucleotide from $[R_L, R_U]$ are retrieved by the biobank. For simplicity of the presentation, we assume $(R_L - \Gamma)$ and R_U are on the same part. Finally, the MK computes the encrypted range $[\mathrm{E}_{\mathrm{OPE}}(K_P^O, \mathfrak{M}(R_L - \Gamma)), \mathrm{E}_{\mathrm{OPE}}(K_P^O, \mathfrak{M}(R_U))]$, and sends this encrypted range to the biobank (with pseudonym of P).
- **Step 7:** The biobank retrieves all the short reads (in the SAM file of patient P) whose encrypted positions $(\mathrm{E}_{\mathrm{OPE}}(K_P^O, \mathfrak{M}(L_{i,j})))$ are in the set $\Delta = \{\mathrm{E}_{\mathrm{OPE}}(K_P^O, \mathfrak{M}(L_{i,j})) : \mathrm{E}_{\mathrm{OPE}}(K_P^O, \mathfrak{M}(R_L - \Gamma)) \leq \mathrm{E}_{\mathrm{OPE}}(K_P^O, \mathfrak{M}(L_{i,j})) \leq \mathrm{E}_{\mathrm{OPE}}(K_P^O, \mathfrak{M}(R_U))\}$.

---

[6] We assume that the biobank has a list of valid MUs, whose requests it will answer.

As OPE preserves the numerical ordering of the plaintext positions, the biobank constructs the set Δ without accessing the plaintext positions of the short reads.
• **Step 8:** The biobank provides Δ along with the corresponding encrypted CSs and the random salt values of the short reads to the MK.
• **Step 9:** The MK decrypts the corresponding positions and the CSs of the retrieved short reads by using K_P^O and $K_{P,CI}$ in order to construct the masking vectors for the biobank. These masking vectors prevent the leakage of out-of-range content (in Fig. 1) and non-consented nucleotides (in Fig. 2) to the MU, as we discussed in Sect. 3. We note that from the positions and the CSs of the short reads, the MK cannot infer the locations or contents of the patient's privacy-sensitive point mutations (e.g., SNPs), which are typically used to evaluate the predispositions of the patients for various diseases. These privacy-sensitive point mutations can only be inferred when the CS is used together with the content of the short read (which is not revealed to the MK).

The MK can determine the actual position of a short read from its mapped position as the MK has the mapping table $\mathfrak{M}_P$ for patient P (i.e., it can infer $L_{i,j}$ from $\mathfrak{M}(L_{i,j})$ using $\mathfrak{M}_P$). Using the position and the CS of a short read, the MK can determine the exact positions of the nucleotides in the content of a short read (but not the contents of the nucleotides, because the contents are encrypted and stored at the biobank). Using this information, the MK can determine the parts in the content of the short read that are out of the requested range $[R_L, R_U]$. Furthermore, the MK can also determine whether the short read includes any nucleotide positions for which the patient P does not give consent. Therefore, the MK constructs binary masking vectors indicating the positions in the contents of the short reads that are needed to be masked by the biobank before sending the retrieved short reads to the MU. We provide the details of the algorithm to construct the masking vectors in [5]. In Fig. 4(a), we illustrate how the masking vector is constructed for the corresponding short read, when the requested range of nucleotides is $[10, 20]$ and for a given set of nucleotide positions for which the patient P does not give consent (as in Fig. 4(c)).

The MK also modifies the CS of each short read (if it is marked for masking) according to the nucleotides to be masked. That is, the MK modifies the CS such that the masked nucleotides are represented with a new operation "O" in the CS. By doing so, when the MU receives the short reads, it can see which parts of them are masked. In Fig. 4(c), we illustrate how the CS of the corresponding short read changes as a result of the masking vector in Fig. 4(a). Then, the MK generates the decryption keys for each short read (whose position is in Δ) by using the master key of the patient (M_P), positions of the shorts read, and the random salt values.[7]
• **Step 10:** The MK encrypts the positions, the (modified) CSs, and the generated decryption keys of the contents of the short reads, using $K_{MK,MU}$. Then, it sends the masking vectors along with the encrypted positions, CSs and decryption keys to the biobank. We note that in this step, the MK encrypts the actual

---

[7] The generation of the decryption keys for the SC is the same as the generation of the encryption keys as we discussed in Sect. 5.1.

positions of the short reads (e.g., $L_{i,j}$ instead of $\mathfrak{M}(L_{i,j})$) as these positions will be eventually decrypted and used by the MU, and the MU does not need to know the mapping table $\mathfrak{M}_P$ of the patient.

• **Step 11:** The biobank conducts the masking by XOR-ing the bits of the encrypted content of each short read (whose position is in Δ) with a random masking string. Each entry (bit) of the random masking string is assigned as follows: (i) If the corresponding entry is set for masking in the masking vector, it is assigned with a random binary value, and (ii) it is assigned with zero, otherwise. We provide the details of the algorithm to perform the masking at the biobank in [5]. Furthermore, in Fig. 4(a), we illustrate how the masked encrypted content for the corresponding short read is constructed by XOR-ing the random masking string with the encrypted content.

• **Step 12:** Finally, the biobank sends the encrypted positions, CSs and decryption keys (generated in Step 10 by the MK) along with the masked contents (generated in Step 11 by the biobank) to the MU. The MU decrypts the received data and obtains the requested nucleotides of the patient.

6   Evaluation

Focusing on the leakage of genomic data, we evaluate the proposed privacy-preserving system by using real genomic data to show (i) how the leakage of genomic data from the short reads threatens the genomic privacy of a patient, and (ii) how the proposed masking technique helps to prevent this leakage. We assume that the MU requests a specific range of nucleotides of patient P (e.g., for a genetic test) from the biobank. In practice, the requested range can include from one to thousands of nucleotides depending on the type of the genetic test.

First, without the masking in place, we observe the ratio of unauthorized genomic data (i.e., number of nucleotides provided to the MU that are out of the requested range) to the authorized data (i.e., number of nucleotides within the requested range) for various request sizes. For simplicity, we assume that all the nucleotides within the requested range are considered as consented data (i.e., the situation in Fig. 2 is not considered); and only those that are out of the requested range (but still provided to the MU via the short reads) are considered as the unauthorized data. For the patient's DNA profile (i.e., SAM file), we use a real human DNA profile [2] (with an average coverage of 8, meaning each nucleotide is present, on the average, in 8 short reads in the SAM file, and each short read includes at most 100 nucleotides) and we randomly choose the ranges of requested nucleotides from the entire genome of the patient. We illustrate our results in Fig. 7. We observe that for small request sizes, the amount of leakage (of unauthorized data) is very high compared to the size of authorized data. As the leakage vanishes (e.g., the ratio in Fig. 7 becomes 0) with the proposed masking technique, we do not show the leakage when the proposed masking technique is in place in Figs. 7, 8, 9, 10.

Using the same DNA profile, we also observe the evolution in the amount of leaked genomic data over time. For simplicity of the presentation, we assume slotted time and that the MU conducts a genetic test on the patient at each time slot (by requesting a particular range of nucleotides from a random part of his genome). In Fig. 8, we illustrate the amount of genomic data (i.e., number of nucleotides) that is leaked to the MU in 100 time-slots. The jumps in the number of leaked nucleotides (at some time-slots) is due to the fact that some requests might retrieve more short reads comprised of more out-of-range nucleotides. As before, leakage becomes 0 when masking is in place, which shows the crucial role of the proposed scheme.

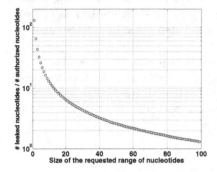

Fig. 7. Ratio of unauthorized genomic data to the authorized data vs. the size of the requested range of nucleotides, when there is no masking in place.

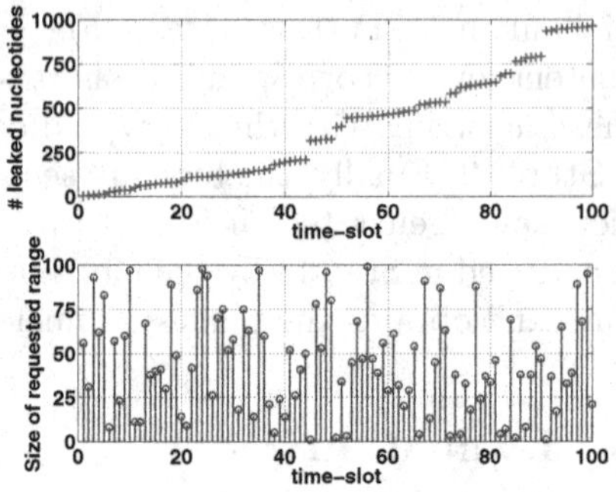

Fig. 8. Number of leaked nucleotides vs. time for various request sizes, when there is no masking in place.

We also study the information leakage, focusing on the leaked single nucleotide polymorphisms (SNPs) of the patient as a result of different sizes of requests (from random parts of the patient's genome). In Fig. 9, we illustrate the number of SNPs leaked to the MU in 100 time-slots. We observe that the number of leaked SNPs is more than twice the number of authorized SNPs (which are within the requested range of nucleotides). When the proposed masking technique is in place, the number of leaked SNPs (outside the requested range) becomes 0 in Fig. 9.

Finally, we study the genomic data leakage (number of leaked nucleotides and SNPs) when the MU tests the susceptibility of the patient [2] to a particular disease (i.e., when the MU asks for the set of SNPs of the patient that are used to test the corresponding disease). For this study, we use real disease markers [1]. We note that for this type of test, the size of the requested range of nucleotides (by the MU) for a single SNP is typically 1, but the SNPs are from several parts of the patient's genome. In Fig. 10, we illustrate the genomic data leakage of the patient as a result of various disease susceptibility tests each requiring a different number of SNPs from different parts of the patient's genome (on the x-axis we illustrate the number of SNPs required for each test). We again observe that the leaked SNPs, as a result of different disease susceptibility tests, reveal privacy-sensitive data about the patient. For example, leaked SNPs of the patient as a result of a test for the Alzheimer's disease could leak information about the patient's susceptibility to "smoking behavior" or "diabetes" (in [5], we list the nature of some important leaked SNPs due to some susceptibility tests in Fig. 10). Similar to the previous cases, the number of leaked nucleotides and SNPs is 0 when masking is in place.

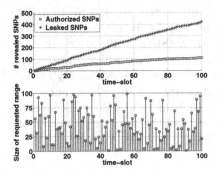 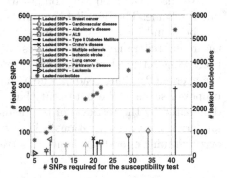

Fig. 9. Number of leaked SNPs vs. time for various request sizes, when there is no masking in place.

Fig. 10. Number of leaked SNPs and nucleotides during the susceptibility test to different diseases when there is no masking in place. The values on the right y-axis correspond to the number of leaked nucleotides.

7   Implementation and Complexity Analysis

We implemented the proposed system and assessed its storage requirement and complexity on an Intel Core i7-2620M CPU with a 2.70 GHz processor under Windows 7, using Java. As before, for the patient's SAM file, we used a real DNA profile [2] including around 300 million short reads (each short read including at most 100 nucleotides).

We used the Salsa20 stream cipher [10] and the implementation of OPE from [15]. We also used CCM mode of AES (with key size of 256-bits) for the secure communication between the MK and the MU, and RSA (with key size of 2048-bits) for the public-key encryption.

We structured the fields in the encrypted short read (in Fig. 5) as follows: We reserved the first 8-bytes for the encrypted position of the short read (via OPE). To save storage, we devoted the next 64-bytes of the encrypted short read to the CS and the content of the short read. As the input size of the stream cipher is 64-bytes, we encrypted the CS together with the content and other (header) information of the short read using the stream cipher. That is, out of the 64-byte input of the stream cipher, we allocated the first 20-bytes for the CS, the next 25-bytes for the content (as each short read in the used DNA profile includes at most 100 nucleotides), and the remaining 19-bytes for the remaining information about the short read (or padding). Finally, the last byte of the short read includes the plaintext random salt. Consequently, we computed the storage cost as 21.6 GB per patient. We note that stream cipher encryption does not increase the size of the data as it is the XOR of the key stream with the plaintext. The storage overhead (due to the proposed privacy-preserving scheme) is due to the encryption of the positions of the short reads by using OPE.

We also evaluated the computation times for different steps of the proposed scheme. The detailed computation times of different steps of the protocol can be found in [5]. Overall, it takes approximately 5 s for the MU to receive the requested range of nucleotides of the patient (Steps 4–12) after privacy-preserving retrieval and masking (for a range size of 100, which includes on the average 23 short reads), which shows the efficiency and practicality of the proposed scheme. We note that the computation time of the whole process is dominated by the retrieval of the reads at the biobank (which does not involve any cryptographic operations). Therefore, we can easily claim that the cost of cryptographic operations is not a bottleneck for the proposed protocol.

8   Conclusion

In this paper, we have introduced a privacy-preserving system for the storage, retrieval, and processing of aligned, raw genomic data (i.e., SAM files). We are confident that the proposed scheme will accelerate genomic research, because clinical-trial participants will be more willing to consent to the sequencing of their genomes if they are ensured that their genomic privacy is preserved.

Acknowledgements. We would like to thank Jurgi Camblong, Pierre Hutter, Zhenyu Xu, Wolfgang Huber, and Lars Steinmetz for their useful comments.

References

1. http://www.eupedia.com/genetics/medical_dna_test.shtml
2. ftp://ftp.1000genomes.ebi.ac.uk/vol1/ftp/data/NA06984/
3. Agrawal, R., Kiernan, J., Srikant, R., Xu, Y.: Order preserving encryption for numeric data. In: Proceedings of the 2004 ACM SIGMOD International Conference on Management of Data, pp. 563–574 (2004)
4. Ayday, E., Cristofaro, E.D., Tsudik, G., Hubaux, J.P.: The chills and thrills of whole genome sequencing. arXiv:1306.1264 (2013). http://arxiv.org/abs/1306.1264
5. Ayday, E., Raisaro, J.L., Hengartner, U., Molyneaux, A., Hubaux, J.P.: Privacy-preserving processing of raw genomic data. EPFL-REPORT-187573 (2013). https://infoscience.epfl.ch/record/187573
6. Ayday, E., Raisaro, J.L., Hubaux, J.P.: Personal use of the genomic data: privacy vs. storage cost. In: Proceedings of IEEE Global Communications Conference, Exhibition and Industry Forum (Globecom) (2013)
7. Ayday, E., Raisaro, J.L., Hubaux, J.P.: Privacy-enhancing technologies for medical tests using genomic data (short paper). In: 20th Annual Network and Distributed System Security Symposium (NDSS) (2013)

8. Ayday, E., Raisaro, J.L., McLaren, P.J., Fellay, J., Hubaux, J.P.: Privacy-preserving computation of disease risk by using genomic, clinical, and environmental data. In: Proceedings of USENIX Security Workshop on Health Information Technologies (HealthTech) (2013)
9. Baldi, P., Baronio, R., De Cristofaro, E., Gasti, P., Tsudik, G.: Countering GATTACA: efficient and secure testing of fully-sequenced human genomes. In: Proceedings of ACM CCS '11, pp. 691–702 (2011)
10. Bernstein, D.J.: The Salsa20 family of stream ciphers. In: Robshaw, M., Billet, O. (eds.) New Stream Cipher Designs. LNCS, vol. 4986, pp. 84–97. Springer, Heidelberg (2008). http://dx.doi.org/10.1007/978-3-540-68351-3_8
11. Chen, Y., Peng, B., Wang, X., Tang, H.: Large-scale privacy-preserving mapping of human genomic sequences on hybrid clouds. In: NDSS'12: Proceeding of the 19th Network and Distributed System Security Symposium (2012)
12. Fienberg, S.E., Slavkovic, A., Uhler, C.: Privacy preserving GWAS data sharing. In: Proceedings of the IEEE ICDMW '11, December 2011
13. Gymrek, M., McGuire, A.L., Golan, D., Halperin, E., Erlich, Y.: Identifying personal genomes by surname inference. Science 339(6117), 321–324 (2013)
14. Jha, S., Kruger, L., Shmatikov, V.: Towards practical privacy for genomic computation. In: Proceedings of the 2008 IEEE Symposium on Security and Privacy, pp. 216–230 (2008)
15. Popa, R.A., Redfield, C.M.S., Zeldovich, N., Balakrishnan, H.: CryptDB: protecting confidentiality with encrypted query processing. In: Proceedings of the Twenty-Third ACM Symposium on Operating Systems Principles (2011)
16. Troncoso-Pastoriza, J.R., Katzenbeisser, S., Celik, M.: Privacy preserving error resilient DNA searching through oblivious automata. In: CCS '07: Proceedings of the 14th ACM Conference on Computer and Communications Security (2007)
17. Wang, R., Li, Y.F., Wang, X., Tang, H., Zhou, X.: Learning your identity and disease from research papers: information leaks in genome wide association study. In: Proceedings of ACM CCS '09, pp. 534–544 (2009)
18. Zhou, X., Peng, B., Li, Y.F., Chen, Y., Tang, H., Wang, X.F.: To release or not to release: evaluating information leaks in aggregate human-genome data. In: Atluri, V., Diaz, C. (eds.) ESORICS 2011. LNCS, vol. 6879, pp. 607–627. Springer, Heidelberg (2011)

Using Search Results to Microaggregate Query Logs Semantically

Arnau Erola$^{(\boxtimes)}$ and Jordi Castellà-Roca

Departament d'Enginyeria Informàtica i Matemàtiques,
UNESCO Chair in Data Privacy, Universitat Rovira i Virgili, Av. Països Catalans 26,
43007 Tarragona, Spain
{arnau.erola,jordi.castella}@urv.cat

Abstract. Query log anonymization has become an important challenge
nowadays. A query log contains the search history of the users, as well
as the selected results and their position in the ranking. These data
are used to provide a personalized re-ranking of results and trend studies. However, query logs can disclose sensitive information of the users.
Hence, query logs must be submitted to an anonymization process to
guarantee that: (a) no sensitive information can be linked to an identity;
(b) the analysis of the anonymized data produces similar results than
the original data, i.e. minimize data distortion. Latest anonymization
approaches utilize microaggregation, a statistical disclosure control technique that provides a privacy comparable with k-anonymity, attempting
to minimize the data distortion. We propose a new method that uses
search results to optimize microaggregation, providing more data reliability than the existing methods.

Keywords: Privacy · Web search · Microaggregation · k-anonymity ·
Query logs · Semantics · Semantic microaggregation

1 Introduction

The query logs stored by Web Search Engines (WSE) contain valuable information for researchers and marketing companies, as they allow the study of
users' behavior or any changes in users' trends [1]. Furthermore, WSE can use
query logs to improve users' experience by providing advanced functionalities
such as personalizing search results (disambiguating terms and predicting user
interests), autocompleting search terms, or correcting spelling mistakes [2].

However, the attractiveness of the advanced functionalities obtained from
storing query logs can be counteracted by the privacy problems they present.
Queries can contain sensitive information (e.g. religion, sexuality, politics etc.)
and can disclose the identity of the user (e.g. a query contains the passport
number). Note that a query itself can contain information about several issues,
for instance, a simple query such as *Drug Clinic Portland* is probably disclosing
that the user lives in Portland and has some problems with drugs. Thus, queries,

J. Garcia-Alfaro et al. (Eds.): DPM 2013 and SETOP 2013, LNCS 8247, pp. 148–161, 2014.
DOI: 10.1007/978-3-642-54568-9_10, © Springer-Verlag Berlin Heidelberg 2014

like microdata (data about an individual), can be classified into the following categories, which are not mutually exclusive, depending on their content:

- **Identifier Queries.** The queries univocally identify the query owner. For example, the query contains the passport number, the credit card number or the full name. Such queries are usually removed because they are not valuable for advanced functionalities and constitute a high privacy threat.
- **Quasi-identifier Queries.** These queries cannot identify a user. However, in combination or with the help of external information (for instance, the information of public databases), they can univocally identify a user. The zip code, age, first name, etc. are some examples.
- **Confidential Queries.** The queries contain sensitive information of the users. For example, queries related with religion, illnesses, investments, etc.
- **Non-confidential Queries.**[1] The queries do not contain sensitive information. Country names and favorite sports can be some examples. However, they can also constitute an identity disclosure risk because in combination they can form a quasi-identifier.

Accordingly, query logs must be submitted to an anonymization process prior to their publication. It involves some data modifications which reduce the probability of disclosing personal information, but at the same time they reduce the data utility. This is a trade-off between utility and privacy, which implies that the greater the privacy, the greater the information loss will be. However, although data have been anonymized, personal information can be inferred from the remaining data. The AOL's case [4], where some individuals were re-identified, is an example.

This study is aimed at exploring the preservation of users' privacy in the dissemination or storage of query logs. To that end, we take the privacy criterion of offering a desired privacy protection. Thus, the main objective is to attain it while maximizing the data utility.

As some authors have stated, the utility in textual data, as query logs are, is related with the semantics [5,6]. To that end, we propose an optimization of the microaggregation method for query logs that groups the users with more similar targets, with the help of the selected results.

The paper is organized in the following sections: Section 2 introduces the related work. The notation used and the similarity metric is presented in Sect. 3. In Sect. 4, we detail our proposal and in Sect. 5 we discuss the evaluation measures. Finally, we present the obtained results and the conclusions in Sects. 6 and 7, respectively.

---

[1] Note that a user can consider some information private or not according to her beliefs, i.e. whereas a user can consider her religion a public issue, another user can consider this information private. Determining what information is private or not is out of the scope of this paper. For this reason, we consider that all the information has the same importance and is private, as is made in [3].

2   Related Work

Microaggregation [7] is a Statistical Disclosure Control (SDC) technique used to prevent re-identification. Although it was initially proposed to protect microdata, it can be adapted to protect query logs [8–11]. It works by creating clusters of at least k users and by replacing their logs by a new log called centroid, which is representative of the group. The centroid is usually created with random queries of the users in each cluster. The privacy achieved is comparable to k-anonymity [12], for the fact that there are at least k users with the same log. While improving privacy, data transformations make data imprecise and distorted, reducing their reliability and utility. Data utility can be defined as their fitness to perform an analysis, i.e. the results obtained from the original data and the transformed data are the same or really close.

However, due to the trade-off between privacy and utility, data utility is usually preserved to perform a specific analysis. In other words, a data set may be useful for some kind of analysis, but not for others. In microaggregation, data utility depends on the clustering method, where the optimum solution is to cluster the users with more similar queries [13]. As k is an input parameter of the method, the only thing that can be done to optimize microaggregation is to maximize data homogeneity [14].

The first approaches to anonymize query logs remove or delete queries in order to avoid identity disclosures [15–17]. However, they only achieve an acceptable level of privacy if the data are deeply perturbed [15].

Recently, microaggregation has been used to anonymize query logs [8–11] and to maximize data utility. Authors in [9] use the edit distance to compute queries' similarities. However, edit distance only takes into account the spelling similarities of the queries, and different queries can point to the same target. For instance, both *Freddie Mercury* and *Queen singer* refer to information about Freddie Mercury.

Authors in [3] use semantic taxonomies to anonymize query logs for the first time. They generalize query terms using WordNet [18]. However, Wordnet is a general-purpose dictionary that can only deal with simple concepts, and proper names are not included. For this reason, a lot of original queries are not published, thus losing a large amount of information. Erola et. al. [10,11] introduces the concept of semantic microaggregation, which consists in clustering users according to what they were looking for. In order to interpret queries, it retrieves the semantics of query terms by using the ODP [19] (see Sect. 3.1), a directory of the Web, as a knowledge source. Note that neither WordNet nor ODP can address sentences, only terms.

Retrieving the semantics of query terms can produce a change or loss in meaning. For example, the ambiguous term *mercury* acquires different meanings in the queries *mercury planet*, *mercury element* and *Mercury, Freddie*. Moreover, the other query terms, such as *Freddie*, can also be ambiguous by themselves. Consequently, clustering query logs according to the semantics of the query terms can increase the information loss. A criterion that can help in achieving better data homogeneity may be to cluster queries searching for the same information. By pursuing this idea, we propose to use the selected results instead of queries in order to retrieve the real interest of the user (query meaning).

3   Notation and Background

For notation purposes, let $U = \{u_1, \ldots, u_n\}$ be a set of n users, being $|U| = n$. Their respective set of queries (logs) are $Q = \{Q(u_1), \ldots, Q(u_n)\}$, where $Q(u_i) = \{q(^1_{u_i}), \ldots, q(^{m_i}_{u_i})\}$ are the set of queries of user u_i and $|Q(u_i)|$, their number.

After the clustering process, the set of clusters $Z = \{z_1, \ldots, z_\gamma\}$ is obtained, being $z_i = \{u(^1_{z_i}), \ldots, u(^{k'}_{z_i})\}$ the set of users that belong to cluster z_i and k' the cluster size, where $2k > k' \geq k$. Let $Cent_{z_i}$ be the centroid of cluster z_i and $|Cent_{z_i}|$ its size, i.e. the number of queries that it contains.

3.1   ODP Similarity Metric

ODP [19] is the most widely distributed database of web content classified by humans. ODP directory is hierarchically structured in themes, and web sites are hand-classified on them, thus forming the ODP tree. Figure 1 shows an example of this classification. Observe that categories can be divided into levels, where the root category is the most generic one.

```
Open Directory Categories  (1-5 of 100)
   1. Recreation: Autos: Makes and Models: Audi (18)
   2. Recreation: Autos: Makes and Models: Audi: Clubs (8)
   3. Recreation: Autos: Makes and Models: Audi: A4 (5)
   4. Recreation: Autos: Makes and Models: Audi: TT (4)
   5. Recreation: Autos: Makes and Models: Audi: Clubs: United Kingdom (2)
```

Fig. 1. Example of ODP query result.

In order to measure the semantic similarity of two queries classified in the ODP hierarchy, we use the measure ODP_{sim} introduced in [11]. To that end, we define a working depth level $l \in \{1, \ldots, L\}$, being L the maximum depth considered. So in Fig. 1, when $l = 1$, we are referring to the root level, i.e. *Recreation*; and the next level is *Recreation : Autos :*; when $l = 2$, and so on.

Let $C_l = \{c(^1_l), \ldots, c(^{m_l}_l)\}$ be the set of possible categories at depth level l in the ODP tree. Let u_i be a user and $Q(u_i) = \{q(^1_{u_i}), \ldots, q(^{p_i}_{u_i})\}$, her set of queries. We denote $C_l(u_i) = \{c_l(^1_{u_i}), \ldots, c_l(^{p_i}_{u_i})\}$ as the set of categories of u_i at level l, being $c_l(^{j_i}_{u_i})$ the category corresponding to the classification of the query $q(^{j_i}_{u_i})$ in the ODP hierarchy at depth level l. $|C_l(u_i)| = p_i$ is the number of categories of user u_i, and $|c_l^{j_i}(u_i)|$ is the number of queries classified in the category $c_l^{j_i}$ that u_i has.

Thus, given two users u_i and u_j, ODP_{sim} is defined as:

$$OPD_{sim}(u_i, u_j) = \sum_{l=1}^{L} \{|c_l| : c_l \in \{C_l(u_i) \cap C_l(u_j)\}\} \tag{1}$$

where $|c_l|$ is the number of categories that users u_i and u_j have in common - the minimum between $|c_l(u_i)|$ and $|c_l(u_j)|$ at level l -. Note that ODP_{sim} returns a similarity value, whose weight is maximum when the matching (similarity) is maximum.

4   Our Proposal in Detail

Previous semantic microaggregation algorithms split queries into terms, thus changing the semantics of the queries and producing an information loss in the protected logs. We propose a semantic microaggregation method to solve this problem. In the first step, we find the semantics of all the queries by submitting them to a WSE (in our case, Google). Then, we classify the search results in the ODP hierarchy and we cluster the users with more common real interests, thus reducing the distortion of the centroid. To that end, we present our system divided in two parts:

1. Semantic interpretation: we obtain the semantics of the query by submitting it to the WSE.
2. Microaggregation using ODP: we cluster the logs according to the classification of the search results and we then aggregate them.

4.1   Semantic Interpretation

Using the search results of a WSE to retrieve meanings is not new, they were already used in [20,21]. However, this is the first time that a WSE is used to anonymize query logs, to the best of our knowledge.

Roughly speaking, this part of the method is a pre-process of the queries for the microaggregation. For each query in the users' logs, we want to obtain the *url* that represents the interest of the user, i.e. the query semantics. Obviously, if this process is made by a WSE, it can select the *url* clicked by the user. Analogously, if we have a query log that contains the *urls* selected by the users, we can also use them.

However, this situation does not always happen. AOL logs are anonymized (most of the *urls* are deleted) and a significant amount of the *urls* are obsolete (AOL logs date from 2006). Therefore, we must redo the search to obtain the *urls* that users had probably selected. To that end, we take into account the work presented in [22], which states that a 68 % of the users of WSEs click a search result within the first page of results. Even more relevant is the fact that a 92 % of the users click a result within the first three pages of search results. Note that WSEs attempt to rank the search results according to the users' interests, i.e. the links which could probably be more interesting for the users appear in the first positions of the rank.

Accordingly, we consider that the first *urls* returned by the WSE are those more reliable according to the interests of the users. Thus, for each query in the users' logs, the query is searched in the WSE, and the first ranked *url*, which is not a sponsored link or a wikipedia link, is stored. Hereafter, we consider that $URL = \{URL(u_1), \ldots, URL(u_n)\}$ are the set of results selected from the Google searches, being $URL(u_i) = \{url(^1_{u_i}), \ldots, url(^{p_i}_{u_i})\}$ the set of *urls* of user u_i, and $url(^{j_i}_{u_i})$ the selected result when query $q(^{j_i}_{u_i})$ was submitted.

4.2   Microaggregation Using ODP

The *urls* are cut at domain name because ODP does not contain all the *urls* of every domain. *Wikipedia* links are not stored because they can contain a large amount of topics and the *url wikipedia.org* is always classified in the same ODP category.

The first step is to obtain the ODP categories for all the *urls* corresponding to the queries in the logs, i.e. the set of categories $C_l(U) = \{C_l(u_1), \ldots, C_l(u_n)\}$ can be obtained at level l. This process is described in Algorithm 1.

Next, we microaggregate the users trying to maintain the maximum data homogeneity. We use Eq. 1 (see Sect. 3) to calculate the similarity between users, where the maximum weight means maximum matching. Thus, we take two steps:

1. Clustering: users are clustered into groups according to their semantics.
2. Aggregation: we calculate the centroid of each cluster and then replace the users' logs with the centroid.

Algorithm 1. Algorithm to classify the *urls* in the ODP

Require: the maximum depth l for the ODP categories
Require: the set of users $U = \{u_i, \ldots, u_n\}$
Require: the set of *urls* $URL(u_i) = \{url(^1_{u_i}), \ldots, url(^{p_i}_{u_i})\}$ of each user u_i
Ensure: the set of categories $C_l(u_i) = \{c_l(^1_{u_i}), \ldots, c_l(^{p_i}_{u_i})\}$ of each user u_i
  for $u_i \in \{u_1, \ldots, u_n\}$ **do**
    for $url(^j_{u_i}) \in URL(u_i) = \{url(^1_{u_i}), \ldots, url(^{p_i}_{u_i})\}$ **do**
      obtain the category $c_l(^j_{u_i})$ at depth l for $url(^j_{u_i})$ using ODP;
    end for
  end for
  return C_l

Clustering. Algorithm 2 describes the clustering process. Briefly, it groups the k most similar users of U. Then, if there are enough users to form a new cluster ($k \leq |U|$), the selected users (the k most similar in U) are deleted from U and a new cluster is formed with the remaining users. It continues until there are not enough users to form a new cluster. If there are users remaining, they are added to the last formed cluster.

Aggregation. Z_i are sets of users and $Q(z_i)$ contains the queries of all users in Z_i. $C_l(z_i)$ is the set of categories of $Q(z_i)$. We use expression 2 to determine which queries of $Q(z_i)$ have to appear in the centroid. We obtain the number of queries classified in category c_l^t, which will appear in the centroid using Eq. 2.

$$|c_l(_{Cent_{z_i}}^t)| = \frac{\sum_{i=1}^{k'} \frac{|c_l(_{u_{z_i}^i}^t)|}{|Q(u_{z_i}^i)|}}{k'} \times |Cent_{z_i}|$$ (2)

being

$$|Cent_{z_i}| = \frac{|Q(z_i)|}{k'}$$ (3)

Therefore, $Cent_{z_i}$ contains $|c_l(_{Cent_{z_i}}^t)|$ queries of the category c_l^t. These queries are selected randomly among those that are in Q_{z_i} and are classified in c_l. As these queries belong to the same category, we can assume they have the same semantics.

Algorithm 2. Algorithm for computing the clusters $Z = \{z_1, \ldots, z_\gamma\}$ of users

---

Require: the maximum depth l for the ODP categories
Require: the set of users $U = \{u_1, \ldots, u_n\}$
Require: the set of categories $C_l(u_i) = \{c_l(_{u_i}^1), \ldots, c_l(_{u_i}^{p_i})\}$ for each user $u_i \in U$
Require: the clusters size k
Ensure: the clusters $Z = \{z_1, \ldots, z_\gamma\}$ of users for $\gamma = \lfloor n/k \rfloor$
    while $|U| \geq k$ **do**
        obtain the cluster z with $2k - 1 > |z| \geq k$ users using Algorithm 3 and $C_l(U)$;
        remove the users $u_i \in z$ from U;
        add z to the set Z
    end while
    return C_l

---

5   Evaluation

We have evaluated our proposal by using a random set of 840 users selected from the AOL files, where each one has submitted between 400 and 600 queries. In total, we have near 400,000 queries. Simulations are performed for cluster sizes k between 2 and 30, and for depth level $l = 5$. We have not considered levels above 5 because only 35 % of the queries can be classified beyond this level [11].

We have chosen Google to perform our tests because of its popularity, but we could have chosen any other web search engine to carry out our experiments.

Next, we present two measures to evaluate the utility and the privacy obtained with the microaggregation.

Algorithm 3. Algorithm for computing a cluster z

Require: the set of categories $C_l(U)$
Require: the clusters size k
Ensure: a cluster z with $2k > |z| \geq k$ users
$\quad z \leftarrow \emptyset$
$\quad$ obtain $u_i, u_j | \max ODP_{SIM}(u_i, u_j)$
$\quad$ add u_j, u_i to the set z;
$\quad C_l(u_i) = C_l(u_i) \cup C_l(u_j)$
$\quad$ remove $C_l(u_j)$
$\quad$ **while** $(|z| < k)$ **and** $|C_l(U)| > 0)$ **do**
$\quad\quad$ obtain $u_j | \max ODP_{SIM}(u_i, u_j)$
$\quad\quad$ add u_j to the set z;
$\quad\quad C_l(u_i) = C_l(u_i) \cup C_l(u_j)$
$\quad\quad$ remove $C_l(u_j)$
$\quad$ **end while**
$\quad$ **if** $(|C_l(U)| < k)$ **then**
$\quad\quad$ add all $u_j \in C_l$ to z;
$\quad$ **end if**
$\quad$ **return** z

5.1   Utility and Privacy

The result of the microaggregation process is a log that contains queries of all the users clustered together. Its utility is conditioned by the data homogeneity, i.e. how similar the original log and the centroid are. This similarity is not conditioned by the spelling mistakes or alternative queries but by the meaning of the queries. Hence, we evaluate the utility of the queries according to their classification in the ODP tree.

We have used three classic similarity coefficients to evaluate the data utility (ODP classification homogeneity): the Jaccard coefficient, the Sokal and Sneath coefficient and the Dice coefficient. Table 1 shows their expressions.

Thus, for cluster sizes (k) between 2 and 30 and maximum level l, we have calculated the three coefficients between the original logs and their corresponding centroids, which are generated with our proposal, the method that also uses ODP to classify the query terms [11], and a random scheme (microaggregation with random clustering). The performance of our scheme can be compared with the performance of two other schemes by dividing the coefficients (see Eq. 4), where the utility of our proposal is the numerator and the utility of the other proposals,

Table 1. Similarity coefficients between two sets S_1 and S_2

Coefficient	Formula
Jaccard	$\frac{|S_1 \cap S_2|}{|S_1 \cup S_2|}$
Sokal and Sneath	$\frac{|S_1 \cap S_2|}{2 \times (|S_1| + |S_2|) - 3 \times |S_1 \cap S_2|}$
Dice	$\frac{2 \times |S_1 \cap S_2|}{|S_1| + |S_2|}$

the denominator. Reference [11] has been selected for comparison as it is the only anonymization method for query logs, which uses the semantics of the queries to cluster the users.

$$Utility_{Coef_y}(C_{prop}, C_x) = \frac{\sum\limits_{i=1}^{n} Coef_y(C_{orig}(u_i), C_{prop}(u_i))}{\sum\limits_{i=1}^{n} Coef_y(C_{orig}(u_i), C_x(u_i))} \tag{4}$$

where C_{orig} are the logs with the original categories, C_{prop} are the generated logs with our proposal, and C_x are the generated logs with the proposal [11] or the random proposal. $Coef_y$ is the coefficient chosen among the three proposed (*Jaccard, Sokal and Sneath, Dice*), which ranges from 0 to 1.

Regarding privacy, a log can be considered private if it does not allow to uniquely identify any user. Microaggregation [12] provides k-anonymity at user level, so the privacy of a user is guaranteed by $k - 1$ other users.

We propose to evaluate the linkability between the original logs and the microaggregated logs by using the previous coefficients with the queries as input data, that is, how many queries of the original log also appear in the microaggregated log. Linkability can be seen as a privacy measure, since it evaluates how many information about a user it is being exposed. The less common queries they have, the more privacy she will achieved. This measure is expressed by Eq. 5. Note that the linkability achieved by our proposal is now the denominator, and the linkability of the other proposals is the numerator.

Another issue of particular interest in query logs privacy is the disambiguation of a user. In a microaggregated log, a user can be disambiguated if her queries can be isolated. Disambiguation means that her queries can be distinguished from the queries of the other users. This is possible if the queries are about different topics, they are in different languages, etc. For instance, consider Bob knows that Alice hates dogs and he saw Alice's anonymized log, which contains the queries *American monster trucks* and *retriever dogs*. Bob can infer that the second query (*retriever dogs*) is not from Alice, as he knows that Alice is not interested in dogs. We think that our approach reduces the possibility to disambiguate the queries of a user, as the queries in the same cluster are more similar.

$$Linkability_{Coef_y}(Q_{prop}, Q_x) = \frac{\sum\limits_{i=1}^{n} Coef_y(Q_{orig}(u_i), Q_x(u_i))}{\sum\limits_{i=1}^{n} Coef_y(Q_{orig}(u_i), Q_{prop}(u_i))} \tag{5}$$

where Q_{orig} is the set of original query logs, $Q_{prop}(i)$ are the logs generated with our proposal and $Q_x(i)$ are the query logs generated with the proposal [11] or the random proposal.

6   Results

Figure 2 shows the comparison of the utility obtained using our method with the method presented in [11] and a random microaggregation (microaggregation with a random clustering). The respective coefficient values are represented in Table 2. The three similarity coefficients used provide close results, thus supporting the validity of the obtained results. When we compare our method with [11] (Fig. 2(a)), the former achieves a maximum of 64 % utility improvement when $k = 15$ (according to the Sokal and Sneath coefficient), although it improves the utility in all cluster sizes. Thus, we can argue that it is easier to match categories using *urls* than query terms, as the latter are difficult to be interpreted or classified in the knowledge base correctly. Moreover, since categories can represent

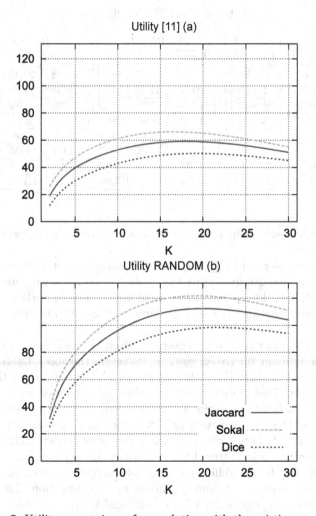

Fig. 2. Utility comparison of our solution with the existing work.

Table 2. Utility coefficients

	Our proposal			SORT [11]			Random		
k	Jaccard	Sokal	Dice	Jaccard	Sokal	Dice	Jaccard	Sokal	Dice
2	42.63	27.6	59.25	35.71	21.78	52.55	32.4	20	47.1
3	30	18	45.37	23.07	13.06	37.41	19.56	11	31.6
4	24.5	14	38.6	17.76	9.76	30.09	14.64	8	24.91
5	21.73	12.5	34.93	14.92	8.08	25.9	12.2	6.6	21.26
10	15.4	8.58	26.1	9.63	5.07	17.5	7.46	3.91	13.69
15	13.16	7.19	22.73	8.04	4.2	14.81	6	3.15	11.29
20	11.75	6.36	20.58	7.24	3.77	13.43	5.39	2.79	10.13
30	9.89	5.26	17.7	6.521	3.38	12.17	4.84	2.49	9.1

Table 3. Linkability coefficients

	Our proposal			SORT [11]			Random		
k	Jaccard	Sokal	Dice	Jaccard	Sokal	Dice	Jaccard	Sokal	Dice
2	24.27	14.32	37.99	33.4	20.07	50.04	33.58	20.19	50.24
3	15.67	8.84	26.24	20.16	11.22	33.51	20.33	11.32	33.77
4	11.05	6.09	19.17	14.44	7.79	25.21	14.69	7.93	25.59
5	8.99	4.95	15.75	11.28	5.98	20.2	11.56	6.13	20.7
10	4.54	2.46	8.16	5.49	2.82	10.39	5.8	2.99	10.94
15	2.73	1.43	5.09	3.67	1.87	7.07	4.02	2.03	7.72
20	2.34	1.23	4.34	2.81	1.42	5.46	3.13	1.59	6.06
30	1.4	0.7	2.68	1.99	1	3.89	2.32	1.1732	4.52

the conceptualizations of the *urls*, this approach enables a semantically-coherent clustering of logs.

We can also observe in Fig. 2(a) that the improvement is higher in cluster sizes between 10 and 20, increasing from 2 to 10 and decreasing above $k = 20$. We presume that working with larger sets of users could outperform the results, because we could presumably find more similar users when the number of users is greater.

Figure 2(b) shows that the improvement of our method is even better compared with a random microaggregation. However, the most interesting is to observe that the method [11] achieves better data utility than the random microaggregation. This is due to the fact that some queries are composed by few terms, and their interpretation in the knowledge base can be correct. In our dataset, 40 % of the queries have 3 or less terms. Thus, we can determine that the interpretation of query terms produces less precise conceptualizations of the queries, but it still works better than a random microaggregation.

Figure 3 shows the linkability reduction of queries using our proposal compared with the proposal [11] and a random microaggregation. The respective coefficient values are represented in Tables 2 and 3. We can observe that our method achieves a significant reduction of the number of real queries that can

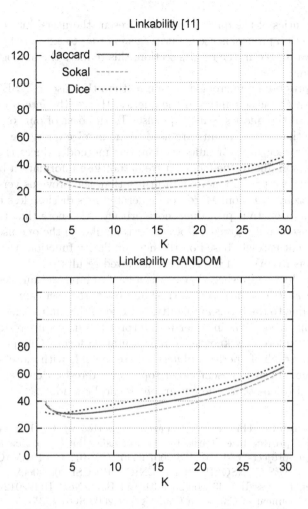

Fig. 3. Linkability comparison of our solution with the existing work.

be found in the original logs as well as in the centroid. In the proposal [11], the reduction is about 30 % in median, and 40 % in the random microaggregation. Thus, it seems clear that our method reduces the risks of privacy disclosures.

It is interesting to observe that [11] only obtains slightly better results than the random microaggregation. This is an effect of the clustering part, which has group users with few common interests, and the aggregation part, which has selected queries at random without taking into account their frequencies.

7   Conclusions

Query logs need to be anonymized in order to guarantee the privacy of the users. However, this process involves data utility loss. Query logs utility is related with the semantics of the queries, which represent the users' interests. Existing privacy-protection proposals use query terms in order to extract their semantics. However, as we stated in the results section, this reduces the homogeneity of the clustered data.

We have proposed a microaggregation method that uses a WSE and ODP in order to interpret the semantics of the queries. Hence, the interpretation of the real meaning of the queries is more precise. To the best of our knowledge, it is the first time that search results are used to anonymize query logs.

As we have seen in the results section, our method reduces the introduced data perturbation due to the fact that we do not lose information by classifying the queries, but we provide more data utility than the previous version [11] and a random microaggregation. Moreover, generated logs disclose less real information about the user, thus providing more privacy. Also note that the clustering heuristic we use is quite greedy. However it is similar to the one used in [11], so our improvement is solely based on the new similarity function. Using a clustering heuristic as MDAV can improve the achieved results.

This study has established that it was a flaw to interpret queries in a knowledge base, because in some cases, the real interest of the user cannot be obtained. It is not only due to the terms ambiguity, but due to the limitations of the knowledge base. The use of *urls* in order to interpret the user's interests give us the possibility to explore new knowledge representation forms. One possibility is to use a bipartite graph of queries and *urls*, where the *urls* with more edges in common (*url* - query) can represent closer topics or interests. However, the amount of data needed to create a coherent graph should be studied.

Acknowledgements. This work was partly supported by the European Commission under FP7 project Inter-Trust, by the Spanish Ministry of Science and Innovation (through projects eAEGIS TSI2007-65406-C03-01, CO-PRIVACY TIN2011-27076-C03-01, ARES-CONSOLIDER INGENIO 2010 CSD2007-00004, Audit Transparency Voting Process IPT-430000-2010-31 and BallotNext IPT-2012-0603-430000) and by the Government of Catalonia (under grant 2009 SGR 1135).

References

1. Richardson, M.: Learning about the world through long-term query logs. ACM Trans. Web **2**, 1–27 (2008)
2. Xiong, L., Agichtein, E.: Towards privacy-preserving query log publishing. In: Amitay, E., Murray, C.G., Teevan, J. (eds) Query Log Analysis: Social and Technological Challenges. A Workshop at the 16th International World Wide Web Conference (WWW 2007) (2007)
3. He, Y., Naughton, J.: Anonymization of set-valued data via top-down, local generalization. Proc. VLDB Endowment **2**(1), 934–945 (2009)
4. Adar, E.: User 4XXXXX9: anonymizing query logs. In: Query Log Analysis: Social and Technological Challenges. A Workshop at the 16th International World Wide Web Conference (WWW 2007) (2007)
5. Jiang, J.J., Conrath, D.W.: Semantic similarity based on corpus statistics and lexical taxonomy (1997)

6. Xu, J., Wang, W., Pei, J., Wang, X., Shi, B., Fu, A.W.: Utility-based anonymization for privacy preservation with less information loss. SIGKDD Explor. Newsl. **8**(2), 21–30 (2006)
7. Defays, D., Nanopoulos, P.: Panels of enterprises and confidentiality: the small aggregates method. In: Proceedings of the 92 Symposium on Design and Analysis of Longitudinal Surveys, Statistics Canada, pp. 195–204 (1993)
8. Hong, Y., He, X., Vaidya, J., Adam, N., Atluri, V.: Effective anonymization of query logs. In: CIKM '09: Proceeding of the 18th ACM Conference on Information and Knowledge Management, pp. 1465–1468 (2009)
9. Navarro-Arribas, G., Torra, V., Erola, A., Castellà-Roca, J.: User k-anonymity for privacy preserving data mining of query logs. Inf. Process. Manage. **48**(3), 476–487 (2012)
10. Erola, A., Castellà-Roca, J., Navarro-Arribas, G., Torra, V.: Semantic microaggregation for the anonymization of query logs. In: Domingo-Ferrer, J., Magkos, E. (eds.) PSD 2010. LNCS, vol. 6344, pp. 127–137. Springer, Heidelberg (2010)
11. Erola, A., Castellà-Roca, J., Navarro-Arribas, G., Torra, V.: Semantic microaggregation for the anonymization of query logs using the open directory project. SORT-Stat. Oper. Res. Trans. **35**(Special issue), 25–40 (2011)
12. Samarati, P.: Protecting respondents identities in microdata release. IEEE Trans. Knowl. Data Eng. **13**(6), 1010–1027 (2001)
13. Domingo-Ferrer, J., Mateo-Sanz, J.M.: Practical data-oriented microaggregation for statistical disclosure control. IEEE Trans. Knowl. Data Eng. **14**, 189–201 (2002)
14. Domingo-Ferrer, J., Sebé, F., Solanas, A.: A polynomial-time approximation to optimal multivariate microaggregation. Comput. Math. Appl. **55**(4), 714–732 (2008)
15. Cooper, A.: A survey of query log privacy-enhancing techniques from a policy perspective. ACM Trans. Web **2**(4), 1–27 (2008)
16. Korolova, A., Kenthapadi, K., Mishra, N., Ntoulas, A.: Releasing search queries and clicks privately. In: WWW '09: Proceedings of the 18th International Conference on World Wide Web, pp. 171–180 (2009)
17. Poblete, B., Spiliopoulou, M., Baeza-Yates, R.: Website privacy preservation for query log publishing. In: Bonchi, F., Malin, B., Saygın, Y. (eds.) PInKDD 2007. LNCS, vol. 4890, pp. 80–96. Springer, Heidelberg (2008)
18. Miller, G.: WordNet - About Us. WordNet. Princeton University, Princeton (2009)
19. ODP. Open directory project (2011)
20. Sætre, R., Tveit, A., Steigedal, T.S., Lægreid, A.: Semantic annotation of biomedical literature using google. ICCSA **3**, 327–337 (2005)
21. Gligorov, R., Aleksovski, Z., Kate, W., F. Van Harmelen, B.: Using google distance to weight approximate ontology matches. In: Proceedings of the WWW-07, pp. 767–776. ACM Press (2007)
22. iprospect.com, inc, iProspect Blended Search Results Study. http://www.iProspect.com (2009)

Legal Issues About Metadata Data Privacy vs Information Security

Manuel Munier[1]([⊠]), Vincent Lalanne[1],
Pierre-Yves Ardoy[2], and Magali Ricarde[3]

[1] University of Pau and Pays Adour, LIUPPA, Mont de Marsan, France
`manuel.munier@univ-pau.fr`
[2] University of Pau and Pays Adour, Pau, France
[3] BackPlan Company, Project Communication Control, Pau, France

Abstract. For the purposes of our work we use the concept of metadata to implement enterprise digital right management mechanisms in an intelligent document environment. Such metadata allows us to firstly define contextual security rules and secondly to ensure the information traceability. However, its use may have legal implications, especially with regard to metadata that can be stored (see personal data, privacy), how it should be stored (see probative value in case of litigation, digital forensics) or computer processing in which it may be involved. Another topical issue is the storage and the processing of data using a service provider: the cloud. We must ensure, however, that this solution does not lead to a loss of information controllability for the company. This article aims to position our work with respect to these legal issues.

Keywords: Privacy · Metadata · Information security · Socio-economic issues

1 Introduction

Whatever business areas, new information technologies (ADSL, laptops, smartphones, tablets,...) lead us to exchange and store more and more information. Their content has also evolved. Data is more and more complex (notions of structured documents, whole archives, or even complete projects). Nowadays, public data is sometimes combined with more confidential data (notion of access restriction). Moreover, we carry our data on usb stick or in our smartphones and share it via (possibly unsecured) wireless communications like 3G, wifi or bluetooth. In the information society, the reliability of the data we handle has become a major issue in terms of security.

Security criteria most commonly used are confidentiality (assurance that information is shared only among authorized persons or organizations), integrity (assurance that the information is authentic and complete), availability (assurance that the systems responsible for delivering, storing and processing information are accessible when needed, by those who need them) and traceability (ability to chronologically interrelate uniquely identifiable entities in a way that is verifiable).

J. Garcia-Alfaro et al. (Eds.): DPM 2013 and SETOP 2013, LNCS 8247, pp. 162–177, 2014.
DOI: 10.1007/978-3-642-54568-9_11, © Springer-Verlag Berlin Heidelberg 2014

Regarding confidentiality, usage control models introduced the notion of context in order to express dynamic security rules in a policy: temporal contexts, spatial contexts, prerequisite contexts, provisional contexts,... To enable or disable these contexts the information system must collect and store various metadata: date, IP address used, user location,... This metadata can later be used for traceability purposes, including use as evidence in case of litigation. Some of this metadata can, however, be considered as personal data of the user and thus bring privacy concerns. Metadata is one of the important keys to the success of the data warehousing and business intelligence effort since the mid nineties of the last century. Data warehouses are designed to manage and store the data whereas the business intelligence focuses on the usage of the data to facilitate reporting and analysis [1,2]. The term metadata refers to "data about data". However, the concept of metadata is not (yet) a well-known concept of the law.

The remainder of this paper is organized as follows: Sect. 2 presents our motivations for the use of metadata and usage control mechanisms to enforce information security; this section also presents a concrete case study in the context of business documents; we developed this example with our partner company BackPlan[TM] [1]; in Sect. 3 we present two areas of our research activities related to information security using the concept of metadata and how metadata can be useful for usage control, traceability and information system monitoring; Sect. 4, using examples of jurisprudence, highlights the need to formalize the metadata necessary to enforce the security policy and the framework in which they can be used order to comply the regulations; Sect. 5 presents some socio-economic issues underlying the storage of data (and metadata) in the today information society; Sect. 6 concludes the paper and presents some of our perspectives.

2   Motivations

As we stated at the beginning of this article, information technology (IT) allows us to share more and more information in the form of documents whose structure becomes more complex. Whether in the context of a "simple" information dissemination (unidirectional communication from a content provider to the users) or a collaborative work environment (several actors interact to complete tasks with a common goal but possibly different objectives), it is therefore necessary to implement security mechanisms that go beyond a simple access control: usage control (how partners can use a document: obligations, workflows, delegation rules,...), information consistency management (e.g. some documents may reference others), traceability (monitoring of actions, metadata attached to information),...

We do not give here all the details of our case study. This section focuses on the use of metadata to improve information security (traceability, usage control) and legal issues that may arise.

---

[1] BackPlan[TM], Project Communication Control
http://www.backplan.fr.

2.1   Sample Application

Consider an Oil & Gas project as the construction of a pipeline or an oil installation. The information system consists of numerous documents, it has a central role, its structure and development evolve along with the progress of the project: the documentation must always precede action (design, work procedures). Documentation is a requirement at the closure of the project along with verifications (records, the minutes,...). The document evolves at the same rate as the project. These documents are specifications, drawings, records of expertise, procedures, records,...

Business Aspects. Such a project obviously involves many partners and subcontractors. Here is a representative example of a project timeline (Fig. 1):

- 1st level design: Basic Engineering. This step is performed by the land surveyor who makes a topographical survey of the site where the work will be done.
- 2nd level design: Detailed Engineering. This is the design phase of the project itself with the aim, in particular, to minimize the environmental and human constraints; it is performed by an engineering company that will plan the work and the construction will be launched from this plan. This level involves various partners (civil engineering, pipefitters, instrumentation engineering, utilities,...) who share many documents.
- Statement of works: numerous buried and air, public or private networks, go through the territory (water, electricity, gases, dangerous products, telecommunications, irrigation,...). Further to accidents, it is imperative to localize very exactly their position. So, during the realization of a project of construction, gas pipeline for example, companies have the obligation to question a centralized information system common to all the French territory.
- Construction phase: it is based on engineering documents and work procedures. It comes with many documents that are intended to demonstrate compliance of the book in terms of quality and regulatory standards (e.g. multifluid standard, water code, capacity under pressure). As-builts will have to justify the differences for the administration.

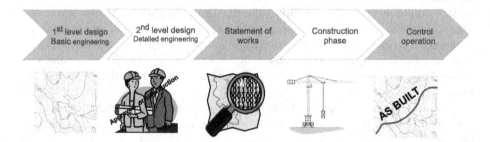

Fig. 1. Oil & Gas project timeline

– At the end of construction the land surveyor will come again, and verify the topographic survey: this is a control operation of a project to verify the differences from the planned location and update the data (to know where everything is). The engineering documents then pass status "As built". This operation can also update the geographic information system (GIS) of the place. As-builts must be attached to requests for authorization to operate sent to administrations (also signed by the legal representative).

As we have stated, the stakeholders will handle many documents. Because of the nature of this type of project, a multitude of corporate associations has to work on the same documents. Where from requires it to manage the communications between these interfaces. Besides, it will be necessary to be able to guarantee that each works with documents "up to date" or that the last modifications in date were well taken into account before the "publication" of certain results (cf. usage control and collaborative work management). There can also occur unforeseen circumstances during the project.

Information Security Aspects. We propose to improve the security of information in two directions: metadata management and usage control.

Metadata. It could be used to "bind" reviews, certifications, good practice guides, standards, and other minutes to design documents and reports within the information system. The aim is to improve traceability, both in the design process (concept of workflow) in case of litigation (concept of proof of conformity, digital forensics). Take for example a phase control such as checking the welding of a pipe[2]; it would be interesting to use metadata to improve the traceability of the process for purposes of validation and/or evidence: photos geotagged (to certify checkpoints), metadata associated with the plans,... Since several partners are working on such a project, everyone could also attach some metadata to the information: confidence and trustworthiness indicators, impact risk of a change,... This metadata would permit to calculate various performance indicators for monitoring the stakeholders' tasks or new metadata for information they produce.

In case of transfer of work this metadata would allow to improve the followup of the project towards the buyer: operations history, context decisions (standards, studies), how and why they have been taken, etc...

Usage Control. Here are some examples of security rules that we would implement to control how partners use documents:

– It is possible to write a deliverable of the project only if confidence in the various technical documents exceeds a certain threshold. It is a dynamic access control based on trust (whether in a document or a stakeholder).

---

[2] The sections of pipe are welded every 12 to 15 m. These welds should be checked: radiography, analysis by a certified individual, hydraulic tests. These controls are spread over time and generate many records that are, once made, a legal value.

- The security rules may prohibit access to parts of the document based on location data. This prevents, for example, on a site (or train) an unknown person takes sensitive information over the shoulder of someone.
- A responsive access control may require a partner (or subcontractor), via a mechanism of pre-obligation to accept the terms of a contract (non-disclosure agreement, delegation of responsibility, deadlines,...) before accessing a plan and contribute to the design.
- A user control would be to require a partner to complete parts of design documents (e.g. inform the radii of curvature of the pipe, write the study of soil before drilling) before a deadline if he wants to stay a project member (notions of punishment and penalty).
- The usage control can also define collective obligations. For example, each stakeholder must have reread each concept study in which they participate at least 7 days before the deadline for validation.

Legal Issues. These are just some examples of opportunities. But the use of metadata is not easy to understand from a legal point of view! First, regarding the collection and storage, some of this metadata can be in the domain of personal data (including geolocation). But their use to enable/disable contextual security policies (permissions, obligations,...) or calculate some indicators (e.g. trust in a stakeholder, document quality) are automatically processes and are therefore subject to a number of regulatory frameworks. Add to that the concepts of accountability and sanctions mentioned above and it is obvious that metadata has now become essential elements of information systems. They should be considered as full data and be secured along with "classic" information.

Section 4 gives more details on requirements to formalize metadata necessary to the security policy and how metadata can be used. One of the objectives is that this metadata can be used as evidence in case of litigation (cf. probative value) while respecting the laws on privacy.

2.2   BackPlan™

BackPlan™ is a French company providing document management services and collaboration workflow applications to improve project communication, transparency across the project, ability to manage schedule and risks, reliable indicators and regulatory compliance. From the engineering phases to the construction phases, projects involve different companies. All of them will use the collaboration solution BackPlan™ to ensure consistency of information across the project and a complete audit trail of project communication. BackPlan™ document management services are currently provided on a server hosted in a data center: the document registry.

Using metadata (as data about data) would allow BackPlan™ to enhance existing services and to offer new services to their customers. During the course of the project, metadata would be used to calculate many indicators for project progress, compliance with deadlines, completion status of the various documents,... Once the project is completed, the company makes and delivers to its customers the case-file containing all the business documents for project traceability. In terms of risk management, in case of litigation this information can be used to identify those responsible for error or prove that during the construction phase of the project the standards in force at that time have been complied with.

3   Metadata and Information Security

Our research activities take place in the field of information system security. Issues related to the legal framework for the use of metadata were raised when we wanted to implement contextual security rules to perform usage control within two areas of research: the development of a secure autonomous document architecture, and the study of service oriented architecture security. This metadata will obviously be used during the life cycle of the document to perform usage control. But they can also be accessed later for traceability of actions performed and thus serve as evidence in case of litigation or for digital forensics.

This section focuses on the use of metadata to improve information security. In our work this "data about data" allows us to implement security mechanisms such as dynamic security policies, collaborative work management, calculation of confidence and trustworthiness indicators,... The use of metadata is not, however, trivial in terms of the law and these technological possibilities must not make us forget the legal issues (see Sect. 4). In addition, this metadata can be more important than the data to which it is associated (see Sect. 5).

3.1   Intelligent Document Architecture

As part of our research we developed a multi-view model for secure data warehouse [3] and we proposed E-DRM[3] architecture based on secure autonomous documents [4]. While "traditional" information systems centralize all the data on a server which users must connect, we have chosen to define an approach where security mechanisms are relocated closer to the user. However, unlike "conventional" DRM architectures that require the use of a dedicated player (which is responsible for enforcing the security policy), we decided to embed these security mechanisms within the document following object-oriented approach: a document is an autonomous entity capable of ensuring by itself the security of the information it contains and controlling how this information is used. Such a document is a kind of information system on its own embedding both a data warehouse and various security modules (access control, usage control, metadata,...). Users can thus exchange the document directly and safely without having to connect to a central site.

The core of our architecture, namely the security kernel, relies on the OrBAC model [5] to express security policies in terms of permissions, prohibitions and obligations between a subject, an object and an action. These security rules are dynamic, that is to say, they can be "adapted" to the context of the actions [6–8]:

---

[3] E-DRM: Enterprise Digital Right Management.

activation or deactivation of rules, the execution of an action triggers the insertion of an obligation,... OrBAC model supports various kinds of contexts: *temporal context* (depends on the time at which the subject is requesting for an access to the system), *spatial context* (depends on the subject (geo)location), *user-declared context* (depends on the subject objective or purpose), *prerequisite context* (depends on characteristics that join the subject, the action and the object) and *provisional context* (depends on previous actions the subject has performed in the system). The embedded information system must therefore provide the information required to check that conditions associated with the context definition are satisfied or not. To do this, either it has direct access to the host system (e.g. a global clock to check the temporal context) or it uses metadata carried by the actions and the nodes contained in the embedded database.

Our approach therefore relies heavily on the concept of metadata, both for collection (traceability) and for context activation (dynamic security rules) or, eventually, computing various indicators throughout the uses (confidence, trustworthiness) as works published in [9–12].

3.2 Service Oriented Architecture Security

Service Oriented Architectures (SOA) offer new opportunities for the interconnection of systems. However, infrastructure design using external services (which we do not control) and/or exposing new services outside the company raises new problems for the information system security because these new technologies introduce new vulnerabilities and therefore new risks. It concerns not only the classical criteria as confidentiality, integrity and availability, but also new concepts like traceability, trustworthiness and controllability. Our work aims to propose an approach for risk management which is based on the ISO/IEC 27005 standard: we propose a development of this standard so that it can fully take into account the type "service" as web services and cloud services [13].

To develop a security model for communications in inter-organisational information systems we also use a usage control oriented approach as presented above. In this context, the use of metadata for traceability of communications (via these services) allow us to compute indicators that will be used to monitor the information system [14]. Our goal is that companies can keep control over their information, despite the use of cloud technologies.

3.3 Data Privacy Concerns

Preliminary tests on our self-protecting document architecture, performed with predefined metadata, allowed us to implement dynamic security rules for usage control. These experiments have also led us to concern ourselves with the privacy of metadata.

According to the ISO 8402 standard, traceability is the ability to trace the history, use or location of an entity by means of recorded identifications. In our architecture, an entity corresponds to an autonomous collaborative work document. History, identification, registration and use are relevant concepts. As we mentioned above, user localization can be an interesting metadata for expressing contextual security rules. But a document could then reveal the presence of a user at a given time in a certain place, or the various revisions which followed one another leading to the final of a contractual document ! So we must not only focus on the metadata that is collected, but also protect it from unauthorized use and control how it can be used (e.g. automatic computation of indicators). Basically, the problem of leakage and/or misuse of information is already known. However, in our approach, the "massive" collection of metadata "of any kind" can effectively exacerbate the problem.

A concrete example is presented in the article [15] entitled "Metadata: the ghosts haunting e-documents". This story demonstrates the risks of exchanging files with embedded data in negotiating a contract. During negotiations, partners used a common word processing program, Microsoft Word, to edit and propose revisions to the contract, and they utilized the program's track changes feature to allow the other side to see the specific changes proposed. They e-mailed the electronic draft, complete with embedded data, back and forth to each other between rounds of revisions. But without using anything but Microsoft Word's inherent functions, someone can reveal hidden internal comments from adverse party concerning terms of the contract, negotiating positions,... In doing so, a stakeholder can be aware of confidential business information and use it to pressure his opponent.

This article also raises an interesting question: is that stakeholder (in this case a lawyer) bound by the same obligations that apply when documents in a misaddressed envelope are received or, conversely, is the stakeholder free to use and review the embedded information?

4   Metadata and Legal Issues

As it has been said from the beginning of this article, our works rely highly on the concept of metadata, both in the collection (traceability) for activation contexts (dynamic safety) and, in the course of time, the computation of various indicators over time (confidence rating or trustworthiness value). Note that, for the moment, the elements of study in this section relate only to the French law. For the scaling of our work, the specificities of each country should obviously be considered.

The concept of metadata is not a well-known concept of the law. Composed of the Greek prefix *meta-* referring to the reference to itself, the term metadata refers to data within data, data which defines limits or describe other data. That data is varied and can include durations, dates, places, elements to identify peo-ple,... In a very precise domain, however law gives a definition to metadata. Article L.127-1, 6° of the Environmental Code actually specifies that it is the *"information describing sets and spatial data services, making possible their dis-covery, their inventory and their use"*. However, this definition, the first one put by a legal text, does not report the diversity which hides under the term of metadata.

Metadata raises three types of difficulties: their collection, their storage and their use. First of all, problems raise with regards to their collection. Very often, its collection is done unbeknown to the authors, at the least in the ignorance of the concerned entities. Concerning the law, this raises the question of the right of access to information contained in metadata and above all the question of the right to know the information is collected. Another difficulty arises straight away: the entity who collects the metadata is not even aware he is making such a collection, it is only, subsequent to the collection, that the meditative elements are discovered and used.

Secondly, metadata raises the question of its storage. This storage implies guaranteeing conservation, not only of the authenticity of the metadata (which refers to the question of the collection and the reliability of the source), but also of its integrity, its stability. What is at the heart of the matter is ultimately to require the reliability of the metadata. It is not only important that it is stored in good conditions, it is also necessary as to ensure its availability, its accessibility, what is needed to be know, by whom, for how long and under which conditions.

Finally, metadata raises the problem of its usage. Such a usage may be done in good faith, as for example in the implementation of security mechanisms, but it can also in bad faith, the metadata being diverted from its original usage or be subject to falsification.

Potentially metadata affects all fields of the law and it is difficult or even useless to apprehend it in the abstract. It consists in identifying areas where the use of metadata is likely to raise specific questions without claiming completeness. Also note that this is a primary questioning limited to the French domestic law.

4.1   Evidence of Law

It is mainly in the field of the law of evidence that the rare decisions of the court of appeal which refers to metadata are found.

In civil law, proof of a legal act can be give by any means, nevertheless within certain conditions. It is in particular required that the evidence be reported fairly and that the type of evidence is reliable. Even if the rules are significantly different from criminal law, the reliability requirement is definitely common to both domains. This reliability requirement is obviously at the heart of the admissibility of an electronic document, proofwise. Article 1316-1 of the Civil Code thus provides that, for proof of legal acts *"the writing in electronic form is admissible in evidence equal to a written document on paper, provided that the person who issued the document and its establiment and storage are executed under the conditions so that its integrity can be duly identified."* It is thus not a surprise that the rare decisions referring to metadata require its reliability.

This is foremost the case of the Ruling of the First President of the Paris Court of Appeal on 25 October 2011, Juris-Data N° 2011-025553 and October 25, 2011 (unpublished, N° 09/14462, 09/14501)[4]. In this specific case, a company

---

[4] See also Orders of November 15, 2011 or August 31, 2012 from the First President of the Paris Court given in matters relating to anticompetitive practices.

filed a legal complaint against the search and seising in its premises authorized by local competent authorities with regards to the investigation of anticompetitive practices. Even if the legal problem did not directly address the issue of metadata, the Court nevertheless adopted the argument of the Competent Authority at the end of which *"the structure of a particular Outlook mail file and the obligation not to change the state of the computer visited nor the characteristics of a file (metadata in the file itself: title, author size, dates, location, and signature,...) necessarily imply the complete seising of the mail file after verifying that it contains elements falling within the scope of the authorization."* In all cases the emphasis is on the requirement that it should seize the entire Outlook messaging so as not to affect the reliability of the input by an alteration of metadata contained in the messages.

In a judgment of the Court of Appeal of Versailles, Ch.1, Sect. 1 of 30 September 2010 (unpublished, N° 09/03831), an applicant pressed on the metadata contained in photographs to prove his position as author of the photographs. The Court retained the metadata elements as evidence noting that these included the identity of the author, the date and time of shooting, the name of the manufacturer of the device, the model of the latter and the description of the camera settings. If metadata may in itself not demonstrate the source of the photographs, it is however the elements which can establish the paternity and can therefore be very useful in the case of a counterfait lawsuit. Within the same context, the Labour Chamber of the Court of Appeal of Rennes retained, in a judgment of 20 September 2011 (unpublished, RG N° 10/05183), that the production of metadata may be used to determine the creation date of an advertising brochure while noting that the reliability of the latter is not discussed.

It is of course conceivable that metadata can serve as evidence in a variety of areas. It can thus be used to prove the absence of an employee. In telework, metadata opens up the possibility to determine whether the employee has met with his working hours. Thus, arise questions of the distinction between personal time and working time, respect of privacy and where the boundaries of the employer's power are situated.

Beyond relations between employer and employees, metadata may be of interest in relationships between business partners or directors of a company. It could for example be used to demonstrate that this officer or that employee was responsible for the disclosure of a trade secret (Article L.621-1 of the Intellectual Property Code and L.1227-1 of the Labour Code).

Moreover, in the context of the mission of prevention and repression measures of illegal downloading which lie within the Hadopi law, metadata can be useful to show which person is actually responsible for downloading illegal copyright protected work. In July 2013, French legislators struck down the heavy-handed Hadopi online copyright law. Under the law's "three strikes" rule, users who violated copyright restrictions three or more times could be punished by having their Internet connections cut. But Hadopi suffered great controversy when France's highest court, the Constitutional Council, declared access to the internet a basic human right. French legislators are now seeking policy reforms that will shift the focus of law enforcement towards commercial piracy issues.

These are obviously only a few possible usages of metadata, an exhaustive list does not seem possible or at least very delicate.

4.2 Privacy and Individual Liberties

Indeed, metadata may contain information about people, whether it concerns identification or location. For instance, a picture of a group of friends can be published on the Internet (we recall that The Internet is a public space) it may contain the names of the people in the picture, the place where it was taken, the date and time of the snapshot (tags on Facebook photos).

So these are issues that concern not only image rights (assuming the image was published without the agreement of different people), but also the respect of someone's privacy set by Article 9 of the Civil Code. For a number of reasons, in fact, a person may want a certain amount of information not to be disclosed. (such date, such time,...).

If the concept of metadata is just beginning to be understood by the law, it has on the other hand understood those of personal data. It concerns information that can directly or indirectly identify individuals (*Information Act N° 78-17 of 6 January 1978, Directive 95/46/EC of October 23, 1995*). The concept of metadata does necessarily correspond to the concept of personal data insofar metadata may contain information which is not necessarily information which can be used to identify a person (information about location, time spent on a file,...). They may, however, raise questions which may be of interest to privacy.

As such, metadata collection is likely to be considered as a collection of personal data. In this sense it seems possible to read Deliberation N° 2011-423 of 15 December CNIL 2011 authorizing the company GEOLSEMANTICS to implement, on a trial basis, as part of a research project, the treatment of personal data, necessary for the development of a tool, called SAIMSI (eng: follow adaptive inter-lingual and multi-source information). The metadata items concerned are those attached to the collected documents, that is to say, those *"corresponding of how the information was collected (if applicable: document URL source, date of registration, date, time and place of the issue body text and the source)"*.

4.3 Digital Protection and Intellectual Creations

The French DADVSI Act of 1 August 2006 introduced the ability to protect intellectual works by systems which limit or prohibit any copying. In French law, these devices are called Technical Protection Measures (MTP), better known by the acronym DRM (Digital Right Management). The Intellectual Property Act has developed a complete,relatively complex system, designed to ensure that such DRM can not be used by producers or publishers aimed at anticompetitive purposes unrelated to the protection of copyrights. The presence of DRM should thus not prevent interoperability, that is to say the ability for the works to be read by the most diverse materials.

5   Metadata and Socio-Economic Issues

In the information society today, metadata becomes sometimes more important than the data which it is associated. Whether in the field of privacy (personal data) or professional (business data of a company), many companies have developed their business on it. Lately, the media focus on large multinational companies such as Google, Facebook or Microsoft regarding the protection of privacy and personal data. This is a hot topic that scares the public. In the professional world, same issues arise about critical data of companies (e.g. research & development, business strategy). This is the case for example of the BackPlan^{TM} company whose business uses metadata on information exchanged between participants for project communication control.

The objective of this section is not to criticize the practices of a particular country or to denigrate the work of a particular company. We just want to highlight the socio-economic issues about information in today's society and the need to harmonize the laws of different countries to define an international legal framework.

5.1   Data are Future's Power

We live in a transitional period, the digitization of everything: people, society, organizations, knowledge, interactions,... Data is the basic building block of the information society. Its quantity is growing exponentially: we are talking about Big Data. The physical infrastructure of the information society, telecommunication systems, storage facilities and data processing, new online services, are industries experiencing unprecedented growth. Data per se offers tremendous potential that we begin to use to generate new knowledge.

Personal data, both that produced by the users (texts, photos, videos,...) and that generated by the systems we use often unknowingly, is the heart of the economy of the information society, and therefore the heart of the economy. Control of the data also allows control of certain markets, which currently are already using U.S. electronic commerce tools in some areas. Control of the information society gives power still difficult to evaluate and far beyond the areas of the market economy.

Data capture is the top priority in some countries such as the United States or China (which hold respectively 72 % and 16 % of the top 50 sites worldwide). In both countries, national data remain under control of the domestic industry. And both aspire to collect the data at the international level.

5.2   Data Location

Geographical location of the cloud provider can have a real impact on the protection and confidentiality of data.

Legal Obligations. Sensitive data can be stored using a cloud computing solution. But for a French company, for example, it is necessary to check that the provider undertakes to keep these documents in France. Otherwise, the company may be unable to ensure that the processing of personal data complies with the legislation in force for it (e.g. in France: duration of data retention, ability to modify and delete information,...).

Similarly, it is generally necessary to comply with certain legal tax obligations: prohibition to store account books outside the European Union, mandatory reporting to the tax authorities in order to store electronic invoices outside the national territory,...

The "USA PATRIOT Act" Dutch legal researchers have published a study [16] that highlights the importance for a European company to choose a European provider to outsource the processing of personal data or information vital to the company. Indeed, since the establishment of the USA PATRIOT Act, U.S. law allows security services to access all personal data [17]:

- data from U.S. companies, even if the data is physically stored on the European territory
- data from their subsidiaries, even if they are located in another country in the world
- data stored on servers that are hosted in the United States, even if the company that owns the servers is of another nationality

The U.S. government has now established a legal arsenal which allows personal data control of foreign citizens, including Europeans, by leveraging its major companies such as Facebook, Google or Microsoft. At the end of 2012, the European Parliament's Committee on Civil Liberties, Justice and Home Affairs ("LIBE") released a study titled "Fighting cyber crime and protecting privacy in the cloud" [18]. Authors denounce the "Foreign Intelligence and Surveillance Act" (FISA). This amendment expressly authorizes U.S. intelligence agencies (NSA, CIA,...) to wiretap (without judicial authorization) U.S. citizens communicating with foreigners suspected of terrorism or spying. Shortly, a secret tribunal is now able to issue a warrant, secret too (the "secret" for actions may be required for an indefinite period), forcing American companies to deliver to U.S. intelligence agencies the private data of foreign users. Therefore your information may be duplicated, stored and disclosed to third parties without notifying you... In December 2012 the amendment was extended until 2017.

Our aim is not to pass judgment on the "USA PATRIOT Act" and other secret projects such as Riot or PRISM (since 2007 and revealed in june 2013 by Edward Snowden). We simply point out that in the current legislation, a European company with strong constraints on the information confidentiality must therefore be vigilant when choosing a service provider (data location and nationality of the provider).

5.3 Towards a European CNIL

The European Parliament has made good progress on the reform of the EU legislation on data protection proposed almost a year ago by the Commission [19].
The United States, which are reforming their own legislation, call for transat-
lantic regulatory convergence, noting that they are just as demanding as the
Europeans in this area. The EU has the ambition to become the global standard
for data protection, suggesting (according to the authors) that the United States
are more lax.

One of the most controversial issues is the requirement of equivalent standards to allow European data transfer to a third country for processing. The
problem also arises for global corporations (e.g. Google), whose processing practices should be approved by the Union, while the United States would continue
to use their codes of conduct.

In January 2013 the European Parliament presented its preliminary report
on the future reform of the EU Directive on the protection of personal data in
response to proposals from the European Commission. Wishing to strengthen the
protection of data of its citizens, Europe is about to start revising the measures
that came into force in 1995 ensuring wanting to replace Directive 95/46/EC on
the protection of data by a European regulation that all Member States should
apply without discussion. This reform will require the creation of an independent
administrative authority, ie a European CNIL, which will enforce the rules on
data protection, which could take the form of an independent agency.

However, for the French Data Protection Authority ("CNIL"), the text proposed by the European Justice Commissioner Viviane Reding "presents considerable progress" but also "elements of concern". The President of the CNIL,
Isabelle Falque-Pierrotin acknowledges that it has the "major advantage" to
submit to the European law all data processing on a European resident by a
company not established in Europe: in other words it is the European law that
would apply to a French victim of abuse by an American internet company,
for example. But, says the President of the CNIL, the European text raises the
problem of the concept of "principal place of business", according to which the
competent regulatory authority in the event of a dispute with a European citizen
is that of the place where the company and not the complainant.

5.4 Synthesis

The political and economic authorities have become aware of the need to establish an international legal framework to control the collection, storage and use
of data. Metadata associated with data is also included. It is indeed value of
the highest importance for companies whose business is the management of
information.

6 Conclusion

Confidence in the data that we handle every day is one of the major challenges of the information society. There are many mechanisms that allow us to

collect, store and process huge amounts of data and especially data on this data: metadata. Metadata is an essential tool for information security: usage control for document sharing and cloud security, digital forensics, evidence in case of litigation,...

Technological possibilities must not however make us forget the legal issues. The objective being to implement a security policy and to ensure information traceability, it is essential to respect existing regulations regarding the metadata that can be stored (see personal data, privacy), how it should be stored (see probative value) and computer processing in which it may be involved.

Through this article we want to raise awareness of potential abuses related to the use of such metadata. Some work has already been done to preserve privacy. An example is the anonymization of data [20,21]. These are not always suitable for our problem of usage control where precisely some indicators should not be anonymous. In the context of E-DRM we talk about business projects between partners. Thus our approach is rather to formalize this "collaboration agreement". For the IT community, this will be in terms of language as specification for metadata to be collected, by what means, how it is stored and what will be the use. For the legal community, it must first qualify the metadata: should it be treated as "traditional" data or should it receive a specific legal regime? Once defined the legal framework, we can study together under what conditions it is possible to use metadata and, in the other way, what are the metadata necessary to apply certain laws. For instance, in the Oil & Gas case study described in Sect. 2.1, it will now be necessary to include in the contract between companies ("collaboration agreements") the insertion or the deletion of this metadata. For instance, should metadata appear within documents delivered at the end of the project?

Finally, in Sect. 5 we discussed some socio-economic issues underlying the mass storage of data (and metadata) in the today information society. Beyond collaboration between partners on a project, we must also study the use of service providers on the "cloud" (storage or processes). These technologies have become unavoidable for companies although they introduce new vulnerabilities for the information security (loss of information controllability). These threats are not just technical (hardware, software, network). They can also be political, which requires the definition of an international legal framework for data protection.

References

1. Inmon, W.H.: Tech topic: What is a data warehouse? Prism Solutions, 1 pp. (1995)
2. Kimball, R., Ross, M., Thornthwaite, W., Mundy, J., Becker, B.: The Data Warehouse Lifecycle Toolkit, 2nd edn. Wiley Publishing, New York (2008)
3. Munier, M.: A multi-view approach for embedded information system security. In: CRiSIS, pp. 65–72. IEEE (2010)
4. Munier, M., Lalanne, V., Ricarde, M.: Self-protecting documents for cloud storage security. In: TrustCom, pp. 1231–1238. IEEE (2012)
5. Kalam, A.A.E., Benferhat, S., Miège, A., Baida, R.E., Cuppens, F., Saurel, C., Balbiani, P., Deswarte, Y., Trouessin, G.: Organization based access control. In: POLICY, pp. 120–131. IEEE Computer Society (2003)

6. Elrakaiby, Y., Cuppens, F., Cuppens-Boulahia, N.: From contextual permission to dynamic pre-obligation: an integrated approach. In: ARES, pp. 70–78. IEEE Computer Society (2010)
7. Cuppens, F., Cuppens-Boulahia, N.: Modeling contextual security policies. Int. J. Inf. Sec. **7**(4), 285–305 (2008)
8. Cuppens, F., Miège, A.: Modelling contexts in the or-bac model. In: ACSAC, pp. 416–427. IEEE Computer Society (2003)
9. Bertino, E., Lim, H.-S.: Assuring data trustworthiness - concepts and research challenges. In: Jonker, W., Petković, M. (eds.) SDM 2010. LNCS, vol. 6358, pp. 1–12. Springer, Heidelberg (2010)
10. Zheng, X., Maillé, P., Le, C.T.P., Morucci, S.: Improving the efficiency of collaborative work with trust management. In: Agoulmine, N., Bartolini, C., Pfeifer, T., O'Sullivan, D. (eds.) Integrated Network Management, pp. 1172–1179. IEEE (2011)
11. Zheng, X., Maillé, P., Le, C.T.P., Morucci, S.: Trust mechanisms for efficiency improvement in collaborative working environments. In: MASCOTS, pp. 465–467. IEEE (2010)
12. Le, C.T.P., Cuppens, F., Cuppens, N., Maillé, P.: Evaluating the trustworthiness of contributors in a collaborative environment. In: Bertino, E., Joshi, J.B.D. (eds.) CollaborateCom 2008. LNICST, vol. 10, pp. 451–460. Springer, Heidelberg (2009)
13. Lalanne, V., Munier, M., Gabillon, A.: Information security risk management in a world of services. In: PASSAT (2013)
14. Jaramillo, E., Munier, M., Aniorté, P.: Information security in business intelligence based on cloud: a survey of key issues and the premises of a proposal. In: WOSIS (2013)
15. Hricik, D., Scott, C.E.: Metadata: the ghosts haunting e-documents. In: FindLaw, March 2008
16. Van Hoboken, J., Arnbak, A., Van Eijk, N.: Cloud computing in higher education and research institutions and the USA PATRIOT Act. Social Science Research Network Working Paper Series, November 2012
17. Lee, L.T.: USA PATRIOT ACT and telecommunications: privacy under attack. Rutgers Comput. Tech. LJ **29**, 371 (2003)
18. EU: Fighting cyber crime and protecting privacy in the cloud. EU Parliament (2012)
19. EU: Proposal for a Regulation of the European Parliament and of the Council on the protection of individuals with regard to the processing of personal data and on the free movement of such data (General Data Protecting Regulation). Comm. European Communities, Bruxelles (2012)
20. Guarda, P., Zannone, N.: Towards the development of privacy-aware systems. Inf. Softw. Technol. **51**(2), 337–350 (2009)
21. Zhou, B., Pei, J., Luk, W.: A brief survey on anonymization techniques for privacy preserving publishing of social network data. SIGKDD Explor. Newsl. **10**(2), 12–22 (2008)

Privacy-Preserving Multi-Party Reconciliation Secure in the Malicious Model

Georg Neugebauer[1]([⊠]), Lucas Brutschy[1], Ulrike Meyer[1], and Susanne Wetzel[2]

[1] Department of Computer Science, RWTH Aachen University, Aachen, Germany
neugebauer@itsec.rwth-aachen.de
[2] Department of Computer Science, Stevens Institute of Technology, Hoboken, USA

Abstract. The problem of fair and privacy-preserving ordered set reconciliation arises in a variety of applications like auctions, e-voting, and appointment reconciliation. While several multi-party protocols have been proposed that solve this problem in the semi-honest model, there are no multi-party protocols that are secure in the malicious model so far. In this paper, we close this gap. Our newly proposed protocols are shown to be secure in the malicious model based on a variety of novel non-interactive zero-knowledge-proofs. We describe the implementation of our protocols and evaluate their performance in comparison to protocols solving the problem in the semi-honest case.

Keywords: Privacy-enhancing technologies · Secure multi-party computation · Cryptographic protocols · Zero-knowledge proofs · Malicious model

1 Introduction

In many applications, multiple parties need to jointly compute a function of their individual inputs, while keeping the inputs to the function private from each other. *Secure multi-party computation* solves this problem without the use of a trusted third party (TTP). Seminal work in this area [2,27] shows that any functionality that can be modeled as a Boolean or arithmetic circuit can be computed in private. As these early generic solutions exhibit a high complexity for the computation of some functionality, a second line of research focuses on developing protocols that can compute only specific functionality but in a very efficient way. Today, both approaches coexist and results arguing in favor developing special purpose protocols [7,8] as well as such arguing in favor of generic approaches have been published recently [10,15].

One such specific functionality is the *reconciliation of ordered sets* first introduced in [19,20] for the two-party case and generalized to multiple parties in [21,23]. As shown in [18], reconciliation of appointments, some types of electronic auctions, and certain e-voting schemes can be reduced to solving this problem. For example, when reconciling an appointment between multiple parties, each party can be considered to have a private input set of possible dates and

J. Garcia-Alfaro et al. (Eds.): DPM 2013 and SETOP 2013, LNCS 8247, pp. 178–193, 2014.
DOI: 10.1007/978-3-642-54568-9_12, © Springer-Verlag Berlin Heidelberg 2014

order these dates according to its individual preferences. A privacy-preserving reconciliation protocol uses these ordered input sets to determine a date which is a *fair* choice given the preferences expressed by each party, *without* revealing anything else about the ordered inputs to the other parties or even to a TTP.

The protocols proposed in [19–21,23] are shown to be secure only in the semi-honest model, that is, under the assumption that all parties follow the prescribed actions of the protocol while trying to extract as much information as possible from their view of the protocol run. In [17] the problem of malicious attackers, i.e. attackers that may deviate from the protocol, is solved for the two-party case. To the best of our knowledge, however, there are currently no multi-party ordered set reconciliation protocols which are secure in the malicious model. This is mainly due to the fact that a straightforward generalization of the two-party protocols is already highly inefficient for the semi-honest case [23]. The semi-honest multi-party protocols introduced in [23] therefore substantially differ in their design from the two-party protocols suggested in [19].

In this paper we propose multi-party protocols solving the reconciliation on ordered sets problem that are provably secure in the malicious model. Our constructions are based on the semantically secure, additively homomorphic Paillier cryptosystem [26] and a series of non-interactive zero-knowledge proofs to provide verifiable set operations. Here, we propose a new homomorphic linear equations proof which enables more efficient verifiable set operations than the ones previously proposed in [16]. In addition, we describe our implementation of the newly proposed protocols and evaluate their performance in comparison to the most efficient currently known semi-honest protocols proposed in [21].

2   Preliminaries

Adversary Models. In secure multi-party computation two adversary models are commonly used: the semi-honest and the malicious model. Both models assume the existence of pairwise encrypted and authenticated channels between the participating parties, such that external attackers do not have to be considered. A semi-honest adversary is an insider attacker that tries to infer as much (secret) information as possible from its view of a protocol run, but strictly follows the prescribed actions of the protocol. A malicious adversary is an insider attacker that can almost arbitrarily deviate from the protocol except refusal to participate in the protocol, manipulation of its own input, and protocol abortion. To prove that a protocol is privacy-preserving in the malicious model the simulation paradigm is used, which compares the real-world execution of the protocol to an ideal-world execution. In the ideal world, all parties provide their inputs to a trusted third party, which computes the correct output and provides the results to each party. In the real world, in addition to the protocol's correct output, the adversary learns all messages exchanged between the parties and all randomness generated during the execution of the protocol. One shows that it is possible to construct a simulator which, given the ideal output, can generate a transcript that is identical to the real protocol execution. If such a transcript can be generated using only the knowledge of the ideal execution, the protocol is privacy-preserving in the malicious model. For a formal definition see [4, 13].

Definition 1 (Ordered Sets and Ranking Functions [21]). *Let D be a set called the* domain. $(S, <) \in 2^D \times 2^{D \times D}$ *is called* ordered set *if $<$ is a strict total order on S. As a shorthand, we write $\{x_1 > ... > x_k\}$ for the ordered set $(\{x_1..., x_k\}, \{(x_j, x_i) \mid 1 \leq i < j \leq k\})$. The ranking function $rank_S : S \rightarrow \mathbb{N}$ is defined by $rank_S (x_i) = k - i + 1$.*

Definition 2 (Composition Schemes [21]). *Let $(S_1, <_1), ..., (S_n, <_n)$ be ordered sets. The ordered set $(S_1 \cap ... \cap S_n, \leq_{\{S_1,..,S_n\}})$ is the combined ordered set of $(S_1, <_1), ..., (S_n, <_n)$ w.r.t. f if $\leq_{\{S_1,..,S_n\}}$ is the order induced by the function $f : (S_1 \cap ... \cap S_n) \rightarrow \mathbb{R}$. The function f is called the* composition scheme. *The* minimum of ranks composition scheme (MR) *is defined by the function $f(x) = min \{rank_{S_1}(x), ..., rank_{S_n}(x)\}$. The* sum of ranks composition scheme (SR) *is defined by the function $f(x) = rank_{S_1}(x) + ... + rank_{S_n}(x)$.*

Definition 3 (Privacy-Preserving Reconciliation on Ordered Sets [21]). *A multi-party reconciliation protocol on ordered sets for an order composition scheme f (MPROS^f) is a multi-party protocol between n parties $P_1, ..., P_n$ each with an input $(S_i, <_i)$ of size k drawn from the same domain D. Upon completion of the protocol, each party learns (X, t) with:*

$$X = \underset{x \in (S_1 \cap ... \cap S_n)}{arg\ max} f(x) \qquad t = \underset{x \in (S_1 \cap ... \cap S_n)}{max} f(x)$$

where $arg\ max_{x \in D} f(x) = \{x \mid \forall y \in D : f(y) \leq f(x)\}$

A protocol run is said to be privacy-preserving in the semi-honest (the malicious) model iff no semi-honest (malicious) party learns anything about the inputs and preferences of the other parties, except what can be deduced from the output (X, t) of the protocol and his own private input set.

The Paillier Cryptosystem. In this paper, we make use of a threshold version of the probabilistic public-key cryptosystem proposed by Paillier [9, 12, 26]. The cryptosystem is additively homomorphic and semantically secure under computational assumptions. Let $E_{pk}(\cdot)$ be the encryption function with public key pk. In an additively homomorphic cryptosystem, there is an operation $+_h$ such that $E_{pk}(a + b) = E_{pk}(a) +_h E_{pk}(b)$ and $+_h$ can be computed efficiently given only $E_{pk}(a), E_{pk}(b)$, and pk. We denote the homomorphic summation by $\tilde{\sum}$.

A (t, n)-threshold cryptosystem is a cryptosystem with a public key pk and n private key shares $sk_1, ..., sk_n$. Using a private key share, a party can compute a *partial decryption* of a ciphertext. To successfully recover the plaintext of a given ciphertext, t of the n key shares are required to compute and combine t decryption shares to obtain the plaintext.

Encryption. $E_{pk}(m) \overset{def}{=} g^m r^N \bmod N^2$ for any plaintext $m \in \mathbb{Z}_N^*$, where $r \in \mathbb{Z}_N^*$ is selected uniformly at random.

Homomorphic Addition. For two ciphertexts $\alpha, \beta \in \mathbb{Z}_{N^2}$, the operation $+_h$ is given by $\alpha +_h \beta \overset{def}{=} \alpha \cdot \beta \bmod N^2$, where $\alpha, \beta \in \mathbb{Z}_{N^2}$.

Homomorphic Scalar Multiplication. For a ciphertext $\alpha \in \mathbb{Z}_{N^2}$ and a scalar $s \in \mathbb{Z}_N^*$, the operation $\times_h$ is defined by $s \times_h \alpha \overset{def}{=} \alpha^s \bmod N^2$.

Privacy-Preserving Multiset Operations. Our protocols make use of the privacy-preserving operations on multisets, i.e., sets in which elements may occur more than once, introduced by Kissner et al. [16]. In these operations a private input multiset $S_i = \{s_{i,1}, ..., s_{i,k}\}$ of party P_i is encoded by the polynomial $f_i(x) = \prod_{j=1}^{k} (x - s_{i,j})$. The coefficients of this polynomial are encrypted with an additively homomorphic cryptosystem.

Union: For an encrypted polynomial ϕ and a plaintext polynomial g, representing the two sets F and G of arbitrary size, a polynomial representation of the union $F \cup G$ can be computed by homomorphic polynomial multiplication: $\phi \times_h g$. The product contains all roots of f and g with the summed up multiplicity. From the decryption of $\phi \times_h g$ one cannot learn more information than from $F \cup G$, as proven in Theorem 1 of [16].

Intersection: For two encrypted polynomials ϕ, γ representing two sets F and G of equal size, the intersection can be computed by the term $\phi \times_h s +_h \gamma \times_h r$. Here, s and r are random polynomials of degree $deg(\phi)$. The roots of the result polynomial are those common to ϕ and γ (with minimum multiplicity) and thus represent the elements of $F \cap G$. Again, from the decryption of the resulting polynomial, one cannot learn more than from $F \cap G$ (Theorem 3 in [16]).

Set Reduction: For an encrypted polynomial γ representing a multiset G one can compute the element reduction $Rd_t(G)$ by the term $\sum_{i=0}^{t} \gamma^{(i)} \times_h F_i \times_h r_i$. Here, each r_i is chosen uniformly at random and each F_i is a fixed polynomial of degree i such that, i.e., $gcd(F_0, ..., F_t) = 1$. The result $Rd_t(G)$ contains all elements $a \in G$ with multiplicity $max\{b - t, 0\}$, if an element a has multiplicity b in G. Again, see [16] for an in-depth discussion of correctness and security.

Privacy-Preserving Reconciliation. The protocols for reconciliation on ordered sets proposed in [21] are based on the privacy-preserving set operations introduced above. In particular, the protocol for the minimum of ranks composition scheme works as follows. Let $S_i = \{s_{i,1} > ... > s_{i,k}\}$ be the input set of party P_i. Then, the protocol operates in rounds. In round $1 \leq l \leq k$ of the protocol, the parties compute $\bigcap_{i=1}^{n} \{s_{i,1}, ..., s_{i,l}\}$. If the resulting set is empty the parties continue with round $l + 1$. If the resulting set is non-empty, the resulting set contains the common elements of all parties with the maximum minimum of ranks value $k - l + 1$. The protocol for the sum of ranks composition scheme computes

$$Rd_t\Big(renc(S_1) \cup ... \cup renc(S_n)\Big) \cap (S_1 \cap ... \cap S_n).$$

Here, $renc\,(S_i)$ denotes an encoding of the multiset S_i in which each element occurs with the multitude indicated by its rank. I.e., the highest ranked element s_{ik} occurs k times while the lowest ranked element s_1 occurs only once. The details of the protocols as well as the proof of correctness and security in the semi-honest model can be found in [21]. We detail how our new protocols differ from these protocols in Sect. 4.

Zero-Knowledge Proofs of Knowledge. Suppose a prover P has knowledge of an x such that $(y, x) \in R$ for some relation R and a public value y. He wants to convince a verifier V of this knowledge without revealing anything but this fact. A protocol that realizes this functionality is called a zero-knowledge proof of knowledge (ZKPK) protocol. Any ZKPK protocol must satisfy three properties: First, it must be *correct,* i.e., if the prover knows x, then the prover can convince the verifier that he knows x. Second, it must be *sound,* i.e., without knowledge of x, a prover can not convince the verifier. Third, it must satisfy the property of *zero-knowledgeness,* i.e., the verifier learns nothing but the fact that P knows an x such that $(y, x) \in R$. For a more formal definition of these properties, see [13]. A well known form of ZKPK protocols are Σ-Protocols, which are interactive two-party protocols in which the verifier generates a random challenge. The so-called *Fiat-Shamir heuristic* [11] is an efficient generalization to the multi-party setting by replacing the challenge generated by the verifier by the result of a hash function. Those protocols are known as *non-interactive* ZKPK protocols. The security of Fiat-Shamir-based proof protocols is given in the random oracle model [1].

Proof of Plaintext Knowledge: In a proof of plaintext knowledge for the Paillier cryptosystem, a prover tries to prove to the verifier that he knows m, r such that $y = g^m \cdot r^N \bmod N^2$ for a known ciphertext y. Interactive variants of the plaintext knowledge proof for the Paillier cryptosystem were proposed in [5,6].

Proof of Correct Multiplication: Suppose two parties know the three ciphertexts α, β, γ. In the proof of correct multiplication, the prover shows that he knows the plaintext m of γ and that $m *_h \alpha = \beta$. Interactive variants of the correct multiplication proof for the Paillier cryptosystem were proposed in [5,6].

Proof of a Subset Relation Using Verifiable Shuffles: Consider a set of plaintext values D. In our setting, the prover selects a subset S of k distinct elements from D in an unknown order and sends encryptions in a verifiable manner to the other parties. More formally, we need a *verifiable shuffle protocol* [14,25]. In our setting, we use a protocol proposed by Nguyen et al. [25], since it can be applied directly in the Paillier cryptosystem, can be made *non-interactive* using the Fiat-Shamir heuristic and runs in linear time in the size of domain D.

Verifiable Threshold Decryption: In order to prove that a party correctly computed the partial decryption in a threshold version for the Paillier cryptosystem, we use an adaption of techniques by Fouque et al. [12].

3 Novel ZK-Proofs

We provide novel non-interactive ZK-Proofs that allow us to specify new protocols for verifiable set union, intersection, and reduction operations. In particular, we convert the interactive proof for plaintext knowledge and correct multiplication [5,6] into non-interactive ZKPK. We present a new ZKPK for homomorphic linear equations and show how this can be used to construct ZKPK for verifiable set operations. We show that these new ZKPKs are more efficient than the ones previously proposed in [16].

Proof of Plaintext Knowledge and Correct Multiplication. We turn the interactive ZKPK's proposed in [6] into *non-interactive* proofs using the *strong* variant of the Fiat-Shamir heuristic. The algorithms and detailed proofs for correctness, special soundness, and special honest-verifier zero-knowledge are given in the extended version of our paper [22].

Proof of a Homomorphic Linear Equation. Assume the following linear equation, where $\alpha_1, ..., \alpha_p, \beta$ are Paillier ciphertexts and $m_1...m_p$ are Paillier plaintexts $m_1 *_h \alpha_1 +_h ... +_h m_p *_h \alpha_p = \beta$. It is possible to construct a proof for the correctness of a homomorphic linear equation, where the scalar factors are only known to the verifier in encrypted form. For an equation with p linear factors we perform p plaintext knowledge proofs in parallel, together with an additional constraint that the given equation holds, similar to the construction proving correct multiplication.

Algorithm 1 lists the steps required to construct and verify the corresponding proof. α_i range over the ciphertext factors involved in the computation, β is the result of the equation, m_i are the secret scalar factors used in the multiplications, r_i the secret randomization factors used for encrypting those to γ_i, and pid_{P_i} is a random value assigned to each party. We use a single challenge, but $p+1$ commitments and $2p+1$ responses in our proof. The algorithms and detailed proofs for correctness, special soundness, and special honest-verifier zero-knowledge are given in the extended version of our paper [22].

Complexity: The proof consists of a hash, p random Paillier plaintexts (with random values) and an additional random value of size b. For p linear factors, we need to perform p binary exponentiations with a Paillier modulus N of size b, thus we have the computation complexities $O\left(p \cdot b^3\right)$.

Next, we show how to construct proofs for computations on polynomials. Basically, the proofs are based on parallel execution of several linear homomorphic equation proofs, but using a common challenge for all protocols. This is commonly referred to as And-Composition of proofs [3].

Proof of Correct Polynomial Operations. We start with the construction of proofs for the correct multiplication of polynomials. For a polynomial f let $E(f)$ denote the coefficient-wise encryption of f and let the corresponding Greek letter

Algorithm 1. Construction and verification of a linear equation proof

Specification:

$$ZKPK \left\{ \begin{matrix} m_1, ..., m_p \\ r_1, ..., r_p, R \end{matrix} \middle| \begin{matrix} [\alpha_1 *_h m_1 +_h ... +_h \alpha_p *_h m_p]_R = \beta \\ \wedge \quad \bigwedge_{i=1}^{p} \gamma_i = E(m_i, r_i) \end{matrix} \right\}$$

Construction:
  (1) Select random $m_i', r_i' \in \mathbb{Z}_N^*$ for $i \in \{1, .., p\}$ and $R' \in \mathbb{Z}_N^*$
  (2) Compute equation commitment $t_R = [\alpha_1 *_h m_1' +_h ... +_h \alpha_p *_h m_p']_{R'}$
  (3) Compute plaintext knowledge commitments $t_i = E(m_i', r_i')$
  (4) Get a challenge $c = h(pid_P, g, \alpha_1, ..., \alpha_p, \gamma_1, ..., \gamma_p, \beta, t_R, t_1, ..., t_p)$
  (5) For $i \in \{1, ..., p\}$, compute responses $m_i'' = m_i' - cm_i \bmod N$
      and $r_i'' = r_i' \cdot r_i^{-c} \bmod N$
  (6) Compute $R'' = R' \cdot R^{-c}$
  (7) Send $(c, m_1'', ..., m_p'', r_1'', ..., r_p'', R'')$

Verification:
  (1) Reconstruct equation commitment
      $t_R' = \beta^c [\alpha_1 *_h m_1'' +_h ... +_h \alpha_p *_h m_p'']_{R''}$
  (2) For $i \in \{1, ..., p\}$, reconstruct plaintext commitments $t_i' = g^{m_i''} r_i''^{N} \gamma_i^c$
  (3) Verify $h(pid_P, g, \alpha_1, ..., \alpha_p, \beta, t_R', t_1', ..., t_p') = c$

ϕ denote the tuple of the encrypted coefficients. Assume we want to prove that $\psi = f *_h \gamma$ for some f and that $\phi = E(f)$. To construct a corresponding proof, we consider the homomorphic polynomial multiplication using the standard long multiplication of polynomials with homomorphic operations. In this expanded form, we get a set of $deg(\psi) + 1 = deg(f) + deg(\gamma) + 1$ homomorphic linear constraints. We can denote this proof in general as listed below.

$$ZKPK \left\{ (f_0, ..., f_{deg(f)}) \middle| \begin{matrix} \bigwedge_{i=0}^{deg(\psi)} \left(\sum_{j=0}^{\tilde{\imath}} \gamma_j *_h f_{i-j} \right) = \psi_i \\ \wedge \quad \bigwedge_{i=0}^{deg(\phi)} \phi_i = E(f_i) \end{matrix} \right\}$$

Here, a coefficient f_j of a polynomial f is considered to be zero $if \; j > deg(f) \, or$ $j < 0$. This enables verifiable set union. The security and correctness of the proof directly follows from the correctness and security of the used sub-protocols for plaintext knowledge, correct multiplication and homomorphic linear equations. This approach can be extended to arbitrary linear expressions of polynomials:

$$\phi_1 *_h f_1 +_h ... +_h \phi_s *_h f_s = \psi$$

The construction is analogous to the construction above, only that we have s as many multiplications in each linear homomorphic constraint.

Verifiable Set Operations. We can construct verifiable set intersection, union, and reduction operations based on verifiable polynomial multiplication. Note that the efficiency of each of these operations depends on the efficiency of the

Table 1. Number of challenges, commitments, and responses for a verifiable polynomial multiplication where each input set consists of k elements

Protocol	Challenges	Commitments	Responses
Several multiplication proofs			
Kissner et al. [16]	$(k+1)^2$	$2k^2 + 4k + 2$	$3k^2 + 6k + 3$
Several linear equation proofs			
Our new approach	$2k+1$	$k^2 + 4k + 1$	$2k^2 + 6k + 3$

polynomial multiplication. Table 1 compares our new verifiable polynomial multi-plication to the approach proposed by Kissner et al. [16]. This previous approach is based on proving the correctness of all involved homomorphic multiplications. This requires the prover to sent all intermediate results to the verifier and pro-vide one proof per homomorphic multiplication. Our generalization of the mul-tiplication proof to arbitrary linear expressions enables more efficient ZKPK on polynomials.

4   MPROS Secure in the Malicious Model

In this section, we propose two new protocols for $MPROS^{MR}$ and $MPROS^{SR}$ and prove their security in the malicious model. Previous multi-party protocols [21,23,24] only provide security in the semi-honest model.

4.1   A Malicious Model Protocol for $MPROS^{MR}$

We first present a malicious model protocol for $MPROS^{MR}$. We use several core techniques to inhibit malicious behavior: Encryptions of all chosen random polynomials, the secret input sets, and all intermediate computation results are broadcasted to all other parties together with ZKPK's proving the correctness of the computations involving those secret values.

Protocol Description: The formal protocol description is shown in Algorithm 2. Encrypted values are denoted by lower case Greek letters, e.g., $\delta_{i,j}$ denotes the encrypted value of $d_{i,j}$. The protocol starts with the distribution of the input sets. Each party computes a shuffle of the domain, such that the first k ele-ments represent its input set and proves the correctness of the shuffle. When all encrypted shuffles have been distributed, the parties verify the proofs of all other parties. Whenever a proof verification fails, the protocol is aborted. In Step 2 and 3, all parties compute the set intersection of the polynomials $\phi_{i,k-t}$, verify the corresponding proofs $\Pi_{\text{INTERSECT},i}$ and decrypt the result π. In Step 4, the result is tested for emptiness. Based on the outcome, one of two actions is performed: If the result is non-empty, we have found the correct result and terminate the protocol. If the result is empty, we repeat the set intersection with a decreased threshold value t. For this purpose, each party adds the next highest ranked element $d_{i,k-t}$ to its current polynomial $\phi_{i,k-t}$ using a simple set union

---

Algorithm 2. Malicious model protocol for $MPROS^{MR}$

Setting: Parties $P_1, ..., P_n$ with ordered input sets, chosen from common domain D, $S_i = \{d_{i,1} > ... > d_{i,k}\}$, $i \in \{1, ..., n\}$. Each party P_i holds a key share for a (n, n)-threshold decryption scheme.

1. Initial Polynomial
   (a) Each party P_i $(i = 1, ..., n)$
      i. Computes an encrypted shuffle $(\delta_{i,1}, ..., \delta_{i,k}, ...)$ of the domain D where the first k elements denote the input set elements.
      ii. Broadcasts the shuffle and correctness proof $\Pi_{SHUFFLE,i}$ (see Sect. 2)
   (b) Each party P_i $(i \in \{1, ..., n\})$ for $j \in \{1, .., n\}$
      i. If $j \neq i$, verifies $\Pi_{SHUFFLE,j}$
      ii. Chooses random polynomial $r_{i,j,1}$ of degree 1
      iii. Computes and commits to $\rho_{i,j,1} = E_1(r_{i,j,1})$
2. Set Intersection (Initially $t = k - 1$. Let $\phi_{i,1} = \left(E(1), \delta_{i,1}^{-1}\right)$)
   (a) Each party P_i $(i = 1, ..., n)$.
      i. Opens the commitment to $\rho_{i,j,k-t}$
      ii. Computes and broadcasts $\gamma_i = \left[\sum_{j=0}^{n} (\phi_{j,k-t} *_h r_{i,j,k-t})\right]_r$
      iii. Broadcasts a proof $\Pi_{INTERSECT,i}$ that γ_i is correctly computed
   (b) Each party P_i $(i = 1, ..., n)$
      i. For $j \in \{1, .., n\} \setminus \{i\}$ verifies $\Pi_{INTERSECT,j}$
      ii. Calculates $\pi = \sum_{i=1}^{n} \gamma_i$
3. Decryption : All parties perform a malicious model threshold decryption of π and obtain the result polynomial p.
4. Emptiness Test / Set Union
   (a) Each party P_i $(i = 1, ..., n)$
      i. Computes the set of elements of S_i which are roots of p:
         $R = \{d \in S_i : (X - d)|p.\}$
      ii. If $R \neq \emptyset$, terminates the protocol with result $(R, t + 1)$
      iii. If $R = \emptyset$ and $t = 0$, terminates the protocol with $(\emptyset, 0)$
      iv. Computes and broadcasts $\phi_{i,k-t+1} = [\phi_{i,k-t} *_h (x - d_{i,k-t})]_r$
      v. Broadcasts a proof $\Pi_{UNION,i}$ that $\phi_{i,k-t+1}$ is correctly computed
   (b) Each party P_i $(i \in \{1, ..., n\})$ for $j \in \{1, .., n\}$
      i. If $j \neq i$, verifies $\Pi_{UNION,j}$
      ii. Chooses random polynomial $r_{i,j,k-t+1}$ of degree $k - t + 1$ and commit to $\rho_{i,j,k-t+1} = E_1(r_{i,j,k-t+1})$
   (c) Proceed with Step 2 using $t - 1$

---

operation, resulting in the polynomial $\phi_{i,k-t+1}$ for the next round. After the verification of the set union operation, the protocol returns to Step 2.

Correctness: We compute the function $Rd_t(S_1 \cap ... \cap S_n)$ as the semi-honest variants discussed in [21,23,24]. Assuming that the zero-knowledge proofs of knowledge are difficult to forge, each party is forced to perform the same computations as in the semi-honest variant of the protocol. Therefore the correctness results from [21] also apply to our malicious model variant.

Security in the Malicious Model

Setting: The ZK proof protocols are based on Σ-Protocols that have been converted into non-interactive protocols using the Fiat-Shamir heuristic. Since the verifier does not interact in the proof generation, it is sufficient to show special honest-verifier zero-knowledge for these protocols, see [13] for more details. We show the security of the protocol against at most $n-1$ attackers. This is achieved with the help of a broadcast of the ZKPK proofs to all $n-1$ other parties.

Table 2. The proofs used in Algorithm 2

$$\Pi_{SHUFFLE,i} = ZKPK \left\{ d_1, .., d_k \left| \{d_1, .., d_k\} \subseteq D \wedge \bigwedge_{i=1}^{k} \delta_i = E(d_i) \right. \right\}$$

$$\Pi_{INTERSECT,i} = ZKPK \left\{ r_{i,1}, ..., r_{i,n}, R \left| \begin{array}{c} \gamma_i = \left[\sum_{j=0}^{\tilde{n}} (\phi_j *_h r_{i,j})\right]_R \\ \wedge \quad \bigwedge_{l=0}^{n} \rho_{i,j} = E_1(r_{ij}) \end{array} \right. \right\}$$

$$\Pi_{UNION,i,t} = ZKPK \left\{ d_{i,k-t}, \phi_{i,k-t}, R \left| \begin{array}{c} \phi_{i,k-t+1} = [\phi_{i,k-t} *_h (x - d_{i,k-t})]_R \\ \wedge \quad \delta_{i,k-t} = E(d_{i,k-t}) \end{array} \right. \right\}$$

ZK-Proofs: Our protocol uses several types of proofs, all of which are listed in Table 2. The proofs for proving the correct set intersection $\Pi_{INTERSECT,i}$ and the proof for correct set union $\Pi_{UNION,i,t}$ directly follow from the proofs outlined in Sect. 3. Note that each union proof $\Pi_{UNION,i,t}$ requires a successful proof verification $\Pi_{UNION,i,t+1}$ with the previously used threshold value $t+1$. Furthermore, we require each party to prove that its chosen subset is part of the domain using a verifiable shuffle and compute a verifiable decryption as described in Sect. 2.

Solving the 0-Polynomial Problem: Malicious attackers can manipulate the protocol by inserting 0-polynomials in the protocol, i.e., polynomials where all coefficients are set to zero. Other parties can not detect these polynomials, as they only receive encrypted versions and by the semantic security of the cryptosystem it is infeasible to check if it encrypts a zero or not. We solve the problem in the following manner: The first coefficient of polynomials that are chosen by a party is always assumed to be a known encryption of 1 (E_1), compare Step 1.b.iii. and 4.b.ii. in Algorithm 2. Since all such computations are reblinded before they are sent to the other parties, this does not reduce the security of the protocol.

Simulation Proof.

Theorem 1. *Assuming that the additively homomorphic, threshold cryptosystem $E(\cdot)$ is semantically secure and the specified ZKPK's and proofs of correct decryption cannot be forged, then in the protocol in Algorithm 2, for any coalition Γ of at most $n-1$ colluding players, there is a player (or group of players) SIM operating in the ideal model, such that the views of the players in the ideal model are computationally indistinguishable from the views of the honest players and Γ in the real model.*

We give the algorithm for a simulator *SIM* in the ideal world that represents one or more honest participants and executes the above protocol with the set of potentially malicious and colluding parties $P_1, ..., P_l$. In addition, the simulator performs the ideal world protocol with the trusted third party *TTP*. The simulator *SIM* acts as a translator between the real world protocol and the ideal world protocol and acts as the honest parties $P_{l+1}, ..., P_n$ in the protocol with the malicious parties. The intuition of the simulation proof is as follows:

If we can generate all protocol messages from only the interaction with the trusted third party, which, in the ideal world, does not leak any information about the private inputs of parties $P_{l+1}, ..., P_n$, then the exchanged protocol messages can not contain more information, than the information provided in the ideal world, i. e., the output of an MPROS protocol, compare Definition 3. We give the simulator the power to extract values from ZKPK's which is a common approach in malicious model security proofs [4,13]. The algorithm for the simulator is given in Algorithm 3. The simulator starts by constructing *random* inputs to the real-world protocol, i.e., selecting a random ordered set of size k and constructing and sending the corresponding encryptions and proofs (Step 1). The random inputs are used in place of the real inputs of the honest parties, which ensures that no information is leaked in the first step.

After receiving the encryptions and the proofs from the malicious parties, the simulator then uses the extractors given in the soundness proofs of the zero-knowledge proof protocols to extract the private sets from the provided proofs (Step 2). This makes it possible to perform the ideal-world protocol with the TTP and the honest parties (Steps 3 and 4). After receiving the result of the protocol from the TTP, the simulator proceeds with the protocol execution in the real model until threshold value $t = m-1$ (Step 5). Then, it inserts a polynomial representation of the result into the real-world protocol execution by choosing the random polynomials $r_{i,j,m-1}$ accordingly (Step 6). Under the assumption of a semantically secure threshold cryptosystem, the views of the players in the ideal model given by the simulator are computationally indistinguishable from the views in the real model. The protocol output is given by Definition 3 and is the same for the ideal and the real model (Step 6).   □

Complexity Analysis. Let n denote the number of parties, k the number of inputs, b the bit size of the modulus, and D the domain of inputs. We have the computation complexity $O\left(\left(|D| + k^3 \cdot n\right) \cdot n \cdot b^3\right)$ for each party. The computations in the malicious model protocol are $O(n)$ more complex compared

---

Algorithm 3. Simulation Algorithm for $MPROS^{MR}$

---

1. For each simulated honest party $P_i \in \Phi$
   (a) Generate an ordered set of random values R_i of size k
   (b) Follow Step 1a) according to the protocol, using R_i as input
2. For each malicious party $P_i \in \Gamma$, extract from the received proof $\Pi_{SHUFFLE,i}$ the private ordered set S_i
3. Send the extracted ordered sets $\{S_i | P_i \in \Gamma\}$ to TTP
   Each honest party $P_i \in \Phi$ sends its set S_i to TTP
4. TTP computes and sends the following results to SIM and the honest players

$$A = \operatorname*{argmax}_{x \in (S_1 \cap \ldots \cap S_n)} \left\{ \min_{1 \leq i \leq n} \operatorname{rank}_i(x) \right\}$$

$$m = \operatorname*{max}_{x \in (S_1 \cap \ldots \cap S_n)} \left\{ \min_{1 \leq i \leq n} \operatorname{rank}_i(x) \right\}$$

5. For $t = k - 1, ..., m$ follow the protocol (Steps 1b-4) for each simulated honest party $P_i \in \Phi$ with input R_i and each malicious party $P_i \in \Gamma$ with input S_i
6. For $t = m - 1$ and each simulated honest party $P_i \in \Phi$ and every $P_j \in (\Phi \cup \Gamma)$
   (a) Select random polynomial s of size $(k - (m - 1) - |A|)$
   (b) Compute polynomial $p = \prod_{a \in A} (x - a) \cdot s$
   (c) Select the remaining polynomials $r_{i,j}$ (of the honest parties) such that $\sum_{i=1}^{n} f_{i,m-1} \left(\sum_{j=1}^{n} r_{i,j,m-1} \right) = p$. See [16], Lemma 2 for a proof that these $r_{i,j}$ exist. Commit to the random polynomials $r_{i,j,m-1}$.
7. Follow and complete the protocol for each party

---

to [21], because we have to verify $n - 1$ proofs in each step. The shuffle proof verification (which depends on the size of the domain D), increases the complexity by a factor of $O\left(|D| \cdot n \cdot b^3\right)$ for $n - 1$ such verifications. The communication of the protocol is tightly coupled with the computation, since each computation needs to be proven by a corresponding proof sent over the network. The size of all messages exchanged over the network is therefore bound by $O\left(\left(|D| + k^3 \cdot n\right) \cdot n \cdot b\right)$. Compared to the semi-honest variants [21], the communication complexity is increased due to the additional transmission of ZK-proofs.

4.2 A Malicious Model Protocol for $MPROS^{SR}$

Similar to the minimum of ranks protocol, a malicious model protocol for ordered set reconciliation with the *sum of ranks* composition scheme can be constructed. The most important difference between the construction of the sum of ranks protocol and the minimum of ranks protocol is that the former also uses set reduction. To compute a set reduction, we need a sum of polynomial multiplications which can be proven secure using the usual zero-knowledge proof construction

Table 3. Overview of MPROS protocols proposed in this paper or previous work

Problem	Model	Comp./Comm. Complexity
$MPROS^{MR}$	Semi-honest, standard model, [21]	$O\left(k^3 \cdot n \cdot b^3\right)$
		$O\left(k^2 \cdot n \cdot b\right)$
	Malicious, random oracle model, Sect. 4	$O\left((|D| + k^3 \cdot n) \cdot n \cdot b^3\right)$
		$O\left((|D| + k^3 \cdot n) \cdot n \cdot b\right)$
$MPROS^{SR}$	Semi-honest, standard model, [21]	$O\left(k^6 \cdot n^4 \cdot b^3\right)$
		$O\left(k^3 \cdot n^3 \cdot b\right)$
	Malicious, random oracle model, Sect. 4	$O\left((|D| + k^5 \cdot n^4) \cdot k \cdot n \cdot b^3\right)$
		$O\left((|D| + k^5 \cdot n^4) \cdot k \cdot n \cdot b\right)$

described in Sect. 3. Otherwise, the protocol is similar to the semi-honest constructions of Neugebauer et al. [21,23,24]. Using the techniques from this paper, a protocol for the sum of ranks composition scheme with computation complexity $O\left((|D| + n^4 \cdot k^5) \cdot n \cdot k \cdot b^3\right)$ and $O\left((|D| + n^4 \cdot k^5) \cdot n \cdot k \cdot b\right)$ communication complexity can be constructed. The formal protocol description is given in the extended version of our paper. Table 3 summarizes the results in theory. All four protocols are polynomial-time bounded with respect to the number of parties n and inputs k.

5 Implementation and Evaluation

Implementation. Our core implementation is written in Java version 1.7.0. We used the GNU Multiple Precision Arithmetic Library (GMP) version 5.0.5 to efficiently compute expensive arithmetic operations such as modular exponentiation using a native C++ library with Java Native Interface (JNI). We implemented the Paillier cryptosystem as the additively homomorphic cryptosystem. Secure channels are established via SSL, threshold key shares are predistributed, and communication is asynchronous. We implemented our ZK-framework for the Paillier cryptosystem, both MPROS protocols presented in [21] as well as our malicious model variants of $MPROS^{MR}$ and $MPROS^{SR}$, see Sect. 4. We evaluate the performance of all four MPROS protocols denoted as MR, MR-zk, SR, and SR-zk with respect to computation and communication overhead. Therefore, we measure the runtime and count the number of bytes transmitted for each party. Whenever possible, we used parallelization by simultaneous computation in threads — depending on the number of available CPU cores.

Test Environment. The setup consists of 10 identical systems each with a 2.93 GHz i7 CPU 870 and 16 GB RAM running a 64-bit Linux with kernel version 3.2.0. All systems are connected via secure channels using TLS. Keys are distributed at start-up. We tested all protocols with up to 10 parties and varied the number of inputs. We tested for a keysize of 1024 and 2048 bit.

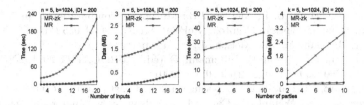

Fig. 1. Comparison of MR-zk and MR for $n = 5$ and $k = 5$

Test Results. In Fig. 1, we present our results for the minimum of ranks with a reasonable keysize of $b = 1024$ bit varying the number of parties or the number of inputs for $n = 5$ and $k = 5$. As expected from theory, the runtime for the malicious model variant MR-zk is higher than for the semi-honest variant MR. For an input domain D of 200 elements and up to 20 inputs k, we have a runtime of up to 4 min for MR-zk and up to 12 s for MR. Also, the amount of data transmitted is higher for the malicious model variants with, e.g., 2.5 MB for MR-zk compared to 0.5 MB for MR in case of 20 inputs. Both protocols MR and MR-zk show linear behavior with respect to the number of parties n due to the parallelized proof verification. The results for the sum of ranks composition scheme can be found in the extended version of our paper. As a conclusion, the notion of a stronger security model comes at the price of slower protocols and the need to transmit more data. The protocol MR-zk is roughly twenty times slower than MR and the transmitted data is ten times higher than in case of MR.

6 Conclusion

We designed and implemented the first multi-party protocols for ordered set reconciliation which are provably secure in the malicious model. Our security proofs are based on a novel framework for secure computation on Paillier-encrypted polynomials which is resistant against malicious attackers. Our theoretical analysis of the asymptotic complexity of our new protocols is confirmed by the practical evaluation of our implementation.

References

1. Bellare, M., Rogaway, P.: Random oracles are practical. In: Computer and Communications Security - CCS 1993, pp. 62–73. ACM (1993)
2. Ben-Or, M., Goldwasser, S., Wigderson, A.: Completeness theorems for non-cryptographic fault-tolerant distributed computation. In: ACM Symposium on Theory of Computing - STOC 1988, pp. 1–10. ACM (1988)
3. Camenisch, J., Stadler, M.: Proof systems for general statements about discrete logarithms. Technical report, ETH Zürich (1997)
4. Canetti, R.: Security and composition of multiparty cryptographic protocols. J. Cryptology **13**, 143–202 (1998)

5. Cramer, R., Damgård, I., Nielsen, J.B.: Multiparty computation from threshold homomorphic encryption. Cryptology ePrint Archive, 2000/055 (2000)
6. Cramer, R., Damgård, I., Nielsen, J.B.: Multiparty computation from threshold homomorphic encryption. In: Pfitzmann, B. (ed.) EUROCRYPT 2001. LNCS, vol. 2045, pp. 280–300. Springer, Heidelberg (2001)
7. De Cristofaro, E., Tsudik, G.: Experimenting with fast private set intersection. In: Katzenbeisser, S., Weippl, E., Camp, L.J., Volkamer, M., Reiter, M., Zhang, X. (eds.) TRUST 2012. LNCS, vol. 7344, pp. 55–73. Springer, Heidelberg (2012)
8. Cristofaro, E., Tsudik, G.: On the performance of certain private set intersection protocols. Cryptology ePrint Archive, Report 2012/054 (2012)
9. Damgård, I., Jurik, M.: A generalisation, a simplification and some applications of Paillier's probabilistic public-key system. In: Kim, K. (ed.) PKC 2001. LNCS, vol. 1992, pp. 119–136. Springer, Heidelberg (2001)
10. Damgård, I., Pastro, V., Smart, N., Zakarias, S.: Multiparty computation from somewhat homomorphic encryption. In: Safavi-Naini, R., Canetti, R. (eds.) CRYPTO 2012. LNCS, vol. 7417, pp. 643–662. Springer, Heidelberg (2012)
11. Fiat, A., Shamir, A.: How to prove yourself: practical solutions to identification and signature problems. In: Odlyzko, A.M. (ed.) Advances in Cryptology-CRYPTO 1986. LNCS, vol. 263, pp. 186–194. Springer, Heidelberg (1986)
12. Fouque, P.-A., Pointcheval, D.: Threshold cryptosystems secure against chosen-ciphertext attacks. In: Boyd, C. (ed.) ASIACRYPT 2001. LNCS, vol. 2248, pp. 351–368. Springer, Heidelberg (2001)
13. Goldreich, O.: Foundations of cryptography: Basic applications, vol. 2. Cambridge University Press, Cambridge (2004)
14. Groth, J.: A verifiable secret shuffle of homomorphic encryptions. J. Cryptology 23, 546–579 (2002)
15. Huang, Y., Evans, D., Katz, J.: Private set intersection: are garbled circuits better than custom protocols. In: NDSS (2012)
16. Kissner, L., Song, D.: Privacy-preserving set operations. In: Shoup, V. (ed.) CRYPTO 2005. LNCS, vol. 3621, pp. 241–257. Springer, Heidelberg (2005)
17. Mayer, D., Wetzel, S.: Verifiable private equality test: enabling unbiased 2-party reconciliation on ordered sets in the malicious model. In: 7th Symposium on Information, Computer and Communications Security, ASIACCS. ACM (2012)
18. Mayer, D.A., Neugebauer, G., Meyer, U., Wetzel, S.: Enabling fair and privacy-preserving applications using reconciliation protocols on ordered sets. In: IEEE Sarnoff Symposium 2011, pp. 1–6. IEEE (2011)
19. Meyer, U., Wetzel, S.: Distributed privacy-preserving policy reconciliation. In: ICC 2007, pp. 1342–1349. IEEE (2007)
20. Meyer, U., Wetzel, S., Ioannidis, S.: New advances on privacy-preserving policy reconciliation. Cryptology ePrint Archive, 2010/064 (2010)
21. Neugebauer, G., Brutschy, L., Meyer, U., Wetzel, S.: Design and implementation of privacy-preserving reconciliation protocols. In: 6th PAIS. ACM (2013)
22. Neugebauer, G., Brutschy, L., Meyer, U., Wetzel, S.: Privacy-preserving multi-party reconciliation secure in the malicious model (extended version). Cryptology ePrint Archive, Report 2013/655 (2013)
23. Neugebauer, G., Meyer, U., Wetzel, S.: Fair and privacy-preserving multi-party protocols for reconciling ordered input sets. In: Burmester, M., Tsudik, G., Magliveras, S., Ilić, I. (eds.) ISC 2010. LNCS, vol. 6531, pp. 136–151. Springer, Heidelberg (2011)

24. Neugebauer, G., Meyer, U., Wetzel, S.: Fair and privacy-preserving multi-party protocols for reconciling ordered input sets (extended version). Cryptology ePrint Archive, Report 2010/512 (2011)

25. Nguyen, L., Safavi-Naini, R., Kurosawa, K.: Verifiable shuffles: a formal model and a paillier-based efficient construction with provable security. In: Jakobsson, M., Yung, M., Zhou, J. (eds.) ACNS 2004. LNCS, vol. 3089, pp. 61–75. Springer, Heidelberg (2004)

26. Paillier, P.: Public-key cryptosystems based on composite degree residuosity classes. In: Stern, J. (ed.) EUROCRYPT 1999. LNCS, vol. 1592, pp. 223–238. Springer, Heidelberg (1999)

27. Yao, A.C.: Protocols for secure computations. In: Symposium on Foundations of Computer Science - SFCS 1982, pp. 160–164. IEEE (1982)

Differentially Private Smart Metering with Battery Recharging

Michael Backes[1,2] and Sebastian Meiser[2](✉)

[1] Center for IT-Security, Privacy and Accountability (CISPA),
Saarbrücken, Germany
[2] Saarland University, Saarbrücken, Germany
`meiser@cs.uni-saarland.de`

Abstract. The energy industry has recently begun using smart meters to take fine-grained readings of energy usage. These smart meters enable flexible time-of-use billing, forecasting, and demand response, but they also raise serious user privacy concerns. We propose a novel technique for provably hiding sensitive power consumption information in the overall power consumption stream. Our technique relies on a rechargeable battery that is connected to the household's power supply. This battery is used to modify the household's power consumption by adding or subtracting noise (i.e., increasing or decreasing power consumption), in order to establish strong privacy guarantees in the sense of differential privacy. To achieve these privacy guarantees in realistic settings, we first investigate the influence of, and the interplay between, capacity and throughput bounds that batteries face in reality. We then propose an integrated method based on noise cascading that allows for recharging the battery on-the-fly so that differential privacy is retained, while adhering to capacity and throughput constraints, and while keeping the additional consumption of energy induced by our technique to a minimum.

1 Introduction

The energy industry has recently begun using smart meters to take fine-grained readings of energy usage, enabling flexible time-of-use billing, forecasting, and demand response [9]. Among enabling dynamic tariffs, the fine-grained metering of energy consumption enables more accurate forecasts, which is expected to lead to an overall saving of energy. Smart metering is currently being widely promoted in the United States, European Union, and Asia as part of the modernization of the electronic grid [1,2]; to this end, 4.3 billion dollars has been allocated by the U.S government for the smart grids [22], with similar programs in progress in the EU and Asia.

In addition to all these undisputed advantages, smart meters also raise serious user privacy concerns [5]: Smart meters provide highly accurate consumption data to the corresponding electricity provider. These data naturally include personal, privacy-sensitive data, e.g., information about when certain devices were active.

J. Garcia-Alfaro et al. (Eds.): DPM 2013 and SETOP 2013, LNCS 8247, pp. 194–212, 2014.
DOI: 10.1007/978-3-642-54568-9_13, © Springer-Verlag Berlin Heidelberg 2014

If metering is performed sufficiently long in small time intervals, personal information can be disaggregated from the overall consumption stream. For instance, non-intrusive appliance load monitoring techniques [16,19,20] already allow for identifying common electronic devices such as personal computers, laser printers, or light bulbs in the overall consumption stream [8], and even to tell apart different TV programs [15].

To address these privacy concerns, privacy-aware solutions for smart metering are currently receiving increasing attention both in the research community and in ongoing standardization processes, e.g., [24]. In fact, the current absence of accepted solutions to tackle these privacy concerns caused a deadlock in the mandatory deployment of smart meters in the Netherlands [10], because of the common belief that smart metering is necessarily privacy-invasive. In this paper, we join the line of research that is working on changing this belief: we present a privacy-aware technique for smart metering that achieves strong privacy guarantees while simultaneously preserving the promises of smart metering.

1.1   Our Contributions

We propose a novel technique for provably hiding sensitive power consumption information in the overall power consumption stream. Our technique relies on a *rechargeable* battery that is connected to the household's power supply, and that appropriately modifies the overall consumption stream by suitably adding or subtracting noise, in order to establish strong privacy guarantees in the sense of differential privacy.

In addition to economic considerations, any solution must respect the fact that a battery adheres to hard resource constraints, such as its capacity (bounding the overall amount of energy that can be stored) and its throughput (bounding the amount of energy that can be charged/retrieved within a given time interval). Moreover, a battery will naturally get depleted over time if it constantly provides energy that is used as noise; a depleted battery will eventually put all privacy guarantees at stake. These limitations in particular render existing general-purpose approaches infeasible, because they typically require higher capacity and throughput than what a real-life battery can offer; moreover privacy-aware battery recharging is not considered in these approaches.

To achieve strong privacy guarantees in such realistic settings, we propose a novel technique for provably hiding sensitive power consumption information in the overall power consumption stream, using a rechargeable battery as a buffer and applying Laplacian noise to the consumption itself by either providing (discharging) or consuming (charging) energy by the battery. We first investigate the influence of, and the interplay between, capacity and throughput bounds of the battery to the overall approach (while still ignoring battery recharging issues), and develop a technique that achieves privacy guarantees in such resource-bounded settings.

We subsequently explore the more involved case of recharging the battery. The complication which arises here is that recharging corresponds to additional energy consumption, which is observable to the adversary by assumption.

We propose an integrated method that allows for recharging the battery on-the-fly so that differential privacy is retained, while adhering to capacity and throughput constraints, and while keeping the additional consumption of energy induced by our technique to a minimum. The central idea is to follow a novel cascading approach for generating differentially private noise: we consider the added noise for recharging the battery as a function that one makes differentially private by appropriately adding (a much smaller amount of) noise. To avoid that this small amount of noise is observable, we impose the assumption that this small additional energy consumption can be hidden in the overall consumption stream. Among other options, this can be achieved by continuously drawing a small, constant amount of energy that is sufficient for the recharging process, and by discarding all energy that exceeds the actual noise demand for recharging the battery in a differentially private manner.[1]

We show that meaningful differential privacy guarantees in such resource-bounded settings can be achieved, in particular using privacy-aware battery recharging. More precisely we focus on a simplistic model that captures all aspects necessary for analyzing the benefits of privacy-aware battery-recharging in smart metering. The privacy guarantee is based on hiding individual device activations in a stream of smart meter data. A more comprehensive model that additionally captures activation patterns of devices over several timeslots or the privacy of consumer behavior patterns is considered future work. Moreover, we provide a correspondence between the parameters of the battery such as capacity and throughput with the obtained privacy guarantees, and we evaluate the applicability of our techniques by means of examples.

1.2 Further Related Work

Privacy concerns in smart metering have been studied in several existing works in the recent past. Anderson and Fuloria [5,6] analyze the security economics of electricity metering, in particular the conflicting interests among stakeholders. Quinn [25] and Cavoukian et al. [9] investigate legal aspects of smart meters. The privacy of billing is investigated by Danezis et al. [18,27] and Molina-Markham et al. [23]. They in particular identify the private information that current meters might leak, and propose protocol adaptations for anonymizing individual measurements. In contrast to our work, these works require a trusted third party for anonymization, as well as changes in the existing communication protocols; moreover, in contrast to differential privacy guarantees, the resulting privacy assurances and the overall consequences are less clear. Similarly, Garcia and Jacobs [14] propose to use homomorphic encryption to achieve privacy for individual measurements, but the lack of a proper perturbation of the aggregate does not make the result differentially private, and the resulting privacy interpretations are again unclear.

---

[1] We stress that we wish to avoid wasting any energy in general. Our solution discards only the small amount of energy that arises for generating the noise of the battery recharging process.

Prior work on differential privacy in smart metering or on the smart use of batteries to achieve privacy guarantees comprises [3, 4, 11, 13, 18, 21, 26, 28, 29].

The paper that we consider most closely related to ours is the promising contribution of Acs et al. [4]. They were first to propose the smart use of a battery in order to achieve and rigorously show differential privacy guarantees. In contrast to our work, they do not consider battery recharging, and hence only obtain meaningful privacy guarantees if battery exhaustion is not an issue, and hence if metering is performed over a short period of time. Moreover, the magnitude of noise that they apply in their Laplacian technique depends on which appliances will be activated in the stream in the future, which only works in settings in which future activations can be accurately predicted, or at least reasonably estimated.

Papers that strive for differential privacy guarantees, yet without considering a battery (and hence in particular without the corresponding benefits gained from privacy-friendly recharging) include [3, 11, 26, 28]. Acs and Castelluccia [3] use aggregation over a large number of smart meters, add noise to the smart meter output, and encrypt the result before delivery to the energy provider. Danezis et al. [11] propose to add noise to customer bills to hide the user consumption behavior. Rastogi and Nath [26] pursue a similar approach but add noise in a distributed manner to improve performance. These approaches require the currently deployed smart meters to be replaced by new, provably trustworthy ones. Shi et al. [28] investigate untrusted aggregators of data. Their approach induces a separation between billing and the actual consumption of electricity; this allows for cheating behaviors, e.g., by applying noise with a slightly positive attitude, corresponding to seemingly increased energy consumption.

The use of a battery for privacy-preserving smart metering is discussed in [21, 29]. Varodayan and Khisti [29] consider a simplistic model where both the battery and the load of the appliances have Boolean state; differential privacy is not considered there. McLaughlin et al. [21] propose to radically smooth the consumption level to counter some common techniques for non-intrusive appliance load monitoring techniques. We consider this a promising approach; however, it currently still lacks any formalized privacy guarantees.

1.3   Outline of the Paper

In Sect. 2, we review the concept and the definition of differential privacy. Section 3 presents our model of privacy-aware smart metering in the presence of a resource-bounded battery. Section 4 investigates differential privacy guarantees in such resource-bounded settings, yet without taking battery recharging into account. Section 5 proposes our technique for privacy-aware battery recharging, and establishes corresponding differential privacy guarantees. Section 6 highlights the relationship between the individual parameters (such as the battery's resource constraints and measurement times) and the obtained privacy guarantees, and explores two concrete use cases. Section 7 discusses our guarantees and the practical feasibility of our approach. Section 8 concludes.

2   Preliminaries

In this paper we use a variant of *differential privacy*, as introduced in [12], as a measurement for the amount of private information leaked by a smart meter. Differential privacy was originally invented as a measurement for the amount of information leaked by answering a statistical query to a database. The notion of differential privacy that we use is *approximate differential privacy*, as introduced in [13]. In contrast to differential privacy, approximate differential privacy allows for an additional error δ.

In the original setting of statistical databases, (approximate) differential privacy intuitively ensures that adding a single entry to the database (or deleting one from it) does not significantly change the answer given to differentially private statistical queries. Usually this is achieved by adding noise to the output. From observing the (noisy) answer to the query, a passive observer cannot determine whether a specific entry is included in the data set or not, no matter which additional information an observer might possess about other entries.

The main difference between the data base setting and the smart meter setting is that we are not interested in single readings of a smart meter, or, more formally, single applications of a function to a specific data set. Instead, we wish to apply a function to a *stream* of data. We hence extend the basic definition of (approximate) differential privacy to streams in a standard way, similar to [17].

Definition 1 ((ϵ, δ)-Differential Privacy on Streams). *A probabilistic algorithm $F : \mathcal{P}(\mathcal{D}) \to \mathbb{R}$ for a set $\mathcal{D}$ provides (ϵ, δ)-differential privacy on streams if for all (possibly countably infinite) streams Φ, Φ' of sets $\mathcal{D}_k, \mathcal{D}'_k \subseteq \mathcal{D}$, differing in at most one element $d \in \mathcal{D}$ at one point i and all sets S of finite and countably infinite streams over $\mathbb{R}$,*

$$Pr[F(\Phi) \in S] \leq e^\epsilon \cdot Pr[F(\Phi') \in S] + \delta,$$

where with $F(\Phi)$ we denote the stream we get when applying F to each element of the stream Φ individually. The probability is taken over the randomness of F.

The smart meter measures the energy load sum in every time interval, so $\mathcal{D}$ corresponds directly to the set of all devices, while $\mathcal{D}_k$ and $\mathcal{D}'_k$ correspond to the devices active in a particular time slot.

3   Privacy-Aware Smart Metering

In this section we present our model of privacy-aware smart metering by means of a battery. We introduce further notation used in the paper, specify the notion of a household, and define the information gained by the smart meter. We finally define two constraints that we focus on in this paper: the battery's resources *throughput* and *capacity*.

Definitions:

Δt Time interval between measurements.

t_i Point in time defined by $t_i = t_0 + i \cdot \Delta t$.

$\mathcal{D}$ Set of all possible devices.

$\mathcal{D}_i$ Set of all active devices in i'th timeslot.

Φ Stream of active devices $\mathcal{D}_1, \mathcal{D}_2, \ldots$

$f(\mathcal{D}_i)$ Consumption of all devices in $\mathcal{D}_i$.

$F(\mathcal{D}_i)$ Noisy version of f; no resource bounds.

$F_b(\mathcal{D}_i)$ F with throughput bounds, and ≥ 0.

$\mathbb{F}(\mathcal{D}_i)$ F with capacity/throughput bounds.
= load measured by the smart meter.

$bl(i)$ Battery level at time t_i.

$\Delta bl(i)$ Battery charging/discharging in step i.

Δf Sensitivity of the function f.

Fig. 1. Notation overview, not including notation for privacy-aware battery recharging (Sect. 5).

3.1 Notation

A household, together with its appliances, is represented by a set of possibly active devices $\mathcal{D}$. We assume this set to be finite, fixed and known to adversaries, i.e., we are able to provide strong privacy guarantees even if $\mathcal{D}$ is known to the adversary. A smart meter measures the energy load on a regular basis. We denote the time interval between two measurements of the smart meter with Δt. Thus, for our model it suffices to consider a starting time t_0 and times $t_i = t_0 + i \cdot \Delta t$ for all natural numbers $i \in \mathbb{N}$.

We assume for simplicity that devices can only be activated/deactivated at times t_i. Thus, a device can be either active (consuming energy) or inactive (not consuming energy) throughout the whole interval. We denote the devices that are active in between t_{i-1} and t_i as $\mathcal{D}_i \subseteq \mathcal{D}$. We write $\Phi = [\mathcal{D}_1, \mathcal{D}_2, \ldots]$ for the list/stream of active devices over time. This assumption does not weaken our guarantees: if a device is only partially active in between two time slots, its consumption will be lower (and deviate from the expected consumption), which makes it harder to link the information to the device.

The consumption function $f : \mathcal{D} \to \mathbb{R}$ assigns to each device $d \in \mathcal{D}$ the amount of energy load it consumes during one time slot (of length Δt). We assume that the consumption of devices d does not vary over time, so $f(d)$ is independent of the time slot i in which the device is active. Although this simplification is in contrast to tome attacks that rely on specific patterns of devices, we can model devices with varying consumption for different time slots by adding one device for each consumption level. The net consumption of all devices in a set $X \subseteq \mathcal{D}$ is expressed by leveraging the function f to the powerset of $\mathcal{D}$, i.e., $f : \mathcal{P}(\mathcal{D}) \to \mathbb{R}$, with $f(X) = \sum_{d \in X} f(d)$.

This quantity is the final output the smart meter can read if no noise is added. To achieve differential privacy, we add noise to the output of f. Without considering the limitations of our battery at this stage, we define a probabilistic function $F : \mathcal{P}(\mathcal{D}) \to \mathbb{R}$ with $F(X) = f(X) + r$ with $r \leftarrow Lap\left(\frac{\Delta f}{\epsilon}\right)$, i.e., where r is the noise we add to $f(X)$.

In our model this noise is drawn from a battery. We denote the battery level at the end of a time slot i (i.e., at time t_i) with $bl(i)$. Thus, the change during a time slot is denoted $\Delta bl(i) = bl(i) - bl(i-1)$ (Fig. 1).

3.2 Modeling Throughput Restrictions

A battery's throughput denotes the amount of energy we can draw out of the battery or recharge into it during one time slot. Since we use the battery only for generating the Laplacian noise that we add to the net consumption, this means that the throughput constitutes an inherent limit for the amount of noise that can be added in one step. For simplicity reasons the battery behavior is considered linear, i.e., the throughput is independent of its current energy level. In practice this can be achieved, e.g., by using a slightly larger battery and ensuring that it is does not reach the non-linear zones.

The Laplacian noise added by F can, although with small probability, reach values of arbitrary magnitude, which cannot be achieved in deployed solutions. We thus define a *throughput-respecting* function F_b based on F that takes into account the throughput bound b of our battery. Moreover, we extend F_b to its *0-bounded variant* $\underline{F}_b$ by capping the load function for the smart meter at 0; this models that we do not permit to sell, discard or waste energy for economical reasons, which in particular excludes trivial approaches that consume enormous amounts of energy to boost the application of noise.[2]

Definition 2 (Throughput-Respecting and 0-Bounded Variant of F).
Given a function F with $F(x) = f(x) + R$ for a deterministic function f and a random variable R. Given a bound for the throughput b, we define the throughput-respecting variant F_b of F as follows:

$$F_b(x) = \begin{cases} F(x) & \text{if } |R| \le b \\ f(x) + b & \text{if } R > b \\ f(x) - b & \text{if } -R > b. \end{cases}$$

We define the 0-bounded variant $\underline{F}_b$ of F_b as $\underline{F}_b(x) = \max(0, F_b(x))$.

3.3 Adding Capacity Restrictions

A battery not only limits the energy output during a specific time interval Δt, but also the total amount of stored energy: its capacity. For the sake of simplicity we consider the capacity to be a fixed value c that does not change over time and that also does not depend on the load drained out of the battery.[3]

---

[2] Selling electricity would be an alternative. However, an accurate treatment would additionally require a detailed cost model; moreover selling electricity after drawing it from the provider is typically not economical. We thus do not further consider this case.

[3] In practice, the amount of energy that a battery can provide usually is slightly smaller when under heavy load; we ignore this here.

The actual output we provide and that is being transmitted by the smart meter depends on the battery's capacity: If the battery is exhausted or fully charged, we naturally cannot add noise in the respective direction to the net load of our devices anymore. Building upon F_b as in Definition 2, we define an overall, *bounded mechanism* $\mathbb{F}$ that, starting with an initial battery level $bl(0)$, adds noise only as long as the capacity is not exceeded in either direction. As soon as the capacity is exceeded, $\mathbb{F}$ stops adding noise and output the net demand f of our devices instead. The output of $\mathbb{F}$ constitutes the output that is transmitted to the energy provider by the smart meter.

Definition 3 (Bounded Mechanism). *Given a function F with $F(x) = f(x) + R$ for a deterministic function f and a random variable R, a capacity bound c and a throughput bound b, we define the corresponding* bounded mechanism $\mathbb{F}$ *as follows, where $bl(i-1)$ is the battery level before step i, R_i the noise added by $\underline{F}_b$ during step i and $s_k = \sum\limits_{j=1}^{k} R_j$ the sum of all noise added until step k:*

$$\mathbb{F}(\mathcal{D}_i) = \begin{cases} f(\mathcal{D}_i) & \text{if } \exists k \leq i.\ s_k > c - bl(0) \vee -s_k > bl(0) \\ \underline{F}_b(\mathcal{D}_i) & \text{otherwise.} \end{cases}$$

The new battery level is $bl(i) := bl(i-1) + (\mathbb{F}(\mathcal{D}_i) - f(\mathcal{D}_i))$.

As soon as the capacity is exceeded, we are facing a situation where our privacy guarantees are at stake. We can, however, give an upper bound for the probability that this happens and integrate it into the overall privacy result that we derive in the upcoming section.

4 Privacy-Aware Smart Metering (Without Battery Recharging)

In this section we investigate the privacy guarantees of our bounded mechanism $\mathbb{F}$, i.e., the privacy guarantees that we obtain in a resource-bounded scenario. To this end, we investigate which probabilities influence the statistical distances between F and $\underline{F}_b$ (the influence of throughput constraints) as well as between $\underline{F}_b$ and $\mathbb{F}$ (the influence of capacity constraints), and develop concrete bounds for these probabilities, depending only on the throughput and capacity values of the battery as well as the magnitude of the noise (specified by Δf and ϵ_1). Finally, we combine these results in order to show that $\mathbb{F}$ is (ϵ_1, δ_1)-differentially private for an arbitrary ϵ_1 and for concrete bounds for δ_1, which depend on the constraints of our battery and the chosen value for ϵ_1. We stress that aside from the fact that the battery can be charged when positive noise is added, battery "recharging", i.e., restoring the battery status to a secure value, is not considered in this section. Thus, we can reach situations in which the battery gets depleted (then yielding trivial privacy guarantees with ϵ_1 or δ_1 greater than 1). Battery recharging, and the benefits that can be drawn from it, are addressed in Sect. 5.

4.1 Differential Privacy and Statistical Distance

We start by exploring the relation between the statistical distance of two functions and differential privacy. First, recall that if our battery was unbounded, we could simply realize the function F by computing $F(\mathcal{D}_i) = f(\mathcal{D}_i) + Lap\left(\frac{\Delta f}{\epsilon_1}\right)$ for sets of devices $\mathcal{D}_i \subseteq \mathcal{D}$, where the Laplacian noise is drawn from the (unbounded) battery and where $\Delta f = \max_{d \in \mathcal{D}} f(d)$ is the sensitivity of the function f to which we add the noise. Adding noise in this manner corresponds to the common approach[4] to guarantee (ϵ, δ)-differential privacy with $\delta = 0$. For $\lambda = \frac{\epsilon}{\Delta f}$, the noise added by the standard technique is $Lap(\frac{1}{\lambda})$, the scaled symmetric exponential distribution with standard deviation of $\sqrt{2}\frac{1}{\lambda}$ with a variance of $2\left(\frac{\Delta f}{\epsilon}\right)^2$. The probability density function is $p(x) = \frac{\lambda}{2} \cdot e^{-|x| \cdot \lambda}$.

We now relate this case to our setting with a resource-bounded battery. To this end, we first show that differential privacy can be transferred between two functions (for increasing values of δ), provided that their statistical distance is sufficiently small.

Definition 4 (Statistical Distance). *The* statistical distance *between two distributions X and Y over a set U is defined as*

$$d(X,Y) = \max_{S \subseteq U}(|Pr[X \in S] - Pr[Y \in S]|).$$

The following lemma relates differential privacy and the statistical distance.

Lemma 1. *Given two probabilistic functions F and G with the same input domain, where F is (ϵ, δ_1)-differentially private. If for all possible inputs x we have that the statistical distance on the output distributions of F and G is: $d(F(x), G(x)) \le \delta_2$, then G is $(\epsilon, \delta_1 + (e^\epsilon + 1)\delta_2)$-differentially private.*

The proofs of all lemmas and theorems are postponed to the extended version for space reasons [7]. We note that this lemma is not tailored to our setting of streams, but applies to arbitrary types of inputs.

4.2 Privacy Guarantees for Throughput Restrictions

For relating the case with unbounded throughput and the throughput-bounded case, we first determine the statistical distance between F and F_b, and subsequently exploit Lemma 1 in a suitable manner. We first observe that if one does not consider streams but only individual timeslots, F_b differs from F if and only if the randomness added by F is of a larger magnitude than the throughput bound b. Consequently, the statistical distance between F and F_b can be bounded as follows:

---

[4] For this work we only consider Laplacian noise. Applying other, e.g., already bounded noise distributions or other masking techniques is considered future work.

Lemma 2. *Given an (ϵ, δ)-differentially private function F with $F(x) = f(x) + R$ for a deterministic function f and a random variable R. Then for all x, the statistical distance between F and F_b is at most $d(F(x), F_b(x)) \leq Pr\left[\|R\| > b\right]$.*

We now derive a concrete bound for this probability, depending on ϵ, the sensitivity Δf of f, and the throughput bound b.

Lemma 3. *Given a function F with $F(x) = f(x) + Lap\left(\Delta f / \epsilon\right)$ for a deterministic function f, and a throughput bound $b \in \mathbb{R}^{+}$, the probability that the Laplacian noise $Lap\left(\Delta f / \epsilon\right)$ applied to f is larger than b is bounded by $Pr\left[\left\|Lap\left(\frac{\Delta f}{\epsilon}\right)\right\| > b\right] = e^{-\frac{b \cdot \epsilon}{\Delta f}}$.*

Moreover, if F_b is (ϵ, δ)-differentially private, then also its 0-bounded variant $\underline{F}_b$ is (ϵ, δ)-differentially private, because one can, without further knowledge, compute $\underline{F}_b(x)$ from $F_b(x)$ for every x.

4.3   Privacy Guarantees for Capacity Restrictions

Including bounds for the capacity requires an approach beyond considering single steps only, since the probability to exceed the capacity in step i also depends on the noise added in previous steps. In fact, if one considered an arbitrarily long time interval during which random Laplacian noise is added, any finite capacity would naturally be exceeded (if there is no recharging). We exclude this case, similar to existing prior works, by restricting us to consumption streams of a certain length n. We exploit how to overcome this restriction by tackling the problem of privacy-aware battery recharging during runtime in Sect. 5.

Similar to how we deal with throughput restrictions, we exploit the statistical distance (now on streams of length n) and subsequently apply Lemma 1. To combine this result with our result on throughput, we immediately bound the distance between $\underline{F}_b$ and $\mathbb{F}$: These functions differ on consumption streams of length n if and only if the capacity is exceeded at least once. Recall that the battery is only used to generate noise added to the net consumption f. We first assume that the battery level is optimally placed at $bl(0) = \frac{c}{2}$ at the beginning of our time interval. Consequently, the probability to exceed the capacity is bounded by the probability that the sum of the noise added in all steps exceeds $\frac{c}{2}$.

Lemma 4. *Given an $(\epsilon_1, 0)$-differentially private function F with $F(x) = f(x) + Lap\left(\frac{\Delta f}{\epsilon_1}\right)$. If the corresponding bounded mechanism $\mathbb{F}$ has capacity bound c and throughput bound b, then for all consumption streams Φ of length n, the statistical distance between $\mathbb{F}$ and $\underline{F}_b$ when starting with battery level $bl(0) = \frac{c}{2}$ is at most*

$$d(\mathbb{F}(\Phi), \underline{F}_b(\Phi)) \leq Pr\left[\exists k \leq n \left|\sum_{j=1}^{k} F_b(\mathcal{D}_j) - f(\mathcal{D}_j)\right| > \frac{c}{2}\right].$$

Recall that we might cap the noise not only at the throughput bound b, but also if the load measured by the smart meter would be negative. Thus, the expected value of the noise is different from zero. We now derive an estimate for the probability to exceed the capacity *at least once*:

Lemma 5. *Given an $(\epsilon_1, 0)$-differentially private function F with $F(x) = f(x) + Lap\left(\frac{\Delta f}{\epsilon_1}\right)$. For all $t > 0$, the probability that the Laplacian noise exceeds the capacity for $c \geq 2(n + t) \cdot \frac{\Delta f}{\epsilon_1}$ in at least one of the n steps is bounded by*

$$Pr\left[\exists k \leq n \left| \sum_{j=1}^{k} F_b(\mathcal{D}_j) - f(\mathcal{D}_j) \right| > \frac{c}{2}\right] \leq \frac{2n}{t^2}.$$

This estimate constitutes a bound for the statistical distance between $\underline{F}_b$ and $\mathbb{F}$.

4.4 Obtaining an Overall Privacy Guarantee

We now combine our results on throughput and capacity constraints to obtain an overall result on differential privacy for $\mathbb{F}$. We consider streams of length n and also impose the assumption that the battery level is set to $bl(0) = \frac{c}{2}$ at the beginning. The following theorem follows directly from the results we have shown in this section.

Theorem 1. *Given an $(\epsilon_1, 0)$-differentially private function F. If the corresponding bounded mechanism $\mathbb{F}$ has capacity bound c and throughput bound b, and $bl(0)$ set to $\frac{c}{2}$, then $\mathbb{F}$ is (ϵ_1, δ_1)-differentially private on all consumption streams of length n with $\delta_1 = (e^{\epsilon_1} + 1) \cdot (P_b + P_c)$ where P_b is the statistical distance between F and F_b and P_c is the statistical distance between $\underline{F}_b$ and $\mathbb{F}$.*

Obtaining concrete bounds for differential privacy can be achieved by plugging in values for P_b (Lemmas 2 and 3) and P_c (Lemmas 4 and 5).

5 Privacy-Aware Smart Metering with Battery Recharging

In the last section, we have established privacy guarantees for settings in which battery recharging is not considered. In this section, we propose an integrated method that allows for recharging the battery on-the-fly, so that meaningful privacy guarantees for more comprehensive use cases can be achieved.

We start with a general explanation what makes privacy-aware battery recharging in the context of smart metering a sophisticated task. After that, we describe our solution to overcome the underlying problems, and which additional assumptions we have to impose.

The General Problem of Privacy-Aware Battery Recharging. We develop a privacy-preserving technique for recharging the battery at runtime, i.e., while using the battery for generating noise. If we simply recharge the battery level to the target level of $\frac{c}{2}$ every n steps via the power line, the energy consumption is modified accordingly and the adversary learns the sum of the noise. This information is sufficient to distinguish the streams, and hence to break differential privacy.

Our Solution: Differentially-Private Noise Generation via Cascading. We pursue the following idea for countering this effect, which constitutes a novel cascading approach for generating differentially private noise: we consider the amount of recharged energy as a function, and make this function differentially private by appropriately adding noise. We show that the additional noise is much smaller than the noise we add directly to the consumption, essentially since the new noise is only used every n steps instead of every step. If desired, this process can be continued, by making this smaller noise differentially private again, and so on. In this paper, we do not formalize this further, i.e., we work with a cascade of depth one.

In a nutshell, this cascading approach transforms the problem of generating a large amount of noise that must be unobservable for an adversary into generating a much smaller, unobservable amount of noise. However, this smaller amount of noise still corresponds to energy consumption that is measured by the smart meter and thus observable by the adversary; hence if we use the battery itself to generate this additional noise, we still leak the amount of noise added by $\mathbb{F}$ in the long run: Assume we restore the battery level to a state $\frac{c}{2} + r$ for a noisy value r. The randomness r hides all but a small part of the information about noise added to the net load in the critical time step i. When we recharge the battery again after n additional steps, information about r is leaked. After recharging the battery sufficiently often, the value of r can be estimated precisely with a high probability, and differential privacy breaks down.

In order to circumvent this inherent problem, we impose the assumption that the amount of additional noise can be hidden in the overall consumption using appropriate techniques. We outline two possible techniques for achieving this in practice. First, one can assume the existence of a distinct, small secondary energy source, e.g., home-owned solar panels, that is unobservable by the adversary and solely used for the recharging process. Second, if we drop the assumption that we do not discard any energy at all, we can simply continuously draw a small, constant amount of energy from the primary source that is sufficient for the recharging process, and discard all energy that exceeds the actual battery recharging demand. For simplicity of notation in the following, we assume that this additional energy is stored in a distinct, small second battery, and then used to recharge the primary battery as described below. (In practice, both batteries would typically coincide.) We stress that the amount of energy that is wasted for the recharging process only depends on the amount of secondary noise, but not on the amount by which the (primary) battery is recharged.

5.1   The Battery Recharging Mechanism

We define the battery recharging mechanism $\mathbb{F}_c$ as follows: it builds on the definition of $\mathbb{F}$, but instead restores its energy every n steps. We additionally reserve an amount $b_{inc} = b$ of throughput. The total amount of throughput for the battery is thus increased to $b_{total} = b + b_{inc} = 2b$, i.e., the total amount of throughput is twice as high as in the restricted setting for n steps without battery recharging. When n steps have passed, we compare the current battery level $bl(i)$ with the target level $\frac{c}{2}$. We do not try to hide the approximate amount of energy that we need in order to restore the battery. The precise value, however, is hidden by Laplacian noise. We postpone the precise definition of $\mathbb{F}_c$ to the extended version [7].

5.2   Differential Privacy of the Battery Recharging Mechanism

To obtain a privacy guarantee for $\mathbb{F}_c$, we employ a conservative approach: We first show that when ignoring the leakage due to recharging, $\mathbb{F}_c$ does not leak more information than $\mathbb{F}$, for which we already gave a privacy guarantee. Then, we calculate the leakage due to recharging and combine both results. An outline of the proof, together with the Lemmas that lead to our final result, can be found in the extended version [7].

   Finally we present the main theorem of this paper. It states that the battery-recharging mechanism $\mathbb{F}_c$ is indeed $(\epsilon_1 + \epsilon_2, \delta_1 + \delta_2)$-differentially private on infinite consumption streams for arbitrary values ϵ_1 and ϵ_2, and we give upper bounds for the values of δ_1 and δ_2, depending on the sensitivity of f (Δf), the privacy guarantee itself (ϵ_1, ϵ_2) and the resource limits of our primary (b, c) and secondary battery (c_{2nd}).

Theorem 2. *Given an $(\epsilon_1, 0)$-differentially private function F with $F(x) = f(x) + Lap\left(\frac{\Delta f}{\epsilon_1}\right)$ for a deterministic function f. If the corresponding capacity-regulating mechanism $\mathbb{F}_c$, when using recharging noise with distribution $Lap\left(\frac{\Delta f}{\epsilon_2}\right)$ has throughput bound $b_{total} = 2 \cdot b = 2 \cdot b_{inc}$ and capacity bound $c_{total} = c + c_{2nd}$, and given a secondary battery that provides at least an amount of c_{2nd} energy every n steps, then for every initial battery level $bl(0)$, $\mathbb{F}_c$ is $(\epsilon_1 + \epsilon_2, \delta)$-differentially private on (possibly infinite) consumption streams with*

$$\delta = (e^{\epsilon_1} + 1) \cdot (P_b + P_c) + (e^{\epsilon_2} + 1) \cdot P_{c_{2nd}}, \text{ where}$$

- P_b *is the statistical distance between F and $\underline{F}_b$.*
- P_c *is the statistical distance between $\underline{F}_b$ and $\mathbb{F}$.*
- $P_{c_{2nd}} \leq e^{-\frac{c_{2nd} \cdot \epsilon_2}{\Delta f}}$ *(more details in the extended version [7]).*

We can formulate several instantiations of this theorem, e.g., by combining the theorem with the concrete bounds for the statistical distances proven in this paper. A corollary for Theorem 2 can be found in the extended version [7].

5.3 Interpretation

We stress that the bounds derived in these results are not necessarily tight, but they allow for a flexible adjustment to different situations. For instance, we can freely decide the amount of noise to be added to the consumption, or to exclude certain devices from the set of devices we wish to hide, e.g., devices with a very high consumption (in this case we just compute the sensitivity Δf over the subset $\mathcal{D}^*$ as $\Delta f = \max_{d \in \mathcal{D}^*} f(d)$). This enables us to derive strong privacy guarantees for those devices that one considers particularly privacy-critical, such as TV, Laptop or other electronic media. Concentrating on particular devices does not require any changes to the physical installation of the battery, but solely a different treatment of the required noise.

If one increases the secondary battery's capacity c_{2nd}, we can further reduce the amount of energy that needs to be drawn unobservably, e.g., by means of a secondary energy source: We can compute the probability that the secondary battery is exceeded over m iterations and get the same privacy guarantee for a smaller share of capacity per iteration. Using this technique and the bounds presented in this paper, the costs for restoring the battery status can (asymptotically) be reduced to $2\frac{\Delta f}{\epsilon_2}$ for each restoring process.

6 Evaluation and Concrete Use Cases

In this section, we further highlight the relationship between the individual parameters (such as the battery's resource constraints and measurement time) and the obtained privacy guarantees. For the sake of illustration, we moreover explore a concrete, realistic use case and analyze which privacy guarantees can be achieved under which resource assumptions.

Figure 2(a) displays the relationship between the required battery capacity and the privacy parameter δ that can be guaranteed by applying Lemma 5. Similarly, Fig. 2(b) shows the relationship between this capacity and the number of steps n for which the capacity has to be provided. In Fig. 2(c) we depict the

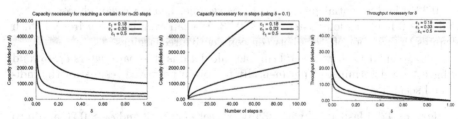

(a) Capacity required for obtaining a privacy guarantee δ during $n = 20$ steps.

(b) Capacity required for obtaining n steps for a privacy guarantee $\delta = 0.1$.

(c) Throughput required for obtaining a privacy guarantee δ.

Fig. 2. Amount of capacity and throughput required, depending on the parameters ϵ, δ and n.

relationship between battery throughput and the obtained privacy guarantees. The values δ in the graphs denote the amount of privacy loss we face for the considered parameters (see Theorem 2). For the graphs, we divided the values for capacity and throughput by the sensitivity Δf of our consumption sum function. This allows to reason about the relation of the different parameters independent from the appliances themselves. If, e.g., a TV with a consumption of 130 W is to be hidden and we aim at $\varepsilon_1 = 0.33$ and $\delta = 0.1$, the battery has to have a throughput of at least about $9 \cdot 130$ W per step (time in between two readings).

6.1   A Concrete Use Case: Hiding TV Activation

For the sake of illustration, we finally investigate the concrete use case of hiding a TV device in the overall consumption stream. We consider three different TV devices with different power consumptions.

We assume a standard American household with an average consumption of about 30 kWh per day, according to the U.S. Energy Information Administration. Within this household, we consider the following three TV devices: (1) a 42" plasma TV with 335 W, (2) a 29" CRT TV with 130 W, and (3) a 19" LCD TV with 36 W. In the following we write $\Delta_1 f$ to denote the sensitivity we have when to hide the plasma TV, and similarly $\Delta_2 f$ for the CRT TV and $\Delta_2 f$ for the LCD TV. We will work with the following parameters: The smart meter sends the current load sum every $\Delta t = 5$ min, which corresponds to one of the most commonly used time intervals in smart metering [21]. We consider an off-the-shelf rechargeable battery, and we assume that the throughput of the battery is sufficiently high so that the battery can be fully discharged within one hour. We consider an additional resource consumption of 3 kWh per day to recharge the secondary battery. Naturally, hiding whether or not the TV is activated also hides which TV program is being watched.

For our computation we hence obtain the following parameters: $\Delta_1 f = 335$ W $\cdot \Delta t \approx 28$ Wh, $\Delta_2 f = 130$ W $\cdot \Delta t \approx 11$ Wh, and $\Delta_3 f = 36$ W $\cdot \Delta t = 3$ Wh. The values for δ heavily depend on the selection of ϵ. Note that the optimal choice of n and the optimal relation of ϵ_1 to ϵ_2 also depend on ϵ; additionally the choice of n can influence the guarantees. We aim to achieve a privacy guarantee of $(0.33, 0.1)$-differential privacy in this example; hence we can choose $\epsilon_1 \geq 0$ and $\epsilon_2 \geq 0$ freely as long as $\epsilon_1 + \epsilon_2 \leq 0.33$. We can even choose n freely, which denotes the number of steps between consecutive rechargings.

We exemplarily show several sample calculations (the parameters ϵ_1, ϵ_2, and n have been determined experimentally to obtain improved results for the individual scenarios):

(1) For the 42" plasma TV with 335 W, we set $\epsilon_1 \approx 0.13$ and $\epsilon_2 \approx 0.20$ and n to 60 (i.e., we restore the battery status every 5 h). We then obtain $(0.33, 0.1)$-differential privacy if one uses a battery with 11 kWh or more.

(2) For the 29" CRT TV with 130 W, we set $\epsilon_1 \approx 0.15$ and $\epsilon_2 \approx 0.18$ and n to 50 (i.e., we restore the battery status every 4.17 h). We then obtain $(0.33, 0.1)$-differential privacy if one uses a battery with 3.7 kWh or more.

(3) For the 19" LCD TV with 36 W, we set $\epsilon_1 \approx 0.21$ and $\epsilon_2 \approx 0.12$ and n to 10 (i.e., we restore the battery status every 50 minutes). We then obtain $(0.33, 0.1)$-differential privacy if one uses a battery with 0.82 kWh or more.

7   Discussion

Adversary Model. In our model, in contrast to other solutions, the smart meter is not trusted. We consider a smart-meter adversary that has access to the power consumption of a household and that can make regular readings of this consumption. This adversary is, in a sense, honest-but-curious. The battery can be bought and installed by the consumer itself, without the need of any cooperation from the smart meter or the electricity company.

Privacy Guarantees. With our solution we can give (mathematically) strong privacy guarantees. However, the interpretation of these results is not trivial.

Formally we can only guarantee to hide a single activation of a single device. In practice, a realistic adversary can not keep track of all other device activations, which means that the uncertainty of an adversary covers more than one activation. However, we can only expect to hide which device (from a set of not-too-greedy devices) was activated and when. If the consumer in question follows a daily routine with almost no variation, our adversary can find out this routine. Moreover our solution does not hide the large bulk of device activations. The adversary might still be able to infer whether or not the consumer is at home (large consumption) or not (small consumption). Our solution does, however, counter many practical attacks, as the addition of random noise makes it hard to analyze the data. The parameters (Δ_f, ϵ) should be modified whenever the privacy policy of a consumer changes, which might be, e.g., after buying a new TV, if this TV consumes more energy.

Hiding the total consumption sum for several (say k) points in time, e.g., by setting $\Delta_f \approx k \cdot$ total consumption, naturally is much more expensive. We consider this out of scope for our solution.

Usefulness. Since our solution adds the noise not to a numerical value, but to the actual consumption of the consumer, the readings of the smart meter are not influenced. In contrast to other works on smart meters, in our case there is no difference between the actual consumption and the smart meter readings (and outputs, if the smart meter is honest).

Thus, in our case the common measure of "usefulness" that is often used when analyzing the practical value of differential privacy should be defined differently. We suggest discussing the practical feasibility of our solution.

Practical Feasibility. The Laplacian noise generation can be done efficiently by applying a relatively simple function to a (normal, uniform) random or pseudorandom variable. The generation of large quantities of noise is stressful for a battery and will in practical use most likely result in a reduced life-time of the battery. We could envision a solution that uses capacitors instead of (or additionally to) a battery to improve the life-cycle of the battery.

In contrast to works that rely on modifying the smart meter, our solution does not come without cost, as installing a sufficiently large battery might be expensive. However, since our solution does not require cooperation, the decision about applying this solution can be made by each individual consumer.

8   Conclusions

We have proposed a novel technique for provably hiding sensitive power consumption information in the overall power consumption stream. Our technique relies on a rechargeable battery that is used to modify the household's power consumption by adding or subtracting noise (i.e., increasing or decreasing power consumption), in order to establish strong privacy guarantees in the sense of differential privacy. To achieve these privacy guarantees in realistic settings, we have investigated the influence of, and the interplay between, capacity and throughput bounds that batteries face in reality. Based on these observations, we have proposed an integrated method based on noise cascading that allows for recharging the battery on-the-fly so that differential privacy is retained, while adhering to capacity and throughput constraints, and while keeping the additional consumption of energy induced by our technique to a minimum.

References

1. Energy Independence and Security Act of 2007. One Hundred Tenth Congress of the United States of America (2007)
2. Directive 2009/72/EC of the European Parliament and of the Council. Official Journal of the European Union (2009)
3. Ács, G., Castelluccia, C.: I have a DREAM! (DiffeRentially privatE smArt Metering). In: Filler, T., Pevný, T., Craver, S., Ker, A. (eds.) IH 2011. LNCS, vol. 6958, pp. 118–132. Springer, Heidelberg (2011)
4. Acs, G., Castelluccia, C., Lecat, W.: Protecting against physical resource monitoring. In: Proceedings of 10th Annual ACM Workshop on Privacy in the Electronic Society (WPES), pp. 23–32. ACM (2011)
5. Anderson, R., Fuloria, S.: On the security economics of electricity metering. In: Workshop on the Economics of Information Security (WEIS) (2010)
6. Anderson, R., Fuloria, S.: Who controls the off switch? In: Proceedings of the 1st IEEE International Conference on Smart Grid Communications (SmartGrid-Comm), pp. 96–101. IEEE Press (2010)
7. Backes, M., Meiser, S.: Differentially private smart metering with battery recharging. Technical report, Saarland University. http://eprint.iacr.org/2012/183 (Online)
8. Baranski, M., Voss, J.: Detecting patterns of appliances from total load data using a dynamic programming approach. In: Proceedings of the 4th IEEE International Conference on Data Mining (ICDM), pp. 327–330. IEEE Press (2004)

9. Cavoukian, A., Polonetsky, J., Wolf, C.: Smartprivacy for the smart grid: embedding privacy into the design of electricity conservation. Identity Inf. Soc. **3**, 275–294 (2010)
10. Cuijpers, C.: No to mandatory smart metering: does not equal privacy. http://vortex.uvt.nl/TILTblog/?p=54 (Online)
11. Danezis, G., Kohlweiss, M., Rial, A.: Differentially private billing with rebates. In: Filler, T., Pevný, T., Craver, S., Ker, A. (eds.) IH 2011. LNCS, vol. 6958, pp. 148–162. Springer, Heidelberg (2011)
12. Dwork, C.: Differential privacy. In: Bugliesi, M., Preneel, B., Sassone, V., Wegener, I. (eds.) ICALP 2006. LNCS, vol. 4052, pp. 1–12. Springer, Heidelberg (2006)
13. Dwork, C., Kenthapadi, K., McSherry, F., Mironov, I., Naor, M.: Our data, ourselves: privacy via distributed noise generation. In: Vaudenay, S. (ed.) EUROCRYPT 2006. LNCS, vol. 4004, pp. 486–503. Springer, Heidelberg (2006)
14. Garcia, F.D., Jacobs, B.: Privacy-friendly energy-metering via homomorphic encryption. In: Cuellar, J., Lopez, J., Barthe, G., Pretschner, A. (eds.) STM 2010. LNCS, vol. 6710, pp. 226–238. Springer, Heidelberg (2011)
15. Greveler, U., Justus, B., Loehr, D.: Hintergrund und experimentelle Ergebnisse zum Thema Smart Meter und Datenschutz. Technical report, Fachhochschule Münster (2011)
16. Hart, G.: Nonintrusive appliance load monitoring. Proc. IEEE **80**(12), 1870–1891 (1992)
17. Hubert Chan, T.-H., Shi, E., Song, D.: Private and continual release of statistics. In: Abramsky, S., Gavoille, C., Kirchner, C., Meyer auf der Heide, F., Spirakis, P.G. (eds.) ICALP 2010. LNCS, vol. 6199, pp. 405–417. Springer, Heidelberg (2010)
18. Kursawe, K., Danezis, G., Kohlweiss, M.: Privacy-friendly aggregation for the smart-grid. In: Fischer-Hübner, S., Hopper, N. (eds.) PETS 2011. LNCS, vol. 6794, pp. 175–191. Springer, Heidelberg (2011)
19. Lam, H., Fung, G., Lee, W.: A novel method to construct taxonomy electrical appliances based on load signatures. IEEE Trans. Consum. Electron. **53**(2), 653–660 (2007)
20. Laughman, C., Lee, K., Cox, R., Shaw, S., Leeb, S., Norford, L., Armstrong, P.: Power signature analysis. IEEE Power Energy Mag. **1**(2), 56–63 (2003)
21. McLaughlin, S., McDaniel, P., Aiello, W.: Protecting consumer privacy from electric load monitoring. In: Proceedings of the 18th ACM Conference on Computer and Communications Security (CCS), pp. 87–98. ACM (2011)
22. Merritt, R.: Stimulus: DoE readies $4.3 billion for smart grid. EE Times (2009)
23. Molina-Markham, A., Shenoy, P., Fu, K., Cecchet, E., Irwin, D.: Private memoirs of a smart meter. In: Proceedings of the 2nd ACM Workshop on Embedded Sensing Systems for Energy-Efficiency in Building (BuildSys), pp. 61–66. ACM (2010)
24. T. S. G. I. Panel. Cyber security strategy and requirements. Technical report 7628, National Institute of Standards and Technology
25. Quinn, E.L.: Privacy and the new energy infrastructure. Soc. Sci. Res. Netw. **09**, 1995–2008 (2009)
26. Rastogi, V., Nath, S.: Differentially private aggregation of distributed time-series with transformation and encryption. In: Proceedings of the 2010 International Conference on Management of Data (SIGMOD), pp. 735–746. ACM (2010)

27. Rial, A., Danezis, G.: Privacy-preserving smart metering. In: Proceedings of the 10th Annual ACM Workshop on Privacy in the Electronic Society (WPES), pp. 49–60. ACM (2011)

28. Shi, E., Chan, T.-H.H., Rieffel, E., Chow, R., Song, D.: Privacy-preserving aggregation of time-series data. In: Proceedings of the 18th Annual Network & Distributed System Security Symposium (NDSS) (2011)

29. Varodayan, D., Khisti, A.: Smart meter privacy using a rechargeable battery: minimizing the rate of information leakage. In: Proceedings of the IEEE International Conference on Acoustics, Speech, and Signal Processing (ICASSP) (2011)

AppGuard – Fine-Grained Policy Enforcement for Untrusted Android Applications

Michael Backes[1,2], Sebastian Gerling[1], Christian Hammer[1], Matteo Maffei[1], and Philipp von Styp-Rekowsky[1(✉)]

[1] Saarland University, CISPA, Saarbrücken, Germany
[2] Max Planck Institute for Software Systems (MPI-SWS), Saarbrücken, Germany
styp-rekowsky@cs.uni-saarland.de

Abstract. Android's success makes it a prominent target for malicious software. However, the user has very limited control over security-relevant operations. This work presents AppGuard, a powerful and flexible security system that overcomes these deficiencies. It enforces user-defined security policies on untrusted Android applications without requiring any changes to a smartphone's firmware, root access, or the like. Fine-grained and stateful security policies are expressed in a formal specification language, which also supports secrecy requirements. Our system offers complete mediation of security-relevant methods based on callee-site inline reference monitoring and supports widespread deployment. In the experimental analysis we demonstrate the removal of permissions for overly curious apps as well as how to defend against several recent real-world attacks on Android phones. Our technique exhibits very little space and runtime overhead. The utility of AppGuard has already been demonstrated by more than 1,000,000 downloads.

Keywords: Android · Runtime enforcement · Security policies · Inline reference monitoring · Rewriting

1 Introduction

The rapidly increasing number of mobile devices creates a vast potential for misuse. Mobile devices store a plethora of information about our personal lives, and GPS, camera, or microphone offer the ability to track us at all times. The always-online nature of mobile devices makes them a clear target for overly curious or maliciously spying apps and Trojan horses. For instance, social network apps were recently criticized for silently uploading the user's entire contacts onto external servers [17,42]. While this behavior became publicly known, users are most often not even aware of what an app actually does with their data. Additionally, fixes for security vulnerabilities in the Android OS often take months until they are integrated into vendor-specific OSs. Between Google's fix with a public vulnerability description and the vendor's update, an unpatched system becomes the obvious target for exploits.

J. Garcia-Alfaro et al. (Eds.): DPM 2013 and SETOP 2013, LNCS 8247, pp. 213–231, 2014.
DOI: 10.1007/978-3-642-54568-9_14, © Springer-Verlag Berlin Heidelberg 2014

Android's security concept is based on isolation of third-party apps and access control [1]. Access to personal information has to be explicitly granted at install time: When installing an app a list of permissions is displayed, which have to be granted in order to install the app. Users can neither dynamically grant and revoke permissions at runtime, nor add restrictions according to their personal needs. Further, users (and often even developers, cf. [23,26]) usually do not have enough information to judge whether a permission is indeed required.

Contributions. To overcome the aforementioned limitations of Android's security system, we present a novel policy-based security framework for Android called AppGuard.

- AppGuard takes an untrusted app and user-defined security policies as input and embeds the security monitor into the untrusted app, thereby delivering a secured self-monitoring app.
- Security policies are formalized in an automata-based language that can be configured in AppGuard. Security policies may specify restrictions on method invocations as well as secrecy requirements.
- AppGuard is built upon a novel approach for callee-site inline reference monitoring (IRM). We redirect method calls to the embedded security monitor and check whether executing the call is allowed by the security policy. Technically, this is achieved by altering method references in the Dalvik VM. This approach does not require root access or changes to the underlying Android architecture and, therefore, supports widespread deployment as a stand-alone app. It can handle even JAVA reflection (cf. Sect. 3) and dynamically loaded code.
- Secrecy requirements are enforced by storing the secret within the security monitor. Apps are just provided with a handle to that secret. This mechanism is general enough to enforce the confidentiality of data persistently stored on the device (e.g., address book entries or geolocation) as well as of dynamically received data (e.g., user-provided passwords or session tokens received in a single sign-on protocol). The monitor itself is protected against manipulation of its internal state and forceful extraction of stored secrets.
- We support fully-automatic on-the-phone instrumentation (no root required) of third-party apps as well as automatic updates of rewritten apps such that no app data is lost. Our system has been downloaded by about 1,000,000 users (aggregated from [5,12,34]) and has been invited to join the Samsung Apps market.
- Our evaluation on typical Android apps has shown very little overhead in terms of space and runtime. The case studies demonstrate the effectiveness of our approach: we successfully revoked permissions of excessively curious apps, demonstrate complex policies, and prevent several recent real-world attacks on Android phones, both due to in-app and OS vulnerabilities. We finally show that for the vast majority of 25,000 real-world apps, our instrumentation does not break functionality, thus demonstrating the robustness of our approach.

Key Design Decisions and Closely Related Work. Researchers have proposed several approaches to overcome the limitations of Android's security system, most of which require modifications to the Android platform. While there is hope that Google will eventually introduce a more fine-grained security system, we decided to directly integrate the security monitor within the apps, thereby requiring no change to the Android platform. The major drawback of modifying the firmware and platform code is that it requires rooting the device, which may void the user's warranty and affect the system stability. Besides, there is no general Android system but a plethora of vendor-specific variants that would need to be supported and maintained across OS updates. Finally, laymen users typically lack the expertise to conduct firmware modifications, and, therefore, abstain from installing modified Android versions.

Aurasium [45], a recently proposed tool for enforcing security policies in Android apps, rewrites low-level function pointers of the libc library in order to intercept interactions between the app and the OS. A lot of the functionality that is protected by Android's permission system depends on such system calls and thus can be intercepted at this level. A limitation of this approach is that the parameters of the original Java requests need to be recovered from the system calls' low-level byte arrays in order to differentiate malicious requests from benign ones, which "is generally difficult to write and test" [45] and may break in the next version of Android at Google's discretion. Similarly, mock return values are difficult to inject at this low level. In contrast, we designed our system to intercept high-level Java calls, which allows for more flexible policies. In particular we are able to inject arbitrary mock return values, e.g. a proxy object that only gives access to certain data, in case of policy violations. Additionally, we are able to intercept security-relevant methods that do not depend on the libc library. As an example consider the policy that systematically replaces MD5, which is nowadays widely considered an insecure hashing algorithm, by SHA-1. Since the implementation of MD5 does not use any security-relevant functionality of the libc library, this policy cannot be expressed in Aurasium. Finally, it is worth to mention that both Aurasium and AppGuard offer only limited guarantees for apps incorporating native code. Aurasium can detect an app that tries to perform security-relevant operations directly from native code, under the assumption, however, that the code does not re-implement the libc functionality. Our approach can monitor Java methods invoked from native code, although it cannot monitor system calls from native code.

Jeon et al. [35] advocate to place the reference monitor into a separate application. Their approach removes all permissions from the monitored app, as all calls to sensitive functionality are done in the monitoring app. This is fail-safe by default as it prevents both reflection and native code from executing such functionality. However, it has some drawbacks: If a security policy depends on the state of the monitored app, this approach incurs high complexity and overhead as all relevant data must be marshaled to the monitor. Besides, the monitor may not yet be initialized when the app attempts to perform security-relevant operations. Finally, this approach does not follow the principle of least privilege since the monitor must have the permissions of all monitored apps, making it a prominent target for privilege escalation attacks [9]. We propose a different approach: Although the security policies are specified and stored within App-Guard, the policy enforcement mechanism is directly integrated and performed within the monitored apps. The policy configuration file is passed as input to the security monitor embedded in each app, thereby enabling dynamic policy configuration updates. This approach does not involve any inter-procedure calls and obeys the principle of least privilege, as AppGuard requires no special permissions. Hence, AppGuard is not prone to privilege escalation attacks.

Table 1. Comparison of Android IRM approaches

Feature	1	2	3	4	5	6	7	8	Runtime Overhead (%)
Aurasium [45]	✓	–	I	◑	✓	–	–	–	14-35
Dr. Android [35]	✓	–	E	◑	◑	–	–	–	10-50
I-ARM-Droid [15]	✓	–	I	–	◑	–	–	✓	16
AppGuard	✓	✓	I	◑	✓	✓	✓	✓	1-12

Legend: 1. No Firmware Mod. 2. On Phone Instr./Updates 3. Monitor
4. Native Methods 5. Reflection 6. Policy Lang. 7. Data Secrecy
8. Parametric Joinpoints; ✓: full support, ◑: partial support

Table 1 compares AppGuard with the most relevant related work that does not modify the firmware. Up to now, no other system can instrument an app and update apps directly on the phone. Dr. Android has an external monitor (E) accessed via IPC; the other three approaches use internal monitors (I). Aurasium can monitor security-relevant native methods, Dr. Android only removes their permissions, which may lead to unexpected program termination, whereas our tool can prevent calls to sensitive Java APIs from native code. Both Aurasium and AppGuard handle reflection; Dr. Android does not handle it; I-ARM-Droid prevents it altogether. AppGuard is the only system that offers a high-level specification language for policies and supports hiding of secret data from e.g. untrusted components in the monitored app. Both Aurasium and Dr. Android only support a fixed set of joinpoints where a security policy can be attached to. In contrast, I-ARM-Droid and AppGuard can instrument calls to any Java method. The last column displays the runtime overhead incurred in micro-benchmarks as reported by the respective authors. AppGuard is competitive in terms of runtime overhead with respect to concurrent efforts. In our previous work [44] we presented the initial idea for diverting method calls in the Dalvik VM with a rudimentary implementation for micro-benchmarks only. It did *not* support a policy language, secrecy, and on-the-phone instrumentation, and did not include case studies. A recent tool paper [3] presented a previous version of AppGuard, which is based on caller-site instrumentation.

2 AppGuard

Runtime policy enforcement for third-party apps is challenging on unmodified Android systems. Android's security concept strictly isolates different apps installed on the same device. Communication between apps is only possible via Android's inter-process communication (IPC) mechanism. However, such communication requires both parties to cooperate, rendering this channel unsuitable for a generic runtime monitor. Apps cannot gain elevated privileges to observe the behavior of other apps.

AppGuard tackles this problem by following an approach pioneered by Erlingsson and Schneider [21] called *inline reference monitor* (IRM). The basic idea is to rewrite an untrusted app such that the code that monitors the app is directly embedded into its code. To this end, IRM systems incorporate a *rewriter* or *inliner* component, that injects additional security checks at critical points into the app's bytecode. This enables the monitor to observe a trace of *security-relevant events*, which typically correspond to invocations of trusted system library methods from the untrusted app. To actually enforce a *security policy*, the monitor controls the execution of the app by suppressing or altering calls to security-relevant methods, or even terminating the program if necessary.

In the IRM context, a policy is typically specified by means of a security automaton that defines which sequences of security-relevant events are acceptable. Such policies have been shown to express exactly the policies enforceable by runtime monitoring [43]. Ligatti et al. differentiate security automata by their ability to enforce policies by manipulating the trace of the program [37]. Some IRM systems [16, 21] implement truncation automata, which can only terminate the program if it deviates from the policy. However, this is often undesirable in practice. *Edit automata* [37] transform the program trace by inserting or suppressing events. Monitors based on edit automata are able to react gracefully to policy violations, e.g., by suppressing an undesired method call and returning a mock value, thus allowing the program to continue.

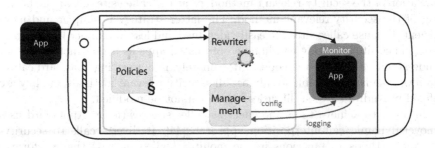

Fig. 1. Schematics of AppGuard

AppGuard is an IRM system for Android with the transformation capabilities of an edit automaton. Figure 1 provides a high-level overview of our system. We distinguish three main components:

1. *A set of security policies.* On top of user-defined and app-specific policies, AppGuard provides various generic security policies that govern access to

platform API methods which are protected by coarse-grained Android permissions. These methods comprise, e.g., methods for reading personal data, creating network sockets, or accessing device hardware like the GPS or the camera. As a starting point for the security policies, we used a mapping from API methods to permissions [23].

2. *The program rewriter.* Android apps run within a register-based Java VM called *Dalvik.* Our rewriter manipulates Dalvik executable (dex) bytecode of untrusted Android apps and embeds the security monitor into the untrusted app. The references of the Dalvik VM are altered so as to redirect the method calls to the security monitor.

3. *A management component.* AppGuard offers a graphical user interface that allows the user to set individual policy configurations on a per-app basis. In particular, policies can be turned on or off and parameterized. In addition, the management component keeps a detailed log of all security-relevant events, enabling the user to monitor the behavior of an app.

3   Architecture

AppGuard [5] is a stand-alone Android app written in Java and C that comprises about 9000 lines of code. It builds upon the *dexlib* library, which is part of the *smali* disassembler for Android by Ben Gruver [30], for manipulating dex files. The size of the app package is roughly 2 Mb.

Instrumentation. IRM systems instrument a target app such that the control flow of the program is diverted to the security monitor whenever a security-relevant method is about to be invoked. There are two strategies for passing control to the monitor: Either at the call-site in the app code, right before the invocation of the security-relevant method, or at the callee-site, i.e. at the beginning of the security-relevant method. The latter strategy is simpler and more efficient, because callee sites are easily identified and less in number [7]. Furthermore, callee-site rewriting can handle obfuscated apps as it does not require to "understand" the untrusted code. Unfortunately, in our setting, standard callee-site rewriting is not feasible for almost all security-relevant methods, as they are defined in Android system libraries, which cannot be modified.

In order to achieve the same effect as callee-site rewriting, AppGuard uses a novel dynamic call-interposition approach [44]. It diverts calls to security-relevant methods to functions in the monitor (called *guards*) that perform a security check. In order to divert the control flow we replace the reference to a method's bytecode in the VM's internal representation (e.g., a virtual method table) with the reference to our security guard. The security guards reside in an external library that is dynamically loaded on app startup. Therefore, we do not need to reinstrument the app when a security policy is modified. Additionally, we store the original reference in order to access the original function later on, e.g., in case the security check grants the permission to execute the security-critical method. This procedure also reduces the risk of accidentally introducing infinite loops by a policy since we usually call the original method.

With this approach, invocations of security-relevant methods do *not* need to be rewritten statically. Instead, we use Java Native Interface (JNI) calls at runtime to replace the references to each of the monitored functions. More precisely, we call the JNI method GetMethodID() which takes a method's signature, and returns a pointer to the internal data structure describing that method. This data structure contains a reference to the bytecode instructions associated with the method, as well as metadata such as the method's argument types or the number of registers. In order to redirect the control flow to our guard method, we overwrite the reference to the instructions such that it points to the instructions of the security guard's method instead. Additionally, we adjust the intercepted method's metadata (e.g., number of registers) to be compatible with the guard method's code. This approach works both for pure Java methods and methods with a native implementation.

Figure 2 illustrates how to redirect a method call using our instrumentation library. Calling Instrumentation.replaceMethod() replaces the instruction reference of method foo() of class com.test.A with the reference to the instructions of method bar() of class com.test.B. The call returns the original reference, which we store in a variable A_foo. Calling A.foo() will now invoke B.bar() instead. The original method can still be invoked by Instrumentation. callOriginalMethod(A_foo). Note that the handle A_foo will be a secret of the security monitor in practice. Therefore, the original method can no longer be invoked directly by the instrumented app.

```
public class Main {
    public static void main(String[] args) {
        A.foo(); // calls A.foo()
        MethodHandle A_foo = Instrumentation.replaceMethod(
            "Lcom/test/A;->foo()", "Lcom/test/B;->bar()");
        A.foo(); // calls B.bar()
        Instrumentation.callOriginalMethod(A_foo); // calls A.foo()
}}
```

Fig. 2. Example illustrating the functionality of the instrumentation library

Policies. We developed a high-level policy language called SOSPoX in order to express and characterize the security policies supported by AppGuard. SOSPoX is based on SPoX [31,32] and is a direct encoding of edit automata. SOSPoX policies enable the specification of constraints on the execution of method calls as well as changes of the control flow. This includes the specification of a graceful reaction to policy violations, e.g., by suppressing an undesired method call and returning a mock value, thus allowing the program to continue. Furthermore, SOSPoX offers support for confidentiality policies. Data returned by method invocations are labeled as either confidential or public: confidential data can only be processed by the methods authorized by the policy. In general, we can specify information flow policies that prevent both explicit flows (i.e., through assignments) and implicit flows (i.e., through the control flow of the program). This can be achieved by a policy disallowing the processing of confidential data. Declassification policies allow selected methods to process confidential data and the returned results are labeled as public. For instance, we can specify that the return value of a function that returns our credit card number is to be kept secret, but that the encryption of the returned credit card number counts as declassification and is no longer secret (cf. Fig. 3). Due to space constraints we omit the technical details of our policies and refer to [2] for a more comprehensive presentation and additional policy examples.

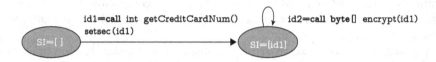

Fig. 3. Security automaton exemplifying declassification by encryption

Rewriter. The task of the rewriter component is to insert code into the target app, which dynamically loads the monitor package into the app's virtual machine. To ensure instrumentation of security-sensitive methods before their execution, we create an application class that becomes the superclass of the existing application class[1]. Our new class contains a static initializer, which becomes the very first code executed upon app startup. The initializer uses a custom class loader to load our monitor package. Afterwards, it calls an initializer method in the monitor that uses the instrumentation library to rewrite the method references.

Separation of Secrets. Policies in our system can specify that the return values of certain functions are to be kept secret. In order to prevent an app from leaking secret values, we control access to these secrets. To this end, the monitor intercepts all calls to methods that the policy annotates as "secret-carrying", i.e. methods that can produce secret output or receive secret input. Whenever the invocation of such a method produces a new secret output, the monitor returns a dummy value, which serves as a reference to the secret for further processing. If such a secret reference is passed to a method that supports secret parameters, the trampoline method invokes the original method with the corresponding secret instead and returns either the actual result or a new secret reference, in case the return value was marked as secret in the policy. The dummy reference values do not contain any information about the secret itself and are thus innocuous if processed by any method that is not annotated in the policy.

Management. The management component of AppGuard monitors the behavior of instrumented apps and offers policy configuration at runtime (cf. Fig. 4). This configuration is provided to the instrumented app as a world-readable file.

---

[1] In case no application class exists, we register our class as the application class.

Its location is hardcoded into the monitor during the rewriting process. This is motivated by the fact that invocations of security-relevant methods can occur before the management app is fully initialized and able to react on Android IPC. The management component provides a log of all security-relevant method invocations for each app (cf. Fig. 4), which enables the user to make informed decisions about the policy configuration. Invocations are reported to the management app using a standard Android Service component. The asynchronous nature of Android IPC is not an issue, since security-relevant method invocations that occur before the service connection is established are buffered locally.

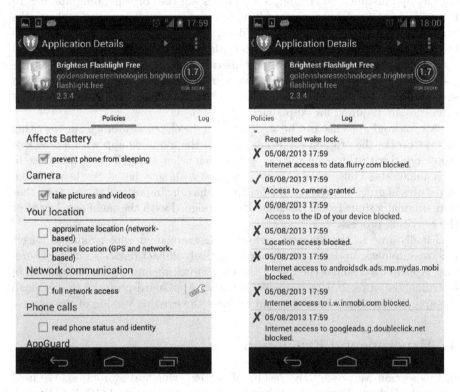

Fig. 4. Screenshots of the AppGuard user interface: Permission configuration (*left*), and log of security-relevant operations (*right*). The *Brightest Flashlight Free* app was chosen for exemplary purposes only, with no further implications to its security.

Monitor Protection. In our system, the inlined monitor is part of the monitored app. A malicious app might try to circumvent the monitor by tampering with its internal state. Furthermore, an app could try to subvert secrecy policies by directly extracting stored secrets from the monitor. Since the monitor package containing secret data and pointers to the original methods is unknown at compile time and due to strong typing, a malicious app would need to rely on reflection to access the monitor. To thwart such attacks, we implement a `ReflectionPolicy` that intercepts function calls to the Reflection API. In particular, we monitor operations that access Java classes and fields like `java.lang.Class->forName()` or `java.lang.Class->getField()` and thereby effectively prevent access to the monitor package.

Deployment. On unmodified Android systems, app sandboxing prevents direct modifications of the code of other apps installed on the device. AppGuard leverages the fact that the app packages of installed third-party apps are stored in a world-readable location in the filesystem. Thus the monitor is capable of inlining any app installed on the device by processing the corresponding `apk` file. In the end, AppGuard produces a self-monitoring app package that replaces the original version. Since stock Android does not allow automatic (un)installation of other apps, the user is prompted to confirm both the removal of the original app as well as the installation of the instrumented app. Moreover, we ask the user to enable the OS-option "Unknown sources: Allow installation of apps from sources other than the Play Store". Due to these two user interactions, no root privileges are required for AppGuard.

All Android apps need to be signed with a developer key. Since our rewriting process breaks the original signature, we sign the modified app with a new key. Apps signed with the same key can access each other's data if they declare so in their manifests. Thus, we sign rewritten apps with keys based on their original signatures in order to preserve the original behavior. In particular, two apps that were originally signed with the same key, are signed with the same new key after the rewriting process.

Finally, due to the different signature, instrumented apps would no longer receive automatic updates, which may negatively impact device security. Therefore, AppGuard assumes the role of the Play Store app and checks for updates of instrumented apps. If a new version is found, AppGuard prompts to download the app package, instruments it and replaces the existing version of the app.

4   Experimental Evaluation

In this section we present the results of our experimental evaluation. We used a Google Galaxy Nexus smartphone (1.2 GHz, two cores, 1 GB RAM) with Android version 4.1.2 for on-the-phone evaluations and a notebook with an Intel Core i5-2520M CPU (2.5 GHz, two cores, hyper-threading) and 8 GB RAM for our off-the-phone evaluations.

4.1   Robustness and Performance Evaluation

Robustness. We tested AppGuard on more than 25,000 apps from two different app markets and report the results in Table 2. The stability of the original apps is tested using the UI/Application Exerciser Monkey provided by the Android framework with a random seed and 1000 injected events (third column).

To evaluate the robustness of the rewriting process we check the validity of the generated dex file (fourth column) and test the stability of the instrumented app using the UI Monkey with the random seed (fifth column). Note that we only consider the stability of instrumented apps where the original did not crash.

The reported numbers indicate a very high reliability of the instrumentation process: we found no illegal dex file and over 99 % of the stable apps were also stable after the instrumentation. The majority of the remaining 1 % does not handle checked exceptions gracefully (e.g. IOException), which may be thrown by AppGuard when suppressing a function call. This bad coding style is not found in popular apps. Other apps terminate when they detect a different app signature. In rare cases, the mock values returned by suppressed function calls violate an invariant of the program. Note, however, that our test with the UI Monkey does not check for semantic equivalence.

Table 2. Robustness of rewriting and monitoring

App market	Apps	Stable	Dex verified	Stable instr.
Google Play	9508	8783	9508 (100 %)	8744 (99.6 %)
SlideMe	15974	14590	15974 (100 %)	14469 (99.1 %)
Total	25482	23373	25482 (100 %)	23213 (99.3 %)

Performance. AppGuard modifies apps installed on an Android device by adding code at the bytecode level. We analyze the time it takes to rewrite an app and its impact on both size and execution time of the modified app. Table 3 provides an overview of our performance evaluation for the rewriting process. We tested AppGuard with 8 apps and list the following results for each of the apps: size of the original app package (Apk), size of the classes.dex file, and the duration of the rewriting process both on the laptop and smartphone (PC and Phone, respectively).

The size of the classes.dex file increases on average by approximately 3.7 Kb. This increase results from merging code that loads the monitor package into the app. Since we perform callee-site rewriting and load the our external policies dynamically, we only have this static and no proportional increase of the original dex file. For a few apps (e.g. Angry Birds) the instrumentation time is dominated by re-building and compressing the app package file (which is essentially a zip archive). The evaluation also clearly reveals the difference in computing power between the laptop and the phone. While the rewriting process takes considerably more time on the phone than on the laptop, we argue that this should not be a major concern as the rewriter is only run once per app.

The runtime overhead introduced by the inline reference monitor is measured through micro-benchmarks (cf. Table 4.) We compare the execution time of single function calls in three different settings: the original code with no instrumentation, the instrumented code with disabled policies (i.e. policy enforcement turned off.), and the incurred overhead. We list the average execution time for

Table 3. Sizes of apk and dex files with rewriting time on PC and phone.

App (version)	Size [Kb]		Time [sec]	
	Apk	**Dex**	**PC**	**Phone**
Angry Birds (2.0.2)	15018	994	5.8	39.3
APG (1.0.8)	1064	1718	0.7	10.1
Barcode Scanner (4.0)	508	352	0.1	2.6
Chess Free (1.55)	2240	517	0.3	4.2
Dropbox (2.1.1)	3252	869	0.5	10.2
Endomondo (7.0.2)	3263	1635	0.7	16.6
Facebook (1.8.3)	4013	2695	1.2	26.4
Instagram (1.0.3)	12901	3292	3.0	44.3
Post mobil (1.3.1)	858	1015	0.2	5.8
Shazam (3.9.0)	3904	2642	1.2	26.1
Tiny Flashlight (4.7)	1287	485	0.1	2.9
Twitter (3.0.1)	2218	764	0.3	8.9
Wetter.com (1.3.1)	4296	958	0.4	10.7
WhatsApp (2.7.3581)	5155	3182	0.8	27.7
Yuilop (1.4.2)	4879	1615	0.8	19.7

Table 4. Runtime comparison with micro-benchmarks for normal function calls and guarded function calls with policies disabled as well as the introduced runtime overhead.

Function call	Original call (ms)	Guarded call (ms)	Overhead (%)
Socket−>< init > ()	0.0186	0.0212	21.4%
ContentResolver−> query()	19.5229	19.4987	0.8%
Camera−> open()	74.498	79.476	6.4%

each function call. For all function calls the instrumentation adds a small runtime overhead due to additional code. If we enabled policies, the changed control flow usually leads to shorter execution times and renders them incomparable. Even with disabled policies the incurred runtime overhead is negligible and does not adversely affect the app's performance.

4.2   Case Study Evaluation

We evaluate our framework in several case studies by applying different policies to real world apps from Google Play [28] (cf. Table 3 for the analyzed versions). As a disclaimer, we would like to point out that we use apps from the market for exemplary purposes only, without implications regarding their security unless we state this explicitly.

For our evaluation, we implemented 9 different policies. Five of them are designed to revoke critical Android platform permissions, in particular the Internet permission (`InternetPolicy`), access to camera and audio hardware (`CameraPolicy`, `AudioPolicy`), and permissions to read contacts and calendar entries (`ContactsPolicy`, `CalendarPolicy`). Furthermore, we introduce a complex policy that tracks possible fees incurred by untrusted applications (`CostPolicy`). The `HttpsRedirectPolicy` and `MediaStorePolicy` address security issues in third-party apps and the OS. Finally, the `ReflectionPolicy` described in Sect. 3 monitors invocations of Java's Reflection API and an app-specific policy. In the following case studies, we highlight 7 of these policies and evaluate them in detail on real-world apps.

Our case studies focus on (a) the possibility to revoke standard Android permissions. Additionally, it is possible to (b) enforce fine-grained policies that are not supported by Android's existing permission system. Our framework provides quick-fixes and mitigation for vulnerabilities both in (c) third-party apps and (d) the operating system[2]. Finally, we present a general security policy that is completely independent of Android's permission system.

Revoking Android permissions. Many Android applications request more permissions than necessary. AppGuard gives users the chance to safely revoke permissions at any time at a fine-grained level.

Case study: Twitter. As an example for the revocation of permissions, we chose the official app of the popular micro-blogging service Twitter. It attracted attention in the media [42] for secretly uploading phone numbers and email addresses stored in the user's address book to the Twitter servers. While the app "officially" requests the permissions to access both Internet and the user's contact data, it did not indicate that this data would be copied off the phone as part of the "Find friends" feature that makes friend suggestions based on the user's address book. As a result of the public disclosure, the current version of the app now explicitly informs the user before uploading any personal information.

To prevent leakage of private information, we block access to the user's contact list. Since friends can also be added manually, AppGuard's `ContactsPolicy` protects the user's privacy while losing only minor convenience functionality. The actual policy enforcement is done by monitoring queries to the `ContentResolver`, which serves as a centralized access point to Android's various databases. Data is identified by a URI, which we examine to selectively block queries to the contact list by returning a mock result object. Our tests were carried out on an older version of the Twitter app, which was released prior to their fix.

Case study: Tiny Flashlight. The app either uses the camera's flash LED as a flashlight, or turns the whole screen white and requests the permissions to access the Internet and the camera. Manual analysis indicates that the Internet permission is only required to display online ads. However, together with the camera, this app could potentially be abused for spying purposes, which would be hard to detect without detailed code or traffic analysis. AppGuard can block Internet access of the app with the `InternetPolicy`, which blocks the in-app ads. We monitor constructor calls of the various `Socket` classes, the

---

[2] By providing policy recommendations based on a crowdsourcing approach, even laymen users can enforce complex policies (e.g. to fix OS vulnerabilities).

`java.net.url.openConnection()` method as well as several other network I/O functions, and throw an `IOException` if access to the Internet is forbidden.

Enforcing fine-grained policies. AppGuard can also add new restrictions to functionalities that are not restricted by the current permission system or that are already protected, but not in the desired way. For example, from the user's point of view most apps should only communicate with a limited set of servers. The wetter.com app provides weather information and should only communicate with its servers to query weather information. The `InternetPolicy` of AppGuard provides fine grained Internet access based on per-app white-listing of web servers. For this app we restrict Internet access with the regular-expression `^(.+\.)?wetter\.com$`, which blocks potentially harmful connections to other servers. White-listing can be configured in the management interface by selecting from a list of hosts the app has already attempted to connect to.

Quick-fixes for vulnerabilities in third-party apps. Although most apps use encrypted `https` for the login procedures to web servers, there are apps that return to unencrypted `http` after successful login, thereby transmitting their authentication tokens in plain text over the Internet. Attackers could eavesdrop on the connection to impersonate the user [36].

Endomondo Sports Tracker returns to `http` after successful login, thereby leaking the authentication token. As the Web server supports `https` for the whole session, the `HttpsRedirectPolicy` of AppGuard enforces the permanent usage of `https`, which protects the user's account and data from identity theft. Depending on the monitored function, we return the redirected `https` connection or the content from the redirected connection.

Mitigation for operating system vulnerabilities. We also found our tool useful to mitigate operating system vulnerabilities. As we cannot change the operating system itself, we instrument all apps with a global security policy to prevent exploits. For example, Android apps do not require a special permission to access the photo storage. Any app with the Internet permission could thus leak private photos without the user's knowledge. We address this problem with a global `MediaStorePolicy` policy that monitors calls to the `ContentResolver` object. Moreover, any app could use the Android browser to leak arbitrary data, by sending an appropriate Intent. The `InternetPolicy` monitors the `startActivity(Intent)` calls and throws an exception if the particular intent is not allowed. It thereby also prevents the local cross-site scripting attack [4] against the Android browser that was present up to Android 2.3.4. Using a combination of `VIEW` intents, it was possible to trick the browser into executing arbitrary JavaScript code within the domain of the attacker's choice, which enabled the attacker to steal login information or even silently install additional apps.

Threats to validity. Like any IRM system, AppGuard's monitor runs within the same process as the target app. This makes it vulnerable to attacks from malicious apps that try to bypass or disable the security monitor. Our instrumentation technique is robust against attacks from Java code, as this code is strongly typed. It can handle cases like reflection or dynamically loaded libraries. However, a malicious app could use native code to disable the security monitor by altering the references we modified or tampering with the AppGuard's bytecode instructions or data structures. To prevent this, we could block the execution of any untrusted native code by intercepting calls to `System.loadLibrary()`, which is, however, not a viable solution in practice. Currently, AppGuard warns the user if an app attempts to execute untrusted native code.

In order to assess the potential impact of native code on our approach, we analyzed the percentage of apps that rely on it. Our evaluation [2] on 25,000 apps (cf. Table 5) revealed that about 15 % include native libraries, which is high compared to the 5 % of apps reported in [46]. We conjecture that this difference is due to the composition of our sample. It consists of 30 % games, which on Android frequently build upon native code based game engines (e.g., libGDX or Unity) to improve performance. Ignoring games, we found only 9 % of the apps to be using native code, which makes AppGuard a safe solution for over 90 % of these apps.

Table 5. Ratio of apps using native code

App market	Overall		Games		No games	
	Apps	Nat. code	Apps	Nat. code	Apps	Nat. code
Google Play	9508	2212 (23 %)	2838	1110 (39 %)	6670	1102 (16 %)
SlideMe	15974	1693 (10 %)	5920	1244 (21 %)	10054	449 (4.5 %)
Total	25482	3905 (15 %)	8758	2354 (26 %)	16724	1551 (9.2 %)

AppGuard monitors the invocation of security-relevant methods, which are typically part of the Android framework API. By reimplementing parts of this API and directly calling into lower layers of the framework, a malicious app could circumvent the security monitor. This attack vector is always available to attackers in IRM systems that monitor method invocations. Furthermore, AppGuard is not designed to be stealthy: due to the resigning of apps, instrumentation transparency cannot be guaranteed. There are many apps that verify their own signature (e.g. from the Amazon AppStore). If they rely on Android API to retrieve their own signature, however, AppGuard can hook these functions to return the original signature, thus concealing its presence. An app could also detect the presence of AppGuard by looking for the presence of AppGuard classes in the virtual machine. In the end, both of these attacks boil down to an arms race, that a determined attacker will win. Up to now, we did not detect any app that tried to explicitly circumvent AppGuard.

Our instrumentation approach relies only on the layout of Dalvik's internal data structure for methods, which has not changed since the initial version of Android. However, our instrumentation system could easily be adapted if the layout were to change in future versions of Android.

Android programs are multi-threaded by default. Issues of thread safety could therefore arise in the monitor when considering stateful policies that take the relative timing of events in different threads into account. While we did not yet experiment with such policies, we plan to extend our system to support *race-free policies* [14] in the future. In contrast, policies that atomically decide whether to permit a method call are also correct in the multithreaded setting.

5   Further Related Work

Researchers have worked on various security aspects of Android and proposed many security enhancements. One line of research [10,18,19,27,41] targets the detection of privacy leaks and malicious third-party apps. Another line of work analyzed Android's permission based access control system. Barrera et al. [6] conducted an empirical analysis of Android's permission system on 1,100 Android apps and suggested improvements to its granularity. Felt et al. [24] analyzed the effectiveness of app permissions using case studies on Google Chrome extensions and Android apps. The inflexible and coarse-grained permission system of Android inspired many researchers to propose extensions [20,29,38–40]. Conti et al. [13] integrate a context-related policy enforcement mechanism into Android. Fragkaki et al. [25] present an external reference monitor approach to enforce coarse grained secrecy and integrity policies called SORBET. In contrast, our intention was to deploy the system to unmodified stock Android phones.

The concept of IRMs has received considerable attention in the literature. It was first formalized by Erlingsson and Schneider in the development of the SASI/PoET/PSLang systems [21,22], which implement IRM's for x86 assembly code and Java bytecode. Several other IRM implementations for Java followed. Polymer [8] is a IRM system based on edit automata, which supports composition of complex security policies from simple building blocks. The Java-MOP [11] system offers a rich set of formal policy specification languages. IRM systems have also been developed for other platforms. Mobile [33] is an extension to Microsoft's .NET Common Intermediate Language (CIL) that supports certified inline reference monitoring. Finally, the S3MS.NET Run Time Monitor [16] enforces security policies expressed in a variety of policy languages for .NET desktop and mobile applications on Windows phones.

6   Conclusions

We presented a practical approach to enforce high-level, fine-grained security policies on stock android phones. It is built upon a novel approach for callee-site inline reference monitoring and provides a powerful framework for enforcing arbitrary security and secrecy policies. Our system instruments directly on the phone and allows automatic updates without losing user data. The system curbs the pervasive overly curious behavior of Android apps. We enforce complex stateful security policies and mitigate vulnerabilities of both third-party apps and the OS. AppGuard goes even one step beyond being capable of efficiently protecting secret data from misuse in untrusted apps. Our experimental analysis demonstrates the robustness of the approach and shows that the overhead in terms of space and runtime are negligible. The case studies illustrate how AppGuard prevents several real-world attacks on Android. A recent release of AppGuard has already been downloaded by more than 1,000,000 users.

Acknowledgement. We thank the anonymous reviewers for their comments. This work was supported by the German Ministry for Education and Research (BMBF) through funding for the Center for IT-Security, Privacy and Accountability (CISPA) and both the initiative for excellence and the Emmy Noether program of the German federal government. Further, we would like to thank Bastian Könings for pointing us to interesting Android apps.

References

1. Android.com: Security and permissions. http://developer.android.com/guide/topics/security/security.html (2012)
2. Backes, M., Gerling, S., Hammer, C., Maffei, M., von Styp-Rekowsky, P.: App-Guard - Fine-Grained Policy Enforcement for Untrusted Android Applications. Technical Report A/02/2013, Saarland University (April 2013)
3. Backes, M., Gerling, S., Hammer, C., Maffei, M., von Styp-Rekowsky, P.: App-Guard - enforcing user requirements on Android apps. In: Piterman, N., Smolka, S. (eds.) TACAS 2013. LNCS, vol. 7795, pp. 543–548. Springer, Heidelberg (2013)
4. Backes, M., Gerling, S., von Styp-Rekowsky, P.: A Local Cross-Site Scripting Attack Against Android Phones. http://www.infsec.cs.uni-saarland.de/projects/android-vuln/android_xss.pdf (2011)
5. Backes SRT: SRT AppGuard : mobile Android security solution. http://www.srt-appguard.com/en/
6. Barrera, D., Kayacık, H.G., van Oorschot, P.C., Somayaji, A.: A methodology for empirical analysis of permission-based security models and its application to android. In: Proceedings of the 17th ACM Conference on Computer and Communication Security (CCS 2010), pp. 73–84 (2010)
7. Bauer, L., Ligatti, J., Walker, D.: A Language and System for Composing Security Policies. Technical Report TR-699-04, Princeton University (January 2004)
8. Bauer, L., Ligatti, J., Walker, D.: Composing security policies with polymer. In: Proceedings of the ACM SIGPLAN 2005 Conference on Programming Language Design and Implementation (PLDI 2005), pp. 305–314 (2005)
9. Bugiel, S., Davi, L., Dmitrienko, A., Fischer, T., Sadeghi, A.R., Shastry, B.: Towards taming privilege-escalation attacks on android. In: Proceedings of the 19th Annual Network and Distributed System Security Symposium (NDSS 2012) (2012)
10. Chaudhuri, A., Fuchs, A., Foster, J.: SCanDroid: Automated Security Certification of Android Applications. Technical Report CS-TR-4991, University of Maryland. http://www.cs.umd.edu/avik/papers/scandroidascaa.pdf (2009)
11. Chen, F., Roşu, G.: Java-MOP: a monitoring oriented programming environment for Java. In: Halbwachs, N., Zuck, L.D. (eds.) TACAS 2005. LNCS, vol. 3440, pp. 546–550. Springer, Heidelberg (2005)
12. Chip: SRT   AppGuard.   http://www.chip.de/downloads/SRT-AppGuard-Android-App_56552141.html

13. Conti, M., Nguyen, V.T.N., Crispo, B.: CRePE: context-related policy enforcement for Android. In: Burmester, M., Tsudik, G., Magliveras, S., Ilić, I. (eds.) ISC 2010. LNCS, vol. 6531, pp. 331–345. Springer, Heidelberg (2011)

14. Dam, M., Jacobs, B., Lundblad, A.: Security monitor inlining and certification for multithreaded Java. In: Mathematical Structures in Computer Science. Cambridge University Press, New York (2011)

15. Davis, B., Sanders, B., Khodaverdian, A., Chen, H.: I-ARM-Droid: A rewriting framework for in-app reference monitors for Android applications. In: Mobile Security Technologies 2012 (MoST 12) (2012)

16. Desmet, L., Joosen, W., Massacci, F., Naliuka, K., Philippaerts, P., Piessens, F., Vanoverberghe, D.: The S3MS.NET run time monitor. Electron. Notes Theor. Comput. Sci. **253**(5), 153–159 (2009)

17. von Eitzen, C.: Apple: future iOS release will require user permission for apps to access address book. http://h-online.com/-1435404 (February 2012)

18. Enck, W., Gilbert, P., Chun, B.G., Cox, L.P., Jung, J., McDaniel, P., Sheth, A.N.: TaintDroid: an information-flow tracking system for realtime privacy monitoring on smartphones. In: Proceedings of the 9th Usenix Symposium on Operating Systems Design and Implementation (OSDI 2010), pp. 393–407 (2010)

19. Enck, W., Octeau, D., McDaniel, P., Chaudhuri, S.: A study of Android application security. In: Proceedings of the 20th Usenix Security Symposium (2011)

20. Enck, W., Ongtang, M., McDaniel, P.: On lightweight mobile phone application certification. In: Proceedings of the 16th ACM Conference on Computer and Communication Security (CCS 2009), pp. 235–245 (2009)

21. Erlingsson, Ú., Schneider, F.B.: IRM enforcement of Java stack inspection. In: Proceedings of the 2002 IEEE Symposium on Security and Privacy (Oakland 2002), pp. 246–255 (2000)

22. Erlingsson, U., Schneider, F.B.: SASI enforcement of security policies: a retrospective. In: Proceedings of the 1999 Workshop on New Security Paradigms (NSPW 1999), pp. 87–95 (2000)

23. Felt, A.P., Chin, E., Hanna, S., Song, D., Wagner, D.: Android permissions demystified. In: Proceedings of the 18th ACM Conference on Computer and Communication Security (CCS 2011) (2011)

24. Felt, A.P., Greenwood, K., Wagner, D.: The effectiveness of application permissions. In: Proceedings of the 2nd Usenix Conference on Web Application Development (WebApps 2011) (2011)

25. Fragkaki, E., Bauer, L., Jia, L., Swasey, D.: Modeling and enhancing Android's permission system. In: Foresti, S., Yung, M., Martinelli, F. (eds.) ESORICS 2012. LNCS, vol. 7459, pp. 1–18. Springer, Heidelberg (2012)

26. Gibler, C., Crussel, J., Erickson, J., Chen, H.: AndroidLeaks: Detecting Privacy Leaks in Android Applications. Technical Report CSE-2011-10, University of California, Davis (2011)

27. Gilbert, P., Chun, B.G., Cox, L.P., Jung, J.: Vision: automated security validation of mobile apps at app markets. In: Proceedings of the 2nd International Workshop on Mobile Cloud Computing and Services (MCS 2011) (2011)

28. Google Play. https://play.google.com/store (2012)

29. Grace, M., Zhou, Y., Wang, Z., Jiang, X.: Systematic detection of capability leaks in stock Android smartphones. In: Proceedings of the 19th Annual Network and Distributed System Security Symposium (NDSS 2012) (2012)

30. Gruver, B.: Smali: a assembler/disassembler for Android's dex format. http://code.google.com/p/smali/

31. Hamlen, K.W., Jones, M.: Aspect-oriented in-lined reference monitors. In: Proceedings of the 3rd ACM SIGPLAN Workshop on Programming Languages and Analysis for Security (PLAS 2008), pp. 11–20 (2008)
32. Hamlen, K.W., Jones, M.M., Sridhar, M.: Chekov: Aspect-Oriented Runtime Monitor Certification via Model-Checking. Technical Report UTDCS-16-11, University of Texas at Dallas (May 2011)
33. Hamlen, K.W., Morrisett, G., Schneider, F.B.: Certified in-lined reference monitoring on.NET. In: Proceedings of the 1st ACM SIGPLAN Workshop on Programming Languages and Analysis for Security (PLAS 2006), pp. 7–16 (2006)
34. Heise: SRT AppGuard. http://www.heise.de/download/srt-appguard-pro-1187469.html
35. Jeon, J., Micinski, K.K., Vaughan, J.A., Reddy, N., Zhu, Y., Foster, J.S., Millstein, T.: Dr. Android and Mr. Hide: Fine-Grained Security Policies on Unmodified Android. Technical Report CS-TR-5006, University of Maryland (December 2011)
36. Könings, B., Nickels, J., Schaub, F.: Catching AuthTokens in the Wild - The Insecurity of Google's ClientLogin Protocol. Technical Report, Ulm University. http://www.uni-ulm.de/in/mi/mi-mitarbeiter/koenings/catching-authtokens.html (2011)
37. Ligatti, J., Bauer, L., Walker, D.: Edit automata: enforcement mechanisms for run-time security policies. Int. J. Inf. Secur. 4(1–2), 2–16 (2005)
38. Nauman, M., Khan, S., Zhang, X.: Apex: extending Android permission model and enforcement with user-defined runtime constraints. In: Proceedings of the 5th ACM Symposium on Information, Computer and Communication Security (ASIACCS 2010), pp. 328–332 (2010)
39. Ongtang, M., Butler, K.R.B., McDaniel, P.D.: Porscha: policy oriented secure content handling in Android. In: Proceedings of the 26th Annual Computer Security Applications Conference (ACSAC 2010), pp. 221–230 (2010)
40. Ongtang, M., McLaughlin, S.E., Enck, W., McDaniel, P.: Semantically rich application-centric security in Android. In: Proceedings of the 25th Annual Computer Security Applications Conference (ACSAC 2009), pp. 340–349 (2009)
41. Portokalidis, G., Homburg, P., Anagnostakis, K., Bos, H.: Paranoid Andoird: versatile protection for smartphones. In: Proceedings of the 26th Annual Computer Security Applications Conference (ACSAC 2010), pp. 347–356 (2010)
42. Sarno, D.: Twitter stores full iPhone contact list for 18 months, after scan. http://articles.latimes.com/2012/feb/14/business/la-fi-tn-twitter-contacts-20120214 (February 2012)
43. Schneider, F.B.: Enforceable security policies. ACM Trans. Inf. Syst. Secur. 3(1), 30–50 (2000)
44. von Styp-Rekowsky, P., Gerling, S., Backes, M., Hammer, C.: Idea: callee-site rewriting of sealed system libraries. In: Jürjens, J., Livshits, B., Scandariato, R. (eds.) ESSoS 2013. LNCS, vol. 7781, pp. 33–41. Springer, Heidelberg (2013)
45. Xu, R., Saïdi, H., Anderson, R.: Aurasium - practical policy enforcement for Android applications. In: Proceedings of the 21st Usenix Security Symposium (2012)
46. Zhou, Y., Wang, Z., Zhou, W., Jiang, X.: Hey, you, get off of my market: detecting malicious apps in official and alternative Android markets. In: Proceedings of the 19th Annual Network and Distributed System Security Symposium (NDSS 2012) (February 2012)

Autonomous
and Spontaneous Security

Reference Monitors for Security and Interoperability in OAuth 2.0

Ronan-Alexandre Cherrueau[1], Rémi Douence[1], Jean-Claude Royer[1]([⊠]),
Mario Südholt[1], Anderson Santana de Oliveira[2], Yves Roudier[3],
and Matteo Dell'Amico[3]

[1] École des Mines de Nantes, Nantes, France
`Jean-Claude.Royer@mines-nantes.fr`
[2] SAP Applied Research, Mougins, France
[3] EURECOM, Sophia Antipolis, France

Abstract. OAuth 2.0 is a recent IETF standard devoted to providing authorization to clients requiring access to specific resources over HTTP. It has been pointed out that this framework is potentially subject to security issues, as well as difficulties concerning the interoperability between protocol participants and application evolution. As we show in this paper, there are indeed multiple reasons that make this protocol hard to implement and impede interoperability in the presence of different kinds of client. Our main contribution consists in a framework that harnesses a type-based policy language and aspect-based support for protocol adaptation through flexible reference monitors in order to handle security, interoperability and evolution issues of OAuth 2.0. We apply our framework in the context of three scenarios that make explicit variations in the protocol and show how to handle those issues.

Keywords: Aspect oriented programming · Interoperability · OAuth protocol · Reference monitor · Security · Type system

1 Introduction

Web services and applications are implemented more and more frequently using open standards for security goals such as WS-policy for SOAP-based services, and, more commonly as part of RESTful APIs, OpenID for authentication as well as OAuth for authorization. OAuth has gained a lot of interest, its 2.0 version recently becoming an IETF standard. All major internet players (Google, Facebook, Microsoft, among others) have already released API's to allow resource access delegation in web applications using this standard.

Although the specifications of the standard are sufficiently clear, developers often have difficulties to correctly implement all of its features. There are

This work has been partially supported by the CESSA ANR project (ANR 09-SEGI-002-01, http://cessa.gforge.inria.fr) and the A4Cloud project (FP7 317550, http://www.a4cloud.eu/).

J. Garcia-Alfaro et al. (Eds.): DPM 2013 and SETOP 2013, LNCS 8247, pp. 235–249, 2014.
DOI: 10.1007/978-3-642-54568-9_15, © Springer-Verlag Berlin Heidelberg 2014

frequently subject to general problems concerning security and interoperability. For example, the design of OAuth 2.0 has put forward simplicity instead of security when choosing to support bearer tokens, which do not require to prove the possession of a cryptographic key. Token confidentiality relies then on storage and transport security (SSL/TLS); therefore, all resources mediated via OAuth 2.0 would be exposed if the transport layer security breaks (in the following, we will use simply "OAuth" instead of OAuth 2.0).

Another problem developers face when using OAuth is to actually produce interoperable implementations. The OAuth standard is not simply an authentication and delegation protocol, but an "authorization framework," whose design was heavily influenced by enterprise use cases. In order to support those use cases, the standard allows for extensibility and defines several components as optional. The standard also specifies several important features only partially, such as client registration, authorization server capabilities, and endpoint discovery, all features that are fundamental to automate service compositions in real implementations.

In this paper we provide a framework that integrates three main features in order to enable programmers to handle such security and interoperability issues, as well as related evolution scenarios: (i) an abstract and typed language for the high-level definition of security policies over service interactions, (ii) the HiPoLDS [10] model for flexible reference monitors, and (iii) aspect-oriented programming techniques for the manipulation of service implementations. More concretely, we provide four corresponding contributions. First, we show how to use a type system with explicit channel types and service subtypes in order to provide correctness guarantees over service compositions and to improve interoperability of the OAuth framework. Second, we harness the high level abstract policy language HiPoLDS for the definition of flexible reference monitors that help enforcing policies on the message level. Third, we leverage a set of aspect-oriented secure software development techniques to manage the evolution of service security capabilities and decouple them from the underlying service implementation; overall, we thus increase the dependability of OAuth deployments. Finally, we apply these techniques in the context of three realistic scenarios that exhibit security, interoperability and evolution issues of the OAuth standard.

This paper is structured as follows. Section 2 introduces the OAuth framework and some of its issues. Section 3 is dedicated to the description of the typed service language and the techniques for service manipulation we use. An application to OAuth in the context of three scenarios is described in Sect. 4. We finish with related work in Sect. 5 and a conclusion.

2 The OAuth 2.0 Authorization Framework

OAuth is an IETF standard devoted to providing authorization to clients requiring access to specific resources over HTTP. The standard was issued as RFC 6749 [22] in October 2012 and is not compatible with the first version. Several web application providers are currently using this framework, among them:

Google, GitHub, Windows Live, and Facebook. OAuth defines several protocols for resource owners to grant third-party access to their resources without exposing their passwords to resource users.

2.1 The Authorization Code Flow Case Study

We will concentrate our study on a central part of the protocol, the *Authorization Code Flow* (or ACF), which is described in Sect. 4.1 of the standard. The general architecture is depicted in Fig. 1. This protocol assumes several parties with different roles. The Resource Owner (RO) is an entity (either a human being, the end-user, or some software he uses) that grants access to some protected resources. A client (C) is a third-party application requesting the use of resources owned by the resource owner. The Authorization Server (AS) is a software application dedicated to checking client rights to access protected resources and delivering related access tokens. The User Agent (UA) is a software application which mediates communications between the client, the resource owner, and the authorization server. The authorization server has two HTTP endpoints: The authorization request (arep) and the token request (trep), while the client requires only one endpoint (crep). There are two types of clients: confidential or public depending if they are capable (or not) of maintaining the confidentiality of their credentials (password, identity, authorization code, token, ...). To get an access token the client C interacts with the authorization server in order to first get an authorization code. This authorization code is delivered by the AS to the client on the behalf of the resource owner. The client and the resource owner do not directly interact in this setting. The protocol assumes that the RO and the clients are registered to the AS. At registration time the confidential client gives an identifier and a URI. For a public client, the authentication method is optional and depends from the AS requirements.

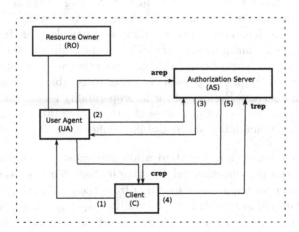

Fig. 1. The Authorization Code Flow (ACF)

The communication steps of the Authorization Code Flow, depicted in Fig. 1, are as follows:

1. C initiates a request and directs UA to AS. C includes its identifier, a state, and optionally a scope and a URI in the message.
2. RO is authenticated via its user agent UA. In this step RO grants or denies access to C.
3. AS replies to C (via UA) with either an authorization code or an error code.
4. C requests an access token from AS. C uses the token endpoint and includes its authorization code, and a URI to redirect the reply.
5. AS authenticates C and checks that the authorization code was previously delivered to C. Authentication is mandatory for confidential clients or if an authentication scheme has been previously established with a public client. AS also checks that if a URI was provided, it is the same as the URI provided when C requested the authorization code. If all these controls are valid, AS sends a token to the redirection URI (and optionally a refresh token).

The OAuth framework specifies further details about the authorization code and token in RFC 6750 [23]. The recommended time life for an authorization code is 10 minutes and it must not be used more than once. Access tokens are credentials used to access the protected resources stored on a resource server and they have a specific scope and a duration limit.

2.2   Interoperability, Security and Evolution Issues

We now present the relevant problems faced by OAuth implementations.

Interoperability. The OAuth standard has been criticized[1] for its likelihood in producing non-interoperable implementations. There are multiple sources for this problem. A large number of components are optional, for example; tokens may assume the "bearer" or "MAC" formats according to the standard, or yet SAML assertions may be used [21]. Furthermore, several components are only partially defined in the standard; this applies, in particular, for the client registration process, server authorization capabilities, and endpoint discovery mechanism. Generally, developers of OAuth client application are interested in creating services that are as flexible as possible in order to be able to access data from multiple resource servers. Because of the interoperability issues, this requires the handling of a large number of distinct settings for each different authorization server, raising maintainability and reusability difficulties.

Evolution. As OAuth is a web authorization framework, its adoption in diverse enterprise scenarios is to be expected. Existing implementations need to be modified in order to cover requirements coming from the enterprise world: resource owners, for example, are unlikely to be individuals but rather organizations. Therefore we envisage in this paper a scenario where authorization needs to be obtained from a user on behalf of its organization.

---

[1] See, e.g., Hammer: http://hueniverse.com/2012/07/oauth-2-0-and-the-road-to-hell.

Security. Several security problems of OAuth are known and the specification warns about a number of potential security issues (Sect. 10 of [22]). Furthermore, threats related to injection attacks and the insufficient protection of credentials have also been investigated [4,12].

3   A Typed Framework for Policy Enforcement

In this section we introduce the framework we leverage to solve the security, evolution and interoperability problems of OAuth. Our solution relies on a typed policy language for service interactions and two main concepts for service manipulations: aspect-oriented programming and reference monitors for policy enforcement.

3.1   Typed Service Interactions

We propose to use a rich type system for service interactions which is sound even in presence of attackers [2]. This type system is defined using so-called semantic typing [5], it supports negation, intersection and union types which are convenient in a query or declarative context. Adding subtyping is important for two main reasons: *(i)* it extends dynamic channel discovery since required services may be provided by more specific ones and *(ii)* it improves interoperability, a client can connect to various compatible services. Since we can discover new channels at runtime, type inference is done at message reception time. Type inference checks that the message is well-formed and computes the types of the discovered channels in the messages.

Concretely, our type system provides the following types: Classic basic types (like `String, Integer, ...`), structured types as labeled type list (`"label"[Type],Type`), record types (`{"label":Type; ...}`) and type for channels (or URIs) that are denoted `<Type>`. We have also negation types (`NOT Type`), union types (`Type + Type`), and intersection types (`Type & Type`). Furthermore we type provided endpoints (channel, URI) as well as required ones. For the definition of the type system, see [2].

This type system has the following benefits: *(i)* it makes explicit a contract that has to be obeyed by servers and clients, *(ii)* it is subject to verification and avoids some ill-formed messages that result from errors or code injection attacks, *(iii)* it provides powerful and declarative means to define properties of data, channels and parties in communications, *(iv)* it supports subtyping which is convenient for more flexible discovery and interoperability. Currently the type system and its machinery has been implemented as a Java library. Work on the integration of the type system in Apache's service framework CXF is on-going.

3.2   Security Domains and Policies

In order to extend OAuth with security policies about resource access, we are using the HiPoLDS language we defined in [10]. Security policies in HiPoLDS rely on the description of the information flows between so-called policy domains. Those domains can capture both component and protocol entities. Policies are expressed using rules that match with the content or with specific properties of the information flow. In particular, HiPoLDS describes patterns in the flow based on the notion of information tag, a construct of the policy language used to annotate the message with security metadata. Some tags can relate to the content of a message payload, at different levels in a protocol stack, like the IP address, some field value at a given offset in the payload, or an encrypted blob in some other part of the message; alternately, other tags refer to more structural component or protocol concepts. In particular, the type system described above can be seen as an example of the latter category: types can be introduced into HiPoLDS rules by annotating the message with a specific information tag. Payload related tags can also be identified through message annotation at the type inference phase. Section 4.2 illustrates both situations.

3.3   Monitors and Aspects

The implementation of both the type system and of policy enforcement at the protocol level can be done with reference monitors [8,18]. Reference monitors represent a flexible solution to evolve existing applications without modifying their code. They act as wrappers around agents and intercept incoming and outgoing messages. Many actions can be associated with messages: control, remove, modify, resend, etc. This is for instance a good way to add extra control on messages to avoid some attacks. In our case, we use monitors, implemented using the HiPoLDS rules, to secure the storage of credentials and to oblige agents to use SSL/TLS connections as advocated by the OAuth standard.

Sometimes we need more intrusive actions to modify the internal code of agents. In this case we propose to use an aspect-oriented approach to complement the monitors. To this end, we have defined a (new) aspect system for Apache's CXF service framework, see [3] for a publicly available implementation. This aspect system enables programmers to statically or dynamically modify service compositions, interceptor definitions and Java-based implementations of CXF services. The events that trigger modifications are defined in terms of finite-state based sequences of service invocations, interceptor calls or features of the service implementation. Once such events are identified, new Java code may be injected or used to replace existing code.

4   Application to OAuth

We now demonstrate how our techniques can overcome the issues impacting OAuth introduced in Sect. 2.2. To this end we consider a workflow from the banking domain, see Fig. 2, as part of which a bank and an insurance company together provide services to private customers.

Alice is a customer of the bank where she has contracted a loan. The bank proposes Alice to use third party services to acquire an insurance concerning her

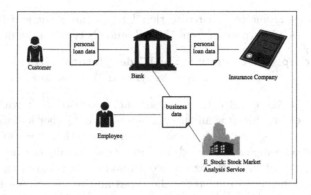

Fig. 2. Enterprise usage of OAuth

loan and buy a share portfolio. For that, Alice uses her web browser to open the web service from the insurance company, which requests access to her loan data stored at the bank. In OAuth terms, Alice is thus the resource owner with her web browser as user agent, the insurance company plays the role of the client, and the bank acts as a resource and an authorization server. Note that Alice is not bound to use only the service of the insurance company (as she is the only responsible for her personal data); she can therefore choose to use any other client registered to the bank's authorization server.

In the following we consider three OAuth-related extension scenarios and show how our framework solves the interoperability and evolution issues raised by these scenarios.

4.1 Type-Based Definition of OAuth-Conform Interactions

Scenario 1. As a first interoperability scenario we assume that the client, the insurance company, was built to work with an existing AS server, e.g., provided by its headquarters, which does not issue refresh tokens. Provided that the same client will request access to resources held in the resource server, the problem now is to equip or modify the client implementation such that it will also be able to use refresh tokens, as imposed by the AS from Alice's bank.

Another token-related interoperability issue consists in different types of access tokens. The OAuth standard allows for bearer and MAC tokens. For instance, the client was built to use bearer tokens, whereas the Bank server requires the MAC token type.

Solution. In order to handle incompatibilities between stakeholders we have to be able to define suitable channel types for the endpoints for OAuth-related interactions and then provide suitable types for the different token types as discussed in Scenario 1 above.

The client endpoint (called redirection URI of the client and noted `crep`) should receive rich information from the AS, and its type can be defined as

$$\text{crep} = < (\ \{\text{"grant"}:\text{AuthCode};\ \text{"state"}:\text{State}\}$$
$$+\ \text{Token} + \text{DenyError}\ )\ \&\ \text{Secure} >$$

On this endpoint the client can receive an authentication code with a state or a token or an error, this is a union type noted `+`. It further specifies that the client should receive secure information with an intersection type (noted `&`). Each type should be as complex as needed, for instance specifying the various cases of errors or the fact that the authorization code and the token have a time duration. Agents are responsible to implement the types and to use values according to their types, types explicit a contract the interacting parties must observe.

The authorization endpoint provided by the bank has type:

$$\text{arep} = < (\ \{\ \text{"id"}:\text{Credents}\ ;\ \text{"state"}:\text{State}\ \}$$
$$\oplus\ \text{Scope}\ \oplus\ \text{C.crep}\ )\ \&\ \text{Secure} >$$

Mandatory information (client identifier, secret and state) are collected in a record type, while optional information (scope and client redirection URI) is typed using the $\oplus$ operator. This is a syntactic sugar for a combination of record and union types defining optional information type. Note that we found the provided `C.crep` type from `C` in `arep` since the client has the option to send its proper URI to the AS.

In the first scenario we need different kinds of token, which can be represented by the subtype hierarchy depicted in Fig. 3. The hierarchy uses unrelated types for "real" tokens and refresh tokens because the latter are not used for resource access but for token management. The client URI should be connected to several servers and with two required endpoints (`AS.crep` (3) and `AS.crep` (5)). Component typing rules imply that these required endpoints should be supertypes of the `C.crep` channel type. For instance, `<(Token + DenyError) & Secure>` or `<MACToken>` are such supertypes (this can be easily shown using the rules in Appendix A Table 1). The type-checking ensures this control and excludes dynamic type errors.

In Scenario 1, the client should receive either tokens from the insurance AS, or tokens and refresh tokens from the bank AS. All of this token information could be secured using either bearer or MAC kinds of token. We have then to change the `crep` type. We can use for instance, one endpoint with the following type:
`crep = <(AuthCode + Token + {"token":Token; "refresh":RefreshToken}` `+ DenyError) & Secure>`.

To evolve the client, we encapsulate it into a reference monitor which manages types, incoming and outgoing messages. To handle the different interoperability situations, the monitor for the client could either have a unique general URI as above or several dedicated URIs connected to each server endpoint. Defining only one endpoint for the client is better at least from a coupling point of view. Decreasing component coupling increases the endpoint type complexity and this requires a powerful type system as the one proposed here. In this case, the

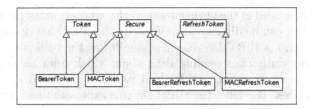

Fig. 3. A UML like hierarchy of tokens

adaptation code checks the dynamic type of the received values in messages and triggers additional codes. This is the place where HiPoLDS rules or aspects can be used as shown below.

4.2   Extending the OAuth Framework Using a Policy

Scenario 2. The OAuth framework describes the overall protocol to grant clients access tokens to the resource server using the Authorization Code Flow. We consider here a scenario in which we need to extend the protocol in order to handle additional security strategies.

Consider that David, a bank employee, needs to analyze the profitability of the fund he manages. In order to do so, he uses an external service from the stock market analysis company E_Stock to evaluate the fund portfolio that contains no personally identifiable information about bank customers. Clearly, E_Stock is acting as a client with respect to the Bank, which still plays the role of a resource server and owner.

The difference to OAuth's standard protocol is here that David cannot be considered as the only resource owner since the actual data owner is the bank. Furthermore, we consider another requirement: banks today typically need to ensure additional accountability guarantees with respect to their employees' behavior. For instance, David should not be able to delegate access to arbitrary external services. He should also not be able to delegate access to stock managed by the bank outside of his fund portfolio.

Solution. The OAuth framework thus has to be extended with the enforcement of a mandatory security policy defined by the bank with respect to its employees' actions. The User Agent's authentication is therefore itself subject to the granting of an authorization by the bank.

The implementation of this mandatory access control on top of OAuth depends essentially on the entity that runs the AS. If it is the bank, then the AS provides a perfect point of enforcement; otherwise, if the AS is managed by a third party, the bank will need to intercept messages between the client and the AS. In the latter case, an aspect based implementation of the reference monitor is necessary as network traffic is likely encrypted (the use of an SSL/TLS secure session being typically recommended in the OAuth framework), whereas in the former case, the reference monitor can be directly introduced by the bank after decryption.

In this scenario, a HiPoLDS reference monitor at the bank would make sure that David only authorizes reading data about stock from his own portfolio, and that the client is an acceptable third party, as identified among a set of authorized services. The following HiPoLDS rule expresses these constraints, by dropping messages not conforming to the policy:

```
m:arep, m.scope.obj in Funds,
  ( m.id not in AuthorizedServices
     or (m.scope.obj not in Portfolio[useragent]) )
=> m is dropped
```

HiPoLDS rules are composed of two parts: the left part, before the '=>' construct, performs pattern matching on messages; the right part defines the security mechanisms that should apply – dropping the message, in this case. The m:arep clause applies when m is annotated with the **arep** information tag. Tags can be associated with a message based on either type inference and/or the structure of the message payload (we do not describe this here for brevity). m.scope.obj and m.id are extracted from the actual message content, part of which can also be identified from the type. In the example, m.scope.obj identifies the list of stocks in the fund E_Stock will be granted access to, and m.id refers to E_Stock. Finally, **Funds** and **AuthorizedServices** are sets, respectively comprising object identifiers on funds and external clients authorized to access fund data. **Portfolio** is a mapping between identifiers of user agents of employees (**useragent**) to the set of object identifiers for fund data.

4.3   Harnessing Types for Aspect-Based Security

Scenario 3. Finally, we consider a scenario that requires some limited invasive modifications by OAuth stakeholders to the implementation of OAuth-related services. The OAuth standard mandates that sensitive data items e.g. authorization grants, tokens, and client credentials are stored securely. Developers frequently fail to adopt the best security mechanisms to protect assets, leading to vulnerable implementations. We consider a scenario in which security-relevant information, such as tokens, have to be stored at a remote user agent.

Solution. The OAuth standard contains a number of prescriptions that do not directly restrict the communication between stakeholders but instead manage security-relevant data has to be handled as part of service implementations. It restricts, for instance, how the user-agent's authenticated state (e.g., session cookie, HTML5 local storage) is to be stored (see OAuth standard, Sect. 10.12). It prescribes that this data has to be kept in a location accessible only to the client and the user-agent. While this may be some common encrypted portion of the memory, it may also involve the use of special-purpose secured storage services, for instance, if the client uses a user agent remotely.

In order to ensure the use of a correct secure storage strategy, a combination of type-based security enforcement and aspect-based adaptation is used: the types that guide service discovery are extended in order to indicate the need of a particular storage strategy depending on the channel configuration between stakeholders and aspects are used to modify the implementation of services in order to use secure storage services if needed.

In the case of a remote user agent, the resource owner has to provide a typed channel for communication between the resource owner and the agent. Its type information makes explicit the need for a particular storage strategy. The strategy is then implemented using an aspect, by statically encapsulating the original token data structure in the user agent by a secure data structure. Alternatively, aspects can be used to dynamically encrypt the tokens and store them in a suitable data structure.

5   Related Work

We discuss related work in this section belonging to four domains: OAuth security issues, types for services, security policy languages, and service evolution, notably using aspects.

OAuth Security Issues. The main document describing OAuth 2.0 is [22] for a comprehensive OAuth security model and analysis. Several classes of attacks are discussed: key and secret storing and transmission, client authentication, token and refresh token, cross-site request forgery, guessing and phishing attacks, clickjacking, open redirectors and code injection. A real example of security problem with Twitter and OAuth 1.0a was described in [16]. Pai et al. [12] uses the specification language Alloy and a SAT solver to discover security counterexample. In [4], the authors claim to find dozens of previously unknown vulnerabilities in connecting social networking like Twitter and Facebook with websites like Yahoo and WordPress.

Types for Services. The type system of [13] is based on a nested record type system with collections and universal polymorphism. This type system is neither recursive nor does it allow channel mobility; its checking algorithm is expensive even in this restricted setting. Sans and Cervesato [17] deal with an abstract model that covers code mobility which we do not address, we are only concerned with remote procedure calls. On the other hand, they consider functions rather than channels and they do not support sum types, nor recursive types. They require a centralized typing table collecting types of services published everywhere in the Internet and assume that this repository can be trusted. A distributed and typed π-calculus for mobile agents is described in [15]. The type system considers malicious agents with erroneous types. Type safety is enforced by dynamically type checking agents when they enter a site. In contrast to our work they do not consider channel discovery or subtyping. The last piece of work is [6] which applies semantics subtyping to the π-calculus. Despite the presence of a precise orchestration, their typing rules for services are similar to ours. We are not concerned with a precise process algebra for agent behaviors and this point is shared with all work on session types. But we focused on typing the communications between several agents leading to similar rules than in component systems (see [19]) and we also consider type attacks from malicious agents.

Security Policy Languages. With respect to security policy languages, HiPoLDS is particularly suited for this setting because it is especially designed for complex distributed architectures, taking into account the fact that different security policies apply in different parts of the distributed system according to its security levels, and not all execution environments where services are running can be controlled. Notice that XACML [11] can be used in conjunction with OAuth 2.0 (e.g. for scope definitions), but it is not suited to describe the reference monitor behavior.

Similarly to HiPoLDS, Law Governed Interactions (LGI) [20] provides a hierarchical way of specifying the architecture of a distributed systems and security policies that apply only to a subset of such a system; policy enforcement is performed by reference monitors. Domains are governed by a mandatory policy, their law. However, the approach fails short to account for multiple stakeholders, since it does not consider that the enforcement might not always be possible - or at least not by an authority that is trusted enough to ensure the application of the law. Thus LGI requires that all reference monitors (running at any location of the distributed system) to be trusted by all participating entities: a strong assumption that cannot be applied in our scenario.

The same assumption is present in SPL [14], a language that like HiPoLDS allows to specify security requirements at different levels of abstraction. In addition to the requirement of trusting reference monitors, SPL is limited to access control policies, and does not allow specifying rules that results in reference monitors altering the messages that are passed between monitors, for example by encrypting content or by adding signatures or other type of security metadata.

The ConSpec language [1] aims at defining the behavior of reference monitors with a simple policy language similarly to our approach. This proposal focuses on the instrumentation of the control flow of an object-oriented program using before- and after- method modifiers. In contrast, our work aims at the high-level description of information flows, in particular materialized by the notions of messages, their types, and information tags. In our approach, a message can be mapped at the instrumentation phase to the interception of a protocol message at a client, a server, or an intermediate party, or to the inlining of a reference monitor controlling inter-component information flows at a protocol endpoint.

Furthermore, ConSpec addresses neither the specification of multiple overlapping security policies, as illustrated in Scenario 2 for instance, nor the definition of roles or groups.

Service Evolution and Aspects. Service evolution can be achieved in a flexible and non intrusive way using reference monitors [18] as long as only the contents and recipients of messages have to be modified. Frequently, these changes are performed using dedicated monitors and reconfigurations of orchestrations, for instance, using aspects that modify BPEL-based service compositions (as, e.g., AO4BPEL [7]). Our approach to service evolution is novel in that our reference monitors are derived from HiPoLDS policy definitions and that our aspect system supports invasive modifications to service interceptors and implementations [9] that are required to resolve some security and interoperability issues of OAuth 2.0 (notably the scenario in Sect. 4.3).

6   Conclusion

The OAuth 2.0 protocol is an IETF standard already adopted by major internet application providers. However, it is often difficult to ensure that the implementation of authorization protocols are secure and interoperable because of the many optional features and different protocol flows of the OAuth framework. In this paper we use a type-based policy language in conjunction with reference monitors and aspect-oriented programming in order to tackle these issues. Types enable the precise definition of communicated data and the rigorous analysis of input data. Further, we integrate a policy language based on security domain and abstract rules to express security. Types and policies are implemented thanks to a reference monitor mechanism which encapsulates the agents that have to be adapted. For advanced evolutions that require invasive modifications of service interceptors and implementations, we use a new aspect-based system for service manipulation. Finally, we have shown three realistic evolution scenarios for which we have solved problems of input validation, interoperability and security issues. Future work is planned on the complete implementation of our framework on top of Apache's CXF web service model and its integration with RESTful service models.

A   Subtyping Rules and Endpoint Types Tables

Table 1 presents the main subtyping rules required in this paper and we give in Table 2 the endpoint types (without the refresh token option) in ACF. In these tables X.name denotes a provided service named name from agent X. The notation X.name (<numbering>) corresponds to a required endpoint connected to X.name.

Table 1. Main subtyping rules

A $\leq$ (A + B) and B $\leq$ (A + B)
(A + B) $\leq$ C $\Longleftrightarrow$ A $\leq$ C and B $\leq$ C
(A & B) $\leq$ A and (A & B) $\leq$ B
C $\leq$ (A & B) $\Longleftrightarrow$ C $\leq$ A and C $\leq$ B
Covariance of record type A $\leq$ A' and B $\leq$ B' $\Longleftrightarrow$ {"a":A; "b":B; ...} $\leq$ {"a":A'; "b":B'}
Channel type contravariance <R> $\leq$ <T> $\Longleftrightarrow$ T $\leq$ R
Compatibility of a required service r connected to a provided one p p:Provided $\leq$ r:Required

Table 2. ACF provided and required endpoint types table

Provided Endpoint Types	
C.crep	<({"grant":AuthCode; "state":State} + Token + DenyError) & Secure>
AS.trep	<(AuthCode $\oplus$ crep) & Secure>
AS.arep	<({"id":Credents ; "state":State} $\oplus$ Scope $\oplus$ C.crep) & Secure>
Required Endpoint Types	
AS.crep (3)	<({"grant":AuthCode; "state":State} + DenyError) & Secure>
AS.crep (5)	<(Token + DenyError) & Secure>
C.trep (4)	<(AuthCode $\oplus$ crep) & Secure>
C.arep (1)	<({"id":Credents ; "state":State} $\oplus$ Scope $\oplus$ C.crep) & Secure>

References

1. Aktug, I., Naliuka, K.: Conspec - a formal language for policy specification. ENTCS **197**(1), 45–58 (2008). (Proceedings of REM 2007)
2. Allam, D., Douence, R., Grall, H., Royer, J.-C., Südholt, M.: Well-typed services cannot go wrong. Rapport de recherche RR-7899, INRIA, May 2012
3. Ascola team. An aspect framework for CXF. http://a4cloud.gforge.inria.fr/doku.php?id=start:aspect4cxf, January 2013
4. Bansal, C., Bhargavan, K., Maffeis, S.: Discovering concrete attacks on website authorization by formal analysis. In: CSF 2012, Cambridge, MA, USA, pp. 247–262. IEEE (2012)
5. Castagna, G., Frisch, A.: A gentle introduction to semantic subtyping. In: Caires, L., Italiano, G.F., Monteiro, L., Palamidessi, C., Yung, M. (eds.) ICALP 2005. LNCS, vol. 3580, pp. 30–34. Springer, Heidelberg (2005)
6. Castagna, G., De Nicola, R., Varacca, D.: Semantic subtyping for the pi-calculus. Theor. Comput. Sci. **398**(1–3), 217–242 (2008)
7. Charfi, A., Mezini, M.: Aspect-oriented web service composition with AO4BPEL. In: (LJ) Zhang, L.-J., Jeckle, M. (eds.) ECOWS 2004. LNCS, vol. 3250, pp. 168–182. Springer, Heidelberg (2004)
8. Chebaro, O., Allam, D., Grall, H., et al.: Mechanisms for property preservation. Technical Report Deliverable D2.4, CESSA Project, July 2012

9. Cherrueau, R.-A., Chebaro, O., Südholt, M.: Flexible and expressive aspect-based control over service compositions in the cloud. In: 4th International Workshop on Variability & Composition (VariComp). ACM DL, March 2013

10. Dell'Amico, M., Serme, G., Idrees, M.S., de Oliveira, A.S., Roudier, Y.: Hipolds: a hierarchical security policy language for distributed systems. Information Security Technical Report (2012)

11. OASIS. eXtensible Access Control Markup Language (XACML) Version 3.0. Technical report, OASIS, January 2013

12. Pai, S., Sharma, Y., Kumar, S., Pai, R.M., Singh, S.: Formal verification of oauth 2.0 using alloy framework. In: CSNT '11, pp. 655–659. IEEE Computer Society, Washington DC (2011)

13. Pu, K.Q.: Service description and analysis from a type theoretic approach. In: ICDE Workshops, pp. 379–386 (2007)

14. Ribeiro, C., Ferreira, P.: A policy-oriented language for expressing security specifications. Int. J. Netw. Secur. 5(3), 299–316 (2007)

15. Riely, J., Hennessy, M.: Trust and partial typing in open systems of mobile agents. J. Autom. Reasoning 31(3–4), 335–370 (2003)

16. Paul, R.: Compromising twitter's oauth security system. Technical report, Ars Technica (2010)

17. Sans, T., Cervesato, I.: QWeSST for type-safe web programming. In: 3rd International Workshop on Logics, Agents, and Mobility (2010)

18. Schneider, F.B.: Enforceable security policies. ACM Trans. Inf. Syst. Secur. 3(1), 30–50 (2000)

19. Costa Seco, J., Caires, L.: A basic model of typed components. In: Bertino, E. (ed.) ECOOP 2000. LNCS, vol. 1850, pp. 108–128. Springer, Heidelberg (2000)

20. Serban, C., Zhang, W., Minsky, N.: A decentralized mechanism for application level monitoring of distributed systems. In: Proceedings of CollaborateCom 2009, pp. 1–10. IEEE (2009)

21. IETF Web Authorization (OAuth) Working Group. SAML 2.0 profile for OAuth 2.0 client authentication and authorization grants. Technical Report V 17, Internet Engineering Task Force (IETF)

22. IETF Web Authorization (OAuth) Working Group. The OAuth 2.0 authorization framework. Technical Report RFC 6749, Internet Engineering Task Force (IETF), October 2012

23. IETF Web Authorization (OAuth) Working Group. The OAuth 2.0 authorization framework: bearer token usage. Technical Report RFC 6750, Internet Engineering Task Force (IETF), October 2012

Remote Biometrics for Robust Persistent Authentication

Mads I. Ingwar$^{(\boxtimes)}$ and Christian D. Jensen

Department of Applied Mathematics and Computer Science,
Technical University of Denmark, Kongens Lyngby, Denmark
{ming,cdje}@dtu.dk

Abstract. This paper examines the problem of providing a robust non-invasive authentication service for mobile users in a smart environment. We base our work on the persistent authentication model (*PAISE*), which relies on available sensors to track principals from the location where they authenticate, e.g., through a smart card based access control system, to the location where the authentication is required by a location-based service. The *PAISE* model is extended with remote biometrics to prevent the decay of authentication confidence when authenticated users encounter and interact with other users in the environment. The result is a calm approach to authentication, where mobile users are transparently authenticated towards the system, which allows the provision of location-based services. The output of the remote biometrics are fused using error-rate-based fusion to solve a common problem that occurs in score level fusion, i.e., the scores of each biometric system are usually incompatible, as they have different score ranges as well as different probability distributions.

We have integrated remote biometrics with the *PAISE* prototype and the experimental results on a publicly available dataset, show that fusion of two remote biometric modalities, facial recognition and appearance analysis, gives a significant improvement over each of the individual experts. Furthermore, the experimental results show that using remote biometrics increases the performance of tracking in persistent authentication, by identifying principals who are difficult to track due to occlusions in crowded scenes.

1 Introduction

What is in a face? Judging by children's drawings, two circles for the eyes, a line for the mouth, and perhaps a dot for the nose makes a face. While seemingly simple, these archetypical features distil faces down to their basic forms and resemble Haar-like features, which are used in face detection methods to find faces in real-time with robust results [1,2].

Christian D. Jensen—The research leading to these results has received funding from the [European Union] [European Atomic Energy Community] Seventh Framework Programme ([FP7/2007-2013] [FP7/2007-2011]) under grant agreement n [242497].

J. Garcia-Alfaro et al. (Eds.): DPM 2013 and SETOP 2013, LNCS 8247, pp. 250–267, 2014.
DOI: 10.1007/978-3-642-54568-9_16, © Springer-Verlag Berlin Heidelberg 2014

Faces are what allow us to differentiate people in a group. It might be a child identifying family members in an old photograph, or security personnel identifying people from their passport photos in the airport. Our faces are the most visible characteristic we have, and together with traits such as fingerprints, palm prints, DNA, and iris patterns possess a high discriminative power. In contrast, hair colour, skin colour, gait, height, and weight all have low discriminative power.

The discriminative power of these traits must be considered in security sensitive biometric applications where the performance of the biometric system is important, for instance in some airports, where holders of biometric passports can go through automated gates that authenticate them using facial-recognition. These security sensitive applications of biometric authentication requires robust and accurate results, but, at the same time they must satisfy user demands of a non-invasive and user friendly authentication process.

In his vision of ubiquitous computing, Mark Weiser states that technology must be *calm* [3,4] in order to allow users to focus on their primary tasks. This implies that any authentication technology should require minimal attention from the users, which excludes the use of many authentication techniques, such as passwords or fingerprints. This lends itself to the use of remote biometrics, that is, biometric characteristics that are measurable from a distance without user interaction, such as facial recognition, appearance or gait analysis.

In this paper we extend our Persistent Authentication model (*PAISE*) [5,6] with continuous authentications using remote biometrics. The *PAISE* model combines traditional authentication mechanisms with location information and tracking of principals. The goal in persistent authentication is to translate user authentication from a single event to a lasting session. The model uses strategically placed authentication points to establish an initial authentication session and principals are then tracked throughout the environment. In this paper we explore the addition of remote biometrics, which are regularly measured to prevent the decay of authentication confidence when authenticated users encounter and interact with other users in the environment. This multi-factor approach gives robust results by utilising the strengths of an interaction-based authentication system with the continuous evaluation of an unobtrusive biometric system.

One of the key applications of persistent authentication is to allow secure provision of location-based services, through calm authentication of mobile users in the smart environment. Indoor location systems have seen an increase in popularity in recent years. In particular, tracking of inhabitants in indoor environments have become vital in hospitals to locate and page staff, in homes for elderly people, and in industry for applications in logistics, warehousing and automation. Persistent authentication extends these applications by utilising the credentials associated with each principal's authentication session. This allows persistent authentication to act as the context manager in a sensor enhanced access control system [7], providing a fine-grained and flexible access control mechanism. The *PAISE* model makes it possible to take informed decisions based on the user's credentials, for instance, detecting that the cleaning personnel are accessing a restricted area, or that the carrier delivering goods is entering the premise through the loading area.

The users credentials are captured by the access control mechanism and provided to the persistent authentication system, which tracks the users and, as needed, verifies the identity of the users based on their biometric characteristics. To do so, a specialised algorithm, known as a biometric expert, processes a sample of the characteristic, referred to as the modality. The expert extracts a small amount of data containing the minutia features of the characteristic, called the biometric signature, which represents the unique aspect of the modality. The biometric signature is compared to a reference database, called the template, which links the true identity of the person to the previously captured biometric samples for that person. A match score is generated between the sample and the template, reflecting the expert's confidence in the identity of the person. Alternatively, the expert can be used for identification purposes, in which the persons signature is compared to all templates and the best match returned, however, in this paper we focus on biometric verification.

The main challenge in biometric verification is that the process is not reliable: an expert may reject a genuine user, or conversely, an expert may accept an impostor. A biometric expert may have insufficient discriminative power, especially within a large group [8], or adverse environmental conditions, such as dust or poor luminosity, can affect the quality of biometric acquisition. These factors are further compounded when using remote biometrics as the quality and resolution of the biometric acquisition is significantly lower due to the uncontrolled acquisition process.

The reliability of remote biometrics can be improved by employing multiple biometric experts and fusing their outputs. In this paper we use *Error-Rate-based Fusion* [9], a novel fusion strategy that transforms individual scores into objective evidences and combines them using Bayesian inference. In more details, let us assume that an expert generates a match score y_i and the expert takes a decision that the claimant is genuine. The false acceptance rate (FAR) at the decision threshold y_i represents the probability that the claimant is an impostor. Similarly, the false rejection rate (FRR) at the threshold y_i represents the intrinsic probability of incorrectly rejecting a genuine user. Bayesian inference is used to combine the false acceptance and false rejection rates of different scores, calculated by different experts, and generate a confidence value representing the probability that claimant is genuine.

We evaluate the performance of our error-rate-based fusion strategy using two biometric experts, facial recognition and appearance analysis, on the publicly available CAVIAR dataset [10]. Our experimental results show a significant improvement in the error rate compared to the performance of each individual expert. In addition, we evaluate the increased tracking accuracy and persistence gained by including remote biometrics in the persistent authentication system. Our results show that including remote biometrics significantly improves tracking by identifying principals who are difficult to track due to environmental factors or occlusions in crowded scenes.

The rest of this paper is organised in the following way: an overview of the remote biometrics used in this paper is given in Sect. 2. Fusion of biometric experts and a quick overview of error-rate-based fusion is presented in Sect. 3. Persistent authentication and the PAISE model are presented in Sect. 4. Our experimental results are presented in Sect. 5 and related work is examined in Sect. 6. Finally, Sect. 7 presents our conclusion and outlines the directions for future work.

2 Remote Biometrics

Compared to their intrusive counterparts, remote biometrics have a lower discriminative power and a higher error rate [11], but they are non-invasive and allow continuous authentication. This ensures a *calm* authentication process without user interaction. The two biometric characteristics we focus on in this paper are facial recognition and appearance analysis based on colour profiles. Our faces possess a high discriminative power, whereas our appearance, in terms of hair and skin colour and the clothes we wear, have a low discriminative power.

For facial recognition we use a linear subspace technique to project high-dimensional data into a lower dimensional subspace by linearly combining features. *Principal Component Analysis* (PCA) [12] and *Linear Discriminant Analysis* (LDA) [13] are well established linear subspace techniques and are considered the most robust methods for face recognition [14].

Consider a set of N facial images $\mathbf{x}_1, \mathbf{x}_2, ..., \mathbf{x}_N$ with values in an n-dimensional image space. A linear transformation maps this n-dimensional image space into a lower m-dimensional feature space $\mathbf{y}_1, \mathbf{y}_2, ..., \mathbf{y}_N$ such that $\mathbf{y}_k$ represents $\mathbf{x}_k$ by introducing a transformation vector W such that:

$$\mathbf{y}_k = W^T \mathbf{x}_k \qquad k = 1, 2, ..., N$$

For the transformation to accurately represent the original data, it is important to retain the highest possible variation, thus the objective is to find a subspace in which the variance is maximised. Let the total scatter matrix S_T be defined as:

$$S_T = \sum_{k=1}^{N} (\mathbf{x}_k - \mu)(\mathbf{x}_k - \mu)^T$$

Where μ is the mean of all the images. The output is a set of n-dimensional eigenvectors $\mathbf{w}_1, \mathbf{w}_2, ..., \mathbf{w}_m$ corresponding to the m largest eigenvalues, which account for the most variance in the training set. Since these eigenvectors have the same dimension as the original images, they are referred to as Eigenfaces [12].

In PCA, classification can be performed in this reduced feature space, for instance using a nearest neighbour classifier. However, a drawback of this approach is, that much of the variation we seek to maximise is caused by illumination changes [15], thus with images of faces under changing illumination the projected feature space will contain variation due lighting and not necessarily due to class separability. Consequently, the points in the projected space will not be well clustered. A better approach is to use Linear Discriminant Analysis, where classification is performed by selecting W in such a way that the ratio of the between-class scatter S_B and the within-class scatter S_W is maximised. With the between-class scatter matrix defined as

$$S_B = \sum_{i=1}^{c} N_i(\mu_i - \mu)(\mu_i - \mu)^T$$

and the within-class scatter matrix defined as

$$S_W = \sum_{i=1}^{c} \sum_{\mathbf{x}_k \in X_i} (\mathbf{x}_k - \mu_i)(\mathbf{x}_k - \mu_i)^T$$

where μ_i is the mean image of class X_i, and N_i is the number of samples in class X_i. A projection, W_{opt} is then found, that maximises the class separability criterion

$$W_{opt} = \arg\max_{W} = \frac{|W^T S_B W|}{|W^T S_W W|}$$

For appearance analysis we use colour profiles, calculated using histogram comparison. Colour histograms are widely used for content-based image retrieval [16] as they are fast to compute, and despite their simplicity, have attractive properties. Since they contain no spatial information they are largely invariant to rotation and translation of objects in the image. Additionally, colour histograms are robust against partial occlusions and changes in camera viewpoint [17].

Colour histograms are typically represented in the RGB colorspace, and the difference between two histograms h_1, h_2 are expressed by the chi-squared distance:

$$\chi^2(h_1, h_2) = \frac{1}{2} \sum_{k} \frac{(h_{1k} - h_{2k})^2}{h_{1k} + h_{2k}}$$

To reduce the error rate of the remote biometric experts, the output of each of these experts are fused, which increases the robustness of the evaluation.

3   Fusion of Biometric Experts

The main challenge in biometric fusion is that different biometric experts generate matching scores in different domains, and that these domains usually follow different probability distributions. Therefore, score normalisation and transformation are required to make the scores compatible, which are error prone processes. Moreover, the existing parametric models assume a certain distribution of scores which also introduces errors in the fusion process.

In our fusion strategy, error-rate-based fusion, we use measures of false acceptances and false rejections, which have the same definitions across different experts, and therefore do not need any normalisation. We work in a nonparametric model, namely we estimate false acceptance and false rejection rates for certain discrete levels of thresholds. Further, the fused output is a confidence measure, which is a continuous probability value; therefore, the decision errors associated with a binary decision do not occur. In the following, we give a brief overview of error-rate-based fusion, and we refer interested readers to the complete algorithm presented in Ingwar et al. [9].

For biometric verification we consider two class labels, A and $\bar{A}$, where A is assigned when the expert concludes that a claimant is genuine, and $\bar{A}$ is assigned if the authentication status of the claimant is unknown. If the claimant is A but the expert wrongly labels him $\bar{A}$ then this event is called a false rejection (FR). Similarly, if the claimant is not A and an expert wrongly labels him A then this event is called a false acceptance (FA). The false acceptance and the false rejection rates (FAR and FRR) correspond to the fractions of FA and FR events taken over all genuine and impostor access.

Let us consider N biometrics experts. The output of the i-th expert is a match score, $y_i \in \mathbb{R}$, where $1 \leq i \leq N$.

For a decision threshold Δ_i, the decision function is defined as follows:

$$decision(\Delta_i, y_i) = \begin{cases} accept & \text{if } y_i \geq \Delta_i \\ reject & \text{otherwise} \end{cases}$$

With the match score y_i, let the functions $FAR(y_i)$ and $FRR(y_i)$ be the false acceptance rate and false rejection rates of the i-th expert with $\Delta_i = y_i$. Since $y_i \in \mathbb{R}$, these functions are continuous, such that $FAR(y_i) \in \mathbb{R}$ and $FRR(y_i) \in \mathbb{R}$. For precise evaluation of $FAR(y_i)$ and $FRR(y_i)$, we use a non-parametric approach, and model them as step functions, in which Δ_i can only take m different values: $\Delta_i \in \{\delta_i^1, \ldots, \delta_i^m\}$, where $\delta_i^1 < \cdots < \delta_i^m$. We call these values of Δ_i error decision thresholds (EDTs). This means that $FAR(y_i)$ and $FRR(y_i)$ are defined over a set of m EDTs.

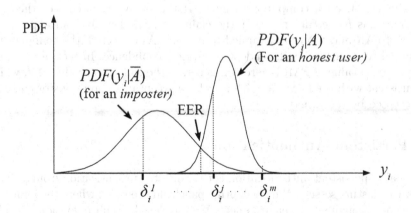

Fig. 1. Error Decision Thresholds (EDTs). Plot of the probability density functions of typical expert scores with the point of Equal Error Rate (EER) shown.

The different values of Δ_i are illustrated in Fig. 1, with a typical plot of the probability density functions (PDF) of expert scores. The figure illustrates that the match score for a genuine user is distributed on larger values as compared to that of an impostor. The figure also shows the point of equal error rate, where the false acceptances and false rejections have the same values.

To illustrate an error-rate-based fusion system, consider a verification system that contains N biometric experts. When biometric data of a claimant is available from the sensors, the system invokes the experts with the claimed identity A. Each expert extracts the relevant biometric signature from the data and compares the extracted signature with the signature templates of A. Each expert then generates a match score y_i, and we compute $FAR(y_i)$ and $FRR(y_i)$ and fuse the match score based on Bayesian inference.

The system has an a-priori confidence that the claimant is A, which is represented as the probability measure, $Pr(A)$. The complementary confidence that the claimant is not A is $1 - Pr(A)$. We compute a-posteriori confidence, $Pr(A|y_i \geq \Delta_i)$, i.e., the probability that the claimant is A after receiving the evidence y_i that meets the decision threshold Δ_i. For brevity, we do not include the decision threshold in the probability expressions, and therefore we write $Pr(A|y_i \geq \Delta_i)$ as $Pr(A|y_i)$. The value of the a-posteriori confidence is computed as follows:

$$Pr(A|y_i) = \frac{TAR(y_i)Pr(A)}{TAR(y_i)Pr(A) + FAR(y_i)(1 - Pr(A))} \tag{1}$$

With TAR being the *true acceptance rate*, i.e. $1 - FRR(y_i)$. Equation 1 allows us to fuse the outputs of N experts, by taking into account the prior confidence level. To get an intuitive feeling of Eq. 1, let us consider a traditional verification expert, which is assumed to be error free, e.g., a password-based authentication of claimant, A, on a computer terminal. If the password is correct then the computer has full confidence that the claimant is A. For such an expert, the values of FAR and FRR are assumed to be zero. As expected, the confidence is evaluated to 1 in Eq. 1 independent of a-priori confidence. In fact, any expert for which the value of FAR is zero will generate the confidence value of 1, which is consistent with the fact that with zero false acceptances no impostor can ever be accepted by the expert.

4   Persistent Authentication

The goal in persistent authentication is to translate authentication from a single event to a lasting session. We track principals from the point where they authenticate and throughout the environment. We use closed-circuit television (CCTV) cameras and image processing algorithms to provide the location data, and then employ filtering techniques to associate the location with target principals in consecutive frames.

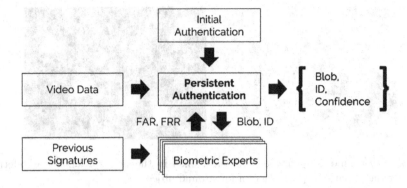

Fig. 2. Overview of the components in the persistent authentication model.

The core component of the *PAISE* model combines data from the authentication system, the smart environment and the biometrics experts, tracks authenticated principals and forwards this information to a location-based service. An overview of the components in the persistent authentication model are shown in Fig. 2. The figure shows how the three components, the authentication system, the smart environment and the biometric experts interface with the core *PAISE* component.

The authentication mechanism handles authentication of principals and provides the initial authentication of the principal. The operation of the authentication mechanism is external to the persistent authentication model, thus *state-of-the-art* solutions are supported, such as intrusive biometrics, smart-cards, wearable tokens, or a combination resulting in multimodal authentication [18].

The smart environment delivers the sensor data needed for tracking. In this paper we use a smart environment that consists of a camera-based location system. CCTV cameras are used to both track principals and to gather remote biometric samples.

The biometric experts process the modalities of the principals captured by the smart environment and returns an estimate of their identity. As mentioned in Sect. 2, the two remote biometrics explored in this paper are facial recognition and appearance analysis.

Finally, the persistent authentication component must: 1. Identify the principals and their locations from the video data and track them throughout the environment, 2. Associate the initial authentication sessions with the corresponding principals, and 3. Continuously provide the biometrics modalities of each tracked principal to the biometric experts and evaluate the feedback. The output is the location of each principal, the associated authentication sessions and the confidence in this assertion.

To identify principals in a video steam, we use image segmentation. In image segmentation objects that share certain characteristics are identified and labeled. In persistent authentication, this means assigning one label to the principals and

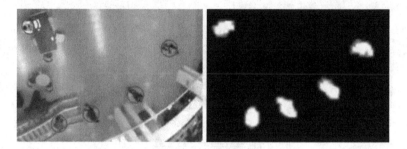

Fig. 3. Background segmentation. For each pixel in the image a label w is inferred denoting the absence or presence of a foreground object.

another label to their surroundings. The principals are then referred to as the image *foreground* and their surroundings as the image *background*.

A binary label $w_i \in \{0, 1\}$ is assigned to each pixel $\mathbf{x}_i$ in the image, indicating whether it is part of a known background ($w = 0$) or if it belongs to the foreground ($w = 1$), determined by the recent history of each pixel $\mathbf{x}_1, ..., \mathbf{x}_n$ modelled as a *Gaussian Mixture Model* [19,20]. The probability that a new pixel $\mathbf{x}$ belongs to the foreground is then given by:

$$Pr(\mathbf{x}|w = 1) = \sum_{k=1}^{K} \lambda_k \mathcal{N}(\mu_k, \Sigma_k)$$

where $\mu_{1...K}$ and $\Sigma_{1...K}$ are the means and covariances of the normal distributions and $\lambda_{1...K}$ are positive valued weights that sum to one. The combination of these normal distributions allows the Gaussian mixture model to describe complex multi-modal probability densities. The Gaussian mixture model is robust to noise and changes in illumination and it handles reflections and shadows well, making it particular suited for indoor surveillance applications. A typical result of the labelling process is shown in Fig. 3. The first image shows a complex scene, captured by a CCTV camera, containing five principals annotated with circles. The second image shows the output of the Gaussian mixture model, a black-and-white binary image. The white pixels in the binary image, also called the blobs, indicate the presence of a principal, and the figure shows that all five principals have been correctly identified.

With the foreground objects identified and labeled, we track them throughout the environment. The objective of the tracking is to associate the location of target principals in consecutive video frames. This association can be especially difficult when multiple users are in the environment, when users are occluded, or when the quality of the images are poor due to environmental conditions. In these situations the tracking system relies on the correlation of principals over time, either inferred from the physical properties of the environment or from a model which describes how the location of the target might change for different possible motions of the principals.

We use a combination of spatial-temporal coherence, filtering and flow techniques to ensure consistent tracking in consecutive frames. The spatial-temporal coherence uses the physical reality of the world to infer correlation. Spatial coherence describes the correlation between signals at different points in space, while temporal coherence describes the correlation between signals observed at different moments in time. In tracking this is used to infer correlation based on the speed and trajectory of the principals, which must be consistent with the physical restrictions of the environment.

In addition to the spatial-temporal coherence, we filter the output of the image segmentation process with the Kalman filter [21, 22], which in essence is a sensor fusion algorithm that uses the system dynamics model to form an estimate of the system's state, which improves tracking under rapidly changing environmental conditions.

Finally dense optical flow [23, 24] is used as a global approach, that is not affected by labelling ambiguities to ensure consistent tracking even in noisy situations. In optical flow it is assumed that when a pixel moves from one frame to another, its intensity or colour does not change. This is a combination of a number of assumptions about the reflectance properties and illumination of the scene and is known as the *brightness constancy*. Solving the brightness constancy results in the magnitude and direction of motion for each pixel in the image. By comparing the displacement to the Kalman filter estimate, tracking becomes possible even when principals are partially occluded, as their direction in the environment helps to differentiate them. Additionally, as the optical flow analysis is applied directly to the image it helps ensure that errors in the labelling process does not carry over into the tracking process.

Tracked principals continuously have their remote biometrics measured and compared to a signature database. This database contains all previous matching signatures and, optionally, high quality enrolment signatures. For each biometric characteristic a set of false acceptance and false rejection rates (FAR and FRR) values are generated. These values are fused, using error-rate-based fusion, which helps reduce the impact of the high error rate of remote biometrics. The result is a biometric confidence score in the identity of the principal, i.e., the confidence on the assertion that a blob has a certain identity. This score is matched with the trackers current confidence score, which turns the confidence into a dynamic value based on positive biometric signatures.

A dynamic score allows the system to take occlusions and other noisy measurements into consideration when determining the confidence in identity, such that, when principal moves through the environment, the confidence in his identity changes based on the quality of the tracking. An example is shown in Fig. 4. The figure shows two paths, a solid line that corresponds to the motion of a principal A and a dashed lined that corresponds the motion of a principal who is not A, denoted, $\bar{A}$. Events on the paths have timestamps, and the time t_0 corresponds to the initial authentication, where A is authenticated using an interactive authentication mechanism, giving an initial confidence of 1.

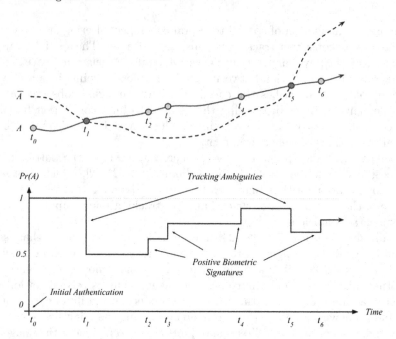

Fig. 4. Confidence in the identity of A. The confidence in A's identity decrease when the paths of A and $\bar{A}$ *intersect and increase with positive biometric signatures.*

The principals are reliably tracked from the point of initial authentication until the time t_1, where occlusions causes ambiguities in the labelling process, which, in turn, causes ambiguity in which of the paths the tracked principal A is following. As a result, the confidence in the identity of A is lowered. How much the confidence is lowered depends on the output of the tracking algorithm, but for the sake of the example, we assume that there is an equal chance of A following either path.

The remote biometrics of A are continuously measured and at time t_2, t_3 and t_4 a positive signature is captured. The resulting biometric confidence score is used to increase the confidence in the identity of A. As A can only follow either the solid line or on the dashed line, the confidence for A on both lines must sum to 1. Therefore, an increase in the confidence on the solid line automatically decrease the confidence that A is following dashed line. The increase in confidence depends on the quality of the biometric sample and the output of the biometric expert. This cycle of decreasing confidence due to noise or occlusions and increasing confidence with positive signatures continues as long as A is in the environment.

5   Experimental Results

In this section we present and discuss our experimental results. We evaluate how remote biometrics, namely facial recognition and appearance analysis, perform when implemented in a persistent authentication system. Both of these characteristics are measured from a distance, and authentication is performed continuously by sampling the modality recurrently.

The data used for the experiments are from the CAVIAR dataset [10]. The dataset comprises of a number of clips that show the frontal view of a corridor in a shopping centre. The clips include people walking alone, meeting with others, conversing, and window shopping. All the video clips are filmed in half-resolution PAL standard (384×288 pixels, 25 frames per second) and compressed using MPEG2.

We track each principal in the video and sample the modalities as they are available. As the setting is a corridor with principals walking in both directions, then principals are not always facing the camera and as a result, the facial expert is only able to extract modalities from a subset of the total principals. In contrast, the appearance expert is always available, though the area that is considered may contain little relevant information due to occlusions of the tracked principal. In the dataset 32 unique principals have been identified by both the facial and the appearance expert, on which we test the performance of our error-rate-based fusion technique. We measure the performance of the tracking by recording the number of frames each principal have been successfully tracked by the persistent authentication system and compare this to the ground truth. In addition, we run the experiments again, this time tracking the principals using only the filtering and flow techniques to evaluate the performance without the biometric experts.

The 32 unique subjects are tracked over multiple video clips, in varying poses and illumination. An example of the captured faces for three principals are shown in Fig. 5. The resolution of the video data is low, and as a result, the resolution of the facial images are very low at 50×50 pixels.

We use the first captured face to construct an initial training set, then for each subsequently captured face, we calculate the error rate using leave-one-out cross-validation, after which the new face is added to the training set. It may happen

Fig. 5. Example of the captured faces for three principals from the CAVIAR dataset.

Table 1. Error rates of the biometric experts

Biometric expert	Error rate
Facial expert	4.72 %
Apperance expert	5.01 %
Error-rate-based fusion	**1.44 %**

that a high number of biometric modalities are captured, thus we limit the size of the training set to the six most recently captured images. In a production system, we recommend using high quality enrolment signatures as the initial training set and augmenting the training set with good quality captured samples. The process is completed for both biometric experts and each step is monitored by a human expert who records the performance of the system and of each biometric experts. The resulting error rates are shown in Table 1.

The table shows that the overall performance of the system when using error-rate-based fusion is significantly lower than any of the individual experts. Our fusion technique has an error rate of 1.44 %, which is expected given the performance of the individual experts and the results are in line with the results published in earlier work [9]. The increase in performance is due to the fact that we weigh the decision given by each expert based on their FAR and FRR values as outlined in Eq. 1; a result, in our error-rate-based fusion strategy, the conflict between experts are more likely to be resolved in favour of the best performing expert.

The individual biometric experts have an error rate of 4.72 % for the facial expert and 5.01 % for the appearance expert. We conjecture that the relatively high error rate of the facial expert is caused by the very low resolution of the training images and the greatly varied poses of the principals. However, this shows that even in adverse conditions the LDA method gives robust results. The performance of the appearance expert is not as affected by the low resolution and thus the results are comparable to our previous studies.

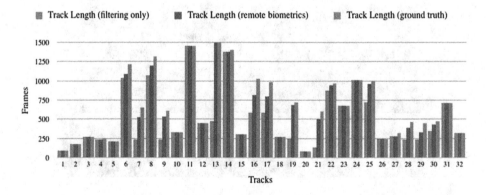

Fig. 6. Computed track lengths vs. ground truth for the CAVIAR dataset

To evaluate the impact of the remote biometrics we compare the performance of the tracking in persistent authentication to the performance without using biometric experts. We use the training data acquired from the CAVIAR dataset and track each of the 32 principals from the point they enter the scene. We measure the number of frames each principal is successfully tracked, with and without the biometric experts, and compare this to the ground truth.

The results are shown in Fig. 6, which charts the results for each the 32 tracks. The majority of the tracks have few or no occlusions and no drop-outs (principals leaving the scene completely), and in these situations both systems achieve near perfect tracking of the principals. The accuracy of the tracking drops when occlusions and drop-outs occur, for instance when principals enter a shop or when multiple principals crowd the scene. The system may completely lose track of a principal, in this case the remote biometrics are used to re-associate the session with the correct principal. As a result, the system using remote biometrics greatly outperforms the other system for a number of the tracks, which is most profound in the tracks 7, 13 and 21.

6 Related Work

In this section, we explore the state of the art related to continuous authentication.

Corner and Noble [25–27] examine the problem of authentication when mobile devices are lost or users leave a workstation logged in. They define traditional authentication mechanisms as *persistent* because they rarely limit the duration that the authentication is valid, so a user may leave a computer logged in for several days. This means that anyone who steals a device that is logged in or gets physical access to the workstation may usurp the authentication of the original user. They define a *transient authentication* mechanism, where all data in the system is encrypted and a small *authentication token*, worn by the user, is needed to provide access to the encrypted data, thus ensuring that access can only be granted when the token is in close proximity to the system. The token stores the cryptographic keys and the proximity mechanism is based on short range wireless communication.

The definitions of persistent and transient authentication by Corner and Noble are device centric, authentication sticks to the device as long as the user is present, so restrictions are put on the users, e.g., they have to wear the authentication token. This creates problems when authentication tokens are forgotten, borrowed or lost. Our definition of persistent authentication is user centric, which means that authentication sticks to the user as long as the tracking is considered reliable. This means that any authentication mechanism, e.g., passwords, PIN or biometrics, can be used and that no additional requirements are placed on the user.

Bardram et al. [28] define a context-aware user authentication mechanism, where users need a smart card to identify themselves to the system and an RFID based tracking system that is used to authenticate the user. This adds complexity for the users, by requiring them to carry two tokens, without offering significantly improved convenience, i.e., the user still has to insert the smart card into the system whenever authentication is required. In comparison, our method removes the need to perform repeated authentication actions.

Klosterman and Ganger [29] define a *continuous biometric-enhanced authentication* mechanism, which uses a biometric authentication module, based on face recognition, to periodically re-authenticate users who are logged in to the system. If, at some point, the biometrics of the user sitting in front of the monitor does not correspond to the biometrics of the authenticated user, re-authentication is required. This means that continuous authentication is achieved without additional requirements placed on the user, but their system authenticate a specific user at a specific location, whereas we propose to track the user so that his authentication may be reused in different locations.

Altinok and Turk [30] present an approach for temporal integration based on uncertainty propagation over time for a multimodal biometric system. Their method operates continuously by computing expected values as a function of time differences. The system generates continuous results in terms of confidence in the identity of the user, which makes it possible to adjust the security level accordingly in real time. Experimental results with simulated data of face, voice, and fingerprints have shown that the system can provide continuous authentication results which are consistently better than the individual components of the system. The authors conclude that comparing these preliminary results to a true multimodal database is very important for continued work in the field.

Sim et al. [31] develop a continuous authentication system based on multimodal remote biometrics in a Bayesian framework that combines both temporal and modality information holistically. This approach allows the system to evaluate the probability that the user is still present even when there is no observation. The authors are successful in integrating results from a fingerprint biometric classifier with a face classifier and develop a model that intuitively separates the uncertainty of the dynamic model from that of the sensor model. Muncaster and Turk [32] take similar approach as [31], but use a Dynamic Bayesian Network to achieve continuous authentication using multimodal biometrics. The advantage of a dynamic Bayesian network is its ability to account for more hidden variables and by modelling more hidden variables, the network is capable of modelling important contextual information. Both approaches focus on a controlled environment, such as a workstation, where an impostor hijacks a logged-in session. In comparison, persistent authentication operates in an uncontrolled and unconstrained environment, where the sessions are user centric, requiring an impostor to displace a legitimate user instead of hijacking an empty workstation.

Niinuma and Park [33] propose a framework for continuous authentication that uses soft biometrics traits, similar to the appearance analysis presented in this paper. The proposed framework automatically registers soft biometric traits every time the user login and fuses soft biometric matching with conventional authentication schemes, namely password and face biometric. The proposed scheme has high tolerance to the user's posture and the experimental results show the effectiveness of the proposed method for continuous authentication. The authors make a number of assumptions about the pose of the users and the location of the body for appearance analysis, furthermore, occlusions are handled on a very ad hoc basis. In contrast, persistent authentication uses image segmentation to locate users which ensures that the regions of interest are correctly identified for appearance analysis, additionally, advance filtering algorithms are used to ensure occlusions does not revert the authentication session and require the user to start over.

7   Conclusion

In this paper we examined the problem of providing a robust non-invasive authentication service for mobile users in a smart environment. We used the persistent authentication model, *PAISE*, to track principals and employed continuous authentication, based on remote biometrics, to identify principals and re-associate lost authentication sessions. The result is a calm approach to authentication, where mobile users are transparently authenticated towards the system, which allows the provision of location-based services.

We used error-rate-based fusion to solve a common problem that occurs in score level fusion, i.e., the scores of individual experts are usually incompatible, as they have different score ranges as well as different probability distributions. In our fusion strategy, we use error rates (false acceptance and false rejection rates), which have the same definitions across different domains, and therefore does not require any normalisation.

We evaluated our error-rate-based fusion strategy on two remote biometric modalities, namely facial recognition and appearance analysis. Our experimental results on a publicly available dataset, show that our fusion strategy gives a significant improvement over each of the individual experts. This increase in accuracy is especially useful for security sensitive biometric applications where the performance of the biometric system is important. We further evaluated the performance of the persistent authentication system with regard to the accuracy of the tracking. Our results show that using remote biometrics help identify principals who are difficult to track due to occlusions in crowded scenes. In addition, remote biometrics allows the system to re-identify principals who drop out of view of the camera and re-enter at a later stage.

Finally, we conclude that the *PAISE* model provides a useful abstraction for authentication systems, which may greatly improve the usability of traditional user authentication.

References

1. Viola, P., Jones, M.: Rapid object detection using a boosted cascade of simple features. In: Computer Vision and Pattern Recognition (2001)
2. Jones, M., Viola, P.: Robust real-time object detection. In: Workshop on Statistical and Computational Theories of Vision (2001)

3. Weiser, M., Brown, J.: Designing calm technology. PowerGrid J. **1**, 1–5 (1996)
4. Weiser, M.: The computer for the 21st century. Scientific American **265**(3), 66–75 (1991)
5. Kirschmeyer, M., Hansen, M.S.: Persistent authentication in smart environments. IMM-THESIS: 2008-16, Technical University of Denmark (2008)
6. Ingwar, M.I., Jensen, C.D.: Towards secure intelligent buildings. In: Proceedings of the 5th Nordic Workshop on Dependability and Security (NODES'11) (2011)
7. Jensen, C.D., Geneser, K., Willemoes-Wissing, I.C.: Sensor enhanced access control: extending traditional access control models with context-awareness. In: Fernández-Gago, C., Martinelli, F., Pearson, S., Agudo, I. (eds.) IFIPTM 2013. IFIP AICT, vol. 401, pp. 177–192. Springer, Heidelberg (2013)
8. Cole, S.: More than Zero: accounting for error in latent fingerprint identification. J. Crim. Law Criminol. (1973-) **95**(3), 985–1078 (2005)
9. Ingwar, M.I., Ahmed, N., Jensen, C.D.: Error-rate-based fusion of biometric experts. In: PST2013 International Conference on Privacy, Security and Trust (PST) (2013)
10. Fisher, R.: CAVIAR Test Case Scenarios (2004)
11. Bhattacharyya, D.: Biometric authentication: a review. Int. J. u-and e-Service **2**(3), 13–28 (2009)
12. Turk, M., Pentland, A.: Eigenfaces for recognition. J. Cogn. Neurosci. **3**(1), 71–86 (1991)
13. Fisher, R.: The use of multiple measurements in taxonomic problems. Ann. Hum. Genet. **7**(2), 179–188 (1936)
14. Belhumeur, P., Hespanha, J., Kriegman, D.: Eigenfaces vs. Fisherfaces: recognition using class specific linear projection. IEEE Trans. Pattern Anal. Mach. Intell. **19**(7), 711–720 (1997)
15. Adini, Y., Moses, Y., Ullman, S.: Face recognition: the problem of compensating for changes in illumination direction. Pattern Anal. Mach. Intell. **19**(7), 721–732 (1997)
16. Flickner, M., Sawhney, H., Niblack, W.: Query by image and video content: the QBIC system. Computer **28**(9), 23–32 (1995)
17. Kakumanu, P., Makrogiannis, S., Bourbakis, N.: A survey of skin-color modeling and detection methods. Pattern Recogn. **40**(3), 1106–1122 (2007)
18. O'Gorman, L.: Comparing passwords, tokens, and biometrics for user authentication. Proc. IEEE **91**(12), 2021–2040 (2003)
19. Stauffer, C., Grimson, W.: Adaptive background mixture models for real-time tracking. Comput. Vis. Pattern Recogn. **2**, 246–252 (1999)
20. Stauffer, C., Grimson, W.: Learning patterns of activity using real-time tracking. IEEE Trans. Pattern Anal. Mach. Intell. **22**(8), 747–757 (2000)
21. Kalman, R.: A new approach to linear filtering and prediction problems. J. Basic Eng. **82**, 35–45 (1960)
22. Welch, G., Bishop, G.: An introduction to the Kalman filter. Technical report, University of North Carolina (1995)
23. Farneback, G.: Fast and accurate motion estimation using orientation tensors and parametric motion models. In: Proceedings of 15th International Conference on Pattern Recognition (2000)
24. Farneback, G.: Very high accuracy velocity estimation using orientation tensors, parametric motion, and simultaneous segmentation of the motion field. In: Proceedings of the Eighth International Conference on Computer Vision 2001, ICCV 2001 (2001)

25. Corner, M., Noble, B.: Zero-interaction authentication. In: Proceedings of the 8th Annual International Conference on Mobile Computing and Networking, pp. 1–11 (2002)
26. Noble, B.D., Corner, M.D.: The case for transient authentication. In: Proceedings of the 10th Workshop on ACM SIGOPS European Workshop: Beyond the PC - EW10 , p. 24 (2002)
27. Corner, M., Noble, B.: Protecting applications with transient authentication. In: International Conference on Mobile Systems, Applications, and Services (MobiSys) (2003)
28. Bardram, J.E., Kjær, R.E., Pedersen, M.Ø.: Context-aware user authentication - supporting proximity-based login in pervasive computing. In: Dey, A.K., Schmidt, A., McCarthy, J.F. (eds.) UbiComp 2003. LNCS, vol. 2864, pp. 107–123. Springer, Heidelberg (2003)
29. Klosterman, A., Ganger, G.: Secure continuous biometric-enhanced authentication. Technical report, Parallel Data Laboratory (2000)
30. Altinok, A., Turk, M.: Temporal integration for continuous multimodal biometrics. In: Proceedings of the Workshop on Multimodal User Authentication (1) (2003)
31. Sim, T., Zhang, S.: Continuous verification using multimodal biometrics. Pattern Anal. Mach. Intell. 29(4), 562–570 (2007)
32. Muncaster, J., Turk, M.: Continuous multimodal authentication using dynamic Bayesian networks. In: Proceedings of the 2nd Workshop of Multimodal User Authentication (2006)
33. Niinuma, K., Park, U., Jain, A.K.: Soft biometric traits for continuous user authentication. IEEE Trans. Inf. Forensics Secur. 5(4), 771–780 (2010)

Classifying Android Malware
through Subgraph Mining

Fabio Martinelli[1], Andrea Saracino[1,2], and Daniele Sgandurra[1(✉)]

[1] Istituto di Informatica e Telematica, Consiglio Nazionale delle Ricerche, Pisa, Italy
{fabio.martinelli,daniele.sgandurra}@iit.cnr.it
[2] Dipartimento di Ingegneria dell'Informazione, Università di Pisa, Pisa, Italy
andrea.saracino@iet.unipi.it

Abstract. Current smartphones are based upon the concept of *apps*, which are lightweight applications that are distributed through on-line marketplaces, such as Google Play (for Android devices). Unfortunately, this market-centric model is affected by several major security and trust issues, due to the fact that anyone can easily create, and deploy through the market, a malicious app that could potentially lead to a massive malware spread.

In this paper, we propose a framework to classify Android malware based upon the concept of common patterns of actions executed by malicious applications. The basic idea is to extract, from known malware, a subset of frequent subgraphs of system calls that are executed by most of the malware. This set of subgraphs constitutes a database of known malicious features. Then, when a new application is downloaded from a market, it is first run in a sandbox to monitor its behavior. This will result in an execution trace that may contain some of the subgraphs previously found in malware. The resulting vector of the found subgraphs is given to a classifier that returns its decision in terms of a likely malware or not. Preliminary tests executed both on known good apps and malware confirm the effectiveness and quality of our proposal.

Keywords: Intrusion detection system · Android · Mobile security · Malware · Classification

1 Introduction

In the last years, smartphones have drastically changed their nature by increasing the number and complexity of their capabilities. In fact, smartphones now offer a larger amount of services and applications than those offered by personal computers. At the same time, an increasing number of security threats targeting smartphones has emerged. Malicious users and hackers are taking advantage of

The research leading to these results has received funding from the EU Seventh Framework Programme (FP7/2007-2013) under grant n. 256980 (NESSoS), n. 257930 (Aniketos), from PRIN Security Horizons funded by MIUR with D.D. 23.10.2012 n. 719, and EIT ICT Labs activity 13077.

J. Garcia-Alfaro et al. (Eds.): DPM 2013 and SETOP 2013, LNCS 8247, pp. 268–283, 2014.
DOI: 10.1007/978-3-642-54568-9_17, © Springer-Verlag Berlin Heidelberg 2014

both the limited capabilities of mobile devices and the lack of standard security mechanisms to design mobile-specific malware that access sensitive data, steal the user's phone credit, or deny access to some device functionalities. In particular, Android is the platform that currently has the highest number of malware. Three factors are the main sources of these security threats: (1) a widespread platform, (2) a readily accessible development tools, and (3) a sufficient attacker motivation (usually, monetary).

To mitigate these security threats, various mobile-specific Intrusion Detection Systems (IDSes) have been recently proposed. Most of these IDSes are *behavior-based*, i.e. they do not rely on a database of malicious code signatures, as in the case of *signature-based* IDSes. A behavior-based (or anomaly-based) IDS is a system that attempts to learn the normal behavior of an application. To this end, the system is firstly trained by receiving as input a set of parameters that describes the way an application normally behaves. Secondly, during the normal usage, the IDS is able to recognize as suspicious any application behavior that strongly differs from those well-known, i.e. learnt during the first phase.

In this paper, we describe *CAMAS*, a framework for Classification of Android MAlware through Subgraphs. CAMAS extracts execution traces from several malicious applications and then it mines common subgraphs from these traces. Meaningful subgraphs are selected through a refinement process. Afterwards, these meaningful subgraphs are searched in the execution traces of newly downloaded applications to discover misbehaviors. In the end, a classifier analyzes these data concerning found subgraphs in the downloaded application to assess if this application should be considered malicious or not.

The main contributions of the paper are the following:

- *CAMAS*, a framework for the Classification of Android MAlware through Subgraphs mining;
- the definition of an app's behavior using a vector of features, where each feature is a subgraph of actions;
- the definition of an algorithm to refine mined frequent subgraphs (*SubGraph-Miner*);
- the definition of an algorithm to find frequent subgraphs in running applications (*SubgraphFinder*);
- an implementation of CAMAS in Java of the tracing, subgraphs mining and classification; graphs are exported in GML (Graph Modeling Language);
- CAMAS has been tested on 12 real malware and good apps.

The rest of the paper is organized as follows. Section 2 introduces CAMAS and discusses its methodology to classify malware. Section 3 reports some preliminary experiments that show the effectiveness of the proposed approach. Finally, after discussing some related works in Sect. 4, Sect. 5 concludes by discussing some future extensions.

2 CAMAS Framework

To identify misbehaviors performed by malicious applications, we need a framework to analyze the application behavior at a lowest possible level, since at the user's level it might by hard to notice malicious actions. The proposed framework *CAMAS* (Classification of Android MAlware through Subgraphs) firstly analyzes malware executions at the lowest level (i.e., at the system call level), and then it mines for common execution subgraphs, by looking for subgraphs that are frequent among the analyzed malware. In the next step, CAMAS analyzes applications that are downloaded from marketplaces and it monitors their executions in a sand-boxed environment. If the analyzed executions contain suspicious subgraphs, the application is considered malicious. This analysis is performed by a classifier, which learns to recognize executions of malicious applications by looking at the suspicious subgraphs that they include. The whole classification process can be summarized in the following steps:

1. Collection of malicious executions extracted from a database of known Android malware (application tracing);
2. Mining of common subgraphs across the malware executions (subgraph features extraction);
3. Extraction of application execution patterns, executed in a sandbox mode (safe application execution);
4. Search of suspicious subgraphs in the extracted application execution (subgraphs locator);
5. Classification of the monitored application (application classification).

In the following, we discuss the methodology and tools that CAMAS uses to extract subgraphs, to perform subgraphs mining and to classify Android applications.

2.1 Malware Subgraphs Mining

To build a representative set of malware behaviors, CAMAS needs to find actions that are frequently performed by malware. In the proposed framework, these actions are represented by subgraphs of system calls. At a high level, the steps performed to extract the common pattern of malware behavior, are the following:

– *Malware monitoring*, through system call tracing;
– *Graph creation*, using cluster of related system calls;
– Common subgraphs extraction (*subgraph mining*) across malware, by carefully choosing the frequency, nodes number and edges number.

These phases are discussed in detail in the following.

Malware Monitoring. In the first phase, a set of known malicious applications are installed on an Android device and are monitored while performing misbehaviors. CAMAS needs to ensure that these misbehaviors are performed during the monitoring phase. To this end, during the training phase only, CAMAS exploits the intrusion detection system MADAM [1], which is able to detect with a good accuracy common Android malware misbehaviors. The monitoring is performed at the system-call level: to perform the monitoring at this level, CAMAS includes a Linux kernel module that hooks the issued system calls and stores the sequence of calls in a shared buffer. Afterward, the shared buffer is analyzed by an Android application, which builds a graph of system calls, which we call *execution trace* (or simply *trace*), which describes the execution of the monitored malware.

Graph Creation. For each malware, multiple traces are collected and then are merged together to build a multi-graph of system calls, i.e. a graph where each node is a system call and the directed edges represent the transition from a system call to the next one. Formally, a system call trace is expressed through an oriented graph $G = (V, E)$, where each system call is a node $v_i \in V$, and edges $e_{i,j} \in E$ represent the transition from a system call v_i into the next one v_j. In the resulting graph, each edge is labelled with a sequence number that represents the position in the trace of a transition from a system call to the next one. The resulting graph may contain more occurrences of the same edge, i.e. $\exists e_{i_1,j_1}, e_{i_2,j_2}$ with $i_1 = i_2$ and $j_1 = j_2$, or edges in-going and outgoing from the same node, i.e. $\exists e_{i,j}$ with $i = j$. This graph type is known in graph theory as *multi-graph*. Several execution traces (i.e. multi-graphs) are merged. The operation of merging two multi-graphs $G_1 = (V_1, E_1)$ and $G_2 = (V_2, E_2)$, returns a new graph $G_3 = (V_3, E_3)$ with $V_3 = V_1 \cup V_2$ and $E_3 = E_1 \cup E_2$.

Both the Linux kernel-module and the Android application that reads the shared buffer are based upon the PICARD framework [2] and are included in the *GraphCreator* CAMAS component. PICARD is the first framework that has introduced the concept of *ActionNode*, i.e. a subgraph of related and consecutive system calls in an execution trace. ActionNodes represent high-level and complex operations (*actions*). The concept of ActionNodes is exploited by the GraphCreator to build execution graphs. To this end, the trace of system calls issued by the tested malware is converted into a multi-graph of ActionNodes, which results more expressive than a graph of simple system calls. Currently, an ActionNode is composed by the automaton of the system calls performed consecutively on the same file. We would like to point out that CAMAS GraphCreator is expressive enough to exploit any relation of system calls and alternative notions of relations among system calls can be used, such as their criticality level. In the end, for each tested malware, the GraphCreator returns a multi-graph of ActionNodes.

Subgraph Mining. After having generated the multi-graphs of ActionNodes from malware executions, CAMAS exploits a mining algorithm to find common execution subgraphs from these multi-graphs. Set of frequent subgraphs with an increasing number of ActionNodes are extracted from the traces using the ParSeMiS [3] toolset. The rationale behind this approach is that malware which perform similar misbehavior should show common actions in their execution graphs. The ParSeMiS toolset returns the set of subgraphs with the same structure, which can be found in at least a chosen (high) percentage of malicious different malware executions. The most important parameter used during this phase is the *frequency* of these subgraphs, i.e. the percentage of malware having the same subgraph in their multi-graphs of ActionNodes. A low number means that the mined subgraphs are found in only some malware, whereas a high number means that the mined subgraphs are found in almost all of the malware. Keep in mind that in this last case also subgraphs that are frequent in any kind of apps (i.e., even good ones) could be found. Hence, it might not be always the case that a high number of frequency means a more representative feature of malware. This is handled by a refinement process.

Some other parameters that can be configured during the subgraph mining are the minimum edge and the minimum node number contained in each mined subgraphs. In fact, the number of common subgraphs mined can be extremely high, in the order of 10^5. Such a number of features is not suitable for a pattern recognition problem, since many subgraphs may be non-representative. For this reason, a fine refinement process is performed on the mined subgraphs, to find those features that are more representative. The refinement process implements these steps:

1. Select subgraphs that exist in at least 50 % of the analyzed malware.
2. Since graphs with few nodes are too generic and non representative of specific behavior, the minimum number of nodes in mined subgraphs is gradually increased, starting from a number of nodes that is set to an acceptable size after a refinement process, so as not to produce too many subgraphs, and gradually increased until common subgraphs are not found anymore.
3. Increase the percentage of analyzed malware required to contain a mined subgraph and go back to step 2.
4. Save common subgraphs in the database in a common format (GML).

A simplified version of the CAMAS algorithm to mine frequent subgraphs in shown in Algorithm 1.

Keep in mind that the algorithm is manually refined at each round to produce a significative number of subgraphs, i.e. features. This means that, for each frequency value, firstly CAMAS tries to discover the number of nodes and edges for which the number of found subgraphs is at an acceptable level.

Set frequency at 50% of the analyzed number of malware;
Set node frequency at an acceptable size after a refinement process;
while *frequency* ≤ *100%* **do**
    mine for commons subgraphs;
    if *there are still subgraphs* **then**
        add found subgraphs to `frequency-node-edges.GML` file;
        increase nodes number;
    else
        increase frequency of 1 step;
        set node frequency at an acceptable size after a refinement process;
    end
end

Algorithm 1: Simplified Algorithm to Mine Frequent Subgraphs

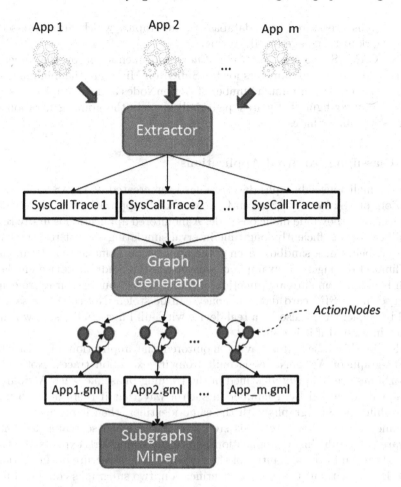

Fig. 1. First part of CAMAS workflow: graph generation and subgraphs mining

Then, it gradually increases these values until subgraphs are not found anymore. This means that, even if the number of subgraphs found is somehow proportional to the number of tested malware, this number is also kept limited in all the configurations in such a way that the number of features is not extremely high.

To further refine the selection process, the subgraphs that are also common to some non-malicious applications are removed. To this end, ActionNodes graphs are also extracted from good applications, i.e. non-infected applications, and then analyzed by CAMAS to mine subgraphs that are in common with malicious applications. Usually, these subgraphs are related to common operations, performed by several applications, and, hence, are not significative in the classification process. In the end, the remaining subgraphs, i.e. those only found in malware, are considered suspicious and meaningful for the classification process.

These graphs are stored in a database of subgraphs, which are expressed in Graph Markup Language (GML) format.

The CAMAS module *SubGraphMiner* implements all of the functions described above. The parameters for the SubGraphMiner are the minimum subgraph frequency, the minimum number of ActionNodes and subgraph edges, and can be easily configured. Figure 1 pictorially depicts the graph generation and subgraphs mining phases.

2.2   Classifying Android Applications

Once the malicious subgraphs database has been created, CAMAS analyzes the behaviors of unknown (e.g., recently downloaded) applications to state if they are infected or they hide malicious code. A monitored application is firstly run in a sandbox for a sufficiently long time interval simulating at best real use-cases. However, being in a sandbox, even if the application is malicious, it can cause only limited damage. An example of sandbox is the Android device emulator, which is able to emulate any function of a real device, but no hardware can be damaged, nor USIM card data or money can be stolen. Notice that a sandbox could be implemented also by a real device with full functionalities, in which we are not interested if it is damaged.

Also in this case, after having monitored the application in a sandbox, a multi-graph of ActionNodes is built from its execution traces. Notice that ActionNodes are uniquely identified in the training phase, i.e. each ActionNode is uniquely identified by a number in such a way that if there are two nodes of two different (sub)graphs with the same identifier, then it means they have the same internal structure. This step is required when searching for known malware subgraphs inside applications, since the framework exploits the GML format that omits the semantics of the node (i.e., the structure of the ActionNodes). Hence, without this unique identification, two subgraphs could end up in being recognized as equal (because they have the same structure), even if only their identification (syntax) is the same, but their semantics (internal structure) is different. Some examples of ActionNodes found in the tested malware set are shown in Fig. 3: each picture is subscribed by the unique ActionNode identifier, where each ActionNode is composed by several system call nodes.

To discover whether the ActionNodes multi-graph of a monitored application includes some malicious subgraphs, a CAMAS application, *SubgraphFinder*, has been implemented. For each malicious subgraph MS_i in the database, SubgraphFinder checks if MS_i exists in the monitored application multi-graph. Then, SubgraphFinder generates a binary vector of n elements, where n is the total number of malicious subgraphs stored in the database of malware. Each element i of this vector is set to 1 if the subgraph MS_i is found in the monitored application, 0 otherwise. At the end, this vector is given to a classifier to test whether the application is considered a malware or not.

Figure 2 pictorially depicts the subgraphs finding and classification phases.

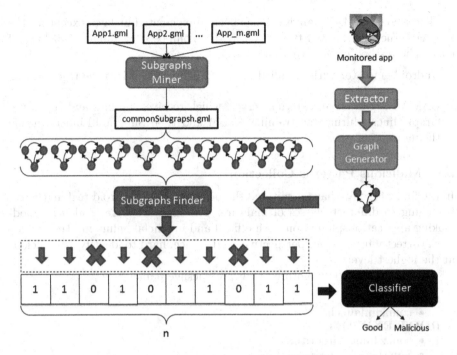

Fig. 2. Second part of CAMAS workflow: subgraphs finding and classification

3   Preliminary Experiments

In this section, we discuss some preliminary results, by showing the various phases of the classification process on some real Android genuine applications and malware. In the malware subgraph mining phase, we have collected representative malicious subgraphs from 12 real malware belonging to the following classes:

- **SMS Trojans:** maliciously send stealthy SMS messages to leak the user credit, maliciously submit the user to premium services, or send to the attacker user's private data.
- **Private Data Trojans:** maliciously retrieve private data like contact lists, IMEI and IMSI codes, received/sent SMS messages. Then, these data are sent to an external server controlled by the attacker through an available Internet connection.
- **Rootkits:** malware that obtain root privileges, exploiting a system weakness, then open a backdoor for the attacker. Installing other malicious applications, send private data to the attacker, or acting as a C&C bot are typical behaviors of a smartphone infected by a rootkit.

The misbehaviors that are made by these malware can be hardly identified by users, since no visible traces are generally left.

The whole CAMAS framework has been implemented in Java, except for the tracing kernel module (written in C), and is composed of about 3,000 lines of code. The testbed of the experiments was:

- Android emulator with modified kernel (2.6.29), which logs the trace system calls on text files;
- CAMAS is run on an external server, which receives log files and runs Sub-GraphMiner (during the training phase) and then SubgraphFinder (during the monitoring phase).

3.1   Malicious Patterns Collection

In the first phase, we have monitored the behavior of 12 Android real malware[1], belonging to different classes of malware. The malware were hidden in good-looking applications, found on both official and unofficial online markets, which work correctly from a user perspective (and, hence, hard to identify as malicious at the highest level).

We report here the monitored malware package name:

- **KMIN**
  - com.km.launcher
- **ROOT EXPLOIT**
  - com.z4mod.z4root:three
  - Super.mobi.eraser
  - com.z4mod.z4root
  - com.zft
  - com.itfunz.itfunzsupertools
  - com.droiddream.android.afdvancedfm
  - com.aps.hainguyen273.app2card
- **SMS TROJAN**
  - tp5x.WGt12
  - com.software.installer
- **MOGAVA**
  - ir.sharif.iranianfoods

As previously said, the CAMAS kernel module logs system calls issued by these applications, by checking if the name of the current process, called current->comm, which is the name of the current running process inside the Linux kernel, is equal to one of the malware names previously reported. Concurrently, a Java activity of a CAMAS module reads periodically from the shared buffer the trace of system calls and generates a file for each application, which contains the traces of all the issued system calls and their parameters. The sequence of systems calls constitutes a graph that, using GraphCreator, (i) is converted into a graph of ActionNodes (ii) is exported using Graph Markup Language (GML) format and stored in a database. Finally, GraphCreator joins all the files together into a single GML file, to facilitate to process of subgraph mining. In the next Section, we discuss how the GML file with all multi-graphs is mined to find frequent subsets.

---

[1] Found at http://contagiominidump.blogspot.it/.

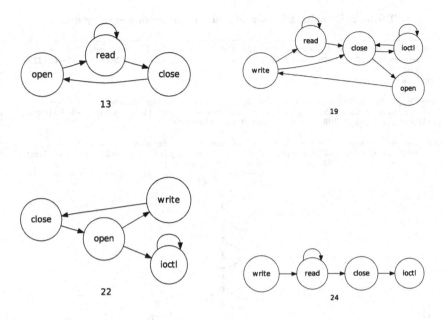

Fig. 3. ActionNodes examples

3.2 Subgraph Mining

From the GML containing all the malware multi-graphs, CAMAS SubGraph-Miner extracts those subgraphs that are common across malware multi-graphs. To this end, CAMAS implements Algorithm 1. To show an example of subgraph mining across malware, Table 1 shows the sequence of commands executed by CAMAS SubgraphFinder on a GML file containing all the 12 tested malware multi-graphs of ActionNodes (in the example, this file is called 12Malware.gml). Each of these commands returns a GML file containing a set of subgraphs with:

- different frequency (parameter --minimumFrequency),
- node count (parameter --minimumNodeCount),
- edge count (parameter --minimumEdgeCount).

To be able to distinguish all the subgraphs that will be used by SubgraphFinder for the vector features, each file has the following name format: 12Malware-*frequency-nodecount-edgecount*.gml. As an example, in Table 1 SubgraphFinder outputs 10 features from the first file, i.e. all the common subgraphs across malware with at least 10 nodes and at least 12 edges and found in at least 7 malware out of 12. In the example, since SubgraphFinder has been scheduled to generate 3 different subgraphs collections (respectively, 12Malware-7-10-12.gml, 12Malware-7-9-14.gml, 12Malware-7-8-14.gml), the length of the feature vector is the sum of all the subgraphs found in these 3 files. Hence, in the end, in this example the vector has length 10 + 15 + 16, i.e. 41.

Figure 4 reports an example of one of the subgraphs found in the GML file: keep in mind that each node identifier (2, 3, 4, etc.) refers to an ActionNode

Table 1. Exploiting SubGraphMiner to find common subgraphs

```
java de.parsemis.Miner —graphFile=12Malware.gml —minimumFrequency=7 —↵
    minimumNodeCount=10 —minimumEdgeCount=12 —outputFile=12Malware—7—10—12.↵
    gml
Complete run took 1.555 seconds; found 10 fragments

java de.parsemis.Miner —graphFile=12Malware.gml —minimumFrequency=7 —↵
    minimumNodeCount=9 —minimumEdgeCount=14 —outputFile=12Malware—7—9—14.gml
Complete run took 1.706 seconds; found 15 fragments

java de.parsemis.Miner —graphFile=12Malware.gml —minimumFrequency=7 —↵
    minimumNodeCount=8 —minimumEdgeCount=14 —outputFile=12Malware—7—8—14.gml
Complete run took 1.708 seconds; found 16 fragments
```

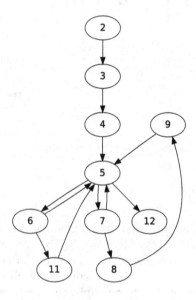

Fig. 4. Subgraph example

identifier. As an example, node 9 of the subgraph shown in Fig. 4 refers to the
ActionNode of Fig. 3 with identifier 9.

After this phase, CAMAS exploits this database of subgraphs to locate malicious subgraphs in the monitored executions of applications. As previously said,
this monitoring is performed in a controlled environment to avoid that unwanted
malicious executions may damage the smartphone.

3.3   Run-Time Classification

When monitoring applications to find subgraphs, the presence or absence of a
subgraph in the monitored execution of an application is used as *feature* to discern between a malicious application and a good one. For each new application,
several graphs are generated that represent the application usage. The union
of these graphs for a new application XYZ is converted into a multi-graph of

ActionNodes and is stored in a file XYZ.gml. After this phase, CAMAS Sub-graphFinder searches if each of the subgraphs stored in GML subgraph files (such as 12Malware-7-10-12.gml, 12Malware-7-9-14.gml, 12Malware-7-8-14.gml of the previous examples) are found in XYZ.gml and then exploits computational intelligence tools, i.e. Bayesian classifiers and artificial neural networks (ANN), to distinguish a malicious execution from a good one. Suppose that the database of malicious features is composed of n elements (41 in the previous example), then SubgraphFinder builds a vector of n elements by searching if each of the n subgraphs is present in the XYZ.GML file. Each element of the vector is set to 1 if the subgraph at the i-th position exists in the XYZ.GML file. The element is set to 0 otherwise.

Following this methodology, we have collected data from 13 malicious applications and 7 good ones. Namely, the genuine applications are the following: AngryBirds, FruitNinja, Google Calendar, Launcher, Android Contact Manager, Calculator and Messages, whereas the malicious applications have been reported previously. We have collected more than 500 distinct runs, and in the end CAMAS has managed to find 80 distinct vectors. From these vectors, there are 33 vectors that are considered as belonging to the malicious class. Hence, the other 47 vectors extracted from runs of non malicious applications are considered genuine. We have used this dataset to extract training and testing sets, using the holdout method, which selects 70 % of the vectors to be used for the training set and the remaining 30 % to be used as testing set. In the experiments, the following classifiers have been used:

- linear discriminant classifier (LDC),
- quadratic discriminant classifier (QDC),
- k-nearest neighbor (K-NN),
- artificial neural networks (ANN).

The K-NN classifier, with a number of neighbors $k = 2$, has produced the best results that we report here in form of a confusion matrix (see Table 2). On the testing set, all the malicious vectors have been classified as malicious, whilst 2 good vectors have been wrongly classified as malicious.

As far as regards the overhead of the whole CAMAS framework, we can partition it in the following classes:

- tracing overhead: less than 1 %;
- graph generation overhead: less than 1 s;

Table 2. Confusion matrix for testing set

	Good	Malicious	
Good	12	2	14
Malicious	0	10	10
	12	12	24

- graph mining overhead: manually tuned to avoid the generation of files with thousand of subgraphs. When refined, usually it takes 1-2 s for each subgraph collection;
- graph searching overhead: order of milliseconds;
- classification overhead: order of milliseconds.

Hence, in the preliminary tests, the framework is able to detect all the executions of malicious applications and the false positive rate can be considered reasonable. The same holds for the run-time and off-line overhead.

4   Related Work

Crowdroid [4] is a machine learning-based framework that recognizes Trojan-like malware on Android smartphones, by analyzing the number of times each system call has been issued by an application during the execution of an action that requires user interaction. A genuine application differs from its trojanized version, since it issues different types and a different number of system calls. Crowdroid builds a vector of n features (the Android system calls). Differently from this approach, in CAMAS the vector of features is composed by n subgraphs of system calls, which better describes the behavior of malware. A similar approach is presented in [5], which also considers the system call parameters to discern between normal system calls and malicious ones. CAMAS exploits system call parameters as well to create ActionNodes, i.e. cluster of file-related system calls, based upon the file descriptor parameter. Another system that exploits system calls and computational intelligence is presented in [1], which is an anomaly-based intrusion detection system that, differently from Crowdroid, monitors the system globally, but it may not be able to detect some trojanized application if their behavior faithfully represents the good ones. Differently from this work, CAMAS is also able to detect the malicious application.

Another IDS that relies on machine learning techniques is *Andromaly* [6], which monitors both the smartphone and user's behaviors by observing several parameters, spanning from sensors activities to CPU usage. 88 features are used to describe these behaviors; the features are then pre-processed by feature selection algorithms. The authors developed four malicious applications to evaluate the ability to detect anomalies. In CAMAS, we have tested only real applications/malware found on online market and/or malware repository.

Similarly to CAMAS sandboxed execution, [7] proposes *AASandbox* to perform static and dynamic analysis on Android apps to automatically detect suspicious applications using a sandboxing. However, in CAMAS user's inputs are not generated by the Monkey tool, but they are part of a analysis phase in which users actively interact with the monitored application. Another work on sandboxed analysis of Android malware is presented in [8]. *DroidAnalytics* [9] is a malware analytic system for malware collection, signature generation and association based on similarity score by analyzing the system at the app/class/method level. CAMAS, on the other hand, works at the system call level and can be extended at any Android level.

Barrera et al. [10] presents a methodology to empirically analyze permission-based security models which makes novel use of the Self-Organizing Map (SOM). The paper analyzes 1,100 Android apps and identifies some trends in how developers use the Android permissions model, such as that while Android has a large number of permissions restricting access to advanced functionality on devices, only a small number of these permissions are actually used by developers. Sanz et al. [11] proposes a methodology for categorizing Android apps through machine-learning techniques that, to represent each application, extracts different feature sets, such as the frequency of occurrence of the printable strings, the different permissions of the application itself and the permissions of the app. The semantics of the features of CAMAS, differently from these approaches, are found at the lowest possible level, i.e. at the kernel-level. This means that even if at the highest-level, i.e. permission-level and/or user-level, a feature may be considered un-harmful, because common among several applications (a permission encompasses several possible usage of the permission itself), at the lowest level it is possible to actually discriminate a good usage of a permission and/or user-level action from a bad one.

Damopoulos et al. [12] introduces *iDMA*, a software for iOS able to dynamically monitor and analyze the behavior of any running application in terms API calls. The authors have created behavioral profiles from tested applications and malware that have been evaluated through machine learning classifiers. Enck et al. and Ongtang et al. [13,14] propose *Kirin* security service for Android, which performs lightweight certification of applications to mitigate malware at install time. Kirin certification uses security rules that match undesirable properties in security configuration bundled with applications. Schmidt et al. [15] performs static analysis on the executables to extract functions calls usage using `readelf` command. Hence, these calls are compared with malware executables for classification. Differently from these approaches, CAMAS performs the analysis of the applications at run-time (in a sand-boxed environment) to be able to spot malicious actions also in obfuscated applications. Finally, [16] surveys some security solutions for mobile devices.

5   Conclusions and Future Work

We have presented CAMAS, a tool for the analysis and classification of malicious Android applications, through pattern recognition on execution graphs. The framework analyzes behaviors at system-call level and exploits the concept of ActionNode to increase the system expressiveness. The framework finds common subgraphs in malware executions and classifies other apps by searching for common patterns of the previously mined subgraphs. The framework is highly configurable and can be easily extended to monitor and analyze other event types.

A future extension considers the detection of high level and security relevant events, such as network actions. We are also planning to increase the number of monitored system calls and explore different relations used to build ActionNodes, such as the criticality class of system calls. Finally, a future extension will include a larger dataset and different types of classifiers and feature-selection algorithms.

References

1. Dini, G., Martinelli, F., Saracino, A., Sgandurra, D.: MADAM: a multi-level anomaly detector for android malware. In: Kotenko, I., Skormin, V. (eds.) MMM-ACNS 2012. LNCS, vol. 7531, pp. 240–253. Springer, Heidelberg (2012)
2. Aldini, A., Martinelli, F., Saracino, A., Sgandurra, D.: A collaborative framework for generating probabilistic contracts. In: Smari, W.W., Fox, G.C. (eds.): Proceedings of the 2013 IEEE International Conference on Collaboration Technologies and Systems, SECOTS 2013, pp. 139–143. IEEE Computer Society (2013)
3. Philippsen, M.: Parsemis: the parallel and sequential mining suite. http://www2.informatik.uni-erlangen.de/EN/research/ParSeMiS
4. Burguera, I., Zurutuza, U., Nadijm-Tehrani, S.: Crowdroid: behavior-based malware detection system for android. In: SPSM '11, October 2011. ACM (2011)
5. Mutz, D., Valeur, F., Vigna, G.: Anomalous system call detection. ACM Trans. Inf. Syst. Secur. $9(1)$, 61–93 (2006)
6. Shabtai, A., Kanonov, U., Elovici, Y., Glezer, C., Weiss, Y.: "Andromaly": a behavioral malware detection framework for android devices. J. Intell. Inf. Syst. $38(1)$, 161–190 (2012)
7. Blasing, T., Batyuk, L., Schmidt, A.D., Camtepe, S., Albayrak, S.: An android application sandbox system for suspicious software detection. In: 2010 5th International Conference on Malicious and Unwanted Software (MALWARE), pp. 55–62 (2010)
8. Reina, A., Fattori, A., Cavallaro, L.: A system call-centric analysis and stimulation technique to automatically reconstruct android malware behaviors. In: Proceedings of the 6th European Workshop on System Security (EUROSEC), Prague, Czech Republic, April 2013 (2013)
9. Zheng, M., Sun, M., Lui, J.C.: Droidanalytics: a signature based analytic system to collect, extract, analyze and associate android malware. In: 12th IEEE International Conference on Trust, Security and Privacy in Computing and Communications (TrustCom 13), Melbourne, Australia, July 2013 (2013)
10. Barrera, D., Kayacik, H.G., van Oorschot, P.C., Somayaji, A.: A methodology for empirical analysis of permission-based security models and its application to android. In: Proceedings of the 17th ACM Conference on Computer and Communications Security, CCS '10, pp. 73–84. ACM, New York (2010)
11. Sanz, B., Santos, I., Laorden, C., Ugarte-Pedrero, X., Bringas, P.: On the automatic categorisation of android applications. In: 2012 IEEE Consumer Communications and Networking Conference (CCNC), pp. 149–153 (2012)
12. Damopoulos, D., Kambourakis, G., Gritzalis, S., Park, S.: Peer-to-Peer Netw. Appl. 5, 1–11 (2012)
13. Enck, W., Ongtang, M., McDaniel, P.: On lightweight mobile phone application certification. In: CCS '09: Proceedings of the 16th ACM Conference on Computer and Communications Security, pp. 235–245. ACM, New York (2009)
14. Ongtang, M., McLaughlin, S., Enck, W., McDaniel, P.: Semantically rich application-centric security in android. In: Proceedings of the 2009 Annual Computer Security Applications Conference, ACSAC '09, December 2009, pp. 340–349 (2009)

15. Schmidt, A.D., Bye, R., Schmidt, H.G., Clausen, J.H., Kiraz, O., Yüksel, K.A., Çamtepe, S.A., Albayrak, S.: Static analysis of executables for collaborative malware detection on android. In: Proceedings of IEEE International Conference on Communications, ICC 2009, Dresden, Germany, 14–18 June 2009, pp. 1–5. IEEE (2009)
16. La Polla, M., Martinelli, F., Sgandurra, D.: A survey on security for mobile devices. IEEE Commun. Surv. Tutorials **15**(1), 446–471 (2013)

Introducing Probabilities in Contract-Based Approaches for Mobile Application Security

Gianluca Dini[1], Fabio Martinelli[2], Ilaria Matteucci[2], Andrea Saracino[1,2], and Daniele Sgandurra[2(✉)]

[1] Dipartimento di Ingegneria dell'Informazione, Università di Pisa, Pisa, Italy
`gianluca.dini,andrea.saracino@iet.unipi.it`
[2] Istituto di Informatica e Telematica, Consiglio Nazionale delle Ricerche, Pisa, Italy
`{fabio.martinelli,ilaria.matteucci,`
`daniele.sgandurra}@iit.cnr.it`

Abstract. Security for mobile devices is a problem of capital importance, especially due to new threats coming from malicious applications. This has been proved by the increasing interest of the research community on the topic of security on mobile devices. Several security solutions have been recently proposed, to address the uprising threats coming from malicious applications. However, several mechanisms may result not flexible enough, hard to apply, or too coarse grained, e.g. several critics have been raised against the Android permission system.

We argue that, it is possible to obtain more flexible security tools and finer grained security requirements by introducing probability measurements.

In this paper we discuss how to introduce probabilistic clauses into the Security-by-Contract and the Security-by-Contract-with-Trust frameworks, revising the main building blocks and providing tools to write probabilistic contracts and policies. A proof-of-concept implementation on Android system has also been presented.

Keywords: Probabilistic contract · Probabilistic policy compliance · Contract-based security approaches · Run-time enforcement

1 Overview

New generation mobile devices (e.g., smartphones and tablets) are becoming day-by-day more powerful and popular. The growth in computing power, ubiquitousness and capabilities of these devices has been parallelized by the growth of available applications, specifically developed for smartphones and tablets. However, these applications may be not completely secure. In fact, malicious developers strive to design and deliver applications that may damage both users and

The research leading to these results has received funding from the EU Seventh Framework Programme (FP7/2007-2013) under grant n. 256980 (NESSoS), n. 257930 (Aniketos), from PRIN Security Horizons funded by MIUR with D.D. 23.10.2012 n. 719, and EIT ICT Labs activity 13077.

J. Garcia-Alfaro et al. (Eds.): DPM 2013 and SETOP 2013, LNCS 8247, pp. 284–299, 2014.
DOI: 10.1007/978-3-642-54568-9_18, © Springer-Verlag Berlin Heidelberg 2014

devices. In particular some applications may hide a Trojan horse that, even if it looks unharmful, in background it performs malicious actions that the users did not expect to happen.

The current security model, which rules (i) if an application can be safely installed on the device, (ii) what kind of actions the application may execute once installed, still suffers from several weaknesses, in particular in its capacity of expressing proper *contracts*. Semantics of current security models is too naïve since it is either based upon trust relationships or upon statements of purpose. In the first case, users accept to run an application if they trust the provider. In the second one, providers state the security relevant actions performed by an application and it is up to the users to decide whether run the application if they consider these operations safe. In the former case the trust level of the trusted entity also determines the code privileges, essentially relegating an application into the "all or nothing" policy, while in the latter case the semantics is too-coarse grained (e.g., Android permissions) or hardly usable. For example, in the Android system, security relevant actions are declared through permissions, which are difficult to understand for average users.

In this paper, we introduce probability aspects into the workflow of two contract-based approaches developed for mobile devices, namely the Security-by Contract [1] (S × C) and the Security-by-Contract-with-Trust [2,3] (S × C × T) frameworks. These two approaches integrate several security techniques to build a chain of trust, which, in the end, ensures that the downloaded application will execute only security actions that are allowed by the user's policy. To this end, we introduce a probabilistic description of the behavior of an application and a more expressive version of the user's security requirements. Indeed, the current models only permit the definition of a set of allowed actions, e.g., the Android permission system (first box of Fig. 1). More expressive policies which take in account a possible action history are modelled through automata that represent allowed executions.

We propose a probabilistic automata-based model that enables the developers to define more expressive contracts through probabilistic clauses, e.g., how often a security-relevant action may happen. The same expressiveness is given to users to specify security policies. Since we include probabilistic clauses in the specification of contracts and policies, the security mechanisms involved into the workflows of S × C and S × C × T has to be redefined. Hence, we present a new workflow for both S × C and S × C × T framework in which each module is updated to support probabilistic functions. The advantage of using probabilities is the possibility of describing more realistic usage scenarios for an application. In fact, many applications depend on user inputs or context information and it is difficult to define realistic policies based upon boolean conditions only. In these models, all the possible execution paths are considered legal. Hence, a low-probability operation is considered valid even if performed several times. For this reason, we introduce probabilities in the definition of security clauses to define more fine-grained contracts and policies. These descriptions better fit real application use

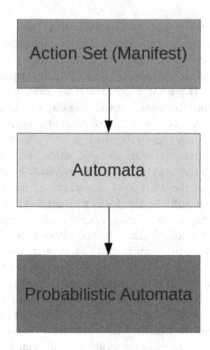

Fig. 1. Graphical representation of the improvement in policies expressiveness.

cases and can be defined without alteration of the Security-By-Contract-with-Trust workflow. Finally, we propose an extension to the Android permission system, which includes the security properties of Probabilistic Security-By-Contract with Trust in the most popular operative system for mobile devices.

The paper is structured as follows. Section 2 introduces the main concepts of contract-based approaches and briefly recalls the Security-by-Contract and the Security-by-Contract-with-Trust frameworks. In Sect. 3, we propose a probabilistic version of both Security-by-Contract and Security-by-Contract-with-Trust. Section 4 presents an application of the proposed approach in Android systems, proposing some extension to the current framework. In Sect. 5, we discuss some related work, while Sect. 6 briefly concludes.

2   Contract-Based Approaches

Contract-based approaches, such as the Security-by-Contract [1] (S × C) and the Security-by-Contract-with-Trust [2,3] (S × C × T) frameworks, have been developed for mobile devices, . They integrate several security techniques to build a chain of trust by sequentially applying them to safely execute applications. The three cornerstones of these security frameworks are application *code A*, application *contract C*, and client *policy P*, where a *contract* is a formal, complete, and correct specification of an application security relevant behavior, e.g., security critical virtual machine API call, or critical system calls [4]. A *policy* is a formal complete specification of the acceptable security-relevant behavior allowed to applications executed on the platform [4]. We assume that both contract and policy are syntactically described by exploiting the same language.

The basic idea of a contract-based approach is the usage of the contract for guaranteeing that security aspects are satisfied. More in detail, using the contract, it is possible to check at deploy time, i.e., before the application execution, if the application satisfies the user policy or not. Let $\preceq$ denote the compliance between two of the previous elements. A contract-based approach guarantees that

$$A \preceq C \preceq P \Rightarrow A \preceq P \tag{1}$$

In the following, we describe the Security-by-Contract (S × C) and the Security-by-Contract-with-Trust (S × C × T) frameworks as approaches that integrate the described techniques to guarantee security at application execution time.

2.1   Towards Security Techniques

Several techniques have been proposed to tackle specific security aspects. Almost all the following are integrated into the S × C or into the S × C × T frameworks.

Application-Contract Matching. It enables statically verification of an application code by using a third-party provided proof and also its validation. The proof is linked to the application code. Verifying the proof validity is more efficient than generating it. The verification procedure follows the steps of the proof and, if all of them are correct, validates its conclusion. Examples of this approach are the *proof-carrying code* [5] and the *model-carrying code* [6] methods.

Contract Policy Matching. It statically analyzes the compliance of a specification, e.g., a contract, with a specified security policy.

Enforcement/Monitoring. The run-time enforcement approach consists of running an application code inside the scope of a *controller* that checks, step-by-step, the executed operations. At each operation, the behavior of the considered application is compared with the consumer policy (*policy enforcement*), and prevents violations by modifying the application behavior at run time, e.g., forbidding non-allowed operations.

This approach differs from monitoring that just observes the behavior of the application and at the end of the executions it could also provide information (e.g., audit, logs) for understanding its behavior, e.g., if the code does not work as described by its contract (*contract* monitoring).

Metrics Manager. Security metrics aim at assessing security threats. For instance, metrics can describe a system in terms of its reputation in a community, number of past, successful interactions or average number of failures per year. Then, these values are exploited for taking security aware decisions. Among the others, *trust*, *risk*, and *probability* aspects are receiving major interest.

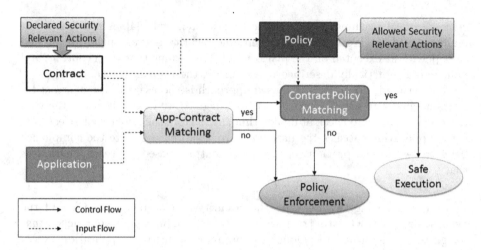

Fig. 2. The Security-by-Contract process.

2.2 Security-by-Contract and Security-by-Contract-with-Trust in a Nutshell

The Security-by-Contract paradigm (S × C) provides a full characterization of the contract-based interaction. It combines different functionalities in an integrated way (see Fig. 2). In particular, it includes a module for automatically checking the formal correspondence between code and contract (*Application-Contract matching*). If the result is negative, then the monitor is run to enforce the policy (*Policy Enforcement*), otherwise a matching between the contract and the policy (*Contract-Policy Matching*) is performed to establish if the contract is compliant with the policy. In this case, the code is executed without overhead (*Safe Execution*), otherwise the policy is enforced again (*Policy Enforcement*).

Along this research line, in [2,3] S × C has been extended in order to deal also with the concept of *trust*. The new framework is named Security-by-Contract-with-Trust (S × C × T) (Fig. 3). S × C × T consists of integrating the S × C paradigm with a monitoring infrastructure for trust management. As a matter of fact, a crucial point of the S × C architecture is the verification of the relation that exists between the application and its contract. Usually, nowadays a mobile application is installed only if its origin is trusted. This means that users can reject or accept the signature of the application provider based upon the trust level. S × C × T extends S × C in two different phases: at deploy-time, replacing the app-contract matching with a *Trust Evaluator* module. This component sets the monitoring state, and at run-time it applies the contract monitoring procedure for tuning the provider trust level. In fact, the S × C architecture has been extended by adding a component for the contract monitoring to check if the contract adheres to the actual execution of the application and, according to the answer, it updates the provider level of trust.

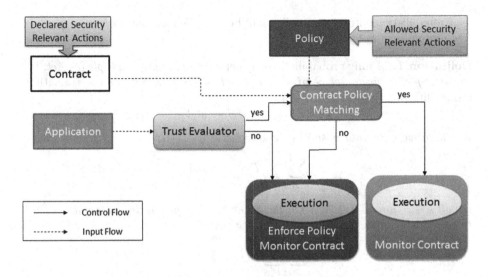

Fig. 3. The Security-by-Contract-with-Trust process.

The advantages of these contract-based frameworks are that they are able to identify unsafe applications before and without running them. In particular, using the contract-policy matching functionality, it checks at deploy-time if the declared behavior of the application is compliant with the required policy. This check, along with the assurance that the application code is compliant with the application contract, which is obtained through the application-contract matching module $(S \times C)$ or by the trust evaluator $(S \times C \times T)$, guarantees that the application satisfies the user requirements. Anytime the contract-policy matching finds that a contract is not compliant with the policy, the application is run in a controlled way through the enforcement module. It is worth noticing that the cost, in terms of energy, of running a contract policy matching is much lower than performing the enforcement. Hence, unsafe applications are not run at all by the user and possible unsafe application are run in a controlled way. This leads to an attack risk reduction.

3 Probabilistic Security-by-Contract and Probabilistic Security-by-Contract-with-Trust

In this section, we describe a probabilistic version of both $S \times C$ and $S \times C \times T$ architectures. It is worth noticing that, in both cases the original workflow is not changed. Only the components are modified in such a way that, on one hand, they are able to cope with probability metrics and, on the other hand, Eq. 1 still holds for an appropriate choice of the notion of compliance.

Let us assume that both probabilistic contract and probabilistic policy are expressed through the same formalism.

Probabilistic contract and policy will be modelled as *(substochastic) generative probabilistic automata* [7,8].

Definition 1. *A* fully probabilistic *or* generative *automata is a tuple* (S, Act, P) *consisting of a finite set* S *of states, a set of actions* Act, *and a* transition probability function

$$P : S \times Act \times S \to [0,1]$$

A generative automata *is said to be* stochastic *if*

$$\sum_{a \in Act} \sum_{t \in S} P(s, a, t) = 1$$

for all $s \in S$ *for all* $a \in Act$. *On the other hand, a generative automata is said to be* semistochastic *or* substochastic *if*

$$\sum_{a \in Act} \sum_{t \in S} P(s, a, t) < 1$$

for all $s \in S$ *for all* $a \in Act$. *For* $C \subseteq S$, *we put* $P(s, a, C) = \sum_{t \in C} P(s, a, t)$. *A state* $s \in S$ *is said to be* terminal *iff* $\sum_{a,t} P(s, a, t) = 0$.

Hereafter, we consider generative automata such that for each action there is only one possible transition for each action $a \in Act$.

3.1 Probabilistic Security-by-Contract Workflow

Being the Security-By-Contract framework modular, introducing probability metrics implies the substitution of some components with their probabilistic counterpart. The Probabilistic Security-by-Contract workflow is depicted in Fig. 4.

Probabilistic application contract matching is verified using some static validation techniques able to deal with probabilistic description of behavior. For instance, as *proof carrying code* [5] is used in S × C, here we can use the *Probabilistic Proof Carrying Code, e.g.,* [9,10]. In particular, this method guarantees that, for all possible k-length execution traces whose probability is calculated as $P_k = \prod_{i=1}^{k} P(s_i, a_i, t_i)$, the application is considered compliant if $P_k > \theta_k$, where θ_k is a given threshold value $0 < \theta_k < 1$ dependent from the length of the execution trace.

Probabilistic contract policy matching is performed by checking the compliance between a contract and a policy. According to the level of required accuracy, several relations can be considered in order to verify the compliance between probabilistic contract and policy. In S × C, the contract-policy matching function checks if the contract and the policy are similar. This means that for each action described in the contract, we check if there exists the same action described in the policy and the description of the transition are similar again. Hence, we assume that the policy specifies a rule for each

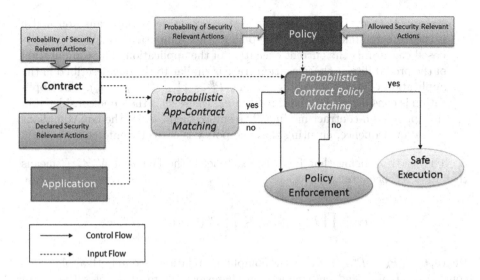

Fig. 4. Workflow for Probabilistic Security-by-Contract

security relevant action, which we call *SecAction*.

Referring to the notion of ε-simulation given in [11], hereafter, we define a slightly different ε-simulation.

Definition 2. *A relation $R \subseteq S \times S$ is a relation of positive ε-simulation, where $\varepsilon \in [0,1]$ if whenever $(s, s') \in R$, then $\forall a \in SecAction$, $\forall W \in S$*

$$\sum_{t \in W} P(s,a,t) \leq \sum_{t' \in R(W)} P(s',a,t') \leq \sum_{t \in W} (P(s,a,t) + \varepsilon)$$

where $R(W)$ is the set of all states that are in relation with states in W trough R. We say that s is ε-simulated by s', written $s \prec_\varepsilon s'$, if $(s, s') \in R$ for some relation of ε-simulation R on S. The idea is that, while the ε-simulation allows a deviation of a values $\varepsilon \in [-1,1]$, here, we are only interested in positive values of ε. Hence, the probabilistic distribution of the contract have to be less than the probability distribution of the policy of, at most, a value ε.

It is worth noticing that, according to our assumptions, having a positive ε-simulation R means that whether $(s, s') \in R$ then, for each action $a \in$ *SecAction*,

$$P(s,a,t) \leq P(s',a,t') \leq P(s,a,t) + \varepsilon$$

and $(t, t') \in R$.

Enforcement of Probabilistic Policies is performed when either the application is not compliant with the contract, or the contract is not compliant with the policy.

At each step, the enforcement computes the probability that the application performs a specific security relevant action a, starting from the current state s, $P^p(s, a, t)$, where t is the destination state of the transition and p is the expected one stated by the policy. This computation exploits history-based concerning the current execution of the application. The computation of the probability of the execution trace is similar to the one described in the application-contract matching module $P_k^p = \prod_{i=1}^{k} P^p(s_i, a_i, t_i)$. The application is considered compliant if $P_k^p > \theta_k$, where θ_k is the same considered in the application-contract module. The enforcement denies the non compliant operation sequence, ensuring that the policy is correctly enforced.

It is worth noticing that Eq. 1 holds. Indeed, the fact that $C \preceq_\varepsilon P$ means that $P_k \leq P_k^p$ because

$$P_k = \prod_{i=1}^{k} P(s_i, a_i, t_i) \leq \prod_{i=1}^{k} P^p(s_i, a_i, t_i) = P_k^p$$

Hence, $\theta_k < P_k \leq P_k^p$ Let $\preceq_\Theta$ be the compliance relation used in both application-contract matching and enforcement mechanisms, where Θ denotes the set of threshold values θ_k for any k-length execution trace, and let us consider to use the positive ε-simulation for the contract-policy matching then the following holds

$$A \preceq_\Theta C \preceq_\varepsilon P \Rightarrow A \preceq_\Theta P$$

3.2 Probabilistic Security-by-Contract-with-Trust

Let us introduce probability also into the S × C × T architecture. Referring to [2,3], the application-contract matching functionality is replaced by the Trust evaluator due to the fact that it is not always possible to statically check the compliance of the application with its contract. Hence, we consider a trusted marketplace that provides trusted information about the compliance between the application and its contract. These measurements are computed using compliance feedback received by remote devices running the framework.

The Probabilistic Security-by-Contract-with-Trust workflow is depicted in Fig. 5 and its components are described hereafter.

Trust Evaluator assesses the trust level of the application to be compliance with its contract. Also in this case, the compliance relation that we consider is the same used in S × C, i.e., $\preceq_\Theta$. Note that even when the developer does not provide a contract for the application, according to [12], it is possible to automatically generate the *probabilistic contract* of an application. Let us assume that the marketplace is able to generate it. In this case the level of trust we consider is the level of reliability of the probabilistic contract as complete description of the application behavior.

    Probabilistic Contract Generation. The contract is generated by analyzing either application executions or the application code [12], i.e., the application control-flow is analyzed to explore all possible executions, and associating to each execution a probability. The union of all the

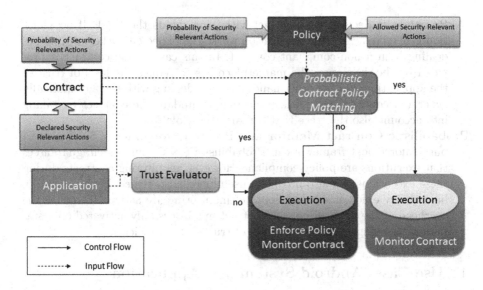

Fig. 5. Workflow for Probabilistic Security-by-Contract-with-Trust

possible executions constitutes all the possible sequences of states that
an application can follow. From these sequences of states, if we only
focus on the security relevant actions executed by an application, i.e.,
SecActions, then the contract is represented by a probabilistic automaton $Q = (V, SecAction, P)$, where the nodes $V = \{v_1, v_2, ..., v_n\}$ is
related to the set of states, $SecAction$ is the set of SecActions performed
by a specific application, and P is the probabilistic transition function
$P : V \times SecAct \times V \rightarrow [0, 1]$ defined as follows: let $mul(v_i, a, v_j)$ be number of times that the action a is executed in the state v_i for reaching the
state v_j and let $mul(v_i)$ be the number of output arcs from v_i. Hence,
for all state $v_i \in V$,

$$P(v_i, a, v_j) = \frac{mul(v_i, a, v_j)}{mul(v_i)}$$

for each v_j reached by v_i through an action a. $P(v_k, a, v_l) = 0$ is associated to any missing edge between v_k and v_l. It is worth noticing that
this model is a generative one.

Probabilistic Contract-Policy Matching. Also in this case, the matching
is performed by checking if there exists a probabilistic simulation relation
or an ε-simulation between the probabilistic contract and the probabilistic
policy. It is worth noticing that, in any case, a probabilistic automata is
returned. Hence, we can exploit the same functionalities we have described
in the Probabilistic Security-by-Contract workflow.

Probabilistic Contract Monitor. The contract monitor is performed when
both the trust level is greater than a policy-defined threshold and the contract policy matching returns a positive answer. This is because, also for

Probabilistic Security-by-Contract-with-Trust holds the Eq. 1. If no violation is detected, then the application worked as expected. Otherwise, we are dealing with a non-compliant contract. In this case, if the contract is provided by the developer, the marketplace has to reduce the level of trust of the application. On the other hand, if we are dealing with the automatically generated contract, the marketplace has to update the contract by taking into account also the trace that contains the violation.

Probabilistic Contract Monitor and Policy Enforcement. Similarly to a pure enforcement framework in Probabilistic S × C, our system guarantees that executions are policy-compliant. However, monitoring contracts during these executions can also provide a useful feedback. Hence, in this scenario, both policy enforcement and contract monitoring are active. To reduce the overhead of the monitoring, the contract monitor is only activated on a statistical base depending on the level of trust of the application.

4   Use Case: Android System and Applications

A possible use-case for the probabilistic contract model is represented by the mobile operative system Android.

Android is an *app-based* mobile operative system: it allows users to download and install applications specifically designed for Android devices. The Android operative system is a complex framework that relies on a generic Linux kernel and several libraries written in high level languages that enable the interaction with all the device components. Applications offer several functionalities exploiting the various interfaces and components of the device, by also accessing resources that are security-critical, such as network interfaces, call dialer, SMS manager, or even private data like contact lists, social network passwords, device IMEI and SIM number. Due to the high number of security-critical resources, smartphones and tablets are susceptible to a higher number of security issues than personal computers. In fact, starting from 2009, the number of attacks targeted to mobile devices has strongly increased [13]. In particular, in 2011 and 2012 several malicious applications (malware) have been developed specifically for Android devices.

Android already includes a contract-like system, based upon the concepts of *permissions* and *manifest*. In Android each application comes shipped with a document called `AndroidManifest.xml` (manifest for short) that describes the application components and declares the security actions performed by the application. If an application has to perform some critical operations, such as to access a device resource, or to read/write sensitive information, this has to be declared it in the manifest file. To enforce this contract, a component on the system-side called *Permission Checker* constantly enforces the policy by denying each operation for which the permission has not been declared in the manifest file. Several criticisms have been raised against this system, which results too coarse-grained [14] and too much reliant on user knowledge and expertise [15].

The main problem of this approach is that the acceptance policy for an application's requested permission is "all or nothing", that is, the user cannot accept only a subset of the required permissions.

We argue that is possible to enhance the Android permission system increasing its expressiveness, including in Android the probabilistic Security-By-Contract model. This is discussed in the next subsection.

4.1   Extended Manifest and Trust Evaluator

The first step to extend the Android permission system is the extension of the manifest file to include a description of the probabilistic automata. The manifest file is written in eXtensible Markup Language (XML), in which the inclusion of additional data is straightforward. Exploiting this feature of the XML language, we extend the manifest introducing a new xml tag: `<contract_clause>`. This tag contains a description of the contract probabilistic automaton in Graph Markup Language (GML). GML gives an XML-like description of a graph or automaton and can be easily embedded in an XML document. In this way, the `<contract_clause>` tag is not analyzed by the Android system, which only checks the ordinary permissions.

Hence, in our proposed framework, the manifest file comes as a contract divided in two parts. The first one is filled by the developer and specifies the application components and permissions. The second part, which can be filled either by the developer or directly by a trusted third party, e.g. the *Google Play* market, contains the probabilistic contract. Since in Android the main vector for application distribution is the on-line marketplace, Google Play, the trust relationship is not directly established between users and developers. Developers build a trust relationship with the market, which decides how much it trusts the applications coming from a developer. This trust value is added to the manifest file. The trust value is analyzed by the Trust Evaluator component, which decides whether the application is trusted or not.

Example 1. "The probability that an SMS is sent to a number not in the contact list is lesser than 3 %". In Android there are several SMS manager applications which can be downloaded and installed, which may automatically send SMS messages (memo or post-poned sending). These applications should send SMS to known numbers and to unknown ones in a limited amount of times only. This avoids, for example the unwilling subscription to premium services. Simply using the Android permissions SEND_SMS and READ_CONTACTS, it is not possible to implement such a policy, that even if simple requires a greater expressivity than the one provided by Android. Using probabilistic automaton, the definition of such a policy is straightforward.

4.2   Policy Manager, Matching and Enforcement

The Policy Manager is used to specify the security policies, which can be either global or per-application. This component presents a simple user interface that allows users to define policies. Moreover this component is able to learn user behaviors concerning security relevant actions, e.g. learning the average of SMS messages sent each day, and to instantiate a proper policy accordingly. In this scenario, the policy manager either receives as input (i) the user-policy, either written in a policy-specification language or even in natural language or (ii) is learnt by monitoring the user behavior. Afterwards, the policy is translated in a probabilistic automata, which can be used for contract-policy matching or policy enforcement.

The contract-policy matching verifies if the policy expressed in the manifest matches the policy provided by the Policy Manager. This control is executed at deploy time. If the contract does not match the policy, the user is prompted to decide if she wants to abort the installation, or install however the application with a run-time policy enforcement. The Security-By-Contract-with-Trust enforcement extends the one performed by the permission checker, ensuring that the defined policies are always enforced. Figure 6 depicts a workflow of the Security-By-Contract-with-Trust extension on Android devices.

Notice that for the sake of clarity, the Application-Contract Matching component has not been included in Fig. 6. This task is, in fact, demanded to the Trusted Third Party.

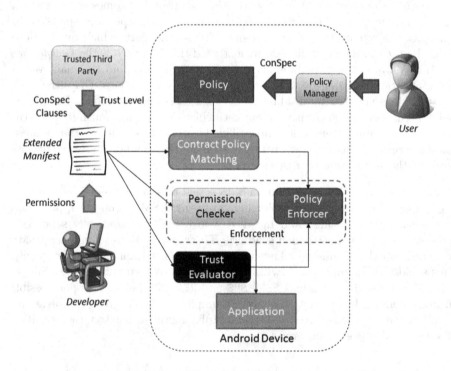

Fig. 6. Inclusion of Security-By-Contract on Android

5 Related Work

In the last decade, the Security-by-Contract framework [1] has been extended and applied in several ways and in different scenarios. For instance, in [2,3] the extension of the Security-by-Contract with Trust manager has been presented. Furthermore, in [3] it has been instantiated in a marketplace scenario and in particular, it is integrated with a trust manager able to manage feedback obtained by the monitoring module. Another application scenario is the one of web service [16,17].

From the quantitative perspective, the problem of finding an optimal control strategy is considered by Easwaran et al. in [18] in the context of software monitoring, where the system is represented as a Directed Acyclic Graph, and where rewards and penalties with correcting actions are taken into account, thus using dynamic programming to find the optimal solution. Similarly, an encoding of access control mechanisms using Probabilistic Decision Process is proposed in [19], where the optimal policy can be derived by solving the corresponding optimization problem. From a different perspective, Bielova and Massacci propose in [20] a notion of distance among traces, thus expressing that if a trace is not secure, it should be edited to a secure trace close to the non-secure one, thus characterizing enforcement strategies by the distance from the original trace they create. A system that exploits system calls to detect non-compliant application is presented in [21]. Referring to probabilistic models, probabilistic contracts has been firstly introduced in [22] for analyzing reliability and availability aspects of systems. The generation of probabilistic contract has been made by analyzing the occurrences of system calls. In [23] a scheme for intrusion detection using probabilistic automata is proposed. This system exploits system calls and hidden Markov models and is able to detect efficiently denial of service attacks. Reference [24] presents another system based upon system calls and Markov models to detect intrusions. This system analyzes the arguments of the system calls but is oblivious of the system call sequence. System call sequence and deterministic automata have been used in [25] to detect anomalies, which are detected when system call sequences differ from an execution trace known to be good. PIGA-virt [26] is a framework devoted on checking the behaviour of programs at run-time based upon administrator expressed security policies.

6 Conclusion and Future Work

In this paper, we have discussed the current limitations of the semantics of the security models for mobile applications. To this end, we have presented a probabilistic version of the Security-by-Contract with Trust, which is able to guarantee definition and enforcement of probabilistic requirements. We have discussed the advantages in terms of expressiveness achieved including probability in the $S \times C \times T$ framework. Finally, we have shown a possible use-case, including $S \times C \times T$ in the Android operative system, showing the feasibility of the proposed approach.

Future extensions to this work will be the definition of probabilistic formalisms and languages, which should be used to programmatically define probabilistic contracts and policies, then to verify their compliance. This language should be equivalent in expressiveness to the probabilistic automata that we have used to express policies and contracts. Furthermore, we are going to include the presented framework in real mobile devices, investigating if it is possible to distribute it as common mobile application, which can give users a way to better handle security on their mobile devices.

References

1. Dragoni, N., Martinelli, F., Massacci, F., Mori, P., Schaefer, C., Walter, T., Vetillard, E.: Security-by-contract (S × C) for software and services of mobile systems. In: At Your Service - Service-Oriented Computing from an EU Perspective. MIT Press, Cambridge (2008)
2. Costa, G., Dragoni, N., Lazouski, A., Martinelli, F., Massacci, F., Matteucci, I.: Extending Security-by-Contract with quantitative trust on mobile devices. In: Proceeding of the Fourth International Conference on Complex, Intelligent and Software Intensive Systems, pp. 872–877. IEEE Computer Society (2010)
3. Costa, G., Dragoni, N., Issarny, V., Lazouski, A., Martinelli, F., Massacci, F., Matteucci, I., Saadi, R.: Security-by-Contract-with-Trust for mobile devices. JOWUA 1(4), 75–91 (2010)
4. Greci, P., Martinelli, F., Matteucci, I.: A framework for contract-policy matching based on symbolic simulations for securing mobile device application. In: Margaria, T., Steffen, B. (eds.) ISoLA 2008. CCIS, vol. 17, pp. 221–236. Springer, Heidelberg (2008)
5. Necula, G.C.: Proof-carrying code. In: Proceedings of the 24th ACM SIGPLAN-SIGACT Symposium on Principles of Programming Languages (POPL '97), pp. 106–119 (1997)
6. Sekar, R., Venkatakrishnan, V., Basu, S., Bhatkar, S., DuVarney, D.C.: Model-carrying code: a practical approach for safe execution of untrusted applications. In: Proceedings of the Nineteenth ACM Symposium on Operating Systems Principles, pp. 15–28 (2003)
7. Hermanns, H., Parma, A., Segala, R., Wachter, B., Zhang, L.: Probabilistic logical characterization. Inf. Comput. 209(2), 154–172 (2011)
8. Baier, C., Engelen, B., Majster-Cederbaum, M.: Deciding bisimilarity and similarity for probabilistic processes. J. Comput. Syst. Sci. 60(1), 187–231 (2000)
9. Sharkey, M.I.: Probabilistic proof-carrying code. Ph.D. thesis, Carleton University (2012)
10. Tsukada, Y.: Interactive and probabilistic proof of mobile code safety. Autom. Software Eng. 12(2), 237–257 (2005)
11. Desharnais, J., Laviolette, F., Tracol, M.: Approximate analysis of probabilistic processes: logic, simulation and games. In: Proceedings of the 2008 Fifth International Conference on Quantitative Evaluation of Systems, QEST '08, pp. 264–273. IEEE Computer Society, Washington DC (2008)
12. Aldini, A., Martinelli, F., Saracino, A., Sgandurra, D.: A collaborative framework for generating probabilistic contracts. In: Smari, W.W., Fox, G.C. (eds.) Proceedings of the 2013 IEEE International Conference on Collaboration Technologies and Systems, SECOTS 2013, pp. 139–143. IEEE Computer Society, San Diego (2013)

13. Juniper Networks Global Threat Center: Malicious Mobile Threats Report 2010/2011 (2011)
14. Zhou, Y., Zhang, X., Jiang, X., Freeh, V.W.: Taming information-stealing smart-phone applications (on android). In: McCune, J.M., Balacheff, B., Perrig, A., Sadeghi, A.-R., Sasse, A., Beres, Y. (eds.) TRUST 2011. LNCS, vol. 6740, pp. 93–107. Springer, Heidelberg (2011)
15. Felt, A.P., Ha, E., Egelman, S., Haney, A., Chin, E., Wagner, D.: Android permissions: user attention, comprehension, and behavior. Technical report, Electrical Engineering and Computer Sciences, University of California at Berkeley (2012) http://www.eecs.berkeley.edu/Pubs/TechRpts/2012/EECS-2012-26.html
16. Dragoni, N., Massacci, F.: Security-by-contract for web services. In: SWS, pp. 90–98 (2007)
17. Gadyatskaya, O., Massacci, F., Philippov, A.: Security-by-Contract for the OSGi platform. In: Gritzalis, D., Furnell, S., Theoharidou, M. (eds.) SEC 2012. IFIP AICT, vol. 376, pp. 364–375. Springer, Heidelberg (2012)
18. Easwaran, A., Kannan, S., Lee, I.: Optimal control of software ensuring safety and functionality. Technical Report MS-CIS-05-20, University of Pennsylvania (2005)
19. Martinelli, F., Morisset, C.: Quantitative access control with partially-observable markov decision processes. In: Proceedings of CODASPY '12, pp. 169–180. ACM (2012)
20. Bielova, N., Massacci, F.: Predictability of enforcement. In: Erlingsson, Ú., Wieringa, R., Zannone, N. (eds.) ESSoS 2011. LNCS, vol. 6542, pp. 73–86. Springer, Heidelberg (2011)
21. Dini, G., Martinelli, F., Saracino, A., Sgandurra, D.: MADAM: a multi-level anomaly detector for android malware. In: Kotenko, I., Skormin, V. (eds.) MMM-ACNS 2012. LNCS, vol. 7531, pp. 240–253. Springer, Heidelberg (2012)
22. Delahaye, B., Caillaud, B., Legay, A.: Probabilistic contracts: a compositional reasoning methodology for the design of stochastic systems. In: 10th International Conference on Application of Concurrency to System Design (ACSD), 2010, IEEE (2010)
23. Hoang, X.A., Hu, J.: An efficient hidden Markov model training scheme for anomaly intrusion detection of server applications based on system calls. In: 12th IEEE International Conferecence on Networks, ICON 2004. vol. 2, pp. 470–474. IEEE (2004)
24. Maggi, F., Matteucci, M., Zanero, S.: Detecting intrusions through system call sequence and argument analysis. IEEE Trans. Dependable Secure Comput. 7(4), 381–395 (2010)
25. Koresow, A.P.: Intrusion detection via system call traces. Software 14(5), 35–42 (1997)
26. Briffaut, J., Lefebvre, E., Rouzaud-Cornabas, J., Toinard, C.: PIGA-Virt: an advanced distributed MAC protection of virtual systems. In: Alexander, M., et al. (eds.) Euro-Par 2011, Part II. LNCS, vol. 7156, pp. 416–425. Springer, Heidelberg (2012)

Advanced Detection Tool for PDF Threats

Quentin Jerome[✉], Samuel Marchal, Radu State, and Thomas Engel

SnT - University of Luxembourg, 4 rue Alphonse Weicker, 2721
Luxembourg, Luxembourg
{quentin.jerome,samuel.marchal,radu.state,thomas.engel}@uni.lu
http://wwwen.uni.lu/snt

Abstract. In this paper we introduce an efficient application for malicious PDF detection: ADEPT. With targeted attacks rising over the recent past, exploring a new detection and mitigation paradigm becomes mandatory. The use of malicious PDF files that exploit vulnerabilities in well-known PDF readers has become a popular vector for targeted attacks, for which few efficient approaches exist. Although simple in theory, parsing followed by analysis of such files is resource-intensive and may even be impossible due to several obfuscation and reader-specific artifacts. Our paper describes a new approach for detecting such malicious payloads that leverages machine learning techniques and an efficient feature selection mechanism for rapidly detecting anomalies. We assess our approach on a large selection of malicious files and report the experimental performance results for the developed prototype.

Keywords: PDF files · Malware detection · Machine learning

1 Introduction

Targeted attacks remain among the highly relevant persistent threat vectors. The past year has seen a dramatic rise in targeted attacks using PDF files as propagation vector[1,2]. Exploiting several zero-day vulnerabilities against popular readers (primarily from Adobe)[3], these attacks are difficult to mitigate for two main reasons. The first is related to users not perceiving the opening of PDF files as dangerous. Browsers plugins that automatically render PDF files make drive-by contamination even easier, since the user merely needs to visit a malicious site in order to get compromised. The second reason is the complex structure of PDF files, which makes their parsing quite challenging. Obfuscation techniques can thwart most of the available PDF parsing libraries, while still allowing error-tolerant readers to parse the file and thus compromise the system. Sometimes,

---

[1] http://thehackernews.com/2013/02/chinese-malware-campaign-beebus-target.html

[2] http://www.securelist.com/en/blog/774/A_Targeted_Attack_Against_The_Syrian_Ministry_of_Foreign_Affairs

[3] http://www.securelist.com/en/analysis/204792255/Kaspersky_Security_Bulletin_2012_The_overall_statistics_for_2012

J. Garcia-Alfaro et al. (Eds.): DPM 2013 and SETOP 2013, LNCS 8247, pp. 300–315, 2014.
DOI: 10.1007/978-3-642-54568-9_19, © Springer-Verlag Berlin Heidelberg 2014

even a slight change in a PDF file can make it unreadable to most libraries and still produce a working exploit for proprietary readers.

In this paper, we consider the mitigation of this attack, which has as major contributions, the followings:

- We propose an n-gram-based application to detect and mitigate attacks leveraging PDF vulnerabilities;
- This method does not rely on semantic parsing and thus is not prone to vulnerability exploitation found in PDF parsing libraries;
- We evaluate the performance of our system on a comprehensive dataset and report very good results for performance, speed and accuracy;
- We compare our tool with academic work;
- We provide a web service implementation of our approach.

Our paper is structured as follows: we start out in Sect. 2 with an overview of malicious PDF files and highlight some of the recent vulnerabilities exploited by this threat. Section 3 details the overall architecture of our system. Section 4 presents the dataset used for the tuning of our approach. We describe the experiments performed and validation in Sect. 5. In Sect. 6, we compare our tool to previous work and we introduce our web service implementation. Section 7 discusses relationships with prior work and we conclude the paper and discuss future work in the Sect. 8.

2 Malicious PDF

In this section, we introduce some lesser-known facts about the PDF language. We first present the basis of the PDF language. We next show some general ways used by rogue authors to craft malicious files. Finally we justify the challenges that our work must address by pointing out the analysis difficulties concerning PDF files.

2.1 PDF, A Programming Language

The PDF language is a PDL (Page Description Language). This type of language was created to avoid dependencies between documents and hardware. Thus, when someone wants to open a PDF document, it has only to own an application known as a Reader in order to interpret and understand the PDF language. This feature provides high portability because the resultant document is not hardware or OS dependant. This interesting property has made PDF an attractive alternative to platform-specific documents like Microsoft Word files. PDF files are now widely used on the Web and unfortunately have also become an attractive vector for malware propagation. Before showing how malicious PDF documents are crafted, we explain the basis of this uncommon language.

We can consider PDF as a collection of various types of object. According to the PDF reference [1], we can enumerate these different types:

- Boolean: Number (integer or real) and String values
- Names
- Array: collection of objects
- Dictionary: collection of objects indexed by their names (type Name)
- Streams: contain encoded data as text or images of the document
- Null objects

To be correctly interpreted and displayed, a PDF must contain some basic parts, ordered as follows.

1. A header, which contains the PDF language version number
2. The document body, which contains all objects
3. A cross-reference table containing offsets of all objects (whether currently in use or deleted by an incremental update) and version number of those objects
4. A trailer containing the cross-reference table offset.

The purpose of the cross-reference table is to retrieve objects efficiently. As mentioned above, it contains versions of objects which can be modified by updates. Once an object is deleted, its current version in the cross-reference table is modified to become the next generation number (version) of this object. Updated objects are appended to the end of the file with a corresponding cross-reference table modification.

Here we enumerate some existing ways to craft malicious documents. Indeed, by design PDF provides a large range of possibilities to create malicious documents. The most-abused features are, for instance, additional features such as JavaScript. Other features proper to a rich language can be used by rogue authors as well. Indeed, because of its popularity, PDF embeds an increasing number of features which offer new possibilities and flaws within the source code. We notice two large categories of attacks relying on PDF language: feature-based and exploit-based attacks. Feature-based attacks leverage only language features such as \OpenAction, which allows a task to be executed when someone opens the document. In [2] the authors illustrate this by crafting phishing attacks relying on such features. Exploit based attacks are more nasty since those rely on vulnerability exploitation. If such an attack succeed, the victim's machine becomes compromised and the attacker can control it remotely. This kind of attacks is even more critical for companies when a workstation becomes infected. We distinguish three families of attacks exploiting vulnerabilities in common PDF readers:

1. Attacks based only on JavaScript, which rely on a flaw in the JavaScript API and need JavaScript to be exploited;
2. Attacks relying on JavaScript only for payload delivery. For instance, before exploitation, a former step of heap spraying [3] can be performed. This technique aims at preparing the heap to control memory allocation and increase the success rate of jumping into the landing zone that the attacker wants;

Table 1. Vulnerabilities

Adobe Reader version(s)	Target	Flaws	CVE-ID
9.1, 8.1.4, 7.1.1 and earlier	JavaScript API getAnnots()	Resource Management Errors (CWE-399)	CVE-2009-1492
8.1.2 and earlier	JavaScript API util.printf()	Stack-based buffer overflow (CWE-119)	CVE-2008-2992
8.1.1 and earlier	JavaScript method in EScript.api	Code Injection (CWE-94)	CVE-2007-5663
10.1.1 and earlier on Windows and Mac OS, 9.x through 9.4.6 on UNIX	U3D	Unknown (probably heap overflow)	CVE-2011-2462
9.x through 9.1.2	authplay.dll	Code injection (CWE-94)	CVE-2009-1862
9.0 and earlier	J2BIG	Heap pointer corruption (CWE-119)	CVE-2009-0658
8.x before 8.3.1, 9.x before 9.4.6, 10.x before 10.1.1	CoolType.dll	Stack-based buffer overflow (CWE-119)	CVE-2011-2441
8.x before 8.2.5 and 9.x before 9.4	ActiveX	Input validation (CWE-20)	CVE-2010-2888
9.x before 9.3.2, and 8.x before 8.2.2	Unspecified	Buffer overflow (CWE-119)	CVE-2010-0198

3. Attacks that do not need JavaScript at all. For instance classical stack based buffer overflow flaws could directly allow arbitrary code execution without a previous heap preparation and thus do not need JavaScript.

In Table 1, we illustrate some real examples of the vulnerabilities cited previously. The information was gathered from the Metasploit[4] database and from the NIST National Vulnerability Database[5]. The CWE – Common Weakness Enumeration – references were retrieved from the MITRE[6] database. We can see in this table that several Reader versions and OSs can be targeted, increasing the attractiveness of such attacks.

2.2   Challenges

As shown in Table 1, several Readers are vulnerable to exploitation. Hence it is very difficult to perform classical dynamic analysis. All the vulnerable software should be grouped in a common monitoring environment in order to cover the

---

[4] http://www.metasploit.com/

[5] http://nvd.nist.gov/

[6] http://cwe.mitre.org/data/slices/2000.html

whole range of threats. Whence choosing a static detection approach is sound in that particular case. However we must face other problems, specific to static analysis.

The PDF language offers its own obfuscation facilities like representing *Name* or *String* objects in hexadecimal form. In addition, another way to obfuscate PDF documents is to use cascade filters to encode Streams objects. In this fashion, the attacker is able to encode the same stream twice or even more with different algorithms. This technique is straightforward to use for an attacker and difficult to reverse engineer. For instance, according to the version 1.7 of the PDF documentation [1], the PDF language provides about 10 filters, including one to encrypt streams.

Object reference can be used to increase the obfuscation level as well. This allows calling an object which is defined elsewhere in the document. It is worth noting that the physical representation of the file does not matter, only the logical structure is important for the Reader.

Another technique often used in malicious files is JavaScript string obfuscation, which has been heavily abused in the past in web based attacks. For instance, using the *eval()* function on an encoded part of the script complicates static analysis.

These aforementioned obfuscation methods are massively used within malicious documents and makes the reverse engineer of files harder. A comprehensive study is performed in [4] and is a relevant example of analysis issues. To avoid time consuming and prone to error desobfuscation, we were motivated to use n-grams as features to represent documents. In addition, extracting n-grams does not require semantic parsing as done in previous works [5,6]. Since the Poppler library used in these approaches can be vulnerable[7], using it for detecting malicious documents is not relevant.

3   Tool Description and Architecture

The ADEPT architecture, presented in this section, is designed to provide both accuracy and performance. A well-known technique for automated detection is machine learning-based classification. This method leverages features associated with malware and benign files and uses them to build a model. The latter is used to classify files depending on their features. Figure 1 shows the architecture of the tool.

3.1   Feature Selection

The first step is to choose relevant features representing both regular and malicious PDF. We choose n-gram to achieve this. N-grams are substrings of length n extracted by sliding over the input character by character. Formally, a n-gram sequence denoted E by :

---

[7] http://www.securityfocus.com/archive/1/526364/30/0/threaded

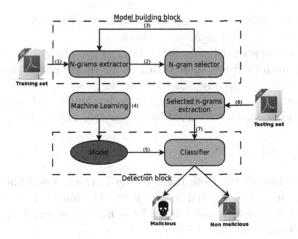

Fig. 1. System architecture

$\forall s \in S^*$, where S^* is the word set of a given alphabet S, $\forall n \in \mathbb{N}^*$, where n is the n-gram length :

$$E = \{s[i; i+n], i \in [0, L-n] \cap \mathbb{N}\}$$

where $s[i; j]$ denotes the substring extracted from s containing characters between indexes i and j. L denotes the length of the string s.

For example, in the string *malicious* and for $n = 3$ we extract the following n-grams set $\{'mal';'\,ali';'\,lic';'\,ici';'\,cio';'\,iou';'\,ous'\}$. The number of n-grams is $N = L - (n-1) \approx L$ and constitutes an upper bound to the number of distinct n-grams that we could extract from a given file.

3.2   Model Building Block

This module extracts relevant features to build the final model used for malware detection. This task is time consuming due to the intensive process of n-grams extraction. However, as the model is built only once, its processing time is not an issue.

N-grams Extractor. This entity parse PDF documents and extracts all n-grams from them. It also permits to gather n-grams for collection of documents.

N-grams Selector. The selector identifies the most relevant n-grams (or features) to include in the model. While, in theory, all features can be used, fast processing of PDF files is possible only when a subset of all possible n-grams is used. Thereby, only the most frequent n-grams are selected among our document corpus. During a preliminary study of our dataset, we noticed that malicious documents are shorter than benign files. To make our approach size independent, we opted for a binary count of n-grams. Hence, each document is represented by a binary vector where each component stands for a n-gram, set to one if the n-gram appears in the document, zero otherwise.

Once features are selected, we need to retrieve the binary occurrence of these features in the initial dataset (step 3 in Fig. 1). In the end of step 3 we get a matrix where each line corresponds to a file and each column to one selected n-gram. This data is ready to train a machine learning algorithm in step 4. We discuss the learning algorithm embedded in our tool in Sect. 5.2.

3.3   Detection Block

Model. This entity results from the machine learning algorithm which builds a model based on data gathered in the preceding block. This model is used now as a classifier input. In order to find the best classifier, we performed the experiments detailed in Sect. 5.

Classifier. Classifier is strongly related to the learning algorithm because it takes a model previously learned as an input parameter for further comparison (step 5). At the same time, it takes a feature vector extracted from a file that we want to classify (step 7). The classifier determines if the feature vector extracted from a file fits a benign or a malicious profile, according to the model that has been learned previously.

4   Dataset Introduction

This section presents the preliminary study made on the dataset detailed in Table 2. In order to compare our findings and benchmark our approach with respect to previous studies we use the datasets introduced in [5]: D1,D2 and D3. The dataset D4 is used further in this paper to evaluate our approach.

Our whole dataset was provided by VirusTotal[8]. For each dataset we have a set of detected files and a set of undetected ones. Files were labelled as detected by Virustotal if at least one anti-virus package among 42 reported an alert. In contrast, all files labelled as undetected passed through anti-virus packages without raising any alert.

While we analyzed some PDF documents manually – with the PDFTool[9] toolkit – we observed that many files had the same structure and almost the same size, but a different hash code. The physical and logical structure of these files were indeed very similar. We assumed that many malicious documents have been generated by exploit kit like BlackHole[10] or Metasploit[11]. Indeed, two hashing values calculated can be very different if only one byte differs between the two files. However this high degree of similarity produces misleading results during the calibration phase of the tool. The reason is that if we have different files with

---

[8] https://www.virustotal.com/
[9] http://blog.didierstevens.com/programs/pdf-tools/
[10] http://en.wikipedia.org/wiki/Blackhole_exploit_kit
[11] http://www.metasploit.com/

Table 2. Datasets introduction

	D1		D2		D3		D4	
	det.	undet.	det.	undet.	det.	undet.	det.	undet.
Date of collection	2010-11-03		2011-01-19		2011-02-17		2012-12-21	
Number of files	7,592	7,768	6,465	9,993	11,634	22,490	3892	3474
Dataset size	873MB	13GB	429MB	13GB	1.5GB	29GB	223MB	3.5GB
Average file size	118KB	1.8MB	67KB	1.4MB	129KB	1.4MB	57KB	1MB
Number of different files	476	unknown	367	unknown	822	unknown	173	unknown

small dissimilarities, the likelihood of taking into account these dissimilarities is low. As a consequence, if we want to evaluate our tool with common machine learning assessment techniques, we would probably test our tool on previously seen instances. Moreover, similarities do not contribute to model building. Therefore we assume that files are different on the PDFID output basis. PDFID is part of the PDFTool toolkit and reflects the internal structure of a given file.

5   Experiments

Here, we present the methodology we follow to find the best classification algorithm for our feature set. To achieve this, we used Weka [7], a well-known machine learning toolkit.

5.1   Experimental Description

In order to find out the best combination of n-gram/classifier, we ran a ten-fold cross-validation test on a labelled – benign or malign – document corpus. We chose to experiment with several well-known classification methods that range from tree and rule based classifiers to Support Vector Machine (SVM). To make an n-fold cross-validation, we firstly partition our dataset into n subsets. We then take $(n-1)$ subsets to train a machine learning algorithm and the remaining one for testing. In order to test each instance available in the dataset we do this n times. Ten folds are most frequently used to obtain significant results[8]. What we want is a classifier that gives the best prediction capabilities. To reach this goal, we must deal with the file similarity problem that we mentioned in Sect. 4. To overcome this issue, we use only different files on the PDFID output basis. By doing this, we provide a *worst case scenario* that gives us a lower bound on detection capability for our tool.

Following we enumerate the settings used for those experiments:

- 843 malicious files gathered from datasets D1 and D2. This is the sum of different files in each dataset;
- 843 regular files randomly chosen in D1 and D2;
- We selected the 10,000 most frequent features in order to build the model. We determined that n-grams occurring less did not contribute to the model significantly.

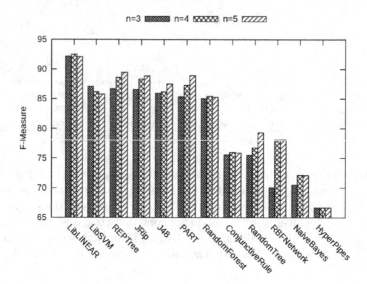

Fig. 2. Classification results for several classifiers

We use a balanced dataset, as recommended by the machine-learning community [9] to avoid over-fitting and under-fitting issues.

Figure 2 depicts classification performances for each combination of n-gram/ classifier that we experimented. On the y axis, we plot the F-Measure also known as F-1 score. The F-Measure is defined as follows:

$$\text{F-measure} = \frac{2(Recall \cdot Precision)}{Recall + Precision}$$

where $\text{Recall} = \frac{\text{Instances in class i classified as belonging to class i}}{\text{Instances in class i}}$

and $\text{Precision} = \frac{\text{Instances in class i classified as belonging to class i}}{\text{Instances classified as belonging to class i}}$.

We used this metric to assess our tool since it evaluates both the retrieving capability of the tool through the *Recall* metric as well as the prediction capability through the *Precision*. Based on the results depicted in Fig. 2, we choose LibLINEAR as classification algorithm coupled with 4-grams to build our detection mechanism since this combination of feature bring the best results with F-Measure = 92.50 %.

5.2 Classifiers Details

This section describes how LibLINEAR [10] works in details. It is an implementation of a support vector machine (SVM) classifier. The aim of SVM classification is to calculate the equation of the boundary between two sets of labelled instances (PDF files in our case) characterized by n features. In this n dimensional problem, it must find the equation of an hyperplane. The shape of the hyperplane can be linear, polynomial, radial or sigmoidal and is determined by a kernel function. The kernel maps data into a space, in which it can be separated by an hyperplane. LibLINEAR is faster than LibSVM because it does not map instances into higher dimensional space, but instead it tries directly to separate instances in the initial vector space [10]. Thus, the computational complexity of the algorithm grows linearly with the number of instances.

More formally, by doing a LibLINEAR classification, the learning algorithm solves the following optimization problem:

$$\min_{w,b} \{\frac{1}{2} \parallel w \parallel^2 + C \sum_{i=1}^{n} \xi(w; x_i, y_i)\}$$

$$\text{subject to } y_i(w \cdot x_i - b) \geq 1 \ \forall \ 0 \leq i \leq n$$

where y_i is the class of instance i
where x_i represents an instance i
and w is the normal to the hyperplane.

The C parameter represents margin rigidity: the higher it is, the softer are margins. This means that we allow misclassified instances to contribute to the model. In contrast, when margins are more rigid, we do not allow those instances to be part of the model. We have to be careful in choosing this parameter because it can lead to under-fitting or over-fitting problems. While the former would represent more our training sample rather than the instance population, the latter would be too general. To find the good value for C, a grid search is usually performed. This consists in varying the parameter and doing a cross validation for each variation. Parameter offering the best cross-validation result is adopted. After a grid search we were able to determine that $C = 0.03125$ is the optimum value. The $\xi(w; x_i, y_i)$ term is the loss function, which approximates the misclassification degree of instance i.

6   Evaluation and Use-Case

We present in this section a real-life use-case for such a detection tool. We firstly define what we mean by such a scenario and then we evaluate our tool. Lastly, we compare our approach with PJScan, another tool aiming at detecting malicious PDF files.

6.1   Real-Life Use-Case

Before going further into this evaluation, we propose to define what we mean by a real-life use-case. Following we point out two points of interest for running our experiments:

1. We must use a training set older than the files we want to detect;
2. We must assess our tool on a realistic dataset of malicious files.

In order to satisfy the first condition, we use the three older datasets introduced in Sect. 4 to train the tool. As a result, we do the training with 24,327 files in

Table 3. Realistic scenario evaluation

	class. as mal.	class. as .reg	Recall	Precision	F-Measure
Malicious	3667	224	97.00%	96.85%	96.92%
Undetected	8	3466			

both classes extracted from D1,D2 and D3. For the evaluation set, we use the most recent dataset, namely D4. In using these settings for the experiments, we also assess the viability of our approach regarding the threat evolution since the training set contains files two years older than files used for testing. Concerning the second requirement, we do not pay attention to the similarity problem between learning and testing. This makes sense since the tool must be able to find threats present in its knowledge base. Moreover, it is possible that some files in the testing set share similarities between them. To quantify the similarity between learning and testing, we found that 50 have the same hashing signature and 416 have a similar PDFID fingerprint. For this experiment we use the settings defined in the previous section.

We can see immediately in Table 3 that the results are better than for the previous experiments. This can be partly explained by the fact that we used many more files than for our evaluation with Weka. Another reason is that in this test case, we did not filter the initial dataset as we did in our first experiment. This allows us to assess the real capabilities of the tool in terms of prediction and identifying known threats. We can also note the low false positive rate – benign files incorrectly classified as malicious – of 0.23 % as well as a very good classification accuracy of 96.85 %. This is a valuable attribute in a detection tool since only few false alarms are raised. Furthermore, we point out that files having the same hashing signature or similar PDFID fingerprint that files in the model were all well classified.

To have a better idea of which files remain undetected by the tool we extracted some pertinent information from misclassified files. The first point of interest is that among these 224 files there are 67 different PDFID outputs. We verified that no file with any of these outputs was in our training data. We can assume that these files are new attacks that our tool did not have in its training set. We also found that 399 files in our evaluation set had one of these PDFID signature. This means that we correctly identified 175 of these files while 224 were misclassified. If these 399 files are really totally new threat, relatively to the tool knowledge, we can not hope detecting new threats with 100 % accuracy.

For sake of space, we do not present the detailed throughput assessment of this detection mechanism. However, it is worth noting that we can process around hundred regular documents per minute on a desktop computer with an Intel Core I5 processor and 8 GB of RAM. We mean by *regular documents* documents that we are used to deal with on a daily basis. Since malicious files are lightweight, the tool performs faster detection on these but a scenario containing only rogue files seems to be unlikely.

Table 4. PJScan evaluation

	class. as mal.	class. as .reg	Recall	Precision	F-Measure
Malicious	209	49	88.89	68.67	77.48
Undetected	3	31			

6.2   Comparisons

In this section we compare our approach with previous academic work in this
area. Therefore, we compare our results against the detection capabilities of
PJScan [5]. To make the comparison as fair as possible we use exactly the same
scenario we defined in the previous section.

Comparison with Academic Work. Here we summarize the experiments
that we ran in order to compare our tool to PJScan. We chose to compare our
tool to PJScan because it is well documented and its source code is open[12].
We do not present a run-time performance comparison with PJScan because
we ran it on a virtual machine due to compatibility issues. Before use, PJScan
needs to be trained on a malicious training sample. As PJScan uses One Class
SVM classification, the model has to be built using only one class. To satisfy
this requirement we fed the model with the malicious files that we used in our
training set. We expected very different results from our own because PJScan
deals only with documents containing JavaScript.

Table 4 summarizes the results provided by PJScan. The tool was only able to
process 3.9 % of the test set. According to the output of the tool, the remaining
files were skipped because no information was found in them. In this situation,
the tool is unable to classify files and thus does not take any decision. However, in
reality we need to take decisions regarding unknown files. Thus, we can conclude
that this tool does not fit well with a real-life scenario. To be fair we compare
both approaches according to the file that PJScan is able to process. From this
comparison, we can conclude that our approach outperforms PJScan since it has
a better accuracy, 96.85 % for ADEPT against 82.19 % for PJScan.

6.3   Web Service Implementation

We briefly present here a web interface implementation of our tool. We developed a front end that makes the tool more user-friendly than the command
line version. The service is hosted at http://www.secan-lab.uni.lu/pdfchecker
and provides a VirusTotal-like graphical interface. The user can choose either
to scan a file or try to retrieve a scan result for a previously scanned file by
providing its SHA-256 signature. The result provides useful information to the
user by showing the first and the last submission date. In addition, we also provide a PDFID-like output from another tool that we have developed. This tool
actually extends the work done for PDFID and does it faster, up to 30 times

---

[12] http://sourceforge.net/p/pjscan/home/Home/

for big files (>25.0 MB). This tool also warns the user when the file he scanned contains dangerous features. This extra-feature is particularly useful when the tool misclassified a document.

7   Related Work

In this section we present the related work concerning PDF analysis and auto-mated PDF detection. We also mention some relevant papers about the general topic of malware detection that drove us to build such a detection mechanism.

7.1   PDF Analysis

Several approaches exist for PDF analysis. We can find both static and dynamic, or even hybrid methods. While our tool addresses the problem of malicious file detection we cite here some analysis tools, helpful when we must deal with unknown threats. Outputs from analysis tools are often used as input for a detection mechanism.

PdfTools[13], developed by Didier Stevens, is an analysis toolkit consisting of PDFID and PDF-PARSER. The former gives statistics about potentially mali-cious features which are embedded in a PDF while the second is a parser that displays the PDF code in a readable format. Another static tool, PDF Struc-tazer, is presented in [2]. It can be used to analyse, create or modify PDF files. In the same paper, the authors show the power of the PDF language by imple-menting phishing attacks using only language features. Itext[14] is an open source and free library providing ways of automating PDF creation and modification. Almost all features provided by the PDF language are supported; References [11] provides an introduction and practical guide.

A dynamic approach is implemented in CWSandbox [12], an application which monitors malware execution in a sandboxed environment. Its dynamic analysis monitors features such as file modification, changes made to the Win-dows registry and processes created. Post execution, the application provides a detailed report directly readable by analysts who can take a decision concerning the file. This tool has been adapted for malicious PDF[15], which is certainly its main problem concerning PDF detection. However, as noted previously, some exploits run only on particular Adobe Reader version. Thus before running a malicious file in a sandboxed environment, we need to know which version is targeted. In [13] the authors introduce MIST, means of interpreting output from online platforms such as CWSandbox. The resulting instruction can subsequently be used for a machine learning based classification.

---

[13] http://blog.didierstevens.com/programs/pdf-tools/

[14] http://itextpdf.com/itext.php

[15] http://honeyblog.org/archives/12-Analyzing-Malicious-PDF-Files.html

7.2   Malicious PDF Detection

A combination of both types of analysis is implemented in MDScan [14] in order to detect malicious PDF files. MDScan first detects malicious code by parsing the document. The extracted code is then monitored in an emulator emulating providing a subset of the functionalities available in the Adobe API. Because some API functions have not yet been implemented; the detection can be defeated if malicious file exploit an unimplemented function. Schmitt *et al.* present PDF Scrutinizer in [15]. The approach combines both static and dynamic analysis to detect malicious PDF files containing JavaScript.

In [5], *Laskov et al.* describe PJScan, a static detection based on machine learning. They focus on malicious PDFs containing JavaScript. They use a JavaScript extractor and then treat extracted code to transform it in a standard token representation. A learning algorithm is then applied to the tokenized sequence in order to detect malicious patterns. The authors leveraged approaches introduced in [16], where lexical analysis associated with a learning method is applied to detect drive-by download attacks.

A recent tool is proposed in [17] where the authors leverage several metadata extraction combined with machine learning in order to determine whether a file is likely to be malicious or not. Another approach, based on the hierarchical structure of PDF documents combined with machine learning has been presented in [6]. Although this approach seems to have good performances, it is still vulnerable to parser vulnerabilities since it uses the libpoppler library.

7.3   Malware Analysis

We have done previous work in machine learning techniques for security in [18–20], but focussed more on the network traffic monitoring and not the system level defines.

In [21] the authors present a detection solution that, like ours, is based on n-gram associated with learning techniques. Their experiments tested different classifiers and different values of n. They address malicious Windows binary (PE files) detection. While their approach targets malicious code in binary format, ours approach deals with ASCII encoded files. Additionally, while their approach leverages information gain in feature selection, ours uses most frequent features.

N-gram analysis is used in [22] in order to detect file types. This type of analysis can be used to tag unknown files or to detect files which try to disquise their content. To reach their goal, the authors firstly obtain n-gram distributions for various file types. Secondly, they compare n-gram distribution of a file under test with known values to determine its real type. Similar work appears in [23], where the authors present a way of detecting embedded files within documents. This method consists in observing variation of n-gram distribution compared to the expected distribution for a given file format. This method can also be used to detect embedded files within PDF files.

Wei-Jen Li et al. [24] present a way to analyse malicious Word documents. Their method is based on static analysis coupled with a dynamic element. Byte distribution is analysed in an initial static analysis step. They further monitor malware behaviour using API hooking techniques. The file is ultimately classified as a result of these two steps.

In term of full dynamic analysis, TTAnalyze, presented in [25] aims to quickly identify malicious PE files. To achieve this, the tool monitors both the Windows API and native API hooks to catch even the stealthiest malware. It evades detection by the rogue program in avoiding both classic API hooking and breakpoint setting.

8   Conclusion

This paper describes an accurate detection tool for malicious payload detection. Our work was motivated by the lack of efficient approaches to mitigate an advanced persistent threat that has had significant impact recently. We proposed a method that leverages machine learning and sequence based features in order to detect malicious PDF files. We have assessed our approach on a very large set of data that was obtained through the courtesy of VirusTotal. The performance in both speed and accuracy are very good since it is able to process hundred files per minutes with 0.23 % of false positives. We plan to extend this work by integrating additional pieces of information, such as entropy and multiple alignment scores. We are also considering to generalize this approach to a larger class of payload types, but obtaining ground truth datasets for each is a particularly challenging.

Acknowledgment. The authors would like to thank Prof. Dr. Pavel Laskov for the support and dataset provided for our experiments. Special thanks also go to the Virus-Total team for giving us access to several datasets.

References

1. Adobe: PDF reference sixth edition, adobe portable document format, version 1.7 (2006)
2. Filiol, E., Blonce, A., Frayssignes, L.: Portable document format (PDF) security analysis and malware threats. J. Comput. Virol. **3**(2), 75–86 (2007)
3. Daniel, M., Honoroff, J., Miller, C.: Engineering heap overflow exploits with JavaScript. In: Proceedings of the 2nd Conference on USENIX Workshop on Offensive Technologies, WOOT'08, pp. 1:1–1:6. USENIX Association, Berkeley (2008)
4. Rahman, M.A.: Getting owned by malicious PDF - analysis. Global Information Assurance Certification Paper (2010)
5. Laskov, P., Šrndić, N.: Static detection of malicious JavaScript-bearing PDF documents. In: Proceedings of the 27th Annual Computer Security Applications Conference. ACSAC '11, pp. 373–382. ACM, New York (2011)
6. Šrndic, N., Laskov, P.: Detection of malicious pdf files based on hierarchical document structure. In: Proceedings of the 20th Annual Network and Distributed System Security Symposium (2013)
7. Hall, M., Frank, E., Holmes, G., Pfahringer, B., Reutemann, P., Witten, I.: The WEKA data mining software: an update. ACM SIGKDD Explor. Newsl. **11**(1), 10–18 (2009)

8. Witten, I., Frank, E., Hall, M.: Data Mining: Practical Machine Learning Tools and Techniques. Morgan Kaufmann, Amsterdam (2011)

9. Akbani, R., Kwek, S., Japkowicz, N.: Applying support vector machines to imbalanced datasets. In: Boulicaut, J.-F., Esposito, F., Giannotti, F., Pedreschi, D. (eds.) ECML 2004. LNCS (LNAI), vol. 3201, pp. 39–50. Springer, Heidelberg (2004)

10. Fan, R., Chang, K., Hsieh, C., Wang, X., Lin, C.: Liblinear: a library for large linear classification. J. Mach. Learn. Res. **9**, 1871–1874 (2008)

11. Lowagie, B.: iText in Action: Creating and Manipulating PDF. Dreamtech Press, New Delhi (2006)

12. Willems, C., Holz, T., Freiling, F.: Toward automated dynamic malware analysis using CWSandbox. IEEE Secur. Priv. **5**, 32–39 (2007)

13. Trinius, P., Willems, C., Holz, T., Rieck, K.: A malware instruction set for behavior-based analysis. In: Proceedings of the Conference Sicherheit Schutz und Zuverlssigkeit SICHERHEIT (TR-2009-07), pp. 1–11 (2011)

14. Tzermias, Z., Sykiotakis, G., Polychronakis, M., Markatos, E.P.: Combining static and dynamic analysis for the detection of malicious documents. In: Proceedings of the Fourth European Workshop on System Security. EUROSEC '11, pp. 4:1–4:6. ACM, New York (2011)

15. Schmitt, F., Gassen, J., Gerhards-Padilla, E.: Pdf scrutinizer: detecting javascript-based attacks in pdf documents. In: 2012 Tenth Annual International Conference on Privacy, Security and Trust (PST), pp. 104–111. IEEE(2012)

16. Rieck, K., Krueger, T., Dewald, A.: Cujo: Efficient detection and prevention of drive-by-download attacks. In: Proceedings of the 26th Annual Computer Security Applications Conference, pp. 31–39. ACM (2010)

17. Smutz, C., Stavrou, A.: Malicious PDF detection using metadata and structural features. In: Proceedings of the 28th Annual Computer Security Applications Conference, pp. 239–248. ACM (2012)

18. François, J., Wang, S., State, R., Engel, T.: BotTrack: tracking botnets using NetFlow and PageRank. In: Domingo-Pascual, J., Manzoni, P., Palazzo, S., Pont, A., Scoglio, C. (eds.) NETWORKING 2011, Part I. LNCS, vol. 6640, pp. 1–14. Springer, Heidelberg (2011)

19. Wagner, C., Wagener, G., State, R., Engel, T.: Malware analysis with graph kernels and support vector machines. In: 2009 4th International Conference on Malicious and Unwanted Software (MALWARE), pp. 63–68. IEEE (2009)

20. Abdelnur, H.J., State, R., Festor, O.: Advanced network fingerprinting. In: Lippmann, R., Kirda, E., Trachtenberg, A. (eds.) RAID 2008. LNCS, vol. 5230, pp. 372–389. Springer, Heidelberg (2008)

21. Kolter, J., Maloof, M.: Learning to detect and classify malicious executables in the wild. J. Mach. Learn. Res. **7**, 2721–2744 (2006)

22. Li, W., Wang, K., Stolfo, S., Herzog, B.: Fileprints: identifying file types by n-gram analysis. In: Proceedings from the Sixth Annual IEEE SMC Information Assurance Workshop. IAW'05, pp. 64–71. IEEE (2005)

23. Stolfo, S.J., Wang, K., Li, W.J.: Fileprint analysis for malware detection. ACM CCS WORM (2005)

24. Li, W., Stolfo, S., Stavrou, A., Androulaki, E., Keromytis, A.: A study of malcode-bearing documents. Detection of Intrusions and Malware, and Vulnerability, Assessment, pp. 231–250 (2007)

25. Bayer, U., Moser, A., Kruegel, C., Kirda, E.: Dynamic analysis of malicious code. J. Comput. Virol. **1**, 67–77 (2006)

Enforcing Input Validation through Aspect Oriented Programming

Gabriel Serme[1], Theodoor Scholte[2], and Anderson Santana de Oliveira[2(✉)]

[1] Eurecom, Biot, France
[2] SAP Labs, Mougins, France
anderson.santana.de.oliveira@sap.com

Abstract. Injection vulnerabilities are still prevalent today, ranking first on OWASP top ten threats to software security. Developers often have trouble to adopt secure coding practices during the software development life cycle, failing to prevent these vulnerabilities. This paper addresses the problem of modular input validation for web applications as a countermeasure to several kinds of code injection attacks. The solution relies on annotations that enrich the metadata concerning the application's input parameters. This information is then used to automatically insert validation code in the target application, using aspect-oriented programming. Our approach allows to mitigate risks and to maintain security functionality separated from the application logic.

1 Introduction

Many web applications and web services are prone to input validation vulnerabilities. Representative examples of this class include cross-site scripting (XSS), SQL Injection and command injection. Although input Validation vulnerabilities are well-known, and have been studied largely in the past decade, vulnerabilities such as SQL Injection and XSS have been dominating the charts for many years. As a matter of fact, these vulnerabilities have been listed among the most relevant threats by Top Ten Project hosted by OWASP[1] since a decade.

Input validation vulnerabilities have the same root cause: improper sanitization of user-supplied input that result from invalid assumptions made by the developer on the input of the application.

Injection attacks, that exploit input validation vulnerabilities, are attacks in which an attacker creates inputs containing special characters and/or markers that alter the behavior of the targeted application in some undesired way. Such attacks can have devastating consequences, ranging from information leakage to privilege escalation in which the attacker can gain full control of the system under attack.

Injection attacks, also called code injection attacks, can take several forms:

---

[1] https://www.owasp.org/index.php/Category:OWASP_Top_Ten_Project

J. Garcia-Alfaro et al. (Eds.): DPM 2013 and SETOP 2013, LNCS 8247, pp. 316–332, 2014.
DOI: 10.1007/978-3-642-54568-9_20, © Springer-Verlag Berlin Heidelberg 2014

- SQL injection is the insertion of a SQL query via the input data from the client to the application. Via this attack, one can obtain sensitive data from the database, to modify it, or to execute administrative operations on it.
- Command Shell injection allows to insert and to execute commands specified by an attacker from the input to a vulnerable application, making it to execute unwanted system commands.
- Cross-site scripting (XSS) attacks: In this type of attack, malicious scripts are injected into the otherwise benign and trusted web sites. Cross-site scripting (XSS) attacks occur when an attacker uses a web application to send malicious code, generally in the form of a browser side script, to a different end user. Cross-Site scripting vulnerabilities are quite widespread and occur whenever a web application uses input from a user in the output it generates without validating or encoding it.
- Other kinds of injection are possible, but the mitigation strategy is similar and covered by the paper. We can mention for instance XML and XPath injection, which occur when a web site uses user-supplied information to construct an XPath query for XML data. By sending intentionally malformed information into the web site, an attacker can find out how the XML data is structured, or access data that he may not normally have access to. He may even be able to elevate his privileges on the web site if the XML data is being used for authentication (such as an XML based user file).

Preventing input validation vulnerabilities is a complex task. Scholte et al. have shown in [27] that despite security awareness programs and tools for detecting input validation vulnerabilities, this class of vulnerabilities is still very prevalent across web applications and the number of reported vulnerabilities is not decreasing. The study [27] also shows that he complexity of the attacks exploiting this class of vulnerabilities remained stable, meaning that hackers do not need to craft more sophisticated injection strings, relying on the easiest vectors to exploit vulnerable applications.

One of the reasons behind the prevalence of input validation vulnerabilities is that the application of any techniques to prevent them, relies entirely on the developers. Although several frameworks do provide libraries containing validation and sanitization functions, these still need to be explicitly called from the application logic in order to validate or sanitize the input provided by users. This has two distinct and important disadvantages: first, developers simply forget (or ignore) to use the already available input validation functionalities. Second, it is hard to maintain, update and evolve the application logic independently - since validation function calls would be scattered along all the application code. Moreover, the validation functionalities built in web application frameworks do not have the necessary degree of granularity to handle the validation of a large number of different data-types an application typically handles.

Since preventing input validation vulnerabilities relies entirely on developers, prevention techniques that are part of the design and implementation phases of the software development lifecycle will help in making web applications and web services more secure.

In order to prevent input validation vulnerabilities, all input read by the program must undergo a validation and sanitization process. This paper focuses on input validation which is, essentially, the process of assigning semantic meaning to unstructured and untrusted inputs to an application, and ensuring that those inputs respect a set of constraints describing a well-formed input. Depending on the data type, additional validation checks might be necessary. For example, a string might contain only allowed characters or the length of the string should stay within certain boundaries. For numerical input, the validation process might check if the value stays within the expected range and if the value is signed or not (positive or negative integer).

We provide a method to prevent input validation vulnerabilities by strictly separating input validation functionality from the application code. In this way, the assignment of data types to input can be enforced while maintaining consistency between input validation and application logic. More specifically, the paper consists in the non-invasive use of Aspect-Oriented Programming in the automatic generation of input validation code, without altering the business logic of the concerned application. We performed an evaluation of our approach under realistic conditions to demonstrate how vulnerabilities can be prevented.

The remainder of the paper is organized as follows:

- Section 2 Explains our methodology to prevent input validation vulnerabilities.
- Section 3 Shows our experimental results.
- Section 4 brings the state of the art in this domain.
- Section 5 summarizes the advantages of the paper focusing on the novelties we introduce.

2   Input Validation Aspects

Our method for mitigating input validation vulnerabilities requires that application developers annotate source code of the application components to be protected. Annotations are a simple way to extend a given programming language in a non-invasive way. In our case, the annotations indicate what are the input parameters and their corresponding enhanced data-types individually. After the programs are annotated, the tool will generate new executable or object code, using aspect-oriented programming techniques(AOP) [18].

The term AOP has been coined around 1995 by a group led by Gregor Kiczales [18], with the goal to bring proper separation of concerns for cross cutting functionalities. The aspect concept is composed of several advice/pointcut couples. Pointcuts allow to define where (points in the source code of an application) or when (events during the execution of an application) aspects should apply modifications. Pointcuts are expressed in pointcut languages and often contain a large number of aspect-specific constructs that match specific structures of the language in which base applications are expressed, such a pattern language based on language syntax. Advices are used to define modifications an aspect may perform on the base application. Advices are often expressed in terms of some general-purpose language with a small number of aspect-specific extensions, such as the *proceed* construct that allows the execution of the behavior of the base application that triggered the aspect application in the first place.

The obtained code will intercept the execution flow whenever an input is received in order to check whether the input is in conformity to some pre-defined format. In the case a non-conform input is read by the application, then a programming exception is raised.

The methodology we propose assumes that all input parameters in the code must be annotated by the developer, otherwise the application will not be executed. However, this feature can be turned off, allowing the developers to partially annotate the code, or to disregard completely the annotation phase. In other words, annotating all input parameters in the source code is mandatory by default.

Correctly annotating the input parameters is critical as it ensures the future verification of all incoming data. An incorrect validation mechanism can compromise the risk mitigation process. In order to bind correctly the parameters and variables of interest, we adopt a semi-automatic approach combining user-based knowledge as well as automatic detection of data types - for instance by using information gathered from model repositories, database schemas, and so on.

At the design phase the developer has to define the enhanced data types, also called Global Data Type, that are used across the application. Enhanced data types have business semantics and provide more precision on the expected user inputs. Therefore, these data types differ from the basic built-in types from the programming language. Examples of enhanced data types or Global Data Types are productID, e-mail address, phone number, address, etc. Abstract types are added in order to obtain a fine-grained and stronger typing related to variables and parameters used in the application.

For instance, in a declaration such as `String email;` the developer would add the annotation `@Email String email;` indicating that only strings obeying a certain pattern for email addresses shall be accepted. The way these patterns are identified are not specific to our approach, and can be combined with machine learning techniques, such as the one introduced in [28]. Here, we consider that the set of enhanced data types is extensible as well as the corresponding validation functionalities for each extended data types.

The tool is built from three main components, illustrated in Fig. 1. The pointcut interface adaptor keeps a mapping between enhanced types and validation functions. This component can also extract data-type information from external knowledge bases to add meta-data information necessary to the input validation. Examples of external information sources are service repositories, such as the SAP Enterprise Services Repository, database schemas, WSDL files, etc. These sources can provide information on the type structure used in the application parameters, such that we can infer enhanced data types associated to them. In these knowledge bases one find further information, such as the required length for data fields, or enumerated values, which can be useful to gain accuracy in the input data validation.

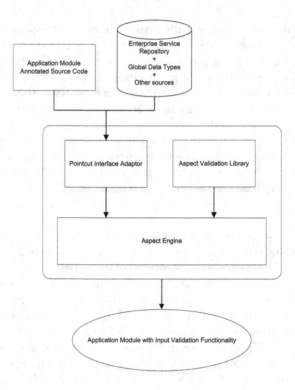

Fig. 1. Architecture of the tool

The Aspect Engine is responsible for the detection of validation points during the execution of the application. The Aspect Engine is capable of modifying the application data flow. It takes into account the type annotations and inserts data validation code whenever there is an assignment for an input parameter, called validation point, that is, whenever data is read from untrusted sources or received from the final users.

A validation point refers to the validation of a specific parameter or variable from the base application. Upon detection of a validation point, the Aspect Engine extracts parameter's data-type and looks for an existing validation library. If the aspect finds a corresponding library, it applies the validation mechanisms described in the module.

The last component in the architecture consists of an extensible aspect library where the validation functions for each enhanced data type are given. This library maps each enhanced data type or Global Data Types, to validation functions that are represented as aspects. The implementation of validation functions have a standardized interface in order to ensure compatibility, and the mapping configuration in the pointcut interface adaptor need to be updated accordingly.

As we presented above, the solution comprises different steps and components to correctly implement an automatic validation during application execution.

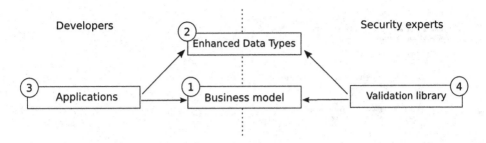

Fig. 2. Components and ideal roles

The Fig. 2 presents the different components, and the ideal separation of roles in the concerns' processing. In the ideal situation, the application has a business model that define all business objects. The automation is made possible through the enhanced data types. Security experts can already propose some enhanced data types, that can be extended over time. The list of enhanced data types can also be extended by any developer, although a security expert would have the most appropriate role to provide clear and accurate information to mitigate risks. The developers are responsible to develop the application, and can use the enhanced data types. Security experts are only responsible of providing a validation library for the enhanced data types, that they can adapt to the business model specificities.

The regular process to create a new enhanced data type is the following. When someone identifies a specific data type, he creates an identifier name for it. This name is released among the application developers and stakeholders. The Listing 1 is an example used in our application to share data types as a Java enum.

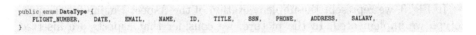

```
public enum DataType {
    FLIGHT_NUMBER,   DATE,   EMAIL,   NAME,   ID,   TITLE,   SSN,   PHONE,   ADDRESS,   SALARY,
}
```

Listing 1: Enhanced Data Types as a Java enum

The new available types can be used to taint variables and parameters along the base application. The Listing 2 shows the different use of our method: the annotations can apply to a method parameter, a constructor argument, or a class variable. It provides a large range of possibilities from application to business model tainting.

In parallel, new names must have their corresponding validation aspects defined in the validation library. It is possible to define multiple validation aspects to a single identifier in the validation library. Nothing prevents one to create different validation mechanisms for a same enhanced data type. The validation behaviour is implemented by the code advice.

```
public class Customer {

    private String name;
    private String firstname;

    @Type(DataType.EMAIL)
    private String email;

    public void setEmail(@Type(DataType.EMAIL) String email) {
        this.email = email;
    }

    public Customer(String name, String firstname,
            @Type(DataType.EMAIL) String email) {
        this.name = name;
        this.firstname = firstname;
        this.email = email;
    }

    /* ... */

}
```

Listing 2: Business model can be annotated

In most cases, the behaviour to validate a type can be given in terms of regular expressions. The handling of regular expressions is frequently provided as a built-in functionality in many programming languages. A deeper test can be introduced as the validation library can access the business model. The validation can therefore validate complex business types, and validate them through different means: functional validation, additional technical checks, etc. For instance, one can verify existence of an e-mail address by contacting mail transfer agents, or wire transfer validation might involve third parties services. More sophisticated attack vectors would require advanced pattern matching, therefore the valid input would need to be specified through XML-Schema validation, for example. This would allow for a more expressive class of languages can be accepted as input, that is, context-free languages. Once the advice code for a specific enhanced data type is created, one needs to encapsulate the validation code in an aspect and to compile it. The generated binaries can then be deployed in the validation aspect library.

In Fig. 3, we represent the implementation of the Aspect Engine for the prototype we implemented. In the picture, we consider that aspects are inserted at run-time into the target application. We assume at this point that several aspects exist in the validation library. The second assumption is that the application about to run has accurate meta-information about enhanced data types.

In this implementation, the Aspect Engine is a specialized class loader who bootstraps all target applications. The first action of the Aspect Engine is to search for available aspects in the aspect library. As the application code is loaded, the Aspect Engine gathers the points in the code that will need the validation and also the applicable validation aspects at those points. If no validation is found for an input parameter, and that the environment is set to enforce validation for all, the application execution is aborted.

Next, the Aspect Engine will proceed with the execution of the application code and observe the application execution until it reaches a validation point. At these points, it detects an enhanced data type annotation used by the base application and searches among the loaded classes one or more corresponding

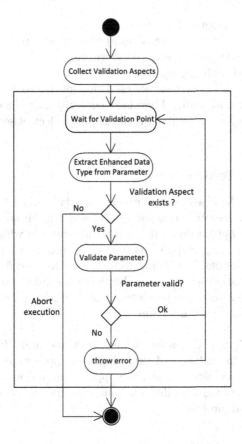

Fig. 3. Input validation flowchart

validation aspects. Then the Aspect Engine applies the validation function for the parameter found. It then loops again to monitor application execution until its termination.

3   Evaluation

The evaluation of our approach is measured by the ability to mitigate input validation vulnerabilities while allowing the normal execution of the web applications. To validate the correct mitigation of security vulnerabilities, we applied a rigorous test on deliberately insecure web applications, and we compared the number of reported vulnerabilities prior and after the correction with input validation aspects. We also made sure that the modifications we bring do not break the normal flow of execution of the application, by manually and intensively testing the validation library.

We used a black-box testing approach, as it allows to analyze the potential application attack surface that would be available for externals security experts.

We avoided the complexity of whitebox analysis, leveraging on the load-time weaving of the cross cutting concerns (validation code) into the application run-time, given that in the present evaluation we want to identify what is the protection rate achieved with our approach.

For the black-box security tests we used two specific tools specialized in web application security and audit. They are classically introduced in penetration testing phase to support automated analysis and collect of security vulnerabilities.

3.1   Penetration Testing Tools

Arachni. Arachni [21] is a web application security scanner framework. It is an open-source ruby framework to assist testers and administrators in evaluating the security of web applications. It provides all features which goes from web application crawling using a spider module to deep packet analysis using blind SQL module for example. The application is able to activate modules for the most common web application vulnerabilities: code injection (through several channels), cross-site scripting, cross-site request forgery, path traversal, remote and local file inclusion, SQL injection, etc..

W3AF. W3AF [25] is a web application attack and audit framework written in Python. It helps in finding and exploring web application vulnerabilities. It comes with several modules to crawl the application and analyze common vulnerabilities. The set of vulnerabilities is similar to the ones covered by Arachni, with some additional modules.

3.2   Analysis

We have applied the steps of our methodology to concrete insecure web applications. We used the *wavsep* project [3] as target for our evaluation. *wavsep* was designed to test web application security scanners, intentionally containing vulnerabilities such as: path traversal, remote file inclusion, reflected XSS, blind and direct SQL injection, and additional flaws. Although *wavsep* has no specific data model with business value, being composed by separated projects with Java Server Pages for each kind of vulnerability, it represents a challenging project to assess our methodology.

We proceeded as follows. First we added Global Data Types where necessary to cover cases that were not already defined in our validation library. *wavsep* uses the following custom types, among others: username, password, target, msgid, transactionDate, minBalance, description, etc.. We enhanced the validation library with these types. Listing 3 presents a simple class validation following our methodology. Second, we created an aspect that wraps around the *request.getParameter()* calls, as shown in Listing 4. The validation library determines the actual Global Data Type from the parameter name (which is a particular behavior of *wavsep*), and validate the input, or aborts the request.

From Fig. 1, it shows how one can replace annotations by another layer to identify the actual enhanced data types.

```
@Validation(value = DataType.NAME)
public class ValidationName implements ValidationInterface {

    final Pattern p = Pattern.compile("\\w{2,15}");
    @Override
    public boolean doProcess(String str) throws Exception {
        Matcher m = p.matcher(str);
        return m.matches();
    }
}
```

Listing 3: Simple validation for a Name data type (used for username for example).

```
@Pointcut("call(* *..HttpServletRequest.getParameter(..))")
    public void pointcutGetParameter() {
}

@Around("pointcutGetParameter()")
public String wavsepCustom(final ProceedingJoinPoint jp) throws Throwable {
    String paramName = (String) jp.getArgs()[0];
    String value = (String) jp.proceed(new Object[] { paramName });
    DataType type = DataType.valueOf(paramName);
    validate(type, value);
    return value;
}
```

Listing 4: Custom adaptation of our methodology to wrap getParameter() inputs for validation.

Table 1 presents the details of our evaluation. We launched the test application on a Tomcat servlet container, without (column "original") and with (column "protected") our validation library. In the second case, we have configured AspectJ to provide load-time weaving of aspects at the start up of the web application. We performed tests using both Arachni and W3af. For simplicity, we retained only the vulnerabilities flagged as critical/high, and discarded reports for the medium or informational issues. The miscellaneous category includes either unclassified vulnerabilities reported "as is" by w3af, or phishing vector and code injection detected by Arachni.

The results show that we can reduce the number of detected vulnerabilities to zero in the XSS, directory path traversal, and the remote file inclusion categories. We have an extremely good rate in the SQL injection category, for which Arachni reports still three vulnerabilities after protection with our library. This is explained by the fact that Global Data Types are efficient when applications use a consistent data model. As *wavsep* provides no data model, but only reflected use of input parameters through the *request.getParameter()* function of the *HTTPServletRequest* object, our pointcut interface adaptor module is probably missing some of the inputs. Our tool was also able to eliminate all reported vulnerabilities by Arachni in the miscellaneous category, corresponding to phishing vector and code injection. w3af still signals a high number of unclassified vulnerabilities, but our tool was able to reduce the original score by almost fifty percent.

Our success rates is partially due to the systematic analysis of the input received by the application, associating to them a precise data type - activity

Table 1. Number of vulnerabilities detected by the Arachni (arac.) and w3af web application security scanners with a black-box approach on original and protected wavsep application.

		Original	Protected
SQL injection	arac.	214	3
	w3af	107	0
Cross site scripting	arac.	185	0
	w3af	119	0
Directory path traversal	arac.	662	0
	w3af	231	0
Remote file inclusion	arac.	120	0
	w3af	0	0
Miscellaneous	arac.	44	0
	w3af	552	278

that developers often neglect. Associated to that, our aspects provide exhaustive validation for all inputs in the application, another point developers tend to underestimate. As a disclaimer, it is important to mention that besides the fact we are confident in the prevention of the vulnerabilities detected by prominent tools such as w3af and Arachni, we cannot state that *wavsep* will be completely free of security bugs by using our approach, as these tools may not uncover all possible vulnerabilities.

4   Related Work

One of the main originalities of the current paper is to addresses the problem of enforcing input validation through a strict separation between data type definitions and application logic. However, in the past decade, much research effort has been spent on making web applications and web services more secure. Researchers have focused on detection mechanisms including static analysis, dynamic taint analysis and client-side security mechanisms. In addition to detection techniques, researchers have also worked on techniques to prevent security vulnerabilities. We give an overview of the different techniques below.

4.1   Static Analysis

The goal of static analysis is to determine whether tainted data, that is data that originate from possibly malicious users, reaches sensitive sinks (e.g. vulnerable points in the program) without being properly sanitized. For this purpose, data flow analysis techniques that operate on the control flow graph are used. Static analysis can be applied in cases where source code or bytecode is available. The advantage it is not necessary to execute the program to detect injection vulnerabilities. Unfortunately, approaches based on static analysis suffer from false positives and false negatives. This is due to imprecise approximations of the control and data flow available at runtime. In addition, false positives might result from runtime validation in which the security label of the data (tainted/untainted) is not changed after the validation.

The WebSSARI project [8] pioneered this line of research. WebSSARI uses a combination of static and dynamic analysis to detect vulnerabilities in PHP code. Jovanovic et al. designed Pixy [16, 17], a static analyzer tool that features a high-precision data flow analysis engine that is flow-sensitive, interprocedural, and context-sensitive and performs alias analysis, literal analysis, and taint analysis. Another approach that tries to overcome some of the limitations of WebSSARI is the work by Xie and Aiken [35], their approach performs interprocedural analysis, is able to model conditional branches and supports dynamic typing. The work by Wassermann and Su [33] employs a string-analysis based approach to detect SQL Injection vulnerabilities. It tracks the source of string values and enforces that user-supplied input is isolated within a SQL query. [34] presents a static analysis approach to detect Cross-Site Scripting vulnerabilities. It also employs string analysis techniques.

The research work on static analysis has not been limited to PHP applications only. Livshits et al. [22] proposed a static analysis approach based on point-to-point analysis to find code injection vulnerabilities in Java applications. The tool implementing these techniques has been made available as Eclipse plug-in.

4.2 Dynamic Taint Analysis

In contrast to static analysis, dynamic taint analysis checks the program at runtime. In general, approaches based on dynamic tainting assign meta-data to user-supplied input. All user-supplied data is set to be tainted. When operations are performed on the input data, this meta-data is preserved. After the sanitization of user-supplied data, the data is set to be 'untainted'. This allows the detection if untrusted data reaches a sensitive sink.

Nguyen-Tuong [23] and Pietraszek [24] worked both independently from each other on dynamic taint propagation. They propose an extension to the PHP interpreter that tracks tainted input data. The extension proposed by Pietraszek can either prevent the execution of code or sanitize the input. The approach proposed by Halfond et al. [6] introduces positive tainting, in this case, only trusted data is tracked.

Dynamic tainting has also its problems. First of all, the techniques has a relative large overhead in terms of performance. Moreover, the input data has to be untainted after a sanitization function. As [1] shows, implementing sanitization functionality is far from trivial. Furthermore, preventing second order attacks is difficult as it requires the tracking of data through persistent data stores.

4.3 Client-Side Security Mechanisms

Unfortunately, not all developers of web applications protect effectively and in-time their applications against Cross-Site Scripting attacks. Therefore, there is a need for client-side solutions to protect users of these web applications. Several approaches exist that aim to provide client-side protection.

In [11], the authors propose a client-side proxy that detects the use of special characters such as ';' in HTTP traffic. When the proxy detects that the application response reflects these presumably malicious requests, the traffic is blocked. Also Noxes [19] is based on the concept of a client-side proxy firewall. However, this approach tries to improve the user experience of personal firewalls by introducing some heuristics. In [32], the authors propose browser plugin that uses static and dynamic tainting techniques to check whether sensitive data is sent to a different domain than where the Javascript code is downloaded from.

BEEP [13] tries to achieve client-side security *by design*. It is a policy-based mechanism that forces the browser to execute only those scripts that are explicitly allowed to run specified by the policy.

4.4   Prevention Techniques

Besides the solutions to detect code injection vulnerabilities, there exist several approaches that prevent code injection vulnerabilities based on sanitization of data. Data sanitization is the process of transforming data such that the resulting data only contains safe characters. In contrast to the traditional practice of sanitization checks that a developer has to implement in an ad-hoc way, these frameworks and/or language extensions ensure that documents and/or queries are automatically protected. Thus, injection vulnerabilities are prevented *by construction* or *by design*.

William Robertson et al. propose in [26] a framework that statically enforces a separation between structure (code) and content (data). In the framework, an (X)HTML document is represented by nodes that are connected to each other. The document is a tree of nodes and each node is an instantiation of the Node type. As a result, the document is strongly typed. Once the document is constructed, a render function converts the document into a string that can be send to the client. The render function automatically sanitizes unsafe characters. The framework also allows developers to specify dynamic SQL queries using an embedded domain-specific language. The only way to execute SQL queries and construct documents is through the interfaces provided by the framework. In this way, sanitization is enforced.

In [15], Johns et al. propose a datatype to enforce the separation between data and code. With this approach, the developer is forced to use the ELET datatype to construct foreign code. Once the developer has specified the foreign code using the ELET datatype, a pre-processor translates the foreign code to an API representation in the hosting language. Data provided by the hosting language can be inserted in the foreign code by using a special function. The main limitation of this approach is that the dynamic construction of foreign code within the foreign code (e.g. JavaScript's eval function) is not supported. Moreover, the dynamic creation of identifier tokens in the foreign language is not supported. In [14], Johns et al. propose a mechanism to secure web applications implemented using an interpreted language. A pre-processor marks foreign code found in the source code as legitimate. After the work performed by the interpreter, a post-processor identifies all the foreign code that has been injected by the user/attacker and masks it such that it will not be executed. The main problem with this approach is that the pre- and post-processors introduce false positives and false negatives.

4.5 Input Validation

Several web application frameworks support input validation through the use of annotations. Frameworks such as Spring MVC [30], Hibernate [12] and Struts 2 [4] support a limited set of input validation types. Hibernate is based on the JSR 303 Bean Validation standard [2]. In contrast to our work, the set of possible input validation types cannot be extended. Furthermore, these frameworks do not support the enforcement of validation functions, e.g. a developer is not forced to validate input. The solutions proposed in [2] and in [7] allow a complete decoupling of validation code and application logic. However, also these solutions do not force the developer to specify the inputs along with the types resulting in less secure applications and a decreased level of quality of data.

Besides frameworks supporting input validation, there exist web application firewalls that are capable of performing input validation. Web application firewalls are placed in front of the web application or web service and all HTTP traffic is routed through the firewall. A firewall can block known malicious requests (blacklist-approach) or only allow known benign requests (whitelist-approach). Scott et al. proposed in [29] to secure web applications using web application firewalls. Since then, the technique has been commercialized and many vendors offer application-level firewalls as appliances [9,10,31]. In contrast to our approach, web application firewalls do not allow to establish and maintain consistency between the input validation specification and the application code. Moreover, application-level firewalls support a very limited set of input types which is not extensible.

Other works have used AOP for validating input to web services. The work presented in [20] uses aspects to improve web service robustness for SOAP based services. Input validation grammars and regular expressions are defined with the help of XML and XPath, what can bring additional vulnerabilities specific to XML parsing. This work is not focused in security, although SQL injection can be prevented with this approach. In [5], aspects are used to introduce security concerns to programs such as authentication, authorization, and input validation. It proposes an architecture, founded on AOP to integrate these security objectives, but no implementation is provided.

5 Conclusions

We presented a method and tool to prevent web applications and services to accept malicious input, which is still today the main vulnerability identified by OWASP. By adding simple and precise type annotations to existing code, our solution brings a lightweight approach to enrich type information concerning the expected input for an application. The work derives validation functions that are modularly integrated into existing applications. The main contributions of the work we present here are :

- Non-invasive use of aspect-oriented programming, which discharges the developers from learning a new programming paradigm;
- High degree of automation and the increase program security with minor effort. Moreover, our approach does not require security expertise from developers;
- Extensibility: allowing developers to create specific enhanced data types and their validation aspects;
- Modular integration of new security functionality without disrupting existing code;
- Security is adopted by design, considering that annotations to all input parameters must be provided, but, in order to provide more flexibility to the solution, an administrator can disable the obligation to annotate all code.

We performed an evaluation of the prototype we implemented, reaching very high success rates in the elimination of injection vulnerabilities, confirming the feasibility and usefulness of the approach.

References

1. Balzarotti, D., Cova, M., Felmetsger, V., Jovanovic, N., Kirda, E., Kruegel, C., Vigna, G.: Saner: composing static and dynamic analysis to validate sanitization in web applications. In: Proceedings of the 2008 IEEE Symposium on Security and Privacy, SP '08, pp. 387–401. IEEE Computer Society, Washington, DC (2008). http://dx.doi.org/10.1109/SP.2008.22
2. Bernard, E., Peterson, S.: JSR 303: bean validation, bean validation expert group. http://jcp.org/aboutJava/communityprocess/pfd/jsr303/index.html (2009)
3. Chen, S.: The web application vulnerability scanner evaluation project - v1.2. https://code.google.com/p/wavsep/ (2012)
4. Foundation, T.A.S.: Struts 2. http://struts.apache.org/ (2011)
5. Hafiz, M., Johnson, R.: Improving perimeter security with security-oriented program transformations. In: ICSE Workshop on Software Engineering for Secure Systems, SESS '09, pp. 61–67 (2009)
6. Halfond, W.G.J., Orso, A., Manolios, P.: Using positive tainting and syntax-aware evaluation to counter sql injection attacks. In: Proceedings of the 14th ACM SIG-SOFT International Symposium on Foundations of Software Engineering, SIG-SOFT '06/FSE-14, pp. 175–185. ACM, New York http://doi.acm.org/10.1145/1181775.1181797 (2006)
7. Hookom, J.: Validating objects through metadata. http://www.onjava.com/pub/a/onjava/2005/01/19/metadata_validation.html (2005)
8. Huang, Y.W., Yu, F., Hang, C., Tsai, C.H., Lee, D.T., Kuo, S.Y.: Securing web application code by static analysis and runtime protection. In: WWW '04: Proceedings of the 13th International Conference on World Wide Web, pp. 40–52. ACM, New York (2004)

9. Imperva: The securesphere web application firewall. http://www.imperva.com/products/wsc_web-application-firewall.html (2011)
10. Inc., B.N.: The barracuda web application firewall. http://www.barracudanetworks.com/ns/products/web-site-firewall-overview.php (2011)
11. Ismail, O., Etoh, M., Kadobayashi, Y., Yamaguchi, S.: A proposal and implementation of automatic detection/collection system for cross-site scripting vulnerability. In: 18th International Conference on Advanced Information Networking and Applications, AINA 2004, vol. 1, pp. 145–151 (2004)
12. JBoss: Hibernate validator. http://hibernate.org/subprojects/validator (2011)
13. Jim, T., Swamy, N., Hicks, M.: Defeating script injection attacks with browser-enforced embedded policies. In: Proceedings of the 16th International Conference on World Wide Web, WWW '07, pp. 601–610. ACM, New York (2007). http://doi.acm.org/10.1145/1242572.1242654
14. Johns, M., Beyerlein, C.: Smask: preventing injection attacks in web applications by approximating automatic data/code separation. In: Proceedings of the 2007 ACM Symposium on Applied Computing, SAC '07, pp. 284–291. ACM, New York (2007). http://doi.acm.org/10.1145/1244002.1244071
15. Johns, M., Beyerlein, C., Giesecke, R., Posegga, J.: Secure code generation for web applications. In: Massacci, F., Wallach, D., Zannone, N. (eds.) ESSoS 2010. LNCS, vol. 5965, pp. 96–113. Springer, Heidelberg (2010)
16. Jovanovic, N., Kruegel, C., Kirda, E.: Pixy: a static analysis tool for detecting web application vulnerabilities (short paper). In: SP '06: Proceedings of the 2006 IEEE Symposium on Security and Privacy, pp. 258–263. IEEE Computer Society, Washington, DC (2006)
17. Jovanovic, N., Kruegel, C., Kirda, E.: Precise alias analysis for static detection of web application vulnerabilities. In: PLAS '06: Proceedings of the 2006 Workshop on Programming Languages and Analysis for Security, pp. 27–36. ACM, New York (2006)
18. Kiczales, G., Lamping, J., Mendhekar, A., Maeda, C., Lopes, C., Loingtier, J.M., Irwin, J.: Aspect-oriented programming. In: Aksit, M., Matsuoka, S. (eds.) ECOOP 1997. LNCS, vol. 1241, pp. 220–242. Springer, Heidelberg (1997)
19. Kirda, E., Krgel, C., Vigna, G., Jovanovic, N.: Noxes: a client-side solution for mitigating cross-site scripting attacks. In: SAC'06, pp. 330–337 (2006)
20. Laranjeiro, N., Vieira, M., Madeira, H.: Improving web services robustness. In: IEEE International Conference on Web Services, ICWS 2009, pp. 397–404 (2009)
21. Laskos, T.: Arachni 0.4.2 - web application security scanner framework. http://www.arachni-scanner.com/ (2013)
22. Livshits, V.B., Lam, M.S.: Finding security vulnerabilities in java applications with static analysis. In: SSYM'05: Proceedings of the 14th Conference on USENIX Security Symposium, p. 18. USENIX Association, Berkeley (2005)
23. Nguyen-Tuong, A., Guarnieri, S., Greene, D., Shirley, J., Evans, D.: Automatically hardening web applications using precise tainting. In: SEC, pp. 295–308 (2005)
24. Pietraszek, T., Berghe, C.V.: Defending against injection attacks through context-sensitive string evaluation. In: Valdes, A., Zamboni, D. (eds.) RAID 2005. LNCS, vol. 3858, pp. 124–145. Springer, Heidelberg (2006)
25. Riancho, A.: W3af 1.0 - open source web application security scanner. http://w3af.org/ (2011)
26. Robertson, W., Vigna, G.: Static enforcement of web application integrity through strong typing. In: Proceedings of the 18th Conference on USENIX Security Symposium, SSYM'09, pp. 283–298. USENIX Association, Berkeley (2009)

27. Scholte, T., Balzarotti, D., Kirda, E.: Have things changed now? an empirical study on input validation vulnerabilities in web applications. Comput. Secur. **31**(3), 344–356 (2012)

28. Scholte, T., Robertson, W.K., Balzarotti, D., Kirda, E.: Preventing input validation vulnerabilities in web applications through automated type analysis. In: Bai, X., Belli, F., Bertino, E., Chang, C.K., Elçi, A., Seceleanu, C.C., Xie, H., Zulkernine, M. (eds.) COMPSAC, pp. 233–243. IEEE Computer Society (2012)

29. Scott, D., Sharp, R.: Abstracting application-level web security. In: Proceedings of the 11th International Conference on World Wide Web, WWW '02, pp. 396–407. ACM, New York (2002). http://doi.acm.org/10.1145/511446.511498

30. Source, S.: Spring web mvc. http://www.springsource.org/go-webflow2 (2011)

31. Trustwave: Trustwave webdefend - web application firewall. https://www.trustwave.com/web-application-firewall.php (2011)

32. Vogt, P., Nentwich, F., Jovanovic, N., Kirda, E., Krügel, C., Vigna, G.: Cross site scripting prevention with dynamic data tainting and static analysis. In: NDSS. The Internet Society (2007)

33. Wassermann, G., Su, Z.: Sound and precise analysis of web applications for injection vulnerabilities. In: Proceedings of the 2007 ACM SIGPLAN Conference on Programming Language Design and Implementation, PLDI '07, pp. 32–41. ACM, New York (2007). http://doi.acm.org/10.1145/1250734.1250739

34. Wassermann, G., Su, Z.: Static detection of cross-site scripting vulnerabilities. In: ICSE '08: Proceedings of the 30th International Conference on Software Engineering, pp. 171–180. ACM, New York (2008)

35. Xie, Y., Aiken, A.: Static detection of security vulnerabilities in scripting languages. In: Proceedings of the 15th Conference on USENIX Security Symposium, vol. 15. USENIX Association, Berkeley (2006). http://portal.acm.org/citation.cfm?id=1267336.1267349

Lightweight Cryptography for Embedded Systems – A Comparative Analysis

Charalampos Manifavas[1], George Hatzivasilis[2](✉), Konstantinos Fysarakis[2], and Konstantinos Rantos[3]

[1] Department of Informatics Engineering,
Technological Educational Institute of Crete, Heraklion, Crete, Greece
harryman@epp.teicrete.gr
[2] Department of Computer and Informatics Engineering,
Eastern Macedonia and Thrace Institute of Technology, Kavala, Greece
{gchatzivasilis,kfysarakis}@isc.tuc.gr
[3] Department of Industrial Informatics,
Technological Educational Institute of Kavala, Kavala, Greece
krantos@teikav.edu.gr

Abstract. As computing becomes pervasive, embedded systems are deployed in a wide range of domains, including industrial systems, critical infrastructures, private and public spaces as well as portable and wearable applications. An integral part of the functionality of these systems is the storage, access and transmission of private, sensitive or even critical information. Therefore, the confidentiality and integrity of the resources and services of said devices constitutes a prominent issue that must be considered during their design. There is a variety of cryptographic mechanisms which can be used to safeguard the confidentiality and integrity of stored and transmitted information. In the context of embedded systems, however, the problem at hand is exacerbated by the resource-constrained nature of the devices, in conjunction with the persistent need for smaller size and lower production costs. This paper provides a comparative analysis of lightweight cryptographic algorithms applicable to such devices, presenting recent advances in the field for symmetric and asymmetric algorithms as well as hash functions. A classification and evaluation of the schemes is also provided, utilizing relevant metrics in order to assess their suitability for various types of embedded systems.

1 Introduction

Embedded computer systems pervade our lives in various forms, from avionics to e-textiles, automobiles, home automation and wireless sensor nodes. Physically, Embedded Systems (ESs) range from miniature wearable nodes to large industrial installations of Programmable Logic Controllers (PLCs).

The security, (i.e. confidentiality, integrity and availability) of networked computer systems is not a novel concern but, in the context of ESs, their various

J. Garcia-Alfaro et al. (Eds.): DPM 2013 and SETOP 2013, LNCS 8247, pp. 333–349, 2014.
DOI: 10.1007/978-3-642-54568-9_21, © Springer-Verlag Berlin Heidelberg 2014

intrinsic and often application specific characteristics render security techniques developed for personal and enterprise systems unsatisfactory or even inapplicable. Such characteristics habitually include resource constraints (namely computational capabilities, memory and power), dynamically formulated and remotely managed or even unmanaged networking as well as operation in hostile environment and time-critical applications.

An additional differentiating factor of ES security is that applications often include direct interaction with the physical world. Consequently, a security incident might lead to asset damage or even personal injury and death. Furthermore, since ESs are often responsible for vital, time-critical applications where a delay or a speed-up of even a fraction of a second could have dire consequences. Mechanisms used to appropriately fortify embedded systems are based on robust cryptographic algorithms. However, the inherent limited capabilities of these resource-constrained devices dictate the use of light schemes.

This paper focuses on the design and implementation aspects of cryptographic mechanisms utilized in resource constrained embedded systems. Similar works on LWC were first carried out in 2007 [7,45]. In [45], the authors evaluate hardware and software implementations for lightweight symmetric and asymmetric cryptography. In [7], the authors investigate lightweight hardware and software solutions for Wireless Sensor Networks (WSNs). In [46], the authors report new trends for lightweight hardware block and stream ciphers. In [47], hardware implementations of block ciphers are examined while in [48], the authors implement and evaluate 12 lightweight block ciphers. Cryptanalytic attacks on lightweight block ciphers were considered in [49].

2   Lightweight Cryptographic Mechanisms

Embedded devices often have inherent limitations in terms of processing power, memory, storage and energy. The cryptographic functionality that ESs utilize to provide tamper resistant hardware and software security functions has direct impact on the system's:

- Size: Memory elements constitute a significant part of the module's surface.
- Cost: Directly linked to the surface of the component.
- Speed: Optimized code provides results faster.
- Power Consumption: The quicker a set of instructions is executed, the quicker the module can return to an idle state or be put in sleep mode where power consumption is minimal.

Traditional cryptography solutions focus in providing high levels of security, ignoring the requirements of constrained devices. Lightweight cryptography (LWC) is a research field that has developed in recent years and focuses in designing schemes for devices with constrained capabilities in power supply, connectivity, hardware and software. Schemes proposed include hardware designs, which are typically considered more suitable for ultra-constrained devices, as well as software and hybrid implementations for lightweight devices.

- Hardware designs implement the exact functionality without redundant components. The main design goal is the reduction of the logic gates that are required to materialize the cipher. This metric is called Gate Equivalent (GE) [12]. A small GE predisposes that the circuit is cheap and consumes little power. For constrained devices an implementation including up to 3000 GE can be considered acceptable while for even smaller devices, like 4-bit microcontrollers, implementations of 1000 GE are being studied [12]. Energy consumption and power constraints are other significant factors. Energy consumption is important when a device is running on batteries while power constraints affect passive devices, like passive RFID tags, that must be connected to a host device to operate. Security attacks and relevant countermeasures that are correlated to power analysis are also considered in hardware designs.
- Software implementations typically only require a microprocessor to operate. The main design goals are the reduction of memory and processing requirements of the cipher. Implementations are optimized for throughput and power savings. Portability is their main advantage over hardware implementations.
- Hybrid schemes combine the two approaches exploiting the best features from both. Hardware implements the basic cipher functionality and software performs the data and communication manipulation. A common practice is the design of cryptographic co-processors. The throughput is mostly affected by the communication bandwidth between hardware and software components. Hybrid implementations target on specific communication applications, like RFID tags, portable devices and Internet servers.

2.1   Symmetric Cryptography

Lightweight and ultra-lightweight ciphers usually offer 80 to 128 bit security [12]. 80 bit security is considered adequate for constrained devices [23], like 4-bit micro-controllers and RFID tags, while 128 bits is typical for mainstream applications [1]. For one way authentication, 64 to 80 bit security would suffice [21].

Three main approaches are followed in implementing lightweight ciphers. In the first case, researchers try to improve the performance of well-known and well-studied ciphers such as AES and DES. A state of the art AES [1] hardware implementation uses 2400 GE and is used as a benchmark for newer ciphers. In the second case, re-searchers design and implement new ciphers, specific for this domain. PRESENT [2] is such an example implemented for lightweight and ultra-lightweight cryptography and is one of the first ciphers that offer a 1000 GE implementation for ultra-constrained devices. In the third case, researchers mix features of several ciphers that are well studied and their individual properties are known.

The absence of decryption is another factor that can reduce the requirements of such ciphers, especially for ultra-lightweight cryptography. Hummingbird-2 [13] is a combination of cipher and protocol and adopts this strategy. This approach is suitable for devices that need only one way authentication. Furthermore, some ciphers like KTANTAN [14] propose that the key should be hard-wired on the device to further reduce the GE due to the absence of key generation operations.

Block Ciphers. DES [15] is a traditional block cipher that can be used in constrained devices although due to its small key sizes, the security level is low. DESL is a lightweight version of the cipher that achieves 20 % size reduction, DESX uses key whitening to increase the security level, while DESXL is the combination of the two variants [15].

Other traditional ciphers that are investigated in this field are AES [1], Camellia [57], CLEFIA [16] and IDEA [48]. Camellia is approved for use by the ISO/IEC and the projects NESSIE and CRYPTREC. The hardware implementation exceeds the 3000 GE bound while the software implementation is fast. CLEFIA is a 128-bit block size cipher and uses 128-, 192- and 256-bits keys. It was designed by SONY and is highly efficient both in hardware and software. It is standardized in ISO 29192-2. IDEA is used in PGP v2.0 and performs well in embedded software.

PRESENT [12] is a milestone in LWC and the comparison unit for lightweight ciphers. It is 128-bit block size cipher and uses 80- and 128-bits keys. It is standardized in ISO 29192-2 and is efficient in both hardware and software. PRESENT's novelties include the replacement of 8 distinct S-Boxes with a carefully selected single one and a fully wired diffusion layer without any algebraic unit.

Hummingbird-2 [13] is a promising ultra-lightweight cipher with a hybrid structure of block and stream cipher. It can optionally produce a message authentication code (MAC) for each message processed and form a one way authentication protocol. It encrypts data in high rates and its performance is better than PRESENT's. Two main drawbacks are the initialization process and the decryption function. In more detail, an initialization process is necessary before en/decryption for its stream property and, moreover, the performance decreases if many small messages are processed. Also, the encryption and decryption operations are different, therefore the en/decryption implementation is 70 % larger than the encryption-only version.

The KATAN and KTANTAN family [14] produces low hardware footprint. KATAN uses a very simple key schedule mechanism and achieves 802 GE. KTANTAN is proposed for devices where the key is initialized once and remains unchanged, achieving 462 GE.

SEA [17] supports a scalable software implementation with low-cost encryption routines. It is parameterized in text, key, and processor size and can produce low memory requirements, small code size and a limited instruction set.

Newer lightweight block ciphers include TWINE [18], Klein [21], LED [20], LBlock [19], PUFFIN-2 [22], Piccolo [23], NOEKEON [48] and ITUbee [50]. TWINE, Klein, LED and LBlock balance tradeoffs between hardware and software implementations. TWINE achieves a good overall status as PRESENT. PUFFIN-2 is faster and more lightweight in hardware than PRESENT for en/decryption implementations. Piccolo is the most lightweight block cipher in hardware and it requires 683 and 758 GE for 80 and 128 bit key size respectively. NOEKEON is reported in LWC for its compact and efficient software implementation. ITUbee is designed for lightweight software and achieves the best overall status in this domain.

SIMON and SPECK [51] have been designed by NSA. The ciphers are recently released, a performance evaluation was presented during the MIT 2013 Legal Hack-a-Thone. Both ciphers perform well in software and hardware. SIMON is better in hardware and SPECK is better in software. Nevertheless, Piccolo achieves a better overall status in hardware.

Furthermore, domain specific ciphers include EPCBC [24] and PRINTcipher [25]. EPCBC is based on PRESENT and targets in Electronic Product Code (EPC) encryption applications. EPC aims to replace bar codes with low-cost passive RFIDS and is an industry standard by EPCglobal. PRINTcipher targets EPC and Integrated Circuit (IC) printing (i.e. used for the production and personalization of circuits).

Stream Ciphers. Stream ciphers are an alternative type of symmetric key ciphers and also well suited to constrained devices. Despite the evolution effort in the field of lightweight stream ciphers, they remain inferior to lightweight block ciphers. Their major draw-back is the lengthy initialization phase prior to first usage. Moreover, there are communication protocols that can't utilize stream ciphers. However, they are still in the foreground due to their simplicity and speed in hardware. They are often used in applications where the plaintext size is unknown.

Traditional stream ciphers RC4, A5/1 and E0 are considered insecure and should not be used in new applications [70]. AES in CTR mode is currently the only secure and widespread solution for stream encryption [70].

As for newer stream ciphers, the most notable are the finalists of the eSTREAM project [26]. eSTREAM was part of the ECRYPT Network of Excellence, targeted to deliver a small portfolio of promising stream ciphers. They considered two profiles of ciphers for different applications. Profile 1, includes ciphers for fast throughput in software, which are faster than the 128-bits AES-CTR. The finalist ciphers are the HC-128 [61], Rabbit [60], Salsa20 [61] and SOSEMANUK [61]. Profile 2, includes ciphers that are suitable for highly constrained environments and are more compact in hardware than the 80 bits AES. The finalists are Grain [3], Trivium [4] and MICKEY 2.0 [53]. All finalists are well-cryptanalyzed and are found secure against all attacks that are faster than the exhaustive key search attack.

In software, Salsa20/12 is reported as the most suitable for constrained devices. It uses 256-bit keys and 128-bit initialization vectors. The cipher utilizes only simple operations of addition, modulo 2^{32}, bit rotation and bitwise XOR, which are efficiently implemented in software. Furthermore the encryption and decryption operations are identical.

In hardware, Grain [3] and TRIVIUM [4] are the more accepted ones and have been reported as the most suitable for constrained devices. The key size of Grain is 80 bits, while the related Grain-128 supports 128-bit keys, and the IV 64 bits and it requires about 1300 GE to implement. TRIVIUM comes up with an 80 bit secret key, an 80 bit IV and about 2600 GE to implement. It was designed as an exercise in exploring how far a stream cipher can be simplified without sacrificing its security, speed or flexibility. It is standardized in ISO 29192-1, as is ENOCORO [5] which has an equivalent GE size in hardware.

Several newer ciphers are proposed based on eSTREAM candidates, like BEAN [43], QUAVIUM [44] and WG-7 [27]. BEAN is based on Grain. It supports binary output production without the need of additional hardware that was needed in Grain. The weak output function leads to an efficient distinguisher and a state-recovery attack [56]. In software, it takes less time to generate the keystream while using the same amount of memory. QUAVIUM is a scalable extension of TRIVIUM. It uses four TRIVIUM-like shift registers in coupling connection instead of three shift registers in series connection of the original TRIVIUM. The hardware implementation is larger than TRIVIUM and the software implementation is faster. WG-7 is the new version of WG cipher that was candidate in eSTREAM. It produces larger throughput than the other candidates and requires less memory. The key size is 80 bits, while the IV is 81 bits and is parameterized for RFID tags [27].

A2U2 [28] is a domain specific stream cipher. It was designed for the extremely resource limited environment of printed electronic RFID tags and is based on the principles of KATAN for efficient hardware. The smaller version requires less than 300 GE.

Hash Functions. Hash functions are another research field of LWC. The standardized or widely-used MD5 (8001 GE) [30], SHA-1 (5527 GE) [29] and SHA-2 (10868 GE) [30] and ARMADILLO (4353 GE) [64] are too large to fit in hardware constrained devices (i.e. more than 3000 GE). After the release of the PRESENT cipher there were many efforts to build novel lightweight hash functions based on PRESENT design principles [31], like C-PRESENT (4600 GE), H-PRESENT (2330 GE) and PRESENT-DM (1600 GE).

The NIST's SHA-3 competition [32] in 2012 defined a new function to replace the older SHA-1 and SHA-2. The finalists [33] were BLAKE, Grostl, JH, Skein and Keccak, with the latter being the winner. Unfortunately, the SHA-3/Keccak and the other finalists aren't much more compact than the previous SHA functions. At this time, all SHA-3 finalists require more than 12000 GE for 128 bit security. The SHA-3 competition has helped our understanding of hash functions significantly and led to a new design trend of hash functions with sponge constructions. Keccak is such a function and a lightweight implementation of a constrained Keccak version [34] was later announced at 2520–5090 GE.

Other new lightweight hash functions with sponge constructions are SQUASH (6328 GE) [35], GLUON (2071 GE) [36], Quark (1379 GE) [37], Photon (1120 GE) [38] and Spongent [39]. Spongent is the most lightweight hash function family known so far. Its smallest implementations require 738, 1060, 1329, 1728 and 1950 GE for 88, 128, 160, 224 and 256 bit respectively. It is based on a sponge construction instantiated with a PRESENT-type permutation, following the hermetic sponge strategy.

All the state of the art ciphers and hash functions that are mentioned should be extensively tested for security vulnerabilities before being widely used.

2.2   Asymmetric Cryptography

Asymmetric algorithms and protocols must also be adapted to operate on devices with the aforementioned resource limitations. This is an elaborate task, since asymmetric ciphers are computationally far more demanding than their symmetric counterparts and are usually used with powerful hardware. The performance gap is wider on constrained devices such as 8-bit microcontrollers. Even an optimized asymmetric algorithm e.g. elliptic-curve cryptography (ECC) is 100 to 1000 times slower than a standard symmetric algorithm like AES which correlates to two or three orders-of-magnitude higher power consumption.

Traditional Asymmetric Cryptosystems. Traditional public key cryptography is based on one-way trapdoor functions. These functions are based on a set of hard mathematical problems. There are three well established cryptosystems:

1. RSA, Rabin [41] - based on the Integer Factorization Problem (FP)
2. ECC [6]/HECC [7] - based on Elliptic Curve Discrete Logarithm Problem (ECDLP)
3. ElGamal [68] - based on the Discrete Logarithm Problem In Finite Fields (DLP)

RSA is the most popular algorithm for asymmetric cryptography and supports key sizes from 1024 to 4096 bits. As such, it is used as a benchmark for the various public key cryptosystems researchers propose. However its large hardware footprint and its resource demanding implementations led researchers to seek for other algorithms for applications in constrained devices.

Rabin is quite similar to RSA. One main difference is the complexity of the factorization problems that they rely upon. Rabin is proven to be as hard as the integer factorizations problem, while RSA is not. Also, the encryption for Rabin is faster but the decryption is less efficient. WIPR [41] is a low-resource implementation of Rabin in hardware. The implementation shares several architectural principles with the SQUASH hash function. It requires 4682 GE and fits on RFID tags and wireless sensor nodes. BluJay [42] is a hybrid Rabin-based scheme that is suitable for lightweight platforms and is based on WIPR and Hummingbird-2. The encryption is significantly faster and more lightweight than RSA and ECC for the same level of security. The hardware implementation requires less than 3000 GE.

ECC [6] and HECC [7] are considered the most attractive cryptosystems for embedded systems. They present smaller operand lengths and relatively lower computational requirements. Their main advantage is the fact that for the same level of security they offer shorter keys compared to RSA, which leads to smaller internal state requirements. As the level of security increases, RSA key sizes grow much faster than ECC. ECC also produces lightweight software implementations due to its memory and energy savings. The most known software implementations [8] are the TinyECC and the WMECC.

HECC is a generalization of elliptic curves. A hyper elliptic curve of genus 1 is an elliptic curve. As the genus increases, the arithmetic of encryption gets more complicated, but it needs fewer bits for the same level of security. HECC's operand size is at least a factor of two smaller than the ECC one. The curves of genus 2 are of great interest for the research community as higher genus curves suffer from security attacks. HECC has better performance than ECC and is more attractive in resource constrained devices.

ElGamal [68] is of no interest for resource constrained platforms. The computation is more intensive than RSA and encryption produces a 2:1 expansion in size from plaintext to ciphertext. It is also considered vulnerable to some types of attacks, like chosen ciphertext attacks.

Alternative Asymmetric Cryptosystems. Alternative public key cryptosystems (APKCs) [9] that are based on other mathematical features have become popular due to their performance and their resistance against quantum computing. These alternative cryptosystems are based on:

- Hash-Based Cryptography. The Merkle signature scheme (MSS) [40] is a crypto-system which uses typical hash functions
- Lattice-Based Cryptography. NTRU [10] is the most popular scheme which is based on the Shortest Vector Problem
- Code-Based Cryptography. McEliece [66] is a popular scheme based on error-correcting codes
- Multivariate-Quadratic (MQ) Cryptography. MQ [67] is based on the problem of solving multivariable quadratic equations over finite fields

An MSS implementation with the AES-based hash function [40] has smaller code size and faster verification process than RSA and ECC. Moreover, the signature generation is faster than RSA and comparable to ECC. MSS may gain ground in lightweight asymmetric cryptosystems due to the evolution of lightweight hash function design.

NTRU [10,11] is the most promising cryptosystem of all APKCs. Encryption and decryption use only simple polynomial multiplications, which makes them very fast compared to traditional cryptosystems. NTRU is highly efficient, suitable for embedded systems and provides a level of security comparable to RSA and ECC. In hard-ware implementations [11], NTRU is 1,5 times faster compared to ECC for the same level of security and only has 1/7 of its memory footprint. The hardware implementation requires almost 3000 GE. In software implementations [10], NTRU is 200 times faster in key generation, almost 3 times faster in encryption and about 30 times faster in decryption compared to RSA. On the other hand, NTRU produces larger output, which may impact the performance of the cryptosystem if the number of transmitted messages is crucial. It is considered safe when the recommended parameters are used [69]. NTRU can be efficiently used in embedded systems because of its easy key generation process, its high speed and its low memory usage. The system is now adopted by the IEEE P1363 standards under the specifications for lattice-based public-key cryptography as well as IEEE P1363.1 and ANSI X9.98 Standard for use in the financial services industry.

The main drawback of McEliece [66] and MQ [67] cryptosystems is the use of large keys. In comparison to 1924 bit RSA, MQ requires 9690 bytes for the public key and 879 bytes for the private key. Key sizes impact on the computations that are performed, the speed, the key storage and the output's size. The advantage of these systems is the fast encryption and decryption process that makes them suitable for high performance applications where messages must be assigned in real time.

3   Evaluation

We analyze the features of different cryptographic solutions and propose the more suitable ones for different types of embedded devices. Based on the devices' capabilities we categorize the solutions in four groups: ultra-lightweight, low-cost, lightweight and specific domain. Ultra-lightweight implementations fit in the most constrained devices (in computation capability, memory, power), like the standard 8051 microcontroller and the ATtiny45. Low-cost devices (e.g. ATmega128) are cheap and perform a little better than ultra-lightweight ones. Lightweight devices include the rest of the devices reported in LWC. As specific domains we consider the EPC encryption applications and IC-printing.

3.1   Hardware Implementations

The hardware implementations are categorized based on chip area. Ultra-lightweight implementations occupy up to 1000 logic gates, low-cost implementations occupy up to 2000 logic gates and lightweight implementations occupy up to 3000 logic gates. The best implementations in each group are selected based on the figure of merit (FOM) metric [64]. FOM is considered as a fair metric to compare the energy efficiency of different implementations; the higher the value, the better.

$$FOM = throughput \ [Kbps]/area \ squared \ [GE^2] \qquad (1)$$

Block ciphers are better than stream ciphers in the three general groups of devices. Hash functions perform efficiently in low-cost and lightweight devices. Asymmetric cryptography is feasible only in lightweight devices. For ultra-lightweight and low-cost devices the key establishment mechanisms based only on symmetric cryptography can be applied. For the domain specific applications, the PRINTcipher achieves a better overall status than EPCBC and A2U2.

For ultra-lightweight devices the block ciphers PRINTcipher, KTANTAN, Piccolo, SIMON, SPECK and LED, and the stream ciphers A2U2 and TRIV-IUM, as well as the hash functions PHOTON and Spongent are implemented. For block ciphers, PRINTcipher is considered insecure for wide use as it is designed for a specific application domain and ignores several types of general attacks.

KTANTAN is only appropriate in applications where the key is hardcoded on the device. SIMON and SPECK are newly proposed ciphers. LED consumes high energy per bit and is inefficient. Piccolo achieves a good overall status and is the most suitable cipher in this category. Regarding stream ciphers, A2U2 achieves the best FOM but as a new cipher it is not extensively cryptanalyzed, therefore the standardized TRIVIUM appears to be the optimal choice. For hash functions, Spongent is the most lightweight choice but PHOTON produces higher FOM.

Targeting low-cost devices, the block ciphers SIMON, SPECK, PRESENT, TWINE, KATAN, Klein, DESL, EPCBC, LBlock, PUFFIN-2, the stream cipher Grain, and the hash functions DM-PRESENT, D-QUARK, and U-QUARK are implemented (as well as the ones for ultra-lightweight devices). For block ciphers, PRESENT is standardized and is considered the best solution. TWINE performs similar to PRESENT but is a new cipher. KATAN, Klein, DESL, EPCBC, LBlock and PUFFIN-2 have worse performance. For stream ciphers, Grain performs better than the ultra-lightweight TRIVIUM. For hash functions, Spongent is the best while DM-PRESENT, D-QUARK, and U-QUARK produce worse FOM metrics.

For lightweight devices, the block ciphers Hummingbird-2, AES, DESXL, DESX and CLEFIA, the stream cipher QUAVIUM, the hash functions H-PRESENT, Keccak, S-QUARK and SQUASH, and the asymmetric cryptosystems NTRUencrypt and GPS-4/4-F are implemented; in addition to the ones for ultra-lightweight and low-cost devices. For block ciphers, AES is the best choice. The standardized PRESENT and CLEFIA are also appropriate. The variants DESXL and DESX can also be applied as they offer higher level of security than DES. Hummingbird-2 is another promising candidate. For stream ciphers TRIVIUM achieves higher FOM than Grain while the new cipher QUAVIUM isn't well cryptanalyzed. The hash function DM-PRESENT achieves by far the best FOM for all the relevant proposals. Keccak as the new SHA-3 function can also be used. S-QUARK and SQUASH produce poor performance. For the asymmetric cryptosystems, NTRU appears to be the most suitable.

Table 1 summarizes the best hardware implementation of each examined cipher that requires less than 3000 GE. The implementations are sorted by the FOM metric.

3.2   Software Implementations

The software implementations are categorized based on the ROM and RAM requirements. Ultra-lightweight implementations require up to 4 KB ROM and 256 bytes RAM, low-cost implementations require up to 4 KB ROM and 8 KB RAM and lightweight implementations require up to 32 KB ROM and 8 KB RAM. The best implementations in each group are selected based on the combined metric (CM) [48]. CM indicates the tradeoff between implementation size and performance and smaller values are better.

$$CM = (code\ size\ [bytes] * encryption\ cycle\ count\ [cycles])/block\ size\ [bits] \quad (2)$$

Table 1. Hardware implementations (<3000 GE)

Cipher	Key Size (bits)	Throughput (Kbps at 100 KHz higher is better)	GE (lower is better)	FOM (higher is better)
Piccolo [23]	80	237.04	1136	1836
SIMON [51]	96	142.2	1216	962
SPECK [51]	96	220.7	1522	953
PRESENT [12]	80	200	1570	811
TWINE [18]	80	178	1503	787
KTANTAN [14]	80	25.1	688	530
PRINTcipher [25]	80	100	503	395
Piccolo [23]	80	14.81	683	317
SIMON [51]	96	15.8	763	271
KATAN [14]	80	25.1	1054	226
Klein [21]	64	30.9	1220	208
HummingBird-2 [13]	128	80	2159	171
SPECK [51]	96	12	884	153
DESL [15]	56	44.4	1848	130
EPCBC [28]	96	12.12	1008	119
LBlock [19]	80	200	1320	115
AES [1]	128	56.64	2400	98
DESXL [15]	184	44.4	2168	95
DESX [15]	184	44.4	2629	64
CLEFIA [16]	128	39	2488	63
PUFFIN-2 [22]	80	5.2	1083	44
LED [20]	80	3.4	1040	32
A2U2 [28]	56	50	284	620
Grain [53]	80	100	1294	597
TRIVIUM [52]	80	100	2017	245
QUAVIUM [44]	80	-	2372	-
DM-PRESENT [31]	64	387.88	2530	605.98
Spongent [39]	88	17.78	1127	139
PHOTON [38]	80	15.15	1168	111.13
D-QUARK [37]	160	18.18	2819	22.88
H-PRESENT [31]	128	11.45	2330	21.09
U-QUARK [37]	128	11.76	2392	20.56
Keccak-f[400] [34]	128	8	2520	12
S-QUARK [37]	224	3.13	2296	5.93
SQUASH [54]	64	0.2	2646	0.29
NTRUencrypt [55]	57	292.2	2850	359
GPS-4 / 4-F (PRESENT) [2]	80	107.23	2143	233

Again, the block ciphers are more efficient than stream ciphers in the three general groups of devices. In software, asymmetric cryptography materializes specific key exchange schemes and communication protocols, like SSL. Due to the complexity of implementing this functionality, cryptographic libraries are utilized to enhance the robustness of an application. Hash functions are embod-

Table 2. Software implementations (<32 KB *ROM*, <8 KB *RAM*)

Cipher	Key Size (bits)	ROM (bytes - lower is better)	RAM (bytes - lower is better)	Throughput (Kbps at 4 MHz higher is better)	CM (lower is better)
SPECK [51]	96	152	108	207.8	2926
SIMON [51]	96	198	168	147	5396
ITUbee [50]	80	400	186	109	14685
AES [59]	128	1912	432	256	29875
TWINE [18]	80	1304	414	118	44173
Hummingbird-2 [13]	128	2227	114	200/172	44400
NOEKEON [48]	128	364	32	21.7	66876
IDEA [48]	128	836	232	31	107765
Klein [21]	80	1268	18	42	120757
PRESENT [45]	80	936	0	23.8	156823
SEA [45]	96	2132	0	39	218663
TWINE [18]	80	792	191	13.6	232575
KATAN [48]	80	338	18	3.5	380582
DESL [58]	56	3098	0	30.6	404918
DESXL [45]	184	3192	0	30.4	425483.6
Hummingbird [63]	256	2950	1064	26.5	445081
DES [48]	56	4314	0	29.6	581918
DESX [58]	184	4406	0	29.4	598871
Camellia [57]	128	1262	12	8	631000
Rabbit [60]	128	1714	216	8421	814
WG-7 [27]	80	1100	0	192	45650
Salsa20 [45]	128	1452	280	111	58181
TRIVIUM [62]	80	424	36	6	281960
Grain [62]	80	778	20	6.4	480026
HC128 [61]	128	23100	4556	189.5/189.6	487446
AES [61]	128	6664	88	40/34	654633

ied to these schemes and protocols. Compact libraries, like CyaSSL [65] which is specifically designed for embedded devices, are suitable for lightweight implementations. Thus, individual primitive implementations are mainly proposed for block and stream ciphers.

For ultra-lightweight devices, the block ciphers SPECK, SIMON, ITUbee, Hummingbird-2, NOEKEON, IDEA, Klein, PRESENT, SEA, TWINE, KATAN, DESL, DESXL and Camellia and the stream ciphers Rabbit, WG-7, TRIVIUM and Grain are implemented. For block ciphers, SPECK achieves the best CM by far. SIMON and ITUbee are also efficient in this domain. Hummingbird-2 and NOEKEON achieve a good overall status. IDEA, Klein, PRESENT, SEA, TWINE, KATAN, DESL, DESXL and Camellia perform poor in such devices. For stream ciphers, Rabbit is the best proposal. WG-7 performs well, but as a new cipher, it isn't well cryptanalyzed. TRIVIUM and Grain have poor performance.

For low-cost devices, the block ciphers AES, TWINE and Hummingbird, and the stream cipher Salsa20 are implemented (in addition to the ones for ultra-lightweight devices). All ciphers perform well but achieve lower CM metric than the proposed ones in ultra-lightweight devices. For lightweight devices, the block ciphers DES and DESX, and the stream ciphers HC128 and AES in CTR mode are additionally implemented. All ciphers perform poor in such devices and are inferior to the proposals in ultra-lightweight and low-cost devices.

Table 2 summarizes the best software implementation of each examined cipher that requires less than 32 KB ROM and 8 KB RAM. The implementations are sorted by the CM metric.

4 Conclusions

The aim of this paper was to provide a comparative analysis on lightweight cryptographic algorithms designed for resource-constrained devices. The inherently limited capabilities of these systems in terms of computing power, memory, storage and energy resources, inevitably limit the effectiveness and the applicability of well-established cryptographic mechanisms designed for systems where such resource constraints are not a significant concern.

Such an extensive analysis is considered essential to those planning on utilizing such mechanisms in newly designed systems or applications running on resource constrained devices. As demonstrated in this work, there is ongoing research on various aspects of lightweight cryptography. The evaluation of the robustness and efficiency of pre-existing as well as newly proposed schemes poses a major challenge to research and development efforts. Overcoming the aforementioned challenges, however, is necessary for realizing the ubiquitous computing future.

Acknowledgement. This work was funded by the General Secretarial Research and Technology (G.S.R.T.), Hellas under the Artemis JU research program nSHIELD (new embedded Systems arcHItecturE for multi-Layer Dependable solutions) project. Call: ARTEMIS-2010-1, Grand Agreement No: 269317.

References

1. Moradi, A., Poschmann, A., Ling, S., Paar, C., Wang, H.: Pushing the limits: a very compact and a threshold implementation of AES. In: Paterson, K.G. (ed.) EUROCRYPT 2011. LNCS, vol. 6632, pp. 69–88. Springer, Heidelberg (2011)
2. Poschmann, A.: Lightweight cryptography - cryptographic engineering for a pervasive world. Ph.D. Dissertation, Faculty of Electrical Engineering and Information Technology, Ruhr-University Bochum, Germany (2009)
3. Hell, M., Johansson, T., Meier, W.: Grain - a stream cipher for constrained environments. Int. J. Wirel. Mob. Comput. **2**(1), 86–93 (2007)

4. De Canniere, C., Prenel, B.: Trivium Specifications. eStream Project. http://www.ecrypt.eu.org/stream/triviump3.html (2008)

5. Watanabe, D., Ideguchi, K., Kitahara, J., Muto, K., Furuichi, H.: Enocoro-80: a hardware oriented stream cipher. In: Third International Conference on Availability Reliability and Security (ARES 08), 4–7 March 2008, pp. 1294–1300 (2008)

6. Hein, D., Wolkerstorfer, J., Felber, N.: ECC is ready for RFID - a proof in silicon. In: Avanzi, R.M., Keliher, L., Sica, F. (eds.) SAC 2008. LNCS, vol. 5381, pp. 401–413. Springer, Heidelberg (2009)

7. Roman, R., Alcaraz, C., Lopez, J.: A survey of cryptographic primitives and implementations for hardware-constrained sensor network nodes. J. Mob. Netw. Appl. **12**(4), 231–244 (2007)

8. Nizamuddin, N., Ashraf Ch, S., Nasar, W., Javaid, Q.: Efficient signcryption schemes based on hyperlliptic curve cryptosystem. In: 7th International Conference on Emerging Technologies (ICET), pp. 1–4 (2011)

9. Guneysu, T., Heyse, S., Paar, C.: The future of high-speed cryptography: new computing platforms and new ciphers. In: Proceedings of the 21st Edition of the Great Lakes Symposium on VLSI (GLSVLSI'11) (2011)

10. Shen, X., Du, Z., Chen, R.: Research on NTRU algorithm for mobile java security. In: International Conference on Scalable Computing and Communications, The Eighth International Conference on Embedded, Computing 2009, SCALCOM-EMBEDDEDCOM'09, pp 366–369 (2009)

11. Kamal, A.A., Youssef, A.M.: An FPGA implementation of the NTRUEncrypt cryptosystem. In: 2009 International Conference on Microelectronics (ICM), pp. 209–212 (2009)

12. Bogdanov, A.A., Knudsen, L.R., Leander, G., Paar, C., Poschmann, A., Robshaw, M.J.B., Seurin, Y., Vikkelsoe, C.: PRESENT: an ultra-lightweight block cipher. In: Paillier, P., Verbauwhede, I. (eds.) CHES 2007. LNCS, vol. 4727, pp. 450–466. Springer, Heidelberg (2007)

13. Engels, D., Saarinen, M.-J.O., Schweitzer, P., Smith, E.M.: The hummingbird-2 lightweight authenticated encryption algorithm. In: The 7th Workshop of RFID Security and Privacy (RFIDSec 2011), Amherst, Massachusetts, USA (2011)

14. De Cannière, C., Dunkelman, O., Knežević, M.: KATAN and KTANTAN - a family of small and efficient hardware-oriented block ciphers. In: Clavier, C., Gaj, K. (eds.) CHES 2009. LNCS, vol. 5747, pp. 272–288. Springer, Heidelberg (2009)

15. Leander, G., Paar, C., Poschmann, A., Schramm, K.: New lightweight DES variants. In: Biryukov, A. (ed.) FSE 2007. LNCS, vol. 4593, pp. 196–210. Springer, Heidelberg (2007)

16. Akishita, T., Hiwatari, H.: Very compact hardware implementations of the blockcipher CLEFIA. Sony Corporation, Technical Paper, June 2011. http://www.sony.co.jp/Products/cryptography/clefia/download/data/clefia-hwcompact-20110615.pdf (2011)

17. Standaert, F.-X., Piret, G., Gershenfeld, N., Quisquater, J.-J.: SEA: a scalable encryption algorithm for small embedded applications. In: Domingo-Ferrer, J., Posegga, J., Schreckling, D. (eds.) CARDIS 2006. LNCS, vol. 3928, pp. 222–236. Springer, Heidelberg (2006)

18. Suzaki, T., Minematsu, K., Morioka, S., Kobayashi, E.: TWINE: a lightweight, versatile block cipher. In: ECRYPT Workshop on Lightweight Cryptography (LC11), 28–29 November, pp. 146–169 (2011)

19. Wu, W., Zhang, L.: LBlock: a lightweight block cipher. In: Lopez, J., Tsudik, G. (eds.) ACNS 2011. LNCS, vol. 6715, pp. 327–344. Springer, Heidelberg (2011)

20. Guo, J., Peyrin, T., Poschmann, A., Robshaw, M.: The LED block cipher. In: Preneel, B., Takagi, T. (eds.) CHES 2011. LNCS, vol. 6917, pp. 326–341. Springer, Heidelberg (2011)

21. Gong, Z., Nikova, S., Law, Y.W.: KLEIN: a new family of lightweight block ciphers. In: Juels, A., Paar, C. (eds.) RFIDSec 2011. LNCS, vol. 7055, pp. 1–18. Springer, Heidelberg (2012). http://rfid-cusp.org/rfidsec/

22. Wang, C., Heys, H.M.: An ultra compact block cipher for serialized architecture implementations. In: Proceedings of IEEE Canadian Conference on Electrical and Computer Engineering (CCECE 2009), St. John's, Newfoundland, May 2009 (2009)

23. Shibutani, K., Isobe, T., Hiwatari, H., Mitsuda, A., Akishita, T., Shirai, T.: Piccolo: an ultra-lightweight blockcipher. In: Preneel, B., Takagi, T. (eds.) CHES 2011. LNCS, vol. 6917, pp. 342–357. Springer, Heidelberg (2011)

24. Yap, H., Khoo, K., Poschmann, A., Henricksen, M.: EPCBC - a block cipher suitable for electronic product code encryption. In: Lin, D., Tsudik, G., Wang, X. (eds.) CANS 2011. LNCS, vol. 7092, pp. 76–97. Springer, Heidelberg (2011)

25. Knudsen, L., Leander, G., Poschmann, A., Robshaw, M.J.B.: PRINTcipher: a block cipher for IC-printing. In: Mangard, S., Standaert, F.-X. (eds.) CHES 2010. LNCS, vol. 6225, pp. 16–32. Springer, Heidelberg (2010)

26. eSTREAM Web Page. http://www.ecrypt.eu.org/stream

27. Luo, Y., Chai, Q., Gong, G., Lai, X.: A lightweight stream cipher WG-7 for RFID encryptionand authentication. In: IEEE Global Telecommunications Conference 2010 (GLOBECOM 2010), pp. 1-6 (2010)

28. David, M., Ranasinghe, D.C., Larsen, T.: A2U2: a stream cipher for printed electronics RFID tags. IEEE International Conference on RFID 2011, 176–183 (2011)

29. O'Neill, M.: Low-Cost SHA-1 hash function architecture for RFID tags. In: Dominikus, S., Aigner, M. (eds.) RFIDSec 2008. http://events.iaik.tugraz.at/RFIDSec08/Papers/ (2008)

30. Feldhofer, M., Rechberger, C.: A case against currently used hash functions in RFID protocols. In: Meersman, R., Tari, Z., Herrero, P. (eds.) OTM 2006 Workshops. LNCS, vol. 4277, pp. 372–381. Springer, Heidelberg (2006)

31. Bogdanov, A., Leander, G., Paar, Ch., Poschmann, A., Robshaw, M.J.B., Seurin, Y.: Hash functions and RFID tags: mind the gap. In: Oswald, E., Rohatgi, P. (eds.) CHES 2008. LNCS, vol. 5154, pp. 283–299. Springer, Heidelberg (2008)

32. SHA-3 Contest. http://csrc.nist.gov/groups/ST/hash/sha-3/Round3/submissions_rnd3.html

33. Gaj, K., Homsirikamol, E., Rogawski, M., Shahid, R., Sharif, M.U.: Comprehensive evaluation of high-speed and medium speed implementations of five SHA-3 finalists using Xilinx and Altera FPGAs. In: The 3rd SHA-3 Candidate Conference, Washington, D.C., 22–23 March 2012 (2012)

34. Kavun, E.B., Yalcin, T.: A Lightweight Implementation of Keccak Hash Function for Radio-Frequency Identification Applications. In: Ors Yalcin, S.B. (ed.) RFIDSec 2010. LNCS, vol. 6370, pp. 258–269. Springer, Heidelberg (2010)

35. Shamir, A.: SQUASH - a new MAC with provable security properties for highly constrained devices such as RFID tags. In: Nyberg, K. (ed.) FSE 2008. LNCS, vol. 5086, pp. 144–157. Springer, Heidelberg (2008)

36. Berger, T.P., D'Hayer, J., Marquet, K., Minier, M., Thomas, G.: The GLUON family: a lightweight hash function family based on FCSRs. In: Mitrokotsa, A., Vaudenay, S. (eds.) AFRICACRYPT 2012. LNCS, vol. 7374, pp. 306–323. Springer, Heidelberg (2012)

37. Aumasson, J.-P., Henzen, L., Meier, W., Naya-Plasencia, M.: QUARK: A

38. Guo, J., Peyrin, T., Poschmann, A.: The PHOTON family of lightweight hash functions. In: Rogaway, P. (ed.) CRYPTO 2011. LNCS, vol. 6841, pp. 222–239. Springer, Heidelberg (2011)

39. Bogdanov, A., Knežević, M., Leander, G., Toz, D., Varıcı, K., Verbauwhede, I.: spongent: a lightweight hash function. In: Preneel, B., Takagi, T. (eds.) CHES 2011. LNCS, vol. 6917, pp. 312–325. Springer, Heidelberg (2011)

40. Rohde, S., Eisenbarth, T., Dahmen, E., Buchmann, J., Paar, C.: Fast hash-based signatures on constrained devices. In: Grimaud, G., Standaert, F.-X. (eds.) CARDIS 2008. LNCS, vol. 5189, pp. 104–117. Springer, Heidelberg (2008)

41. Oren, Y., Feldhofer, M.: WIPR - a low-resource public-key identification scheme for RFID tags and sensor nodes. In: Basin, D.A., Capkun, S., Lee, W. (eds.) WISEC, pp. 59–68. ACM (2009)

42. Saarinen, M.-J.O.: The BlueJay ultra-lightweight hybrid cryptosystem. In: 2012 IEEE Symposium on Security and Privacy Workshops (SPW), 24–25 May 2012, pp. 27–32 (2012)

43. Kumar, N., Ojha, S., Jain, K., Sangeeta, L.: BEAN: a lightweight stream cipher. In: Proceedings of the 2nd International Conference on Security of Information and Networks (SIN '09), pp. 168–171 (2009)

44. Tian, Y., Chen, G., Li, J.: QUAVIUM - a new stream cipher inspired by TRIVIUM. J. Comput. 7(5), 1278–1283 (2012). doi:10.4304/jcp.7.5.1278-1283

45. Eisenbarth, T., Paar, C., Poschmann, A., Kumar, S., Uhsadel, L.: A survey of lightweight cryptography implementations. IEEE Des. Test Comput. 24(6), 522–533 (2007)

46. Paar, C., Poschmann, A., Robshaw, M.J.B.: New design in lightweight symmetric encryption. RFID Secur. 3, 349–371 (2009)

47. Kitsos, P., Sklavos, N., Parousi, M., Skodras, A.N.: A comparative study of hardware architectures for lightweight block ciphers. J. Comput. Electr. Eng. 38(1), 148–160 (2012)

48. Eisenbarth, T., et al.: Compact implementation and performance evaluation of block ciphers in ATtiny devices. In: Mitrokotsa, A., Vaudenay, S. (eds.) AFRICACRYPT 2012. LNCS, vol. 7374, pp. 172–187. Springer, Heidelberg (2012)

49. Anjali, A.P., Saibal, K.P.: A survey of Cryptanalysis attacks on lightweight block ciphers. IRACST - Int. J. Comput. Sci. Inf. Secur. (IJCSITS) 2(2), 65 (2012)

50. Karakoç, F., Demirci, H., Harmancı, A.E.: ITUbee: a software oriented lightweight block cipher. In: Avoine, G., Kara, O. (eds.) LightSec 2013. LNCS, vol. 8162, pp. 16–27. Springer, Heidelberg (2013)

51. Beaulieu, R., Shors, D., Smith, J., Treatman-Clark, S., Weeks, B., Wingers, L.: The SIMON and SPECK families of lightweight block ciphers. IACR, Cryptology ePrint Archive, 2013. http://eprint.iacr.org/2013/404.pdf (2013)

52. Mentens, N., Genoe, J., Preneel, B., Verbauwhede, I.: A low-cost implementation of Trivium. In: ECRYPT Workshop, SASC - The State of the Art of Stream Ciphers, pp. 197–204 (2008)

53. Good, T., Benaissa, M.: Hardware performance of eStream Phase-iii stream cipher candidates. In: State of the Art of Stream Ciphers Workshop (SASC 2008), February 2008, pp. 163–173 (2008)

54. Zhilyaev, S.: Evaluating a new MAC for current and next generation RFID. Master thesis, University of Massachusetts Amherst (2010). http://scholarworks.umass.edu/cgi/viewcontent.cgi?article=1477&context=theses

55. Gaubatz, G., Kaps, J.-P., Sunar, B.: Public key cryptography in sensor networks—revisited. In: Castellucia, C., Hartenstein, H., Paar, C., Westhoff, D. (eds.), ESAS 2004. LNCS, vol. 3312, pp. 2–18. Springer, Heideberg (2005)

56. Agren, M.: On some symmetric lightweight cryptographic designs. Ph.D. dissertation, Department of Electrical and Information Technology, Faculty of Engineering, LTH, Lund University (2012).

57. Cakiroglu, M.: Software implementation and performance comparison of popular block ciphers on 8-bit low-cost microcontroller. Int. J. Phys. Sci. **5**(9), 1338–1343 (2010)

58. Rinne, S., Eisenbarth, T., Paar, C.: Performance analysis of contemporary lightweight block ciphers on 8-bit microcontrollers (2011)

59. Bos, J.W., Osvik, D.A., Stefan, D.: Fast implementations of AES on various platforms. In: SPEED-CC - Software Performance Enhancement for Encryption and Decryption and Cryptographic Compilers (2009)

60. Boesgaard, M., Vesterager, M., Christensen, T., Zenner, E.: The stream cipher rabbit 1. http://www.ecrypt.eu.org/stream/p3ciphers/rabbit/rabbit_p3.pdf (2010)

61. Meiser, G., Eisenbarth, T., Lemke-Rust, K., Paar, C.: Software implementation of eSTREAM profile I ciphers on embedded 8-bit AVR microcontrollers. In: Workshop Record State of the Art of Stream Ciphers (SASC 07). Also submitted in: The eSTREAM Project (2007)

62. Otte, D.: AVR-Crypto-Lib. http://www.das-labor.org/wiki/AVR-Crypto-Lib/en (2009)

63. Engels, D., Fan, X., Gong, G., Hu, H., Smith, E.M.: Hummingbird: ultra-lightweight cryptography for resource-constrained devices. In: Sion, R., Curtmola, R., Dietrich, S., Kiayias, A., Miret, J.M., Sako, K., Sebé, F. (eds.) FC 2010 Workshops. LNCS, vol. 6054, pp. 3–18. Springer, Heidelberg (2010)

64. Badel, S., Dağtekin, N., Nakahara Jr, J., Ouafi, K., Reffé, N., Sepehrdad, P., Sušil, P., Vaudenay, S.: ARMADILLO: a multi-purpose cryptographic primitive dedicated to hardware. In: Mangard, S., Standaert, F.-X. (eds.) CHES 2010. LNCS, vol. 6225, pp. 398–412. Springer, Heidelberg (2010)

65. Gaubatz, G., Kaps, J.-P., Sunar, B.: Public Key Cryptography in Sensor Networks Revisited. In: Castellucia, C., Hartenstein, H., Paar, C., Westhoff, D. (eds.), Proceeding of the 1st European Workshop on Security in Ad-Hoc and Sensor Networks ESAS 2004. LNCS, vol. 3312, pp. 218. Springer-Verlag (2004)

66. Shoufan, A., Wink, T., Molter, G., Huss, S., Strentzke, F.: A novel processor architecture for McEliece cryptosystem and FPGA platforms. In: Proceedings of the 20th IEEE International Conference on Application-specific Systems, Architectures and Processors (ASAP 2009), pp. 98–105 (2009)

67. Yang, B.-Y., Cheng, C.-M., Chen, B.-R., Chen, J.-M.: Implementing minimized multivariate PKC on low-resource embedded systems. In: Brooke, P.J., Clark, J.A., Paige, R.F., Polack, F.A.C. (eds.) SPC 2006. LNCS, vol. 3934, pp. 73–88. Springer, Heidelberg (2006)

68. Gamal, T.E.: A public key cryptosystem and a signature scheme based on discrete logarithms. IEEE Trans. Inf. Theor. **31**(4), 469–472 (1985)

69. Howgrave-Graham, N., Silverman, J.H., Whyte, W.: Choosing parameter sets for NTRUEncrypt with NAEP and SVES − 3. In: Menezes, A. (ed.) CT-RSA 2005. LNCS, vol. 3376, pp. 118–135. Springer, Heidelberg (2005)

70. Bjorstad, T.E.: An introduction to new stream cipher designs. In: 25th Chaos Communication Congress (2008)

Short Papers

A Simulation of Document Detection Methods and Reducing False Positives for Private Stream Searching

Michael Oehler[(✉)] and Dhananjay S. Phatak

Cyber Defense Laboratory, Department of Computer Science and Electrical Engineering, University of Maryland Baltimore County, Baltimore, Maryland
{oehler1,phatak}@umbc.edu

Abstract. Private stream searching is a system of cryptographic methods that provide a search facility while preserving the confidentiality of the search criteria and matching documents. This research analyzes the original documentation detection method of the private search system, defines a new detection method based on an appended hash, and presents an analysis of false positives occurring in both methods. Our method offers a lower false positive rate than prior work, and integrates seamlessly into an implementation of private stream searching.

Keywords: Private stream search · Data privacy · Oblivious transfer · Simulation

1 Introduction

Rafail Ostrovsky and William Skeith created a Private Stream Search (PSS) system that conceals the search criteria, performs a search on the encrypted criteria, and returns matching documents in an encrypted buffer [1]. This private search system preserves the confidentiality of the search criteria and the search results from external entities.

We define a new method for document detection that demonstrates a lower false positive rate than the original method. Our method utilizes a hash of the document stored to the output buffer, and differs from prior attempts that measure a Hamming weight. This is an aspect of private searching that has not been discussed previously. We then adapt our detection method and the iterative recovery technique presented by Danezis and Diaz [2]. Our improved detection method reduces the occurrence of a non-recoverable error for this iterative technique. Our results are thus, relevant for implementers and those researching private stream searching.

2 Private Stream Search

The private search system created by Ostrovksy [1] is based on the asymmetric cryptosystem defined by Paillier [3], and utilizes the additive homomorphic

J. Garcia-Alfaro et al. (Eds.), DPM 2013 and SETOP 2013, LNCS 8247, pp. 353–361, 2014.
DOI: 10.1007/978-3-642-54568-9_22, © Springer-Verlag Berlin Heidelberg 2014

property of the cryptosystem. The private search system involves two parties: a client and an information provider. A client constructs a query. The provider performs the search, delivers a result, and gains no knowledge of the query or response. Although the process for private searching is conceptually similar to a general search, the structures for the query and results differ. There is an encrypted filter, an output buffer, and computational facets to describe.

If we define Paillier's encryption routine as $E : \mathbb{Z}_N \to \mathbb{Z}_{N^2}$ and the decryption routine as $D : \mathbb{Z}_{N^2} \to \mathbb{Z}_N$, relative to a public and private key, then the homomorphic property can be expressed as: $D(E(x) \times E(y)) = x + y$, for plaintext messages x and y. Notice that $\prod_k E(x) = E(kx)$, and clearly, $E(x)^k = E(kx)$ for some constant value $k \in \mathbb{Z}_N$.

The ciphertext from the Paillier cryptosystem is randomized. An encrypted value is indistinguishable from another, even for the same encrypted value using the same public key. An encryption of $E(1)$ is indistinguishable from another value of $E(1)$.

The Query: In Ostrovsky's system, the client creates a query by selecting a public dictionary of words $D = \{w_1, w_2, w_3, \ldots\}$ and a set of private keywords $K \subseteq D$. The client then constructs an encrypted filter $F = \{f_1, f_2, f_3, \ldots, f_{|D|}\}$, where $f_i = E(1)$ for an associated keyword $w_i \in K$. Otherwise, $f_i = E(0)$. This encrypted filter establishes a one-to-one association between words of interest and all other words in a dictionary without exposing the private keywords. The client sends the encrypted filter and dictionary to the information provider.

The Search: The information provider creates an output buffer of tuples $B = \{(E(0), E(0)), (E(0), E(0)), \ldots\}$, and processes a search as follows:

For each document, d that exists in a data source, extract a set of words W from d such that $W \subseteq D$. Compute the encrypted value $s = \prod_{|W|} f_i = E(m)$ where every value of f_i (from F) associates with a corresponding word $w_i \in D$. The value s is the encrypted match value (the client will decrypt this value to recover the number of distinct keywords present in the document $m = |W \cap K|$.) The provider then computes the exponentiation $r = s^d$. The encrypted search result r is either $E(m \times d)$, or $E(0)$ when no keywords occur in the document.

Note that a document d is a numeric representation of a textual document, network packet, database record, file, etc. For long documents, d may be partitioned. Last, a matching document d is *scaled* by the match value m.

The provider then saves the result $\{s, r\}$ to the output buffer. Specifically, the provider selects random buffer positions $B' \subseteq B$, and performs a (pairwise) modular multiplication, $B' = B' \times \{s, r\}$. The new values for B' are then reassigned to their associated positions in B. When no keywords appear in a document $\{s, r\} = \{E(0), E(0)\}$, the plaintext values of the buffer remain unchanged. Otherwise, multiple copies of the encrypted match value and the scaled document value $\{s, r\} = \{E(m), E(m \times d)\}$ are stored in the buffer.

The provider returns the encrypted buffer to the client when done.

The Result: To recover a document, the client decrypts the buffer, performs an integer division, and initiates a document detection routine. Document detection is discussed further in Sect. 3.1.

Intuitively, the selection of a few random buffer positions perpetuates the survival of at least one document copy (Ostrovsky formally presents this idea as the color survival theorem.) However, and at a buffer's capacity, the majority of buffer positions are chosen multiple times eliminating surviving copies. The private search system thus, has a non-zero probability that some documents will not survive. Large buffers may minimize this condition, but this results in storage inefficiencies that are suboptimal.

3   Related Work

Researchers recognized that a collision of multiple documents in a buffer position did not entirely destroy information; a collision only obscures a document. In fact, a collision produces a linear combination of documents. For example, if n documents are stored at a buffer position b_x, then the value of b_x is $\{E(\sum_{i=0}^{n} m_i), E(\sum_{i=0}^{n}(m_i \times d_i))\}$. Research has thus, qualified external structures, additional processes, and leveraged the redundancy of multiple copies to extract documents that were not recoverable in the original approach.

Bethencourt presented an algorithm for document storage that passes (encrypted) knowledge of a matching document's index to the client [4,5]. The client uses this knowledge to solve a system of linear equations. Specifically, the provider constructs a second encrypted output buffer, known as the matching-indices buffer M, and saves the result of a search to buffer positions in M designated by hash values of the document's index.

When decrypted, the client uses the matching-indices buffer as a Bloom filter to validate a document's membership in the output buffer, and to establish a set of linear equations to solve. Bethencourt recognizes that the matching-indices buffer (a Bloom filter) introduces the possibility of a false positive, complicating a solution [4,5]. Finiasz has also remarked on the asymptotic cost of solving a system of linear equations with a large number of terms [6].

Danezis and Diaz introduced a simple iterative method for document recovery that does not incur significant computational cost or the cost of an additional buffer [2]. In this method, the provider and client use a (truncated) hash of incremented document values to generate a list of buffer positions: $positions = \{H(d_i), H(d_i + 1), \ldots, h(d_i + l)\}$, for each document d_i and for l document copies.

Using these l positions, the provider stores a copy of the result $\{s, r\}$ to each buffer position via a modular multiplication. The method replaces Ostrovsky's random selection. The salient point is that the client can reconstruct the same positions, subtract the newly discovered document values from those l. positions, and repeat until no further documents are discovered or the buffer is empty.

There is a final issue: the provider must encode a document such that the client can detect a document's occurrence in the output buffer. This is addressed in the Sect. 4.

3.1   Document Detection by $k/3$ Triples

Ostrovsky defines a probabilistic method that distinguishes a document from a collision of documents in a buffer position [1].

In this method, the provider appends k-bits to each document, partitions these bits into $k/3$ triples, and randomly sets a bit in each triple to 1. The provider then uses this modified document d' in the search $r = s^{d'}$. As before, the provider stores multiple copies of the result $\{s, r\} = \{E(m), E(m \times d')\}$ via modular multiplication to the output buffer.

After decrypting the buffer, the client detects a document if a buffer position has non-zero values, the number of matching keywords and the scaled document value, $(m, m \times d')$ are divisible $m | (m \times d')$, and each $k/3$ triple has a Hamming weight of one. Otherwise, the buffer position stores the sum of 2 or more documents; a collision.

As an example, assume that the provider searches two documents. The first document $d_1 = 576_8$ is tagged with three randomly selected triples: 4_8, 2_8, and 1_8 when $k = 9$. The provider appends these triples to the document: $d'_1 = 576421_8$. If this document (privately) matched two keywords then $s_1 = E(2)$ and $r_1 = E(2)^{d'_1} = E(2 \times 576421_8)$. The search result would be: $\{s_1, r_1\} = \{E(2), E(1375042_8)\}$.

The provider performs a second search on $d_2 = 675_8$, and appends the triples 1_8, 2_8, and 4_8. The modified document is: $d'_2 = 675124_8$. If this document matched five keywords, the result would be: $\{s_2, r_2\} = \{E(5), E(4261644_8)\}$.

To demonstrate a false positive, assume that the provider saves both results to the same buffer position b_0. Recall that modular multiplication in the encrypted domain produces a summation of plaintext values. When the provider multiplies the encrypted results to the buffer, the tuple at b_0 becomes $E(2 + 5)$ and $E(1375042_8 + 4261644_8)$, specifically: $b_0 = \{E(7), E(5656706_8)\}$.

After decryption, the client divides $5656706_8 / 7 = 653212_8$, detects that the three triples, 2_8, 1_8, and 2_8 have a Hamming weight of one, and falsely retrieves a document $d = 653_8$.

We must assure that the occurrence of a false positive in each buffer position is a rare event. Otherwise, when executing Danezis's iterative method for document recovery, the client would compute incorrect buffer positions, subtract an incorrect value from these positions, and induce a non-recoverable error.

4   New Method for Document Detection

In our detection method, the provider calculates a hash of the document, appends k-bits of this hash to the document, and then uses this modified document in the search: $d' = d || (H(d) \& mask)$ where $mask = 2^k - 1$ and $r = s^{d'}$. The provider then saves multiple copies of the result $\{s, r\}$ to the buffer, as before. When the client retrieves a non-zero value from the buffer, the client removes k-bits, calculates a hash, and then compares that result with previously removed bits (the hash calculated by the provider.) If the two hash values match, the client returns the document as a search result. Otherwise, the client knows that the buffer position contains a linear summation (collision) of documents.

This subtle change imputes a dependency between the document and the appended bits used to verify that document. Our method is still probabilistic, and a false positive is still possible. We expect a hash function to provide a uniform distribution; one collision in $1/2^k$ for k appended bits.

5   A Simulation of Document Detection Methods

We present two simulations that measure the number of false positives from sets of collisions. In the first, documents are not scaled by m, the number of matching keywords. This provides a fundamental assessment of the $k/3$ appended triples and our appended hash methods. These results are shown in Tables 1 and 2.

The results of the second simulation are presented in Tables 3 and 4, and reflect the number of false positives in practice. That is, when documents are scaled by m, and the divisibility of the linear combination of documents is addressed.

These tables depict the minimum, mean, and maximum number of false positives. A lower value is better. Simulations were conducted in *Mathematica*.

To assess the number of false positives, we executed ten trials that randomly created 1000 documents with values $0 < d < 2^{64}$, and one to five equally sized sets of colliding-documents. We appended k-bits to all documents such that the documents held either $k/3$ triples or k-bits of an MD5 hash. This produced a set of 1000 collisions for each method. We used the same documents to minimize the variation any document may have on each detection method.

There are three remaining conditions: The size of k, the number of colliding documents, and whether documents are scaled by m. We varied k from 9 to 24 bits, and created collisions with 1 to 5 documents. In the second simulation, the number of matching keywords m was randomly selected from a range, 1 to 10.

To clarify the construction of a collision, consider the summation of three documents where three triples are used: $d'_0 = 11111_8$, $d'_1 = 22121_8$, and $d'_2 = 55212_8$. The resulting collision is $d = \sum_{i=0}^{2} d'_i = 11111_8 + 22121_8 + 55212_8 = 110444_8$. Since two documents are added to the initial, this is a *2 Document Collision*. As this example shows, the three triples 444_8 have a Hamming weight of one. This false positive would contribute to the results presented under the column titled, "2 Document Collision" and along the first row since $k = 9$.

5.1   Comparing Detection Methods

We begin with an assessment of Ostrovsky's original detection method that appends $k/3$ triples and notice the following: a summation of two unit vectors in $\mathbb{Z}_2^3$ results in another unit vector two out of nine times (a false positive.) That is, if we add 1, 2, or 4, there are two such additions that lead to another unit vector: $1+1$ and $2+2$. The probability that a false positive occurs in $k/3$ triples after a single summation is simply $(2/9)^{k/3}$.

Table 1. False positives for a summation of $k/3$ triples per 1000 collisions

$k/3$ appended triples	1 Document collision			2 Document collision			3 Document collision			4 Document collision			5 Document collision		
	Min	$\overline{M}$	Max	Min	$\overline{M}$	Max	Min	$\overline{M}$	Max	Min	$\overline{M}$	Max	Min	$\overline{M}$	Max
9, 3 triples	4	9.4	13	26	32.1	36	61	77.6	93	43	51.5	58	42	51.5	64
12, 4 triples	1	3.1	6	5	9.3	16	18	33.8	40	14	18	23	6	14.7	21
15, 5 triples	0	0.7	3	0	2.2	5	10	17.2	24	2	6.4	10	4	6.7	10
18, 6 triples	0	0.1	1	0	0.8	3	6	8.4	14	0	2	5	0	2.1	4
21, 7 triples	0	0.1	1	0	0.2	1	0	2.4	6	0	0.8	3	0	0.4	1
24, 8 triples	0	0	0	0	0.1	1	0	1.6	3	0	0.1	1	0	0.4	1

Table 2. False positives for a summation of k-Bit hash values per 1000 collisions

k-Bit appended hash	1 Document collision			2 Document collision			3 Document collision			4 Document collision			5 Document collision		
	Min	$\overline{M}$	Max	Min	$\overline{M}$	Max	Min	$\overline{M}$	Max	Min	$\overline{M}$	Max	Min	$\overline{M}$	Max
9	0	.5	2	0	0.2	1	0	0.3	1	0	0	0	0	0.1	1
12	0	0.1	1	0	0.1	1	0	0	0	0	0	0	0	0	0
15	0	0	0	0	0	0	0	0	0	0	0	0	0	0	0
18	0	0	0	0	0	0	0	0	0	0	0	0	0	0	0
21	0	0	0	0	0	0	0	0	0	0	0	0	0	0	0
24	0	0	0	0	0	0	0	0	0	0	0	0	0	0	0

The result of this first summation leads to six possible states: A triple is either 0, 2, 3, 4, 5, or 6. Thereafter, the summation of additional unit vectors produces a result in $\mathbb{Z}_8$, and a cycle is formed. That is, any unit vector in $\mathbb{Z}_2^3$ added to a member of $\mathbb{Z}_8$ produces a result in $\mathbb{Z}_8$. In this cycle, there are 9 summations out of the 24 possible summations of unit vectors that lead to a false positive. The probability of a false positive thus, increases to $(9/24)^{k/3} = (3/8)^{k/3}$, and as the number of summations in a collision increases.

We observed this effect in our simulation. Table 1 shows that the number of false positives increases after a collision of two or more documents: when $k = 9$, every triple had one bit set, at a minimum, 4, 26, 61, 43, and then 42 times out of a thousand collisions for 1 to 5 summations of documents respectively.

We present this effect, because the number of false positives for *scaled* $k/3$ triples actually decreased as the number of summations increases. See Table 3. This may confuse implementers, leading to an incorrect conclusion about these detection methods in practice. We discuss why this occurs next.

5.2 Detection Methods in Practice

Recall that the provider saves a result $\{s, r\}$ to a buffer position where s is the encrypted number of matching keywords, and r is the scaled value of the document, namely $s = E(m)$ and $r = s^{d'} = E(m \times d')$. When a document matches more than one keyword, the document and appended bits are scaled

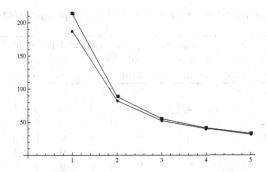

Fig. 1. Number of divisible results vs. Number of summations in a collision

by m. After decryption, the client can only initiate detection if the number of keywords is a divisor of the document $m|(m \times d')$.

We now consider the number of divisors that occur as a result of a collision of scaled documents. In this instance, we are looking for a sum of matching keywords that divides the linear combination of scaled document values: $\sum_{i=0}^{n} m_i | \sum_{i=0}^{n} (m_i \times d_i')$.

Figure 1 presents the average number of divisors found in a set of 1000 collisions and for 1 to 5 document collisions. The line with the square and circular plot-marks represent the number of divisors when the document is appended with triples and a k-bit hash respectively. Both lines exhibit the same rate of decay, regardless of the appended detection method. More importantly, the number of collisions (samples) used in our simulations decreases significantly as the number of summations in a collision increases.

This means that both detection methods consider fewer candidate collisions as the number of summations increases. For instance, Fig. 1 shows that when a single document is added to our initial set of 1000 documents, these summed and scaled documents ($m_0 d_0' + m_1 d_1'$) are divided by the sum of their matching keyword values ($m_0 + m_1$) approximately 200 times. After four summations, our experiments considered only 50 collisions.

Tables 3 and 4 present the results of the the detection methods in practice. For $k/3$ triples, we observe that when $k = 9$, every triple had one bit set, at a minimum, 14, 3, 2, 0, and 0 times out of a thousand collisions and for 1 to 5 summations (Table 3.) This number of false positives is significantly less than that observed in Table 1. We emphasize then that the reduction in false positives for the summation of scaled $k/3$ triples is a result of the reduced dataset size, and not as a result of the detection method itself.

When comparing Tables 3 and 4, our appended hash method produces fewer false positives overall. We observe that no false positives occurred when 18 bits were appended. We emphasize that our method is still probabilistic and that no singular value for k will suffice. If the output buffer is expected to store several thousand documents, the size for k must be commensurate with that buffer size.

Table 3. False positives for sums of scaled $k/3$ triples per 1000 collisions

$k/3$ appended triples	1 Document collision			2 Document collision			3 Document collision			4 Document collision			5 Document collision		
	Min	$\overline{M}$	Max	Min	$\overline{M}$	Max	Min	$\overline{M}$	Max	Min	$\overline{M}$	Max	Min	$\overline{M}$	Max
9, 3 triples	14	19.6	28	3	5.5	8	2	4.7	6	0	1.8	4	0	1.3	3
12, 4 triples	5	9.1	14	1	2.6	7	0	1.3	4	0	0.2	1	0	0.3	2
15, 5 triples	3	4.2	7	0	0.6	2	0	0.5	1	0	0.4	0	0	0.2	1
18, 6 triples	0	1.9	6	0	0.1	1	0	0.3	1	0	0	0	0	0	0
21, 7 triples	0	0.5	2	0	0.2	1	0	0	0	0	0.2	1	0	0.1	1
24, 8 triples	0	0.9	3	0	0	0	0	0	0	0	0	0	0	0	0

Table 4. False positives for sums of scaled k-Bit hash values per 1000 collisions

k-Bit appended hash	1 Document collision			2 Document collision			3 Document collision			4 Document collision			5 Document collision		
	Min	$\overline{M}$	Max	Min	$\overline{M}$	Max	Min	$\overline{M}$	Max	Min	$\overline{M}$	Max	Min	$\overline{M}$	Max
9	0	1.7	4	1	1.4	3	0	1.2	2	0	1.4	4	1	2	3
12	0	0.3	2	0	0.1	1	0	0.4	2	0	0.4	1	0	0.4	2
15	0	0.1	1	0	0.1	1	0	0	0	0	0.1	1	0	0	0
18	0	0	0	0	0	0	0	0	0	0	0	0	0	0	0
21	0	0	0	0	0	0	0	0	0	0	0	0	0	0	0
24	0	0	0	0	0	0	0	0	0	0	0	0	0	0	0

However, selecting greater values of k will deduct from the possible number of bits used to store a document (or partitions of a document.) If the modulus of the public key is 1024-bits, the implementer deducts k-bits of document storage per position in the output buffer. Selection of k will be application dependent.

6   Closing Remarks

This research was motivated by seemingly spurious and non-recoverable errors. We implemented Ostrovsky's private search, integrated Danezis's iterative document recovery, and created a private packet filtering system [7]. During testing, our prototype occasionally produced extraneous *documents*. False positives do occur. Our immediate recourse added additional triples. However, this reduced the size of the document stored in a buffer position. We sought an alternative.

Integration of our appended hash method was seamless, produced an immediate improvement, and the analysis presented validates this observation. Implementers should incorporate our appended hash method for document detection, and benefit from our shared experience.

References

1. Ostrovsky, R., Skeith III, W.E.: Private searching on streaming data. In: Shoup, V. (ed.) CRYPTO 2005. LNCS, vol. 3621, pp. 223–240. Springer, Heidelberg (2005)
2. Danezis, G., Diaz, C.: Space-efficient private search with applications to rateless codes. In: Dietrich, S., Dhamija, R. (eds.) FC 2007 and USEC 2007. LNCS, vol. 4886, pp. 148–162. Springer, Heidelberg (2007)
3. Paillier, P.: Public-key cryptosystems based on composite degree residuosity classes. In: Stern, J. (ed.) EUROCRYPT 1999. LNCS, vol. 1592, pp. 223–238. Springer, Heidelberg (1999)
4. Bethencourt, J., Song, D., Waters, B.: New construction and practical applications for private stream searching. In: Security and Privacy (SP'06), pp. 132–139 (2006)
5. Bethencourt, J., Song, D., Waters, B.: New techniques for private stream searching. ACM Trans. Inf. Syst. Secur. (TISSEC) **12**(3), 1–32 (2009)
6. Finiasz, M., ramchandran, K.: Private stream search at the same communication cost as a regular search: role of LDPC codes. In: ISIT'12, pp. 2566–2570 (2012)
7. Oehler, M., Phatak, D.: A private packet filtering language for cyber defense. In: Annual Symposium on Information Assurance (ASIA'13), pp. 46–55 (2013)

Dynamic Anonymous Index
for Confidential Data

Guillermo Navarro-Arribas[1]($\boxtimes$), Daniel Abril[2], and Vicenç Torra[2]

[1] Department Enginyeria de la Informació i de les Comunicacions (DEIC),
Universitat Autònoma de Barcelona (UAB), Campus de la UAB,
08193 Bellaterra, Catalonia, Spain
gnavarro@deic.uab.cat

[2] Institut d'Investigació en Intel.ligència Artificial (IIIA), Consejo Superior de
Investigaciones Científicas (CSIC), Campus de la UAB,
08193 Bellaterra, Catalonia, Spain

Abstract. In this paper we introduce a k-anonymous vector space model,
which can be used as an index of a set of confidential documents. This
model allows to index, for example, encrypted data. New documents can
be added or removed while maintaining the k-anonymity property of the
vector space.

1 Introduction

We tackle the problem of storing confidential documents in a cloud computing
scenario, where the server storing the documents is not the owner of the documents. In such cases, users might like to protect their documents by, for example,
encrypting them. This will ensure that the document remains confidential in the
server. It is not only protected from other users, but also ensures that any intrusion performed in the systems or security breach will not lead to the disclosure
of the contents of the document.

At the same time, in some scenarios it will be desirable to provide some form
of index or metadata about the stored documents. The metadata could be used
to perform queries on a given set of documents, but also for other information
retrieval tasks. Ideally these metadata should preserve to some extent the privacy
provided by encrypting the documents.

Instead of relying on a strictly cryptographic solution, in this paper we
explore a novel approach inspired by the application of SDC (*Statistical Disclosure Control*) and PPDM (*Privacy Preserving Data Mining*) techniques to
information retrieval. Our approach is to provide public metadata about the
encrypted documents. The metadata must ensure that a minimum degree of
privacy and anonymity is provided about the documents while presenting some
useful information about them. We have chosen to represent these metadata as a
document vector space model (VSM) [8], which is normally used in information
retrieval systems. In a vector space model, it is common to represent a document
as a vector of terms with an associated frequency-based weight.

J. Garcia-Alfaro et al. (Eds.): DPM 2013 and SETOP 2013, LNCS 8247, pp. 362–368, 2014.
DOI: 10.1007/978-3-642-54568-9_23, © Springer-Verlag Berlin Heidelberg 2014

In Sect. 2 we introduce the motivating scenario. Section 3 introduces the k-anonymous VSM, and its protection is described in Sect. 4. Finally, Sect. 5 provides some evaluation results and Sect. 6 concludes the paper.

2   Scenario Description

We contextualize our proposal in a typical cloud computing system or more precisely as a cloud storage service. We consider a repository of documents, where each document belongs to a different user. Examples could be a repository of electronic patient health record, papers submitted to a conference, or a repository of research project proposals.

We do not deal here with the concrete protocols and processes to implement the interaction with the user. Intuitively, the user submits an encrypted document together with the document vector representing the document. The user (or client software) is free to apply any desired pre-anonymization to the document vector. Then the server adds the document vector to the VSM. This process requires, as we will see, the anonymization of such vector. The user can, on request, delete his document from the server, and its corresponding document vector is deleted from the VSM.

It is important to note that we consider the server as trusted. That is, the users trust it to correctly perform the anonymization process. Once a document vector is anonymized to be included in the VSM, it is deleted by the server. The fact that the server does not keep the original vectors ensures an additional level of security in case of an intrusion.

The main objective of our proposal is to anonymize the VSM. Compared to typical datasets used in SDC and PPDM, the VSM as presented in this work can be considered a *dynamic* dataset. We consider that there can be discretionary insertions and deletions of documents in the server, which has the implications that document vectors can be added to or removed from the VSM. There are some proposals dealing with stream data [2,4–7,9,17], which only contemplate insertions in the dataset. Moreover streaming data assumes that new records will be inserted in a timely basis, allowing the buffering of new records to be inserted. The concrete case of dynamic data has scarcely been treated in [15,16]. We depart from these works to introduce the dynamic anonymization using microaggregation, and it application to VSM.

3 k-Anonymous VSM

In order to maintain the document based anonymity of the VSM, we introduce the idea of k-anonymous VSM as analogous to classical k-anonymity with respect to quasi-identifiers in SDC [12,14]. We will introduce the k-anonymous VSM together with some notation. Given a set of documents D we denote as $\boldsymbol{V}(d_i)$ the vector for document d_i, such that $\boldsymbol{V}(d_i) = (w_{1,i}, \ldots, w_{M,i})$, where $w_{j,i}$ is the weight associated to term j in document i. The set of document vectors $\mathcal{D} = \{\boldsymbol{V}(d_1), \ldots, \boldsymbol{V}(d_n)\}$ forms the *vector space model (VSM)*. The weight is normally taken to be a frequency based metric associated with the term [8].

Definition 1. *A VSM* $\mathcal{D}$ *is a k-anonymous VSM if and only if for every document vector* $\boldsymbol{V}(d_i)$ *in* $\mathcal{D}$ *there exists at least* $(k-1)$ *other document vectors in* $\mathcal{D}$ *that are indistinguishable from* $\boldsymbol{V}(d_i)$.

In this paper we deal with dynamic data, and its protection if it is not done properly can lead to inference.

3.1   Inference on Multiple Anonymizations of Dynamic Data

Several works show inference attacks on data with multiple anonymizations, including streaming data, in terms of l-diversity [2,16]. We do not deal with confidential attributes, so l-diversity does not apply.

Even so, our VSM data can be vulnerable to inference through intersection of equivalence classes. This is a common problem in clustering based anonymization when multiple anonymizations of the same data are released [9,13]. An attacker can reduce the cardinality for some given quasi-identifier values by intersecting different equivalence classes that contain some common records, thus, breaking k-anonymity.

In [13] the authors show that intersection can easily happen in the context of generalization. The same can be applied to microaggregation. Consider for instance the generic example from Table 1. For simplicity we will consider a single numeric attribute in the dataset (age). Note also that the record identifier r_i is given only as a reference to help understand the example, the actual anonymized dataset (VSM in this case) has only quasi-identifiers, and no other identifiers is given.

We have an original dataset T with two different 2-anonymous microaggregated versions T_1, and T_2. An attacker with knowledge of both tables, and knowledge of the aggregation applied (in this case the arithmetic mean) can easily infer information about the record r_3. Given the aggregation operator $\mathbb{C}$, if $\mathbb{C}(r_1, r_2, r_3) = 15$ in T_1 and $\mathbb{C}(r_1, r_2) = 12$ in T_2, it yields $r_3 = 21$. Depending on the aggregation operator in use, it might not be so easy to infer the value of r_3 and maybe the attacker can only give an estimation or approximate value.

This same problem can arise in the case of dynamic data, so the operations to insert and remove elements should take it into account.

Table 1. Example of intersection in microaggregated tables.

Record	Age	Record	Age	Record	Age
r_1	12	r_1	15	r_1	12
r_2	12	r_2	15	r_2	12
r_3	21	r_3	15	r_3	27
r_4	30	r_4	30	r_4	27
r_5	30	r_5	30	r_5	27

(a)   Original table T (b)   Microag-gregated table T_1 (c)   Microag-gregated table T_2

4 Dynamic Microaggregation of VSM

We introduce our anonymization process by defining the insertion and deletion operations on the VSM. The data are statically anonymized (see [1]), and then records can be added or removed. The static anonymization through microaggregation can be described as a two step process:

- *Partition*: Define a partition P on the original data $\mathcal{D}$, where each cluster has at least k elements. This partition tries to ensure a minimum information loss.
- *Aggregation*: For each cluster $c_i \in P$, substitute each element in the cluster by its cluster representative or centroid. Usually, an aggregation operator $\mathbb{C}$ is used to compute the centroid $\hat{c}_i = \mathbb{C}(\{V(d_j) \mid V(d_j) \in c_i\})$.

We will use following cosine distance function between document vectors:

$$d(V(d_1), V(d_2)) = 1 - \frac{V(d_1) \cdot V(d_2)}{|V(d_1)||V(d_2)|} \tag{1}$$

where $\cdot$ is the dot product of the vectors. For the aggregation of the microaggregation step we use a component-wise mean to aggregate vectors:

$$\mathbb{C}(\{V(d_1), \ldots V(d_n)\}) = \frac{1}{n}(\sum_{i=1}^{n} w_{i,1}, \ldots, \sum_{i=1}^{n} w_{i,M}) \tag{2}$$

Depending on the concrete application other distances and aggregation operators could be used.

4.1 Simple Document Vector Insertion

Given a k-anonymous VSM $\mathcal{D}' = \{V'(d_1), \ldots, V'(d_n)\}$, which forms a partition $P(\mathcal{D}') = \{c_1, \ldots, c_v\}$, we want to insert a new document vector $V(d_*)$. $\hat{c}_i$ denotes the centroid of the cluster c_i. In order to do so we follow the procedure:

1. Find the cluster $c_i \in P(\mathcal{D}')$ such that $d(V(d_*), \hat{c}_i) \leq d(V(d_*), \hat{c}_j)$ for all $c_j \in P(\mathcal{D}')$.
2. Add the new vector $V(d_*)$ to the cluster c_i by applying the perturbation $V'(d_*) = \hat{c}_i$ to the new vector.

The second step is important in order to prevent inference by intersection. Computing a new centroid for the cluster will reduce the information loss but will also lead to inference attacks as the one described in Sect. 3.1.

4.2 Simple Document Vector Deletion

Given a k-anonymous VSM $\mathcal{D}' = \{V'(d_1), \ldots, V'(d_n)\}$, which forms a partition $P(\mathcal{D}') = \{c_1, \ldots, c_v\}$, we want to remove a document vector $V'(d_*) \in \mathcal{D}'$. The deletion has the following steps:

Table 2. Example of deletion.

Record	Age
r_1	10
r_2	10
r_3	21
r_4	21
r_5	30
r_6	30

(a) T_1

Record	Age
r_1	10
r_2	10
r_3	21
r_4	21
r_5	21

(b) T_2

1. Identify the cluster c_i such that $\mathbf{V}'(d_*) \in c_i$, and delete the vector from the cluster.
2. If $|c_i| < k$ find another cluster c_j such that $d(\hat{c}_i, \hat{c}_j) \leq d(\hat{c}_i, \hat{c}_l)$ for all $c_l \in \mathcal{D}'$ and $l \neq i \neq j$.
3. Add the vectors of the cluster c_i to the cluster c_j. To do so all vectors $\mathbf{V}'(d_i) \in c_i$ are perturbed as $\mathbf{V}'(d_i) = \hat{c}_j$.

Steps 2 and 3 are equivalent to the insertion of elements, no new centroid is re-computed to avoid inference. There is however an important point to consider with respect to inference and deletion.

For example, Table 2 shows the deletion of the record r_6 from the 2-anonymous table T_1 resulting into table T_2. An attacker knowing both tables T_1 and T_2 will know that one of the records with value 30 has been deleted and the other has been merged into the cluster of records with value 25. No record can be identified or distinguished from the rest with probability higher than $1/k$. This is true if the user has no other knowledge from the records other than the quasi-identifiers.

5   Evaluation

To provide an initial evaluation of the perturbation introduced by our proposal we rely mainly in observing the within cluster homogeneity (SSE). Given a protected VSM $\mathcal{D}' = \{\mathbf{V}'(d_1), \dots, \mathbf{V}'(d_n)\}$, with a partition into clusters $P(\mathcal{D}') = \{c_1, \dots, c_v\}$, and its respective original VSM $\mathcal{D} = \{\mathbf{V}(d_1), \dots, \mathbf{V}(d_n)\}$, where $\mathbf{V}'(d_i)$ is the protected version of the vector $\mathbf{V}(d_i)$, we can compute an SSE as:

$$SSE(\mathcal{D}') = \sum_{c_i \in P(\mathcal{D}')} \sum_{\mathbf{V}(d_j) \in c_i} d^2(\mathbf{V}(d_j), \hat{c}_i)$$

where d is the cosine distance. In order to compare sets of documents with different size, we will divide the SSE by the number of documents in the set to give a normalized SSE with respect to the number of documents.

We selected 1000 random documents from the R8 subset of the Reuters-21578 dataset [11], containing a collection of classified Reuters news. Stop-words are removed from the document as well as terms with two or less letters. Once the

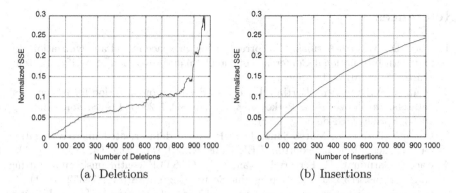

Fig. 1. Normalized SSE for deletions and insertions on the 5-anonymous dataset.

documents are cleaned we apply the Porter stemming algorithm [10], which considers all words with the same stem as the same word, producing a reduction in the size of the feature set.

From the initial set of documents we start by generating a 5-anonymous version of the set applying the MDAV algorithm [3]. With this set we first apply consecutive deletion of random elements and then, starting again from the protected 1000 set, we insert new documents. Figure 1 shows the evolution of the normalized SSE as elements are deleted or inserted from the 5-anonymous version of the dataset.

Note that the values are very low because SSE is divided by the number of elements in each case. The values of SSE for greatest number of insertions and deletions give an idea of the SSE value for maximum perturbation. So if we consider a maximum value of 0.3, then values of 0.1 and 0.05 represent approximately and respectively the 33 % and 17 %.

6   Conclusions

We have introduced the anonymization of a dynamic vector space model based on microaggregation. The vector space model can be used as the metadata of encrypted documents in a typical cloud storage service. The VSM is ensured to be k-anonymous with respect to the documents, and this property is maintained while documents can be inserted and deleted from the set. We have presented here an initial work which can be further developed. We plan to explore the application of other data privacy techniques and the improvement on reducing the information loss during insertions and deletions.

Acknowledgments. This Work is partially funded by projects TSI2007-65406-C03-02, ARES-CONSOLIDER INGENIO 2010 CSD2007-00004, TIN2010-15764, and TIN2011-27076-C03-03 of the Spanish Government, and by project FP7/2007-2013 (Data without Boundaries). work contributed by one of the authors was carried out as part of the Computer Science Ph.D. program of the Universitat Autònoma de Barcelona (UAB).

References

1. Abril, D., Navarro-Arribas, G., Torra, V.: Vector space model anonymization. In: Sixteenth International Conference of the Catalan Association of Artificial Intelligence (CCIA 2013) (to appear)
2. Byun, J.-W., Sohn, Y., Bertino, E., Li, N.: Secure anonymization for incremental datasets. In: Jonker, W., Petković, M. (eds.) SDM 2006. LNCS, vol. 4165, pp. 48–63. Springer, Heidelberg (2006)
3. Domingo-Ferrer, J., Mateo-Sanz, J.M.: Practical data-oriented microaggregation for statistical disclosure control. IEEE Trans. Knowl. Data Eng. 14, 189–201 (2002)
4. Cao, J., Carminati, B., Ferrari, E., Tan, K.-L.: CASTLE: continuously anonymizing data streams. IEEE Trans. Dependable Secure Comput. 8(3), 337–352 (2011)
5. De Capitani di Vimercati, S., Foresti, S., Livraga, G.: Privacy in data publishing. In: Garcia-Alfaro, J., Navarro-Arribas, G., Cavalli, A., Leneutre, J. (eds.) DPM 2010 and SETOP 2010. LNCS, vol. 6514, pp. 8–21. Springer, Heidelberg (2011)
6. Iwuchukwu, T., Naughton, J.F.: K-anonymization as spatial indexing: toward scalable and incremental anonymization. In: Proceedings of the 33rd International Conference on Very Large Data Bases, Vienna, Austria, pp. 746–757 (2007)
7. Li, J., Ooi, B.C., Wang, W.: Anonymizing streaming data for privacy protection. In: IEEE 24th International Conference on Data Engineering, ICDE 2008, pp. 1367–1369 (2008)
8. Manning, C.D., Raghavan, P., Schütze, H.: An Introduction to Information Retrieval. Cambridge University Press, Cambridge (2009)
9. Pei, J., Xu, J., Wang, Z., Wang, W., Wang, K.: Maintaining K-anonymity against incremental updates. In: 19th International Conference on Scientific and Statistical Database Management, SSBDM 2007 (2007)
10. Porter, M.F.: An algorithm for suffix stripping. Program 14(3), 130–137 (1980)
11. Reuters Ltd., Reuters-21578, Distribution 1.0 (2004). http://www.daviddlewis. com/resources/testcollections/reuters21578
12. Samarati, P.: Protecting respondents identities in microdata release. IEEE Trans. Knowl. Data Eng. 13(6), 1010–1027 (2001)
13. Stokes, K., Torra, V.: Multiple releases of k-anonymous data sets and k-anonymous relational databases. Int. J. Uncertain. Fuzziness Knowl.-Based Syst. 20(06), 839–853 (2012)
14. Sweeney, L.: k-anonymity: a model for protecting privacy. Int. J. Uncertain. Fuzziness Knowl.-Based Syst. 10(5), 557–570 (2002)
15. Truta, T.M., Campan, A.: K-anonymization incremental maintenance and optimization techniques. In: Proceedings of the ACM Symposium on Applied Computing, pp. 380–387 (2007)
16. Xiao, X., Tao, Y.: M-invariance: towards privacy preserving re-publication of dynamic datasets. In: Proceedings of the ACM SIGMOD International Conference on Management of Data, pp. 689–700 (2007)
17. Zakerzadeh, H., Osborn, S.L.: FAANST: fast anonymizing algorithm for numerical streaming DaTa. In: Garcia-Alfaro, J., Navarro-Arribas, G., Cavalli, A., Leneutre, J. (eds.) DPM 2010 and SETOP 2010. LNCS, vol. 6514, pp. 36–50. Springer, Heidelberg (2011)

Are On-Line Personae Really Unlinkable?

Meilof Veeningen[1]([✉]), Antonio Piepoli[1,2], and Nicola Zannone[1]

[1] Eindhoven University of Technology, Eindhoven, The Netherlands
m.veeningen@tue.nl
[2] Politecnico di Bari, Bari, Italy

Abstract. More and more personal information is available digitally, both collected by organisations and published by individuals. People may attempt to protect their privacy by avoiding to provide uniquely identifying information and by providing different information in different places; however, in many cases, such profiles can still be de-anonymised. Techniques from the record linkage literature can be used for pairwise linking of databases, and for cross-correlation based on these pairwise results. However, the privacy implications of these techniques in the on-line setting are not clear: existing experiments depend on quasi-identifiers and do not focus on cross-correlation. This paper studies the problem of de-anonymisation and, in particular, cross-correlation of multiple databases using only non-identifying information in an on-line setting.

1 Introduction

As more and more personal information is available digitally, privacy risks are becoming a major concern. On the one hand, enterprises and government agencies gather personal information to provide personalized services; on the other hand, individuals share more and more information about themselves using social networking. To protect their privacy, individuals often create multiple digital representations of themselves. They may use different nicknames and provide different identity attributes to different organisations, or even provide different values for the same attribute. We call one such representation of an identity a *persona*. Intuitively, a persona consists of a set of attributes characterizing a particular "view" on the individual. Therefore, knowing a persona of an individual only provides a partial knowledge on that individual.

People's on-line behaviour suggests a belief that using different personae prevents linking and hence protects their privacy; however, in reality, personae can be linked using various techniques [13]. In particular, the pairwise linking problem, i.e., deciding whether or not two given personae are about the same individual, has attracted attention ever since the seminal paper of Fellegi and Sunter [12]; see [16] for a recent survey. Multiple personae can be grouped together based on pairwise decisions using domain-dependent [3,21,24,28] or domain-independent [4,7] algorithms. Recently, also promising results have been reached using more fundamental statistical techniques [27].

J. Garcia-Alfaro et al. (Eds.): DPM 2013 and SETOP 2013, LNCS 8247, pp. 369–379, 2014.
DOI: 10.1007/978-3-642-54568-9_24, © Springer-Verlag Berlin Heidelberg 2014

On the other hand, the privacy community has focused on preventing such linking. As a first step, identifying information should not be not shared, or only shared using communication protocols that employ appropriate cryptographic primitives [29]; the fact that links remain hidden can then be shown using formal techniques (e.g., [5,10,30]). However, as argued above, also non-identifying information can cause privacy leakage: this can be assessed using statistical frameworks like differential privacy [11], k-anonymity [9], ℓ-diversity [18], t-closeness [17] and (ρ, α)-anonymisation [2].

Recent works study the privacy implications of techniques for linking in the on-line social networking setting [14,22,23]. One particular example is the dataset used by Netflix to improve its recommendation system: although the dataset was anonymised, it has been de-anonymised using a statistical approach [22]. More general works try to recover on-line identities from people search engines [14] or social networking sites [23]. However, these works essentially rely on quasi-identifiers (rare movies in [22]; names in [14,23]), and do not consider clustering of information of several sources into one user profile. Koot [15] experimentally assesses privacy leakage by estimating how many people share a given set of attributes; however, this does not directly give insight into what links can actually be recovered when such a set of attributes is available.

In this paper, we investigate to what extent multiple personae of an individual can be linked together using limited information. In particular, we show how to reconstruct an individual's identity from personae at different service providers (e.g., social networks) that do not share any identifiable information (e.g., email address). We apply existing pairwise linking techniques, and use their output to cluster different personae using graph-based techniques. To obtain insight into the difficulty of the linking problem, and to study the robustness of our approach, we perform a number of experiments.

2   An Illustrative Case Study

To illustrate the privacy implications of sharing personal information on-line, we consider a scenario consisting of four service providers, namely a music community site, a movie community site, and two social networks that resemble Last.fm, IMDb, Facebook and LinkedIn, respectively. Each service provider stores certain information about the user (see Fig. 1): e.g., Last.fm stores users' nickname, country, gender, and favourite band; IMDb stores nickname, first name, country of origin, age, and favourite film.

Reconstructing identities from such databases is challenging for several reasons. Clearly, the amount of overlapping attributes between Last.fm and IMDb (i.e., nickname and country) is not sufficient to reliably determine whether personae from Last.fm and IMDb belong to the same individuals; similarly for other providers. In addition, users can provide different values for the same attribute: e.g., a user may specify a favourite movie on Facebook and another on IMDb, or use different nicknames at different providers. Also, the information in the databases may contains typos, which makes it difficult to correlate entries stored in

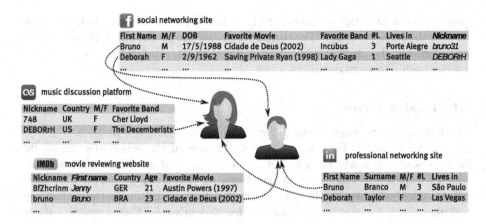

Fig. 1. User personae stored at different service providers. M/F denotes gender; #L denotes number of languages spoken. Italic attributes do not occur in the low-quality scenario.

different databases. Finally, the number of personae that each user has is not known a priori: in our cases, a user can have accounts at any combination of one, two, three, or four of the above service providers.

Given these challenges, one may think that the availability of different personae with partially overlapping attributes does not pose a privacy threat. In this paper, we analyse if this is true by performing experiments to cross correlate non-identifiable information.

3 Approach

To evaluate the feasibility of building profiles of individuals by linking different personae, we present a general approach based on well-known techniques from the literature. We assume that the personae are stored in a number of databases at different service providers. Databases have different, but not mutually disjoint, sets of attributes.

The approach consists of two separate phases (Fig. 2): the *linking phase* and the *clustering phase*. The objective of the linking phase is to determine the *profile*

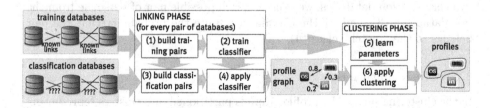

Fig. 2. Our approach for building individuals' identities by linking their personae.

graph for a set of personae, assessing the pairwise probability that two personae refer to the same person. In the clustering phase, the profile graph is partitioned into identities (i.e., sets of personae belonging to the same individual). We now discuss both phases in detail.

3.1   Linking Phase

The linking phases assesses the pairwise probability that two personae refer to the same individual. For this, we use the values of the attributes shared by both personae. Because the number and type of attributes shared depends on which database the two personae are stored in, this phase is executed for each pair of databases separately. We adapt standard probabilistic record linkage techniques [12] for the linking phase. The idea of probabilistic record linkage is to compare the values of all overlapping attributes of a record pair: similar values increase the link probability, different values decrease it. From now on, we assume two databases with a non-empty set of overlapping attributes.

Pairwise similarity between attribute values is determined using "similarity scores" between 0 and 1. For instance, the similarity score of surnames "Smith" and "Snith" should be close to 1, but the similarity score of surnames "Smith" and "Jones" should be close to 0. The similarity score should be chosen depending on the type of attribute, e.g., exact match for attributes with finitely many values (i.e., score 1 if two attribute values match, and 0 otherwise), or Jaro-Winkler distance [31] for textual attributes.

Given these similarity scores, probabilistic record linkage can be seen as a classification problem from machine learning. *Classification* is the task to determine, given a training set of observations and the class they belong to, a decision procedure that assigns classes to new observations. An algorithm that solves the classification problem is called a *classifier*. Typically, it first performs a "training stage" in which it determines internal parameters based on the training set; and then a "classifier stage" in which it uses the obtained parameters to classify new observations. In our case, observations are the similarity scores for record pairs; the classes are "match" and "non-match".

Thus, we determine the pairwise linking probabilities using a classifier as follows (steps (**1**)–(**4**) in Fig. 2). First, given two training databases and their known links, we generate a representative number of pairs of records and compute their similarity scores (**1**). We then run the training stage of the classifier (**2**). (This can be done once independently from the classification databases.) Given two classification databases, we generate each possible pair of personae from the two databases (**3**), and let the classifier compute the probability that the pair belongs to the "match" class (**4**).

3.2   Clustering Phase

In the clustering phase, the profile graph is partitioned into clusters representing profiles of personae about the same individual. We use two different clustering algorithms. In general, these algorithms consist of two steps (steps (**5**)–(**6**) in

Fig. 2): a *training step* (**5**) in which parameters are learned from the training databases, and a *clustering step* (**6**) in which the profile graphs corresponding to classification databases are clustered.

Our first clustering algorithm is *threshold transitive closure*, a very simple algorithm against which the performance of other clustering methods can be measured. The algorithm is parametric in *threshold* p_{tct}. Given a profile graph, the clustering step is as follows: (i) construct the undirected, unweighted graph G containing all nodes of the profile graph, and all edges with weight $\geq p_{tct}$; (ii) return as identity the set of personae corresponding to each connected component of G.

Our second clustering algorithm is *community detection*, an algorithm that recursively applies community detection to cluster personae into profiles. Many graphs that model real-life phenomena (e.g., friends on social networks, citations in academia) have a "community structure" in that they contain clusters that have "dense" connections (i.e., with high-weight edges) between nodes inside the cluster, and "sparse" connections between nodes from different clusters. Community detection algorithms aim to find such clusters. In particular, we use the Louvain method [6], a heuristic algorithm aiming to optimize the modularity score, a popular metric for community structure.

In practice, it turns out that just using the Louvain method to cluster the profile graph does not work very well: the communities it finds are too large, leading to poor results. Therefore, we consider a recursive variant that repeatedly runs the Louvain method until it provides a stable result. More precisely, we apply the Louvain method to the complete profile graph. We then recursively apply the Louvain method to any subgraphs that it produces, until running Louvain no longer changes the graph; the clusters found in this way are returned as identities. As we show later, this algorithm does produce reasonable results. For this algorithm, no parameters need to be learned in the training phase.

4   Experiments

In this section, we present experimental results obtained using our approach. We first describe our experimental set-up and evaluation framework (Sect. 4.1); then discuss our main findings (Sect. 4.2). Implementation details, data sets, and source code are available [25].

4.1   Evaluation Framework

The aim of our experiments is two-fold: we both evaluate the difficulty of building profiles based on non-identifiable information, and compare the performance of approaches in various circumstances. In the remainder of this section, we present the metrics used to evaluate our experimental results and the analysed scenarios.

To compare different approaches, we apply the standard statistical metrics of *precision*, *recall*, and *f-measure* [19] on pairwise links. Precision specifies what proportion of found links are real; recall specifies what proportion of real links are found; f-measure (the harmonic mean of precision and recall) measures overall performance. These metrics also work for pairwise linking methods that do not return clusters. We compare the values of the metrics after the linking phase to the values after the clustering phase.

To assess the difficulty of building user profiles, we use the *entity distribution* (ED) and *entity composition* (EC) measures proposed in [20]. These metrics give more insight into how many identities can be recovered than the standard comparison metrics presented above. The ED value for an actual identity is the number of clusters that contain a persona belonging to the identity; we provide a histogram of ED values of all identities. The EC value for a cluster is the number of different identities that the personae in the cluster belong to; we provide a histogram of EC values of all clusters.

To assess how different circumstances influence the ability to link data and the performance of different methods, we perform several experiments. We consider generated datasets corresponding to four databases, shown in Fig. 1, in three different scenarios:

- In the **baseline** scenario, we consider 500 different identities, and a realistic amount of overlap between attributes from the four databases (all attributes in Fig. 1);
- In the **large** scenario, we consider 1000 different identities to see how the number of identities influences performance, while keeping the amount of overlap the same;
- In the **low-overlap** scenario, we consider 500 identities, but reduce the overlap between partial identities by using only the non-italic attributes in Fig. 1.

In each scenario, we vary the amount of personae per identity: in the **dense** variant there are on average three partial identities per identity; in the **sparse** variant, there are two. Furthermore, in the **non-perturbed** variant we assume that data are not affected by perturbations; in the **perturbed** variant we allow both spelling mistakes and altogether different attribute values. We get twelve experiments in total; we repeat each 10 times.

4.2   Results

Building User Profiles. The ED and EC metrics capture to what extent the profiles of individuals have been recovered. Figure 3 reports average ED and EC for 10 runs of each experiment. The x-axis shows the number of actual identities in a profile (for EC) or profiles for an identity (for ED). The y-axis shows the relative frequencies with which the values occurred. Note that ED and EC represent a trade-off: the more identities we want to fully recover (hence low ED values), the more easily wrong personae will also be linked together (hence high EC values). When the two different clustering methods give a different kind of trade-off, we discuss both possibilities.

The results suggest that it is possible to recover identities with a fair amount of accuracy. In the baseline scenario, almost 90 % of identities can be fully recovered (i.e., ED = 1), with an accuracy (i.e., proportion of profiles that have EC = 1)

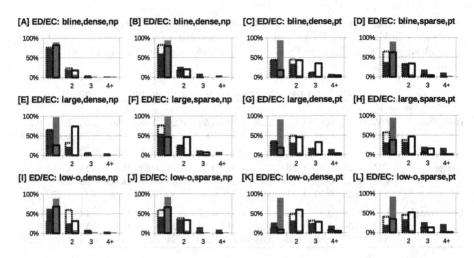

Fig. 3. ED/EC results of our experiments. Left bars show community detection: blue bar is ED, dashed bar is EC. Right bars show threshold transitive closure: orange bar is ED, solid bar is EC. Abbreviations: bline = baseline, low-o = low-overlap, np = non-perturbed, p = perturbed.

of over 80 % (graph [A]). At the same time, the results clearly show that both introducing perturbation and reducing the amount of overlapping attributes make linking more difficult. This is to be expected as both reduce the amount of information available for linking. When perturbations are introduced, the number of fully recovered profiles decreases to 45 % (at 44 % accuracy; graph [C]). When the amount of overlapping attributes is reduced, still 88 % of profiles can be recovered, but accuracy drops to 69 % (graph [I]). The effect of decreasing density is mixed: while community detection generally gives decreased recovery at similar accuracy (hence more difficulty in linking), threshold transitive closure in many cases gives higher accuracy at similar recovery (hence less difficulty in linking); we discuss this later when comparing the two methods.

The worst results are found for the perturbed low-overlap case; interestingly, they occur in the dense variant. Although denseness should make linking easier, it also means that profiles are larger and thus harder to reconstruct. Apparently, the second effect outweighs the first: while a 90 % recovery rate is still possible, this gives an accuracy of 35 % in the sparse case (graph [L]), but of only 9 % in the dense case (graph [K]).

When considering a larger dataset for our experiments, i.e., in the large scenario, the percentage of recovered profiles drops from 80 % to 65 % with 65 % accuracy for community detection (and 97 % with 26 % accuracy for threshold transitive closure; graph [E]). This is probably due to the fact that the more personae there are, the more personae of different identities may inadvertently share similar attribute values.

Finally, even when profiles cannot be fully recovered, partial recovery of profiles is almost always possible. Especially in the baseline and large scenarios,

Table 1. Average precision ("p")/recall ("r")/f-measure ("f") results of our experiments after linking phase ("PW"); community detection ("CD"); and threshold transitive closure ("TC"). Boldfaced f-measures indicates significantly best result(s). "Pt" means perturbation.

		Dense, no pt			Sparse, no pt			Dense, pt			Sparse, pt		
		p	r	f	p	r	f	p	r	f	p	r	f
Baseline	PW	0.37	0.83	0.51	0.38	0.83	0.52	0.24	0.68	0.36	0.25	0.68	0.37
	CD	0.75	0.84	**0.79**	0.50	0.82	0.62	0.48	0.58	**0.52**	0.35	0.60	**0.44**
	TC	0.49	0.91	0.63	0.62	0.83	**0.70**	0.57	0.30	0.39	0.28	0.60	0.38
Large	PW	0.23	0.83	0.36	0.24	0.83	0.37	0.14	0.68	0.23	0.14	0.68	0.23
	CD	0.64	0.76	**0.69**	0.42	0.74	0.53	0.35	0.48	**0.40**	0.26	0.51	**0.34**
	TC	0.52	0.50	0.51	0.91	0.42	**0.57**	0.20	0.32	0.24	0.41	0.25	0.31
Low overlap	PW	0.26	0.67	0.38	0.26	0.67	0.37	0.14	0.43	0.21	0.14	0.44	0.21
	CD	0.50	0.44	0.47	0.32	0.51	0.39	0.20	0.23	0.22	0.15	0.27	0.20
	TC	0.45	0.85	**0.58**	0.58	0.71	**0.64**	0.34	0.22	**0.26**	0.38	0.22	**0.28**

identities seldom end up in more than two profiles. In the best case, 96 % of all identities are recovered into one or two profiles (at 82 % accuracy; graph [A]); in the worst case, we still get 58 % (and 63 % of profiles consist of at most two identities; graph [K]). Thus, even with our general techniques, many links can be made based on non-identifiable information.

Comparison Between Approaches. We compared the two clustering methods (community detection, CD, and threshold transitive closure, TC) both to each other and to pairwise (PW) linking. Note that PW is not able to compile personae into a profile; actually, pairwise decisions may be incompatible (e.g., profile #1 is linked to #2 and #3, but #2 and #3 are not linked). Thus, we use precision, recall and f-measure (that are also defined in the pairwise case) for the comparison. The averages over 10 runs of our experiments are shown in Table 1. In each experiment, the metrics are computed after the linking phase; and after applying community detection or transitive closure. Bold indicates the method(s) that returns the statistically significant highest f-measure.

TC and CD have higher f-measures than PW in all experiments; almost always significantly so. Reducing the amount of overlap or introducing perturbation makes the results of pairwise matching drop considerably. However, the effect of applying clustering after pairwise matching does not diminish: although the TC and CD statistics also drop, the difference between TC/CD and PW generally remains considerable. Thus, exploiting links between more than two profiles clearly helps to increase performance.

CD generally produces better results than TC in the baseline and large scenarios, while TC provides better results in the low overlap scenario. Since the baseline and large scenarios are characterized by the availability of "enough" linking information, this suggests that CD is "smarter" in exploiting such information; however, TC is more robust than CD when the amount of overlap decreases. When TC has a higher f-measure than CD, TC usually has a higher precision than CD (in half of the cases, it also has a higher recall). This observation can be explained by the very high threshold for TC (always ≥ 0.90) chosen to maximise its f-measure.

The density/sparseness of the dataset also has an effect on the performances of the considered approaches. Unsurprisingly, the results for PW when reducing density are generally the same because it considers every pair independently. More surprisingly, reducing density also hardly reduces the f-measure for TC; for CD however, there is always such a drop. This can be explained by noting that CD depends more on the overall structure of the graph, whereas the clustering of a particular persona in TC is only influenced by a few other persona that it is strongly linked with.

5 Conclusions and Future Work

In this paper, we studied the feasibility of reconstructing individuals' identities by linking only non-identifiable information. In particular, we presented a generic approach for building individuals' identities from personae stored in different databases based on two well-known techniques: record linkage and graph clustering. We applied the approach to several scenarios. The experiments suggest that even without identifiable information, identities can be compiled with reasonable accuracy.

Although the methods and experiments in this paper already yielded insightful results, both also lead to interesting directions for future work. Possible improvements to the method include the use of other community detection methods; iterative approaches to resolve clusters and improve classification; and non-supervised learning techniques. We did not focus on a computational evaluation in this work; in fact, our current implementation is at least quadratic in the number of the personae considered. Well-known blocking techniques from record linkage [16] may be used to increase scalability. Concerning the experiments, one important step would be to consider (much) larger and real (i.e., non-generated) datasets, or more accurate perturbation [8]. Precision/recall trade-offs may be studied using generalised community scores [1, 26]. Privacy effects of deliberately introducing inconsistencies in on-line profiles can be studied by looking at the performance of perturbed versus non-perturbed data in a mixed dataset.

Acknowledgements. We thank the anonymous reviewers for their useful comments. This work is funded by the Dutch Sentinel Mobile IDM project (#10522), and the Dutch national program COMMIT through the THeCS project.

References

1. Arenas, A., Fernández, A., Gómez, S.: Analysis of the structure of complex networks at different resolution levels. New J. Phys. **10**(5) (2008)
2. Baig, M.M., Li, J., Liu, J., Ding, X., Wang, H.: Data privacy against composition attack. In: Lee, S., Peng, Z., Zhou, X., Moon, Y.-S., Unland, R., Yoo, J. (eds.) DASFAA 2012, Part I. LNCS, vol. 7238, pp. 320–334. Springer, Heidelberg (2012)

3. Bhattacharya, I., Getoor, L.: Collective entity resolution in relational data. ACM Trans. Knowl. Discov. Data 1(1) (2007)
4. Bilenko, M., Basu, S., Sahami, M.: Adaptive product normalization: Using online learning for record linkage in comparison shopping. In: Proceedings of the Fifth IEEE International Conference on Data Mining, pp. 58–65. IEEE (2005)
5. Blanchet, B., Abadi, M., Fournet, C.: Automated verification of selected equivalences for security protocols. J. Log. Algebr. Program. 75(1), 3–51 (2008)
6. Blondel, V.D., Guillaume, J.L., Lambiott, R., Lefebvre, E.: Fast unfolding of communities in large networks. J. Stat. Mech.-Theory Exp. 2008(10) (2008)
7. Chaudhuri, S., Ganti, V., Motwani, R.: Robust identification of fuzzy duplicates. In: Proceedings of the 21st International Conference on Data Engineering, pp. 865–876. IEEE (2005)
8. Christen, P., Pudjijono, A.: Accurate synthetic generation of realistic personal information. In: Theeramunkong, T., Kijsirikul, B., Cercone, N., Ho, T.-B. (eds.) PAKDD 2009. LNCS, vol. 5476, pp. 507–514. Springer, Heidelberg (2009)
9. Ciriani, V., de Capitani di Vimercati, S., Foresti, S., Samarati, P.: k-anonymity. In: Yu, T., Jajodia, S. (eds.) Secure Data Management in Decentralized Systems. Advances in Information Security, 323rd edn, p. 353. Springer, Heidelberg (2007)
10. Delaune, S., Ryan, M., Smyth, B.: Automatic verification of privacy properties in the applied pi calculus. In: Proceedings of IFIPTM 2008: Joint iTrust and PST Conferences on Privacy, Trust Management and Security, IFIP, vol. 263, pp. 263–278. Springer, Heidelberg (2008)
11. Dwork, C.: Differential privacy. In: Bugliesi, M., Preneel, B., Sassone, V., Wegener, I. (eds.) ICALP 2006, Part II. LNCS, vol. 4052, pp. 1–12. Springer, Heidelberg (2006)
12. Fellegi, I.P., Sunter, A.B.: A theory for record linkage. J. Am. Stat. Assoc. 64(328), 1183–1210 (1969)
13. Getoor, L., Machanavajjhala, A.: Entity resolution: theory, practice & open challenges. Proc. VLDB Endow. 5(12), 2018–2019 (2012)
14. Gupta, M., Wu, Y.M., Joshi, S.S., Tiwari, A., Nair, A., Ilangovan, E.: On the linkability of complementary information from free versions of people databases. SIGMETRICS Perform. Eval. Rev. 40(4), 96–100 (2013)
15. Koot, M.R.: Measuring and predicting anonymity. Ph.D. thesis, University of Amsterdam (2012)
16. Köpcke, H., Rahm, E.: Frameworks for entity matching: a comparison. Data Knowl. Eng. 69(2), 197–210 (2010)
17. Li, N., Li, T., Venkatasubramanian, S.: t-closeness: privacy beyond k-anonymity and ℓ-diversity. In: Proceedings of International Conference on Data Engineering, pp. 106–115. IEEE (2007)
18. Machanavajjhala, A., Kifer, D., Gehrke, J., Venkitasubramaniam, M.: ℓ-diversity: privacy beyond k-anonymity. ACM Trans. Knowl. Discov. Data 1(1) (2007)
19. Menestrina, D., Whang, S.E., Garcia-Molina, H.: Evaluating entity resolution results. Proc. VLDB Endow. 3(1–2), 208–219 (2010)
20. Michelson, M., Macskassy, S.A.: Record linkage measures in an entity centric world. In: Proceedings of the 4th workshop on Evaluation Methods for Machine Learning (2009)
21. Méray, N., Reitsma, J., Ravelli, A., Bonsel, G.: Probabilistic record linkage is a valid and transparent tool to combine databases without a patient identification number. J. Clin. Epidemiol. 60(9), 883–891 (2007)

22. Narayanan, A., Shmatikov, V.: Robust de-anonymization of large sparse datasets. In: Proceedings of IEEE Symposium on Security and Privacy, pp. 111–125. IEEE (2008)

23. Northern, C.T., Nelson, M.L.: An unsupervised approach to discovering and disambiguating social media profiles. In: Proceedings of Mining Data Semantics Workshop (2011)

24. Singla, P., Domingos, P.: Multi-relational record linkage. In: Proceedings of the KDD-2004 Workshop on Multi-Relational Data Mining, pp. 31–48. ACM (2004)

25. Piepoli, A., Veeningen, M.: Implementation of identity clustering accompanying paper "are on-line personae really unlinkable?" (version 1.0). http://www.mobiman.me/downloads/

26. Reichardt, J., Bornholdt, S.: Statistical mechanics of community detection. Phys. Rev. E **74**, 016110 (2006)

27. Sadinle, M., Fienberg, S.E.: A generalized fellegi-sunter framework for multiple record linkage with application to homicide record systems. arXiv 1205.3217 (2012)

28. Sapena, E., Padró, L., Turmo, J.: A graph partitioning approach to entity disambiguation using uncertain information. In: Nordström, B., Ranta, A. (eds.) GoTAL 2008. LNCS (LNAI), vol. 5221, pp. 428–439. Springer, Heidelberg (2008)

29. Troncoso, C.: Design and analysis methods for privacy technologies. Ph.D. thesis, KU Leuven (2011)

30. Veeningen, M., de Weger, B., Zannone, N.: Formal privacy analysis of communication protocols for identity management. In: Jajodia, S., Mazumdar, Ch. (eds.) ICISS 2011. LNCS, vol. 7093, pp. 235–249. Springer, Heidelberg (2011)

31. Winkler, W.E.: String comparator metrics and enhanced decision rules in the fellegi-sunter model of record linkage. In: Proceedings of the Section on Survey Research, pp. 354–359 (1990)

On the Privacy of Private Browsing –
A Forensic Approach

Kiavash Satvat, Matthew Forshaw, Feng Hao$^{(\boxtimes)}$, and Ehsan Toreini

School of Computing Science, Newcastle University, Newcastle, UK
kiavash.satvat@gmail.com,
{m.j.forshaw,feng.hao,Ehsan.Toreini}@ncl.ac.uk

Abstract. Private browsing has been a popular privacy feature built into all mainstream browsers since 2005. However, despite its prevalent use, the security of this feature has received little attention from the research community. In this paper, we present an up-to-date and comprehensive analysis of private browsing across four most popular web browsers: IE, Firefox, Chrome and Safari. We report that all browsers under study suffer from a variety of vulnerabilities, many of which have not been reported or known before. Our work highlights the complexity of the subject and calls for more attention from the security community.

1   Introduction

In 2005, Safari first introduced private browsing, a feature that enables a user to surf the Internet without leaving traces on her local computer, such as history, cookies and temporary files [5]. All other mainstream browsers have since added the feature, including Internet Explorer (IE) [4], Chrome [1] and Firefox [2].

Although the basic aim of private browsing is the same, the implementations vary greatly across different browsers. This adds significant complexity to the subject. So far only few researchers have attempted to investigated the subject. In 2010, Aggarwal *et. al.* first initiated the security analysis of private browsing in [5]. In particular, they defined a threat model, surveyed the main usage of private browsing, reviewed the open source code of Firefox, and studied the effect of Firefox extension on private browsing. In 2011, Said *et al.*continued the investigation by examining the content in the volatile memory and they found artifacts left in memory about user activities in the private session even after the session had been closed [6]. Apart from these two publications [5,6], the subject of the security of private browsing seems to have been mostly neglected by the research community.

In this paper, we extend the earlier works in several aspects. First, we refine the threat model in [5] to capture more realistic threats in practice. Second, we carry out more extensive experiments than [5]: covering not only Firefox, but also IE, Chrome and Safari. Third, we scrutinise artefacts left from private browsing from all angles: not only in memory as in [6], but also in disk and network traffic.

J. Garcia-Alfaro et al. (Eds.): DPM 2013 and SETOP 2013, LNCS 8247, pp. 380–389, 2014.
DOI: 10.1007/978-3-642-54568-9_25, © Springer-Verlag Berlin Heidelberg 2014

2   Research Methodology

In this research work, we took a forensic approach to collect and analyse residual data left on the host computer after the private browsing session. Virtualisation was used to prevent any cross-contamination between experiments. In particular, VMware Player (a free version of VMware) was installed [10]. Windows 7 was chosen based on its popularity among the Internet users. The latest versions of the four most popular browsers (as in April, 2013 [9]) were installed: Mozilla Firefox (19.0), Apple Safari (5.1.7), Google Chrome (25.0.1364.97) and IE (10.0.9200.16521).

For each experiment, a fresh Windows installation with a single web browser was used. The experiments were carried out for each browser to investigate possible residual data left in memory or disk after private navigation. To allow other researchers to easily replicate the experiments, we only used *freely* available forensic tools. Finally, all the software tools developed during the course of this research are released as open source (see [20]). We hope this would help browser vendors evaluate the security of their products and improve accordingly.

3   Threat Model

Same as in [5], we categorise attackers into two types: local and remote. A local attacker is someone who has physical access to a user's machine. The threat model defined in [5] restricts the local attack to "after the fact" forensics. On the other hand, it is acknowledged in [5] that the user may have installed third-party browser extensions before the private session. Our model about a local attacker is essentially the same as that in [5] but with one difference: we explicitly assume at least one of the installed third-party extensions were written by an attacker. Instead of surveying the third-party extensions and speculating their behavior as in [5], we write our own extensions as if from an attacker's perspective. This allows capturing the exact impact of extensions more directly.

For remote attacks, we assume the attacker is capable to engage with the user in a web browsing session over HTTP(S). This typically happens when a user navigates to a web site that is controlled by an attacker, whose goal is to detect whether the user is in the private mode[1]. As compared with the model in [5], we have excluded the threat of remote websites tracking users (e.g., based on IP addresses [7] or unique browser fingerprints [14]). This is because private browsing has never been designed to prevent web tracking [1–4]. (We refer interested readers to other privacy-preserving tools such as TOR [15] for the prevention of web tracking.)

---

[1] Given the often negative connotation of using the private mode for viewing adult websites (see [5]), we consider the fact of using the private mode a privacy feature by itself. If the remote website learns the user is in the private mode, it may push more adult-oriented advertisement to the user.

Table 1. List of attacks and their applicability to each browser. Those marked with * contain new results discovered by our study, while others correspond to attacks that have been previously known but validated again by our study.

	Firefox	Chrome	IE	Safari
Domain name system	√	√	√	√
Memory inspection	√	√	√	√
File timestamp	–	√	–	√
Index.dat *	N/A	N/A	√	N/A
SQLite database crash *	√	√	N/A	√
SQLite added bookmark *	√	√	N/A	√
Extension *	√	√	–	√
Cross-mode Interference *	N/A	√	N/A	N/A
Hyperlink attack	√	√	√	√
Timing attack *	√	√	–	√

Against the defined thre at model, we conducted a series of experiments to assess the security of private browsing among the four most popular browsers: Firefox, Chrome, IE and Safari. Table 1 summarises the attacks, and their applicability to specific browsers.

4   Local Attacks

4.1   Summary of Previously Known Attacks

Domain Name System (DNS). DNS caching has long been known as a major threat to private browsing [5]. This vulnerability is caused due to the operating system caching all DNS queries sent by a web browser. We confirm that this vulnerability still persists in all browsers three years after it was reported in [5]. Third-party extensions have been developed to address this issue [11,12], but none of them has been adopted by browser vendors.

Memory Inspection. In 2011, Said *et al.* reported that artifacts from a private browsing session were found in the main memory after the end of the session [6]. We have verified that the same vulnerability still exists in the latest versions of all fours browsers. After navigating a few websites in the private mode and closing the session, we inspected the content in RAM and discovered traces of private navigation, including visited URLs, password and cookies.

File Timestamp. In [5], the authors compared the "last modified date" of files in the Firefox profile directory before and after private browsing. They found the timestamps had been changed while file sizes remained the same, which allows deducing the occurrence of a private session in the past. Our experiments show the vulnerability has been fixed in the latest version of Firefox (and also IE), but it still exists in Chrome and Safari.

4.2   Index.dat

The Index.dat files are binary format log files used by IE to store the user's browsing history, cookies, temporary files, etc. We analyse these files in order to evaluate the correlation between IE's InPrivate mode and Index.dat files. After the navigation of the targeted websites in the private mode, we scrutinise residual traces left in the files. Unlike in some earlier versions of IE, the latest version has successfully removed the traces of visited websites in the private mode.

However, we found that adding bookmarks in the IE private mode could lead to information leakage. Bookmarks added during a private session were stored as standalone files with corresponding creation timestamps. On the other hand, there is no matching URL for the added bookmark in `Histoy.IE5\index.dat`. A comparison between these files could allow an attacker to deduce that the bookmark was added in the private mode and when. False positives may occur if the user added a bookmark in the usual mode without visiting the page (e.g., right-click over a hyperlink to add it to the bookmarks). However, the false negatives are always zero.

4.3   SQLite Database

SQLite databases are used by Firefox, Chrome and Safari to store historical records of browsing activities [13]. We study the correlation between private browsing and the underlying SQLite database and reveal two vulnerabilities: one related to the application crash, and the other related to adding bookmarks.

Application Crash. There are many reasons why a browser program may terminate in an unexpected way, e.g., sudden power loss or system crash. The critical question is that: if the program terminates in an unexpected way, will it leave unexpected evidence on disk?

In Firefox, the SQLite database uses the Write Ahead Logging (WAL) mode to implement database transactions such as atomic commit and rollback. In the event of application crash, database connections are not closed cleanly and the WAL files will remain on disk until the browser is restarted. We observed that the WAL files left from the private mode always had the zero size (since there were not database updates), while the WAL files left from the usual mode had non-zero size. Hence, based on the size of a WAL file and its timestamp, an attacker will be able to deduce that a private session occurred at a specific time.

Chrome implements the SQLite database transactions using Journal files instead of the WAL files. To speed up the loading, the browser uses two SQLite databases to store the history records; a primary "History" database and monthly digests in the form of "History Index YYYY-MM". In the usual mode, the browser uses a journal file for each database. However, in the private mode, it just uses one journal file for the "History" database only. All journal files will remain on disk in the event of application crash or power loss. Based on the existence of only one journal file, an attacker can deduce that a private session occurred and the timestamp of the file reveals when. Similar to Firefox, restarting the browser in the usual mode will remove the evidence.

The case of Safari is more serious. Unlike Firefox and Chrome that only use in-memory SQLite database for private browsing, Safari first writes records of the visited websites to the database file and then removes them after the browser is closed normally. We found that if the browser was closed in an abnormal way (e.g., manual termination), the records of visited websites in the private mode would remain in the database. The residual data persists on disk even after the browser is restarted, which poses a serious threat to the user's privacy. As a countermeasure, we recommend Safari to adopt in-memory SQLite updates, like Chrome and Firefox.

Adding Bookmarks. In Firefox, after visiting targeted websites and adding a bookmark in the private mode, we examine the `places.sqlite` SQLite database, which contains records of all visited URLs and added bookmarks. Our investigation revealed that a bookmark added during the private mode was recorded with empty "title" and "last_visit_date" fields, disclosing that the bookmark was added during the private mode at a specific time. It is worse than the earlier IE case, since the evidence is definite: i.e., zero false positive and zero false negative. The case of Chrome is similar. The URL for bookmarks added in the private mode could be found in the "`history`" SQLite database. Unlike a bookmark recorded in the usual mode, the "visit_count" field was always set to 0 and the "hidden" field set to 1.

The case of Safari is the most problematic. Under the normal operation, Safari removes the browsing history in the private mode when the program is closed. However, we found that as long as the user added one bookmark during the private navigation, all the websites that were visited during the private session would remain in the SQLite database. (A bug report on this issue has been filed to Apple.)

4.4   Extensions

Chrome Extension. We developed a Chrome extension (the source code in [20]) that, once enabled in the private mode, was able to record detailed user activities for the duration of a private browsing session. This includes when the tabs were opened and closed, which web pages were visited and at which time, how the user moved between tabs and windows, etc. In the latest version of Chrome, extensions are disabled in the private mode by default. This "disable-by-default" policy significantly alleviates the threat. However, the fact that Chrome allows the private and usual modes to run in parallel renders this policy ineffective, as we will explain in Sect. 4.5.

Internet Explorer Extension. We developed an IE extension [20] to obtain the URL and the content of the HTML pages based on using the Browser Helper Object (BHO) class. Like Chrome, IE disables extensions in the private mode by default. However, even after we manually enabled extensions in the private mode, we found the extension had only restricted privilege: in particular, it could no longer invoke the BHO class. Hence, our attack did not work on IE.

Safari and Firefox Extensions. We developed similar extensions for Safari and Firefox [20], which were able to record details of the user's activities within a private session [20]. In both Safari and Firefox, extensions are enabled by default in the private mode. Hence, they are vulnerable to extension attacks. The countermeasure we recommend is to disable extensions by default in the private mode, just like in IE and Chrome.

4.5   Cross-Mode Interference

While extensions in Chrome are disabled by default in the private mode, Chrome allows the usual and private modes to run in parallel, providing the attacker an opportunity to exploit cross-mode interference.

The attack was motivated by the following observation: the `Chrome://memory` page displays all the opened tabs in the browser regardless if they are in the usual or private mode. Accordingly, we developed an extension [20] using the standard Chrome extension APIs [18].

The attack works as follows. In the usual mode, the extension is enabled by default and it is able to invoke standard APIs to list all tabs, each having a unique ID. If the tab is in the usual mode, the extension can obtain further details about the tab, such as the page title and URL. However, if the tab is in the private mode, no response will be given. This lack of response provides an indication that the queried tab is in the private mode. By periodically polling the tabs, the extension can detect the existence of a private browsing session, the number of active tabs opened in the private mode, and when those tabs are opened and closed.

Chrome also provides experimental APIs (which are enabled in `chrome://flags`) to further enforce the extension's functionality [19]. In particular, it provides the following additional information about each tab: the CPU consumption, network bandwidth and Frames Per Section (FPS). This information is obtainable even for tabs in the private mode.

The extra information allows the attacker to draw an even more fine-grained profile about the user activities within a private session. Figure 1 shows how the user's activities are correlated with the CPU consumption and network bandwidth usage. Loading new pages increases the CPU and bandwidth usage at the same time while scrolling pages only affects the CPU consumption. When one is watching an HTML5 video, there is a substantial increase of both the CPU usage and network bandwidth. As a countermeasure, we recommend the browser should always be run in a single mode. This applies to all other browsers.

5   Remote Attacks

5.1   Hyperlink Attack

A conventional technique adopted by all browsers to distinguish visited links from unvisited ones is by changing colour, hence improving the user's browsing

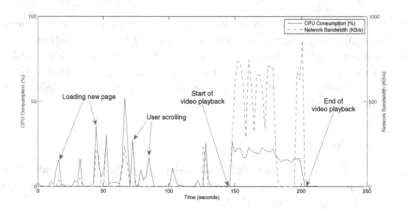

Fig. 1. Profiling the user activities in the private mode

experience [8]. However, there are noticeable deviations for the same mechanism to work in the private mode. As we have tested, all browsers started a new private session with all hyperlinks displayed in blue. Furthermore, in Chrome, Firefox and Safari, the hyperlink never changes colour even after the user has clicked the link or visited the URL. (One might argue that this has the benefit of making it more difficult for the remote website to track the visited pages than in the usual mode since the color of the hyperlink does not change much; however, it is worth noting that defence against web tracking is not within the threat model of private browsing.)

These deviations create an exploit path for a remote attacker. Based on the difference in the hyperlink colours, the remote attacker is able to tell a private mode apart from a usual mode. For example, since in Chrome, Firefox and Safari, the hyperlinks are persistently blue in the private mode, a remote website can use JavaScript to check the colour of the hyperlinks and easily tell if the user is currently in the private mode. This vulnerability was first reported in [5] and we find it still exists in the latest versions of the browsers. However, the case of IE is different from the rest browsers; the colour of the hyperlink does change based on the user's clicking just like in the usual mode. However, the private mode still deviates from the usual mode in that the former always displays all hyperlinks in blue in the beginning of the session. Hence, if the remote attacker is able to regularly engage with the user in more than one sessions (e.g., the remote attacker controls a news website), he can easily tell if the user is in the private mode.

As a countermeasure, we suggest to remove deviations of how hyperlinks are colored between the usual and private modes. The only difference should be that the private mode does not save any information about visited links after the session is closed.

5.2 Timing Attack

In this section, we describe a novel timing attack, which is able to remotely detect the private mode based on measuring the time of writing a large number of cookies. We developed a simple PHP and MySQL application to measure the time taken to write a predefined number of cookies, and then store these results to a database for further analysis. The Selenium testing framework [17] was used to automate testing for large-scale experimentation.

We collected extensive timing measurements for the usual and private modes (100 samples per mode per browser) as training data (see Fig. 2). We then collected further 100 timing measurements for each browser for each mode for evaluation. The evaluation is based on using a standard z-test [16] (details can be found in the full version of the paper [20]). There are two types of errors in the evaluation. One is the False Acceptance Rate (FAR), that is the rate of a usual session being characterised as the private mode. The other is False Rejection Rate (FRR), that is the rate of a private session being characterised as the usual mode. The two error rates vary according to the threshold. Hence, in the evaluation, we used the Equal Error Rate (EER) where the FRR and FAR curves intersect. In the ideal case, the EER should be close to 50 %: i.e., the chance for the attacker to detect the private/usual mode is no better than tossing a coin. However, as shown in Table 2, with the exception of IE, a remote attacker is able to correctly identify the browsing mode with high accuracy.

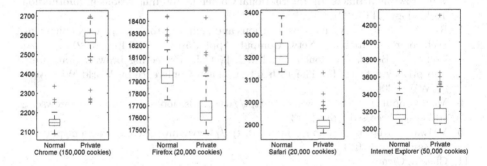

Fig. 2. Box plots representing timing data collected for browsers under test.

Table 2. Equal Error Rates for detecting the private mode

Browser	Equal Error Rate (EER) (%)	Threshold (t)
Google Chrome	1	0
Mozilla Firefox	9	0
Internet Explorer	63	−0.0002
Apple Safari	1	0.0055

6 Conclusion

We have revealed a range of vulnerabilities in the existing implementations of private browsing. The problems are generally caused by the following factors: a lack of understanding of the threat model (especially in relation to remote attacks), a lack of appropriate control of running extension in the private mode (and neglect of the cross-mode interference) and a lack of rigorous and systematic test (especially in edge cases such as program crash and adding bookmarks).

References

1. Chrome Private Browsing Mode. https://support.google.com/chrome/bin/answer.py?hl=en&answer=95464&p=cpn_incognito. Accessed April 2013
2. Mozilla Firefox Private Browsing Mode. http://support.mozilla.org/en-US/kb/private-browsing-browse-web-without-saving-info. Accessed April 2013
3. Safari Private Browsing Mode. http://support.apple.com/kb/PH5000. Accessed April 2013
4. Internet Explorer Private Browsing Mode. http://windows.microsoft.com/en-us/windows-vista/what-is-inprivate-browsing. Accessed April 2013
5. Aggarwal, G., Burzstein, E., Jackson, C., Boneh, D.: An analysis of private browsing modes in modern browsers. In: The 19th USENIX Symphosium on Security (2010)
6. Said, H., Mutawa, A.H., Awadhi, A.I., Guimaraes, M.: Forensic analysis of private browsing artifacts. In: International Conference on Innovations in Information Technology (IIT) (2011)
7. Ruiz-Martínez, A.: A survey on solutions and main free tools for privacy enhancing Web communications. J. Netw. Comput. Appl. 35(5), 1473–1492 (2012)
8. Collin, J., Bortz, A., Boneh, D., Mitchell, C.J.: Protecting browser state from web privacy attacks. In: The 15th International Conference on World Wide Web (WWW) (2006)
9. Most Popular Web Browsers. http://www.w3schools.com/browsers/browsers_stats.asp. Accessed April 2013
10. VMware Player Version 4.0.0. http://www.vmware.com/products/player/. Accessed April 2013
11. Click & Clean. https://chrome.google.com/webstore/detail/ghgabhipcejjmhhchfonmamedcbeod?utm_source=chrome-ntp-icon. Accessed April 2013
12. Clear DNS Cache. https://addons.mozilla.org/en-us/firefox/addon/clear-dns-cache/. Accessed April 2013
13. Jeon, S., Bang, J., Byun, K.: A recovery method of deleted record for SQLite database. Pers. Ubiquit. Comput. 16(6), 707–715 (2011)
14. Eckersley, P.: How unique is your web browser? https://panopticlick.eff.org/browser-uniqueness.pdf. Accessed April 2013
15. The Official Website for the TOR Project. https://www.torproject.org/. Accessed April 2013
16. Kreyszig, E.: Introductory Mathematical Statistics. Wiley, New York (1970)
17. Selenium. http://seleniumhq.org/. Accessed April 2013

18. Standard Chrome Extension API. http://developer.chrome.com/extensions/. Accessed April 2013
19. Experimental Chrome Extension API. http://developer.chrome.com/extensions/experimental.html. Accessed April 2013
20. Open-Source Software Tools Developed for the Research of Private Browsing. http://homepages.cs.ncl.ac.uk/m.j.forshaw1/privatebrowsing/

Privacy-Preserving Trust Management Mechanisms from Private Matching Schemes

Oriol Farràs$^{(\boxtimes)}$, Josep Domingo-Ferrer, and Alberto Blanco-Justicia

Department of Computer Engineering and Maths, UNESCO Chair in Data Privacy,
Universitat Rovira i Virgili, Av. Països Catalans 26, 43007 Tarragona, CA, Spain
{oriol.farras,josep.domingo,alberto.blanco}@urv.cat

Abstract. Cryptographic primitives are essential for constructing privacy-preserving communication mechanisms. There are situations when two parties that do not know each other need to exchange sensitive information over the Internet. Trust management mechanisms make use of digital credentials in order to establish trust among these strangers. We present a method to reach an agreement on the credentials to be exchanged in which the parties can control the disclosure of their credential preferences. Our method is based on secure two-party computation protocols for set intersection.

Keywords: Trust management · Secure two-party computation · Set intersection · Privacy

1 Introduction

Interactions between parties that involve exchanging sensitive information are part of everyday life. Taking a medical test, paying with a credit card or asking for directions are examples of such interactions. In all of these cases an individual or organization C reveals some information to another individual or organization S so that S can provide a service to C. Clearly, an exchange of personal information is more likely to take place if there is trust between the interacting parties. For instance, people agree on revealing medical data to a doctor in a medical center, but not to anyone or anywhere. These interactions are easy to carry out face to face and in a specific context, but they are challenging if performed over the Internet, where personal identification is not obvious and the physical context is simply not there.

This work was partly supported by the Government of Catalonia under grant 2009 SGR 1135, by the Spanish Government through projects TIN2011-27076-C03-01 "CO-PRIVACY" and CONSOLIDER INGENIO 2010 CSD2007-00004 "ARES", and by the European Comission under FP7 project 'Inter-Trust'. The second author is partially supported as an ICREA Acadèmia researcher by the Government of Catalonia; he is with the UNESCO Chair in Data Privacy, but he is solely responsible for the views expressed in this paper, which do not necessarily reflect the position of UNESCO nor commit that organization.

J. Garcia-Alfaro et al. (Eds.): DPM 2013 and SETOP 2013, LNCS 8247, pp. 390–398, 2014.
DOI: 10.1007/978-3-642-54568-9_26, © Springer-Verlag Berlin Heidelberg 2014

A first approach is securing the communication using cryptographic protocols. Using these techniques in combination with public key infrastructures provides users interacting with remote parties with the certainty that they are communicating with the real service provider. Furthermore, encrypting communication prevents third parties from eavesdropping on the transmitted contents. This has been the basis of secure digital communications and e-commerce, but recent reports show that authentication is not always enough for users to trust service providers [17,23].

The special Eurobarometer on data protection and electronic identity [23] shows that the majority of Europeans are concerned about their behavior being recorded via payment cards, mobile phones or mobile Internet. Moreover, 43 % of the respondents claim they have been asked more personal information than necessary in order to access online services.

Therefore, there is a need to design new access control systems in which not only the identity of the parties is revealed and assured, but trust is built through the exchange of valid credentials that contain attributes of the parties. Trust management mechanisms make use of digital credentials in order to establish trust between strangers. Trust negotiation schemes are protocols for establishing trust between parties unknown to each other through the exchange of credentials and personal information; in such negotiation protocols, the disclosure of this information is performed according to access control policies determined by the parties.

Trust management is a building block of many industry-led frameworks. One example is the Interoperable Trust Assurance Infrastructure (Inter-Trust, [12]), a project that seeks to develop a framework to support trustworthy applications in heterogeneous networks and devices, based on the enforcement of interoperable and changing security policies [2]. Trust negotiation (Fig. 1) is essential in Inter-Trust to reach agreements on the security policies, the so-called Service Level Agreements (SLAs). Inter-Trust will incorporate trustworthiness by integrating legal, social and economic concerns, thereby allowing applications and devices to negotiate and be constrained by such concerns.

A critical issue in trust management is to preserve the privacy of the users. During the trust establishment process, the parties can try to learn information about each other. On the one hand, the service requesters can try to obtain information about the preferences of the service providers: if the requesters indicate their wish to use specific options, the server is forced to show the different acceptable options. Since the revealed options may reflect the business model and the target customers considered by the provider, service providers are reluctant to show full descriptions of their access policies. On the other hand, requesters do not want to provide information on the credentials they own unless those credentials are essential for the transaction.

In summary, service providers are reluctant to show their access policies, and clients want to disclose as little private information as possible. Therefore, during the trust establishment process no party should learn any information about the access policies or preferences of the other parties beyond what is

SERVICE REQUESTER   SERVICE PROVIDER

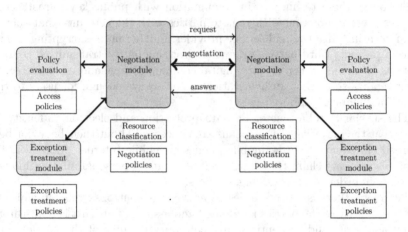

Fig. 1. Negotiation module of Inter-Trust

strictly required for trust establishment. Solutions based on trust negotiation mechanisms [7,10,14–16,20,24,26] control the disclosure of user preferences by showing the access control policies in a sequential way. However, trust negotiation mechanisms are oriented to controlling credential disclosure, but the users may obtain information on the access control policies by playing with the system. Trust management mechanisms based on secure multiparty computation [18,21, 28] provide higher privacy protection.

1.1 Our Results

We address the problem of constructing a privacy-preserving mechanism for choosing the credentials to be exchanged. Moreover, we consider that privacy preservation should be achieved as effortlessly as possible. Therefore, our goal is to come up with an efficient and privacy-preserving mechanism to determine the optimal set of informations to be disclosed, according to the preferences of the two parties. We present a method that is based on secure two-party computation protocols for set intersection. Specifically, it is constructed from the private matching schemes in [9].

In our proposal, the client sends a list of options to the server in a private way. Each option is a combination of credentials the client would agree to show. The server has a correspondence list that, for each accepted combination of client credentials, specifies the credentials the server would show. Using secure multiparty computation techniques, client and server compute the matching options. Then the server sends to the client the options that match the client's preferences. In this way, the server does not learn the preferences of the client, and the client only learns the specific access policies that match her selected options.

Using the Paillier homomorphic cryptosystem [22], the total number of exponentiations needed is $O(s + t \ln \ln s)$, where s and t are the number of options specified by the client and the server, respectively.

The rest of this paper is organized as follows. In Sect. 2 we present an introduction to trust management. Section 3 is devoted to private matching schemes. We present our results in Sect. 4. Section 5 lists conclusions and open problems.

2   Trust Management

Remote communications over the Internet often require the interacting parties to trust each other, especially when the communication involves the exchange of private, confidential, or sensitive information. Traditional approaches to establish trust assume that the parties are known to each other before the communication takes place. Organizations often sign a SLA and collaboration contracts before engaging in the exchange of services and information. This approach is not always possible, because the assumption that the parties are known to each other is not always true, especially in open environments such as the Internet and the Web [26].

Secure Sockets Layer (SSL) and its successor Transport Layer Security (TLS) are cryptographic protocols that provide trust and security to communications over the Internet. These protocols begin with a negotiation or *handshake* phase in which the two parties (normally a client and a server) agree on an encryption algorithm and a shared key to encrypt the communication. Also, during this phase the two parties exchange digital certificates in order to authenticate each other. Even though the use of TLS is widespread, users do not fully trust Internet service providers, as discussed in the previous section. Therefore, there is a need to improve existing strategies and/or devise new methods for establishing trust.

More recent approaches to establishing trust are the *Automatic Trust Negotiation* (ATN) protocols. ATN is based on the exchange of digitally signed credentials to establish trust and make access control decisions. Digital credentials are an extension of traditional electronic certificates that only prove the identity of a user. Credentials can include additional attributes, and hence they can certify more properties of that user, such as age, permission to perform a certain activity, membership to a certain organization, etc. In the full version of this paper [8] we provide an introduction to cryptographic credentials, access control policies, negotiation techniques, and secure multiparty computation.

3   Private Set Intersection

Secure multiparty computation allows a set of parties to compute a joint function of their inputs in a secure way without requiring a trusted third party. During the execution of the protocol the parties do not learn anything about each other's input except what is implied by the output itself.

There are two main adversarial models: honest-but-curious and malicious. In the former model, the players follow the protocol instructions but try to obtain information about other players' inputs from the messages they receive. In the latter model, the adversary may deviate from the protocol in an arbitrary way. Aumann and Lindell [1] introduced a new model, the covert adversary model. A covert adversary may deviate from the protocol in an attempt to cheat, but such deviations are detected by honest parties. In this context, the parties may be considered rational, that is, acting according to their interests. In game-theoretic terms, it is assumed that players only try to maximize their utility functions; hence, all possible deviations from the correct protocol execution have this goal.

The intersection of two sets can be obtained by using the generic constructions based on Yao's garbled circuit [27]. This technique is very generic, because it allows computing any arithmetic function, but for most of the functions it is inefficient. Many of the recent works on two-party computation are focused on improving the efficiency of these protocols for particular families of functions. Freedman, Nissim, and Pinkas [9] presented a more efficient method to compute the set intersection that was called *private matching scheme*. The idea of Freedman, Nissim, and Pinkas [9] was used in many other works to improve the computation of set operations. Kissner and Song [13] presented secure multiparty computation protocols for computing set intersection, multi-set intersection and other combinatorial operations. They presented constructions for honest-but-curious adversaries and malicious adversaries. Hazay and Lindell [11] presented a construction that is secure in the covert model. There are also other interesting constructions, such as [4,19].

4   A Privacy-Preserving Trust Management Scheme

In this section we present a new mechanism for privacy-preserving trust management. We consider the following situation. A client C wants to buy a service from a server S. S needs some personal and financial information about C to perform the transaction. However, C is reluctant to show private information to S, because C is not sure that S is trustworthy.

The mechanism we construct is a protocol based on the private matching scheme of Freedman, Nissim, and Pinkas [9]. Our protocol is secure in the honest-but-curious model.

Our proposal allows parties C and S to agree on the information they have to exchange to perform the transaction in a private way. Broadly speaking, C first sends an encrypted message to S that declares which credentials and personal information she would be inclined to reveal to S. S cannot read the message, but he can create an encrypted message containing the options declared by C in which he agrees, and the information S would reveal in each case. The interest of our protocol lies in the protection of the preferences of each party. That is, S does not learn the preferences of C, and C only learns the specific access policies that match her selected options.

Let E_C and E_S be the domains of credentials and personal data of C and S, respectively. Define $D_C = \mathcal{P}(E_C)$ and $D_S = \mathcal{P}(E_S)$, where, for any set A, $\mathcal{P}(A)$ is the power set of A.

First C defines different combinations of elements from E_C that she would be ready to show to S. Let $X = \{a_1, \ldots, a_s\} \subseteq D_C$ be the set of such options. Independently, S defines $Y = \{(b_1, c_1), \ldots, (b_t, c_t)\} \subseteq D_C \times D_S$, the acceptable combinations $(b_i, c_i) \in D_C \times D_S$ according to his preferences. That is, for every acceptable combination of elements b_i from D_C, S would show $c_i \in D_S$. Observe that $(b_i, c_i) \neq (b_j, c_j)$ for every $1 \leq i < j \leq s$, but b_i and b_j (or c_i and c_j) may be equal.

Our scheme can be constructed by means of the Paillier cryptosystem [22]. It exploits its homomorphic property whereby, given three elements m_1, m_2, m_3, it is possible to compute efficiently $Enc(m_1 + m_2)$ and $Enc(m_1 \cdot m_3)$ from $Enc(m_1)$, $Enc(m_2)$, and m_3. Our protocol is as follows:

1. C computes the polynomial $p(x) = \prod_{i=1}^{s}(x - a_i)$.
2. C sends $Enc(p_0), \ldots, Enc(p_s)$ to S, where p_i is the coefficient of degree i of p.
3. For every $1 \leq j \leq t$, S picks a random element $r_j \in \mathbb{Z}_n$ and computes $Enc(r_j \cdot p(b_j) + (b_j \| c_j))$. Then S sends the ciphertexts to C.
4. C decrypts the t ciphertexts.

The result of each decryption is an element from X attached to an element of D_S or a random element.

4.1 Discussion

The parameters for the Paillier cryptosystem are $n = p \cdot q$, where p and q are large primes satisfying the properties in [22]. Then we describe $X \in \mathbb{Z}_n$ and $Y \subseteq \mathbb{Z}_n \times \mathbb{Z}_n$. A way to encode an option in $\mathbb{Z}_n$ is the following. First, we establish an order among the credentials. Given an option $\{\mathrm{cred}_{i_1}, \mathrm{cred}_{i_2}, \ldots, \mathrm{cred}_{i_u}\}$ for some $i_1 < i_2 < \ldots < i_u$, we consider $x = \sum_{j=1}^{u} 2^{i_j}$. If the domain D_C (or D_S) is much larger than the number of realistic options, we can use a hash function [9]. The amount of exponentiations needed is $O(s \cdot t)$, and it can be reduced to $O(s + t \ln \ln s)$ [9].

The protocol is secure in the honest-but-curious adversary model. Following [9] we can create a protocol that is secure in the malicious adversary model by means of zero-knowledge proofs. The resulting protocol is much less efficient.

We consider that the previous solution is to be deployed in the typical client-server context, where the client is usually at a disadvantage. Hence, we offer higher protection to the client's privacy than to the server's privacy. However, there are other situations in which we need to guarantee a more equitable treatment. In this case, private matchings also provide a natural solution for privacy-preserving trust management. A solution would be a private matching in which the inputs contain the preferred options about one's own credentials and the other party's credentials. That is, $X, Y \subseteq D_C \times D_S$. A solution along this line was presented in [18].

In this work we present a method for agreeing on the credentials to be exchanged, but we do not analyze the way the credentials are exchanged and disclosed. There are many schemes for *fair exchange* of information between different parties. Some recent proposals consider schemes that are secure in the covert model, as for instance [3,5,6].

5   Related Work

Yao *et al.* [28] presented Point-Based Trust, a trust management mechanism built from a tailored secure multiparty computation protocol. The owner of a resource values the amount of sensitive information of each credential, and the output of the protocol provides an acceptable combination of the credentials that minimizes the owner's privacy loss. A drawback of this scheme is that this quantitative approach does not take into account the dependencies among credentials. For instance, a credential A may be useless without a credential B, or A and B may contain the same information.

In a privacy-reconciliation protocol [18,21], each party holds a private input set in which the elements are ordered according to the party's preferences. The goal of a reconciliation protocol on these ordered sets is to find all common elements in the parties' input sets that maximize the joint preferences of the parties. The main drawback of these schemes is efficiency. The computation of the best option is, in general, a hard problem and so the protocols are less efficient than the scheme presented here. Moreover, adding privacy protection to reconciliation protocols can increase their running time by two orders of magnitude [18,25].

6   Conclusions

In this paper we have presented a privacy-preserving mechanism for trust management. This work is restricted to the two-party case. Given the preferences of each party on credential disclosure, our method provides a proposal on the credentials to be exchanged that is consistent with the parties' preferences. The privacy of the parties is preserved because their preferences are protected by a secure two-party computation protocol for set intersection that is secure in the honest-but-curious model.

Future work might consider the combination of this trust management method with fair exchange mechanisms and the integration of these building blocks into more general frameworks. Moreover, it would be interesting to extend this construction to the covert adversarial model.

References

1. Aumann, Y., Lindell, Y.: Security against covert adversaries: efficient protocols for realistic adversaries. J. Cryptology **23**(2), 281–343 (2010)
2. Autrel, F., Cuppens, F., Cuppens-Boulahia, N., Coma, C.: MotOrBAC 2: a security policy tool. In: Third Joint Conference on Security in Networks Architectures and Security of Information Systems (SARSSI), pp. 273–287 (2008)

3. Buttyán, L., Hubaux, J.-P.: Rational exchange - a formal model based on game theory. In: Fiege, L., Mühl, G., Wilhelm, U.G. (eds.) WELCOM 2001. LNCS, vol. 2232, pp. 114–126. Springer, Heidelberg (2001)
4. Dachman-Soled, D., Malkin, T., Raykova, M., Yung, M.: Efficient robust private set intersection. In: Abdalla, M., Pointcheval, D., Fouque, P.-A., Vergnaud, D. (eds.) ACNS 2009. LNCS, vol. 5536, pp. 125–142. Springer, Heidelberg (2009)
5. Domingo-Ferrer, J.: Rational privacy disclosure in social networks. In: Torra, V., Narukawa, Y., Daumas, M. (eds.) MDAI 2010. LNCS, vol. 6408, pp. 255–265. Springer, Heidelberg (2010)
6. Domingo-Ferrer, J.: Coprivacy: an introduction to the theory and applications of co-operative privacy. SORT-Statistics and Operations Research Transactions, special issue, pp. 25–40 (2011)
7. Dong, C., Dulay, N.: Privacy preserving trust negotiation for pervasive healthcare. In: Pervasive Health Conference and Workshops, pp. 1–9 (2006)
8. Farràs, O., Domingo-Ferrer, J., Blanco-Justicia, A.: Privacy-preserving trust management mechanisms from private matching schemes. http://arxiv.org/abs/1308.2435
9. Freedman, M.J., Nissim, K., Pinkas, B.: Efficient private matching and set intersection. In: Cachin, Ch., Camenisch, J.L. (eds.) EUROCRYPT 2004. LNCS, vol. 3027, pp. 1–19. Springer, Heidelberg (2004)
10. Frikken, K.B., Li, J., Atallah, M.J.: Trust negotiation with hidden credentials, hidden policies, and policy cycles. In: NDSS (2006)
11. Hazay, C., Lindell, Y.: Efficient protocols for set intersection and pattern matching with security against malicious and covert adversaries. In: Canetti, R. (ed.) TCC 2008. LNCS, vol. 4948, pp. 155–175. Springer, Heidelberg (2008)
12. Interoperable Trust Assurance Infrastructure (Inter-Trust). EU Project FP7-ICT 317731, 2012–2014. http://www.inter-trust.eu
13. Kissner, L., Song, D.: Privacy-preserving set operations. In: Shoup, V. (ed.) CRYPTO 2005. LNCS, vol. 3621, pp. 241–257. Springer, Heidelberg (2005)
14. Lee, A.J., Winslett, M., Basney, J., Welch, V.: Traust: a trust negotiation based authorization service. In: Stølen, K., Winsborough, W.H., Martinelli, F., Massacci, F. (eds.) iTrust 2006. LNCS, vol. 3986, pp. 458–462. Springer, Heidelberg (2006)
15. Lee, A.J., Winslett, M., Perano, K.J.: TrustBuilder2: a reconfigurable framework for trust negotiation. In: Bertino, E., Ferrari, E., Karabulut, Y., Li, N. (eds.) IFIPTM 2009. IFIP AICT, vol. 300, pp. 176–195. Springer, Heidelberg (2009)
16. Li, J., Li, N., Winsborough, W.H.: Automated trust negotiation using cryptographic credentials. ACM Trans. Inf. Syst. Secur. 13(1), art. no. 2 (2009)
17. MEF Global Privacy Report 2013
18. Meyer, U., Wetzel, S., Ioannidis, S.: Distributed privacy-preserving policy reconciliation. In: ICC, pp. 1342–1349 (2007)
19. Miyaji, A., Rahman, M.S.: Privacy-preserving two-party rational set intersection protocol. Informatica 36(2), 277–286 (2012)
20. Nejdl, W., Olmedilla, D., Winslett, M.: PeerTrust: automated trust negotiation for peers on the semantic web. In: Jonker, W., Petković, M. (eds.) SDM 2004. LNCS, vol. 3178, pp. 118–132. Springer, Heidelberg (2004)
21. Neugebauer, G., Brutschy, L., Meyer, U., Wetzel, S.: Design and implementation of privacy-preserving reconciliation protocols. In: EDBT/ICDT Workshops, pp. 121–130 (2013)
22. Paillier, P.: Public-key cryptosystems based on composite degree residuosity classes. In: Stern, J. (ed.) EUROCRYPT 1999. LNCS, vol. 1592, pp. 223–238. Springer, Heidelberg (1999)

23. Special Eurobarometer 359: Attitudes on Data Protection and Electronic Identity in the European Union, June 2011
24. Squicciarini, A., Bertino, E., Ferrari, E., Paci, F., Thuraisingham, B.: PP-trust-X: a system for privacy preserving trust negotiation. ACM Trans. Inf. Syst. Secur. 10(3), art. no. 12 (2007)
25. Voris, J., Ioannidis, S., Wetzel, S., Meyer, U.: Performance evaluation of privacy-preserving policy reconciliation protocols. In: POLICY, pp. 221–228 (2007)
26. Winsborough, W.H., Seamons, K.E., Jones, V.E.: Automated trust negotiation. In: DISCEX, vol. 1, pp. 88–102 (2000)
27. Yao, A.C.-C.: How to generate and exchange secrets. In: FOCS, pp. 162–167 (1986)
28. Yao, D., Frikken, K.B., Atallah, M.J., Tamassia, R.: Point-based trust: define how much privacy is worth. In: Ning, P., Qing, S., Li, N. (eds.) ICICS 2006. LNCS, vol. 4307, pp. 190–209. Springer, Heidelberg (2006)

Author Index

Abril, Daniel   362
Ardoy, Pierre-Yves   162
Ayday, Erman   133

Backes, Michael   194, 213
Baquero, Carlos   51
Barni, Mauro   66
Bernaschi, Massimo   66
Blanco-Justicia, Alberto   390
Brutschy, Lucas   178

Castella-Roca, Jordi   100, 148
Cherreau, Ronan-Alexandre   235
Coan, Brian   114

Dell'amico, Matteo   235
Di Crescenzo, Giovanni   114
Dini, Gianluca   284
Domingo-Ferrer, Josep   390
Douence, Remi   235

Engel, Thomas   300
Erola, Arnau   148

Farras, Oriol   390
Ferrer-Gomila, Josep-Lluis   100
Forshaw, Matthew   380
Fysarakis, Konstantinos   333

Gerling, Sebastian   213
Goncalves, Nelson   51

Hajny, Jan   17
Hammer, Christian   213
Hao, Feng   380
Hatzivasilis, George   333
Hengartner, Urs   133
Hubaux, Jean-Pierre   133

Ingwar, Mads Ingerslew   250

Jensen, Christian Damsgaard   250
Jerome, Quentin   300
Jose, Rui   51

Kammüller, Florian   83
Kogure, Jun   34
Koshiba, Takeshi   34

Lalanne, Vincent   162
Lazzeretti, Riccardo   66

Maffei, Matteo   213
Malina, Lukas   17
Manifavas, Charalampos   333
Marchal, Samuel   300
Martinasek, Zdenek   17
Martinelli, Fabio   268, 284
Matteucci, Ilaria   284
Meiser, Sebastian   194
Meyer, Ulrike   178
Molyneaux, Adam   133
Munier, Manuel   162
Murdoch, Steven J.   3
Mut-Puigserver, Macia   100

Navarro-Arribas, Guillermo   362
Neugebauer, Georg   178

Oehler, Michael   353

Payeras-Capella, M. Magdalena   100
Phatak, Dhananjay S.   353
Piepoli, Antonio   369
Pignata, Tommaso   66
Preibusch, Soren   83

Raisaro, Jean Louis   133
Rantos, Konstantinos   333
Ricarde, Magali   162
Roudier, Yves   235
Royer, Jean-Claude   235

Sabellico, Alessandro   66
Santana De Oliveira, Anderson   235, 316
Saracino, Andrea   268, 284
Satvat, Kiavash   380
Scholte, Theodoòr   316
Schultz, John   114
Serme, Gabriel   316
Sgandurra, Daniele   268, 284
Shimoyama, Takeshi   34
State, Radu   300
Styp-Rekowsky, Philipp von   213
Sudholt, Mario   235

Tethal, Ondrej   17
Toreini, Ehsan   380
Torra, Vicenç   362
Tsang, Simon   114

Veeningen, Meilof   369
Vives-Guasch, Arnau   100

Wetzel, Susanne   178
Wright, Rebecca N.   114

Yasuda, Masaya   34
Yokoyama, Kazuhiro   34

Zannone, Nicola   369